S0-AJD-087

AMERICAN
MULTINATIONALS
AND AMERICAN
INTERESTS

C. FRED BERGSTEN
THOMAS HORST
THEODORE H. MORAN

AMERICAN MULTINATIONALS AND AMERICAN INTERESTS

THE BROOKINGS INSTITUTION
Washington, D.C.

338.8
B499

169461

Copyright © 1978 by
THE BROOKINGS INSTITUTION
1775 Massachusetts Avenue, N.W., Washington, D.C. 20036

Library of Congress Cataloging in Publication Data:

Bergsten, C. Fred, 1941–
  American multinationals and American interests.
  Includes bibliographical references and index.
  1. International business enterprises.
2. Corporations, American. I. Horst, Thomas,
joint author. II. Moran, Theodore H., 1943–
joint author. III. Title.
HD2755.5.B46   338.8'8   77-91786
ISBN 0-8157-0920-X
ISBN 0-8157-0919-6 pbk.

9 8 7 6 5 4 3 2 1

Board of Trustees

Robert V. Roosa
Chairman

Louis W. Cabot
Vice Chairman;
Chairman, Executive Committee

Vincent M. Barnett, Jr.
Barton M. Biggs
Edward W. Carter
William T. Coleman, Jr.
Lloyd N. Cutler
Bruce B. Dayton
George M. Elsey
John Fischer
Huntington Harris
Roger W. Heyns
Carla A. Hills
Luther G. Holbrook
Lane Kirkland
Bruce K. MacLaury
Robert S. McNamara
Arjay Miller
Barbara W. Newell
Herbert P. Patterson
J. Woodward Redmond
Charles W. Robinson
Warren M. Shapleigh
Phyllis A. Wallace

Honorary Trustees

Arthur Stanton Adams
Eugene R. Black
Robert D. Calkins
Colgate W. Darden, Jr.
Douglas Dillon
John E. Lockwood
William McC. Martin, Jr.
H. Chapman Rose
Robert Brookings Smith
Sydney Stein, Jr.
J. Harvie Wilkinson, Jr.

THE BROOKINGS INSTITUTION is an independent organization devoted to nonpartisan research, education, and publication in economics, government, foreign policy, and the social sciences generally. Its principal purposes are to aid in the development of sound public policies and to promote public understanding of issues of national importance.

The Institution was founded on December 8, 1927, to merge the activities of the Institute for Government Research, founded in 1916, the Institute of Economics, founded in 1922, and the Robert Brookings Graduate School of Economics and Government, founded in 1924.

The Board of Trustees is responsible for the general administration of the Institution, while the immediate direction of the policies, program, and staff is vested in the President, assisted by an advisory committee of the officers and staff. The by-laws of the Institution state: "It is the function of the Trustees to make possible the conduct of scientific research, and publication, under the most favorable conditions, and to safeguard the independence of the research staff in the pursuit of their studies and in the publication of the results of such studies. It is not a part of their function to determine, control, or influence the conduct of particular investigations or the conclusions reached."

The President bears final responsibility for the decision to publish a manuscript as a Brookings book. In reaching his judgment on the competence, accuracy, and objectivity of each study, the President is advised by the director of the appropriate research program and weighs the views of a panel of expert outside readers who report to him in confidence on the quality of the work. Publication of a work signifies that it is deemed a competent treatment worthy of public consideration but does not imply endorsement of conclusions or recommendations.

The Institution maintains its position of neutrality on issues of public policy in order to safeguard the intellectual freedom of the staff. Hence interpretations or conclusions in Brookings publications should be understood to be solely those of the authors and should not be attributed to the Institution, to its trustees, officers, or other staff members, or to the organizations that support its research.

Foreword

THE multinational corporation has become one of the most controversial economic and political institutions of our time. What international investment does to jobs, exports, prices, income distribution, access to raw materials, taxes, and market power is debated in host and home countries alike. To some observers, multinationals threaten the international economic and political system; to others, they stabilize international relations. In one view, they are engines of progress; in another, agents of exploitation. Controversy over the causes and effects of foreign investment has frustrated the development of coherent government policies. Disagreements stem from inadequate data, inappropriate theories and analytical methods, and complex interactions between the economics and the politics of foreign investment.

On one point, everyone agrees: the role of multinationals has grown tremendously in the last two decades. Americans are accustomed to thinking of the U.S. economy as large and self-sufficient, but in recent years over a fifth of corporate profits have been earned abroad and a fourth of all new corporate investment has been made in foreign countries.

In 1973 the authors of this book began an extensive study of the effect of American multinationals on the U.S. economy and U.S. foreign policy. This task required them to study, as well, the effect of foreign investment on host countries and on other home countries. In attempting to find answers to old questions, the authors raise some new ones. Yet they have adhered to their original purpose of identifying the important questions, applying rigorous methods to recent data, drawing conclusions, and making policy recommendations.

Their work on this book was done while the authors were part of the

Brookings Foreign Policy Studies program—C. Fred Bergsten as a senior fellow and Thomas Horst and Theodore H. Moran as research associates. The authors record here their gratitude to the scores of friends, colleagues, students, and critics who reviewed the work as it progressed. In particular, they thank Richard E. Caves, Harry Grubert, Gary Hufbauer, George Kopits, Guy Stevens, and Raymond Vernon. If these failed to save the authors from error, it was not for want of trying. The authors are also grateful for the help of Karen Anderson, Thomas Popovich, Thomas Pugel, Robert Owen, and Claudette Simpson. The manuscript was edited by Diane Hammond and data were verified by Penelope S. Harpold. Florence Robinson prepared the index and the charts were drafted by the Ford Studios.

The study was financed by a grant from the Sloan Foundation. The U.S. Department of Labor, the U.S. Department of the Treasury, and the U.S. Agency for International Development gave supplemental grants to analyze some of the narrower issues.

The views expressed in this book are solely the authors' and should not be ascribed to the trustees, officers, or other staff members of the Brookings Institution. Nor do they reflect the views of the Sloan Foundation, the agencies of the U.S. government that provided assistance, or the agencies and institutions with which the authors became affiliated after their work at Brookings.

BRUCE K. MAC LAURY
President

January 1978
Washington, D.C.

Contents

Appendix Tables

Figures

PART ONE

Analysis

CHAPTER ONE

American Multinationals, Center of a Storm

THE INFLUENCE of American multinational corporations on the American economy and foreign policy has been a major issue of the seventies. The business community and others contend that foreign investment promotes American interests. World production is more efficient, American exports are increased, the quantity and quality of employment is augmented, and American access to raw materials at reasonable prices is improved. Furthermore, American investment contributes to the economic growth of foreign countries, strengthening their balance of payments and raising their employment. It widens economic relations between the United States and communist countries. The competitive position of the United States in world markets and its economic growth at home, they say, depends on the continued expansion of overseas investment. United States policy should support existing investments and promote future investments.

The American multinationals have, however, many domestic opponents who believe that foreign direct investment hurts American interests. By producing abroad, they export American jobs; by transferring technology to overseas affiliates, they undermine domestic economic growth. They alter the distribution of national income, away from labor and toward capital; they erode labor's bargaining power by supporting non-union operations overseas; they siphon revenues from the U.S. treasury. Rather than promoting American foreign policy interests, they interfere by becoming excessively involved in the internal politics of other coun-

3

tries. They pervert international relations through bribes and kickbacks; and they generally dictate the course of U.S. foreign policy. They distort the economic development of poorer countries by promoting inappropriate production and consumption patterns and by draining their all-too-limited human and financial resources. The firms, it is said, speculate in foreign-exchange markets, attacking weak currencies and destabilizing currency values.

A central issue is the distribution of costs and benefits arising from foreign direct investment. The distributional issue has two dimensions: distribution of the costs and benefits (a) between home and host countries and (b) among groups, especially labor and capital, within a country. Distributional problems exist even when the investment increases total welfare, but they become acute when the net effect on world welfare is uncertain, as it might be when the investment is induced by high tariffs on U.S. exports or lower taxes than those paid in the United States. One focus of this book is the efforts of various groups to tilt the benefits in their direction and to minimize their share of the costs. Such efforts often limit others' gain or threaten international tranquility and, thus, should be a concern of policy. Two kinds of conflicts are notable: those between the host and home governments (mainly the United States), and those between the multinationals and the governments of home or host countries.[1]

What is striking about the debate on multinationals is the complete lack of agreement between the sides. Claims are made that foreign direct investment creates jobs and that it exports jobs, that it helps the balance of payments and that it hurts it, that it promotes U.S. foreign policy, that it subverts U.S. foreign policy, that it fosters economic development, and that it depresses economic development. These differences reflect value judgments, the bases for which were formed long before multinational enterprises became a central issue. Labor has always been more concerned than management (and than most economists) with the adjustment costs of changing production patterns. Proponents of active U.S. engagement in world affairs, of course, look more favorably on multi-

1. Host countries are those in which the foreign branches, subsidiaries, and affiliates of multinationals operate. Home countries are those in which multinationals are headquartered. Many countries (including the United States) are both home (to IBM, for example) and host (to Shell, for example), but there remains a conceptual distinction between the two.

nationals than do those who would limit U.S. involvement overseas. Multinationals have become the new focus of an old debate because of their size, pervasiveness, and susceptibility to national policies.

Contradictions multiply when one considers attitudes in other countries toward American multinationals. Host countries frequently charge that the firms hurt their balance-of-payments positions, drain their treasuries of tax revenues, cost them jobs through the use of inappropriate technology, and exploit their raw materials for the benefit of consumers. Yet it is highly unlikely that foreign direct investment hurts the balance of payments of both home and host countries or drains tax revenues from both, unless third countries (tax havens in the latter case) benefit at the expense of both home and host countries. It is more plausible that such investments create or destroy jobs in both home and host countries, but the conditions are rare under which both lose, in the aggregate.

The two views can be reconciled to some extent by disaggregation of the universe of foreign direct investment: investments in some industries may export U.S. jobs, or hurt the U.S. balance of payments, or foul U.S. foreign policy; and investments in others may have opposite effects. To be useful, disaggregation may have to be at the level of individual firms or even individual investments. Indeed, a recurring theme of this book is the need to disaggregate the phenomenon, both to understand its effects and to devise sensible policies to deal with it. But to formulate policy, one also must judge the overall effect.

The objective of this book is to provide a basis for American policy toward American multinationals by analyzing the whole array of their effects on the U.S. economy and on U.S. foreign policy. The intensity of the competing views is not the only roadblock to the development of a coherent U.S. policy. The intellectual problems are also formidable. Indeed, some of the contentious issues have not been subjected to serious analysis; definitive answers even for those that have been studied carefully are elusive because of problems of data and methodology.

In the field of international trade, certain accepted concepts undergird the policy of the United States and most other countries. Even in the field of international monetary relations, where a systemic shift from fixed to flexible exchange rates was accomplished in the early 1970s, underlying concepts are clear.

No such intellectual consensus exists regarding foreign direct investment. There are at least two competing economic models and four competing political models that seek to explain the phenomenon. Traditional economic analysis views foreign direct investment as motivated by differences in the return on capital in different countries. But product cycle and industrial organization analyses, developed in the 1960s, emphasize technological and marketing know-how rather than the abundance of capital. The emphasis on oligopolistic aspects of foreign investment plays down the significance of returns on investment in home versus host countries.

On the political side, there are four conventional schools of thought. The imperialist as well as the mercantilist points of view argue that there is a joint, and often successful, effort by American multinationals and the U.S. government to dominate the world both economically and politically. In contrast, the sovereignty-at-bay thesis,[2] which developed in the early 1970s and is associated with the product cycle approach, posits that multinational firms have become dominant over all nation-states—both the host countries in which they operate and the home countries, including the United States, where they are based—with largely beneficial effects on all concerned. Most recently, the global reach school,[3] while agreeing that the firms have become dominant, concludes that the effects are negative on home and host countries alike, including the United States.

With the realization that disagreement over the economic and political results of foreign direct investment bring corresponding disagreement on policy, we examine each school of thought in this volume. The economic models are presented in part two, the political models in part three. We conclude that they all have weaknesses and that a new approach is needed to understand the issue and to provide a basis for sound policies.

The central question in assessing the impact on the U.S. economy of foreign investment is how the actual event compares with what would have happened otherwise. Organized labor believes that production in the United States could have continued, at least in most instances, if foreign direct investments had not been made. Multinational enterprises believe that the investments were necessary to avoid losing their market positions. Competing claims can be reconciled only by knowing which premise is correct.

2. After Raymond Vernon, *Sovereignty at Bay: The Multinational Spread of U.S. Enterprises* (Basic Books, 1971).
3. After Richard J. Barnet and Ronald E. Müller, *Global Reach: The Power of the Multinational Corporations* (Simon and Schuster, 1974).

There is no way to know for sure. However, this study pursues several approaches in pursuing a correct judgment. First, a review of the literature presents the analytical issues: the relation between exports from the United States and foreign production by the subsidiaries, the implications of that relation for American jobs and income distribution, the role of the firms in providing the United States with access to raw materials, the effects of current taxation of foreign direct investment on U.S. Treasury revenues, the impact of foreign direct investment on the market power of the firms within the United States, their role in the international monetary and trading systems, and their effect on development in the poorer countries.

Second, we have undertaken original studies of several issues: the relation between exports and foreign production, the effects of U.S. tax policy, the relation between foreign direct investment and the firms' domestic market power, the effect of foreign direct investment on U.S. access to raw materials, and the effect of multinationals on the functioning of the international economic system. In carrying out these studies we encountered many problems familiar to researchers in this field: serious gaps in the data, confidentiality requirements which severely limit disaggregation of data to the level of individual firms or even of industries, long time lags in data availability, and the perennial question of what would have happened in the absence of foreign direct investment, for which data will never be available.

Our third methodological approach is reviewing case studies. There is an enormous and growing literature on the effects of foreign direct investment on specific host countries, industries, and firms. Little of this work deals with the effects of investment on the United States (or other home countries) but inferences can be drawn from these studies. This approach is particularly fruitful in assessing foreign direct investment in raw materials but also yields insights in several manufacturing industries. A conformity of conclusions based on different data and different methods provides a surer foundation for U.S. policy than could be gained from relying on any one alone.

The Growth of American Multinationals

As long ago as 1970, one-third of the work force of several hundred multinationals surveyed by the Department of Commerce were employed

Table 1-1. *Sales by Majority-Owned Foreign Affiliates as a Share of Total Foreign Sales of American Multinationals, 1966–73*

| Year | Foreign market (billions of dollars) | | | Foreign affiliate share (percent) |
	Total	Exports from United States	Foreign affiliate sales	
1966	127.1	29.3	97.8	77.0
1967	139.2	30.7	108.5	78.0
1968	154.4	33.6	120.8	78.2
1969	170.7	36.4	134.3	78.7
1970	197.8	41.9	155.9	78.8
1971	227.2	42.8	184.4	81.2
1972	261.1	48.8	212.3	81.3
1973	361.8	70.3	291.5	80.6

Source: *Survey of Current Business*, vol. 55 (June 1975), p. 26; ibid., vol. 55 (August 1975), p. 23; ibid. vol. 56 (June 1976), p. 32.

abroad.[4] In a survey of manufacturing firms, the ratio was 29.8 percent of the work force at the end of 1969 and 34 percent at the end of 1973.[5]

Over 80 percent of the foreign sales of American multinationals now derive from the production of their majority-owned foreign affiliates and less than 20 percent from exports from the United States (see table 1-1). Over 20 percent of U.S. exports in 1970 represented sales of U.S. parent companies to their foreign subsidiaries, up from perhaps 17 percent in 1966.[6] Over 27 percent of 1970 gross sales of the firms in the Department of Commerce survey were accounted for by their majority-owned foreign affiliates, up from 23 percent in 1966.[7]

4. The sample size is 298. Calculation is based on data in *Survey of Current Business*, vol. 53 (October 1973), p. 37.

5. Calculated from a survey of 111 firms, *The Effects of U.S. Corporate Foreign Investment 1970–73* (New York: Business International, December 1975), p. 29.

6. Sales in 1970 totaled $8.6 billion for the 298 multinational enterprises sampled by the Department of Commerce (*Survey of Current Business*, vol. 53, January 1973, p. 37). Total U.S. exports that year were $41.9 billion. The comparable figures for 1966 were $5 billion in sales, $29.3 billion total. U.S. affiliates of multinationals based in other countries accounted for 24 percent of 1966 U.S. exports (statement of Milton A. Berger before the Subcommittee on Foreign Commerce and Tourism of the Senate Commerce Committee May 3, 1976; processed, p. 5). Hence, in 1977 American-based and foreign-based multinationals probably account for at least half of all U.S. exports.

7. Based on data in *Survey of Current Business*, vol. 53 (January 1973), p. 37.

Table 1-2. *Foreign Expenditure as a Share of Total Plant and Equipment Expenditure by American Corporations, 1960 and 1966–76*

| | Plant and equipment expenditure (billions of dollars)ª | | | Foreign share |
Year	Total	Domestic	Foreign	(percent)
1960	40.6	36.8	3.8	9.4
1966	72.2	63.5	8.7	12.0
1967	75.2	65.5	9.7	12.9
1968	77.8	67.8	10.0	12.9
1969	87.2	75.6	11.6	13.3
1970	93.8	79.7	14.1	15.0
1971	97.5	81.2	16.3	16.7
1972	105.1	88.4	16.7	16.0
1973	120.3	99.7	20.6	17.2
1974	138.2	112.4	25.8	18.5
1975	139.5	112.8	26.7	19.2
1976	146.4	120.5	25.9	17.8

Sources: *Economic Report of the President, January 1976* (GPO, January 1976), p. 216; *Survey of Current Business*, vol. 56 (March 1976), pp. 19–24; and ibid., vol. 57 (March 1977), pp. 31, 33.

a. Data on domestic and foreign expenditures are not precisely comparable, because (a) property expenditures are included in the foreign series but not the domestic series, and (b) foreign expenditures include only those by majority-owned foreign affiliates of American multinationals, ignoring altogether expenditures in enterprises where they are minority owners. The growth rates of the two series are thus more strictly comparable than their absolute magnitudes.

In 1975, foreign investments of American multinationals accounted for over 19 percent of their total plant and equipment expenditures, double that of 1960 (see table 1-2).

In 1974, the foreign earnings of American multinationals accounted for 26.9 percent of their total earnings, up from 8.6 percent in 1957 (see table 1-3). The 1957 and 1974 figures are inflated by abnormally high profits for oil companies; however, the ratio for manufacturing, alone, more than quadrupled in the eighteen years. The ratios of gross foreign earnings (before foreign taxes) to gross total earnings (before U.S. taxes) are even higher; one estimate is 23.1 percent in 1971, 22.6 percent in 1972, and 26.1 percent in 1973.[8] Income on foreign direct investment, plus fees and royalties from affiliated foreigners, contributed over $21 billion to the U.S. balance of payments in 1974, almost as much as total U.S. exports of capital goods (excluding automobiles).

8. Adolphe J. Warner and David W. Bodenberg, "International Comments" (Becker Securities Corporation, September 26, 1975; processed).

American Multinationals and American Interests

Table 1-3. *Foreign Earnings as a Share of Total Earnings of American Corporations, 1957 and 1966–74*

Billions of dollars unless otherwise stated

Year	Earnings in all industries			Earnings in manufacturing		
	Total[a]	Foreign[b]	Foreign share (percent)	Total[a]	Foreign[b]	Foreign share (percent)
1957	45.4	3.9	8.6	24.0	1.0	4.2
1966	78.6	5.2	6.7	41.6	1.9	4.6
1967	75.6	5.5	7.3	37.9	1.9	5.0
1968	82.1	6.5	7.9	41.2	2.4	5.8
1969	77.9	7.5	9.6	36.8	3.1	8.4
1970	66.4	8.0	12.1	27.1	3.1	11.5
1971	76.9	9.0	11.7	32.4	3.5	10.8
1972	89.6	10.8	12.1	40.6	4.8	11.7
1973	98.6	16.9	17.2	43.8	6.7	15.3
1974	93.6	25.1	26.9	37.4	6.5	17.4

Sources: *Economic Report of the President, January 1976*, p. 256; *Survey of Current Business*, vol. 55 (October 1975), p. 51; for 1957, Department of Commerce, *U.S. Business Investments in Foreign Countries* (GPO, 1960), p. 124.

a. Profit is calculated before U.S. taxes, with inventory valuation adjustment, and without capital consumption adjustment.

b. Earnings are calculated after foreign taxes.

Foreign incomes of individual firms are even more impressive than the aggregate figures. Eight of the top ten U.S. firms in *Fortune*'s industrial 500 earned at least 49 percent and as much as 87 percent of their total 1974 income from foreign branches, affiliates, and subsidiaries (see table 1-4). And for seventeen of the top one hundred companies for which data are available, at least half of total 1973 or 1974 income was derived from overseas operations.[9] The trend since 1965 is also notable. Of the thirty-five firms for which we have data, twenty-nine experienced a rise in the share of their total income derived from overseas operations.

9. Many companies do not report their foreign operations with enough precision to permit the calculation of the ratio of foreign income to total income. According to our calculations, which also include ratios of foreign sales to total sales, foreign operations account for at least a quarter of the total operations of seventy of *Fortune*'s industrial 500.

Table 1-4. *Income from Foreign Investments as a Share of Total Income, Selected American Multinationals, 1965 and 1970s*

Multinational and 1974 rank by sales	1974 financial data (millions of dollars)		Share of total income from foreign investments (percent)	
	Total sales	Total income	1965	1970s[a]
Exxon (1)	42,061,336	3,142,192	60	83.0
General Motors (2)	31,549,546	950,069	10	17.1
Ford Motor (3)	23,620,600	369,900	12[b]	48.6
Texaco (4)	23,255,497	1,586,441	25	81.8
Mobil Oil (5)	18,929,033	1,047,446	52	87.2
Standard Oil of California (6)	17,191,186	970,018	43	77.1
Gulf Oil (7)	16,458,000	1,065,000	29	86.7
General Electric (8)	13,413,100	608,100	18[c]	17[d]
International Business Machines (9)	12,675,292	1,837,639	30	49.1
International Telephone and Telegraph (10)	11,154,401	451,070	60	63.1
Chrysler (11)	10,971,416	(52,094)	25[c]	47.4
Continental Oil (16)	7,041,423	327,609	9	66.0[e]
du Pont (17)	6,910,100	403,500	17[c]	27.6[c]
Occidental Petroleum (20)	5,719,369	280,677	n.a.	50.0[e]
Union Carbide (22)	5,320,123	530,058	22	41.4
Goodyear (23)	5,256,247	157,461	34	36.0[c]
International Harvester (26)	4,965,916	124,053	19	75.1[e]
Dow Chemical (27)	4,938,483	557,457	42[d]	45.8[c,e]
Procter and Gamble (28)	4,912,279	316,695	18	28.5
Radio Corporation of America (31)	4,594,300	113,300	5	19.2[c]
Eastman Kodak (32)	4,583,629	629,519	15	24.6
Kraftco (33)	4,471,427	94,627	n.a.	21.0[c]
Caterpillar Tractor (36)	4,082,127	229,181	43[c]	53[c,f]
Firestone Tire and Rubber (40)	3,674,890	154,025	26	39[f]
Xerox (41)	3,576,442	331,083	n.a.	48.9
Monsanto (43)	3,497,900	323,200	21[c]	31[c,f]
W. R. Grace (44)	3,472,291	130,558	34[c]	39[c,f]
R. J. Reynolds (48)	3,229,668	310,698	n.a.	36.4[c]
Continental Can (52)	3,087,448	119,449	n.a.	25[d]
Ralston Purina (55)	3,073,210	90,691	n.a.	21.9[c]
International Paper (56)	3,042,235	262,600	15[c]	27.0[c]
General Foods (58)	2,986,692	119,480	7[b]	25.3[c]

Table 1-4 (*continued*)

Multinational and 1974 rank by sales	1974 financial data (millions of dollars)		Share of total income from foreign investments (percent)	
	Total sales	Total income	1965	1970s[a]
Minnesota Mining & Manufacturing (59)	2,936,959	301,739	30[c]	39.2
Marathon Oil (60)	2,882,174	170,493	10[c]	78.3
Singer (66)	2,661,700	(10,100)	52[c]	75[e,f]
Honeywell (68)	2,625,683	75,768	23[c]	43.2
Colgate-Palmolive (69)	2,615,448	118,698	n.a.	55.3[e]
Sperry Rand (70)	2,613,486	112,558	28[c]	52.8
Consolidated Production Corp. Int. (71)	2,570,273	99,153	47	56.4
Weyerhauser (73)	2,529,013	276,197	n.a.	34.0[c]
Coca Cola (74)	2,522,150	195,972	n.a.	59.0[e]
Deere (75)	2,495,086	164,311	16[b,c]	26.4[c]
Uniroyal (82)	2,300,533	48,630	n.a.	53.3
Owens-Illinois (88)	2,116,436	83,472	10	23.2[c]
General Mills (94)	2,000,103	75,137	n.a.	16.7[c]
National Cash Register (97)	1,979,003	87,165	47	36[d]
Johnson and Johnson (99)	1,937,211	161,620	25	51.5
Raytheon (100)	1,928,855	57,751	10[c]	26.8[c]
Warner-Lambert (102)	1,911,046	155,323	37	30[d]
American Cyanamid (107)	1,779,872	154,724	22	49.1[e]
Borg-Warner (108)	1,767,801	50,840	7	30.3
National Lead (124)	1,597,474	77,921	n.a.	62.5
Texas Instruments (126)	1,572,487	89,621	20[c]	38[c]
Pfizer (130)	1,541,673	135,267	56	74.3
Burroughs (134)	1,510,836	142,937	69	32.8
H. J. Heinz (139)	1,438,251	64,320	65	45.9
Merck (152)	1,329,550	210,492	31	45.0[e]
Avon Products (159)	1,260,292	111,755	17	42.7[c]
Gillette (160)	1,246,422	87,739	35[a]	65.2
Otis Elevator (179)	1,108,942	43,529	35	59.8[e]
Corning Glass (190)	1,050,962	48,125	7	32[c]
Kellogg (200)	1,009,818	72,031	n.a.	34.1[c]
Hewlett-Packard (225)	884,053	84,022	12	42.0[c]
Foster Wheeler (228)	875,704	12,701	64	41.6[e]
Crown Cork and Seal (248)	776,158	39,663	33	40.4
Polaroid (253)	757,296	28,387	18[b]	37.0[c]
Sunbeam (258)	739,879	31,365	19	40.3[e]
Schering-Plough (266)	703,797	123,978	56[g]	41.0[e]

Table 1-4 (*continued*)

Multinational and 1974 rank by sales	1974 financial data (millions of dollars)		Share of total income from foreign investments (percent)	
	Total sales	Total income	1965	1970s[a]
Black and Decker (278)	641,971	44,569	22	54.0[e]
USM (281)	634,602	19,680	62	114.0[e]
Searle (288)	621,310	72,421	n.a.	50.0[e]
Chesebrough-Pond's (309)	561,257	43,611	42	29.5
Norton (311)	558,332	25,118	n.a.	61.4
Stanley Works (318)	545,017	19,908	19	43.9[e]
Addressograph Multigraph (321)	540,833	308	13	216.0[e]
Sybron (343)	491,581	22,436	n.a.	46.6[e]
AMP (348)	482,107	46,226	25	57.2[e]
Outboard Marine (350)	480,142	16,704	18[c]	60.6[e]
Libby, McNeill, and Libby (363)	464,710	13,520	18	62.0[b,e]
Inmont (397)	413,584	14,217	n.a.	49.4[e]
Signode (403)	404,795	23,939	23[c]	36.1[c,e]
Miles Laboratories (420)	386,167	15,978	23[c]	59.0[e]
H. H. Robertson (444)	338,573	7,282	55	40.4[e]
Jonathan Logan (456)	322,545	6,149	n.a.	45.1[e]
Ferro (457)	322,328	17,749	n.a.	77.8[e]

Sources: "The Fortune Directory of the 500 Largest Industrial Corporations," *Fortune*, vol. 91 (May 1975), pp. 210–28, for rank, sales, and income; foreign income based on authors' interpretations of data from: Securities and Exchange Commission 10-K forms (1974 foreign income); *Fortune*, vol. 90 (November 1974), p. 175 (1973 foreign income); *Fortune* staff (1970 and 1972 foreign income); and Nicholas K. Bruck and Francis A. Lees, "Foreign Investment, Capital Controls and the Balance of Payments," *The Bulletin* (Institute of Finance, Graduate School of Business Administration, New York University), nos. 48 and 49 (April 1968), pp. 69–81 (1965 foreign income).
n.a. Not available.
a. Data are for 1974 unless otherwise noted.
b. Excluding Canada.
c. Sales, including exports from United States.
d. Figure is for 1972.
e. Figure is for 1973.
f. Figure is for 1970.
g. Schering only.

Defining America's Position

Multinationals have become a force to reckon with, not only because of the size of American firms but because of the growth of multinational firms worldwide. As the largest trading and investing nation, the United States is materially affected by the influence of multinationals on the international economic system.

Foreign direct investment affects the international economic system and is affected by that system. The activities of multinationals are influenced by national trade policies, by exchange rates, by attitudes and policies toward foreign investment itself, and even by political situations, such as the assertiveness of the developing countries and détente between the United States and the Soviet Union. Since major changes are occurring in the international milieu, one can expect major changes in the role and operations of multinational enterprises. Such changes intensify the need for new national policies toward foreign direct investment and for new international arrangements, both to head off conflicts between governments and to enable governments to countervail the power of the multinationals and their ability to evade the jurisdiction of any single government.

The United States must define its own policy and play a leading role in international economic arrangements for reasons beyond its size and traditional leadership position. First, the United States is by far the largest home country for multinationals. In 1971, American-based firms accounted for 52 percent of the stock of all foreign direct investment, down from 55 percent in 1967 but still far above the 14.5 percent of second-place Britain and even farther ahead of the home countries whose foreign direct investment was rising most rapidly (Germany, at 4.4 percent, and Japan, at 2.7 percent; see table 1-5). Second, and less widely recognized, the United States is the second largest host country for foreign direct investment (Canada is first).[10]

Finally, many countries are suspicious of official U.S. attitudes toward foreign direct investment and harbor the imperialist/mercantilist view of U.S. foreign direct investment. They interpret the absence of clear-cut U.S. policies as confirming their suspicions that the United States uses American multinationals to pursue national and, especially, foreign policy goals. Before they will agree to limit their own freedom regarding foreign direct investment, these countries need to be convinced that the United States has a balanced national position. The United States must, therefore, arrive at a clear view of what it wants from foreign direct invest-

---

10. The book value of foreign direct investment in the United States totaled $26.5 billion at the end of 1974 (see statement of Berger, p. 3); the book value of U.S. foreign direct investment in Canada was $24.4 billion at the end of 1974; the United States has in recent years accounted for about 77 percent of all such investment in Canada, which therefore presumably totaled about $32 billion (ibid., p. 13).

Table 1-5. *Distribution of Stock of Foreign Direct Investment, Home Country, 1967 and 1971*

Home country	Book value (millions of dollars)		Share of total (percent)		Per capita value, 1971 (dollars)
	1967	1971ᵃ	1967	1971ᵃ	
United States	59,486	86,001	55.0	52.0	415
United Kingdom	17,521	24,019	16.2	14.5	422
France	6,000	9,540	5.5	5.8	186
Germany	3,015	7,276	2.8	4.4	119
Switzerland	4,250	6,760	3.9	4.1	1,070
Canada	3,728	5,930	3.4	3.6	275
Japan	1,458	4,480	1.3	2.7	43
Netherlands	2,250	3,580	2.1	2.2	272
Sweden	1,514ᵇ	3,450ᶜ	1.4	2.1	425
Italy	2,110	3,350	1.9	2.0	62
Belgium	2,040	3,250	0.4	2.0	335
Australia	380	610	1.9	0.4	48
Portugal	200	320	0.2	0.2	33
Denmark	190	310	0.2	0.2	63
Norway	60	90	0.0	0.0	23
Austria	30	40	0.0	0.0	5
Other	4,000	6,000	3.7	3.6	...
Total	108,200	165,000	100.0	100.0	...

Sources: United Nations, *Multinational Corporations in World Development*, ST/ECA/190(1973), p. 139; for population data, *World Bank Atlas* (International Bank for Reconstruction and Development, 1973).

a. Except for United States, United Kingdom, Germany, Japan, and Sweden, 1971 figures are estimates derived by applying the average 1966–71 growth rate of the United States, the United Kingdom, and Germany.

b. 1965 current price for assets of majority-owned manufacturing subsidiaries.

c. 1970 current price for assets of majority-owned manufacturing subsidiaries.

ment and how to go about obtaining it. This is a minimum requirement for reaching international accords.

Chapter two takes a broader look at what U.S. policy toward foreign investment has been and how that policy compares with that of other home countries facing the same challenges.

American Policy toward American Multinationals: An Overview

THE UNITED STATES has no consistent, coherent policy toward foreign direct investment and multinational enterprises. Nor has it ever had one. But many specific policies have a major impact on foreign direct investment, and most of them have a proinvestment orientation. The tilt began to change in the past few years, as both the administration and Congress began to respond to mounting internal criticism of multinationals.

Most of the individual measures directed explicitly at foreign direct investment were developed within the context of a particular functional issue: tax policy, foreign policy, trade policy, balance-of-payments policy. There has been little effort to relate one policy to another or to any overall approach to foreign direct investment. Indeed, there has been no agency in the U.S. government to coordinate the different policies affecting foreign direct investment: the Treasury Department largely determines tax and balance-of-payments policy, the Department of State usually determines expropriation policy and aid-related measures, the Overseas Private Investment Corporation has the major role in shaping investment insurance and guarantees, and the Department of Justice, Federal Trade Commission, and Securities and Exchange Commission have their respective functional responsibilities. Domestic macroeconomic policy and trade policy, which have major effects on foreign direct investment, are separate

16

responsibilities and are made with little attention to their implications for foreign direct investment.

Such an evolution in policymaking is understandable. Many policies, particularly in the tax area, were formulated before multinational enterprises became important to U.S. economic and foreign policy. Later, when multinationals grew to be a potent force, government policy usually focused on dealing with short-term crises—political relations with an expropriating country, a balance-of-payments deficit, domestic economic decline—rather than the long-term, structural issues regarding foreign direct investment. Even today, many policymakers (including those engaged in international economic policy, let alone the majority, whose orientation is primarily domestic) have little awareness of the foreign investment impact of their policies.

The new importance of the activities of these firms (as demonstrated in chapter one), however, brings into question the appropriateness of existing policies. It also suggests the need to develop an overall policy toward multinational enterprises and the need to coordinate that policy with other U.S. economic and foreign policies. The sharp increase in the flow of direct investment into the United States by foreign-based multinational enterprises (toward which U.S. policies are also largely ad hoc) adds to the importance of assessing U.S. policy.

The Policy Prescriptions of Traditional Analysis

Classical international investment theory suggests that the United States, as a home country, could pursue one of two basically different goals. One is to *maximize global economic welfare*. This is the focus of most economic analysis, which avoids explicit treatment of distributional issues, either among or within countries.

Adoption of a global welfare goal, however, does not determine the specific nature of policy. If all markets were perfectly competitive and no externalities existed, the government's role would be abstention from interference with foreign direct investment. But because much investment is carried on by firms in oligopolistic industries, the market is not perfectly competitive. Further distortions are caused by market interventions by other home and host governments. In addition, important externalities— such as pollution and international politics—are often related to such investments. Therefore, maximizing the contribution of foreign direct investment to global economic welfare may require active national policies on a wide range of specific issues.

Second, the United States could seek to *maximize its national economic welfare.*[1] This could require the application of optimum capital controls, either taxes or quantitative limits on foreign direct investment. (Limits could apply to not only capital but technology and other factor flows, as well.) Such controls would be primarily for limiting the level of investment to increase the returns from each unit. Controls might also be used to alter the industry composition of investment. In practice, there are two constraints on the use of optimum capital controls: the user must be large enough to significantly affect the rate of return on its overseas investments, and offsetting retaliation must be avoided or at least limited.[2]

The United States might be able to overcome both constraints. Though its previous near-monopoly position as a home country for multinational enterprises is eroding, the United States still has a far greater share of foreign investment than any other country. In addition, foreign retaliation is less likely than retaliation against efforts to install an optimum tariff on imports of goods. Indeed, some countries seek to reduce incoming direct investment and might welcome U.S. limitations. At a minimum, the schizophrenic attitude with which most host countries view U.S. investment limits the likelihood of their reacting sharply, as was indeed the case when the United States limited capital exports by American-based firms from 1965 to 1974 for balance-of-payments purposes. Finally, no international rules or institutions authorize retaliation to new barriers to foreign direct investment similar to those authorized by the General Agreement on Tariffs and Trade regarding new barriers to international trade.

1. Some analysts argue that the national welfare of the world's dominant economic power is maximized by a free international economic system, because the dominant power is best able to exploit its opportunities. They reject the distinction between national and global welfare, at least for the United States at the present time and Britain in the nineteenth century. An important empirical question is whether the United States does exercise dominant world economic power in any meaningful sense.

2. Host countries, recognizing that the United States or a small group of home countries possess such power, recommended (through the United Nations Group of Eminent Persons, whose conclusions they dominate) "that home countries do not hamper the process of transfer by multinational corporations of the production of labor-intensive and low-skill products to developing countries, and that they protect the domestic work force displaced by this transfer, through adjustment assistance measures." United Nations, *The Impact of Multinational Corporations on the Development Process and on International Relations,* ST/ESA/6 (May 1974), p. 75.

There are several ways that unrestricted foreign direct investment could lower the national welfare of the United States and thus call for optimum capital controls. Traditional economic analysis focuses on comparative rates of return on alternative investment opportunities; it thus regards the higher pretax rates on foreign (than on domestic) investment as evidence that foreign investment promotes world welfare. From the national standpoint of the home country, however, the comparison should be made between domestic earnings and foreign earnings *after the payment of foreign taxes,* which represents the return on the investment to the home country.[3] Thus some analysts recommend that foreign earnings be denied the foreign tax credit.[4]

In addition, an individual firm contemplating an investment abroad may ignore the impact of its activity on the return on other U.S. foreign direct investment.[5] When the outstanding stock is already quite large, as is the case for the United States, the reduction in income of other investors could offset the return on the new investments.[6] This consideration is most

3. Considerable amounts of foreign direct investment by U.S.-based firms might, on this criterion, still be viewed as promoting the national interest of the United States. Glenn P. Jenkins and Brian D. Wright, "Taxation of Income of Multinational Corporations: The Case of the United States Petroleum Industry," *The Review of Economics and Statistics,* vol. 57 (February 1975), p. 10, conclude that "although the U.S. petroleum corporations paid no U.S. tax on their foreign income over the years 1969 to 1972 the rate of return net of foreign taxes from their foreign investments compares favorably with the gross rate of return on domestic corporate investment." Transfer pricing and tax considerations would have to be taken into account, however, before one could conclude that these rates of return were fully comparable.

4. Murray C. Kemp, "Foreign Investment and the National Advantage," *Economic Record,* vol. 38 (March 1962), p. 62; Paul B. Simpson, "Foreign Investment and the National Economic Advantage: A Theoretical Analysis," in Raymond F. Mikesell, ed., *U.S. Private and Government Investment Abroad* (University of Oregon Books, 1962), p. 504; Mordechai E. Kreinen, "Direct Foreign Investments and the American Interest," *Economia Internazionale,* vol. 20 (August 1967), p. 507; and J. Carter Murphy, "International Investment and the National Interest," *Southern Economic Journal,* vol. 27 (July 1960), pp. 11–17.

5. A. E. Jasay, "The Social Choice Between Home and Overseas Investment," *Economic Journal,* vol. 70 (March 1960), p. 107; Kemp, "Foreign Investment and the National Advantage," p. 56.

6. In 1973, the book value of foreign direct investment by U.S.-based firms rose by about $12.9 billion. Given a 10 percent return on those investments in their first year—a generous assumption—they produced earnings of about $1.3 billion. The book value outstanding at the end of 1972 was $94.3 billion, on which earnings in 1972 were $11.5 billion. Thus, if the new investments reduced the rate of return on the outstanding stock by 12 percent, they would adversely affect overall earnings. *Survey of Current Business,* vol. 54 (August 1974), p. 16.

relevant for perfectly competitive industries; it is less applicable to the oligopolistic industries that characterize much of foreign direct investment.

A third consideration of national interest is that foreign investments (direct or portfolio) are subject to default, confiscation, repudiation, or other forms of host-country manipulation which, unlike domestic defaults or bankruptcies, can negate the whole worth of the investment from the standpoint of the home country.[7] This risk alone does not appear insignificant; slightly more than $2 billion of U.S. foreign direct investment has been so lost during the entire postwar period.

Finally, an important element in traditional analysis is the impact of foreign direct investment on the terms of trade of the home country. For example, in this view, the major benefit that Great Britain derived from its heavy foreign investment in the years before 1914 is the development of cheap sources of raw materials and the railroads to transport them efficiently.[8] The development of other foreign factors of production, including labor, can have similar effects. But foreign investment can lead to reduced export prices for the home country if it generates new competition for home-country production.[9] Hence the net impact of foreign direct investment on the home country's terms of trade is positive in some cases and negative in others.

Traditional economics does point to certain clear benefits to the home country from foreign direct investment. Exports of capital increase the returns on capital invested at home.[10] By increasing foreign incomes, they

7. This point was raised originally by J. M. Keynes, "Foreign Investment and the National Advantage," *The Nation and the Atheneum,* vol. 35 (August 9, 1924), p. 586.

8. See Alexander K. Cairncross, *Home and Foreign Investment 1870–1913* (Cambridge: Cambridge University Press, 1953).

9. A home country can, in theory, cope with unfavorable effects of foreign direct investment on its terms of trade by placing an optimum tariff on the trade flows, themselves. Sophisticated analyses of foreign direct investment by traditional economists integrate the concepts of optimum tariffs and optimum capital controls in arriving at an overall optimizing foreign economic policy for an individual country. See Murray C. Kemp, "The Gain from International Trade and Investment: A Neo-Heckscher-Ohlin Approach," *American Economic Review,* vol. 56 (September 1966), pp. 788–809; Ronald W. Jones, "International Capital Movements and the Theory of Tariffs and Trade," *Quarterly Journal of Economics,* vol. 81 (February 1967), pp. 1–38; Franz Gehrels, "Optimal Restrictions on Foreign Trade and Investment," *American Economic Review,* vol. 61 (March 1971), pp. 147–59.

10. Jasay, "The Social Choice Between Home and Overseas Investment," p. 112,

improve the demand for home-country exports. In addition, they may raise the level of total world savings and investment and, hence, the future level of sustainable consumption.[11]

There are many shortcomings in the traditional approach. Most analyses assume, explicitly or implicitly: perfect competition, complete knowledge of foreign and domestic investment opportunities, no externalities, no foreign retaliation, perfect substitutability between domestic and foreign investments, full employment (or at least no concern about transitional adjustment problems), and balance-of-payments equilibrium. Yet many of these conditions are not met in the real world. Once they are abandoned, "it is impossible to say with certainty whether . . . investing abroad is preferable to investing at home. . . . Much depends on the industries and the conditions in which the investment takes place."[12]

The most important shortcoming is the static nature of traditional analysis. Yet multinational enterprises argue that merely maintaining static foreign direct investment would reduce the rate of return over time and, thus, weaken their global competitive position. On the other hand, the dynamic effects of foreign direct investment, many argue, have been unfavorable to the home country. This is because the "developmental benefits of capital accumulation," including technological progress and increases in productivity, accrue to the host country.[13] The argument takes contemporary form in the charge by the AFL-CIO that foreign direct investment is eroding the industrial bases of the American economy.

Given the conflicting effects, traditional, general equilibrium eco-

---

regards the impact of foreign direct investment on the domestic rate of return as the most important test from the standpoint of the home country. Having earlier concluded that any home country is likely to get "too much foreign and too little domestic investment" in terms of the impact on overall rates of foreign return, because of the effect on intramarginal investments, he balances his final judgment with a view that foreign investment may be too small to optimize the return on domestic investment.

11. Takashi Negishi, "Foreign Investment and the Long-Run National Advantage," *Economic Record*, vol. 41 (December 1965), pp. 628–32.

12. Thomas Balogh and Paul B. Streeten, "Domestic Versus Foreign Investment," *Oxford University Institute of Statistics Bulletin*, vol. 22 (August 1960), p. 223.

13. Marvin Frankel, "Home Versus Foreign Investment: A Case Against Capital Export," *Kyklos*, vol. 18, fasc. 3 (1965), pp. 411–33. He estimates that this factor alone assures a negative impact of foreign direct investment on the home country unless its yield is at least 250 percent of the available return on domestic investment.

nomics cannot provide guidance in finding policies which would maximize the gain from foreign direct investment. As Jasay concluded in
1960:

A conflict between private and social investment optima is entirely possible;
what appears impossible is to *establish the presumption of a general bias* for
private overseas investment to be either too large or too small. Nor can therefore a general recommendation be made for public policy in this regard.[14]

Present Policy

The deficiencies in traditional analysis of international investment help
explain why home countries such as the United States have been reluctant
to accept its policy prescriptions without qualification. The alternative is
not, however, another logically coherent theory, but rather an eclectic,
ad hoc approach. Sometimes the goal may be global or national welfare,
as measured by a traditional analyst; but often the goal lies outside the
classical realm, for example promoting domestic employment, maintaining the balance of payments, or improving access to raw materials. In
some instances, the conclusion is that foreign investment should be encouraged; in others, the opposite prescription is reached. Because ad hoc
analyses are often the rationalizations for current policies, a review of
their effect on international investment follows.

Present U.S. policy deals directly with foreign direct investment in three
areas: taxation of foreign income, insurance against noncommercial risks
faced by foreign direct investment in particular countries, and expropriation. In addition, capital outflows to finance foreign direct investment were
limited from 1965 until early 1974 by quantitative controls aimed at
strengthening the U.S. international financial position.

Beyond these specific measures, a number of general U.S. policies affect foreign direct investment by U.S.-based firms. Antitrust policy extends to at least some of their foreign operations. The National Labor
Relations Act, which provides much of the framework for labor-management negotiations, covers foreign direct investment as well as domestic
investment. Several aspects of trade policy directly affect foreign direct
investment. The international monetary policy of the United States has
had several important effects on multinational enterprises. In a broad

14. "The Social Choice Between Home and Overseas Investment," p. 113.

sense, all national policies—growth policy, industrial policy, manpower policy, the level and structure of taxation, indeed all efforts to maintain political and social stability—have an impact on investment decisions.[15]

In addition, the United States is a participant in several international agreements that affect foreign direct investment: the articles of agreement of the International Monetary Fund (IMF), the code of liberalization of capital movements of the Organisation for Economic Co-operation and Development (OECD), and the International Center for the Settlement of Investment Disputes (ICSID) managed by the World Bank. Further-more, the United States has in recent years participated in a series of inter-national discussions aimed at forging new arrangements regarding multi-national enterprises. The most important of these is the Committee on International Investment and Multinational Enterprises (CIME) estab-lished in the OECD, which in mid-1976 promulgated guidelines for multinational enterprises, a decision on national treatment, and a decision on international investment incentives and disincentives. None of these international efforts, however, has significantly affected U.S. policy to-ward foreign direct investment.

American *taxation* of foreign direct investment has two main features: (1) the foreign tax credit through which income, withholding, and certain other taxes paid to foreign central governments are credited against U.S. tax liabilities; and (2) tax deferral, through which no U.S. tax is levied on the income of subsidiaries incorporated in other countries until that in-come is repatriated. Other features of the U.S. tax code that have an impor-tant impact on foreign direct investment are the investment tax credit and the provision for domestic international sales corporations, both of which reduce effective tax rates on domestic investment. (President Carter has proposed the elimination of both tax deferral and the domestic interna-tional sales corporations.)

The basic tax laws covering foreign income were adopted without any systematic reference to home-country policy toward foreign direct invest-ment. These provisions clearly did not aim at maximizing U.S. national

15. Structural differences among countries' wage rates or taxation are generally reflected in the exchange-rate relations among their currencies, especially with to-day's highly flexible exchange rates. To be sure, different industries can be affected differently by a combination of tax structures and offsetting exchange-rate moves. And changes in historical patterns can produce new disequilibria, which may take time to offset. But structural differences among economies should not have a major impact on foreign direct investment.

welfare. This would have called for full taxation of foreign income without any credit against taxes paid abroad. Indeed, giving credit for foreign taxes suggests that the economic rationale was promotion of world welfare by avoiding tax distortions on the global allocation of capital.

Tax deferral, however, is counter to both national and global welfare. Its apparent aim was to preclude disadvantage for American-based companies competing with local firms (or multinationals based elsewhere, since all other home countries practice deferral or exemption). The analysis in chapter six shows, however, that the overall U.S. tax system no longer provides any net incentive to invest abroad rather than at home. Current policy in this key area is roughly neutral toward foreign direct investment, the proinvestment tilt of the past having declined sharply since the early 1960s.

The postwar U.S. programs of *investment insurance and guarantees* for foreign direct investment sought to promote development in certain foreign countries. Several minor provisions of the tax code also had such a purpose, but the insurance program was the major policy instrument for implementing a cardinal tenet of postwar U.S. foreign policy: that American foreign direct investment could spur economic development around the world and was, thus, a major component of U.S. foreign assistance. The purpose of the program was to insure foreign direct investment against some of the noncommercial risks of investing in the countries covered: the threat of war, expropriation, and currency nonconvertibility. It began as a component of the Marshall Plan, to induce U.S. investment in Western Europe.[16] Since 1959, however, it has been limited to the developing countries. Until 1971, the insurance and guarantees were administered by the successive U.S. foreign aid agencies, as part of overall assistance policy.

Since 1971, the program has been managed by the Overseas Private Investment Corporation (OPIC), an independent government corporation.[17] Congress has increasingly required OPIC to focus on financial rather than developmental principles. In practice, OPIC's emphasis has shifted from the development of poorer countries and support for multinationals toward protecting other short-run U.S. economic interests,

16. The early history is traced in Marina von N. Whitman, *The United States Investment Guaranty Program and Private Foreign Investment,* Princeton Studies in International Finance, no. 9 (Princeton University, 1959).

17. A good survey of recent OPIC activities is *The Overseas Private Investment Corporation: A Critical Analysis,* prepared by the Congressional Research Service for the House Committee on Foreign Affairs (Government Printing Office, 1973).

Table 2-1. *Share of Overseas Private Investment Corporation (OPIC) Insurance Coverage in Third and Fourth Worlds, November 1973 and February 1976*

Percentage

Insurance program[a]	Third World[b]		Fourth World[c]	
	November 1973	*February 1976*	*November 1973*	*February 1976*
Inconvertibility	56.9	73.0	43.1	27.0
Expropriation	51.5	55.4	48.5	44.6
War risk	49.4	55.1	50.6	44.9
Total	51.6	58.4	48.4	41.6

Source: Author calculations, based on OPIC data obtained through private communication.
a. Current (as opposed to contingent or maximum) coverage.
b. All of South America except Bolivia and Paraguay; all of East Asia; Yugoslavia, Portugal, Greece, Turkey, Iran, and Israel.
c. All of Africa, South Asia, Central America, and the Caribbean.

particularly jobs and the balance of payments. Indeed, each corporate application for OPIC coverage must estimate the "U.S. effects" of the proposed investment, and OPIC has turned down requests because an adverse impact on U.S. employment or the trade balance seemed likely.

In addition, as the incidence of foreign expropriations rose, OPIC insurance fees increased and its terms hardened. It has financed few extractive investments in recent years, both because fewer projects have been undertaken by American-based multinationals and because OPIC has reduced the share of such ventures in its portfolio because of the risk. And the proportion of its insurance directed to the poorest countries has declined in recent years (see table 2-1).

The ostensible goal of OPIC insurance is global welfare, attained by offsetting some of the peculiar noneconomic risks that discourage foreign direct investment. Its record of financial self-sufficiency suggests that it does not represent a net subsidy to U.S.-based firms. In recent years, however, its goals have become increasingly nontraditional (notably, U.S. employment), and it may no longer equate the conditions of domestic and foreign investment. It has certainly become less attractive, in general, to the multinational enterprises. Its primary goal has never been to maximize the national economic welfare of the United States.

The third major policy explicitly directed at foreign direct investment relates to *expropriation* without fair, prompt, and adequate compensation. The United States traditionally has taken a dim view of such actions, on two grounds: that defense of U.S. nationals in their activities abroad (as tourists, missionaries, or investors) was a responsibility of U.S. foreign policy; and that "arbitrary" foreign seizure of private U.S. property retards the free flow of international investment. American multinationals occasionally sought such retaliation in earlier periods but have seldom done so in recent years; their earlier fear that any single expropriation would trigger additional expropriations was replaced by the fear that U.S. retaliation would trigger more expropriations.[18]

In 1962, Congress added the Hickenlooper amendment to the Foreign Assistance Act. The amendment required the United States to automatically cease all bilateral aid to any country that expropriated private U.S. property without fair compensation or without taking the appropriate steps. In 1972, through the Gonzalez amendment, Congress applied the same principle to U.S. support for soft loans from the Inter-American Development Bank, the allocation of import quotas for sugar, and all U.S. contributions to the international lending institutions (World Bank, International Development Association, Inter-American Development Bank, Asian Development Bank).

In practice, however, the principle of automatic retaliation has been administered quite flexibly. The Hickenlooper amendment was applied only once, and the Gonzalez amendment has never been formally applied, though both have been used as levers to achieve U.S. objectives in a few investment disputes. In 1973, the Hickenlooper amendment lost much of its force when automaticity was eliminated by providing for a presidential waiver of its aid cut-off. A similar change was implicitly added to the Gonzalez amendment. And in 1974, when Congress extended the possible scope of sanctions against expropriation, the President was free to designate countries for preferences, even if they violated sanctions against appropriation, if he should determine "that such designation will be in the national economic interest" (88 Stat. 2067–68).

The fourth area in which the United States directly addresses foreign direct investment is *balance-of-payments* policy. From February 1965 through January 1974, first (through 1967) on a voluntary basis and then

18. A useful summary of U.S. policy in that area, and its application in one major case, is in Jessica Pernitz Einhorn, *Expropriation Politics* (Lexington Books, 1974). The history of the Hickenlooper and Gonzalez amendments and U.S. corporate attitudes is traced in Charles H. Lipson, "Corporate Preferences and Public Policies: Foreign Aid Sanctions and Investment Protection," *World Politics,* vol. 28 (April 1976), pp. 396–421.

on a mandatory basis, the amount of capital that U.S.-based multinational enterprises could export from the United States was limited to reduce the deficit in the U.S. balance of payments. The program did not limit foreign plant and equipment expenditures by American-based firms but only the ways in which such investment could be financed.[19] The program was administered by the Office of Foreign Direct Investment (OFDI) within the Department of Commerce.

The controls were instituted in an effort to offset the effects on the U.S. balance of payments of the growing overvaluation of the dollar.[20] The overvaluation itself provided an increasing incentive for U.S.-based firms to invest abroad rather than in the United States, because of the improving competitive position of other countries. Thus the controls were in reality a second-best (or third-best) policy, adopted to restore the status quo ante rather than to achieve any positive goal. Indeed, the controls were removed soon after the second devaluation of the dollar and the widespread adoption of flexible exchange rates.

Even so, the controls sparked conflict between the United States and several host countries (notably Canada, Australia, and France), which recognized that the U.S. action threatened to deprive them of some of the benefits (capital inflows and reinvested earnings) of foreign direct investment. Hence they became concerned about the effects of the U.S. action on their balance-of-payments positions and capital markets. And they worried politically about the extraterritorial reach of U.S. policy implied by its effort to dictate to subsidiaries (including those in which U.S. par-

19. Some observers argue that foreign direct investment was thus favored over foreign portfolio and bank lending, which were checked by the interest equalization tax and the Federal Reserve Board's voluntary foreign credit restraint program. In practice, however, the commercial banks, and to a lesser extent, the investment banks, circumvented the controls by operating in the Eurobond and Eurocurrency markets.

20. The *net* reduction in the U.S. balance-of-payments deficit probably fell far short of the *gross* shift of corporate financing to foreign capital markets, because of offsetting capital flows induced by the higher interest rates abroad triggered by the increase in foreign borrowing by U.S. firms. See Martin F. J. Prachowny, *A Structural Model of the U.S. Balance of Payments* (Amsterdam: North Holland, 1969), and David Morawetz, "The Effect of Financial Capital Flows and Transfers on the U.S. Balance of Payments Current Account," *Journal of International Economics,* vol. 1 (November 1971), pp. 426–27. For a contrary view, see Peter H. Lindert, "The Payments Impact of Foreign Investment Controls," *Journal of Finance,* vol. 26 (December 1971), pp. 1083–99.

ents were minority owners) how they should divide their earnings between reinvestment and repatriation to the United States.[21]

In addition to these policies aimed directly at foreign direct investment, there have been a series of attempts by the U.S. government throughout the postwar period to control specific activities of the foreign subsidiaries of U.S.-based firms to promote U.S. foreign policy or internal economic objectives. In implementing its policy of controlling exports to the communist countries, the United States restricted sales of foreign subsidiaries through its leverage over their U.S. parents. Some of these restrictions were coordinated through the coordinating committee of NATO (COCOM), but several of the U.S. efforts triggered clashes with host countries. In recent years, this policy has been attempted infrequently (and carried through even more infrequently)[22] because of the general easing of U.S. trade policy toward the communist countries and the growing ability of host countries to reject U.S. efforts to control firms incorporated in their territories.

The United States has also on occasion tried to apply its antitrust policies and securities disclosure policies in other countries.[23] Several U.S. efforts to apply its antitrust law have triggered conflicts with other countries, particularly in Canada and Western Europe. In one recent case, the Federal Trade Commission argued that competition in the domestic U.S. photocopier market could be increased if Xerox Corporation spun off its European and Japanese subsidiaries, since Xerox's own subsidiaries were

21. In calculating net capital outflows, the OFDI included repatriated earnings as well as gross outflows; otherwise, a firm could simply cut the former to offset the required cutback in the latter. But a problem of extraterritoriality was thus raised. Major controversy was avoided, however, for three reasons. Some large host countries had been urging the United States to lessen its balance-of-payments deficits, preferably by limiting capital outflows; the international capital markets became the main source of new financing, making it impossible to discover the geographical sources of the borrowed money; and other adjustments in the capital account limited the effects on the balance-of-payments positions of both the United States and the host countries.

22. During 1974, the United States sought to block sales to Cuba of locomotives from Argentina and trucks from Canada manufactured by subsidiaries of U.S.-based multinational enterprises. In both instances, the United States backed down when it became clear the countries intended to proceed.

23. For a complete typology of the securities issue see Paul M. Goldberg and Charles P. Kindleberger, "Toward a GATT for Investment: A Proposal for Supervision of the International Corporation," *Law and Policy in International Business,* vol. 2 (Summer 1970), pp. 313–17.

potential competitors in the U.S. market. No spin-offs were required in the consent decree ending the case, however. At the same time, domestic antitrust policy has probably increased the level of foreign direct investment by U.S.-based firms and brought on the emergence of conglomerates in the 1960s, by precluding both further market expansion by U.S. firms and takeovers of competitors in their own industries.

The National Labor Relations Act, along with several other pieces of legislation, governs labor-management relations in the United States by requiring management to negotiate with legally constituted labor unions and to provide them with adequate data as a basis for such negotiations. The act applies in principle to international as well as domestic operations. However, the several efforts by labor to use it to defend its interests vis-à-vis the multinational enterprises (to restrain foreign direct investment) have failed totally (see chapter four). Labor law has had no impact thus far on foreign direct investment.

The international monetary policy of the United States can have an important effect on foreign direct investment. In the late 1960s, the United States permitted the dollar to become overvalued because it viewed devaluation as disruptive both to the functioning of the international monetary system and its leadership of the noncommunist world. The overvaluation heightened the incentive for U.S.-based multinational enterprises to invest abroad rather than in the United States (and for foreign-based multinational enterprises to invest at home, or in third countries, rather than in the United States). Subsequent devaluations of the dollar and adoption of flexible exchange rates restored equilibrium in national competitive positions.

Facets of U.S. trade policy also affect foreign direct investment. Its generally liberal treatment of imports permits the foreign affiliates of U.S.-based firms to sell to the U.S. market, though its high effective tariffs and nontariff barriers discourage such activities in a few industries (including some processed raw materials, textiles, and benzenoid chemicals). Its exemption from duties of U.S.-made components of imports, in sections 806.30 and 807 of the Tariff Schedule, facilitates the assembly of finished products abroad. On the other hand, the steady U.S. effort to negotiate reductions in the trade barriers of other countries has reduced the incentive for investing behind tariff and nontariff walls.

Several provisions of the Trade Act of 1974 addressed problems raised by multinational enterprise. The program of trade adjustment assistance, inaugurated in the Trade Expansion Act of 1962 to assist workers displaced by imports to adjust into new endeavors, was extended to provide for assistance to communities where "the transfer of firms or subdivisions of firms located in such area to foreign countries have contributed importantly" to job layoffs.[24] A new section of the law requests that "firms relocating in foreign countries" provide at least sixty days' advance notice to their workers and to the Secretary of Labor and Secretary of Commerce, make maximum use of adjustment assistance, offer new jobs to employees "who are totally or partially separated as a result of the move," and "assist in relocating employees to other locations in the United States where employment opportunities exist."[25]

In addition to its national policy measures, there are international measures that the United States has agreed to. The Articles of Agreement of the International Monetary Fund, developed in Bretton Woods in 1944–45, permit individual countries to control capital movements (in contradistinction to current account transactions, which could be checked only when the international community agreed that such checks were needed for balance-of-payments reasons). The architects of the Bretton Woods Agreements were thinking primarily of portfolio investment, not multinational enterprises. By the middle 1950s, the United States sought international support for freeing the flow of foreign direct investment. The Organisation for European Economic Co-operation adopted a code of liberalization of capital movements, which was incorporated in the OECD with its creation in 1960.[26] The United States launched a further effort in the OECD in 1973 to assure "national treatment" for direct investors in all member countries and to limit the use of disincentives to such investment maintained by member countries. The OECD countries agreed in 1976 to notify each other of deviations from the newly agreed norms and new consultative procedures. Simultaneously, the United States has taken a largely skeptical view of the efforts by the United Nations, beginning in 1973 with the appointment of its Group of Eminent Persons, to implement mandatory international checks on the activities of multinational enterprises without parallel agreements on the policies of governments toward foreign direct investment.

24. 88 Stat. 2035–36.
25. 88 Stat. 2041.
26. The history is in Henry G. Aubrey, *Atlantic Economic Cooperation: The Case of the OECD* (Praeger, 1967), pp. 64–65 and 109–10.

In the OECD negotiations of 1973–76, the United States also sought checks on certain host-country incentives, particularly tax concessions, to foreign direct investment. The agreement is quite weak, however; for example, incentives in the guise of regional policies, not aimed explicitly at foreign direct investment, are exempt. So U.S. policy in international forums still largely supports foreign direct investment and freedom of action for multinational enterprises, unlike its retrenchment in taxation, OPIC insurance, and trade policy. Indeed, the U.S. opposition to the proposals of the Group of Eminent Persons, for example, is couched in terms of "assuring the rights of multinational corporations."[27]

This review of U.S. policy points to several conclusions. First, there is no coordinated overall program. Each individual measure affecting foreign direct investment, either directly or indirectly, has developed largely in a separate functional area, in response to problems in that area at a particular point in time. The government is not organized to coordinate the separate policies, and each agency is largely autonomous in managing the impact on foreign direct investment of policies within its area of responsibility.

Second, these individual policies display a common theme: support of foreign direct investment by U.S.-based multinational enterprises, both by encouraging the investment itself and by defending the firms against adverse treatment in host countries. The traditional government attitude is that there is a high coincidence between the interests of the multinational enterprises and the country as a whole.

In practice, the specific policy measures adopted toward foreign direct investment point toward different underlying objectives. Some seek to promote world welfare. Some seek to promote nontraditional objectives of the United States. Views vary as to the motives underlying the proinvestment U.S. approach. Interestingly, there has been no effort to apply optimum capital controls to promote the national economic welfare.

Third, in a number of areas the proinvestment tilt is being reduced. Doubts about the identity of interests between the firms and the country are increasingly translated into law. The changes implemented so far limit support to the firms, rather than actually restrict their activities.

27. Department of State, "The Views of the United States Government Concerning the Report of the Group of Eminent Persons on The Impact of Multinational Corporations on the Development Process and on International Relations" (November 6, 1974; processed), p. 3.

The Policies of Other Home Countries

Other home countries have the same policy options as does the United States. They can seek to promote global welfare, their national welfare, or more immediate goals through either supporting or restricting foreign direct investment. With the exception of Japan, other home countries have been no more coherent than the United States in formulating such policies. As in the case of the United States, some of their macroeconomic policies, particularly regarding exchange rates, have had a major impact on the level of their foreign direct investment.

Eleven home countries accounted for over 95 percent of the stock of all foreign direct investment by market economies in 1971; the United States alone accounted for 52 percent (see table 1-5). The United Kingdom, the original leader in this area, still is the second largest home country by a wide margin (14.5 percent, compared to 5.8 percent for France).[28] The most rapid growth is exhibited by Germany and Japan. Germany increased its share of the world stock of foreign direct investment from 2.8 percent in 1967 to 4.4 percent in 1971, and Japan more than doubled its share from 1.3 percent to 2.7 percent during the same period. Indeed, from 1967 to 1971, Japanese and German foreign direct investment grew at average annual rates of 28.3 percent and 22.8 percent, respectively, compared to U.S. and U.K. rates of 9.2 percent and 6.5 percent, respectively. Among firms based in various countries, there are important differences in the structure as well as the magnitude of foreign direct investment. For example, about 60 percent of the foreign affiliates of U.S.-based multinationals are wholly owned by the parent, compared to under 30 percent of the affiliates of Japanese-based parents.[29]

The importance of foreign direct investment to a home (or host) country should be judged in comparison to the size of the country, not in absolute terms. Switzerland had over $1,000 foreign direct investment per capita, more by far than any other country in 1971 (see table 1-5). Sweden was second ($425), slightly ahead of the United States and the

28. The U.K. case is analyzed by John H. Dunning, "The Costs and Benefits of Foreign Direct Investment to the Investing Country," in Dunning, ed., *Studies in International Investment* (London: Allen and Unwin, 1970).

29. Richard D. Robinson, "From Multinational Corporation to World Government?" in C. G. Alexandrides, ed., *International Business System Perspectives* (Georgia State University, School of Business Administration, 1973), p. 285.

United Kingdom ($415 and $422, respectively). Canada, the Netherlands, and Belgium had around $300; France, $186; Germany, $119; and Italy and Japan, around $50.

There is some similarity between this measure of openness and openness in terms of international trade. Switzerland, Sweden, the United Kingdom, Canada, and the Low Countries are relatively open on both counts, while France and Japan are relatively closed. However, there are several notable exceptions: the United States is far more open in terms of international investment than international trade, while Germany and Italy are much more trade-oriented. In 1971, the international production of U.S.-based firms was almost four times larger than U.S. exports, whereas international production by firms based in Germany, Italy, and Japan were only about 40 percent of the exports of those countries (see table 2-2).

The three countries (the United States, the United Kingdom, and Switzerland) which loom largest by far, both in absolute terms and relative to their national exports, are also the three whose exchange rates were demonstrably overvalued, in terms of the international competitive positions of their economies, throughout much of the era of fixed exchange rates.[30] The two countries whose foreign production ranged farthest beneath their exports in 1971, Germany and Japan, had the most demonstrably undervalued exchange rates during the 1960s, the boom period for foreign direct investment.[31] Hence there is a priori evidence that exchange rates affect trade and investment patterns. The acceleration of foreign direct invest-

30. The British pound may have been overvalued before World War I; it was clearly overvalued during 1925–31, as well as in most of the postwar period. Some observers argue that the dollar was overvalued as early as 1960; the overvaluation grew rapidly from 1965 to 1971. For both countries, the international roles of their currencies provided financing for the resulting balance-of-payments deficits and enabled them—indeed, induced them—to maintain overvalued exchange rates. Even when their balance-of-payments deficits could be reconciled with international financial equilibrium, the international competitive position of their domestic production eroded and foreign direct investment grew. Switzerland, the only other country whose foreign production exceeded its exports, also experienced steady capital inflows over time and hence developed an exchange rate overvalued in terms of the international competitive position of its economy. For a complete analysis of these international monetary phenomena see C. Fred Bergsten, *The Dilemmas of the Dollar: The Economics and Politics of United States International Monetary Policy* (New York University Press, 1975).

31. Italy, whose foreign production was also less than 50 percent of its exports, also maintained what some observers maintain was an undervalued exchange rate.

Table 2-2. *Exports of Major Home Countries Compared to Estimated Foreign Production of the Multinationals Based in Each, 1971*

		Estimated foreign production	
Home country	Exports in millions of dollars	In millions of dollars[a]	As percentage of exports
United States	43,492	172,000	395.5
Switzerland	5,728	13,500	235.7
United Kingdom	22,367	48,000	214.6
France	20,420	19,100	93.5
Sweden	7,465	6,900	92.4
Canada	17,582	11,900	67.7
Belgium	12,392	6,500	52.4
Netherlands	13,927	7,200	51.7
Italy	15,111	6,700	44.3
Japan	24,019	9,000	37.5
Germany	39,040	14,600	37.4

Source: UN, *Multinational Corporations in World Development*, ST/ECA/190 (1973), p. 159.
a. Estimated foreign production equals the book value of foreign direct investment multiplied by the factor 2. The factor was derived as follows: the ratio of foreign sales to book value of foreign direct investment was estimated from 1970 U.S. data on gross sales of majority-owned foreign affiliates and book value of U.S. foreign direct investment. Gross sales of majority-owned foreign affiliates (approximately $157 billion) includes transactions between foreign affiliates and parent corporations (approximately $20.3 billion) and interforeign affiliate sales (approximately $28.1 billion), which together account for about 30 percent of gross foreign affiliate sales. The book value of U.S. foreign direct investment in 1970 amounted to $78.1 billion. The resulting ratio of gross sales to book value is 2:1.

ment by multinational enterprises based in Germany and Japan since the realignment of exchange rates beginning in 1971, and the sharp increase in the role of the United States as a host country, adds credence to this observation.[32]

The international monetary policies of home countries thus appear to have an important bearing on their patterns of foreign direct investment. In addition, all home countries must decide how to tax the income on foreign direct investment; most have provisions similar to those of the United States for crediting taxes paid abroad against tax liabilities at home. Germany exempts income from countries with whom it has tax treaties and has a tax-sparing credit for income from developing countries. France exempts 95 percent of all foreign income from any taxation in

32. Some analysts argue that foreign direct investment caused the overvaluation of the dollar and sterling. Aside from the inherent impossibility of attributing such causality to any single component of a country's balance of payments, it is the maintenance of disequilibrium exchange rates that generates such changes. If parity changes had kept pace with the exchange-rate effects of foreign direct investment that were motivated by factors other than competitive relations among countries, they would have avoided the distortion of investment patterns.

Table 2-3. *Foreign Direct Investments Insured by Guarantee Agencies of Home Countries, 1971–73*[a]
Millions of dollars

Home country	1971	1972	1973
Australia	4.5	2.8	4.4
Austria	n.a.	13.6	2.6
Belgium	...	0.2	0.5
Canada	3.6	3.6	15.0
Denmark	4.3	1.4	3.3
Germany	72.4	41.3	80.7
Japan	90.0	89.2	167.0
Netherlands	8.2	1.0	4.2
New Zealand	...	...	0.2
Norway	0.3	0.5	0.5
Switzerland	10.3	4.3	n.a.
United Kingdom	...	...	12.9
United States	239.2	223.6	215.8

Source: OECD, *Development Co-operation, 1974 Review* (Paris: OECD, November 1974), p. 143.
n.a. Not available.
a. Data from France's program are not available. Multinationals in Sweden have not used Sweden's insurance program because of its strict eligibility requirements.

France. A couple of small home countries exempt all foreign income from domestic taxes, while others deduct foreign income taxes from taxable income rather than credit them against domestic taxes.[33]

Fifteen home countries also insure and guarantee some foreign direct investment by their firms in developing countries (see table 2-3). Most programs focus on the developmental effects of proposed investments in the host countries. A few, including Australia's, seek to promote the type of investment that meets host-country preferences by offering premium rates for joint ventures. However, several of the programs (including the Japanese and Australian) are not limited to covering investments in developing countries.

In addition, a number of the programs (including France's) explicitly link the extension of insurance to an expansion of home-country exports. The Japanese program originally was limited to investments that would help the balance of payments.[34] Several (including the Canadian, Jap-

33. For a useful compilation see Price Waterhouse, *Corporate Taxes in 80 Countries* (New York: Price Waterhouse, January 1975). An excellent comparative analysis of European practices is Bernard Snoy, *Taxes on Direct Investment Income in the EEC: A Legal and Economic Analysis* (Praeger, 1975).
34. OECD, *Liberalisation of International Capital Movements: Japan* (Paris: OECD, 1968), p. 16.

36 American Multinationals and American Interests

anese, and British) are managed by the export promotion agencies of their governments. The Japanese scheme, in addition, applies to portfolio investment in non-Japanese companies if the investment is used to develop mineral resources for import by Japan under long-term supply contracts. All of the national insurance and guarantee programs are, of course, selective, and support specific projects that meet their criteria.

Virtually all home countries, for balance-of-payments reasons, have controlled exports of capital to finance foreign direct investment. Several (the United Kingdom, Japan, France, Sweden) used such controls regularly, applying them in response to the immediate balance-of-payments situation. None has tried to use its controls to maximize its national welfare (indeed none, with the exception of Britain in earlier periods, has had enough market power to contemplate doing so). The objective was simply to limit the immediate balance-of-payments deficit.

Though the United States is historically hostile to such controls, it applied them when it was concerned with its balance of payments. The United Kingdom, which generally permitted outflows despite its exchange controls, also tightened its rules considerably during the 1960s. Germany and Japan, on the contrary, tried to increase their foreign direct investment outflows in the late 1960s and early 1970s, to reduce their balance-of-payments surpluses and avoid adjusting their current account positions. Their efforts failed to prevent sizable revaluations of both currencies.

There have also been efforts by home countries to use their multinational enterprises in the extractive industries to assure access to imported raw materials. Some of these efforts—particularly in France, the United Kingdom, and Japan—are discussed in chapter five, which concludes that they have been almost wholly unsuccessful. Indeed, none of the home countries of the multinational oil companies appeared to do any better than other oil-importing countries during the OPEC production cutback (and embargo) in 1973–74, whether or not they actively sought preferential treatment from their firms (as did the United Kingdom and, probably, France).[35]

35. Robert B. Stobaugh, "The Oil Companies in Crisis," *Daedalus* (Fall 1975), pp. 179–202, finds that Royal Dutch/Shell cut U.K. oil supplies by 10–15 percent despite government demands. Petrofina and ten other companies boycotted Belgium to force the government to permit them to charge higher prices; France got better treatment from American-based firms than from French companies, despite its efforts to gain preferential treatment from the latter; the United States, home base to most of the companies, got the poorest treatment of all.

Two home countries, Japan and Sweden, instituted fairly comprehensive policies regarding foreign direct investment by firms based within their jurisdictions. Throughout most of the postwar period, Japan exercised tight control over outgoing (and incoming) foreign direct investment. In 1968, it officially sought to promote various national goals through foreign direct investment.[36]

The Ministry of Finance is required to issue a permit for any foreign direct investment by Japanese firms. Before 1971, no permit was issued until the Ministry of International Trade and Industry (MITI) certified that no Japanese workers would be displaced. The firms had to submit their own calculations of expected results plus the relevant regulations of the host country. If differences of opinion existed between the investor and the government, the government prevailed, the assumption being that it was in a better position to judge both the national interest and the interest of the firm.

Surveillance by the Japanese government continued after a foreign direct investment was made. Declared earnings and the proceeds of disinvestments were to be repatriated without delay unless they were reinvested in the same enterprise, though enforcement was not strict and considerable delays reportedly occurred in practice. These policies apparently worked: surveys by the Export-Import Bank of Japan in 1968 and 1969 indicate that more than 50 percent of all such investments were undertaken to maintain or increase exports from Japanese parent firms, and a large part of the rest were to develop sources of raw materials.[37]

In the early 1970s, Japan made major changes in its policy toward outgoing foreign direct investment. Since 1971, MITI does not review manufacturing investments case by case. In 1970 Japan announced a policy of exporting low-productivity, polluting industries as part of a revised industrial strategy. It also sought to step up its foreign direct investment to reduce its greatly enlarged foreign exchange reserves and to head off a second revaluation of the yen. It instituted more generous tax treatment

36. OECD, *Liberalisation of International Capital Movements: Japan*, p. 18. It also reports, however, that Japanese foreign direct investment has prompted "some replacement of Japanese exports by local manufacturing." The following paragraphs draw heavily on this document, especially pp. 37–41.
37. The evidence is summarized in Lawrence B. Krause, "Evolution of Foreign Direct Investment: The United States and Japan," in Jerome B. Cohen, ed., *Pacific Partnership, United States-Japan Trade—Prospects and Recommendations for the Seventies* (Lexington Books, 1973).

of income from foreign direct investment, accelerated grants of investment insurance, and made approval from the Ministry of Finance virtually automatic.[38] As a result of these policy changes—and the revaluations of the yen, the threat of trade protectionism in the United States, and the maturing of the Japanese firms—there was a sharp increase in the level of Japanese foreign direct investment in 1972 and 1973, more than doubling the value of the previously outstanding stock.

The balance-of-payments rationale for the new policy fell when the increase in oil prices threatened the stability of the Japanese balance of payments. The recession of 1974–75 raised opposition to deliberate export of industries. MITI now tries to control investments in the extractive industries, both informally and through government policy (including credits and investment insurance). In 1975, the government proposed changes in the Antimonopoly Act, which would enable it to restrain Japanese-based multinationals from anticompetitive acts. Hence present Japanese policy, while more liberal in comparison to postwar policy, has the same ambivalence that U.S. policy has.

Sweden also has a comprehensive public policy toward foreign direct investment. It has had more outward foreign direct investment per capita than any country in the world except Switzerland and has investigated more thoroughly than any other home country the impact on its economy of its multinational enterprises.[39] As a result of those studies, plus political pressure from labor organizations, Sweden became the first home country to enact comprehensive legislation governing foreign direct investment by

38. Though denials were still made for foreign policy reasons and to avoid "grave adverse effects on the Japanese economy." For a short analysis see Richard D. Robinson, "National Efforts to Establish Guidelines for the Behavior of Multinational Corporations," a report prepared for the Bureau of International Labor Affairs (1975; processed), pp. 10.2–10.4.

39. A study undertaken for the Swedish government by Nils Lundgren is summarized in English in *Internationella Koncernen i industriläner. Sam Lällsekononisha aspehler* [betänhande or Koncentration Sutredningen, SON 1975:50] (Stockholm, 1975), pp. 297–1324. See also Birgitta Swedenborg, *Den Svenska Industrins Investeringar i Utlandet 1965–70*, with a summary in English (Uppsala: Almquist and Wicksell, 1973), which reveals, p. 152, a high degree of inverse correlation between the rates of growth of Swedish exports and the increase in foreign production by subsidiaries of Swedish-based firms, in six regional markets between 1965 and 1970. The new Swedish policy resulted from deliberations by a government-appointed committee headed by a cabinet minister, Carl Lidbom; see *The Economist* (April 13, 1974), p. 10. Much information in the following paragraphs is based on author interviews with Swedish government, labor, and industry leaders.

domestic firms. The major concern of Sweden's blue-collar unions was investment in low-wage countries, notably Finland, Ireland, and Portugal. White-collar workers feared the export of Swedish technology. Both concerns developed during 1971–73, when there was recession in Sweden and a sharp increase in foreign direct investment by Swedish-based firms.

The Swedish law became effective in July 1974. It authorizes the government to block a foreign direct investment when necessary to achieve the objectives of economic policy.[40] Such investments traditionally required approval on balance-of-payments grounds, so a procedure for government review was established. A key innovation of the law was that the application must include the view of the labor union or unions (Sweden has separate organizations for blue-collar and white-collar workers) representing workers of the firm proposing to make foreign investments.

Proposals are screened by a committee of representatives of the Ministry of Labor, Ministry of Industry, and the two labor organizations. Three of these officials and three of the directors of the Swedish Central Bank (which reviews all foreign exchange expenditures) must approve all applications. Denials can be appealed to the board of directors of the bank, but the veto power of labor remains if the Labor party controls the Riksdag (because a majority of the board is appointed by the majority party).

As of mid-1975, no application for foreign direct investment had been denied.[41] In fact, the same two people in the Central Bank who, for many years, had weighed applications against the balance-of-payments criterion were the sole staff for considering whether they met the new criteria—

40. The bill originally proposed by the Labor government referred specifically to unemployment, but the Conservative opposition, arguing that restrictive legislation would violate Sweden's international commitments under the OECD code of liberalization of capital movements, was able to generalize the language during parliamentary consideration. The bill was literally passed by the casting of a lot, the Swedish procedure for breaking a tie vote in the Riksdag. The Conservative opposition was managed by Staffan Burenstam Linder, whose *An Essay on Trade and Transformation* (Uppsala: Almquist and Wiksell, 1961) was one of the intellectual forerunners of the product cycle explanation of foreign direct investment subsequently developed by Raymond Vernon and others.

41. The major Volvo investment in the United States was approved before the new law was passed. However, Volvo workers agreed with management that the step was necessary to preserve jobs in Sweden, so the application would presumably have been approved in any event. Swedish firms generally believe that the unions will take similar positions when foreign direct investment is clearly needed to preserve the position of a firm.

suggesting little government interest in using the legislation to restrain foreign direct investment.

It can also be argued that the new law represents no real change in policy. Most Swedish-based multinationals are already so deeply involved abroad that they could finance most planned investments without transferring additional capital out of Sweden. Swedish unions were already represented on corporate boards. But media criticism, which triggered the legislation, seems to have been satisfied by the new law.

On the other hand, the Swedish Confederation of Trade Unions maintains its attack on multinationals and calls for still tighter government regulation.[42] And interviews with top officials of the Swedish government suggest that, when the Labor party is in power, the unions will play a pivotal role in determining which individual foreign direct investments are permitted. Swedish labor leaders are aware of the potential of their power in their negotiations with Swedish firms over the whole range of labor-management issues. Hence the new law may have important effects in determining the nature of foreign direct investment, even if no investment application is ever denied.

Conclusion

With the exception of Japan and possibly Sweden, home countries have not adopted coordinated policies toward foreign investment. Most home-country policies are remarkably similar. Virtually all of them permit foreign tax payments to be credited against domestic tax liabilities (or exempt foreign income from taxation altogether) and defer taxation on foreign income until it is repatriated. Most have programs to insure foreign direct investment in developing countries. Most maintain at least standby balance-of-payments controls on capital outflows to finance foreign direct investment. Since the policies are so similar, no home country has gained much competitive advantage for its multinational enterprises, nor is there much conflict among home countries regarding those firms.

Japan is the one important home country that has a comprehensive national policy toward outward foreign direct investment designed to promote national economic objectives. Some of these goals were tradi-

---

42. The confederation's "Preparation Report on Multinationals," is summarized in *News From the Federation of Swedish Industries*, no. 2 (October 1975), p. 2.

tional: improving the terms of trade by improving access to foreign raw materials, meeting an increasing share of home demand in some industries from cheaper sources abroad, and avoiding further pollution and intensity of land use in the home islands.

The basically laissez-faire attitudes of other home countries developed during an earlier era when host countries had similarly laissez-faire policies. Now, host countries increasingly are able to tilt the benefits of foreign direct investment in their direction. Whether home countries will maintain their traditional policies when host countries seek to maximize their national gain—and whether domestic political forces within home countries will enable them to do so—remains to be seen.[43] The decline in support for foreign direct investment in U.S. and Swedish policy may be a partial response to this changed environment.

Answers to these questions turn on the impact of both foreign direct investment and new host-country policies on home countries. Part two of this book presents a comprehensive analysis of American investment abroad and the U.S. economy. Part three looks at its effect on U.S. foreign policy, with particular emphasis on the economic and political implications for the United States of host countries' increasing capability to harness the firms. In part four, implications for U.S. policy are derived and recommendations offered for extensive changes in the current approach.

43. Stefan H. Robock, "The Case for Home Country Controls over Multinational Firms," *Columbia Journal of World Business*, vol. 9 (Summer 1974), wonders "why should there be any dispute about the general principle that home countries should establish controls over the multinational operations of enterprises whose headquarters are located in that country?" (p. 76) and concludes that "a review of the case for home country controls leads me to wonder why the issue has been so long in coming to the forefront" (p. 77).

PART TWO

Domestic Policies

CHAPTER THREE

Exports, Imports, and the Balance of Payments

WHEN AMERICAN MANUFACTURERS set up Mexican assembly plants just across the Rio Grande or factories in Singapore and South Korea and export back to the United States, do they add to the flood of American imports and take jobs away from American workers, or do they, through their foreign presence, expand markets for American exports and protect the domestic market from a larger flood of imports? Of all the questions raised by American investments abroad, few provoke such acrimonious debate as this one. While we neither endorse the mercantilistic tone of the question nor give it primary importance, we address it first to clear the discussion of American multinationals of its most emotional aspect.

Multinationals affect the U.S. balance of payments not only through their exports and imports but also through capital transfers and repatriation of dividends, royalties, and head-office fees. However, the relation between capital outflows and repatriation of earnings is highly predictable, varying only marginally with the rate of return on the investments and the share of earnings repatriated. So we focus on the impact of foreign direct investment on exports and imports, because it is potentially larger, more volatile, and more wide-ranging than its impact on other components of the balance of payments. The effects of foreign direct investment on U.S. jobs, though they derive largely from the impact on U.S. trade, are considered in the following chapter along with the other issues of special concern to U.S. labor.

45

Déjà Vu

A brief discussion of the historical record and the foreign literature is in order; for, just as the multinational firm itself is not new, neither is public concern for its impact on the U.S. economy. In the late 1920s, the United States was engaged in a public policy debate spurred largely by the American Federation of Labor's concern that the branch plants American industry built abroad were reducing employment for American workers at home. Out of that debate came two Senate resolutions, two inconclusive Commerce Department studies, a vehement denial of any wrongdoing by the multinationals, and some studies by the academic community.

The most comprehensive and informative volume is Frank Southard's *American Industry in Europe,* published in 1931.[1] Besides presenting a wealth of information, this study both in its research design and its principal conclusions is the prototype for much subsequent research. According to Southard, analysis must go beyond a simple demonstration that firms invest abroad because it is profitable and address itself to the more difficult question of why it is more profitable than simple exporting.

Southard found eight factors that induce American foreign commerce away from exporting and toward investing: (1) high tariffs imposed by most European countries after the First World War; (2) high transport costs for bulky, fragile, or perishable products (Southard's examples: automobiles, which take ten times the cargo space when assembled than when unassembled, and shredded wheat biscuits); (3) loss of scale economies of American production through idiosyncracies of foreign markets that dictate product modifications (for example, high taxes on gasoline and on large automobiles, which dispose most Europeans toward small, low-horsepower cars); (4) patent laws that protect only if the patent is worked locally (for example, Libby Owens's glass-making processes); (5) the threat of entry into the U.S. market by foreign producers, which can often be forestalled by taking over foreign production (for example, the General Electric's assumption of minority positions in several Euro-

---

1. Frank A. Southard, Jr., *American Industry in Europe* (Houghton Mifflin, 1931). Southard subsequently enjoyed a distinguished career as an international financial official at both the U.S. Treasury Department and the International Monetary Fund and retired as Deputy Managing Director of the Fund in 1975.

pean electrical equipment companies, and Alcoa's control of Norwegian aluminum production); (6) discrimination in government purchasing (especially among defense and communication agencies) against foreign-produced goods but not against foreign-owned subsidiaries; (7) discrimination by consumers against imported goods (fueled by such slogans as Adam Opel's "Sie müssen nicht unbedingt Opel kaufen, aber ein deutscher Wagen muss es sein" or "You don't have to buy an Opel, but it must be a German car"; ironically, Adam Opel was sold to General Motors); (8) the relationship between local service facilities (sales and repair) and the highly customized products it services (for example, machinery tailored to exact specifications and requiring trained repairmen).[2]

Offsetting these incentives are certain advantages of exporting: the economy of scale in American plants, lower economic and political risk, and access to skilled and motivated labor. The decision whether to export or produce overseas must take into account the advantages of each. But one wonders how much discretion firms have in making the choice. Do firms invest abroad only when exports are or will soon become unprofitable? Or do they invest abroad whenever investing is more profitable than exporting? Southard concludes

If the European market can be more profitably served from a European plant, it will be so served.

To imply, however, that the American corporation is given a choice in the matter is scarcely accurate. Export of goods to Europe, or to parts of Europe, may be partially or entirely impossible or unprofitable, due to high tariffs, heavy transport costs, or any of the other factors . . . which have driven American industry to Europe. Thus the International Telephone and Telegraph Corporation insists that . . . "if the International Corporation should close up its factories abroad, it would merely mean that German and Swedish factories, our chief competitors, and the other American-owned factories in Europe would divide the foreign field and that no more American communication equipment would go from this country than goes at the present time. As a matter of fact, the chances are there would not as much go, for there would be no coördination, as there is today, between the European sales and the export business." . . .

Under such circumstances, the effect on American exports is not to be attributed so much to the actual migration of American industry as to the production and marketing conditions which made the migration necessary. The

2. Ibid., pp. 113–32.

Detroit automobile workers or the Akron tire-makers may as well attempt to prevent the establishment of branch plants in California as to prevent their establishment in Europe. Many of the causal factors in the two situations are identical.[3]

Southard's conclusion, in short, is that American firms never freely choose foreign production over exporting, that substitution of foreign for American production is never willful. If this is true, there is little chance that an American policy to discourage foreign investment would promote exports. But Southard's conclusion does not necessarily follow from his evidence. Theoretically, an American manufacturer faces one of four circumstances: (1) exporting and foreign subsidiary production are both profitable; (2) exporting is profitable, foreign production is not; (3) foreign production is profitable, exporting is not; and (4) neither is profitable. Southard concludes that the first possibility, where both are profitable and an American firm can freely choose between the two, never arises. Indeed, if the economists' assumption of perfect competition were satisfied, he would be right. But as several other authors show, and we confirm in chapter seven, American multinationals are likely to have competitive advantages that free them from the necessity always to produce wherever costs are lowest. Southard's conclusion can be supported only if he shows that American firms always export when the choice is really theirs, which needs far more evidence than even Southard gives. His evidence leads only to a Scotch verdict, not proven.

Five years after Southard's original study, he produced with Herbert Marshall and Kenneth Taylor a companion volume entitled *Canadian-American Industry*.[4] Since both the research strategy and the principal conclusions are the same as the earlier work, a summary of the essential differences between American investment in Canada and in Europe will suffice here: (a) natural-resource extraction was far more important in Canada than in Europe; (b) Canadian production was entitled to British Commonwealth tariff preferences; (c) Canadian tastes were closer to American tastes, alleviating a need for special foreign-market products; and (d) transport costs were substantially less to Canada than to Europe.[5]

3. Ibid., pp. 198–99.
4. Herbert Marshall, Frank A. Southard, Jr., and Kenneth W. Taylor, *Canadian-American Industry: A Study in International Investment* (Yale University Press, 1936).
5. Ibid., pp. 198–217.

The Canadian study also showed how Canadian tariff policy encouraged investment:

There can be no question that in planning its tariff policy Canada has, throughout at least the past 35 years, been perfectly aware of the relation between the branch plant movement and tariffs. . . . In 1931 the *Financial Post* could without exaggeration print an article headlined: "Claim Tariff Brings Canada 90 New Plants; Government Points with Pride to Long List." Whatever may be the effect of tariffs on branch plant development, recent Canadian governments have been convinced both that the relation is close and direct and that the more branch plants the better.[6]

American investment in Canadian industry, far from being an unintended side-effect of Canadian tariff policy, was its conscious and deliberate objective. Supporters of this high-tariff policy included not just Canadians anxious to promote employment of Canadian workers, but established American subsidiaries as well:

Another result of branch factory expansion is the vested interest that those plants come to have in the tariff *status quo*. True, it may be that in the beginning many of them were established reluctantly by American companies who would have much preferred to export finished articles to Canada. Once in operation on a reasonably profitable basis, however, there may be almost equal reluctance to abandon them should tariffs be lowered. It was reported that more than one of the lobbying firms at the Ottawa Conference in 1932 were American subsidiaries anxious that "Empire content" rules be stiffened and that other protection be maintained or increased to retain their Empire markets.

In general the management of American-owned plants in Canada will be found supporting a protectionist tariff policy, not only because that is part of the traditional habit of mind of manufacturers on this continent, but because if an American company has established a Canadian plant to serve the Canadian market, it is naturally anxious to retain a substantial tariff against its competitors in the United States which have not established branches.[7]

In two short paragraphs, Marshall, Southard, and Taylor raise three critical propositions, which such a study could easily pass over: first, that an American firm's preference for exporting over investing may disappear or even reverse itself after investments are made; second, that American multinationals may have substantially different policy objectives from American exporters; and, third, that multinationals may themselves be instrumental in maintaining or even raising barriers to American exports.

6. Ibid., pp. 274–77.
7. Ibid., p. 275

The British Experience

During the economic and political dislocations of the 1930s, 1940s, and early 1950s, foreign investment waned as an economic phenomenon and a political issue. Nevertheless, in the mid-1950s an interesting study appeared, by T. E. Pennie, concerning the failure of British exporters to maintain their traditional share of the Canadian market after the Second World War.[8] It is relevant here both because the British experience foreshadows the American and because it offers some direct insight into the nature of American investment abroad. Its thesis is that British exports to Canada are highly differentiated products: consumer goods in which styling and design are important, or producer goods with sophisticated sales and servicing requirements. Establishing and maintaining a substantial market for these types of products require a substantial sales effort by the manufacturer, and entrusting that responsibility to an independent agent is difficult and often impossible. American goods are Britain's chief competitors in Canada. And because Commonwealth tariff preference for years favored British imports over American, it has in effect encouraged American firms to establish manufacturing plants in Canada, and, more important, to acquire and develop marketing facilities. The paradox is that

In the long run, trade and investment may be complementary, not competitive. (a) Subsidiaries may manufacture most of the products sold, but the proportion which is imported from the parent company, although small relative to total sales, might be significantly larger than would exist in the absence of a local factory. The large British chocolate manufacturers, for example, produce their staple lines in Canada and import the more specialized products, such as boxes of chocolates, from the parent companies. The bulk lines advertise the imported goods and the local organization provides distributive arrangements for a complete range of products. . . . (b) The establishment of a manufacturing plant calls for the initial export of capital equipment.[9]

The declining share of British goods in world trade and the simultaneous expansion of British manufacturing subsidiaries abroad was a source of increasing concern for public policy in Britain in the early 1960s. But as the situation worsened, the argument grew that the exports of British

8. "The Influence of Distribution Costs and Direct Investments on British Exports to Canada," *Oxford Economic Papers,* vol. 8 (October 1956).
9. Ibid., p. 242.

overseas investors were as high as they could be. S. J. Wells, in fact, saw advantages for Britain in the very process of substituting British subsidiary production for British exports, beginning with the establishment of a sales and service facility, then a firm to assemble British-made components, then the foreign production of some components, and so on.[10] Eventually, the subsidiary's distribution network would promote other exports from the parent firm and the subsidiary would buy its capital equipment from the firm that supplied its British parent. However, Wells concludes in his final analysis:

On balance, however, most British firms do not engage in local overseas manufacture in order to reap such benefits as these. They do so because they have to. Although there are clearly the compensating advantages we have outlined, it is probably true to say that most firms look upon the substitution of overseas for domestic manufacture as a necessary evil rather than as a means of reaping economies. . . . although a number of advantages have accrued to certain companies who have developed overseas organizations . . . in many cases the decision to transfer production abroad has been forced upon British firms. Often the choice has been either acceptance of overseas manufacture or the more or less complete loss of a market.[11]

In short, even though foreign investing is often highly profitable, British firms prefer to export; they invest abroad only to avoid losing a foreign market altogether and to promote the export of British goods.

In a 1967 study commissioned by the Confederation of British Industry, W. B. Reddaway agrees with Wells.[12] Rather than assessing the opportunities of both exporting and manufacturing abroad, Reddaway assumes that exporting is infeasible:

Our basic assumption (in the absence of any reason to the contrary) was that if, for example, the British company had not established a factory to produce pharmaceuticals in New Zealand, then a factory with roughly the same capacity would have been established by a non-U.K. company to make the same type of products.[13]

Thus, in calculating the balance-of-payments consequences of foreign

10. *British Export Performance: A Comparative Study* (London: Cambridge University Press, 1964). As noted in chap. 2, more eclectic views about the overall value of foreign direct investment to the home country were raised in theoretical articles by several British economists during the period of active foreign direct investment by British firms.
11. Ibid., pp. 45–46.
12. Reddaway and others, *Effects of U.K. Direct Investment Overseas* (London: Cambridge University Press, 1967).
13. Ibid., p. 23.

investing, Reddaway initially ignored the potentially large displacement
of British exports and concentrated on the export of machinery, components, raw materials, and finished goods produced by the parent and
distributed by the subsidiary. But all these associated exports, as they
came to be called, seemed small. Machinery exports to British overseas
affiliates were less than 2.5 percent of total British machinery exports and
less than 10 percent of the affiliates' plant and equipment expenditures;
exports of raw materials, components, and finished goods for immediate
resale averaged less than 3.5 percent of the affiliates' total sales.[14] Since
the advantages of associated exports are small, even a modest displacement of exports by affiliates' sales results in a net displacement. The Reddaway study of British investments comes to the same conclusion as the
contemporary Hufbauer-Adler study of American investments (see
American Views, below): the effect of foreign investment on the balance
of trade and the balance of payments depends largely on the extent to
which the parents' exports are displaced.

Host-Country Views

Some of the earlier studies of postwar American foreign investments
came not from American scholars but from those in foreign countries
where American investment was large, such as Canada and Australia.
A. E. Safarian's *Foreign Ownership of Canadian Industry* and Donald T.
Brash's *American Investment in Australian Industry* are two of the better
known. Both examine the importing and exporting practices of American-
owned subsidiaries, comparing their volume of trade with domestically
owned Canadian and Australian manufacturers. They find that American-owned subsidiaries initially import more than their local competitors,
and they explain the phenomenon by the "similarities of product, specification of standards, and similar factors,"[15] and by the fact that "so many
American ventures begin life in Australia as primarily assembly or packaging operations."[16]

14. Ibid., pp. 62, 68.
15. Safarian, *Foreign Ownership of Canadian Industry* (Toronto: McGraw-Hill
of Canada, 1966), p. 158.
16. Brash, *American Investment in Australian Industry* (Canberra: Australian
National University Press, 1966), p. 206.

As the subsidiary ages, however, the tendency to import diminishes:

Many of the officers of the firms interviewed pointed to the Canadian tariff and related regulations as a key factor limiting their imports from the parent or other sources abroad, particularly where a specific Canadian content to production is required. . . . The progressive development of economical alternative sources of supply in Canada as the volume required of the item expands is a potent force transferring purchasing to domestic sources. . . . It was a common experience of many of the firms in this study to import a component or commodity until the increase in the size of the Canadian market for it, the acquisition of the necessary skills of production, the development of domestic sources of supply, or a favourable change in some cost component—sometimes accompanied by an adjustment in the tariff—permitted its economical production or purchase in Canada.[17]

Both Safarian and Brash attempted to investigate whether the subsidiaries gave preference to imports from the United States and from the parent in particular. Brash, however, was skeptical of what he was told in interviews:

During early interviews conducted as part of the present survey, participating companies were asked a series of questions on their use of Australian-made materials and components. As time went on, however, it became increasingly apparent that most of the questions were inadequate to elicit much useful information on this topic and several of them were not asked in later interviews. Too often, executives stated that "we buy locally wherever possible," in deference, it is thought, to current popular opinion.

John Lindeman and Donald Armstrong found the same difficulty in their study of American investment in Canada. "Of course all company executives interviewed expressed a strong preference for Canadian-made goods and services; it would take an unusually frank man to express any other view. However, further investigation showed that there were degrees of preference."[18]

A strong preference for *Canadian*-made goods and services? Multinationals obviously cater to their foreign as well as their American audiences. The safest conclusion is probably that drawn by the skeptical foreigners: multinationals differ among themselves in their eagerness or reluctance to substitute foreign for American production when and if they have a meaningful choice.

17. Safarian, *Foreign Ownership of Canadian Industry*, pp. 148–49.
18. Brash, *American Investment in Australian Industry*, pp. 206–08; his quotation is from Lindeman and Armstrong, *Policies and Practices of United States Subsidiaries in Canada* (U.S.: National Planning Association; Canada: Private Planning Association of Canada, 1960).

American Views

The Organic Theory

In the 1960s, American economic concern about foreign investments initially focused on the balance of payments. In a study for Congress, Phillip W. Bell calculated payout recoupment periods (the time between a foreign investment and the repatriation of an equivalent sum of money in dividends, interest, royalties, and fees) and found that ten to twenty years could pass before foreign investment benefited the U.S. balance of payments.[19]

However, Bell's assumption that the effect of foreign direct investment on American exports could be ignored was challenged by Judd Polk, Irene W. Meister, and Lawrence A. Veit in their study for the National Industrial Conference Board.[20] Drawing upon confidential data supplied by multinational firms, the Board argued the organic theory of foreign direct investment, that American multinationals are rarely able to choose exporting over foreign production:

In many less-developed countries local manufacturing is initiated by residents or other foreign companies, and U.S.-company exports to a given market are rendered noncompetitive by protective devices. In developed areas, notably in Europe, the emphasis is on local and foreign competitors, who, having plants on the spot, are in a position to take advantage of changes in terms of volume and type of products demanded, and can supply customers faster and better than a company that depends on slower and costlier long-distance supply lines. . . .[21]

. . . When questions about trade were raised at company interviews, there was near unanimous agreement that "foreign presence" was an important long- and short-term support for maintenance of exports at a high level. . . .

19. "Private Capital Movements and the U.S. Balance-of-Payments Position" in *Factors Affecting the United States Balance of Payments,* compilation of Studies Prepared for the Subcommittee on International Exchange and Payments of the Joint Economic Committee (GPO, 1962), pp. 395–481. Martin F. J. Prachowny and J. David Richardson, "Testing a Life-Cycle Hypothesis of the Balance-of-Payments Effects of Multinational Corporations," *Economic Inquiry,* vol. 13 (March 1975), p. 93, validate Bell's conclusion. They estimate that the financial flows generated by the average American foreign direct investment reach a break-even point, from the standpoint of the balance of payments of the United States, after 13½ years.

20. *U.S. Production Abroad and the Balance of Payments: A Survey of Corporate Investment Experience* (National Industrial Conference Board, 1966).

21. Ibid., pp. 43–44.

Companies repeatedly pointed out that at the time they made their foreign investments competitive pressures in the relevant market were causing a decline of exports, that the only means of maintaining their market position was production "on the spot," and that by undertaking foreign production they assured a future flow of U.S. exports (raw materials, capital goods, and other products) to, and income receipts from, a market whose potential for absorption of final product exports from the United States would otherwise have become nil.[22]

This argument, nothing more nor less than Southard's thesis of thirty-five years earlier, was pushed to its logical extreme (and, some would say, beyond) by its modern proponents:

The failure to supply new investment funds would result in a complete loss of earnings even in the short-run—a run as short, say, as the usual one-year accounting period of the national balance of payments. . . .

In the almost universal judgment of producers, maintaining competitive position requires continuing investment. Growth is considered indistinguishable from earning ability; "to stand still is to lose."[23]

But the Polk, Meister, and Veit study offers little evidence beyond the statements of the multinational firms. The Scotch verdict stands.

The Behavioral Theory

Also published in 1966 was Yair Aharoni's *The Foreign Investment Decision Process*.[24] Inspired by Herbert Simon's pioneering work on behavioral theories of the firm, Aharoni investigated the foreign investment process from the viewpoint of the businessmen making the critical decisions. Since exogenous factors may give firms a real choice between foreign and American production, the emphasis here was less on such factors as tariffs and transport costs, the size of the foreign markets, and so forth, and more on the endogenous decisionmaking process of the multinational firm.

Aharoni looked inside the firm to see how the choice is resolved. Among the more interesting of his findings are:[25]

1. Because foreign market opportunities are well outside the day-to-day experience of the typical American businessman, potential profit is

22. Ibid., pp. 115–16.
23. Ibid., p. 133.
24. *The Foreign Investment Decision Process* (Harvard University Press, Graduate School of Business Administration, 1966).
25. Ibid., pp. 49–61, 182–90, 115–16.

a weak incentive. Other stimuli are usually behind even a decision to explore foreign investing: the threat of losing an established export market because of a new tariff or a new competitor; the prodding of a customer, supplier, or other respected source; a sudden fancy on the part of a top executive.

2. The perceived risk diminishes and the willingness to explore new countries increases as a firm gains foreign experience. Part of the cause is expertise; part is the bureaucratic interest of a firm's now-established international division in promoting foreign investment.

3. Foreign investment proposals are usually considered first by the lower management echelons and, if favorably reviewed, work their way up the management hierarchy. But once a lower echelon decides to recommend an investment, it overstates benefits and understates costs, and its report resembles a selling document rather than "a reflection of the way in which the recommendations were determined. . . . It is interesting to note that the higher the echelon to which the report is submitted, the more 'accuracy flavor' the report has."[26] In other words, top levels of management may be misled into believing there is no choice.

The Product Cycle Theory

Product cycle studies, and in particular the contributions of Raymond Vernon, argue that American firms operating in a high-income, high-wage market have strong incentives to develop products for leisure time or that save labor.[27] Foreign markets for such goods are initially small and local competition undeveloped, so exporting is a feasible method of supplying foreign demands. As time passes, the technology of production stabilizes, foreign demand grows, foreign competition grows, and the firm establishes production facilities abroad to maintain its erstwhile export market:

Overseas investment eventually comes into the picture partly because the large-scale marketing of technically sophisticated products demands the existence of local facilities and partly because the protection of the oligopoly position of

26. Ibid., p. 116.
27. Vernon, "International Investment and International Trade in the Product Cycle," *Quarterly Journal of Economics,* vol. 80 (May 1966), pp. 190–207; and William Gruber, Dileep Mehta, and Raymond Vernon, "The R&D Factor in International Trade and International Investment of United States Industries," *Journal of Political Economy,* vol. 75 (February 1967), pp. 20–37.

EXPORTS, IMPORTS, BALANCE OF PAYMENTS 57

the U.S. producer eventually requires such investment. The threat of competition in foreign markets may come from local sources or from other outside producers, as the original technology-based oligopoly position of the U.S. producer in any given product begins to be eroded. At this point, with profits on exports being threatened, the U.S. company may see a high prospective marginal yield in an investment in local facilities, provided such facilities will help to buttress its existing market position.[28]

Product cycle analysis explains the shift from exporting to foreign production over the life of the product. When products are very new and close substitutes are hard to find, exporting is easy and foreign production is difficult; when products are old and both the product itself and its manufacturing process have been standardized, exporting is uneconomical and foreign production is economical.

At the beginning of the cycle and at the end, an American manufacturer may indeed have little real choice about where to produce. But the choice remains when to make the transition from exporting to foreign investment, and it depends on the firm's expectations about the growth of the foreign market, its experience in investing abroad, its ambitions for growth, and the foreign investment policies of the United States and other governments. The fact that foreign markets for any given product may eventually be lost to American exports is a constraint on U.S. policy, but it hardly renders moot the question of export displacement.

Export Displacement

The U.S. balance of payments remained in deficit throughout the 1960s, and the continuing outflow of capital to finance American investments abroad was widely viewed as the major cause. The multinationals' rejoinder was that without their foreign investments the deficit would have been even larger.

Gary Hufbauer and Michael Adler, in a 1968 study, ask the key question: What is the alternative to investment, exporting or local production within the foreign country by a foreign-owned firm?[29] Without directly answering their question, Hufbauer and Adler investigated the implications for the balance of payments of both alternatives. The difference is

28. Gruber and others, "The R&D Factor in International Trade," p. 21.
29. G. C. Hufbauer and F. M. Adler, *Overseas Manufacturing Investment and the Balance of Payments,* U.S. Department of Treasury, Tax Policy Research Study no. 1 (GPO, 1968).

striking. If exporting is the alternative to U.S. investment, the positive contribution of repatriated dividends, royalties, and fees is swamped by the negative impact of displaced exports.[30] The initial capital outflow is recovered only after fifteen or twenty years, if ever. If production by a foreign-owned firm is the alternative, the displacement of exports is inevitable. Although stopping the foreign investment would prevent the initial capital outflow, it would preclude repatriation of dividends, royalties, and fees as well as the small associated exports; within three to five years of the initial capital outflow there is a cumulative contribution to the balance of payments. Though the Hufbauer-Adler study analyzes both alternatives, it does not indicate which is the more likely.

Until the late 1960s export displacement was primarily a balance-of-payments issue. At this point the AFL-CIO renewed its historic charge that foreign investment is the runaway shop on an international scale.[31] In the 1960s the U.S. balance of trade deteriorated substantially, as U.S. exports failed to keep pace with the growth in world exports and U.S. imports surged. While import competition was particularly acute in certain industries (cameras, tape recorders, typewriters, television sets) imports grew faster than exports even in the machinery industries, where the U.S. export performance has traditionally been strongest. According to estimates by the Bureau of Labor Statistics, the growth of imports relative to exports translates into a net loss of 500,000 jobs between 1966 and 1969 and another 400,000 jobs between 1969 and 1971. Besides contributing to domestic unemployment, imports undermine the unions' ability to negotiate increases in wages and fringe benefits for American workers.

Rather than ascribing the loss of exports to the overvaluation of the dollar or to the growing efficiency of European and Japanese competitors, the AFL-CIO blames it on the commercial policies of national govern-

30. Virtually all studies show associated exports to be a small percentage of the total sales of the foreign subsidiaries. See especially Reddaway, *Effects of U.K. Direct Investment Overseas;* Hufbauer and Adler, *Overseas Manufacturing Investment and the Balance of Payments,* p. 24; and Benjamin I. Cohen, *Multinational Firms and Asian Exports* (Yale University Press, 1975), p. 115, which concludes from a series of case studies that local firms import more than the subsidiaries of multinationals in Taiwan, about the same in Singapore, and less in Korea.

31. Nathaniel Goldfinger gives labor's position in "An American Trade Union View of International Trade and Investment," in Duane Kujawa, ed., *American Labor and the Multinational Corporation* (Praeger, 1973), pp. 28–53.

ments and the conscious decisions of multinational firms. While the United States has steadily reduced tariff barriers, foreign governments are said to subsidize exports to the United States and limit imports from the United States with quotas, government buying preferences, and other nontariff barriers. More important, American multinationals exploit American technology in foreign markets through patent licensing and foreign direct investment rather than through exports. While licensing and investing may be more profitable than exporting, the consequences for U.S. trade and employment have been devastating.

Devaluation of the U.S. dollar, while badly overdue, "cannot possibly be viewed as a significant solution to the export of U.S. technology, capital, and jobs, with their accompanying deterioration of the U.S. position in world trade."[32] Rather, the United States must (1) tighten its tax treatment of income from foreign direct investment (see chapter six); (2) repeal sections 806.30 and 807 of the U.S. Tariff Schedule, which enable American firms to ship American raw materials and components out of the country for assembly and then ship the finished goods into the United States, paying import duty on only the foreign value added; (3) place direct controls on the multinationals' export of capital and technology through licensing and direct investment; and (4) impose import quotas to prevent disruptions in any one industry.

Case Studies

A study commissioned by the U.S. Department of Commerce and undertaken by Robert B. Stobaugh and his associates at the Harvard Business School counters labor's position.[33] Since knowing what would have happened if an American firm had not invested abroad is the only way to judge the impact of the investment on exports, imports, employment, the balance of payments, and so forth, Stobaugh narrowed the focus to nine investment projects. The AFL-CIO had followed a similar procedure, pointing out specific investments that had allegedly exported jobs. Stobaugh selected an investment project from each of the nine manufacturing industries listed in the Department of Commerce foreign investment statistics: food processing, chemicals, paper manufacturing,

32. Ibid., p. 48.
33. Stobaugh and others, *Nine Investments Abroad and Their Impact at Home* (Harvard University Press, Graduate School of Business Administration, 1976).

American Multinationals and American Interests

petroleum, rubber products, primary and fabricated metals, machinery, electrical goods, and transportation.

The nine case studies chronicle the uncertainties behind the decision to invest. The firms acted upon educated guesses rather than upon sure information about what would maximize their profits or maintain their share of the market. Even if their objective were to maximize American exports or employment, they still could not be sure when to go abroad and when to stay at home. In some of the cases, such as a fruit cannery in Africa or petroleum transportation facilities linking Europe and the Middle East, the foreign investment had little to do with American exports or imports. In other cases, the firms seemed to have to choose between making the investment or losing the market altogether. In only two of the nine cases, a tire plant in Canada and a radio factory in Taiwan, does Stobaugh find that the firm could have opted for American production, and even here the options would have expired within five to ten years. Stobaugh concludes that, in general, American firms have little choice but to invest abroad and that the investments contribute to a balance-of-payments surplus and to U.S. employment.

The data, however, could also support alternative conclusions. Stobaugh concludes, for example, that the investment of $54.4 million to expand tractor production in Europe would have had a negative effect on the U.S. trade balance and employment level after the first five years of operation, except that it generated export of loss leaders, creating a market for new products. In addition, the negative effects would have been much larger if it were not assumed there were a large number of associated exports (admittedly sheer guesses). The study reveals that the subsidiary was still running at a loss after five years.[34]

David Schwartzman also studied European investments by North American farm machinery manufacturers, and his findings only heighten the doubts about Stobaugh's analysis.[35] Schwartzman's study questions the value to the United States and Canada of foreign direct investment by farm-machinery firms. Because of the higher return on domestic North American investments and other factors, he concludes that European investment left producers with too many plants to avail themselves fully of the economies of scale. World welfare, as well as North American

34. Ibid., chap. 6.
35. *Oligopoly in the Farm Machinery Industry,* Report for the Canadian Royal Commission on Farm Machinery (Toronto: 1970).

exports and jobs, would have gained from expansion of North American output rather than creation of overseas capacity.[36] Furthermore, the parent corporations barred sales to North America from the new European subsidiaries, keeping home-country consumers from benefiting from lower European prices.

Another case study in Stobaugh's work—an investment in Taiwan for manufacturing automotive radios—reveals negative effects on the U.S. economy.[37] The investment was made to preempt Japanese competition in the United States, but the shift in production out of the United States was made five years before the Japanese would have posed a threat to the firm's U.S. production. The investment, then, reduced U.S. exports and jobs for at least five years.

An investment by a U.S.-based tire company, which Stobaugh studied, triggered a conflict between the United States and Canada.[38] Stobaugh concedes that the investment reduced U.S. exports and jobs and that it would have helped the balance of payments only if no U.S. capital were involved and if all raw materials were imported from the United States. The fear that foreign multinationals would invest if the American firm did not, developing economies of scale which would enable them to compete effectively in both the United States and Canada, was the primary motivation for this investment. As it turned out, the American company could not preempt either the Canadian or the American tire market with this strategy. The Canadian plant was built, but France's Michelin tire company established a radial-tire plant in Nova Scotia anyway. Nova Scotia is remote from the industrial heartland of Canada (southern Ontario and western Quebec) but is within easy shipping distance of the

36. A broader study of American foreign direct investment in the United Kingdom comes to the same conclusion—that subsidiaries of American firms are less productive than their parents, mainly because of their smaller scale of operations and consequent lack of mechanization. John H. Dunning, *The Role of American Investment in the British Economy*, Broadsheet 507 (London: Political and Economic Planning, February 1969), esp. pp. 136–37, 184–85, 193.

37. The same case was studied by Richard W. Moxon, *Offshore Production in the Less Developed Countries: A Case Study of Multinationality in the Electronics Industry*, bulletin of the New York University Graduate School of Business Administration, nos. 98–99 (July 1974). His analysis essentially replicates Stobaugh's but disaggregates even further and suggests (a) that the trade effects of such investments far outweigh the importance of related financial flows and (b) the job effect in the United States is more likely to be negative for investments in computer cores and semiconductors than in consumer electronics.

38. Stobaugh and others, *Nine Investments Abroad*, chap. 3.

eastern United States; and, most important, the Canadian government offered regional subsidies for new investment. The U.S. manufacturers complained about these subsidies, and the United States placed a counter-vailing duty on imports. Subsequently, Michelin also established a plant in South Carolina, which, like Canada, subsidizes local investment. In the end, the American company's Canadian investment precluded neither Canadian nor American investment by the French manufacturer.[39] This case study is a classic example of the uncertainty of international invest-ment planning and a sober reminder of the pitfalls in the case-study method.

There are many other sources of case-study evidence. Du Pont's analy-sis of its own experience concludes, not surprisingly, that its foreign in-vestment has a positive effect on the U.S. economy.[40] The study reveals a spurt of U.S. exports to an overseas market after du Pont announced plans to invest in that market, because, the report says, foreign importers viewed du Pont as a local supplier. When the company reversed a deci-sion to invest, exports fell sharply. Union Carbide, a competitor of du Pont, tells a similar story.[41] While recognizing that some exports were lost by foreign direct investment, the Union Carbide study concludes that the net effect was likely to be positive. A study of the pharmaceutical in-dustry by Robert E. Lipsey and Merle Yahr Weiss finds that "U.S.-owned nonmanufacturing affiliates are associated with comparatively large U.S.

39. Canadian tariff and nontariff barriers were also important in meeting Cana-dian demand. As noted, however, the American firm was more concerned with the loss of its U.S. market than its Canadian market. In addition, a large share of Canadian tire sales is for the original tires for new cars made by the three largest U.S. automakers, which standardize their requirements to the products of American tire companies.
40. "Positive Effects of Manufacturing Abroad on Domestic Employment in the du Pont Company" (August 1972; processed).
41. "Union Carbide's International Investment Benefits the U.S. Economy" (updated November 1975, first issued October 1972; processed). Union Carbide estimates that its exports in 1974 would have totaled $304 million—up from $45 million in 1951—even in the absence of any foreign investment, but that the remain-ing $162 million of actual exports were caused by that investment. Over the entire period, $1.01 billion of additional exports were attributed to the firm's foreign invest-ment (p. 4). Individual analyses for particular products in particular countries reveal cases in which (a) local content requirements forced local investments that promoted U.S. exports (Mexico); (b) local content requirements induced local investments and a decline in U.S. exports (Japan); and (c) local content requirements forced a withdrawal from an investment that led to a decline in U.S. exports (pp. 25–29).

exports of all pharmaceuticals."[42] An Upjohn study, using regression analysis, attributes over $30 million of its $40 million exports in 1971 to its foreign direct investment.[43] Interviews with twelve U.S. subsidiaries in Spain indicate that a good share of their $25 million of imports from the United States "could be bought from a local supplier."[44]

Case-study material has been compiled also by the Overseas Private Investment Corporation (OPIC). The corporation is required by law to estimate the effect on the U.S. economy and on the host country of all insured investments. Firms applying for insurance must make a five-year projection of the effects of the proposed investment on U.S. trade, on the U.S. balance of payments, and on employment in the United States and compare those effects with the most plausible alternative to that investment. OPIC also investigates the alternative of U.S. production, particularly when exports to the United States are planned. OPIC's conclusions are thus highly relevant to the broader policy issue. And the OPIC conclusion is that the overall effects of foreign investment are generally favorable to both the U.S. balance of payments and U.S. employment. Of the fifty applications that OPIC formally rejected between January 1971 and May 1973, eleven were deemed adverse to U.S. economic interests.[45] Four of the eleven proceeded without OPIC insurance and presumably the United States realized the projected adverse effects. In addition, OPIC frequently discourages formal applications when informal analyses suggest that the proposed investments would have negative effects on the U.S. balance of trade.

Each rejection, formal or informal, represents an instance, in which impartial analysis projects an adverse effect on the U.S. trade balance (and hence on U.S. jobs). As with all case studies, however, it is difficult to

42. "Exports and Foreign Investment in the Pharmaceutical Industry," Working Paper no. 87 (National Bureau of Economic Research, 1975; processed), p. 29.
43. "The Upjohn Company: Social and Economic Benefits to the United States from Foreign Investment" (June 1973; processed). It compares actual results in 1971 with the situation before 1952, when Upjohn made its first foreign investments. However, there are several serious methodological problems with the analysis.
44. Pedro Nueno, "U.S. Exports and U.S. Direct Investment in Spain: A Comparative Study of their Effects upon the Economies of Both Countries" (paper presented at the Academy of International Business, Dallas, December 1975; processed), p. 18.
45. Carl H. Middleton, "Analysis of OPIC Insurance Rejections" (May 1973; processed). The value of rejected applications ($570 million) exceeded the value of those that were accepted ($457 million), although this comparison is skewed by the rejection of one huge ($400 million) project.

generalize from the results. On the one hand, they represent a minority of the total applications submitted to OPIC. And OPIC receives applications only for foreign direct investment in developing countries, so the evidence does not necessarily apply to the much larger body of U.S. foreign direct investment in the industrialized countries. On the other hand, the OPIC policy of rejecting projects with adverse effects on the U.S. economy probably deters many proposals.

In 1971, OPIC contracted with Harbridge House, Inc., for a study of twenty U.S. private investment ventures in four developing countries (Colombia, India, Thailand, and Venezuela), in an effort to assess both their developmental effects and their impact on the U.S. balance of payments.[46] Harbridge House does not draw generalizations from any of the cases, but the overall results are an interesting addition to case-study information. Of its twenty cases, five appear to have had a clearly positive effect on U.S. exports, four others were positive only because host-country import-substitution policies made exports impossible, three had neither positive nor negative effects, five were associated with declines in U.S. exports that, because of competition, might have occurred anyway, one clearly reduced U.S. exports, and two could not be classified. In addition, eight of the twenty had a positive effect on the capital account, and the rest had a negative effect, either because of operating losses (five) or high rates of reinvestment related to the newness of the project. Meshing the two calculations for thirteen ventures (those less than ten years old and hence roughly comparable), Harbridge House finds that the impact on the overall U.S. balance of payments was clearly positive in four cases, probably positive in three more because of what might have happened otherwise, and negative in four cases; two remained unclassified.

For all their usefulness, however, case studies invite dangerous generalizations.[47] The results themselves cannot be treated as factual data, and

46. "U.S. Investment Ventures in Developing Countries" (study prepared for the Overseas Private Investment Corporation, 1972; processed). The results are summarized on pp. S-30 to S-32.

47. An egregious example is a study by Robert B. Stobaugh, Piero Telesio, and others, "The Effect of U.S. Foreign Direct Investment in Manufacturing on the U.S. Balance of Payments, U.S. Employment, and Changes in Skill Composition of Employment," Occasional Paper no. 4 (Washington: Center for Multinational Studies, 1973; processed). It assumes that the Stobaugh case studies "are a representative cross section of U.S. foreign investment in manufacturing" (p. 16) and extrapolates from them the conclusion that only 2.3 percent of the sales of foreign affiliates of American multinationals displace exports.

differences of interpretation can produce sharply divergent conclusions. Any simple generalization can be proven or disproven with the "right" cases.

Statistical Analyses

Several examinations of aggregate export, import, and foreign investment statistics show that multinationals contribute to the balance of trade. Two multinational groups, the Emergency Committee for American Trade, and Business International, surveyed their members and found that their employment, exports, and contribution to the balance of payments increased faster during the 1960s than those of American manufacturing as a whole.[48] Robert G. Hawkins, working with published industry statistics, found that U.S. imports were increasing in virtually every industry, but those dominated by the multinationals grew no faster than the others and, further, the multinationals' performance was notably stronger than the others on the export and employment accounts.[49] The U.S. Tariff Commission, using unpublished statistics collected by the Department of Commerce for 1966 and 1970, found that multinational exports and imports grew faster than nonmultinational trade (table 3-1). The multinational-generated surplus of exports over imports increased slightly, while that of nonmultinationals was almost eliminated. (Multinational exports include not only the parent companies' exports but exports to their affiliates from other American firms.)

Whether the simple comparisons in these studies point to the correct conclusions is difficult to say. Multinationals are often the largest firms in the most technologically advanced industries; export markets are easier for them to find, and imports are easier to avoid. Their growth and pro-

48. Emergency Committee for American Trade, "The Role of the Multinational Corporation in the United States and World Economies" (February 1972; processed); and two studies by Business International: *The Effects of U.S. Corporate Foreign Investment 1960–1972* (New York: Business International, 1972), and *The Effects of U.S. Corporate Foreign Investment 1970–1973* (New York: Business International, 1975). Of the seventy-three firms polled by ECAT on the probable effect on their exports if they had no foreign investments, 24 percent said exports would have been much smaller, 21 percent said somewhat smaller, 42 percent said they would have been the same, and 12 percent thought they would be larger (p. 35 and table 43), though only 7 percent thought their "foreign investments had adversely affected their domestic investment programs" (p. 21).

49. "U.S. Multinational Investment in Manufacturing and Domestic Economic Performance," Occasional Paper no. 1 (Washington: Center for Multinational Studies, 1972; processed).

Table 3-1. *Comparison of Exports and Imports, American Multinationals and Nonmultinationals, 1966 and 1970*

Millions of dollars

Type of sale	Multinationals		Nonmultinationals	
	1966	*1970*	*1966*	*1970*
Exports	7,826ᵃ	12,988ᵃ	21,461	28,975
Imports	5,803	10,940	19,660	28,859
Trade surplus	2,023	2,048	1,801	116

Source: *Implications of Multinational Firms for World Trade and Investment and for U.S. Trade and Labor,* prepared by the U.S. Tariff Commission for the Senate Finance Committee (GPO, 1973), p. 173.
a. Includes, also, exports to their foreign subsidiaries from firms other than the parent firm.

vision of jobs, both at home and abroad, is almost certain to be above the national averages in all countries where they operate. If trade performance is to be judged not on an absolute scale but relative to each firm's potential, statistics like those in table 3-1 tell us very little. If account is taken of the greater technical sophistication of the multinationals compared to the nonmultinationals, the multinationals' performance might appear worse than that of nonmultinationals.

Several econometric analyses have been made of the all-too-crude data describing American trade and investment patterns. Thomas Horst presented evidence that exporting and foreign investing are alternative methods of exploiting American technological advantages abroad and that high foreign tariffs discourage American firms from exporting.[50] Andrew Schmitz and Jurg Bieri found that the increasing share of American investments and the decreasing share of American exports to the Common Market countries after 1957 reflect the Common External Tariff's discrimination against U.S. exports,[51] but Anthony E. Scaperlanda and Laurence J. Mauer reached the opposite conclusion.[52] Robert

50. "The Industrial Composition of U.S. Exports and Subsidiary Sales to the Canadian Market," *American Economic Review,* vol. 62 (March 1972), pp. 37–45. Dale Orr, working with more disaggregated data, was unable to confirm the ability of Canadian tariffs to discriminate against U.S. exports, but that failure may have been caused by an implicit reweighting of the data. See Orr, "The Industrial Composition of U.S. Exports and Subsidiary Sales to the Canadian Market: Comment," *American Economic Review,* vol. 65 (March 1975), pp. 230–34; and, also, Thomas Horst, "Reply," ibid., p. 235.
51. "EEC Tariffs and U.S. Direct Investment," *European Economic Review,* vol. 3 (November 1972), pp. 259–70.
52. "The Determinants of U.S. Direct Investment in the E.E.C.," *American Economic Review,* vol. 59 (September 1969), pp. 558–68.

E. Lipsey and Merle Yahr Weiss conclude that American investments promote U.S. exports and, in the less-developed countries at least, displace the exports of foreign competitors.[53] Michael Adler and Guy V. G. Stevens tried without success to estimate cross-elasticities of demand between American exports and foreign subsidiary production, which would indicate whether one is a substitute or a complement for the other.[54]

Given the complexity of the foreign investment process (revealed in the case studies) and the crudeness of available foreign investment and trade statistics, statistical studies can do little more than verify that foreign market size and growth, technological sophistication, tariff levels, and other broad factors help shape American export patterns. The effect of subtler factors, such as the effect of firms' foreign investment experience or the impact of foreign competitors' behavior, have yet to be established. Econometric studies of such factors are probably far in the future and yet are probably the only way to establish inferences about what would happen if American firms did not invest abroad.

A Conceptual Framework

In putting the concepts discussed above into a useful frame, let us begin by stressing the role of the individual investor in the interplay between overseas investment and U.S. exports or imports. Such a microeconomic orientation contrasts with traditional general-equilibrium analysis, which economists typically use in analyzing international trade and investment problems.[55] In traditional analysis, a firm can invest as much abroad as it wants and not be concerned with the effect on its own exports; the trade-off between exporting and investing exists only for the economy as a whole. The literature surveyed above, in contrast, assumes that the

53. "Exports and Foreign Investment in Manufacturing Industries," Working Paper no. 131, revised (National Bureau of Economic Research, May 1976; processed).

54. "The Trade Effects of Direct Investment," *Journal of Finance*, vol. 29 (May 1974), pp. 655–76.

55. See, for example, Robert A. Mundell, "International Trade and Factor Mobility," *American Economic Review*, vol. 47 (June 1957), pp. 321–35; Murray C. Kemp, "The Gain from International Trade and Investment: A Neo-Heckscher-Ohlin Approach," *American Economic Review*, vol. 56 (September 1966), pp. 788–809; and Ronald W. Jones, "International Capital Movements and the Theory of Tariffs and Trade," *Quarterly Journal of Economics*, vol. 81 (February 1967), pp. 1–38.

primary effect of foreign investment is on the investor's own exports and imports and ignores the aggregate effect.

There are several possible explanations for a microeconomic trade-off. One possibility is that the firm itself has limited capital available for investment, so that more invested abroad implies less invested at home. A second possibility is that product markets, rather than capital markets, constrain investment behavior. Say that an American firm manufactures a product different from that of its competitors (maybe the firm has a secret formula, a patent, or a better reputation with consumers) and decides to manufacture that product abroad. When IBM decides to build its computers in Europe, or RCA decides to import its television sets from Taiwan, U.S. exports may fall or imports rise because no other American producer has the right to use the company's patents, trademarks, or distribution network. This possibility, which squares well with all our evidence on why firms invest abroad, certainly permeates the literature surveyed above.

Another point is that a modern American manufacturing corporation does much more than produce commodities. It recruits and trains workers, researches and develops new products, seeks out new customers through advertising and other marketing activities, finances and distributes its products, provides technical assistance to users, and maintains repair, service, and spare-parts facilities for old customers. These activities are often critical to a manufacturer's success not only in maintaining its market at home but in entering a market abroad. Recognition of these ancillary activities is critical because published foreign investment statistics include these operations and because our public policy toward foreign investment rarely discriminates between manufacturing and ancillary operations. For example, the balance-of-payments guidelines of 1965–74 and the foreign tax credit make no distinction between these operations. A broader definition of foreign investment will help us understand why statistical analyses come out the way they do and will also help us formulate effective foreign investment policies.

Factors in the Production Decision

Let us analyze the decision to establish a foreign manufacturing plant to supply an export market. In our initial analysis, demand for the product is fixed and given, so that the decision to produce within the foreign country implies a comparable reduction in American exports.

The choice between exporting and producing abroad is based on several factors. If a firm has little experience operating foreign plants it will be conservative about investing abroad. It will export, for example, as long as it can maintain its foreign market from its American base.[56] Since American wage rates until recently have been higher than those in Canada and Western Europe, to say nothing of Latin America and the Far East, for exporting to be feasible, tariffs and transport costs would have to be low and the product would have to be rather distinctive or have a significant cost advantage (such as that lent by a large-scale operation or a highly skilled labor force). Exporting from the United States is always difficult, and is altogether impossible in the absence of one or more of these advantages.

While foreign production saves on the tariffs and transport costs of exports and allows the American firm to use cheaper foreign labor, there are disadvantages. Most important are the start-up and overhead costs of establishing foreign plants. The American firm may be able to export using existing U.S. plant capacity, but foreign production usually entails additional property, plant, and equipment charges. More important (if less tangible) foreign production may bring a host of hidden learning costs as the investor discovers how to deal with and train a foreign work force. An American investor is more willing to undertake foreign production when it has already spent time, effort, and money establishing its name with foreign customers, when the foreign market is substantial or looks like it soon will be, or when the firm has had experience in adapting its manufacturing operations to other foreign environments.

The decision by an American firm to replace its own exports with foreign-produced goods may be precipitated by several factors: (1) an increase in the tariff on its exports; (2) other host-country incentives to local production (discussed in chapter nine); (3) high U.S. labor and materials costs relative to those abroad; (4) devaluation of the foreign currency against the U.S. dollar; (5) competition in the foreign market, forcing the use of cheaper foreign production; (6) growth of the foreign market to a point where start-up and overhead costs are relatively minimal; and (7) the firm's gratuitous reassessment of foreign production

56. See Aharoni, *The Foreign Investment Decision Process.*

relative to exporting. In each of these cases, foreign production takes the place of American exports. Given a limit on how much the American firm can sell abroad, more foreign production is bound to mean less exporting, whatever the reason for substitution.

Even for a simple manufacturing investment, in which the substitution of foreign production for domestic production is straightforward, we have no simple answer to the question: What would have happened had the American firm not invested abroad? The answer depends on what factor or factors precipitated the foreign investment. In some cases, such as an increased tariff, changes in other host-country policies, inflation of U.S. wage rates, devaluation of the foreign currency, or an increase in foreign competition, the only alternative to foreign investing may be withdrawal from the foreign market. In other cases, however, such as growth of the foreign market (unaccompanied by increased competition) or a firm's own reconsideration of the pros and cons of foreign investing, exporting may be a viable although less profitable alternative to investing.

The factors that favor investing for the purpose of exporting back to the U.S. market are similar to those for investments to serve the foreign market. American production is protected from import displacement not only by economic and psychological inertia—why close an American plant as long as it is making money?—but also by tariffs, transport costs, shipping delays, and all the other impediments to international trade. For an American firm to shut down domestic operations and import from its foreign subsidiary, trade barriers would have to be low and the differential in labor costs high, as they often are in the manufacture of shoes, electronics, textiles, and other products that use unskilled labor. And since an American firm is more likely to import when threatened by outright losses than when merely enticed by a higher return, competitive imports by either foreign firms or by other American multinationals may be a necessary spur to this type of investment.

But, as with export replacement, the investment could be precipitated by (1) U.S. tariff reductions (negotiated multilaterally through General Agreement on Tariffs and Trade or bilaterally, as in the Canadian-American Automotive Agreement of 1965); (2) explicit or implicit subsidies by foreign governments; (3) high U.S. wage costs relative to foreign costs; (4) devaluation of the foreign currency; (5) competitive pressure to use the lowest cost production; and (6) a gratuitous reassessment by the firm of the pros and cons of foreign investing.

Factors in Nonproduction Decisions

Our simple model of the trade-offs between foreign and domestic production does not characterize all types of foreign investment. American operations abroad also include sales and servicing, distribution, product modification and adaptation, and a host of other activities. Foreign investment statistics, even those for manufacturing affiliates, typically include a wide spectrum of manufacturing and nonmanufacturing activities. By any other standard than the economic measure of value added, the manufacturing operations may be the ancillary activity. Comparing U.S. exports or imports to these foreign investment statistics is like comparing a basket of apples to a basket of apples, oranges, and mangoes. While the absence of more precise statistics may force us to make such comparisons, we should at least be aware of the consequences of using heterogeneous foreign investment data.

Let us consider one nonmanufacturing activity, wholesale distribution. As a general principle, the distribution of products from manufacturers to retail outlets is subject to substantial overhead and low variable costs. The economies of scale come from various indivisibilities in the construction and maintenance of warehouses, automation in the handling of goods and the control of inventories, the scheduling and routing of deliveries, and so on. The independent wholesaler keeps his costs and commission charges down by handling the goods of several manufacturers simultaneously. Although manufacturers may insist that the distributor not handle directly competing products, the independent wholesaler is rarely dependent on any one manufacturer for his livelihood and can usually turn to other manufacturers for new business. In consequence, the distributor is less anxious about the success of any one product than the manufacturer is. While the manufacturer can try to negotiate a contract with the distributor requiring top performance, in reality, deficient performance is difficult to anticipate, difficult to detect, and difficult to remedy.

The alternative to relying on independent distributors is for the firm to establish its own distribution network. With its own sales and deliverymen in the field, quick delivery of undamaged goods can be assured, information about new customers or new markets more faithfully and accurately communicated back to the manufacturer, and buyer reactions to new products quickly assessed. The drawback, of course, is that the overhead costs which otherwise fall on several manufacturers fall on one firm, alone. Research on domestic marketing shows that American corporations with fragile or perishable products are readier to distribute their own products than are other firms, and that larger firms are more willing to shoulder the cost of a distribution network than are smaller firms. And, as Pennie and others show, an exporter will undertake more responsibilities for foreign distribution as foreign sales expand.[57]

As with wholesale distribution, so with other nonmanufacturing activities. An American manufacturer may be willing to provide maintenance, repair, and spare-parts facilities, to adapt its product to local standards or tastes, and to provide technical assistance to its customers. The likelihood depends on whether the industry manufactures durables or nondurables, producer or consumer goods, new products or old, and within any given industry, whether the firm is large or small. The critical difference between ancillary activities and manufacturing is that the former tend to expand the foreign market for the firm's product, be they American exports or locally produced goods; the latter merely switches production from one location to another. Market-expanding investments tend to promote U.S. exports.[58]

Assembly operations fall between the two extremes of simple manufacturing and market-oriented ancillary activities. When an American firm establishes a subsidiary to assemble U.S. parts and components for local sale, U.S. exports of finished goods are displaced, but U.S. exports of parts and components may be enhanced. If U.S. parts and components are assembled abroad for export back to the United States, there is a decrease in American assembly operations but an increase in the production of parts and components. Notice that if assembly operations use much more labor than the manufacture of parts and components, the U.S. trade balance could benefit but U.S. employment suffer.

That American multinationals engage in a mix of manufacturing and

57. "The Influence of Distribution Costs and Direct Investments on British Exports to Canada."
58. There is one catch. Recall the economic affinity of foreign production for large foreign markets: all other things equal, the more a firm can sell abroad, the larger the production volume over which start-up and overhead costs can be spread. The more willing a firm is to distribute its own product abroad, the more incentive it has to manufacture abroad. Conversely, the more it is willing to manufacture abroad, the more sense it makes to distribute its own product, to adapt its product to local conditions, to advertise it heavily, and so on. This domino effect, whereby one type of foreign investment encourages another, means that the market-oriented ancillary investments are not as neutral as they at first appear. They may promote U.S. exports, but they heighten the incentives to manufacture abroad as well.

nonmanufacturing activities has obvious implications for analyzing American export and foreign investment statistics. If manufacturing were the only activity of American firms operating abroad, then we would expect increasing foreign production, whatever its cause, to be matched by diminishing American exports or expanding American imports. The substitution of foreign for American production might not be willful, but as one went up the other would have to come down. If, to the contrary, distribution, sales, servicing, and other market-expanding activities were the only reason for investing abroad, then more foreign investment might well imply more exporting. In practice, of course, we get an unknown mix of the two effects, and the net effect on U.S. trade could be positive or negative.

The heterogeneity of American investment abroad has implications, too, for the formulation of public policy toward that investment. None of the U.S. policies outlined in chapter two differentiate between the manufacturing and nonmanufacturing activities of a foreign affiliate. While it may be difficult to discriminate between the different activities of a foreign investor, policies that encourage or discourage foreign investment without discrimination are bound to have an uncertain effect on U.S. exports, imports, and the balance of payments.

At this point we can see why it is so difficult to offer a simple answer to the question of what would happen if U.S. firms were prevented from investing abroad. The answer depends first on what type of investment is being prevented: manufacturing? assembly? sales and service? some unspecified combination of the three? Even if we can be certain that only manufacturing investments are to be stopped, we must still inquire why the firm wants to make the investment. Has the tariff gone up? other policies changed in host countries? the foreign currency devalued? the foreign market grown? foreign competition increased? Sometimes U.S. trade would benefit from stopping foreign investment, sometimes not. Formulating public policy toward U.S. investments abroad would surely be simpler if we had a simpler answer to these questions.

New Empirical Evidence

As the previous section demonstrates, the relation between trade and investment is heterogeneous; only in certain cases does foreign production imply displacement of U.S. production, and even then displacement may or may not be willful on the part of the American firm. In reading or conducting foreign investment case studies, this heterogeneity is manifest.

But if both economic theory and individual case studies preclude our drawing inferences free of qualification or exception about foreign investment and U.S. trade, it is still possible that aggregate export, import, and foreign investment statistics may support some general inferences. If the AFL-CIO argument that U.S. investments abroad displace American jobs is wrong in some cases and right in others, the latter cases may still be numerous or important enough to produce a statistically significant relation between U.S. investments abroad and U.S. exports or imports. Or if the multinationals are generally correct in emphasizing cases where their overseas investments promote U.S. exports or minimize U.S. imports, then the merit of their argument may be revealed in aggregate statistics even though exceptions to their general rule can be found.

Statistical Sources

In our efforts to verify either hypothesis, we analyzed the Internal Revenue Service's statistics prepared from corporate income tax returns. These data are carefully prepared and processed, and disaggregate the American manufacturing sector into seventy-five industries. Indeed, they are the only source of foreign investment statistics with such industry detail.

However, the foreign investment activities of the firms in an industry must be inferred from their foreign dividends and tax credits. While data on sales or assets of foreign affiliates would have been highly preferable, they are unavailable.[59] Our proxy for a firm's foreign investment level is its foreign subsidiary's dividends plus foreign tax credits deflated by the parent's total assets (which includes the book value of its investment in its overseas affiliates, but not the affiliates' assets financed through foreign borrowing).[60] In theory, our proxy is so riddled with distortions and errors as to be almost unworthy of further consideration. In practice, however, it appears to be considerably more reasonable. In table 3-2,

59. The Department of Commerce statistics on foreign affiliate assets and sales are much less disaggregated than the Internal Revenue Service statistics, are available for only 1966 and 1970, and do not seem to be collected with the same thoroughness and accuracy as the IRS statistics.

60. The sources and definitions of our data are described in appendix A. One industry of the seventy-six was dropped for our purposes.

seventy-five industries are ranked according to the average value of our foreign investment proxy over the seven-year interval, 1965–71. As one can see, the top industries (toiletries, drugs, soft drinks, computers and office machinery, photographic equipment) are those which are led by the best known American multinationals (Proctor and Gamble, Eli Lilly, Coca Cola, IBM, and Eastman Kodak). The industries on the bottom of the list—clothing, furniture, wood—consist largely of small, anonymous producers, few of which have national, much less multinational, operations. While our proxy may give too much credit to the highly profitable, highly advertised products and too little to less profitable, more mature products (for example, rubber, farm machinery, metal cans), it seems to work in spite of these deficiencies.

If the AFL-CIO is substantially correct, then industries investing more abroad should exhibit lower export and/or higher import levels than industries investing less. In fairness to its thesis, allowance must be made for spurious factors, such as American technological know-how. American multinationals with technological advantages over their foreign competitors may simultaneously export more and invest more than more traditional firms, but to credit the multinationals' superior export performance to their foreign investment would not be accurate. To know whether more foreign investment causes more exports and fewer imports (as the multinationals suggest) or fewer exports and more imports (as the unions suggest) technology and any other spurious considerations must be held constant. Thus, export and import statistics on industry characteristics are needed.

Our measure of an industry's export and import performance is the ratio of its exports or competing imports to domestic industry shipments averaged over the seven-year interval, 1965–71 (see table 3-2). For example, toiletries producers exported 1.92 percent of their domestic shipments, while imports of competing products (perhaps, but not necessarily, by these producers from their overseas affiliates) averaged 0.32 percent. Changes in export and import performance over the seven-year period are measured by the increase in the export or import share between the first three years, 1965–67, and the last three, 1969–71. Toiletries exports were 0.11 of a percentage point lower (as a share of the industries' domestic shipments) in 1969–71 than they had been in 1965–67, while imports grew by 0.01 of a percentage point between the same periods. Finally, the ratio of scientists and engineers to total employment in 1970

Table 3-2. *Trade Characteristics of Seventy-five U.S. Manufacturing Industries, Ranked by Foreign Investment*

Percentage

Industry IRS number and name	Foreign investment proxy[a]	Export share[b]	Import share[c]	Change in export share[d]	Change in import share[e]	Technical intensity[f]	Advertising intensity[g]
2840 Toiletries	3.30	1.92	0.32	−0.11	0.01	4.45	16.96
2830 Drugs	2.93	6.80	2.20	0.31	0.38	8.09	11.71
2086 Soft drinks	2.77	0.87	0.19	0.05	−0.02	1.31	8.46
3570 Office machines	2.70	15.12	4.87	7.77	2.96	9.36	0.79
3860 Photography	2.59	9.32	4.41	1.08	1.43	8.64	2.65
2910 Petroleum	2.22	2.51	5.90	−0.22	1.17	8.37	0.43
3420 Hardware	1.80	3.94	3.21	0.13	1.63	2.03	4.60
3830 Optical and medical	1.63	8.07	5.03	0.74	0.89	4.42	4.59
2040 Grain mill	1.53	5.56	0.43	−0.33	0.03	1.59	7.19
3010 Rubber	1.36	2.56	3.31	−0.14	2.64	3.37	2.23
3660 Radio and television	1.24	3.90	6.18	0.86	4.84	10.93	2.40
2698 Paper	1.21	1.17	0.29	0.16	0.14	1.33	0.98
3710 Motor vehicles	1.16	5.71	7.87	2.14	7.68	3.12	1.20
3298 Minerals	1.16	3.95	5.10	0.41	1.38	2.51	1.01
3530 Construction equipment	1.04	20.97	1.68	1.98	0.89	5.03	0.80
3630 House appliances	0.99	3.05	3.61	−0.34	2.51	2.92	3.15
3330 Nonferrous metals	0.89	3.12	8.54	0.85	−0.74	3.33	0.43
2810 Chemicals	0.79	9.35	3.07	1.08	1.31	8.76	1.18
2850 Paints	0.75	1.77	0.04	0.30	0.00	5.80	2.31
3410 Metal cans	0.74	0.41	0.14	−0.22	0.06	2.47	1.05

2020	Dairy	0.72	1.20	0.76	0.04	0.09	0.64	3.87
3430	Heating and plumbing	0.68	3.14	0.39	0.28	0.22	2.47	1.41
2898	Other chemicals	0.66	9.32	2.34	0.51	0.27	5.70	1.81
2712	Periodicals	0.64	2.51	0.26	-0.03	0.29	0.36	2.12
3550	Special machinery	0.59	17.84	6.98	3.74	4.04	4.50	1.14
2098	Other food	0.58	5.97	2.60	0.34	0.11	1.70	6.64
3698	Other electrical products	0.53	6.22	2.78	0.77	1.41	7.28	1.62
3210	Glass	0.51	4.04	3.67	-0.15	0.95	2.17	0.95
3560	General machinery	0.49	10.03	3.80	1.69	2.04	4.50	1.19
2030	Canned foods	0.48	2.92	2.92	-0.18	0.36	1.30	3.97
3810	Scientific equipment	0.46	15.15	1.92	1.97	0.89	9.42	1.39
3598	Misc. machinery	0.45	7.95	1.71	-1.26	0.20	5.10	1.28
3310	Ferrous metals	0.43	2.46	5.92	1.22	2.42	2.48	0.24
2050	Bakery	0.39	0.09	0.36	-0.38	0.15	0.57	4.95
3520	Farm machinery	0.39	10.10	6.99	-2.12	0.55	3.56	1.06
3440	Structural metal	0.38	2.48	0.39	-0.34	0.29	2.78	0.70
3580	Service machinery	0.35	8.48	0.57	-0.40	0.52	4.50	1.62
3540	Metalworking	0.34	7.53	3.08	0.94	0.66	3.82	1.14
2620	Pulp, paper	0.24	7.11	14.86	1.71	-0.86	2.43	0.84
3990	Misc. manufacturing	0.24	4.90	9.93	0.86	3.43	1.08	3.22
3270	Concrete	0.22	0.14	0.11	0.00	0.01	2.07	0.54
3461	Metal stamping	0.21	4.71	0.34	0.79	0.23	1.90	0.99
2711	Newspapers	0.19	0.05	0.08	-0.00	0.04	0.08	0.45
3870	Watches	0.19	1.55	17.44	0.22	2.09	2.38	6.89
2998	Other petroleum	0.19	14.85	0.08	-0.05	0.07	3.89	1.33

Table 3-2 (continued)

Industry IRS number and name		Foreign investment proxy[a]	Export share[b]	Import share[c]	Change in export share[d]	Change in import share[e]	Technical intensity[f]	Advertising intensity[g]
3240	Cement	0.18	0.32	1.72	-0.08	1.13	2.07	0.16
2100	Tobacco	0.18	3.16	0.21	0.84	0.15	1.41	6.92
2715	Books	0.17	3.63	2.06	0.46	0.28	0.36	3.68
3662	Electronics	0.17	7.41	2.99	5.38	1.86	7.28	1.00
3798	Transportation equipment	0.16	3.26	7.06	-1.04	3.96	1.95	0.68
2410	Logging	0.15	7.06	9.73	2.63	1.88	0.38	0.29
2310	Men's clothing	0.14	0.80	3.29	0.28	2.25	0.21	1.92
3930	Ordnance	0.13	12.29	1.84	-4.64	0.38	14.72	1.67
3720	Planes	0.13	10.67	1.31	6.18	0.26	14.63	0.28
3498	Misc. fabricated metals	0.12	4.65	3.65	0.39	1.33	2.47	1.00
2084	Liquors	0.12	0.88	27.31	-0.08	2.66	1.31	3.72
2228	Weaving	0.11	2.86	4.65	0.11	0.92	0.92	0.71
2798	Printing	0.10	0.66	0.27	-0.25	0.12	0.36	0.88
2060	Sugar	0.09	0.34	26.89	0.09	2.72	2.13	0.53
2430	Plywood	0.09	0.81	6.03	0.28	0.77	0.46	0.68
3450	Screws	0.09	2.18	3.19	0.59	1.64	2.05	0.72
2010	Meat	0.08	1.55	3.75	-0.07	0.94	0.58	2.18
3140	Footwear	0.08	0.28	9.24	-0.02	9.16	0.28	2.55
2398	Misc. textiles	0.07	2.35	1.08	-0.97	0.13	0.46	1.09
2298	Other textiles	0.07	2.02	7.45	-0.17	-1.74	0.96	0.83

2250	Knitting mills	0.06	0.74	4.15	−0.04	2.60	0.33	1.68
2082	Beer	0.06	0.18	0.97	−0.07	−0.02	1.31	9.86
2330	Women's clothing	0.05	0.51	3.45	0.03	2.25	0.21	1.97
2590	Other furniture	0.04	0.81	1.83	0.05	1.24	0.65	1.49
3098	Plastic products	0.04	2.25	2.21	1.14	0.93	2.35	1.22
2510	House furniture	0.04	0.43	1.83	−0.11	1.24	0.65	2.34
2498	Other wood	0.02	1.41	4.99	0.09	0.82	0.67	0.95
3198	Other leather	0.01	2.65	10.06	0.12	3.72	0.69	2.25
2380	Other apparel	0.01	0.83	7.96	−0.06	3.43	0.21	1.73
3730	Ships, boats	0.01	2.30	0.90	1.26	0.71	4.31	0.85

Sources: U.S. Internal Revenue Service, *Sourcebook of Statistics of Income, Corporations, 1965 through 1971* (computer tape records, stored at U.S. National Archives); U.S. Internal Revenue Service, *Statistics of Income, 1966, Corporation Income Tax Returns* (GPO, 1970), and ibid. for 1967–71 (GPO, 1971–76); U.S. Office of Management and Budget, *Standard Industrial Classification Manual, 1967* (GPO, 1968); U.S. Commerce Department, *Annual Survey of Manufactures* (GPO, 1967–73); U.S. Census Bureau, *Exports of Domestic Merchandise, S.I.C. Based Products and Area Report, FT 610, Annual 1965* (U.S. Census Bureau, 1967) and ibid. for 1966–71 (Census Bureau, 1968–72); U.S. Census Bureau, *U.S. Imports for Consumption and General Imports, S.I.C. Based Products and Area Report, FT 210, 1965 Annual* (Census Bureau, 1967) and ibid. for 1966–71 (Census Bureau, 1968–73); U.S. Census Bureau, *Census of Population: 1960*, PC(2) *Subject Reports* 1C, 5B, 6A, 7A, 7B, 7C, 7E, and 7F (GPO, 1962); U.S. Census Bureau, *Census of Population: 1970*, PC(2) *Subject Reports* 1A through 1G, 5B, 5C, 6A, 7A, 7B, 7C, 7F, 8B (GPO, 1972). See table A-1 for a concordance among Internal Revenue Service, Standard Industrial, and Census Bureau industry classifications.

a. Foreign dividends plus tax credits as a percentage of firms' assets, the percentage averaged over seven years, 1965–71.
b. Exports as a percentage of the industry's domestic shipments averaged over seven years, 1965–71.
c. Comparable U.S. imports as a percentage of domestic shipments averaged over seven years, 1965–71.
d. Change of average 1969–71 export share in relation to average 1965–67 export share.
e. Change of average 1969–71 import share in relation to average 1965–67 import share.
f. Number of scientists and engineers as a percentage of total employment in 1970.
g. Advertising expenditures as a percentage of total assets averaged over the seven years, 1965–71.

and the ratio of advertising expenditures to total assets show that the toiletries industry is characterized by high technology and very high advertising.

Export performance can be analyzed using the cross-tabulations shown in table 3-3. Each of the seventy-five industries is classified according to several criteria: its foreign investment proxy, its employment of scientists and engineers, its advertising intensity, and so forth. The first statistic in the last row of the table indicates that between 1965 and 1971 the average industry exported 4.5 percent of its domestic shipments. Reading across, the next four statistics reveal that industries in the first quartile of foreign investors (the first eighteen in table 3-1) exported 6.0 percent of domestic shipments on average, that those in the second quartile exported 5.7 percent on average, and so forth. Thus, by reading across the rows, one can see how export performance varies with the level of foreign investment.

However, averages for all industries take no account of the technological intensity or other characteristic of the industries. Accordingly, the first two rows contrast the export performance of high- and low-technology industries. Across the board, the high-technology industries exported 8.1 percent of domestic shipments, while low-technology industries averaged only 2.3 percent; high-technology industries in the first quartile of foreign investors exported 7.6 percent, compared to 9.7 percent for those in the second quartile. Thus, reading down a column gives a rough idea of how export performance varies with the characteristics of the industries, because the foreign investment level is held more or less constant.

Several features of table 3-3 are striking. Export performance is clearly stronger in the high-technology and machinery industries; the former averaged exports equal to 8.1 percent of domestic shipments and the latter 10.6 percent. These industries employ proportionately higher numbers of educated, skilled, and experienced workers. While these characteristics of U.S. industries with strong export records have been noted frequently, table 3-3 reveals the separate contribution of foreign investing to exporting. Reading across the rows, one sees the marked difference between the top three quartiles and the bottom quartile. Industries with little or no foreign investment export only 1.4 percent of domestic shipments (bottom row, last column), a performance that cannot be attributed to low technology, or a poorly educated or low-skilled labor force, or any other attribute. A modest amount of foreign investment, perhaps in the form of overseas sales and service affiliates—enough to place an industry in the

Table 3-3. *Export Performance[a] of Industries by Foreign Investment Level and Other Characteristics, 1965–71*

Percentage

Characteristic	All industries	Foreign investment quartile[b]			
		First	Second	Third	Fourth
Technology[c]					
High	8.1	7.6	9.7	7.8	2.3
Low	2.3	3.5	2.5	3.0	1.3
Advertising[d]					
High	3.1	4.6	2.4	2.8	1.0
Low	5.0	7.7	7.5	4.8	1.4
Machinery[e]					
High	10.6	18.0	11.0	8.4	2.3
Low	3.0	4.5	3.6	4.1	1.2
Education[f]					
High	6.5	6.6	7.9	6.2	1.0
Low	2.2	3.1	2.5	2.9	1.4
Earnings[g]					
High	5.7	6.9	6.4	5.0	1.3
Low	2.4	4.3	3.0	3.0	1.3
Experience[h]					
High	4.5	4.1	5.2	5.1	1.4
Low	4.2	8.9	6.7	3.3	1.3
Professionals[i]					
High	7.5	8.7	8.8	6.1	1.5
Low	2.6	3.3	3.3	3.2	1.3
Managers[j]					
High	4.6	5.8	7.5	2.3	1.0
Low	4.2	6.1	4.1	5.7	1.5
Clerks[k]					
High	6.9	7.4	8.9	5.2	1.4
Low	2.6	4.3	2.5	3.6	1.3
Salespeople[m]					
High	3.1	5.6	3.5	1.7	0.7
Low	5.0	6.2	7.0	6.1	1.5
Crafts workers[n]					
High	4.9	7.6	6.0	4.0	1.3
Low	3.9	5.2	5.8	4.7	1.3
Operatives[p]					
High	3.0	3.4	4.3	4.3	1.4
Low	5.7	7.7	7.1	4.2	1.1
Laborers[q]					
High	2.9	3.4	4.3	2.8	0.9
Low	5.0	6.7	6.6	5.1	1.5

Table 3-3 (*continued*)

Characteristic	All industries	Foreign investment quartile[b]			
		First	Second	Third	Fourth
Whites[r]					
High	6.0	6.9	6.7	5.7	1.3
Low	2.1	3.7	2.9	2.3	1.3
Males[s]					
High	4.9	6.8	5.8	5.0	1.1
Low	3.4	4.3	6.1	3.1	1.5
Unionization[t]					
High	4.4	3.8	4.4	5.5	1.9
Low	4.3	7.8	7.0	3.2	1.3
Average, all industries	4.5	6.0	5.7	4.4	1.4

Sources: U.S. Internal Revenue Service, *Sourcebook of Statistics on Income Corporations, 1965 through 1971* (computer tape records, stored at U.S. National Archives); U.S. Census Bureau, *Census of Population: 1960*, PC(2) *Subject Reports* 1C, 5B, 6A, 7A, 7B, 7C, 7E, 7F (GPO, 1962); U.S. Census Bureau, *Census of Population: 1970*, PC(2) *Subject Reports* 1A through 1G, 5B, 5C, 6A, 7A, 7B, 7C, 7F, 8B (GPO, 1972); L. W. Weiss, unpublished appendix to "Concentration and Labor Earnings," *American Economic Review*, vol. 56 (March 1966). See table A-1 for a concordance among Internal Revenue Service, Standard Industrial, and Census Bureau industry classifications.

Note—These notes also pertain to tables 3-4, 3-5, and 3-6.

a. Weighted by average 1965–71 shipments, thus deflating total exports of individual industries by total shipments. (Because of the difficulty in assigning exports and imports to an appropriate Standard Industrial Classification, we have in a few instances given less than full weight to industries whose statistics were not considered fully reliable.)

b. The first quartile of foreign investors are those ranked from one through nineteen in table 3-1. The second quartile are those ranked nineteen through thirty-seven, and so on.

c. Scientists and engineers were 0–3.2 percent of total 1970 employees (Low), or over (High).

d. Advertising expenditures, 1965–71, were 0–2 percent of total assets (Low), or over (High).

e. Firms high in machinery are those that, based on our own assessment, manufactured durable capital equipment for other producers (see appendix A). Such distinctions as raw materials versus capital equipment and producers versus consumers are impossible to draw exactly.

f. Median educational level of employees in 1970 was 0–12 years (Low), or over (High).

g. Median yearly earnings of employees in 1970 was up to $7,000 (Low), or over (High).

h. Workers aged 30–54 years were 0–55 percent of total 1970 employees (Low), or over 55 percent (High).

i. Professional, technical, and kindred workers were 0–8.8 percent of total 1970 employees (Low), or over (High).

j. Managers and kindred workers were 0–5.8 percent of total 1970 employees (Low), or over (High).

k. Clerical and kindred workers were 0–12.5 percent of total 1970 employees (Low), or over (High).

m. Sales workers were 0–3.0 percent of total 1970 employees (Low), or over (High).

n. Crafts, foremen, and kindred workers were 0–19.2 percent of total 1970 employees (Low), or over (High).

p. Operatives were 0–43.2 percent of total employees (Low), or over (High).

q. Laborers were 0–5.0 percent of total 1970 employees (Low), or over (High).

r. Race of employees was 0–90.5 percent white (Low), or over (High).

s. Sex of total 1970 employees was 0–71.9 percent male (Low), or over (High).

t. In 1970, in those industries with more than 70 percent of employees working in plants, union contracts covered 0–50 percent of production workers (Low), or over 50 percent (High).

third quartile—may be a prerequisite to exporting. However, beyond this, further increases in foreign investment are not matched by comparable increases in U.S. exports.

The relation between foreign investment and imports, analyzed in table 3-4, is somewhat opposite that of investment and exports. Imports

Table 3-4. *Import Performance of Industries, by Foreign Investment Level and Other Characteristics, 1965–71*

Percentage

Characteristic[a]	All industries	Foreign investment quartile[b]			
		First	Second	Third	Fourth
Technology					
High	3.2	4.1	3.0	1.9	0.9
Low	4.8	3.0	1.7	7.0	5.6
Advertising					
High	4.6	2.9	1.2	11.4	5.2
Low	4.1	4.7	2.9	3.6	5.4
Machinery					
High	3.0	3.3	3.0	3.3	0.9
Low	4.5	3.7	2.1	6.3	5.6
Education					
High	3.8	3.8	2.7	6.7	0.7
Low	4.7	2.9	1.8	4.9	6.2
Earnings					
High	3.5	4.0	2.4	5.0	1.3
Low	5.4	2.9	2.0	6.8	6.4
Experience					
High	3.9	4.2	2.5	2.7	11.3
Low	4.5	2.9	2.1	8.9	4.2
Professionals					
High	2.5	3.7	2.3	1.6	0.6
Low	5.3	3.6	2.4	8.0	5.9
Managers					
High	3.9	2.7	2.0	5.6	7.1
Low	4.5	4.3	2.8	5.7	4.7
Clerks					
High	3.4	3.4	2.7	4.5	1.7
Low	4.9	4.0	1.9	6.5	5.7
Salespeople					
High	3.7	1.9	1.1	5.2	8.0
Low	4.5	4.8	2.9	6.0	4.6
Crafts workers					
High	3.6	5.0	2.5	4.7	1.6
Low	4.8	3.0	2.1	6.9	6.6
Operatives					
High	4.7	4.6	2.5	6.6	4.9
Low	3.8	3.1	2.2	4.9	6.4
Laborers					
High	5.9	3.6	3.0	7.7	8.5
Low	3.6	3.7	2.0	4.4	4.2

Table 3-4 (*continued*)

Characteristic[a]	All industries	Foreign investment quartile[b]			
		First	Second	Third	Fourth
Whites					
High	3.5	3.8	2.2	5.0	3.7
Low	5.2	3.4	3.0	6.6	5.7
Males					
High	4.4	4.1	2.3	5.9	5.6
Low	4.1	2.9	2.4	5.1	5.1
Unionization					
High	4.3	5.1	2.9	4.7	3.5
Low	4.2	2.5	2.0	6.5	5.5
Average, all industries	4.2	3.7	2.3	5.6	4.8

Source: Same as table 3-3.
a. See table 3-3, notes c–t, for explanation of characteristics.
b. See table 3-3, notes a and b, for explanation of quartile rank and weighting of factors.

are higher in industries marked by low foreign investment, low technology, low education, low annual earnings, a low percentage of professional, technical, and kindred workers, a high percentage of operatives, and a high percentage of nonwhite workers. While this pattern probably reflects more the cheap-labor or natural-resource characteristics of certain industries (for example, pulp and paper, watches and clocks, liquors, sugar, furniture, and leather goods) than the absence of foreign investment per se, the evidence does not support the conclusion that foreign investment leads to higher than average imports.

Looking only at the levels of U.S. exports and imports and their relation to foreign investment, one might wonder why the AFL-CIO has been so upset. Tables 3-5 and 3-6 make the reasons more apparent. They show the increases in U.S. exports and imports as a percentage of domestic shipments between the periods 1965–67 and 1969–71. According to our way of measuring export or import growth, an increase in one or the other from, say, 5 percent to 6 percent of domestic shipments, would be shown as an increase of one percentage point. According to table 3-5, the average industry increased its exports by only one-half of a percentage point between 1965–67 and 1969–71. As for variations around this low average, the traditionally strong export industries—the high-technology industries and the machinery manufacturers—showed the largest increases. The low-technology industries barely maintained their low export ratios

Table 3-5. *Export Growth of Industries between 1965–67 and 1969–71,*
by Foreign Investment Level and Other Characteristics

Percentage

Characteristic[a]	All industries	Foreign investment quartile[b]			
		First	Second	Third	Fourth
Technology					
High	1.03	1.14	0.58	1.56	1.27
Low	0.22	0.32	0.09	0.50	0.04
Advertising					
High	0.19	0.23	0.07	0.46	0.03
Low	0.67	1.56	0.44	0.89	0.16
Machinery					
High	1.46	4.88	1.09	0.36	1.27
Low	0.30	0.31	−0.03	0.89	0.04
Education					
High	0.79	0.94	0.42	1.25	0.31
Low	0.21	0.24	0.15	0.44	0.07
Earnings					
High	0.74	1.16	0.38	0.92	0.38
Low	0.17	0.13	0.04	0.54	0.03
Experience					
High	0.50	0.33	0.23	1.05	0.20
Low	0.50	1.60	0.43	0.48	0.09
Professionals					
High	1.12	1.50	0.81	1.18	0.51
Low	0.16	0.14	−0.12	0.55	0.06
Managers					
High	0.64	1.17	0.78	0.26	0.20
Low	0.41	0.60	−0.19	1.16	0.07
Clerks					
High	0.89	1.27	0.52	1.05	0.17
Low	0.25	0.25	0.11	0.58	0.10
Salespeople					
High	0.45	1.23	0.19	0.24	0.08
Low	0.53	0.56	0.38	1.17	0.15
Crafts workers					
High	0.54	0.71	0.23	0.87	0.31
Low	0.47	0.87	0.45	0.65	0.03
Operatives					
High	0.30	0.22	−0.16	1.31	0.03
Low	0.70	1.20	0.67	0.39	0.33
Laborers					
High	0.29	0.12	−0.02	0.36	0.14
Low	0.59	1.11	0.33	0.82	0.12

Table 3-5 (*continued*

Characteristic[a]	All industries	Foreign investment quartile[b]			
		First	Second	Third	Fourth
Whites					
High	0.68	0.97	0.32	0.95	0.36
Low	0.26	0.43	0.34	0.55	0.04
Males					
High	0.54	1.05	0.26	0.56	0.24
Low	0.44	0.35	0.45	1.15	0.01
Unionization					
High	0.44	0.19	−0.03	1.11	0.26
Low	0.54	1.32	0.58	0.48	0.09
Average, all industries	0.53	0.88	0.34	0.78	0.21

Source: Same as table 3-3.
a. See table 3-3, notes c–t, for explanation of characteristics.
b. See table 3-3, notes a and b, for explanation of quartile rank and weighting of factors.

over this seven-year interval. Here, as before, industries in the lowest quartile of foreign investors had slower growing exports than those in the top three quartiles. But, generally speaking, the relation between foreign investment levels and export growth is random.

Table 3-6. *Import Growth of Industries between 1965–67 and 1969–71, by Foreign Investment Level and Other Industry Characteristics*
Percentage

Characteristic[a]	All industries	Foreign investment quartile[b]			
		First	Second	Third	Fourth
Technology					
High	1.14	1.44	1.11	0.65	0.71
Low	1.39	1.91	0.50	1.33	1.72
Advertising					
High	1.50	1.44	0.17	1.73	3.01
Low	1.20	1.85	1.07	0.95	1.18
Machinery					
High	1.46	1.93	1.52	1.32	0.71
Low	1.27	1.58	0.45	1.11	1.72
Education					
High	1.14	1.74	0.94	0.66	0.27
Low	1.47	1.05	0.52	1.51	1.93

Table 3-6 (continued)

Characteristic	All industries	Foreign investment quartile[b]			
		First	Second	Third	Fourth
Earnings					
High	1.08	1.88	0.89	0.67	0.61
Low	1.62	1.10	0.22	1.98	1.95
Experience					
High	1.10	1.85	0.71	0.46	1.77
Low	1.47	1.26	0.88	1.92	1.65
Professionals					
High	1.04	1.55	1.08	0.51	0.42
Low	1.45	1.70	0.53	1.53	1.81
Managers					
High	0.90	0.78	0.86	1.04	0.92
Low	1.57	2.16	0.71	1.24	1.93
Clerks					
High	1.16	1.44	1.03	1.06	0.88
Low	1.40	1.85	0.52	1.22	1.76
Salespeople					
High	0.68	0.63	0.16	0.98	0.94
Low	1.62	2.25	1.08	1.28	1.86
Crafts workers					
High	1.12	1.99	0.98	0.83	0.99
Low	1.45	1.44	0.52	1.59	1.90
Operatives					
High	1.51	2.18	0.47	1.31	1.89
Low	1.10	1.27	1.01	1.04	1.04
Laborers					
High	0.69	0.16	0.71	0.72	1.05
Low	1.56	2.04	0.82	1.40	1.89
Whites					
High	1.20	1.34	0.79	0.93	2.96
Low	1.44	2.35	0.77	1.45	1.32
Males					
High	1.17	1.77	0.84	0.98	1.12
Low	1.51	1.32	0.67	1.45	2.15
Unionization					
High	1.25	2.44	0.76	0.60	1.29
Low	1.33	0.97	0.81	1.65	1.71
Average, all industries	1.28	1.48	0.75	1.15	1.47

Sources: Same as table 3-3.
a. See table 3-3, notes c–t, for explanation of characteristics.
b. See table 3-3, notes a and b, for explanation of quartile rank and weighting of factors.

Table 3-6 shows the growth in U.S. imports between 1965–67 and 1969–71. Imports were clearly growing much faster than exports: the average increase for imports was 1.28 percentage points, or two and a half times the comparable increase in exports. As the table makes abundantly clear, this growth was not in a few isolated industries. Virtually every industry experienced an increase of one to two percentage points. Perhaps the most interesting variation around this high average is among the eighteen industries in the top quartile of foreign investors. Within this group, imports were growing especially quickly in industries whose workers had more education, higher earnings, and more experience and were operatives, nonwhite, and unionized.

Of course, the statistics do not indicate whether foreign investment was the *cause* of this rapid growth of imports. Looking back to table 3-2, one can see that the industries with high increases in import share were motor vehicles; radio, television, and communications equipment; office machinery; and rubber products. Although one would have to undertake detailed industry studies to determine the role of foreign investment in promoting imports in these industries, casual evidence suggests that the relation between foreign investment and importing varies from industry to industry.

A substantial portion of the increased imports of motor vehicles came from the Canadian subsidiaries of the Big Three U.S. automobile producers and was induced by the tariff reductions of the Canadian-American Automotive Pact of 1965. This would seem to be a classic case of the substitution of foreign for domestic investment induced by a tariff reduction.

One should not ignore, of course, the growing automotive exports of Japanese and German companies to the United States. In radio, television, and communications equipment, the growth of imports was probably due to the growing competitiveness of Japanese products (Sony, Panasonic, and so on) and the induced export of production and jobs by U.S. companies to the Far East. In this instance, U.S. investments abroad appear to be more defensive than they were in the case of automotive imports. Finally, the growth of U.S. imports of rubber products probably consisted largely of radial tires from European producers, and the correlation with U.S. investments abroad may well be spurious. One must be wary of drawing any simplistic conclusions from these sorts of statistics.

Additional Evidence

Rather than relying on data from the Internal Revenue Service, alone, we also analyzed the more familiar foreign investment statistics collected by the U.S. Department of Commerce. The most detailed available from the Commerce Department were statistics furnished the Tariff Commission in conjunction with the latter's report to the Senate Finance Committee. The Commerce statistics are drawn from a 1966 benchmark census of U.S. firms with foreign affiliates of more than nominal size, and from a 1970 sample survey for which a response was not mandatory. These data have obvious appeal: rather than making do with foreign dividend and tax credit statistics, the Commerce Department reports foreign affiliate sales and assets, and foreign trade and investment statistics are broken down into major countries or regions. Unfortunately, lurking just below this appealing surface are several severe problems. To avoid disclosing individual firm activity, the Commerce Department furnished the Tariff Commission with tables in which firms had been aggregated into thirty-two industries and eight major areas or countries. (One entry, for example, is the transportation equipment industry in the Common Market countries.) Despite this level of aggregation, sometimes only one or two firms report activity in certain industries and certain areas. Following the so-called rule of three, the Commerce Department censored any statistic representing three or fewer positive contributions. And then, because industry and area totals were published, other entries had to be suppressed to prevent the Tariff Commission or other users from deducing the tainted statistics. As a result, in many Commerce Department tables, more entries are suppressed than presented. Because of the Tariff Commission's objection to the censorship, the Commerce Department agreed to indicate with a letter code the approximate size of the suppressed entry (A = $0–$9 million, B = $10–$24 million, and so on). Using these letter codes and the industry and area totals, we reconstructed an approximation to the original tables. While this is a poor (and time-consuming) substitute for the original statistics, our estimates are probably not far off the mark.[61]

61. Letter coding prevents any one estimate from being too far off the mark, while industry and area totals guarantee that the total algebraic errors for any given industry or area equals zero. Thus we cannot systematically overstate or understate the values of exports, and so on, for any industry or any area.

But the problems did not end here. Comparing the Commerce Department statistics on the total assets of the American firms with foreign affiliates to the presumably larger IRS statistics on the total assets of all American firms in the comparable industry, we were dismayed to find that the former were sometimes larger than the latter. The plausible and charitable explanation is that the Commerce Department had trouble classifying highly diversified investors (such as du Pont, General Electric and International Telephone and Telegraph) and followed procedures different from those followed by the Internal Revenue Service and other agencies. We further aggregated the Commerce Department statistics, reducing the number of industries from thirty-two to twenty-three, considerably fewer than the seventy-five shown in the IRS publications.[62] While the details of gathering and processing statistics would normally go into an appendix, the deficiencies in this primary American source of foreign investment statistics are of general concern.

Table 3-7 defines the variables constructed from the data. Total exports by American multinational parents deflated by the estimated total shipments of these firms, XM, includes both exports to the firms' affiliates and exports to independent foreign buyers; no distinction is made between intrafirm and arm's-length trade. Because industry groupings can be as broad as "transportation equipment" or as narrow as "grain products," export statistics must be deflated by some measure, such as total production or shipments. Unfortunately, the Commerce Department provided only the total assets of the parent firms, which we converted to estimated shipments by multiplying the total assets by the ratio of industry assets (using IRS data) to industry shipments (using Census Bureau statistics).[63] To avoid a spurious correlation between our export and our foreign investment variables, we subtract from the foreign affiliates' sales

62. The twenty-three industries are grain products; beverages; other food; paper; drugs; cosmetics and toiletries; other chemicals; rubber; primary metals excluding aluminum; copper and brass; fabricated metal products; farm machinery; industrial machinery; office and other machinery; household electrical appliances; other electrical goods; transportation equipment; textiles and clothing; wood and furniture; publishing; stone, clay, and glass products; instruments; and all other manufacturing. The eight countries or regions are Canada; United Kingdom; Common Market (original six); other European; white Commonwealth; Japan; Latin America; and other African, Asia, and the Far East.

63. Mixing statistics from different sources is, regrettably, sometimes the only course open.

Table 3-7. *Variables Used in Regression Analysis*

Symbol	Definition	Source
XM	Exports of American multinationals to own affiliates and independent foreign importers, deflated by estimated multinational shipments (domestic assets times the ratio of 1967 industry shipments to industry assets)	TARIFF, COMMERCE, IRS
SM	Sales of foreign affiliates less imports from U.S. parents, deflated by estimated U.S. shipments of parents	TARIFF, COMMERCE, IRS
XI	Exports of all American firms deflated by total industry shipments	UN, TARIFF, COMMERCE
SI	Sales of foreign affiliates less imports from U.S. parents deflated by total U.S. industry shipments	TARIFF, COMMERCE, IRS
RD	Research and development expenditures as percentage of sales	NSF
DMACH	Dummy variable denoting machinery industry	Authors
P	Dummy variable denoting producer goods industry	Authors
AD	Advertising expenditure as percentage of sales	IRS
SZ	Estimated total assets of a median sized plant constructed by multiplying number of employees in a median sized plant by ratio of shipments to employees by ratio of total assets to receipts	COMMERCE, IRS
GNP	Gross national product of region in 1966	IMF
CONS	Consumption expenditure per capita	IMF
US	Ratio of commodity imports from U.S.A. to total commodity imports	UN, IMF

Sources: U.S. Tariff Commission, worksheets on foreign affiliate sales (n.d.; processed) [TARIFF]; U.S. Commerce Department, *Annual Survey of Manufactures, 1967* (GPO, 1969) [COMMERCE]; U.S. Internal Revenue Service, *Statistics of Income, 1967, Corporation Income Tax Returns* (GPO, 1971) [IRS]; United Nations *Yearbook of International Trade Statistics, 1967* (1968) [UN]; National Science Foundation, *Research and Development in Industry, 1966* (GPO, 1968) [NSF]; International Monetary Fund, *International Financial Statistics* (IMF, monthly) [IMF].

the value of their imports from their own parents, which is why we refer to *SM* as subsidiary *net* sales.

By relating *SM* to *XM*, we hope to gain some additional insight into the relation between exporting and foreign investing. For public policy purposes, however, we should also be interested in how foreign investment affects all U.S. exports, not just those of the parent firms. A multinational's foreign investment might promote its own exports but displace other manufacturer's exports. Accordingly, we collected statistics of total exports in the twenty-three manufacturing industries, *XI*.

Here, as before, comparisons between export and investment levels must be corrected for spurious correlations. To account for differences among industries, we constructed measures of several industry characteristics: *RD* is company-sponsored research and development expenditures as a percentage of sales, one measure of technological intensity; *DMACH* is a dummy variable indicating the capital equipment industry where the U.S. competitive strength has traditionally been at its very strongest; *P* is also a dummy variable indicating producer, rather than consumer, goods; because consumer goods often are more difficult to adapt to local market conditions and tastes, American penetration of these foreign industries may be more difficult. The American advantage in consumer industries lies, if anywhere, with highly differentiated and advertised goods, which is proxied by *AD*, the IRS estimate of advertising expenditures as a percentage of total receipts from sales. Finally, if American firms have better access to capital than foreigners do, they may be at a comparative advantage where capital requirements are stiff; *SZ* is an estimate of the asset value of a median sized plant in the industry. We expect that in a statistical analysis, American exports and foreign subsidiary net sales should both be larger, ceteris paribus, in industries marked by high values of *RD, DMACH, P, AD,* and *SZ.*

Unlike IRS statistics, Commerce Department statistics distinguish among foreign countries or regions. The economic sizes of foreign markets differ from one region to another, and we tried to capture this effect with an estimate of an area's total gross national product, *GNP.* Because American goods are particularly attractive to other high-income consumers, we measure levels of economic development with estimates of consumption expenditures per capita, *CONS.* And finally, since American firms seem more attuned to market opportunities in Canada, Latin America, and Western Europe than elsewhere, we must take some account of the apparent differences in geographical, political, and cultural proximity: *US* is the ratio of a country or region's total commodity imports coming from the United States, which seems to reflect this notion of proximity.

The rationales for the variables are mixed, some weak, some strong: *RD,* for example, has precedents; *P, SZ,* and *US,* may not have. Our concern is the effect that foreign investment has on U.S. exports, not spurious associations between the two. To guard against these, all relevant variables have been included.

As long as no account is taken of industry and area characteristics, the correlation between exporting and investing is positive. The simple correlation between multinational exports, XM, and foreign affiliate net sales, SM, is 31 percent, while that between industry exports, XI, and comparably defined affiliate net sales, SI, is 28 percent. But as the equations in table 3-8 indicate, each of these correlations can be partially accounted for by the underlying differences in technology, level of development of the various geographical reasons, and so on.

While some equations fit the export or subsidiary net-sales data better than others do, and although a few of the coefficients are insignificant or incorrectly signed, the results contain few real surprises. Note the stronger performance of AD in foreign investment than in the export equations, which seems to indicate that highly advertised consumer goods lend themselves strongly to foreign production, but not to exporting. (Of course the structure of import tariffs, exchange restrictions, and other trade barriers could also be the causes.) By contrast, $DMACH$ is more significant in trade than in investment, implying good exporting opportunities compared to investing opportunities. The strong performance of consumption per capita, $CONS$, suggests that as countries or regions become more highly developed, American firms substitute production for exporting. What we do not know, of course, is whether this substitution is voluntary, as it might be if the firms were simply revealing a preference to be closer to high-income markets, or involuntary, as it could be if foreign competition in these markets was stronger than in less-developed regions.

But as interesting as an exploration of the American advantage in exporting and investing might be, it is only a preliminary attraction. What one really wants to know is, holding all these industry and area characteristics constant, what the remaining correlation is between XM and SM or XI and SI. To find that out, we add SM and SI to the equations having XM and XI as the dependent variables (see table 3-9). The coefficients of SM and SI are positive and statistically significant, indicating that the partial correlation between exporting and investing is also positive. The source of this positive correlation is revealed in the last two equations, because the negative and significant coefficients on SM^2 and SI^2 indicate a clear tendency for the positive relation between exporting and investing to flatten out as investing increases. In short, this regression analysis confirms the threshold effect uncovered by the simpler cross-tabulations used in table 3-3. Here, as there, it appears that a modest amount of foreign in-

Table 3-8. *Effect of Industry and Area Characteristics on American Multinationals' Exports, Total Industry Exports, and Net Sales of Foreign Affiliates, 1967*

Dependent variable	Independent variable[a]								Regression statistic[b]		
	RD	DMACH	P	AD	SZ	GNP	CONS	US	R^2	F	Degrees of freedom
XM	0.0006 (2.0)	0.008 (6.8)	0.0006 (0.7)	-0.0002 (-0.9)	0.04 (2.9)	0.017 (3.6)	0.0007 (1.0)	0.013 (6.9)	0.46	19.0	175
SM	0.0011 (0.7)	0.005 (0.8)	0.0043 (1.0)	0.0015 (1.7)	0.12 (1.2)	0.088 (3.5)	0.023 (6.1)	0.042 (4.1)	0.34	11.0	175
XI	0.0013 (3.5)	0.008 (5.6)	0.0018 (1.8)	-0.0002 (-1.3)	0.00 (0.0)	0.020 (3.4)	0.0003 (0.4)	0.015 (6.3)	0.43	16.7	175
SI	0.0022 (2.5)	0.005 (1.4)	0.0034 (1.5)	0.0018 (3.9)	0.10 (2.0)	0.063 (4.7)	0.013 (6.3)	0.023 (4.3)	0.45	18.0	175

Source: See table 3-7.
a. Numbers in parentheses are t statistics.
b. R^2 is not corrected for degrees of freedom. F is for the equation as a whole.

Table 3-9. *Effect of Industry and Area Characteristics, Net Sales of Foreign Affiliates, and Net Sales Squared, on American Multinationals' Exports and Total Industry Exports, 1967*

Dependent variable	Independent variable[a]										Regression statistic[b]		
	RD	DMACH	P	AD	SZ	GNP	CONS	US	SM or SI	SM² or SI²	R^2	F	Degrees of freedom
XM	0.0006 (2.0)	0.008 (6.7)	0.0005 (0.6)	−0.0002 (−1.1)	0.04 (2.2)	0.015 (3.0)	0.0001 (0.2)	0.013 (6.0)	0.026 (9.8)	...	0.47	17.4	174
XI	0.0012 (3.3)	0.008 (5.4)	0.0017 (1.8)	−0.0003 (−1.3)	−0.003 (−0.1)	0.018 (2.9)	0.0000 (0.0)	0.014 (5.8)	0.029 (0.9)	...	0.44	15.0	174
XM	0.0005 (1.5)	0.008 (6.7)	0.0004 (0.05)	−0.0003 (−1.5)	0.041 (2.3)	0.012 (2.4)	−0.0004 (−0.4)	0.012 (5.6)	0.093 (2.8)	−0.44 (−2.3)	0.49	16.6	173
XI	0.0010 (2.7)	0.008 (5.7)	0.0015 (1.5)	−0.0003 (−1.5)	−0.003 (−0.1)	0.016 (2.7)	−0.0007 (−0.7)	0.014 (5.3)	0.019 (2.4)	−2.13 (−2.2)	0.45	14.3	173

Source: See table 3-7.
a. Numbers in parentheses are t statistics. SM and SM² are used only when XM is the dependent variable, SI and SI² only when XI is the dependent variable.
b. R^2 is not corrected for degrees of freedom. F is for the equation as a whole.

vesting is highly complementary to U.S. exporting but that higher levels of foreign investment have no strong or consistent impact on U.S. exports.[64]

Summary and Conclusion

To design effective public policy to improve the impact of American investments abroad on U.S. exports, imports, employment, the balance of payments, or virtually any other focus of public concern, one must know what would have happened if American firms had not or could not invest abroad. Would U.S. exports have expanded or imports diminished? Or would foreign competitors have moved in to fill the economic vacuum? As eager as the AFL-CIO has been to conclude that U.S. employment suffered as foreign investment grew, and as the multinationals have been to argue the converse, neither conclusion does even rough justice to such a complex question. Whether employment and the balance of trade benefit or whether they suffer depends on the nature of the investment. Both historical and case-study literature reveal the heterogeneous economic circumstances in which foreign investment takes place and the variety of possibilities that could have happened had the investment not been made.

In an empirical analysis of foreign trade and investment statistics, one looks not for rules admitting no exceptions but for general tendencies—propositions that hold true more often than not. The drawback to utilizing aggregate statistics is that one loses sight of both the specific nature or composition of foreign investment and the triggering mechanisms. Aggregate foreign investment statistics do not reveal whether foreign subsidiaries are seeking new markets for the multinationals' products, assembling components manufactured in the United States, or are wholly unrelated to imports and exports. Nor do aggregate statistics reveal why investments were made: growing markets, new foreign competition, higher tariffs, exchange-rate changes, or other reasons. Although industry and geographical data can account for differences in technological know-how among industries or differences in market size among countries, the triggering mechanism is blurred.

64. Using simple rank order correlations for the nineteen manufacturing industries in Commerce Department data, Hawkins, in "U.S. Multinational Investment in Manufacturing and Domestic Economic Performance," found "no systematically observable relation between intensity of foreign investment and changes in the ratio of sales to imports or exports," p. 17.

But if one cannot determine either the type of foreign investment or the triggering mechanism, nonetheless, one may draw some inferences about both from the statistical analysis. If most foreign investment displaces U.S. investment, as the AFL-CIO thesis implies, then whatever the triggering mechanism—tariffs, exchange rates, foreign competition— more foreign investment should be accompanied by shrinking U.S. exports and/or growing U.S. imports. On the other hand, if most foreign investment expands foreign markets for U.S. exports or minimizes U.S. imports, as the multinationals imply, foreign investment should be accompanied by growing exports and/or shrinking imports. Finally, if foreign investment includes both types or is unrelated to U.S. production—as most of the literature suggests—a haphazard relation between trade and investment patterns would be expected.

Our empirical analysis suggests the relation between foreign investment and exports or imports is largely haphazard. Cross-sectional analysis of two sets of data, however, suggest certain exceptions. In industries or countries with minimal American investment, an expansion of U.S. investment is likely to be matched by an expansion of U.S. exports. The apparent complementarity between exporting and investing is probably because subsidiaries focus their initial activity on marketing and assembling their U.S. parents' products rather than on producing a full product line, themselves. At modest-to-high levels of foreign investment, complementarity lessens.

We also uncovered some evidence that certain industries marked by high foreign investment (motor vehicles; radio, television, and communications equipment; office machinery; and rubber products) did experience faster than average import growth between 1965 and 1971. Without more detailed industry studies, however, it is impossible to determine the extent to which foreign investment was the cause, the effect, or merely a spurious correlate of the growth of imports.

The general thrust of our cross-sectional evidence seems consistent with inferences drawn from product cycle studies. The initial investments of an American manufacturer tend to promote exports by developing foreign markets for U.S. products. Over time, however, foreign investment becomes less and less the complement of, and more and more the substitute for, U.S. exports. At any given point, the relation between trade and investment is a complex aggregation of simpler connections. Simple conclusions cannot give full justice to the substantial differences among industries, among firms within the same industry, or even among the different product lines and geographical markets of the same corporation.

In analyzing the data, a de facto statistical relation must not be confused with the causal relation on which economic policy should be based.[65] No finding in our empirical analysis should be mistaken for a conclusion of what would have been—or might yet be—given other economic conditions or other foreign investment policies. The general lack of strong statistical relations between foreign trade and investment levels reflects not only poor data and inexact methods but also the simultaneous presence of complementary and substitutional relations. The most one can infer is that these forces tend to offset one another. Any theory that presumes the presence of one and the absence of the other cannot be squared with the evidence.

We thus conclude that broad restrictions on—or subsidies to—American investments abroad, such as controls on capital outflows or preferential tax treatment of foreign-source income, are bound to be clumsy and inefficient instruments for affecting U.S. employment or the balance of payments. If foreign investment policy is to promote either of these objectives, it should be, at the very least, highly selective. Considerable care should be taken to distinguish one type of foreign investment from another and to determine if American production is likely to be a continuing alternative to foreign manufacturing. A foreign investment policy that is unselective or based on inappropriate criteria could easily do more harm than good, even in terms of its own objectives.

65. Robert F. Frank and Richard T. Freeman, "Multinational Corporations and Domestic Employment" (Cornell University, 1975; processed), argue that our finding of complementarity at low levels of exporting and foreign investment does not necessarily imply that U.S. exports would be lower if foreign investment were restricted. We agree, since it is wholly conceivable that American firms, confronted by such restrictions, would find ways of maintaining traditional export markets. We do believe, however, that Frank and Freeman's analysis is fundamentally misleading in focusing on foreign manufacturing and ignoring the market-expanding aspects of direct investment. Their analysis, although seeming to rest on an empirical base, assumes that foreign investment can only displace U.S. exports. Given that assumption, they seek to determine how much U.S. exports might rise if foreign investment were curtailed. Our point is that foreign investment is heterogeneous—it displaces exports in some instances, promotes them in others, and is unrelated to them in still others. Frank and Freeman's analysis is a sophisticated extension of Hufbauer and Adler's hypothesis (*Overseas Manufacturing Investment and the Balance of Payments*), but Frank and Freeman offer no evidence that it is the right hypothesis.

CHAPTER FOUR

Labor

AMERICAN LABOR has several concerns about foreign direct investment: first, that it exports jobs. If production that could have remained competitive at home is transferred abroad, there is an immediate loss of jobs. And if, over time, the investment erodes the home country's competitive strength, including its technological or capital bases, there will be long-term job losses.

Labor believes, also, that foreign direct investment erodes labor's share of national income. Traditional economics suggests that export of capital reduces the stock of capital in the home country and enhances its returns at the expense of labor; some argue that the income shift in recent years has been sizable. Both of these issues pit workers in home countries against workers in host countries. Host-country labor benefits not only from the jobs and technology exported from the home country but also from the larger national income that results from a flow of capital to their country from the home country. So important differences between the attitudes of home-country and host-country labor toward multinational enterprises are to be expected.[1]

There are other concerns, however, that are common to labor in both home and host countries. One is the threat that multinationals pose to labor's ideological and institutional position. Labor in all countries is affected when multinationals do not recognize host-country unions, invest

1. B. C. Roberts and Jonathan May, "The Response of Multinational Enterprises to International Trade Union Pressures," *British Journal of Industrial Relations*, vol. 12, no. 3 (November 1974), conclude that "conflicts of interest between unions in home and host countries of multinational enterprises . . . at bottom are probably the main obstacle to effective international union collaboration," p. 416.

in anti-union countries, exploit host-country workers by evading local work standards, invest in countries without such standards, pay substandard wages, or support regimes that have policies opposed by labor (such as apartheid in South Africa and suppression of human rights in post-Allende Chile). Home-country labor may oppose the low wages and weak unions of host countries for pragmatic reasons, too, thinking that they attract investment and add to the export of jobs.

Finally, labor is intensely concerned over the effect on its bargaining position of the internationalization of business. Blue-collar labor is essentially immobile, internationally. There are exceptions within Europe and between Canada and the United States, but the importance of family and community ties to most workers limits their mobility even in those areas. And labor is almost wholly immobile across oceans and between northern and southern hemispheres, for reasons of both geographical distance and cultural (including linguistic) differences. Capital and management, on the other hand, are highly mobile across national boundaries. Runaway plants can now run halfway around the globe, but strikes by national unions affect only portions of the earnings of a multinational, in contrast to the total earnings of a firm that operates completely within a single country.

The importance of this concern to labor in the United States is confirmed by the apparent antipathy of the AFL-CIO to foreign direct investment in the United States by foreign-based multinationals. Logically, the AFL-CIO should see such investment as a means of importing jobs, consistent with its view that outgoing foreign direct investment exports jobs. However, the increase in jobs is not, in American organized labor's view, a welcome trade-off for a decrease in bargaining position. The leadership of the AFL-CIO—where concern for bargaining power is most manifest within the U.S. labor movement—is apparently no more eager to deal with a multinational Mitsubishi than with a multinational Dow Chemical.

Unions in countries that traditionally play host to subsidiaries share the view of the AFL-CIO. The international mobility of plants means the prospect of loss of jobs. Negotiating with the management of a subsidiary seems pointless, because the firm's decisions are made in the home country. And, though the multinational may pay higher wages than local employers, it may ignore local labor practices and traditional working conditions.

The mobility of multinational enterprises, in fact, may not be as great as labor believes. As the International Labour Office, itself, points out, most production runs in most industries are based on long-term investments which cannot be easily shifted, excess capacity is frequently unavailable in alternative sites, and large investment losses and large severance payments would be incurred by precipitate shifts.[2] Indeed, a multinational may be *more* susceptible to labor action than a nonmultinational, because its national components often depend heavily on each other. The Labour Office also points out that subsidiaries are subject to local laws, that personnel officials are almost always drawn from the local population, and that the corporate interests within a multinational are so similar that the actual locus of decisionmaking—whether the parent or the subsidiary—may not matter to the negotiations.

Nevertheless, international shifts of production within an existing family of plants is, by definition, unique to multinationals. And the power of this unique position can manifest itself in practices that are threatening to labor: substituting overtime for excess capacity, for example, or effecting changes in local laws that have hitherto deterred a multinational's flexibility. Hence, relative mobility and its effect on relative bargaining positions is the root of labor's antagonism toward multinational enterprises.[3] Before we turn to the alternatives available to labor in dealing with multinationals, the issues of job displacement and income distribution must be placed in perspective.

Job Displacement

The AFL-CIO cites numerous instances of job losses because of foreign investment, but it does not ask whether these jobs could have been maintained without the foreign investment. The multinationals cite their growing domestic employment, but they do not ask whether it would rise even faster without foreign investment. Neither labor's nor the multinationals' argument takes into account all the information necessary to trace the effect of foreign direct investment on U.S. employment.

2. "Industrial Relations in a Multinational Framework," *International Labour Review*, vol. 107 (June 1973), esp. pp. 496–500.

3. This issue is cited as the most important concern of host-country labor by David H. Blake, "Trade Unions and the Challenge of the Multinational Corporation," *The Annals of the American Academy of Political and Social Science*, vol. 403 (September 1972), pp. 36–37.

But the job effect of foreign direct investment cannot be ignored. It is impossible to fulfill desired employment levels through macroeconomic policy. As the recent past illustrates, macroeconomic policy is not flexible, the forecasts it relies on often go awry, and the inflationary costs of a policy devoted fully to reducing unemployment may be simply too high for society to pay. Even if macroeconomic policy could ensure full employment, foreign direct investment can still cause transitional costs by triggering a shift in the structure of the work force.

Recent Studies

There have been three comprehensive efforts to estimate the effect of foreign direct investment on U.S. employment. Because none of these studies successfully resolves the prior issue of the effect of U.S. exports and imports, each is forced to make one or more assumptions about "what would have happened otherwise."

The staff of the U.S. Tariff Commission (now the U.S. International Trade Commission), working under the direction of Robert Cornell, concludes that the cumulative total of all foreign direct investment by American multinationals through 1970 would have created a gross job loss of 2.4 million if the consumers of all of the foreign production could have been served by U.S. exports instead—an obviously unrealistic assumption but one which is useful in deriving an upper limit for the possible effects of the phenomenon.[4] Against this, the commission offset a gain of 1.1 million jobs because of (a) exports to the foreign affiliates, (b) a growth in exports to the foreign market, (c) a growth in the home office to manage the subsidiaries, and (d) investment in the United States by foreign-based multinationals (assuming that freedom for American firms to invest in foreign countries encourages freedom for firms in those countries to invest in the United States). Thus the Tariff Commission estimates a maximum of 1.3 million jobs lost from the cumulative total of foreign direct investment through 1970.

The commission makes two alternative estimations using other bases. Assuming that only 50 percent (instead of 100 percent) of the foreign markets would have been served by U.S. exports, the net job loss falls to

4. U.S. Tariff Commission, *Implications of Multinational Firms for World Trade and Investment and for U.S. Trade and Labor*, report to the Senate Committee on Finance (Government Printing Office, 1973), pp. 645–72.

about 400,000, because the rest of the sales would have been lost in any event. And, finally, assuming that U.S. exports would have kept only their 1960-61 share of world trade in manufacturing, the commission finds that the gains exceed the loss, producing a net increase of 500,000 jobs.

Using similar data and assumptions, Robert G. Hawkins calculates that the net effect ranges from a net loss of 660,000 jobs to a net gain of 240,000 jobs for the cumulated total of U.S. foreign direct investment through 1970. His judgment is that the most probable effect was "approximately a wash," that is, net displacement or creation of 25,000 or fewer jobs.[5] The relevance of both the Tariff Commission and Hawkins estimates is limited, of course, because they compare actualities with simple alternative scenarios rather than with close-to-factual analyses of what might have happened otherwise.

The most recent and detailed study is by Robert F. Frank and Richard T. Freeman.[6] On the assumption that exports could substitute for all foreign affiliate production, they seek to measure the probable extent of that substitution given the inferior cost competitiveness of domestic production. They measure the annual effect of foreign direct investment, not the effect of several years. And they include in their calculation (through the use of input-output tables) the indirect effects on suppliers in addition to the direct effect on the investing industries. Finally, they include changes in the labor market to assess the real impact on workers, including both employed workers and potential workers.

Frank and Freeman find that the annual effect ranges between the creation of a small number of jobs (about 11,000) and the displacement of a sizable number (about one million) and conclude that the annual loss is 120,000–260,000 jobs, 70 percent in the investing industry and the remainder in supplying industries. There are large differences among the twenty-one industries disaggregated by their data, but in none is creation of jobs more likely than displacement. They go on to minimize the net effect, however, by citing an increase of one week in the average period of unemployment and an average of seven weeks before the majority of workers who lost their jobs because of foreign direct investment were re-

5. "Job Displacement and the Multinational Firm: A Methodological Review," Occasional Paper no. 3 (Center for Multinational Studies, June 1972; processed), p. ii.
6. "The Impact of United States Direct Foreign Investment on Domestic Unemployment" (May 1975; processed).

employed. Thus, even Frank and Freeman's pessimistic assumption that foreign investment substitutes for U.S. exports suggests that one should look at factors like macroeconomic policy rather than foreign investment to explain the high rates of domestic unemployment experienced in the 1970s.

Distribution of Income

Even if exchange rate adjustments or some combination of monetary and fiscal policy offset loss of jobs, the question of who benefits from foreign direct investment would remain. Because the distribution of national income between labor and capital has received so much attention from economic theorists, let us review the principles of the traditional analysis and fit some data to them.

The Traditional Model

Although international trade theory usually assumes that only commodities move in international exchange, several writers consider the economic consequences of the international movement of capital and labor. As early as 1904, Arthur C. Pigou argued that a tariff protecting domestic labor from cheap imports could be undermined by domestic capitalists investing abroad.[7] If the tariff succeeded in raising the wages of labor and depressing the return on capital, foreign investment opportunities would become more attractive and domestic labor would suffer as domestic capital was transferred overseas. The relation between international trade and investment was further explored in 1919 by Eli Heckscher, who reasoned that international trade (disregarding tariffs and transport costs) could actually equalize both wage rates and the returns on capital between two trading countries.[8] Even though one country might start with more capital and, consequently, higher wages than the other country, trade between the two would lower wages in one country and raise them in the other until they were equal. The first country's wages

7. *Protective and Preferential Import Duties* (London: McMillan, 1904), pp. 59–60.
8. "The Effect of Foreign Trade on the Distribution of Income," in *Readings in the Theory of International Trade*, vol. 4, Blakiston Series of Republished Articles on Economics (Blakiston, 1950), pp. 272–300.

fall because it imports goods that take advantage of cheap labor and exports goods that take advantage of abundant capital. Thus if international trade were completely free of tariffs and transport costs, the original differences in national wage rates and returns on capital would disappear and, with them, the economic incentive to international investment or emigration.

Fourteen years after the Heckscher study, Bertil Ohlin backpedaled a bit by denying the possibility of *complete* equality in wage rates and returns on capital. However, he reaffirmed the general principle:

> The exchange of goods cannot bring about a complete equalization of factor prices. Interregional differences remain, and call forth factor movements, whenever the difference is great enough to overcome the obstacles. Factor prices are in this way brought into completer harmony as between regions; the need for interregional trade, and consequently its volume, are reduced. Thus factor movements act as a substitute for the movements of commodities.[9]

But in 1948, Paul A. Samuelson showed that under the conventional (if strict) assumptions, complete equalization is a distinct possibility.[10] It remained, however, for Robert A. Mundell in 1957 to show the exact theoretic relation between international trade and investment: either free trade or free investment equalizes wages and capital returns, and barriers to one will only stimulate the other.[11]

If one were to apply the traditional theory to U.S. investment and labor, the effect of foreign investment on income distribution would be very small because international trade would adjust to offset the effect. To compensate for the loss of capital, the United States would cut both exports of capital intensive goods and imports of labor intensive goods, and the terms of trade, labor's wage, and labor's share of national income would remain unchanged. While labor must adjust by transferring from one industry to another, the burden is transitional, not permanent.[12]

If international trade cannot or will not adjust, however, fewer laborers

9. *Interregional and International Trade* (Harvard University Press, 1935), p. 169.
10. "International Trade and the Equalisation of Factor Prices," *Economic Journal*, vol. 58 (June 1948), pp. 163–84.
11. "International Trade and Factor Mobility," *American Economic Review*, vol. 47 (June 1957), pp. 321–35.
12. These transitional costs can be significant in the short run, however. See Stephen P. Magee, "The Welfare Effects of Restrictions on U.S. Trade," *Brookings Papers on Economic Activity 3:72*, pp. 678–86.

would have to switch from one industry to another, but labor's real wages and its share of national income would suffer permanent harm from the foreign investment. An extreme example is considered by Lester C. Thurow.[13] With only one commodity produced at home or abroad, no international trade would flow except as return on international investment. Foreign investment cannot, by assumption, be offset by switching production from the exported to the imported commodity. Thus the real wage of labor must fall until the substitution of labor for capital within the industry can compensate for the loss of domestic capital.

According to Thurow's estimates, the free international flow of capital would raise the real income of all Americans by less than 1 percent if the rest of the world had as much labor but only half as much capital as the United States. The redistribution of income within the United States would be substantial, however: the real income of labor would fall by over 8 percent while the real return on capital would jump by more than 22 percent.[14] With the opportunities for substitution between commodities ruled out, the estimated swings in the distribution of income from labor to capital are substantial.

Similar calculations have been made by Peggy B. Musgrave. Using a one-sector model like Thurow's, and including the tax consequences of foreign investment, Musgrave estimates that domestic utilization of the entire $80 billion of American capital invested abroad through 1968 would have raised labor's share from 72.2 percent to 79.4 percent of national income and diminished capital's from 22.8 percent to 20.6 percent, a shift of about $25 billion, or $125 per American, in 1974.[15] While this estimate is not as large as Thurow's, it also implies that foreign investment significantly reduces labor's share of U.S. national income.

There are three severe limitations on the usefulness of the Thurow-Musgrave analysis. The first is the omission of international trade adjustments which, as just noted, can wholly compensate for any shift in in-

13. "Multinational Companies and the American Distribution of Income" (1973; processed).

14. Ibid., table 4, p. 13.

15. *Direct Investment Abroad and the Multinationals: Effects on the United States Economy,* report prepared for the Subcommittee on Multinational Corporations of the Senate Foreign Relations Committee (GPO, 1975), p. 97. Estimates are based on an elasticity of substitution between capital and labor of 0.75 and on a definition of capital which includes structures, equipment, and inventory, but not land or cash.

come distribution triggered by the foreign investment. Second is the failure to recognize that foreign direct investment by American multinationals does not equate to net capital outflow from the United States, both because those firms finance a majority of their investments with foreign capital and because whatever export of funds takes place tightens the U.S. capital market and attracts incoming capital. Third, they give short shrift to the transfer of technology.[16] Thurow considers the possibility that American foreign investment increases foreign productivity but assumes that the benefits are shared by all factors generally, including foreign capital, rather than by American capital in particular.[17]

Testing the Model

According to at least the simpler traditional models of international investment and income distribution, the substantial flow of U.S. investment abroad over the last few decades should have brought about substantial redistribution of income from domestic labor to internationally mobile capital and management. One can test these models against the actual experience of the last thirty years, using statistics on the overall distribution of U.S. income as well as data on labor earnings in different manufacturing industries.

Let us begin with the distribution of income between labor and capital. "Income" in this instance includes not only the returns to labor and capital generated by domestic production but also the earnings from foreign investment. With U.S. capital seeking higher returns abroad, it is altogether possible that capital's share of domestic income is falling even as its share of total income (from domestic plus foreign investment) is rising. The Department of Commerce publishes annual statistics on national income, which include employee compensation, proprietors' income, rental income, corporate profits, and net interest. Included in corporate profits are foreign branch earnings and subsidiary dividends after foreign taxes.

16. Musgrave, *Direct Investment Abroad and the Multinationals*, p. 97, notes the existence of technology transfer but assumes that its significance is limited to the multinationals' repatriation of royalties and fees. This seems an understatement, since the higher-than-average returns earned by foreign investors may include an imputed return on know-how.
17. Thurow, "Multinational Companies and the American Distribution of Income," pp. 18–22.

Figure 4-1. *Share of Labor and Capital in Total U.S. National Income, 1946–76*

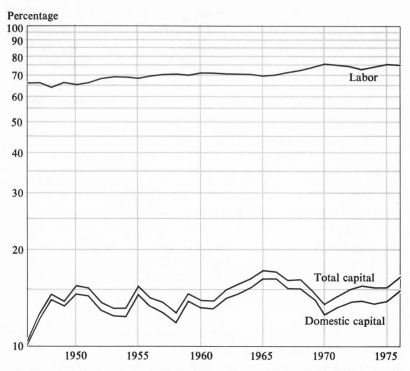

Sources: *The National Income and Product Accounts of the United States, 1929–1974: Statistical Tables,* a supplement to the *Survey of Current Business* (GPO, 1977), pp. 36–37; *Survey of Current Business,* vol. 54 (August 1974), pt. 2, p. 16; and ibid., vol. 55 (November 1975), p. 9; and ibid., vol. 57 (August 1977), p. 43, and (November 1977), p. 6; U.S. Commerce Department, *Balance of Payments of the United States, 1919–1953* (GPO, 1954), p. 155; U.S. Commerce Department, *Balance of Payments: Statistical Supplement,* rev. ed. (GPO, 1963), pp. 184, 202–07; U.S. Bureau of Economic Analysis, "Statistics on Earnings, Dividends, and U.S. Direct Investments Abroad, 1960–1971" (July 24, 1974; processed); *Multinational Corporations: A Compendium of Papers Submitted to the Subcommittee on International Trade of the Committee on Finance of the United States Senate* (GPO, 1973), p. 56.

By adding foreign subsidiaries' retained earnings to this measure of national income, we can calculate total national income.[18]

Figure 4-1 traces the fluctuations in labor and capital share of total national income as defined. According to traditional theory, the share of

18. The data are from *Survey of Current Business* (August 1974), table 9, p. 16; ibid. (October 1974), table B, p. 40; and *National Income Product Accounts of the United States, 1929–1965* a supplement to *Survey of Current Business* (GPO, 1966).

employee compensation and domestic capital should fall and total capital should rise over the period. As figure 4-1 shows, the actual experience does not bear this out. Over the thirty-one years depicted, the share of employee compensation edged slowly upward from 66 percent to 75 percent. There was a detectable decline during 1972–73, perhaps caused by rapid inflation of prices and the presence of wage-price controls rather than by foreign direct investment.

As figure 4-1 indicates, corporate profits tend to fluctuate much more over the course of the business cycle than do employee earnings. But, apart from the rapid rise in corporate profits from their artificial low after the Second World War, the fluctuations are around a more or less stable mean. (The relative gain in employee compensation came at the relative expense of proprietors' and rental income.) Corporate profitability rose rapidly in the early and middle 1960s, dropped rather precipitously during the late 1960s, and only recently began to recover. Until 1972–73, foreign investment made a steady but comparatively small contribution to total capital returns. In 1972–73, however, the fluctuation in total capital returns came primarily from foreign earnings.

The statistics lend little support to the notion that the surge in foreign direct investment over the last decades significantly affected income shares. These aggregate statistics, of course, could be masking important shifts at a lower level of aggregation. The better-compensated employees of multinational firms—managers, scientists, and other professionals— may have gained as ordinary laborers lost.

Table 4-1 presents estimates of the income shares of families divided by quintile, with separate estimates for the top 5 percent. The most striking feature of this table is how little the distribution of income has changed over the last twenty-five years, despite the growth of the American economy. The only significant change is a small erosion of the share of the top 5 percent. These statistics hardly suggest big gains for top managers and engineers and losses for everyone else as foreign investments increased.

One must be wary of drawing conclusions on the basis of aggregate statistics and simplistic tests of hypotheses. But the share of labor in total national income has increased somewhat over the last two decades, and the total share of capital has fluctuated around a relatively stable mean. And while chapter seven gives ample evidence that foreign earnings can stabilize a multinational's consolidated profits, the earnings do not fully

Table 4-1. *Percentage*[a] *of Income Before Taxes Received by Families in Six Income Brackets, Selected Years, 1947–72*

Year	Income rank					
	Lowest fifth	Second fifth	Third fifth	Fourth fifth	Highest fifth	Top 5 percent
1947	5.1	11.8	16.7	23.2	43.3	17.5
1950	4.5	11.9	17.4	23.6	42.7	17.3
1960	4.8	12.2	17.8	24.0	41.3	15.9
1966	5.6	12.4	17.8	23.8	40.5	15.6
1972	5.4	11.9	17.5	23.9	41.4	15.9

Source: *Economic Report of the President, 1974* (GPO, 1974), p. 140.
a. Amounts are rounded.

compensate for declining domestic profits. All in all, the link between foreign investment and the distribution of U.S. income appears to be extremely tenuous.

Alternative Labor Strategies

Though it is doubtful that multinational enterprises export significant numbers of jobs from the United States or adversely affect labor's share of American income distribution, some jobs are exported (see chapter three), and the position of labor in collective bargaining is weakened by the multinationalization of business. In addition, labor's belief, whether well-founded or not, that jobs are exported has led it to search for effective means to countervail the perceived power of multinational enterprises.

These efforts follow two broad strategies: reducing the mobility of the multinational enterprises and increasing labor's own ability to counter that mobility. Tactically, labor can pursue these strategies either through purely national efforts, usually in league with their own governments, or internationally, by coordinating the activities of labor across borders or by promoting intergovernmental agreements. Table 4-2 displays specific approaches and examples of each. In any approach, home-country and host-country labor may seek to promote their own interests, the interests of each other, or both. And a labor union can pursue different approaches simultaneously, for no single approach could achieve all of labor's objectives.

Table 4-2. *Examples of Four Labor Strategies for Countervailing Power of Multinationals*

	Strategy	
Tactic	*Reducing multinationals' power*	*Increasing labor's power*
National effort	U.S. Burke-Hartke bill; Swedish insurance program	Germany's Mitbestimmung (codetermination); Swedish requirement for union approval of investment
International effort	Attempts toward U.N. guidelines and GATT clause on fair labor standards	Genk strike, Saint-Gobain strike, Michelin strike (solidarity action); U.S.-Canada Automotive Pact (international collective bargaining)

Reducing Multinationals' Power through National Effort

The most serious efforts by national labor to check the power of multinational enterprises have been made in the United States and Sweden. In 1969 and 1970, two major U.S. unions challenged foreign investment by the firms under the authority of the National Labor Relations Act (NLRA), which compels business to bargain with labor over its investment decisions that affect employees in the bargaining unit.[19] They were unable to demonstrate that the investments caused an actual reduction in U.S. employment, however, or even that foreign investment data were germane to collective bargaining. Since these failures, U.S. labor has made no effort to use the NLRA to strengthen its position vis-à-vis multinational enterprises.

The AFL-CIO in 1971 developed and sponsored an alternative approach, the Burke-Hartke bill, which sought to legislate four major new constraints on multinational enterprises. First, it would increase the taxation of their foreign income by eliminating the deferral of taxation of

19. The International Union of Electrical, Radio, and Machine Workers (IUE) raised the subject of foreign investments with General Electric during negotiations for their 1969–72 labor agreement, and in 1970 the United Auto Workers attacked Ford Motor's decision to produce Pinto engines and gear boxes at its English and German subsidiaries. The cases are traced and the applicability of the National Labor Relations Act is analyzed in Duane Kujawa, "Foreign Sourcing and the Duty to Bargain Under the NLRA," in Duane Kujawa, ed., *American Labor and the Multinational Corporation* (Praeger, 1973), pp. 253–58.

such income until it is repatriated to the United States and by permitting them to treat payment of foreign taxes only as deductions, rather than credits, against their U.S. tax liabilities.[20] Second, it would require presidential licensing of all foreign direct investments and exports of technology, with decisions based on a number of criteria including the effect on U.S. jobs. Third, more complete corporate disclosure of international activities would be required. Fourth, U.S. imports, especially those produced abroad with American-made components, would be curtailed, partly to prevent American firms from meeting domestic demand through foreign production.[21] As noted in chapter one, changes in the U.S. tax code in 1975 accomplished a small part of the first of these union objectives. However, the other components of the Burke-Hartke approach were rejected by both the administration and Congress.

Sweden is the only other home country in which labor has made a major effort to check locally based multinationals through national legislation, and it has succeeded in structuring two Swedish laws relating to multinational enterprises.[22] First, Swedish legislation authorizing government insurance for foreign direct investment in developing countries requires that the insured firm meet specific standards in such matters as collective bargaining rights; compensation, for wage losses during illnesses, injuries, and layoff; pensions; and several other health and welfare matters. This law sought to help labor in host countries, rather than in Sweden, and pursues interests common to home-country and host-country labor. Swedish-based firms ignore the insurance program, however, rather than meet its conditions.

Swedish unions have also increased the power of home-country labor to cope directly with multinationals. As outlined in chapter two, Sweden

20. The implementation of both proposals would probably have a much more limited effect in cutting foreign direct investment by U.S. firms than is usually supposed; see chap. 6. At the time the bill was proposed, however, the AFL-CIO, the multinationals, and conventional economic wisdom, all suggested that it would have a massive impact.
21. For the conceptual underpinning of these proposals see Stanley H. Ruttenberg and others, *Needed: A Constructive Foreign Trade Policy*, a report prepared for the Industrial Union Department, AFL-CIO (Washington: October 1971). The policy proposals are on pp. 122–28. The United Auto Workers had previously proposed the first three steps; it opposed import quotas throughout the congressional debate on trade policy in 1973–74, however.
22. The Trade Union Congress in the United Kingdom voiced some hostility toward multinationals in the early 1970s and again in 1975, but no legislation or other operative regulatory device has been proposed at the time of this writing.

in 1974 adopted legislation requiring all capital outflows for foreign direct investment by Swedish-based firms to be approved by the Swedish government. All corporate applications for such permission must be accompanied by statements on the proposed investment from both blue-collar and white-collar unions. But no applications have been denied, and it is too early to know how much advantage Swedish labor will derive from their opportunity.

Increasing Labor's Power through National Effort

Workers in Germany, and to some extent other continental European countries and Great Britain, are going a different route to improve their power to countervail the power of multinationals. Rather than allying with the home-country government to overturn corporate decisions that are already made, these unions have for many years sought national and European Community legislation giving them equal representation with management on all supervisory boards—Mitbestimmung, or codetermination. This effort, motivated by a wide range of concerns, preceded the present attention to multinationals and, indeed, since the 1950s has gone forward in a few industries. The most concrete success to date of codetermination vis-à-vis foreign investments came in Germany in early 1975, when the opposition of Volkswagen workers to the firm's proposed investment in the United States helped delay the project and forced the retirement of the management that proposed it.

American unions show little interest in codetermination. (For different reasons, neither do the communist-dominated unions of Italy and France.) Indeed, this is the only one of the four possible strategies U.S. unions have not pursued. Their history of arm's-length confrontation with industry and the hostility to labor of many U.S. firms make the unions wary of any cooperative steps. The clout of the AFL-CIO is largely based on its representation of a distinctive part of the body politic and on the collective power of member unions, which would become diluted through codetermination. Indeed, AFL-CIO leadership views labor representatives on the boards of German firms as being co-opted by management.

Increasing Labor's Power through International Effort

The Volkswagen case also provides a fascinating instance of informal transnational union cooperation, because the opposition of the Volkswagen workers to the investment was at least partly stimulated by Leonard Woodcock, president of the United Auto Workers (UAW) of the United States, during a week-long visit to Wolfsburg. To Woodcock, Volkswagen investment in the United States would have meant simply a shift of jobs from the three large American automakers to Volkswagen, rather than a creation of additional jobs, because demand in the industry at that time was depressed. And in reaching this conclusion he was no doubt in agreement with the appraisal of VW management—that U.S. investment was necessary to retain its share of the U.S. market.[23]

Secretary-General Charles Levinson of the International Federation of Chemical and General Workers' Unions (ICF), suggests that multinational collective bargaining will evolve through three stages: "company-wide support of a single union in one country" in a dispute with a foreign subsidiary or parent firm, "multiple negotiations with a company in several countries at the same time," and finally "integrated negotiations around common demands."[24] The ultimate objective would presumably be multinational collective bargaining, with a single multinational union composed of members from all relevant countries confronting each multinational enterprise (or industry), and operating under the requirements of international law.

National unions have already taken action within each stage. British and American unions supported their Belgian counterparts in a strike against a Ford Motor plant in Genk in 1968, in pursuit of efforts by the International Metalworkers Federation to achieve "upward harmonization of wages."[25] French, German, Italian, and American glass workers simultaneously struck the Saint-Gobain group of companies in early 1969. French and Italian workers, supported at least morally by other European rubber-worker's unions, struck Michelin in 1971 to protest new invest-

23. Subsequently, when demand for automobiles revived with the recovery of the world economy in late 1975 and 1976, both the German auto workers and the UAW withdrew their objections to the investment.

24. Charles Levinson, *International Trade Unionism* (London: Allen and Unwin, 1972), pp. 110–11. See, esp., chap. 4.

25. These and other examples are drawn largely from David C. Hirschfield, *The Multinational Union Challenges the Multinational Company*, Report no. 658 (New York: Conference Board, Inc., 1975), pp. 22–39. He lists (p. 4) the seventeen international trade secretariats and their respective memberships, which total over 53 million workers and range from 11.5 million in sixty-five countries for the International Metalworkers Federation to 10,350 in six countries for the Universal Alliance of Diamond Workers.

ments in Canada.[26] The International Federation of Air Line Pilots Associations staged the world's first multinational, multicompany, shutdown in 1972 when it blocked much of the world's air transportation for a day in an effort to persuade the United Nations to adopt sanctions against countries that harbored skyjackers.[27] American and Canadian auto workers bargained jointly with Chrysler (and simultaneously with General Motors and Ford) within the context of U.S.-Canada automotive pact, achieving wage parity across national borders. In all of the other cases, however, it is unclear whether labor's efforts significantly affected the eventual outcome.[28]

Coordinating and implementing international efforts require certain effort on the part of labor, such as collecting data on the profits and practices of all the subsidiaries of individual firms. The most advanced effort is that of the International Metalworkers' Federation, which has a computer bank on wages and working conditions at forty-seven representative

26. These are the same Michelin investments against whose output the U.S. government applied countervailing import duties (see chap. 3). In this case, the United States as a home country and the rubber workers of France and Italy were allied against a multinational and, implicitly, against the Canadian government and Canadian workers.

27. This was not an action directed against the airline companies, but it demonstrates the possible scope of coordinated union activity.

28. Commenting on the Saint-Gobain effort, Hirschfield, *The Multinational Union Challenges the Multinational Company,* concludes that it "ended up essentially on a national basis" (p. 28). Blake, "Trade Unions and the Challenge of the Multinational Corporation," finds that although the "united front did break down, there was some uniformity of timing and tactics" (p. 43–44). For negative readings on the overall effectiveness of the International Federation of Chemical and General Workers' Unions, see Herbert R. Northrup and Richard L. Rowan, "Multinational Collective Bargaining Activity: The Factual Record in Chemicals, Glass, and Rubber Tires," *Columbia Journal of World Business,* vol. 9 (Spring 1974), pp. 112–24; and "Multinational Collective Bargaining Activity: The Factual Record in Chemicals, Glass, and Rubber Tires, Part II," *Columbia Journal of World Business,* vol. 9 (Summer 1974), pp. 49–63. They do conclude, however, that ad hoc groupings of European unions were "able to force a multinational company to alter drastically a plan of action" in the AKZO case in 1972 (pt. 2, p. 53) and suggest that joint action by communist unions in Europe also represent potential avenues for effective labor cooperation across national borders. The International Federation of Petroleum and Chemical Workers achieved some of the safety and health procedures sought in the strike of their U.S. union in 1973 but none of the desired pension improvements; Shell labeled the efforts of the IFPCW completely unproductive. The International Federation of Airline Pilots Associations got no skyjack treaty, but most countries did significantly tighten their security procedures.

plants of fifteen world auto companies. The secretariats transmit data and technical advice to member unions to help them in specific negotiations, and work generally to strengthen individual unions.[29] Company councils are formed by unions in different countries, and meetings are sought with management to discuss both specific issues and overall corporate investment policy.[30] Common termination dates are sought for labor contracts in different countries, making simultaneous strikes possible. When "solidarity action" is actually needed, unions in nonstriking countries may refuse to work overtime or to otherwise help to offset declining output, and may give financial assistance to the strikers. Almost 25 percent of a group of American multinationals and 40 percent of a group of foreign-based multinationals, responding to a poll in early 1975, reported that they had already experienced at least some of these types of union solidarity.[31]

There are a number of fundamental structural differences among labor organizations in different countries, however, which make the multinationalization of labor extremely difficult. One difference is bargaining method: some are highly decentralized and operate mainly at the firm or even plant level, as in the United States; some operate at the industry level, as in Western Europe; and some are highly centralized, engaging in national bargaining across all industries, as in Sweden. (Only the U.S. model appears widely applicable on the international level.) Another difference is the degree of unionization within a country: less than 25 percent of American workers are unionized, whereas almost all Scandinavian workers are union members. In countries where union membership is

29. For example, in "Main Bargaining Points for Negotiations with the Singapore Subsidiary of Caterpillar," a document prepared by the International Metalworkers Federation Social and Economic Research Department (Geneva, November 1973), detailed and sophisticated information is provided on the global profitability and outlook for Caterpillar, the importance of Singapore to its global operations, the outlook for demand in the Far East, the contribution of labor to Caterpillar's profits, the failure of wages to rise as fast as profits, productivity gains recorded by Caterpillar's workers, the importance of looking at the global operations of the firm in framing labor's position on wages and other issues, and the progress of unions in other countries in their negotiations with Caterpillar. Similar documentation has been prepared for member unions in several industries in other countries.

30. Philips Lamp agreed in 1969 to give its unions advance notice of all production transfers within the European Community—and did so six times in the next four years. Hirschfield, *The Multinational Union Challenges the Multinational Company*, p. 25.

31. Ibid., pp. 7–9.

nonuniversal, any skewness in union composition will affect strategy.[32] Too, ideological differences among unions in different countries remain: some are still dedicated to gaining control of their governments or of achieving broad objectives such as codetermination. And most of them harbor the bureaucratic fear that internationalization would weaken them.

In addition, workers compare their position to other workers within their own countries, rather than to workers in their industry in other countries.[33] This is particularly true of multinational workers in developing countries, whose pay is usually high by national standards though low in comparison to workers in the same industries in the industrialized countries.

There have been recent disagreements between national unions in different countries, triggered by the differences outlined here.[34] Canadian members of the AFL-CIO, for example, denounced the federation's pursuit of tight quotas on U.S. imports and foreign direct investments and threatened to leave the federation unless Canada were exempt from any such steps. In 1974, Japanese auto workers rejected United Auto Worker requests for their help in persuading Japanese auto firms to accept voluntary export restraints on their sales to the United States. The United Rubber Workers supported countervailing duties on U.S. sales of Michelin tires. The International Federation of Petroleum and Chemical Unions opposed the ICF stress on company councils on the grounds that low-paid workers in developing countries could not be asked to help high-paid workers in industrial countries.

Despite the difficulties, a number of U.S. unions participate in efforts

32. The membership of the AFL-CIO is in fact quite unrepresentative of the overall U.S. labor force. See C. Fred Bergsten, "The Costs of Import Restrictions to American Consumers," in Robert E. Baldwin and J. David Richardson, eds., *International Trade and Finance* (Little, Brown, 1974).

33. See Lloyd Ulman, "Multinational Unionism: Incentives, Barriers, and Alternatives," *Industrial Relations*, vol. 14 (February 1975), esp. pp. 10–13. He argues that elements that prompted development of national unions—job insecurity in some regions and the ability of firms to counter strikes by moving production—are also present internationally. However, the critical ingredient, a general decline in wages, is missing at the moment. He thus concludes that "the prospects for such developments are not favorable at this time" (p. 1), though "in the long run international unionism might not be dead" (p. 30).

34. For a remarkably candid statement by a labor official of differences between national unions see Masao Aihara, "Multinational Companies and Trade Unions: A Japanese View," in C. Fred Bergsten, ed., *Toward a New World Trade Policy: The Maidenhead Papers* (Lexington Books, 1975), esp. pp. 167–69.

118 American Multinationals and American Interests

to multinationalize labor, both to help unions in other countries and to seek help for their own activities; on the other hand, virtually all of these unions also supported the Burke-Hartke efforts to slash foreign direct investment by American firms, which would hurt labor in other countries. Solidarity actions obviously will be combined with other strategies in union confrontation with the power of multinationals.

Reducing Multinational Power through International Effort

For many years, labor groups have sought to add to international trade agreements (General Agreement on Tariffs and Trade) requirements covering working conditions and pay. (Such requirements were included in the charter of the stillborn International Trade Organization.) More recently, some labor groups have been in the forefront of the efforts to use the United Nations to set new international rules, or at least guidelines, on the operations of multinational enterprises.

Summary and Conclusions

Though none of the four strategies available to labor has achieved dramatic success, all are building toward it. And though many multinationals are skeptical that international collective bargaining will ever occur, others see it as inevitable.[35] But internationalization of labor has progressed very slowly compared with internationalization of business, and it is viewed even by its most ardent devotees—the dedicated people who manage the international trade secretariats in Geneva—as requiring a decade or more to become a significant force in world industrial relations.[36] In any event, eventual multinationalization appears to be a component of labor's strat-

35. Hirschfield, *The Multinational Union Challenges the Multinational Company;* Roberts and May, "The Response of Multinational Enterprises to International Trade Union Pressures."
36. Author interviews. Hirschfield, "Highlights for the Executive," *The Multinational Union Challenges the Multinational Company* (unnumbered preliminary page) agrees that "the immediate prospects for actual multinational coordinated collective bargaining seem remote. Multinational labor organizations must overcome legal barriers, nationalism, union rivalries, a tendency toward bargaining at the plant level, and resistance by the multinational companies to the very concept of multinational bargaining."

egy, both to gain psychic redress against the superior mobility of capital and management and to defend its more tangible economic interests.[37]

This analysis suggests that labor's primary recourse, particularly in the short run, is to governments of both host and home countries; indeed much of labor's success in countervailing the power of corporations within national borders has come through influencing government policy. National legislation is required to regulate working standards, minimum wages, bargaining with representative unions, and allowing actions by labor such as strikes. Though collective bargaining in the United States first occurred before the 1930s, it was the legislation of that and subsequent periods that enabled U.S. labor to begin to exercise effective countervailing power.

Just as labor within individual countries once had to both organize itself and get government help to cope with the national spread of industry, so must world labor organize itself internationally and get help from both home and host governments, through both national and international policies, to cope with the multinationalization of the corporate sector. We should thus expect it to pursue a two-track strategy, with a heavy emphasis in the immediate future on seeking government help.

Two specific U.S. policy changes could be sought. Though sympathy strikes across national borders may be effective in keeping a firm from increasing production in one country to offset the production cutback of a struck plant in another country, such strikes are illegal in the United States and many other countries. Legalizing sympathy strikes in the United States would permit workers of the parent company to support strikes by workers in its foreign subsidiaries and would enable American labor to play a larger role in international union cooperation.

Second, the jurisdiction of the National Labor Relations Board could be extended to cover foreign direct investment. This could raise problems of extraterritoriality, because data might be required from subsidiaries incorporated in other countries. On the other hand, the board could get

37. William J. Curtin, "The Multinational Corporation and Transnational Collective Bargaining," in Kujawa, ed., *American Labor and the Multinational Corporation,* is probably right in concluding that labor can get the most mileage from "multinational cooperation in the utilization of the economic weaponry of collective bargaining," which the unions refer to as "solidarity action" (p. 219). Correspondingly, Roberts and May, "The Response of Multinational Enterprises to International Trade Union Pressures," report that American multinationals are most worried about this type of labor action (p. 411).

information from the parent regarding its transactions with the subsidiary, and penalties could be applied simply to the parent.

In closing, it must be added that labor's interests and priorities may in some cases run counter to national interests. Multinational labor may benefit only the relatively elite workers, while national labor may simply protect positions already acquired; in either case, the conditions for the majority of workers could well be worsened.[38] Hence labor can no more be permitted to dictate national policy than can business.

Widespread controls over foreign direct investment, as advocated by the AFL-CIO and as effected in Sweden, could adversely affect the national economic welfare of the home country (as well as welfare in host countries). Codetermination, in practice, could bring either co-option of labor by business, reducing labor's countervailing power, or collusion of labor and business against broad public interests.

38. See Robert W. Cox, "Labor and the Multinationals," *Foreign Affairs*, vol. 54 (January 1976), pp. 363–65.

CHAPTER FIVE

Access to Raw Materials

OVER 30 PERCENT of U.S. foreign direct investment is in the extractive industries, although that share has been declining in recent years. At the same time, national concern over access to raw materials has risen sharply. In 1975 the United States depended on imports for at least 25 percent of its consumption of each of thirty key minerals and metals (see tables 5-1 and 5-2), and this percentage is rising for virtually all of them. America's access to raw materials, then, must be one of the important considerations in constructing a national policy toward multinationals.

Since the industrial revolution, the need for raw materials has been a concern of the major powers of Europe and Asia and was an element in their formal and informal empire-building. Until recently, however, shortages in the United States have been short-term, although shortages during wartime have provoked the panicky reaction that America (or the world) was running out of supplies. During the period of American postwar leadership in international affairs raw materials were abundant, with new geological discoveries and new extraction techniques keeping prices relatively low.

In the 1970s, however, the availability and cost of raw materials are again major concerns. Are lessons drawn from periods of apparent abundance good guides to the future? Can market forces by themselves correct short-term disequilibria to ensure that extractive industries function smoothly and efficiently? There have been fundamental changes in the structure of international natural resource industries. They have changed the role that multinational corporations will, or can, play in keeping commodity markets competitive, and they have profound impli-

121

122   *American Multinationals and American Interests*

Table 5-1. *Percentage of Key U.S. Minerals and Metals Supplied by Imports, and Their Major Foreign Sources*

Mineral	Percentage imported[a]	Major foreign sources
Columbium	100	Brazil, Thailand, Nigeria
Mica (sheet)	100	India, Brazil, Malagasy
Strontium	100	Mexico, United Kingdom, Spain
Manganese	99	Brazil, Gabon, Australia, South Africa
Cobalt	98	Zaire, Belgium-Luxembourg, Finland, Norway, Canada
Tantalum	95	Thailand, Canada, Australia, Brazil
Chromium	91	South Africa, Soviet Union, Turkey, Rhodesia
Asbestos	86	Canada, South Africa
Aluminum (ores and metals)	85	Jamaica, Surinam, Australia, Dominican Republic
Fluorine	82	Mexico, Spain, Italy
Bismuth	80	Peru, Japan, Mexico, United Kingdom
Platinum group (metal)	80	South Africa, United Kingdom, Soviet Union
Tin	75	Malaysia, Thailand, Bolivia
Mercury	73	Canada, Algeria, Mexico, Spain
Nickel	71	Canada, Norway
Zinc	64	Canada, Mexico, Australia, Honduras, Peru
Tellurium	59	Peru, Canada
Selenium	58	Canada, Japan, Mexico
Antimony	56	South Africa, People's Republic of China, Bolivia, Mexico
Tungsten	54	Canada, Bolivia, Thailand, Peru
Cadmium	50	Mexico, Canada, Australia, Belgium-Luxembourg
Potassium	49	Canada
Gold	45	Canada, Switzerland, United Kingdom, France
Gypsum	39	Canada, Mexico, Jamaica
Vanadium	36	South Africa, Chile, Soviet Union
Barium	35	Ireland, Peru, Mexico
Petroleum (incl. natural gas)	35	Canada, Venezuela, Nigeria, Saudi Arabia
Silver	30	Canada, Mexico, Peru
Iron	29	Canada, Venezuela, Japan, European Economic Community
Titanium (ilmenite)	28	Canada, Australia

Source: U.S. Bureau of Mines, *Minerals and Materials: A Monthly Survey* (GPO, June 1976), p. 3.
a. Total consumption equals U.S. primary and secondary production plus net import reliance. Net import reliance equals imports minus exports plus or minus government stockpile and industry stock changes.

Table 5-2. *U.S. Imports and Exports of Raw and Processed Minerals,*
1975 and 1976
Billions of dollars

Mineral	1975	1976
Imports		
Crude oil	18.3	22.9
Refined petroleum	6.5	6.8
Iron and steel	4.7	3.8
Chemicals	2.9	3.6
Natural gas	1.4	2.0
Iron ore	0.9	0.5
Bauxite and alumina	0.6	0.6
Aluminum	0.4	0.5
Nickel	0.5	0.4
Copper	0.4	0.7
Tin	0.3	0.3
Chrome and alloys	0.3	0.2
All others	2.8	3.7
Total	40.0	46.0
Exports		
Chemicals	5.6	6.3
Coal	3.3	2.5
Iron and steel	2.5	1.9
Plastics	1.2	1.6
Petroleum products	0.9	1.0
Iron and steel scrap	0.8	0.6
Aluminum	0.4	0.5
Copper	0.3	0.3
All others	3.0	3.3
Total	18.0	18.0
Imports minus exports	22.0	28.0

Source: U.S. Bureau of Mines, *Minerals and Materials: A Monthly Survey* (GPO, June 1976), p. 4.

cations for the relations between producer and consumer countries and
among consumer states, themselves.

Defining the Issue

Large consumer states should design policies toward home-based extractive multinationals to achieve certain objectives. After more than a

century of debate, the appropriate objectives and appropriate policies are still opaque. A definition of the issue may cast some light. It has two parts: the price of raw materials to the home country and their availability to the home country.

Basically, the price of an industrial commodity consists of the production costs plus the profit of the producer. A public policy designed for the benefit of consumers would encourage competition to keep the price as close as possible to the production costs, over the long term. Access, too, can be expressed as a cost: the cost of influencing how suppliers will distribute output when there is not enough to go around, or the cost of influencing how suppliers will ration output on terms different from those the market would otherwise produce. The cost can be levied with either an economic or a noneconomic price tag and, under certain circumstances, can approach infinity (that is, a consumer may be unable to get any more supply "at any price" or may be willing to pay "any price" to get additional supply).

In general, access is a question of who gets supplies at a price lower than where the market clears. But this is clearly too narrow a definition if individual suppliers have discretion about the level as well as the disposition of output that would maximize their returns. Under these conditions, access includes both the cost of influencing who will get available supply and the cost of influencing how much supply will be available. Access can be measured on a scale that estimates the cost of influencing suppliers to act against their economic self-interest when they have any discretion about price or volume. A national policy designed for the benefit of consumers should aim to minimize that cost while still ensuring access at some predetermined level (perhaps a certain share of all available output, perhaps a level unchanged in absolute terms despite supply cutbacks).

If natural resource industries were highly competitive, if the sources of raw materials were widely dispersed geographically, and if new supplies could be developed rapidly in response to a rise in prices, the problems for consumers of price and access would be minor. No producer would be able to raise the price by restricting his own output. Cartels of either companies or producing countries or both would be difficult to form or maintain. Sudden shortfalls would put producers in the position of rationing output for only a brief period of time. Consumers would have little incentive to prefer one supplier (for example, one of their own nationality) over others. The discipline of the market would solve the problem of access at the same time it pushed price toward cost.

But scale factors in natural resource industries are large, lead times for the development of new output are long, and sources of supply are frequently concentrated in a few regions. To the extent that these factors limit competition, they provide both the power to raise prices by restricting production and the power to allocate supplies.

Strategies of the Past

Governments of major consuming states can deal with oligopoly in the extractive industries by means of public policies directed at its causes (to improve competition) and public policies directed at its consequences (to ensure that the discretion about production, price, and access falls as little as possible into the hands of outsiders). These strategies are not mutually exclusive, but when given a choice, the major consumer states have shown a consistent preference for dealing with consequences. Their efforts to avoid being dependent on the good will or the whim of "outsiders" for raw materials has traditionally taken three forms: developing domestic self-sufficiency, acquiring colonies, and promoting foreign direct investment in order to have their "own" companies as suppliers.

Domestic Self-Sufficiency

Producing all supplies internally may appear to be the ultimate solution to the problem of access. It provides the consuming state with control over the disposition of output, albeit at the cost of forgoing lower prices available elsewhere. Stockpiling is another form of domestic self-sufficiency. Enough materials are stocked to last through possible cutbacks in supplies, this time at the cost of acquiring and maintaining the stocks. Looking at the problem historically, for most countries the possibility of domestic self-sufficiency through internal production did not last long into the twentieth century. In the second half of the nineteenth century, well before resources of copper, nickel, tin, bauxite, oil, coal, and iron ore were exhausted, the marginal cost of domestic output became too high for Japan, Great Britain, France, and even Germany to compete commercially with powers that availed themselves of cheaper resources outside their own borders. The United States at that time still had an economic choice between local and foreign production. Now, in the last quarter of the twentieth century, the United States finds itself increasingly reliant on external sources for many materials; the alternative is high prices plus social costs such as environmental damage.

Domestic self-sufficiency is deceptive, anyway. To some extent, it merely disguises the problems of access and price by transferring the power to withhold supplies and/or raise prices to local rather than foreign groups (coal miners, oil companies, copper workers, bureaucrats) and shifts the burden of influencing that power to the domestic political system. Unless domestic suppliers (and domestic labor) are highly competitive among themselves, the security of supply in a self-sufficient system is only as great as the willingness of the state to compel its members to act in the interest of consumers. Thus it does not eliminate the vulnerability of supply to the power of suppliers, as Britain found in the coal strike of 1974. Moreover, whatever degree of access this system may provide in a crisis becomes more costly over time as the country depletes its cheaper sources of raw materials. A country using a strategy of self-sufficiency risks eventually being more dependent than ever on foreigners, as local reserves become exhausted.

Colonization

At one time, the acquisition of empire (backed by military protection of trade routes) assured a flow of raw materials to consuming countries (copper from Northern Rhodesia, oil from Java, bauxite from Guinea, rubber from Malaya). Colonization was an international extension of domestic self-sufficiency, and its effectiveness depended upon the ability of the home government to get colonial administrators and colonial companies to act in accordance with its desires.[1] The assumption of the large industrial powers of Europe and Asia that raw materials markets were highly imperfect (composed, that is, of oligopolists of either their own or other consuming states) suggests that imperialist expansion was rationally

1. The companies demanded special concessions for their products before allowing Britain a trade monopoly, thus shattering Joseph Chamberlain's plans for protection and imperial preference in the early 1900s. See E. J. Hobsbawm, *Industry and Empire: The Making of Modern English Society,* vol. 2, *1750 to the Present Day* (Pantheon Books, 1968), p. 124.

self-interested. Indeed, the debate about whether the colonies of the British, French, Russians, or Dutch "paid" for themselves by generating a net economic gain to the home country is misdirected.[2] Neither established imperialists nor the late-coming Germans and Japanese could weigh the costs of empire purely against the financial benefits derived from overseas possessions. They had also to weigh the costs of empire against the costs of being at the mercy of suppliers who could manipulate the flow of raw materials. Reducing reliance on the discretion of outsiders may have made empire worthwhile even if the costs of maintaining it were greater than the direct benefits.

Foreign Direct Investment

But the vast paraphernalia of formal empire was not necessary to ensure access to cheap raw materials. Until quite recently, the same result could be had at much less cost through direct foreign investment. From the end of the Second World War, the main benefit consuming countries derived from foreign direct investment was not preferred treatment but a smoothly functioning, multilateral, nondiscriminatory supply system in which new entrants or the threat of new entrants at the production stage prevented the abuse of market power by existing suppliers.

However, industrial home countries did not explicitly seek maximization of competition.[3] In Europe, national support of large extractive companies (frequently created through the consolidation of existing companies) was predicated upon the acceptance of oligopoly in international markets and upon the desire to create a powerful oligopolist to call one's

2. See Leonard S. Woolf, *Empire and Commerce in Africa: A Study in Economic Imperialism* (London: Allen and Unwin, 1919); Eugene Staley, *War and the Private Investor: A Study in the Relations of International Politics and International Private Investment* (University of Chicago Press, 1935); Michael Barratt Brown, *After Imperialism* (London: William Heinemann, 1963).
3. There have been exceptions. In the mid-sixties the Japanese, to ensure supplies of iron ore and copper, signed long-term contracts, many with small companies or new industry entrants who used them as collateral to finance expansion of their market shares. The effect was a decrease in concentration. In 1955 the U.S. government insisted that eight American oil companies be included in the reconstituted Iranian Consortium. Although restrictive off-take arrangements by the major partners hindered the growth of the independents' market share, Atlantic, Richfield, and Getty did expand their activities overseas. See Mira Wilkins, *The Maturing of Multinational Enterprise: American Business Abroad from 1914 to 1970* (Harvard University Press, 1974), p. 323.

own. In the United States, foreign investment policy has encouraged all investors (which, in industries with high barriers to entry, are the established companies) to invest in any way, or in any combination, or in any place that they deemed best for maximizing their own profits. As long as production is reasonably competitive as a by-product of the foreign investment process, such policies can be labeled a success. But the rationale with which they ordinarily have been justified (that is, to provide secure access to raw materials in case of shortage) depends upon the same conditions as the colonial system: effective exercise of sovereignty by the companies over their foreign operations and the ability of the home government to compel or persuade the companies to put that sovereignty at the service of home-country goals.

To strengthen their influence over company affairs, European governments frequently sought an ownership share. "The price of oil does not depend wholly, or even mainly, on the ordinary workings of supply and demand,"[4] Winston Churchill, as First Lord of the Admiralty, argued in 1914. To "acquire proper bargaining power and facilities with regard to the purchase of oil" for the Royal Navy, he urged the House of Commons to take a majority stake in the Anglo-Persian Oil Company, which then served as the instrument of the home state. Not only did the company supply British military and civilian needs during the First World War while keeping Iranian oil out of the hands of the Germans and Austro-Hungarians, it followed British Treasury instructions to limit dividend payments (and hence Iranian revenues) despite a previous understanding with the Iranian government that it would raise local revenues as sales rose.

The United States, on the other hand, has benefited from home-company sovereignty over foreign sources of raw materials without the need for government participation in the workings of those companies. In normal times, with abundant domestic supplies and low strategic vulnerability to cutoffs in foreign supplies, American policymakers devoted less attention to both the threats and the opportunities of resource diplomacy than did their counterparts in Europe and Asia. In times of crisis, however, the United States has used its power over companies of American nationality to serve the interests of the nation, just as the governments of

4. Quoted material from Elizabeth Monroe, *Britain's Moment in the Middle East 1914–1956* (London: Chatto and Windus, 1963), p. 98. For similar sentiments on the part of German and French officials, see Staley's account of the Mannesmann mining company, *War and the Private Investor*, pp. 178–95.

other industrial countries have. In the Second World War, Great Britain
and the United States together set price ceilings for the output from the
countries where their home companies were located, negotiating only with
the firms.[5] Host countries in the Third World, unable to market the output themselves, claimed that, in terms of lost earnings, they contributed
as much as the main combatants to the war effort.[6]

America's only aggressive venture into resource diplomacy (when it
threatened to deny petroleum supplies to Great Britain, France, and
Israel during the Suez invasion of 1956 if they did not withdraw their
forces) also required the exercise of American sovereignty via companies
of American nationality. With the Suez canal closed and the Syrian pipelines destroyed, Europe was 64 percent short of its usual petroleum requirements. Rationing had already begun in both France and Great Britain. There was spare capacity available in Venezuela, owned by Gulf Oil
and Creole Petroleum (Standard Oil Company of New Jersey, now Exxon); but President Eisenhower and Secretary of State John Foster Dulles
warned the British and the French that additional supplies from these
sources would not be forthcoming until they agreed to total withdrawal.

If the nationality of ownership of petroleum companies in Venezuela
were crucial in determining who got Venezuelan oil, one must assume that
the penalties the United States could levy on the American parent corporations for selling new output to the Europeans were greater than the
benefits the companies would gain from the sales and greater than the loss
Venezuela could threaten them with if they did not expand production.
The European countries had prepared an international oil allocation plan
to expand the oil available to France and Great Britain in which the

5. See S. McKee Rosen, *The Combined Boards of the Second World War: An
Experiment in International Administration* (Columbia University Press, 1951).

6. In Chile, for example, export revenues for copper would have been $107 mil-
lion greater if the country had received the price allowed for subsidized mines in
the United States; see Theodore H. Moran, *Multinational Corporations and the
Politics of Dependence: Copper in Chile* (Princeton University Press, 1974), p. 61.
These revenues would have been $500 million more if Chile had received Europe's
free market price; see Markos Mamalakis and Clark Winton Reynolds, *Essays on
the Chilean Economy* (Irwin, 1965), p. 240.

Throughout this book the Third World refers to developing countries whose economic progress moved them into a new international middle class (virtually all of
the Middle East, Latin America, and East Asia). The Fourth World includes those
countries, mainly in Africa and South Asia, with a per capita income below $400;
it equates roughly with the 35–45 countries the World Bank and the United Nations
consider the most seriously affected by the energy crisis.

American oil companies showed a willingness to participate.[7] But the Justice Department ruled that the companies needed an antitrust exemption to do so, and no exemption was forthcoming from the Eisenhower administration until the invasion forces were withdrawn. It is not certain whether Venezuela protested being denied the opportunity to sell added output at premium prices in Europe. But it had no alternative except to go along with the decisions of the American companies. Its foreign exchange reserves were low, its dependence upon petroleum earnings was great, and it did not have (and could not hire) the skills needed to manage the production, refining, and transport of the oil.

This incident demonstrates both the strength and the weakness of using direct foreign investment as a means of controlling access to output in highly imperfect markets. The system depends on a world, whether called neocolonial or not, in which host governments (by choice or necessity) permit investors to respond to the needs of the home country, even when better terms are available elsewhere, and in which investors, whether by choice or necessity, accede to the demands of their home countries. This world existed for the first five or six decades of this century. It no longer does.

The Obsolescing Bargain

What has happened to that comfortable world of resource procurement? The images of Anaconda, British Petroleum, and Alcan, long the symbol of invulnerability in their relations with host countries, are shattered. In the petroleum industry, the major corporations are in the process of being transformed, with or without nationalization, from independent and dominant actors into junior partners of the host governments; and they are virtually helpless to prevent it. These changes are being duplicated across the spectrum of direct investment in the extractive industries.

The power of the natural resource companies of Europe and North America sprang from their ability to dictate terms at the beginning of an investment. Scale factors were large; Aramco's first refinery at Ras Tanura in 1945, Anaconda's shift to sulphides at Chuquicamata in 1948, and

7. Author interview, January 16, 1975, with Angus Beckett, chairman, Organisation for Economic Co-operation and Development oil committee, Turin, Italy.

Bethlehem and U.S. Steel's mining operations in the Orinoco basin in 1951, all cost more than $100 million to construct (a figure that would have to be multiplied by four or five, for the same capacity in current costs).[8] The technologies of exploration, extraction, and processing, were tightly held. Support industries worked almost exclusively for the investors.

The investments had to be made in lump sums and under great uncertainty. As a consequence, firms were unlikely to make an investment unless they were promised substantial discretion in how they conducted their operations and high returns if they were successful. With weak competition among investors and little if any ability to exploit their resources themselves, host governments had little choice but to accept foreign investors on their own terms or to do without any investment. General Juan Vicente Gómez, for example, allowed the Creole Petroleum Corporation (Standard Oil Company of New Jersey) to write its own legislation as a condition of entry into Venezuela after the First World War.[9] In the same period, Kennecott paid taxes to the Chilean government of only 0.8 percent in sales.[10] This type of agreement, so generous to investors, was typically for a forty-year, sixty-year, or ninety-nine year period—or even for perpetuity.

Once the investments were made and the mines or wells successfully working, however, such long-term agreements could not be enforced without the use of gunboats (or the covert equivalent of gunboats) by the home governments of the investors. The high fixed costs, which gave foreign companies such strength at the beginning of the investment, became a source of vulnerability afterwards. With their capital sunk, foreign investors could be trapped into continuing production as long as they were recovering their variable costs. However, through the first four decades

8. On the background of Aramco in Saudi Arabia, see Edith T. Penrose, *The Large International Firm in Developing Countries: The International Petroleum Industry* (Massachusetts Institute of Technology Press, 1968) and Wilkins, *The Maturing of Multinational Enterprise*. On Anaconda in Chile, see Mamalakis and Reynolds, *Essays on the Chilean Economy,* and Moran, *Multinational Corporations and the Politics of Dependence.* On Bethlehem and U.S. Steel in Venezuela, see Henry Gomez, "Venezuela's Iron Ore Industry," in Raymond F. Mikesell and others, *Foreign Investment in the Petroleum and Mineral Industries* (Johns Hopkins University Press for Resources for the Future, 1971).

9. Edwin Lieuwen, *Venezuela,* 2nd ed. (London: Oxford University Press, 1965), pp. 47–48.

10. Mamalakis and Reynolds, *Essays on the Chilean Economy,* p. 226.

of this century, two factors besides the threat of gunboats gave stability to long-term agreements: docile host-country leaders, who accepted the status quo (or who accepted private payments to preserve the status quo); and a lack in the host country of expertise to oversee and supervise the operation of the foreign companies.

The result was that the terms of the initial agreements were rarely renegotiated. In Venezuela, the successor to Gómez, Eleazar López Contreras, passed a law for the country's petroleum industry in 1938, calling for higher payments to the government, but the major oil companies disputed its legality and ignored its consequences.[11] López did not press the issue. In Chile in the 1920s, the reform administration of Arturo Alessandro raised the tax on the country's copper industry from 6 percent to 12 percent (but with great temerity lest Anaconda and Kennecott withdraw). The Chilean government had no firm data on the companies' after-tax rate of return; for Kennecott it was about 40 percent per year.[12]

Host-country leadership and expertise began to change after the Second World War. The growing demands of urbanization and social mobilization made acquisition of hard currency revenues a priority of Third World governments in the postwar period. Their extractive sectors, dominated by foreign firms, became a focus for nationalistic demands of an intensity rare in the tranquil oligarchic societies of earlier periods. This produced classic confrontations—such as Mossadeq's insistence on higher revenues from the Anglo-Iranian Oil Company to finance the country's First Development Plan, and the struggle of the Kinshasa government to use earnings from the copper mines of Katanga to pay for postindependence development of the Congo—confrontations that escalated to nationalization.

More pervasive than confrontation was the host country's improvement of its economic, financial, and accounting skills, so that it could monitor industry more closely and force the renegotiation of terms when conditions permitted. Saudi Arabia began to train national administrators and strategists at the Harvard Business School, the Johns Hopkins School of Advanced International Studies, and other American institutions. (Zaki Yamani, Minister of Petroleum, and Suleman Soliam, Minister of Com-

11. Lieuwen, *Venezuela*, p. 55.
12. Since Anaconda had bought its Chuquicamata property as a going concern in 1923 the return on book value averaged only 14 percent. For these calculations, see Moran, *Multinational Corporations and the Politics of Dependence*, pp. 22–23.

merce and Industry, were trained in this period.) Chile created an independent staff to oversee the operations of its North American mining companies, instead of solely relying, as it had in the past, on advisories of New York brokerage houses regarding market conditions and corporate activities in the international copper industry.

As late as 1958, the transfer price received by Venezuela for its iron ore "was determined solely by the companies [U.S. Steel and Bethlehem] on the basis of criteria that each deemed as relevant."[13] The same was true for Liberia.[14] But by the late 1960s and early 1970s, producer organizations—the Intergovernmental Council of Copper Exporters (CIPEC), the International Bauxite Association (IBA), and the Association of Iron Exporting Countries—were formed, as OPEC had been a decade earlier, to share information on terms of concession, on pricing formulas, and on strategies to strengthen the hand of local negotiators.

A host country's need for higher revenues and the development of its bargaining skills produced a new interaction between the host country and the natural resource investor, an interaction that Raymond Vernon calls the obsolescing bargain.[15] A foreign company is enticed by terms that outweigh the drawbacks of committing large lump sums of capital under conditions of great uncertainty. Once the uncertainty is dissipated and the project is profitable, the original terms appear to be overgenerous to the company, who, because it now cannot withdraw, must accept the stricter conditions of a new bargain. This process has a cyclical character: to attract new investors or new commitments from old investors (for greater capacity, more processing, new technologies), the climate might improve for a period. But the new bargains, too, obsolesce.[16]

13. Gomez, "Venezuela's Iron Ore Industry," p. 327.
14. Author interviews with industry officials.
15. Raymond Vernon, *Sovereignty at Bay: The Multinational Spread of U.S. Enterprises* (Basic Books, 1971), pp. 46–59.
16. The cycle would not be affected by type of investor (a state agency or a private company) or by type of home-country government (socialist or capitalist). A state agency that invests directly in foreign natural resources, and wants to be compensated for the initial risk and uncertainty, is subject to the same vulnerabilities and instabilities as a private investor. A state agency established to serve the needs of the home country would be inclined to keep prices low at the production stage. Of course, a state agency established to aid the host country would be inclined to accommodate to the obsolescing bargain. But if Soviet natural resource investments like the Dabele bauxite mine in Guinea happen to generate less tension than multinational investments, it is probably not because they are state run but because they operate on a coproduction basis rather than on a direct ownership basis.

Dividing the Shares

In democratic systems, the competition of political parties limits the period of stability after new investments are in place. For example, in 1969 President Eduardo Frei of Chile was pushed from a program of chileanization of Anaconda to one of nationalization by a rebellion in his own Christian Democratic Party. All of the major candidates for president the following year (including the conservative Jorge Alessandri, long a friend and admirer of Anaconda's management) pledged to uphold the nationalization.[17]

Regardless of political persuasion, host governments are seldom impervious to the appeal of increased revenues from their foreign-dominated extractive sector. In Venezuela, a military junta overthrew Rómulo Betancourt twelve days after he announced a mandatory 50-50 profit split. Though it promised a more friendly environment for the oil companies, the new regime kept the profit formula, and in 1956–57 the new strongman, Marcos Pérez Jiménez, shook the entire industry by revoking unworked concessions of the major oil companies and calling for new bids to finance his plans for urban construction. In Iran, Mossadeq was overthrown after he nationalized the Anglo-Iranian Oil Company in 1951. But the regimes that followed pressed successfully for higher returns from the reconstituted consortium. In Chile, the military successors to Allende promised generous treatment for new foreign investors but have upheld the nationalization of Anaconda and Kennecott and compensated the former owners at less than book value.[18] Thus, the apparent exceptions to economic nationalism frequently prove the nationalistic rule.

In the international oil industry, competition among investors for new concessions was used by host governments to revise the terms of agree-

17. Evaluation of Alessandri's relations with Anaconda derived from author interviews with Anaconda officials, New York and Santiago, 1969–70.

18. The book values for the properties of Anaconda and Kennecott in Chile were disputed. Anaconda put its losses in 1972 at $474 million but accepted a settlement of $253 million from Chile in 1974 (plus a contested insurance claim against OPIC for $160 million). The comptroller general of Chile set the book value for El Teniente (49 percent owned by Kennecott) at $319 million as of 1970. In 1974, Kennecott settled for $54 million. See "Anaconda Says Chile to Pay It $253 Million Sum," *Wall Street Journal*, July 25, 1974; Gene Smith, "Kennecott Accepts Pact With Chile," *New York Times*, October 25, 1974; Kennecott Copper Corporation, *Confiscation of El Teniente*, supplement no. 2 (New York: Kennecott, 1972).

ments with established investors to the benefit of the host governments. J. Paul Getty's Pacific Western Oil Company (the precursor to Getty Oil) bought into Saudi Arabia in 1949 by offering larger tax payments than the established oil companies were then willing to pay, upsetting the stability of existing agreements.[19] Equilibrium was restored in 1952 only after Venezuela's 50-50 profit-sharing formula—the most favorable terms enjoyed by any host country—spread throughout the Persian Gulf. This formula raised the revenues of oil exporting governments by 300–400 percent, largely at the expense of the U.S. Treasury, because the firms were able to credit their higher tax payments to the host countries against their tax liabilities in the United States.[20] Independent firms with a great deal to gain from new sources of crude oil and little to lose from the revision of existing concessions, were a constant threat to the major oil companies. Italy's Ente Nazionale Idrocarburi (ENI) and the Standard Oil Company of Indiana enabled Iran in 1957 to breach the 50-50 formula and the resistance of the majors, the so-called Seven Sisters, to equity participation.[21] In a similar fashion and at about the same time, the Arabian Oil Company of Japan underbid the majors for the offshore rights of Kuwait and Saudi Arabia in the neutral zone between the two countries.[22]

Libya provides the classic example of the successful manipulation of independents for national advantage. In the 1960s, King Idris used Continental Oil and Occidental Petroleum (which did not have large European sales and were therefore less averse than the majors to cutting product prices) to speed the development of Libyan reserves and to move more Libyan crude oil into the continental market. Idris' successor,

19. Zuhayr Mikdashi, *A Financial Analysis of Middle Eastern Oil Concessions: 1901–1965* (Praeger, 1966), p. 136.
20. Estimate of Henry Cattan, *The Evolution of Oil Concessions in the Middle East and North Africa* (Oceana Publications, 1967), p. 10. Wilkins, *The Maturing of Multinational Enterprise*, p. 321, suggests that Standard Oil of New Jersey encouraged the use of the 50-50 formula in the Middle East to expand host-country revenues at no cost to the U.S. oil companies, which could claim foreign tax credits. As we see in chap. 6, the decision to qualify these tax payments for the foreign tax credit was made by the National Security Council for reasons of foreign policy.
21. Penrose, *The Large International Firm in Developing Countries*, p. 74. The Seven Sisters are Exxon, Royal Dutch/Shell, British Petroleum, Gulf Oil, Texaco, Standard of California, and Mobil.
22. Ibid.

Colonel Qaddafi, then carried the manipulation a step further, threatening the same independents with production cuts. They gave in to demands for higher taxes, because (unlike the majors) they did not have alternative sources of crude oil.[23]

In other natural resource industries, the effect of competition among companies to push into the domains of others by underbidding established investors has been more subdued, perhaps because the spread between price and cost is less than for oil. But they have been squeezed in the same manner by their host countries. The Anglo-American Corporation of South Africa and the Roan Selection Trust (42 percent owned by American Metal Climax) held their Zambian copper concessions in perpetuity before Zambia's independence in 1964, with free remittance of all profits.[24] In 1968, President Kenneth Kaunda announced that only 50 percent of after-tax profits could be sent abroad; the remainder had to be invested in Zambia. The following year, in the first Mines and Minerals Act in the country's history, all mineral rights were assumed by the state, and on January 1, 1970, the government took over 51 percent of both companies. The resulting joint ventures were taxed at 73 percent, with 51 percent of the remaining 27 percent—for a total of 87 percent—going to the government. To encourage expansion of output, however, the government decided to allow management and sales contracts that restored much of the prior cash flow to the parent corporations.[25] But as the expansion projects neared completion in the early 1970s, President Kaunda began to tighten the cash flow again. In 1974 he forced revision of the contracts, five years early.

Cycles similar to Zambia's could be traced for the other major copper-

23. In 1971, independent and major firms (with the blessing of the U.S. government) formed the London Policy Group to try to guarantee supplies of crude oil to independent companies. But John Irwin, U.S. under secretary of state, undermined these efforts by concluding that Iran's demands would bring price stability. (Author interviews with industry sources. See also Edith Penrose, "The Development of Crisis," *Daedalus,* Fall 1975, pp. 39–44.)

24. Republic of Zambia, *Prospects for Zambia's Mining Industry* (Lusaka; Zambia: 1970); Mark Bostock and Charles Harvey, eds., *Economic Independence and Zambian Copper: A Case Study of Foreign Investment* (Praeger, 1972); and Raymond F. Mikesell, "Recent Developments in the Zambian and Zairian Copper Industries" (paper prepared for U.S. State Department, Bureau of Intelligence and Research, January 3, 1972; processed); Richard L. Sklar, *Corporate Power in an African State: The Political Impact of Multinational Mining Companies in Zambia* (University of California Press, 1975).

25. *Engineering and Mining Journal,* vol. 170 (December 1969), p. 12.

producing countries, Chile, Peru, and Zaire.[26] As with oil, there is evidence of a cumulative tightening of terms for the benefit of the host country, in part, because the host countries gain expertise (or hire it) in taxation, finance, and accounting; in part, because growing domestic capabilities in supervising production, processing, and marketing make nationalization a credible threat. In the Chilean case, Kennecott, in 1964, agreed to sell 51 percent of its shares to the government to escape a tax burden above 80 percent. However, chileanization speeded the entry of nationals into areas that were previously the monopoly of foreigners. And by 1970, at the time of the nationalization of the industry, there were only two Americans (ten non-Chileans) out of a total of ten thousand employees on Kennecott's payroll.[27]

Moreover, companies that are latecomers to a particular country start with tighter terms than early investors and find themselves squeezed more rapidly. In Liberia, Republic Steel began to mine iron ore in the late 1940s with a concession that included no income tax, no control over transfer prices for the output, and only a small royalty per ton.[28] In 1952, the terms were renegotiated with an income tax replacing the royalty. The income tax was steadily raised over the course of the subsequent decade. In 1967, Bethlehem Steel and a consortium of Swedish and Canadian investors opened a Liberian mine on terms only slightly more generous than Republic was receiving. By 1974 it had a renegotiated contract that left it with a greater tax burden and greater host-country control over export pricing than Republic had had to face at the end of the earlier cycle.[29]

Host countries that are latecomers to the natural-resource business begin with better bargaining skills than their predecessors and learn from

26. On Chile, see Mamalakis and Reynolds, *Essays on the Chilean Economy;* and Moran, *Multinational Corporations and the Politics of Dependence.* On Peru, see Raymond F. Mikesell, *Foreign Investment in Copper Mining: Case Studies of Mines in Peru and Papua New Guinea* (Johns Hopkins University Press for Resources for the Future, 1975), pp. 39–77. On Zaire, see Mikesell, "Recent Developments in the Zambian and Zairian Copper Industries"; and Rupert Emerson, *Africa and United States Policy* (Prentice-Hall, 1967), pp. 59–94

27. Kennecott Copper Corporation, letter to stockholders, December 30, 1964. The figures on non-Chilean employment come from Kennecott Copper Corporation, *Expropriation of the El Teniente Copper Mine by the Chilean Government* (New York: Kennecott, 1971).

28. Author interview with industry officials.

29. Most of the burden was borne by the Swedish, Canadian, and U.S. treasuries through their foreign tax credits.

the successes of experienced host countries. Colombia signed its first investment agreement for nickel with Hanna Mining in the late 1960s, and before the project was in full operation, the Colombian Minister of Mines prepared to revise the terms of the contract by hiring the same American consultants who had helped Liberia renegotiate with Bethlehem. (His aim, for political reasons as well as reasons of national interest, was to be able to announce the conclusion of the most advantageous mining agreement in that industry in the world.) Malaysia's 1971 negotiations with a consortium of Japanese copper investors were informed by an analysis of the terms in Chile and Peru over the preceding two decades.[30] In 1974, Jamaica multiplied by six its revenue from bauxite, learning strategies from Guyana's nationalization of Alcan in 1971.[31] And also in 1974, Papua New Guinea, one of the poorest of the newly sovereign nations, by playing off competing teams of American and Peruvian consultants, was able to negotiate exceedingly favorable terms with Rio Tinto Zinc to develop its copper resources.

Nor has this dialectic, the process of renegotiation, been confined to the Third World. After the mining boom in British Columbia and Ontario in the late 1960s, provincial and federal governments in Canada competed with each other to raise the combined tax burden to 60 percent, with some surtaxes going to 100 percent.[32] In Australia, the primary focus of the Labor government elected in both 1972 and 1974, was greater equity participation for nationals.[33]

Controlling Prices and Markets

Not only has the obsolescing bargain meant the transfer of a larger share of the returns from the extractive sector to host governments, it has

30. See Louis T. Wells, Jr., David N. Smith, and Theodore H. Moran, *Malaysia's Copper Development Policy*, a study prepared under the auspices of Harvard University Development Advisory Service for the Malaysian government (Kuala Lumpur, Malaysia: 1972).

31. Author interviews with Jamaican officials, 1974–75.

32. "British Columbia Passes Controversial Minerals Royalties Act," *Engineering and Mining Journal*, vol. 175 (August 1974), p. 23; "Doubling of Ontario Mining Profits Tax May Yield $50 Million," *Engineering and Mining Journal*, vol. 175 (November 1974), pp. 28–29; "Stale Canada Mine Sector Seen," *Journal of Commerce* (March 10, 1975).

33. "Changes in Australia's Mineral Policy Proposed by the Labor Government Will Emphasize Maximum Ownership of Resources," *Engineering and Mining Journal*, vol. 175 (January 1974), p. 40.

also meant, for many raw materials, the transfer of effective control over price and marketing policy as well. Beginning in the 1960s, governments that export raw materials began to unilaterally increase prices when market conditions permitted. And, with their fixed investments held hostage, foreign companies had no choice but to collaborate.

IRON ORE. The mining boom in Australia began in 1964 with an American-British-Australian consortium at Hamersley accepting letters of intent from the major Japanese steel manufacturers to buy half a billion dollars worth of ore over a sixteen-year period.[34] Less than two years later, when the stipulated price was lower than market quotations in Europe, the federal government of Australia overrode the constitutional prerogative of the state governments and refused to grant export licenses for the ore unless the price was raised.

COPPER. Major exporting countries refused to go along with the informal price ceilings that the U.S. government had imposed on American mining companies at the beginning of the Vietnam War. In 1966, President Lyndon Johnson dispatched Averell Harriman to Chile to offer a 40-year $10 million Agency for International Development (AID) loan at less than 1 percent interest if Chile would permit Anaconda to sell 100,000 tons of its output in the United States at the domestic producers' price of 36 cents per pound, rather than at a price over twice as high on the London Metals Exchange (LME).[35] Though President Frei assented, once the transaction was completed he instructed Anaconda and Kennecott to use the higher LME price for further output. Since they would be taxed on that basis in any case, the companies complied.

BAUXITE. In 1974, Jamaica began pegging its tax on bauxite to the aluminum ingot price in the United States, effectively eliminating the previous power of the companies to set their payments to the host country by determining the export price; the immediate result was a sixfold rise in Jamaican revenues, and most of the other bauxite producers shortly followed Jamaica's lead.

OIL. The OPEC countries in 1974 dropped even the pretense of negotiating with the foreign companies as market conditions changed, preferring to dictate price and tax levels on a take-it-or-leave-it basis. And

34. Hamersley Holdings, Ltd., "Prospectus," and "Hamersley Iron Ore Contract" (Hamersley Holdings, Ltd., April 1965; processed).

35. Thomas O'Hanlon, "The Perilous Prosperity of Anaconda," *Fortune,* vol. 73 (May 1966), p. 119.

the loss of multinational control has affected the position of the home countries. The United Kingdom, though owner of 49 percent of British Petroleum, appears to have fared worse during the crisis than did Japan (with no controlling shares in oil companies) or the embargoed United States, though it fared better than France (with home-based companies) and Germany (with none).[36]

The Intergovernmental Council of Copper Exporters (CIPEC), the International Bauxite Association (IBA), and the Association of Iron Exporting Countries (AIEC) were established, like OPEC, to give host countries sovereignty over the prices of their exports. The transfer of sovereignty over the price of exports does not, of course, signify that exporters will get any price they want, but it does mean that direct foreign investment has gone the way of empire and no longer provides large industrial states with a vehicle for dealing with the consequences of oligopoly power in commodity markets. These countries must now deal with the causes of oligopoly power at the production stage. Can foreign direct investment function effectively to keep the production stage competitive? Our analysis of the obsolescing bargain calls that into doubt. Should the industrial countries therefore anticipate the proliferation of producer cartels in other raw materials along the lines of OPEC? Or is oil truly an exception?

Producer Cartels

The Argument Against

Producer cartels have two basic weaknesses. Though over the short run its members may gain by limiting production and dividing the market, any one member can gain more—can expand its market share—by discounting the cartel price (provided it doesn't, by this action, cause the breakup of the cartel). Once a member starts to cheat, moreover, any member that does not will lose out. Over the long run, the high prices of a successful cartel merely stimulate the search for new sources of supply and substitutes. Members may be worse off than before. The debate

36. Robert B. Stobaugh, "The Oil Companies in the Crisis," *Daedalus* (Fall 1975), p. 189; Stobaugh estimates the following percentage differences in actual consumption for petroleum for January–March 1974 from the preembargo forecast: Japan, −3; United States, −11; United Kingdom, −12; France, −21; Netherlands, −22; West Germany, −26 (pp. 192–93).

about the proliferation of cartel-like behavior has focused on the question of whether, in the light of OPEC's successes in increasing its revenues from oil, there may be some new willingness among exporters of other raw materials to take risks to alter the terms of trade in their direction. There may be some new discipline to keep them from cheating on each other as they try to restrict production, and to help them collude in the face of past failures.

Those who argue that "oil is the exception" assert that demand for petroleum is more price-inelastic than for other raw materials.[37] It is vital to industrial and consumer activities, it cannot be recycled, and the price of substitutes is high (especially for some uses, like transportation). Furthermore, some of the countries that initially took the risk in boosting oil prices (Saudi Arabia, Kuwait, the Gulf Emirates) had, at the time of the 1973 oil embargo, large financial reserves and small populations. The producers of other primary products (India and Mauritania, iron ore; Jamaica and Guinea, bauxite; Zaire and Peru, copper) might be more reluctant to risk losing buyers. Finally, the Arab core of the petroleum cartel had a common political commitment (their enmity toward Israel) that inspired them to act in concert, a commitment that is missing elsewhere.

The Argument For

Each argument discounting the threat of producer cartels has its counter argument.[38] Though past estimates of price elasticity of demand for industrial commodities are subject to error, some studies show that demand

37. See Stephen D. Krasner, "Oil Is the Exception," *Foreign Policy,* no. 14 (Spring 1974), pp. 68–84; Stephen D. Krasner, "A Somewhat Different View of the Crisis," in Allan Roth, ed., *The Crisis in World Materials: A U.S.-Japanese Symposium* (Rutgers University Graduate School of Business Administration, 1974); Bension Varon and Kenji Takeuchi, "Developing Countries and Non-Fuel Minerals," *Foreign Affairs,* vol. 52 (April 1974), pp. 497–510; and Simon D. Strauss, "Strategic Materials: More Vulnerable Bottlenecks Ahead?" *Defense Planning for the 1980s and the Changing International Environment, Proceedings of National Security Affairs Conference* (Washington: National War College, 1975), pp. 53–69.

38. C. Fred Bergsten, "The Threat From the Third World," *Foreign Policy,* no. 11 (Summer 1973), pp. 102–24; C. Fred Bergsten, "The Threat is Real," *Foreign Policy,* no. 14 (Spring 1974), pp. 84–90; C. Fred Bergsten, "The New Era in World Commodity Markets," *Challenge,* vol. 17 (September–October 1974), pp. 34–42; and Zuhayr Mikdashi, "Collusion Could Work," *Foreign Policy,* no. 14 (Spring 1974), pp. 57–68.

for petroleum may be more price elastic than has been assumed (especially in the United States, where conserving gasoline may be economically feasible) and that demand for other commodities, particularly in the short run, is price-inelastic.[39] Substitutes have taken the place of commodities other than oil only after shifts in relative prices lasted long enough to give the appearance of a new equilibrium. But if the prices of substitutes were to fluctuate widely, or rise jointly, or become uncertain, even long-run demand for the original product would be price-inelastic. And the econometric technique of projecting future relationships from historical data will not show it. In addition, substitutes for a product whose price had been raised through cartel action may not attract new investment, because cartel prices could fall (either to compete with the substitutes or because the cartel weakens).

In any case, even short-term price inelasticities of demand provide both the incentive and the opportunity for market manipulation. Whether politicians in producing countries choose to maximize current revenues, at the possible cost of losing markets later, depends on how heavily they discount the future. Political and economic tension may lead political leaders to adopt strategies inimical to a long-run view of the national interest.[40] Indeed, it is often rational for developing countries to discount the future more highly than industrialized countries and thus seek to maximize immediate returns.[41] The condition of depending upon the export of one or two products to support large populations with pressing domestic needs may, therefore, lead not to a moderate resource policy but to short-term risk-taking. Our analysis of the political dynamics driving the obsolescing bargain supports this contention.

39. Charles River Associates, Inc., *An Economic Analysis of the Copper Industry,* Department of Commerce, Publication PB 189 927 (GPO, 1970); and Charles River Associates, Inc., *An Economic Analysis of the Aluminum Industry* (Cambridge: Charles River Associates, March 1971); Franklin M. Fisher and Paul H. Cootner, in association with Martin Neil Baily, "An Econometric Model of the World Copper Industry," *The Bell Journal of Economic and Management Science,* vol. 3 (Autumn 1972), pp. 568–609.

40. When he announced a sixfold increased in bauxite levies to the Jamaican parliament in March 1974, Jamaican Prime Minister Michael Manley acknowledged such an intertemporal trade-off: "The time may not be too distant when technological progress will begin to yield substitutes for bauxite." Jamaican Parliament news release, May 15, 1974, p. 2.

41. Harry G. Johnson, *Economic Policies Toward Less Developed Countries* (Brookings, 1967), p. 155.

Shared political causes are not necessary to successful producer cartels. OPEC was a success before the war of Yom Kippur. Furthermore, it includes countries (Iran and Venezuela) that are not inimical to Israel, the Arab states were serious rivals, and most members had low levels of monetary reserves. But OPEC was a huge economic and political success. Statements by representatives of undeveloped nations suggest that they share a strong desire to confront the industrial world over control of natural resources. Expression of solidarity is a point of national dignity in the international arena; because of this, leaders or parties that abandon that solidarity could lose domestic political support.

Of course, no other producer cartel, no matter how successful, can shift as much wealth to host exporters as a petroleum cartel can, nor can it have as much impact on world politics. But resource diplomacy—the attempt by producers to manipulate short-term inelasticities of demand, unilaterally or collusively, for maximum economic and political gain—is quite likely to be a feature of international trade in the foreseeable future. And the probability of its success, at least in the short run, is high.

Constraint on Investment

Resource diplomacy can lead to problems between developed and developing countries, among developed countries, and for those developing countries in the Third and Fourth Worlds that are not rich in natural resources. The magnitude and seriousness of these problems depend on whether market forces counter market power at the production stage— whether high prices stimulate investment, creating new supplies and new suppliers.

The obsolescing bargain constitutes a fundamental structural change in natural-resource industries that renders the traditional market force, via direct foreign investment, obsolete. Direct foreign investment in natural-resource development has been based, since at least the end of the Second World War, on a myth, the myth of the sanctity of the long-term concession contract. It is a myth in the sense that it continues to be believed and acted upon even when the empirical probability of its being observed has dropped nearly to zero. Combining optimism with naiveté, the myth holds that what happened in the Chilean copper industry or the Venezuelan iron ore industry in one decade will not happen in the Peruvian copper industry or the Brazilian iron ore industry in the next, and that the nationalism of Surinam and Indonesia is not the same as the nationalism of Canada and Australia.

The dynamics of the obsolescing bargain leads to somber conclusions, not necessarily because nationalization is inevitable but because it *is* inevitable that six or eight or twelve years after capital is sunk in large successful extractive operations, tax rates will rise to 60–70 percent (with careful scrutiny of transfer pricing and other interaffiliate transactions) and supervision of price and marketing policy will pass to the hands of host-country officials.[42]

The traditional optimism of U.S. government agencies about the extent of reserves and about elasticities of supply if prices rise in no way takes into account the obsolescing bargain and obsolescing foreign direct investment.[43] The complacency about resource availability is based on geologic calculations of direct production costs in relation to hypothetical price levels, with past investment behavior projected uncritically into the future. Though such projections include the caveat that political uncertainties in countries where the deposits are located might hamper the investment process, there is really very little political uncertainty. It is a virtual political *certainty* that an investment agreement in an extractive industry will be revised to the level of mature concessions elsewhere a short time after the mine begins to produce. This is the "discount factor" that must be applied to the estimate of commercially feasible reserves

---

42. Vernon notes that tax rates on "mature concessions" in the copper and oil industries were 10–15 percent in the 1920s, 50–55 percent in the 1950s, and nearly 70 percent by the late 1960s (*Sovereignty at Bay,* pp. 53–55). As the revenues to investors drop from 30 percent to 20 percent of gross profits, a company would have to be willing to invest enough to expand output by half to offset the effects of the declining share. See Raymond Vernon, "Foreign Enterprises and Developing Nations in the Raw Materials Industries," *American Economic Review,* vol. 60 (May 1970), p. 125. Since 1970 there have been nationalizations in petroleum, copper, iron ore, and bauxite, with tax rates in some mature concessions rising above 80 percent.

43. See recent projections in U.S. Bureau of Mines *Commodity Data Summaries* (GPO, annual); and U.S. Interior Department, *Annual Report of the Secretary of the Interior under the Mining and Minerals Policy Act of 1970* (GPO, 1972) and ibid., *1973–1976.* See also U.S. National Commission on Materials Policy, *Material Needs and the Environment Today and Tomorrow: Final Report, June 1973* (GPO, 1973); and Council on International Economic Policy, *Special Report: Critical Imported Materials* (GPO, 1974), which fails, however, to draw the proper conclusions from its own analysis.

available for development in the Third World, Canada, and Australia, and to the estimates of price elasticity of supply for actual development via direct foreign investment.

Direct foreign ownership by large extractive companies exacerbates the problem of future cartelization. One, their very size and apparent power heighten the political pressure on host-country governments to exercise countervailing power. Two, the oligopolistic market structures created by the companies provide the means for host countries to control markets by effectively controlling the companies.

Host governments anxious to attract new investment may attempt to restore faith in long-term contracts. They may loosen terms, improve the political climate, and solemnly swear to potential investors that their promises will never be revoked. The government of Chile, for example, advertises that future investors in the mineral sector can keep full equity control indefinitely. Canada, with combined federal and provincial taxes too high to justify further investments in low-grade copper deposits in British Columbia and medium-grade iron ore deposits in Ontario might, sometime, again welcome U.S. mining companies. Australia might try to rekindle that country's natural resource boom by relaxing its strictures on foreign ownership.

But investors must weigh periods of relaxation and promises of stability against the record of the past and against domestic political pressure for revision of the agreement. In the petroleum industry, of course, the spread between cost and price may return enough on investments before the bargain is obsolete to justify investors taking a risk. But the spread between cost and price for other minerals does not allow such quick returns.[44]

The Outlook for Copper

By geologic estimates, copper might be considered scarce. Like tin and tungsten, proved reserves (at 1972 market prices) are about half of

---

44. CIPEC production costs in 1969 were 24 cents a pound in Chile, 30 cents a pound in Zambia, 33 cents a pound in Congo (Zaire), and 21 cents a pound in Peru; 1967–70 copper prices on the London Metals Exchange stayed consistently below one dollar a pound (*Metal Bulletin*, vol. 58, October 22, 1971, p. 29).

cumulative demand projected to the year 2000.[45] In the past, however, new methods of large-scale, low-grade mining have more than made up for the depletion of the richer reserves. In the United States the grade of mined copper ore dropped by half between 1950 and 1970 (from about 1 percent copper content to less than 0.5 percent), without an appreciable increase in real production costs; world reserves during that same period doubled.[46] A tripling of prices from the 1972 level may again double reserves, which include some copper-bearing nodules on the seabed whose production costs are little known.[47] On the basis of experience, then, it is not realistic to say that the world is, in some absolute sense, running out of copper. The answer to the question of supply depends on location of reserves and the costs of developing them.

Investment outside the United States

Most of the world's copper lies in low-grade porphyry deposits along the rims of the Pacific (touching Chile, Peru, the western United States, British Columbia, Malaysia, Indonesia, and Oceania), in the mountains of central Asia (including Iran), and in the copper belt in Africa. Development costs average over $3,000 a ton (in 1972 prices), or over $300 million for a medium-sized mine of 100,000 tons a year.[48] Development averages five years. A corporation contemplating a new investment in copper outside the United States, therefore, must decide whether to commit massive amounts of funds in its own name with a highly uncertain payback period and (except for U.S. mines) in regions where economic nationalism, with or without nationalization, has a long tradition.

At the margin, the outlook for new mineral investments is not good.

45. Sources: proved reserves, U.S. Bureau of Mines, *Commodity Data Summaries, 1974* (GPO, 1974); and ibid. *1975* (GPO, 1975), projected at 1972–73 market prices; estimated cumulative demand, from Brookings Institution, *Trade in Primary Commodities: Conflict or Cooperation?* (Brookings, 1974), p. 16.
46. Calculated from data in Orris C. Herfindahl, *Copper Costs and Prices: 1870–1957* (Johns Hopkins University Press for Resources for the Future, 1959), pp. 14, 15, 220–27, and National Commission on Materials Policy, *Material Needs and the Environment Today and Tomorrow*, p. 4B-16.
47. International Bank for Reconstruction and Development, *Report on the Limits to Growth* (Washington, D.C.: IBRD, September 1972), p. 7.
48. National Commission on Materials Policy, *Material Needs and the Environment Today and Tomorrow*, p. 4B-17.

In 1967 in the South Pacific, Rio Tinto began a $300 million project on Bougainville (Papua New Guinea).[49] By the year of completion (1974) the original concession had been renegotiated twice, each time raising the tax and widening the definition of taxable income. The nationalistic stance of the Papua New Guinea government led Kennecott to abandon a prospective mine at OK Tedi. In Mexico, American Smelting and Refining began work in 1974 on the $500 million La Caridad mine after a three-year delay caused by Mexico twice adjusting its equity share (from 10 percent to 33 percent to 44 percent).[50]

In Peru, financing was delayed six years (from 1969 to 1975) before Southern Peru Copper could raise $620 million for the 970,000 ton Cuajone project.[51] Only by skillful pressure (that is, loss of depletion allowance on one mine already in operation unless the funds were invested in new facilities) were the Peruvian authorities able to get Southern Peru's parent corporations (American Smelting and Refining, Cerro, Newmont, and Phelps Dodge) to move ahead at all.[52] Southern Peru illustrates what even a leisurely progression of the obsolescing bargain can imply for future investment decisions. From 1960–71, taxes took 38 percent of net returns, and the Cuajone project was commonly considered one of the best around. But by the mid-1970s taxes had risen to 68 percent, and the internal rate of return to the investors amounted to only 13.5 percent.[53] This shows the difficulty in reconciling the host country's idea of fair return on investment to the return necessary to attract investment. To Peru, Southern Peru was a symbol of exploitation.[54] Even after the 1966

49. *Bougainville Copper Ltd. (B)*, Case study 4-174-104 (Harvard University Graduate School of Business Administration, 1974).

50. "Mexican Copper Project Begins After Long Delay," *New York Times*, January 20, 1974.

51. "Southern Peru Gets Financing for Copper Mine," *Wall Street Journal*, January 6, 1975.

52. Mikesell, *Foreign Investment in Copper Mining*, pp. 53–55, 65.

53. Raymond F. Mikesell, "Southern Peru Copper Company's Profits from Toquepala: An Economic and Normative Analysis" (March 1973; processed). The internal rate of return, of course, takes into account the sequence in which expenditures are made and returns received. For Southern Peru, the rate thus includes the six-year development period (1955–60) in which $182 million was invested but no earnings were generated.

54. See Carlos Malpica, *El Mito de la Ayuda Exterior* (Lima: Francisco Moncloa Editores, 1967); Claes Brundenius, "The Anatomy of Imperialism: Multinational Mining Corporations in Peru," *Journal of Peace Research*, no. 3 (1972), pp. 189–207.

changes in the country's mining code, Southern Peru earned over 18 percent a year in the subsequent four years and by the early 1970s had recovered all its invested capital through depreciation, depletion, and amortization. Still, a 13.5 percent rate of return is not sufficient to justify the investment from the point of view of investors. Taking into account the discounted value of returns in relation to expenditures since the beginning of the mine's development, the project could reach the parent investors' target of a 15 percent return a year by 1980 (twenty-five years after the beginning of the investment) only if favorable assumptions are made about copper prices and if Peruvian authorities do not raise taxes in proportion to the increase in the company's profitability.

Copper consumption is growing 5 percent a year. To meet the demand, investment commitments must be made for four 100,000 ton mines each year, and this projection assumes, optimistically, that expansion of existing facilities will compensate for the depletion of older mines.

Investment within the United States

If the prospect of revised contracts and 60–70 percent tax rates deter copper investments outside of the United States, will not normal market forces redirect those investments to Utah, Montana, or Arizona? The U.S. Department of the Interior describes American copper reserves as vast. But the average ton of ore processed in the United States contains only eight to ten pounds of metal, a grade of 0.4–0.5 percent, about half the richness of deposits in Latin America (more than 1.0 percent), and a sixth that mined in Africa's copper belt (2.7 percent).[55] The ore in Duval's 1970 Sierrita mine (65,000 tons a year) has as little as 0.3 percent copper, or less than seven pounds of copper per ton of waste.[56] The tons of waste are left in slag heaps, or "restored" into the Arizona landscape. Anaconda's Twin Buttes, Montana, project (80,000 tons a year in 1970) has a higher metal content (0.68 percent), but before production could begin, 236 million tons of overburden (over two-thirds that exca-

55. For the United States: National Commission on Materials Policy, *Material Needs and the Environment Today and Tomorrow*, p. 4B-16; for Africa: Mikesell, "Recent Developments in the Zambian and Zairian Copper Industries," p. 7; for Latin America: *Engineering and Mining Journal*, various issues.

56. George P. Lutjen, "Open-Pit Guide: Sierrita Makes it with Big Equipment," *Engineering and Mining Journal*, vol. 171 (August 1970), pp. 70–73.

vated for the Panama Canal) had to be removed.[57] Besides waste disposal and land restoration problems, concern over the emission of sulphur into the air has delayed construction of new smelter facilities in the United States and could force early closure of others.[58] Many more projects such as Sierrita and Twin Buttes would be economically feasible only with high and stable copper prices, of course, but even then, the social and environmental costs could cause substantial delays.

As for recycling, physical estimates of scrap availability suggest that no more than 10 percent of the country's requirements could be met from an active recovery program.[59] The cost of the recycling program was not estimated. The same study does suggest that contamination will impose severe technical limitations on reuse.

The Outlook for Iron Ore

World deposits of iron ore are much more abundant than copper, with proved reserves equaling almost five times estimated cumulated demand until the year 2000.[60] Arm's-length prices show a remarkable stability from the end of the Korean War until the present, with quotations not deviating more than 10 percent below or 11 percent above the average price (in constant dollars).[61] Prices during the 1960s, measured by spot prices in Rotterdam and payments on long-term contracts in Japan, went down slightly (less freight costs, which also declined), despite the efforts of some of the large exporters to renegotiate long-term sales contracts. This was caused, in large part, by an explosive growth in iron ore exports between 1950 and 1970: 14 percent a year, compared to 5.8 percent aver-

57. George P. Lutjen, "Twin Buttes Solves the Problems of Great Depth, Low Grade, Complex Orebody," *Engineering and Mining Journal*, vol. 171 (August 1970), pp. 74–78.
58. U.S. Bureau of Mines, *Commodity Data Summaries, 1974;* and ibid., *1975.*
59. Hans Landsberg, "Comments on 'Strategic Materials: More Vulnerable Bottlenecks Ahead?,'" note 50 (July 9, 1974; processed); and Leonard Fischman and Hans Landsberg, "Adequacy of Nonfuel Minerals and Forest Resources," in Ronald G. Ridker, ed., *Population Resources and the Environment*, vol. 3 (GPO, 1972), pp. 96–98.
60. Proved reserves: U.S. Bureau of Mines, *Commodity Data Summaries, 1974;* and ibid., *1975* projected at 1972–73 market prices; estimated cumulative demand: Brookings Institution, *Trade in Primary Commodities: Conflict or Cooperation?*
61. U.S. Interior Department calculations, 1974.

age annual growth of world steel consumption. Australia's iron ore exports went from zero in 1960 to 41 million metric tons in 1970; Brazil's went from 5 to 28 million tons; Liberia's, from 3 to 24 million tons; India's, from 9 to 20 million tons; Canada's, from 17 to 39 million tons. By 1974, these five countries plus Venezuela accounted for 33 percent of world production, and almost 70 percent of world exports. They hold 73 percent of the world's reserves of recoverable iron (at 1972 prices).

Investment outside the United States

Even more than in the copper industry, scale factors make investment in iron ore mining highly vulnerable to the obsolescing bargain. The capacity of the great Australian mines (Hamersley, Mount Newman, Robe River, Mount Goldsworthy) range from 10 million to 38 million tons a year and cost (in 1975 prices) from $250 million to over $1 billion. In Brazil, Marcona's joint venture at Germano, with an output of 10 million tons a year, will cost at least $400 million; and U.S. Steel's 45-million-ton-a-year operation at Carajas, well over a billion dollars.

Economic nationalism has been uneven: strong in Venezuela, Liberia, Peru, and Mauritania and weak thus far in Canada, Australia, and Brazil. But continued investment in the latter countries depends on continued low comparative taxes and continued sources of capital for investment. If the investment outlook does change, the principal geologic alternatives are Angola, Chile, and India, hardly havens from the threat of economic nationalism.

Investment within the United States

If growth rate of output slows and prices rise in the five primary exporting countries (with or without collusion), how easily can production in the United States be brought on-stream to equilibrate the market? America's high-grade iron ores are virtually depleted, and its nine billion tons of low-grade taconite ore are only 22 percent recoverable at 1972 prices. These ores (about 80 percent concentrated in the Lake Superior region of Minnesota and Michigan) are approximately one-half to one-third the richness (21–29 percent iron content) of the large mines in Australia and Brazil (59–64 percent iron content) and require extensive beneficiation and agglomeration before they can be used. To produce 7.5

million tons of pellets that are 64 percent iron from a typical large taconite operation, 17 million tons of overburden must be removed and 27
million tons of waste rock disposed of.[62] Thus, production of a ton of
iron generates 2.5 to 3.5 tons of tailings. U.S. Steel's 12.5 million-ton-per-
year Minntac operation in Minnesota disposes of 52 million tons of waste,
or the equivalent of the Panama Canal excavation, every six years.[63]

Seven new operations the size of Minntac would be required for the
United States to raise its share of the world's iron ore production by 1
percent. Four new Minntacs a year would be needed to supply the new
demand generated by a 5 percent yearly growth in steel consumption.
Such additions are not feasible, given not only the problem of waste disposal but other environmental problems such as the dust that is dumped
into the air and the asbestos-like matter that is dumped into Lake Superior.[64] Thus, the assertion that price increases in world markets could
easily and rapidly be countered by expansion of American production requires unrealistic assumptions about public acceptance of massive environmental damage and/or about the industry's ability to repair or
prevent it.

As for recycling iron, estimates of physical feasibility are not encouraging. In automotive scrap, for example, there are severe technical constraints due to quality considerations, such as contamination.[65] In general,
neither economic incentives nor civic enthusiasm will increase the recycling of iron appreciably.[66]

Supplies of copper and iron ore have always been highly inelastic in
the short term. Long-term inelasticity, which our analysis suggests may
be the trend, could lead to a closer fit between capacity and demand in
these notoriously cyclical industries and an end to the recent buyers'
market. One or two major exporters, acting alone, might be able to lead
the way in raising prices. Such groups as CIPEC and the Association of
Iron Exporting Countries might then be able to act in concert with a high

62. U.S. Interior Department estimates, 1973.
63. Calculated from "Minntac Preparing for Second Major Expansion," *Engineering and Mining Journal,* vol. 175 (November 1974), p. 106.
64. U.S. Bureau of Mines, *Commodity Data Summaries, 1974;* and ibid., *1975.*
65. James W. Sawyer, Jr., *Automotive Scrap Recycling: Processes, Prices and
Prospects* (Johns Hopkins University Press for Resources for the Future, 1972).
66. Landsberg, "Comments on 'Strategic Materials: More Vulnerable Bottlenecks Ahead?' "; Fischman and Landsberg, "Adequacy of Nonfuel Minerals and
Forest Resources," p. 98.

degree of impunity. Neither traditional direct foreign investment nor domestic investment offers a system that adjusts to price changes smoothly enough to assure reasonable prices or secure access.[67]

The Outlook for Bauxite

Cartel-like behavior in the bauxite industry is much more possible than in copper or iron.[68] The structure of the industry is like the petroleum industry, and in fact, concentration is substantially higher. The ten members of the International Bauxite Association (IBA) account for about 70 percent of noncommunist production, with two of them (Australia and Jamaica) producing 45 percent. The thirteen members of OPEC, in contrast, produce 61 percent of noncommunist oil, with Saudi Arabia and Iran (as of 1972) accounting for 25 percent. The supplies of bauxite are funneled through a tightly constricted industrial structure in which six companies (Alcoa, Alcan, Kaiser, Reynolds, Pechiney, and Alusuisse) account for about 60 percent of the noncommunist aluminum market. The Seven Sisters of the oil industry account for 71 percent of noncommunist oil output.

Investment outside the United States

The obsolescing bargain came late to the aluminum industry.[69] There is virtually no arm's-length market for bauxite. Almost all of the material used for metal (as opposed to refractories or abrasives) traditionally comes from excavations owned by the major aluminum companies. Ex-

67. The new militancy of American Indian tribes with regard to natural resource concessions on their lands could reinforce long-term inelasticity, though it is not clear how great their claims are. See Americans for Indian Opportunity, *Real Choices in Indian Resource Development* (Washington, D.C.: AIO, 1975).

68. For further details, see C. Fred Bergsten, "A New OPEC in Bauxite," *Challenge,* vol. 17 (July–August 1976), pp. 12–20. See also Henri A. M. Guda, "Organization and Priorities of the International Bauxite Association" (paper presented at the May 1975, meeting of the Geological Society of Jamaica; processed).

69. Sterling Brubaker, *Trends in the World Aluminum Industry* (Johns Hopkins University Press for Resources for the Future, 1967); Martin S. Brown and John Butler, *The Production, Marketing, and Consumption of Copper and Aluminum* (Praeger, 1967); and Zuhayr Mikdashi, *The International Politics of Natural Resources* (Cornell University Press, 1976); Isaiah A. Litvak and Christopher J. Maule, "Nationalisation in the Caribbean Bauxite Industry," *International Affairs,* vol. 51 (January 1975), pp. 43–59.

port earnings for the producing countries have been determined, therefore, by the transfer-pricing strategies of those companies.

Jamaica, in response to both the transfer-pricing and revenue issues, set a production levy as a percentage (7.5 percent in 1974, 8.5 percent by 1976) of the published price of aluminum ingots in the United States, tying its income to the end product sold by the companies. To prevent the companies from offsetting the levy elsewhere, Jamaica set a minimum production level, took majority interest in the companies, and created the International Bauxite Association. Other IBA countries have since adopted similar formulas. By taxing the ingot price (much as OPEC countries tax the posted price of petroleum), IBA countries leave to the companies the decision on whether to either pass the tax (to the final consumers or the U.S. Treasury through the foreign tax credit) or try to defeat IBA's strategy by undertaking the necessary investments. Bauxite accounts for only 10–20 percent of the final cost of aluminum products, but the added cost of imports to the United States still totaled about $200 million in 1974 as a result of IBA actions.

In the short run, of course, the companies have no choice but to try to raise product prices to offset as much of the higher net tax burden as possible. They raised them in 1974 and, after a lag caused by the recession in 1975, again in 1976. The Department of the Interior thus concluded in early 1975 that "the United States is already in the early stages of a monopoly pricing action,"[70] and the Council on International Economic Policy in the White House publicly recognized the "artificial increase [of bauxite] prices to a level well beyond those that would occur under free market conditions."[71]

It may seem that over the long term, in response to rising taxes at the production stage, companies could develop new sources of bauxite and refuse the role of tax collectors for the IBA countries. Though most of

70. Office of Minerals Policy Development, U.S. Interior Department, *Critical Materials: Commodity Action Analyses* (GPO, 1975), p. 33. The study also concludes "there are . . . at least three reasons why the aluminum companies may not have a strong incentive to do research into domestic resources and may not view the threat of a commodity action with the same seriousness as the government might like." The three reasons are their sunk investments in Jamaica and other foreign countries, "their ability to pass on the cost increases in the form of higher prices," and the fear that "opening up production from domestic resources may lead to an increase in the competitiveness of the industry" (pp. 40–42).

71. Council on International Economic Policy, *Special Report: Critical Imported Materials*, p. 17.

the world's reserves of bauxite (66 percent) are located in five IBA countries (Australia, Guinea, Guyana, Jamaica, and Surinam, with the first two alone accounting for 54 percent),[72] a determined program of new investments would increase production, reducing dependence on current IBA output, and making collusion more difficult.

Development of new sources of bauxite, even if cheaper, would be complicated by several factors, however. First, a company's smelting capacity is geared to specific bauxites available only from specific countries; in this sense, U.S. as well as foreign investments are hostage to host-country actions with regard to the utilization of existing plants. Second, companies will have to produce the minimum levels of bauxite specified by the IBA countries. (Only Jamaica has such a requirement at present, but Secretary-General Henri Guda of IBA predicts that similar requirements will be adopted by other member countries in the future.) Third, the firms will have to raise their final prices to support the higher tax load levied by the countries. Indeed, it is not hard to imagine the largest IBA members devising a system of fines for refusal to meet quotas and/or a system of compulsory reinvestment of profits to create new capacity at a certain rate within their own countries, which would deter aluminum companies from creating new capacity elsewhere.

Investment within the United States

There are, in the United States, nonbauxite sources of alumina—kaolin clays, anorthosite, and alunite, for example. Very little is known about their production costs,[73] and even if current pilot projects indicate that costs are cheaper than for bauxite, processing would require large new expenditures for refinery and smelter technology. It would take at least six to eight years to begin supplying consumers. In the meantime, the mining companies may be compelled, as noted above, to invest in more bauxite capacity in IBA countries.

Less than 20 percent of aluminum demand is filled by recycled metal. Resources for the Future estimates that, in physical terms, the proportion could climb to more than 40 percent, but it did not calculate costs.[74] And incentive to invest in experimental recovery programs would be low

72. U.S. Bureau of Mines, *Commodity Data Summaries, 1974;* and ibid., *1975.*
73. Author interviews with aluminum executives, 1974–75.
74. Landsberg, "Comments on 'Strategic Materials: More Vulnerable Bottlenecks Ahead?' "; Fischman and Landsberg, "Adequacy of Nonfuel Minerals and Forest Resources," pp. 96–98.

for companies trying to keep the price of aluminum high (to recover the high tax per pound) while being forced to absorb a large quantity of bauxite.

Under such circumstances, there is little reason to expect established companies to make massive investments in new bauxite projects, or to undertake a rapid and expensive conversion to nonbauxite sources, or to increase the use of recycled aluminum on a massive scale. They have not done so during the first few years since the initial IBA actions, and they have even abandoned efforts to have nationalization decrees rescinded through international arbitration. These firms, like oil companies, are more likely to implicitly help the producing countries, allocating market shares among themselves while testing elasticity of demand to discover how to maximize their joint monopoly rents. Like the members of OPEC, the IBA countries are fully aware of their own interest in maintaining the firms' profits, which deters them from anticartel behavior. The path of least resistance for the direct investor is thus likely to run from confrontation through co-optation to eventual collaboration with the export cartel.

But will not market forces undermine a successful IBA cartel by bringing into the industry new companies, unencumbered by a need to protect assets and earnings in the IBA countries? The aluminum industry at the smelter (or reduction) stage is one of the most capital-intensive and energy-intensive industries in the world. It requires three to five times as much investment per unit of output as steel.[75] The capital cost of a single 150,000-ton smelter is approximately $400 million in 1975 prices. None of the major companies has less than six times that capacity; Alcoa has thirteen times as much. Many of the larger smelters of Alcoa and Alcan have private fuel sources. These barriers, which kept the aluminum industry highly concentrated even when energy was cheap, are more intimidating now that energy is expensive and investments are politically and financially more risky.

The Outlook for Producer Cartels

Aluminum has, for three decades, been the spoiler for copper, tin, lead, zinc, and (to a certain extent) steel, growing faster than they have (8 percent per year), eating into their traditional uses, and acting as a brake

75. Zuhayr Mikdashi, "Aluminum," in Raymond Vernon, ed., *Big Business and the State: Changing Relations in Western Europe* (Harvard University Press, 1974), p. 172.

on their prices. Thus the IBA seems a good candidate to duplicate some of the successes of OPEC, and over the long term, in fact, it might be more successful than OPEC in coordinating production. Its success will be an important stimulus to other producer associations.

Successful price manipulation by the Council of Copper Exporters (CIPEC) and the Association of Iron Exporting Countries (AIEC) is more uncertain, especially during recession periods of the international business cycle. Major producers (Chile, Zambia, Liberia, and India) must maintain export earnings and government revenues and may not agree to allocations of excess capacity.[76] However, successful price leadership by major exporters during periods of economic expansion seems reasonably predictable and could lead to ever more effective cartel behavior.[77] The limitations on expanding capacity make coordination of production easier than history may suggest. Capacity constraints, by lowering the likelihood that cartel members will unilaterally increase output, lowers the risk to all of them of ending up worse off because of collusion.

Resource diplomacy is the manipulation of market imperfections by exporting countries, alone or in concert, for maximum economic and political gain. Competition for raw materials among large industrial states could create division among the United States, European countries, and Japan, and promote the influence of the Soviet Union.[78] (The initial reaction of most importing countries to the oil embargo, for example, was to deal privately with individual exporting countries.) Resource diplomacy would simply exacerbate relations between industrial and developing countries, causing a North-South confrontation.[79] It would reinforce

76. On the other hand, CIPEC achieved its first real successes at the bottom of the 1974–75 recession, cutting production jointly and negotiating a cessation of Japan's disruptive sales of stockpiled copper. See Karen A. Mingst, "Cooperation or Illusion: An Examination of the Intergovernmental Council of Copper Exporting Countries," *International Organization*, vol. 30 (Spring 1976), esp. pp. 285–87. The proper measurement of collusive strength, of course, is not whether a cartel keeps prices as high during recessions as during booms but whether it prevents price declines from being as severe as they otherwise would be.

77. For example, though Australia and Canada (and perhaps even Brazil) may not lead in raising prices, they may follow the lead of others, as Canada did with petroleum prices. Australia is a full member of both IBA and AIEC and an associate member of CIPEC.

78. Helmut Schmidt, "The Struggle for the World Product," *Foreign Affairs*, vol. 52 (April 1974), pp. 437–51.

79. Moreover, rising prices for primary products would shift income from poorer to richer countries within the South and from the underprivileged to the privileged in all countries.

the pressure for export controls among those countries that had or could get access to resources, undermining three decades of progress toward liberal trade. Finally, it would intensify the struggle among the major consumers for spheres of influence in the Third World.

Balance-of-Payments Effects

Though American multinationals may no longer ensure raw materials to the United States, they do pass on a share of the rents and may provide markets for American capital equipment and ancillary services (such as engineering contracts). Earnings remitted to the United States by American multinationals in 1973 totaled $4.5 billion for petroleum alone (including fees and royalties) and $0.5 billion more for the other extractive industries (excluding fees and royalties, which are not disaggregated for this sector).[80]

But the structure of the multinationals has helped producing countries to raise prices: the U.S. petroleum import bill, for example, rose from under $3 billion in 1970 to $27 billion in 1975 to $45 billion in 1977. The effect of American oil companies on the U.S. balance of payments has not been positive. In the future, the share of the industry rents accruing to the multinationals will decline as bargains continue to obsolesce.

Thus balance-of-payments considerations, like aggregate welfare considerations, argue for maximizing competition in the extractive industries. Though a classic argument in favor of foreign direct investment is to improve the home country's terms of trade by lowering the cost of imports, we find that the extractive multinationals are no longer able to do so.

American Policy Options

The role of direct foreign investment has been doubly transformed in the past twenty-five years. It can no longer assure preferred access for customers in the home country during a period of shortage (real or contrived) without the assent of the host country. And it is increasingly unable, in its traditional form, to develop new supplies and new suppliers so as to solve the problems of price and access.

80. *Survey of Current Business*, vol. 55 (October 1975), pp. 49, 58.

Domestic Self-Sufficiency

For some minerals, U.S. self-sufficiency is physically impossible. For many others, the costs, including environmental costs, would be substantial. Even if domestic self-sufficiency were feasible it would not assure access to raw materials. It would merely bring market power to local groups. In periods of crisis, the American government would confront American business and labor groups instead of foreign governments. But the results could be as unhappy as in Britain's 1974 confrontation with its coal industry, which reduced the country to a three-day workweek.

Furthermore, development of American resources would lead to depletion and, ultimately, greater dependence on foreign suppliers, unless technology provides alternative substances in sufficient quantity to offset depletion.

Even if the social costs and abuses of domestic market power could be handled, many international problems would remain. Domestic self-sufficiency is impossible for Japan and the industrial states of Europe. Competition among them would be fierce for the remaining pool of supplies, and that pool might be more easily manipulated when, after American withdrawal, only highly vulnerable consumers remain.

Moreover, domestic self-sufficiency dashes hope for an open world economy. In the first place, import protection is needed to develop self-sufficiency. Second, national sacrifices are needed, and they may make the country unwilling to share its supply during shortages, which would lead to export controls. Furthermore, because local production would be costly, domestic goods would be costly and would need a protected market.

Economic Stockpiles

Economic stockpiles of raw materials that are subject to fluctuating supply would be more helpful to consumer countries than self-sufficiency. Stockpiles lessen the reward, and hence the incentive, for short-term market manipulations by producers, yet support prices during slumps and protect access during booms. If established on an international basis, economic stockpiles could mute the competition among consuming states. They could be made part of a package that would include prohibitions on export controls, further assuring access to supplies for importing countries.

But stockpiles are expensive to create and likely to be underfinanced. The International Tin Agreement, the only international buffer stock ever maintained for an extended period, has not been financed sufficiently since it was established. In addition, stockpiles can cause misallocation of resources by distorting market signals that stimulate technological change and substitution. Moreover, they do not resolve the misallocation that is a by-product of economic nationalism and the obsolescing bargain. Hence, stockpiles would not free multinational mining companies to develop the huge reserves of the globe. They would not improve the chances for the Third and Fourth World countries with untouched deposits to market their resources. Finally, they would not dissipate the political tensions between home and host governments that accompany the obsolescing bargain.

Nonequity

What is clearly needed is a way for natural resource companies to use their scarce talents and valuable skills for the extraction of raw materials and to respond quickly to market signals, without being vulnerable to the ravages of the obsolescing bargain. The national interest of the United States lies in maximizing the amount of industrial materials produced and in diversifying the sources that produce them. This calls for a formula other than equity investment.

UNBUNDLING SERVICES. American companies have experimented with one method of spreading risk: "unbundling" corporate services. They have separated the provision of capital from the provision of corporate responsibilities like managerial experience, production technology, and marketing expertise. At the first credible postwar threat of nationalization, in the mid-1960s, investors in the copper, petroleum, natural gas, iron ore, and nickel industries began to raise more of their overseas capital by various forms of project financing. They contracted with customers to buy the bulk of the output of a future project; to raise the capital for the project, they sold collection rights on the contracts (at a discount) to financial intermediaries.[81]

81. For evidence, see Theodore H. Moran, "Transnational Strategies of Protection and Defense by Multinational Corporations: Spreading the Risk and Raising the Cost for Nationalization in Natural Resources," *International Organization,* vol. 27 (Spring 1973), pp. 273–87; Ralph M. Dorman, "The Influence of Expropriation on Mining Company Investments," *Mining Congress Journal,* vol. 59 (October 1973), pp. 38–40. For an analysis of the political economy of this corporate strategy, see chap. 10.

Sharing capital commitments with processors and consumers helps investors spread risk but not avoid it. Unbundling has, in fact, left U.S. investors more vulnerable than ever; there are American natural resource companies operating in South Asia with debt-equity ratios of five to one, and all output for the estimated life of the project is already sold to consumers in Europe and Japan.[82] The customers, Norddeutsch and Sumitomo, share with the local subsidiary the risk of price fluctuation and responsibility for the debt. And the U.S. corporations are, in a sense, service contractors for Norddeutsch or Sumitomo. Yet, because they formally own the local property, they are still vulnerable to nationalistic moves by the host country.

CONTRACTING SERVICES. American policy should take unbundling one step further. It should abandon entirely the idea of direct ownership of foreign mineral rights or subsoil resources and encourage the provision of production and marketing skills through service or management contracts in developed countries (for example, Canada and Australia) as well as developing countries. Natural resource companies that are now operating without equity under management contracts, service contracts, or co-production agreements, in petroleum (Peru, Indonesia), copper (Iran, Zaire, Poland), bauxite (Guinea), and coal (Poland) are proof that such contracts, because they offer a highly leveraged return on corporate assets, can be extraordinarily lucrative.[83] They do not offer, of course, a perpetual stream of return reflecting the initial risk, as an equity investment is supposed to do. But that is, as we have seen, unrealistic. Nevertheless, with limited exceptions, American policy continues to support the traditional equity involvement and even to discourage new approaches.

To be sure, management or service contracts, like any other arrangement with host countries, are subject to the obsolescing bargain. But they can adapt to it more easily than direct investments. Contractual arrangements generate less tension than equity investments, because they avoid

---

82. See "Freeport's Erstberg is a Real Bargain," *Engineering and Mining Journal,* vol. 172 (July 1971), p. 85.

83. Author interviews with management of participating companies, 1974–75. For more on nonequity projects, see Louis Kraar, "Oil and Nationalism Mix Beautifully in Indonesia," *Fortune,* vol. 88 (July 1973), pp. 98–103; Robert Fabrikant, "Production Sharing Contracts in the Indonesian Petroleum Industry," *Harvard International Law Journal,* vol. 16 (Spring 1975), pp. 303–51; and Allan T. Demaree, "Aramco is a Lesson in the Management of Chaos," *Fortune* (February 1974), p. 162.

the sensitive issue of foreign ownership of subsoil rights and they do not require the host government to cede ownership of a producing facility for a sustained, often indefinite, period of time.

But the argument for service contracts is not simply that it avoids tension, but that companies would actually be in better bargaining positions. Fewer of their assets would be committed. They could, if need be, more credibly threaten to withdraw from the management of any single project. Service or management contracts can be limited in duration and be based on payment for services rendered; and they can more easily be renegotiated as competition for the services changes. They can include performance bonuses, which provide incentive (at least as effective as ownership shares) for fast and efficient services.

MORTGAGING THE PRODUCT. A shift from direct investment to service contracting in the extractive industries would require development capital in the form of debt to future customers and financial intermediaries. Protection of their credit would be as important as protection of equity investments. We would expect that the long-term safety of capital loaned to a state mining or petroleum agency would be greater than capital loaned to a private foreign equity investor, who might well be nationalized or expropriated. The safety of the creditors could be furthered by engaging international financial institutions as intermediaries in raising capital. An existing institution could be used, such as the International Finance Corporation of the World Bank; or a new institution could be created, such as the International Resources Bank proposed by the United States at the 1976 United Nations Conference on Trade and Development.

In addition, nations where most consumers and creditors are located could agree that creditors whose loans were in default have the right to sue in the national courts of the countries where the output is sold for either possession of the output or custody of the payments. Such a "hot products" convention, covering the treatment of claims against the output of state-owned properties whose debts were not being paid, would force exporting governments to respect the commitments they or their predecessors made, whether or not they agreed to the hot-products convention. The feasibility of a mining project, itself, would be determined by a reputable international company (as it is now) but the project would be owned by a state development agency, like Algeria's Sonatrach, Zaire's Gécomines, or Iran's Sar Chesmeh Mining Company. A creditor who wanted more assurance could require the contractors to invest some capital as part of the total debt. No change in the packaging of capital can eliminate the commercial risk in the extractive industries. But the nonequity arrangement we propose would reduce the political risk to the company and the creditors and would spread the commercial risk among the company, the creditors, the processors, the buyers, and the host government.

The shift out of equity would protect the interests of the companies and of the creditors, restore ownership of the national patrimony to the exporting governments, enable them to develop their resources, and reduce tension in relations between the United States and the developing world.

Most important, however, from the point of view of consumers, a nonequity system would make it easier for foreign companies to undertake new projects in response to a rise in prices. It would make sources of commercially exploitable raw materials, now closed off by economic nationalism, available for development. It would make producer cartels harder to form and harder to hold.[84] It would encourage both new production companies and new producing countries to enter the market, which is essential to competition. For example, nonequity bauxite production would eliminate the threat of complete nationalization, which now prevents aluminum companies from creating competitive national suppliers at the production stage. And the nonequity approach would enable countries with iron or copper reserves to begin production or expand their market shares more easily. Many countries with large mineral reserves (Peru, Chile, Zaire, Mexico, Brazil, Indonesia) want to expand capacity. They would rather increase export earnings by expanding production than by reducing it, especially if it can be done in a way that satisfies national pride—that does not relinquish the national heritage to foreign investors.

The most straightforward way to hasten the shift from the direct equity formula to management or service contracts is to change the U.S. tax treatment of the foreign income of American extractive multinationals.

---

84. If American oil companies were not equity holders but simply marketers of the cheapest oil available, they would have no need to help major producers maintain stable market shares. This would help prevent OPEC from monitoring oil production and oil prices. The uncertainty of the OPEC members about what the others were doing could be enhanced by auctioning, through sealed bids, import tickets for the U.S. market. All oil-exporting countries could then cheat on the rest without being observed. See M. A. Adelman, "Oil Import Quota Auctions," *Challenge,* vol. 18 (January–February 1976), pp. 17–22.

Earnings on nonequity contracts should continue to be eligible for the full foreign tax credit. Earnings from equity holdings should gradually be made ineligible for the foreign tax credit.[85]

Alternatively, a per-country calculation of foreign tax credit should be required. Some firms now lose nothing from increased tax rates in producing countries because they combine all of their foreign earnings and tax liabilities, the so-called overall method. A 70 percent tax in one host country, for example, may be offset by a 26 percent rate in another country, negating all of a firm's U.S. tax liabilities. Using the per-country approach would mean that taxes paid to any individual country above the U.S. rate (48 percent) could be counted only as a deduction and not as a credit against tax liability in the United States; and since the taxes of most producing countries on foreign direct investment in the extractive industries are above 48 percent, such a move by the United States should provoke a rapid shift out of equity. As a further inducement, subsidiaries providing management services could be permitted to continue using the overall method. But even with a per-country limitation, the fees in a service agreement could be structured to embody a tax rate no higher than the U.S. level.[86]

Any of these changes represent a dramatic shift in U.S. tax policy, which traditionally has subsidized the obsolescing bargain by allowing increasing host-country taxes to be credited against U.S. taxes. Recent tightening of the tax treatment of petroleum multinationals simply compounds the mistake; what is needed is more exploration in more diverse locations. Penal-

85. The U.S. Congress limited the amount of foreign taxes eligible for crediting on "foreign oil and gas extraction income" (Tax Reduction Act of 1975), which may deter, somewhat, the equity approach in that industry. For explanation, see Jerome B. Libin, "Significant Changes in United States Taxation of Foreign Income," *Bulletin for International Fiscal Documentation*, vol. 29 (July 1975), pp. 269–72.

86. American tax policy toward petroleum multinationals takes the opposite approach. The Tax Reduction Act of 1975 requires companies to calculate tax by the overall method, so that they can no longer both offset foreign losses against U.S. income and also credit foreign taxes against overall tax payments, including those in profitable countries. Our proposed policy would allow the netting of foreign losses against domestic income but would ban the netting of taxes against the foreign tax credit, extending the present limitation on the amount of foreign taxes eligible for credit. See chap. 6 for detailed discussion. For more on overall method and the petroleum industries' use of it, see Glenn P. Jenkins and Brian W. Wright, "Taxation of Income of Multinational Corporations: The Case of the United States Petroleum Industry," *Review of Economics and Statistics*, vol. 57 (February 1975), p. 3.

izing foreign earnings may be counterproductive.[87] Tax policy should alter the incentives among the types of foreign investment so as to promote non-equity involvement and discourage equity involvement. This might well amount to tax liberalization for the oil multinationals and tax tightening for multinationals in the other extractive industries.

As a further inducement for American companies to abandon direct foreign ownership, the U.S. government could deny insurance through the Overseas Private Investment Corporation (OPIC) to equity investment in raw materials but allow full OPIC coverage for nonequity operations. And the lower risks of nonequity might justify lower insurance rates. In addition, the United States could use OPIC to guarantee the debt advanced by American institutions.

Host countries may push the extractive multinationals part of the way into nonequity involvement. In 1975, Saudi Arabia began a 100 percent takeover of Aramco, which is in the national interest of the United States when compared with the alternatives.[88] But Jamaica limited its bauxite nationalizations to 51 percent, clearly to maintain the firms' equity and, thus, their interest in holding prices high and production down. Jamaica's more sophisticated approach appears likely to be emulated by other host countries in the extractive industries.

For the United States and other importing countries, the Jamaican approach is the worst possible. U.S. policy should encourage total nonequity, which would refocus the goals of American multinationals to parallel those of the home country. Their interest would be to maximize the returns on their technical and managerial skills by diversifying the sources and increasing amounts of raw materials available for world markets.

87. Japan, for example, taxes its multinationals preferentially. See Greyson Bryan, "The Tax Implications of Japanese Multinational Corporations," *Journal of International Law and Politics*, vol. 8 (Fall 1975), p. 189.

88. However, the companies nationalized by Saudi Arabia still have equity in oil production elsewhere in the world and thus are interested in optimizing world oil prices and avoiding excessive world output. Saudi Arabia is living in the best of both worlds as a result of its nationalization, though nationalization by the other major producing countries would undermine Saudi Arabia's advantage and jeopardize the symbiotic relation between the companies and the producing countries.

CHAPTER SIX

Tax Issues

TAX POLICY is the most tangible expression of the official U.S. attitude toward the foreign direct investment of American corporations. Although the Internal Revenue Code as it applies to the foreign-source income of corporations is all but incomprehensible to the laity, the economic and political questions it raises are clear. Does it encourage firms to invest abroad rather than in the United States? Can American multinationals avoid taxes by shifting income from the United States into tax-haven countries? If the foreign tax credit were repealed, would American firms seriously lessen their foreign investment? Would they increase investment in the United States? Would certain tax changes lessen the competitiveness of American firms in world markets? Would such changes hurt the economies of other countries, thereby disturbing the world economy and U.S. foreign policy?

This chapter begins with a summary of American taxation of foreign-source income, to explain what U.S. policy is and from whence it came.[1] After a review of the economic literature on the taxing of foreign investment income, we indicate the inadequacies of the conventional approach,

1. For a complete survey see Lawrence B. Krause and Kenneth W. Dam, *Federal Tax Treatment of Foreign Income* (Brookings Institution, 1964); Peggy B. Musgrave, *United States Taxation of Foreign Investment Income: Issues and Arguments* (Harvard Law School, 1969). For a detailed study on the foreign tax credit see Elisabeth A. Owens, *The Foreign Tax Credit: A Study of the Credit for Foreign Taxes Under United States Income Tax Law* (Harvard Law School, 1961); Elisabeth A. Owens and George Ball, *The Indirect Credit* (Harvard Law School, 1975). Most studies of the historical background of current policy draw directly or indirectly on Jacob Stewart Seidman, *Legislative History of Federal Income Tax Laws, 1938–1861* [sic] (Prentice-Hall, 1938).

and in the sections that follow we analyze U.S. taxation of American manufacturing multinationals and recommend changes.

Current U.S. Tax Policy

When the corporate income tax was imposed in 1913, the rate was set at 1 percent of income, which may explain why no one worried too much about details. Rather than taxing only income from domestic operations, the United States taxed foreign-source income as well. The earnings of an unincorporated foreign branch of an American company were taxed as they were earned, but the comparable earnings of a subsidiary incorporated in a foreign country could be reinvested abroad without incurring any immediate U.S. tax liability. Taxes were payable only when an American investor paid itself a dividend. This deferral of U.S. taxes on retained earnings was consistent with the practice of taxing individuals' dividend income and not their pro rata share of a corporation's retained earnings. Whether corporate investors should be treated as private individuals was quickly resolved at the outset, and the deferral accorded to U.S. investors has remained a cornerstone of tax policy ever since.

For the first five years of income taxation, the United States taxed all income of its residents net of foreign taxes; foreign tax payments were simply deducted from the taxable income of the investor. The investors were paying higher total taxes than their foreign competitors, and the additional burden became heavier as the American tax rate went up.[2] After five years of this double taxation, one witness before the House Ways and Means Committee asked for a tax exemption for foreign-source income or, that failing, a lower tax rate. Although he was the only witness to address himself to the issue, the Ways and Means Committee, the House, the Senate and the President accepted a foreign tax credit as a good compromise. Foreign taxes, rather than constituting a mere deduction from taxable income, could now be credited directly against the U.S. income-tax liability. Thus, in 1918 the second cornerstone of U.S. tax policy, the foreign tax credit, became firmly entrenched.[3]

2. See Krause and Dam, *Federal Tax Treatment of Foreign Income*, pp. 27–43.
3. Suppose that a foreign affiliate of a U.S. firm earns $100 from its local operations and that the foreign and U.S. corporate income tax rates are 10 percent and 25

Because the foreign-tax credit is basic to U.S. policy, we should note its more important features. First and foremost, only taxes on the income of American investors can be credited against the American tax liability; excise, sales, value added, and other such taxes cannot. This distinction derives from the notion that the burden of an income tax is borne by the investor, but that of a sales or similar tax is passed on to customers.[4]

While distinguishing an income from a sales tax may appear easy, in actual practice one can be made to pass for the other. The most notorious

---

percent, respectively. Suppose that $50 is reinvested locally, and the balance repatriated to the parent firm. Under all conditions and assumptions, the foreign government gets $10, the $50 is reinvested, and the remaining $40 is split between the U.S. investor and the U.S. government. Before 1918, if the affiliate were an unincorporated branch, the U.S. Internal Revenue Service would have allowed the $10 deduction for foreign taxes and collected 25 percent of the remaining $90, which amounts to $22.50. The parent's after-tax income would, thus, have been $17.50. If the affiliate were separately incorporated, the United States would have applied its 25 percent to only the $40 dividend, kept $10 in taxes, and left the U.S. investor with $30.

In 1918, a foreign tax credit was extended to taxes paid to foreign governments by U.S. corporations and to taxes deemed paid through their majority-owned affiliates. For an unincorporated branch, this meant that its potential U.S. tax liability was 25 percent of the pretax $100, but this $25 liability was reduced $10 for taxes paid to the foreign government, so the branch paid only $15 instead of $22.50 and the parent's after-tax income was $25 instead of $17.50. The potential tax liability of the separately incorporated subsidiary was 25 percent of its $40 dividend, or $10, against which 4/10 (the ratio of dividends to pretax foreign earnings) of the foreign tax payments, or $4, could be credited. U.S. taxes were thus reduced to $6 and the parent's receipts increased to $34.

Under this formula, the subsidiary has an advantage over the branch even if all foreign earnings are paid out as dividends and $50 is reinvested from after-tax U.S. earnings. Such is the case because the subsidiary's potential tax liability is 25 percent of $90 (instead of $100). Although the parent can claim only 9/10 of the $10 as foreign taxes deemed paid, it still comes out ahead ($22.50 less $9 is $13.50 in U.S. taxes), compared to the $15 paid by the branch. This situation was changed in 1962 for subsidiaries in the developed countries by requiring investors to gross foreign income by foreign taxes deemed paid before computing their U.S. tax liability (and at the same time allowing them to make an analogous adjustment in their foreign tax credit). After 1962, the $40 dividend would be grossed up by 4/9 (ratio of dividends to after-tax earnings) of the $10 in foreign taxes deemed paid, so that the U.S. potential tax liability would be $11.11 (25 percent of $44.44), against which the $4.44 could be credited. The resulting $6.67 paid in U.S. taxes is, thus, somewhat higher than the $6 paid before 1962 and in less-developed countries from 1962 to 1976.

4. The distinction is not supported by empirical research on tax incidence. See Richard A. Musgrave and Peggy B. Musgrave, *Public Finance in Theory and Practice,* 2nd ed. (McGraw-Hill, 1976), chap. 18.

case in point has been the income taxes based on posted prices set by the oil-exporting countries. Had these taxes been based explicitly on the value or the quantity of crude oil extracted, they would not have qualified for a tax credit in the United States. Had the oil-exporting countries employed a simple income tax, they would have had to police the transfer prices used by the integrated oil companies (the lower the price of crude oil exports to downstream affiliates, the less the taxable income of the oil-exporting countries). In 1950 the United States, anxious to encourage petroleum companies to invest in friendly countries, allowed oil-exporting countries to base an income tax on a posted price, whose only real function was to inflate taxable income (and hence provide a mechanism for transferring U.S. financial assistance without congressional approval). As the posted price bore less and less relation to the market price, this income tax became a per-barrel royalty in disguise.[5] Although this particular subterfuge was consciously initiated by the United States, the general problem of distinguishing one type of tax from another can occur whenever any foreign country tries to protect or increase its tax revenues by setting transfer prices on intrafirm exports of American multinationals. This distinction between taxes and other payments eligible and ineligible for the foreign tax credit is becoming increasingly blurred as foreign tax authorities become more sophisticated in taxing investment income.[6]

A second critical feature of the foreign tax credit is that it cannot exceed the taxes tentatively due the U.S. Treasury on foreign-source income alone. Thus the foreign tax credit cannot be used to reduce an American corporation's taxes on its domestic income. This limitation has a very pragmatic rationale. If a dollar paid in taxes to a foreign government can be offset by a dollar not paid to the U.S. Treasury, American investors have no incentive to resist higher foreign taxes. The U.S. Treasury, not the investors, would bear the burden of increased foreign taxes. A limitation on the foreign tax credit caps the revenue loss of the U.S. Treasury, a loss which otherwise could be massive.

5. In July 1976, the IRS announced that it would henceforth investigate whether these payments did represent direct taxes eligible for the foreign tax credit. In January 1978, Saudi Arabian and Libyan taxes based on "posted prices" were ruled not creditable.

6. For evidence on the similarity of treatment toward export platform investments see Grant L. Reuber and others, *Private Foreign Investment in Development* (Oxford: Clarendon Press, 1973), pp. 299–300.

Although as of 1976, U.S. investors must use an overall method in determining the limitation on their foreign tax credit, the per-country method has been used in the past and remains an option for the future.[7] If the per-country method were used, an American investor would first calculate its tentative U.S. tax rate and then multiply that tentative tax rate by its income from each foreign country to determine the allowable credit for each. The tentative tax rate is the ratio of total taxes tentatively due the U.S. Treasury (before deducting the various tax credits) to the global income of the U.S. corporation. For a corporation with no capital gains or other income taxed at an advantageous rate, the tentative U.S. tax rate would be the 48 percent statutory tax rate. With capital gains and other such income, the tentative tax rate may drop below 48 percent. Whatever the investor's tentative tax rate turns out to be, it determines the maximum tax credit that can be claimed for income from each foreign country.

Alternatively, the American investor could use the tentative tax rate to calculate a single, overall limitation on its total foreign tax credits from all countries. An American investor could thereby combine income and tax payments from different countries. The accounting requirements imposed on the multinational firms and the Internal Revenue Service auditors are greatly reduced by this averaging, for transfer prices for transactions between affiliates have little effect on the tax credit.

This accounting simplicity has its economic cost, however. An American investor with sizable investments in high-tax countries may be greatly tempted by tax holidays or low tax rates in other countries. After paying the minimal foreign taxes, all after-tax income may be repatriated without incurring any additional U.S. tax liability, for the U.S. taxes tentatively due may be offset by excess tax credits from the high-tax countries. Furthermore, the high-tax countries may feel that they have little to gain by reducing their taxes on U.S. investments since, through the overall credit mechanism, such tax cuts may be automatically offset by higher taxes owed to the U.S. Treasury. Although it streamlines the accounting and auditing requirements, the overall method modifies and complicates the effect of national taxes on international investment behavior.

---

7. Since passage of the Tax Reduction Act of 1975 (89 Stat. 54–65), the overall approach must be used on all "foreign oil-related income." Laws pertaining to manufacturing firms have required one or the other calculation method but at one time required the calculation yielding the larger tax liability.

Why, then, did any corporation ever choose the per-country limitation over the overall limitation, since the latter allowed the firm to use excess tax credits from high-tax countries while the former did not? The answer to this question is intimately associated with that to another: why would a firm ever have an unincorporated branch, rather than a locally incorporated affiliate, since the latter allows the firm to defer U.S. taxes while the former does not?

If all foreign investments earned profits, subsidiaries would be preferable to branches for tax avoidance, and the overall limitation would be superior to the per-country limitation. But not all foreign investments earn profits, not in the short run and certainly not as far as the tax accounts are concerned. Particularly notable exceptions are natural-resource investments, which often show huge losses (often accounting phenomena due to treating exploration, drilling, and other development costs as current expenses rather than capital costs subject to depletion or depreciation) during their first years of operation. Analogous losses, though less spectacular and prolonged, are incurred by manufacturing investments with high start-up expenditures. The tax implication is that losses of an unincorporated branch could be subtracted from the domestic earnings of the American parent and thereby used to reduce U.S. taxes. But, to do this, the American investor had to use the per-country method. If it elected the overall method, it had to combine its foreign gains and losses and deduct only its net foreign losses from its domestic income. If its foreign gains exceeded its foreign losses, the investor would pay foreign taxes on all its profitable investments and be unable to deduct its losses from any of its taxable income, foreign or domestic.[8]

In the early 1960s, U.S. taxation of foreign investment income became a major domestic political issue. With the surge of American investment in Europe widely regarded as a major cause of the U.S. balance-of-payments deficit in the late 1950s, the Kennedy administration proposed eliminating the deferral of taxes on unrepatriated income. The Treasury argued that eliminating deferral would discourage capital outflows and encourage firms to repatriate a higher proportion of their foreign investment earnings. The elimination of deferral was a much larger step than Congress was willing to take, however, and the Revenue Act of 1962 simply limited its scope in several respects.

The most straightforward change the Tax Reform Act of 1962 brought

8. This was one aim of the Tax Reduction Act of 1975 (see note 7).

about is the grossing-up requirement, which raised the effective rate of taxation on foreign-source income. Before 1962, foreign-source income and applicable tax credit were based on a subsidiary's income after the foreign income tax; since 1962, foreign-source income has been grossed up to include taxes paid by the subsidiary. Grossing up guarantees that a subsidiary repatriating all its earnings as dividends will bear the same tax burden as an unincorporated branch. The increase in taxes from grossing up depends on the foreign income tax and the dividend payout rates. The maximum impact comes when a foreign subsidiary pays 24 percent of its income in taxes to the foreign country and repatriates the remaining 76 percent. If grossing up is not required, the U.S. tax liability amounts to an additional 18.2 percent of pretax income; if grossing up is required, the U.S. tax liability is 24 percent of pretax income. Grossing up thus increases total taxes from 42.2 percent to 48 percent of the pretax income from such an affiliate. To encourage direct investment in developing countries, they were exempted from the 1962 grossing-up requirement.

The Revenue Act of 1962 also sought to limit the accumulation of taxable income in tax-haven subsidiaries. Rather than defining tax-haven countries, the act defined base-company income: it arises from an affiliate organized with tax avoidance as a significant purpose; it is generated by buying or selling within the multinational or is passive income such as dividends and royalties from affiliated companies. An example is the income earned by a Swiss affiliate used as a financial intermediary between an American parent and a German or French subsidiary. After 1962, the commissions and fees received by the Swiss affiliate could be classified as base-company income and deemed a dividend to the U.S. parent and subject to U.S. taxation. Base-company income was then no longer fully entitled to deferral.[9]

9. The Revenue Act did, however, create significant exceptions to the base-company income rules. If the hypothetical Swiss and German affiliates together made sufficient dividend distributions to bring the average tax rate up to a specified minimum, the deemed distribution of base-company income could be reduced or eliminated. This was called the minimum-distribution exception. Likewise, if base-company income were reinvested in qualifying investments in less-developed countries, no dividends were deemed distributed to the American parent. Third, if base-company income were less than 30 percent of the affiliate's total income (it might have additional income from manufacturing), no dividends were deemed distributed. Finally, income from shipping and air transport were specifically excluded from base-company income. These rules were tightened considerably in the Tax Reduction Act of 1975.

If the base-company income rules can limit the abuse of deferral, tax avoidance will remain an issue as long as national income tax rates differ and investors have some flexibility in their intrafirm accounts. If the transfer price assigned to intrafirm exports can be lowered, the use of interest-bearing debt minimized, or charges for head-office or technological services pared, taxable income can be shifted from the parent to its overseas affiliates. The multinationals do not have a free hand in avoiding taxes, however. Under section 482 of the Internal Revenue Code, the Service can challenge any intrafirm transfer price or charge it believes does not conform to the arm's-length standard (that which would prevail between an independent buyer and seller). But the arm's-length standard is ambiguous and difficult to administer. In buying and selling complex products or their components, an objective measure of an arm's-length price may be impossible to find. Likewise, many activities jointly benefit foreign and domestic operations. Research efforts, for example, may be directed at developing new products for both domestic and foreign markets. While such joint costs must be apportioned between the beneficiaries, the proper formula for allocating such costs may be ambiguous. To avoid unnecessary U.S. taxes or to satisfy foreign demands, the multinationals may resolve the arm's-length ambiguity in favor of their foreign affiliates.[10]

An alternative to monitoring transfer prices was considered by the House of Representatives in 1962. Rather than trying to determine an appropriate price for every intrafirm transaction, global income could be allocated in proportion to assets, sales, or some other stable base. (The income tax payments of U.S. corporations to the different states in which they operate within the United States are often allocated on the basis of the shares of their payroll, capital, and sales in each.) For example, if two-thirds of a multinational's sales were in the United States and one-third abroad, then two-thirds of its global income would be attributed to

10. By 1968, there had been 800 challenges. See Treasury Department, "Summary Study of International Cases Involving Section 482 of the Internal Revenue Code" (January 1973; processed). Manipulative transfer pricing in the oil industry cost consuming countries a minimum $205 million tax loss in 1966 and $240 million in 1970, according to the implications in Glenn P. Jenkins and Brian D. Wright, "Taxation of Income of Multinational Corporations: The Case of the United States Petroleum Industry," *Review of Economics and Statistics*, vol. 57 (February 1975), pp. 3–10.

the U.S. parent for tax purposes. Such an allocation formula would greatly reduce a multinational's ability to avoid taxes, but the resulting allocation of taxable income might be rather arbitrary. Different formulas give rise to different geographical allocations of taxable income and become a bone of contention among local tax authorities, as occurred among the states of the United States in administering their "three-factor formula."[11] In the end, the House scrapped any use of formulas and encouraged the Internal Revenue Service to use its existing authority to monitor transfer prices more closely than it had in the past.

The Revenue Act of 1962 also included an investment tax credit, which was not extended to overseas investment.[12] In the hope of stimulating domestic economic growth and improving the international competitiveness of production in the United States, Congress authorized American investors to credit an amount equal to 7 percent of their new capital equipment against their income taxes.[13] The investment tax credit has had an on-again, off-again history: it was passed in 1962, liberalized in 1964, suspended in 1966, reinstituted in 1967, repealed in 1969, brought back in 1971, and increased to 10 percent in 1975. Because Congress was not particularly concerned by slow growth abroad, and even hoped that the measure would strengthen the U.S. trade balance, the investment tax credit has never applied to the foreign investments of American firms.[14]

Faced with a large and growing balance-of-trade deficit in 1971, and arguing that deferral encouraged foreign production at the expense of U.S. exports, President Nixon proposed in his new economic policy of August 15, 1971, not to eliminate deferral but to create a similar advantage for American exporters: domestic international sales corporations, or DISCs. (As with the investment tax credit in 1962, it was also argued that other countries used similar devices so that such a step by the

11. A view sympathetic to income allocation (and yet recognizing that technical problems must be resolved in constructing the formula) is taken in Gerard M. Brannon, "National Shares of Multicompany Income" (paper prepared for the Organisation for Economic Co-operation and Development, 1973; processed).

12. 76 Stat. 962–73.

13. The success of the investment tax credit is a matter of some debate. See Gary Fromm, ed., *Tax Incentives and Capital Spending* (Brookings Institution, 1971).

14. Tax treaties negotiated in the mid-1960s with several developing countries to extend the investment tax credit to earnings from investments in those countries were not approved by the Senate.

United States would simply offset what others were already doing.)[15] A DISC is essentially a dummy corporation to which export profits can be ascribed. While 50 percent of such profits must be paid out to the owners and thereby subject to normal U.S. taxation, the remaining 50 percent are tax-deferred as long as those earnings are reinvested in export-related projects. Furthermore, American exporters are not bound by the usual arm's-length standard in determining how to allocate total profits between manufacturing and exporting; instead, they can use special rules, which guarantee a high return for the DISC and, thus, low taxes on U.S. exports.

In the early 1970s, the AFL-CIO lobbied hard, but unsuccessfully, to get Congress to eliminate both deferral and the foreign tax credit. Without a foreign tax credit, all foreign-source income would be taxed by foreign governments and then again by the United States. The unions hoped that this double taxation would limit American firms' willingness to invest abroad and enhance the unions' bargaining strength in wage negotiations. Whether the impact would have been as labor hoped, Congress refused to vote such legislation.

But the Tax Reduction Act of 1975 indicates that the unions, and others who wish to tighten the tax treatment of foreign income, have made some headway. The U.S. Senate actually voted to end deferral, the first time that either legislative branch has done so, though it was reinstated in the Senate-House conference committee. The most significant changes in the act affected the multinational petroleum firms.[16] To force these companies to pay higher U.S. taxes, Congress modified their foreign tax credit in two ways. First, a separate limitation was placed on the foreign tax credits deriving from the extraction of oil. In 1975 only 52.8 percent of income from oil extraction could be claimed as a tax credit; the limit dropped to 50.5 percent in 1976 and 50 percent thereafter. In short, the high payments to oil-exporting countries offer far fewer U.S. tax

15. See Gary C. Hufbauer, "The Taxation of Export Profits," *National Tax Journal*, vol. 28 (March 1975), pp. 43–59.

16. *Tax Reduction Act of 1975: Law and Explanation* (Commerce Clearing House, 1975), pp. 47–48. The act tightens the rules pertaining to base-company income, making it harder for the multinationals to exploit tax-haven situations. Both the minimum distribution exception, by which deemed distributions could be reduced through actual dividend payments, and the option of reinvesting earnings in less-developed countries, are eliminated entirely. Furthermore, dividends are deemed paid when base-company income exceed 10 percent (instead of 30 percent) of the affiliate's total income.

credits than heretofore. Second, the per-country method can no longer be used for any oil-related income. Having no choice but to use the overall method, the petroleum companies have to offset foreign drilling and exploration expenses with other foreign-source income rather than against domestic U.S. income.

The Tax Reform Act of 1976 has a variety of provisions affecting U.S. taxation of foreign-source income. The exemption from grossing up of income from less-developed countries was terminated; income from these countries is now taxed in the same manner as income from developed countries. The deferral of U.S. taxes on export income allocated to a DISC is restricted to income from exports over and above a base value (which, in turn, equals 67 percent of the average value of exports during an earlier, four-year base period). By limiting DISC benefits in this way, Congress hoped to stem loss of tax revenues without destroying incentives to make new exports. An exemption for a portion of the income of a western hemisphere trade corporation, which some U.S. investors use to export or invest in Canada or Latin America, will be phased out by 1980. All U.S. investors, not just the oil companies, must henceforth use the overall method of calculating the limitation on the foreign tax credit. And finally, the act denies both deferral and the foreign tax credit to certain income of U.S. companies participating in or complying with an international boycott, such as that Arab countries imposed against Israel.

After an extended debate, the Treasury recently issued new guidelines for administering sections 861 and 863 of the Internal Revenue Code.[17] These guidelines describe the proper allocation of research and development, interest, and stewardship expenses among foreign and domestic affiliates in determining the overall limitation on the foreign tax credit. Under the new guidelines, U.S. manufacturers deduct a higher portion of these domestic expenses from their foreign-source income, reducing the ceiling on the foreign tax credit. Unless the investor has a deficit of foreign tax credits, its foreign tax credit will fall and its U.S. tax payments rise. The only way the investor can avoid a comparable increase in its global tax burden is by passing on the higher charges to the foreign affiliates, thereby reducing foreign tax payments. The multinationals argue that foreign tax authorities will not allow higher deductions for

17. U.S. Office of the Federal Register, *Federal Register,* vol. 42 (January 6, 1977), pp. 1195–1214.

U.S. expenditures, and that the new guidelines, therefore, subject the disputed income to double taxation.

To summarize: the basic foundations of U.S. tax policy, deferral and the foreign tax credit, were laid down fifty years ago and, although modified several times, have remained more or less intact ever since. It was only in the 1960s, when the U.S. Treasury proposed eliminating deferral to help the balance of payments, that tax policy became controversial. It has, in the 1970s, become very controversial indeed. Congress chose not to eliminate deferral or the foreign tax credit but rather to offset their unwanted effects through a variety of compensating measures. An investment tax credit was given to domestic, but not foreign, investment (1962); the Internal Revenue Service stepped up its policing of transfer-pricing practices; deferral was extended to export earnings through domestic international sales corporations (1971) and then modified (1976); the per-country method of calculating the limitation on the foreign tax credit was eliminated for the oil companies (1975) and then for all investors (1976); income from developed countries was no longer exempt from grossing up (1962), nor that from less-developed countries (1976); the eligibility of base-company income for deferral was limited (1962 and, especially, 1975), and new guidelines were issued for allocating R&D, interest, and stewardship expenses among domestic and foreign affiliates (1977). Most recently, President Carter in early 1978 proposed the elimination of both deferral and the DISCs. Maintaining the foundations of a policy, but making one qualification after another, has made it difficult to determine the real thrust of U.S. policy, much less whether it promotes the national interest of the United States.

Tax Policy and Traditional Economic Theory[18]

Traditional economic analysis of taxation is everything that actual U.S. policy is not: clean, coherent, and reasonably easy to understand. It ignores the balance-of-payments, unemployment, and other "short-run" concerns and focuses on "long-run" issues, such as the distribution of income between capital and labor or efficiency in the international location of capital. Such theory is too ethereal to be of much use in drafting

18. Peggy B. Musgrave, *Direct Investment Abroad and the Multinationals: Effects on the United States Economy,* a study prepared for Senate Foreign Relations Committee (GPO, 1975), chap. 7, surveys this literature.

tax legislation, but the way it relates policy to goal is in refreshing contrast to actual practice.

The conclusions of the analysis can be easily stated. A basic theorem is that both the home and the host country benefit from international investment and that the welfare of both is maximized by unrestricted investment. This proposition in investment theory is analogous to Ricardo's theorem that two countries can benefit from international trade predicated on comparative advantage and that free trade maximizes world welfare. But any one country may benefit by restricting international exchange: home countries can benefit by limiting capital exports to force a higher return, host countries by limiting capital imports to lower borrowing costs. Restrictions by either are, however, beggar-thy-neighbor policies, since the country imposing restrictions gains less than its investing partner loses.

Traditional theory also explores the impact of international investment on the distribution of national income between labor and capital in both the home and the host countries. In the home country, the export of capital hurts domestic labor by making it less productive and helps domestic capital by lessening competition. Wages fall, and the return on capital rises. In the host country, the opposite happens, wages rise and the return on capital falls. Local labor becomes more productive when it works with more capital, while locally owned capital suffers from increased competition. Thus, in each country, one faction will tend to support foreign investment and the other to oppose it, as long as the issue revolves around these purely economic considerations.

If either the home or the host country taxes the income of capital, the pattern of international investment may be distorted, and some of the potential global benefits may be lost. In fact, investment decisions will be distorted unless capital export neutrality prevails (that is, unless an investor pays the same total tax on foreign investment as it does on domestic investment). Capital export neutrality can be achieved in a variety of ways. If the host country refrains from taxing foreign investment, then the home country can tax its domestic and its foreign investors at the same rate. Alternatively, if the host country taxes foreign-owned investments, the home country can give a full tax credit to its foreign investors for taxes paid in host countries. The critical difference between these two methods is who collects the taxes, the home country or the host country.

From a national standpoint, taxes paid abroad are hardly as good as taxes paid at home. In traditional analysis, the national gain from foreign investment for the home country is measured by the sum of the returns of the foreign investors and the revenues of the home treasury; national benefits include both public and private gains. Because taxes paid to the foreign government have no benefit for the home country, it has no reason to give its investors a tax credit for foreign taxes paid. The national gain is maximized by disallowing any credit for foreign taxes and allowing only a simple deduction for foreign taxes paid, as was done in the United States from 1913 until 1918.[19]

National neutrality, as opposed to capital export neutrality, prevails when investors have no incentive to invest abroad when the national interest would be better served by domestic investment. The proposal to eliminate the foreign tax credit and allow only a simple deduction for foreign taxes paid has been justified as maximizing U.S. gains from international investment.[20] We hasten to add, however, that this argument presumes that tax policy of other countries is fixed. If foreigners retaliate by changing their tax laws, both home and host countries may wish the tax war had never started.[21]

We should also define capital import neutrality (or competitive neutrality), a standard often advocated by the multinationals. Under this approach, American investors would pay the same taxes on their overseas income as their foreign competitors do. An easy and obvious way of providing capital import neutrality would be for the host country to tax foreign capital at the same rate as locally owned capital and then for the home country to exempt foreign investment income from taxation.[22]

19. The social cost of foreign direct investment to the United States, based on this concept, is estimated at about $2.5 billion annually in Wilson E. Schmidt, "U.S. Capital Export Policy: Backdoor Mercantilism," in *U.S. Taxation of American Business Abroad* (American Enterprise Institute, 1975), pp. 28–31.

20. See Peggy B. Musgrave, "Tax Preferences to Foreign Investment," *Economics of Federal Subsidy Programs, Part 2: International Subsidies,* papers submitted to Joint Economic Committee (GPO, 1972), pp. 176–219; and her comments in *Tax Subsidies and Tax Reform,* Hearings before the Joint Economic Committee, 92:2 (GPO, 1973), pp. 192–96, 200–02.

21. See Koichi Hamada, "Strategic Aspects of Taxation on Foreign Investment Income," *Quarterly Journal of Economics,* vol. 80 (August 1966), pp. 361–75.

22. France and the Netherlands follow this practice. It is advocated for the United States by Norman B. Ture, "Taxing Foreign-Source Income," in *U.S. Taxation of American Business Abroad,* pp. 37–66.

These simple conclusions about national tax policy depend on simple assumptions about the international investment process. The most dramatic qualifications of the simple traditional theory come not from introducing new wrinkles but from altering the fundamental assumptions about the foreign investment process. Suppose, first, that foreign investment entails the transfer of technology rather than capital. Unlike a capital outflow, the international transfer of technology does not inhibit domestic production. While traditional economists have studied this sort of international exchange,[23] the implications for taxing foreign investment income have not been widely appreciated. If technology can indeed be transferred to foreign production without materially harming domestic production, the national interest in taxing this foreign-source income evaporates, because nothing is gained from trying to keep it at home. On the other hand, nothing is lost in taxing that income, because the foreign investor will make the transfer despite the tax. In the short run, the home country's tax policy affects only the distribution of the benefits between the public and the private sector; in the long run, high taxes may discourage R&D spending.

Another modification of the simple conclusions adduced above comes from opening a second channel for international capital flows. Traditional analysis assumes that foreign investment entails only equity capital, not debt. The distinction between the two is critical, because the two types of income are taxed in very different ways. Equity income is taxed primarily in the host country, with the home country giving a foreign tax credit, while interest income is typically subject to a small withholding tax in the host country and bears the full income tax in the home country.

If foreign investment can be either debt or equity, the investors' choice between the two may be determined largely by tax or other policy considerations. For example, American multinationals sharply increased the use of debt to finance their foreign operations during the period of the U.S. balance-of-payments controls on outflow of U.S. capital to finance foreign direct investment. If the home country eliminates its foreign tax credit, the primary impact may be to encourage the substitution of debt for equity in international capital flows. A seemingly substantial reform in national tax policy may change the form, but not the volume, of international lending.

23. Michael Connolly, "Trade in Public Goods: A Diagrammatic Analysis," *Quarterly Journal of Economics*, vol. 86 (February 1972), pp. 61–78.

Assessing Current U.S. Tax Policy

Traditional tax theory suggests three standards by which U.S. policy might be judged: national neutrality, capital export neutrality, and competitive neutrality. National neutrality, aimed at maximizing the national advantage, allows U.S. investors to deduct foreign taxes from their taxable income but denies a tax credit. Capital export neutrality, which should maximize the global benefits of international investment, could be obtained by eliminating deferral but giving an unlimited foreign tax credit. Competitive neutrality, which achieves tax equity between investors of different nationalities, requires an exemption of foreign investment income from U.S. taxes.[24] Accordingly, the current U.S. policy of exempting subsidiaries' income from U.S. taxation until dividends are paid and then giving a foreign tax credit has been characterized as a hybrid of competitive and capital export neutrality.[25] With a foreign tax credit at its base, U.S. policy falls short of national neutrality.

This characterization of U.S. policy is, at best, a rough one. The difference between competitive and capital export neutrality can be substantial, so knowing that U.S. policy falls somewhere in between is useful but hardly definitive. How much difference in actual practice is there between competitive and capital export neutrality? How much difference does deferral really make? How much of that difference is offset by the U.S. investment tax credit or DISC, neither of which applies to foreign investment? The complexity of the U.S. and foreign tax systems and the diversity of investors' tax circumstances make it difficult to offer more than rough answers. Nevertheless, we attempt in this section to evaluate the overall thrust of existing tax policy.

The best sources of information on the income and taxes of individual corporations are the 10-K forms filed annually with the U.S. Securities

24. Tax analysts sometimes relate tax liabilities to services provided the taxpayer by the government collecting the revenue. We assume no relation between them.

25. See Krause and Dam, *Federal Tax Treatment of Foreign Income,* pp. 53–54; Musgrave, *United States Taxation of Foreign Investment Income,* pp. 120–21; and Gary C. Hufbauer, "A Guide to Law and Policy," in *U.S. Taxation of American Business Abroad* (American Enterprise Institute, 1975), pp. 1–6. Full capital import neutrality would require host countries to avoid any levies on foreign companies, such as withholding taxes on remitted dividends, which they did not levy on local firms.

and Exchange Commission. Until recently, these forms provided minimal information about foreign versus domestic sales, assets, income, and taxes. Most corporations published only consolidated statistics for global operations. Under pressure from the Securities and Exchange Commission to present disaggregated financial statistics and to reconcile book income reported to shareholders and taxable income reported on tax forms, however, American corporations give more detailed data on their global operations. We have thus been able to compile basic tax and financial statistics from the 1974 10-K forms for six large petroleum companies and thirty-six large manufacturers, all of which have substantial foreign operations. Although many corporations did not report certain data, and definitions vary from one corporation to another, some basic patterns of multinational behavior are revealed (table 6-1).

In columns 1 and 2 we show U.S. and foreign income taxes payable in 1974 as a percentage of book income before taxes in the respective areas. Columns 3 and 4 show taxes payable plus taxes deferred as a percentage of book income before taxes.[26] Tax burdens vary substantially from one corporation to another. For example, International Business Machines paid U.S. income taxes equal to 51.3 percent of its U.S. book income before taxes, while International Telephone and Telegraph paid only 19.7 percent. The twenty-four manufacturing corporations reporting the relevant tax and income data paid U.S. taxes averaging 30.7 percent of U.S. book income, slightly higher than the 28.5 percent average for the six petroleum companies but well under the statutory 48 percent rate, reflecting the combined impact of accelerated depreciation, the investment tax credit, DISC, the favorable tax treatment of capital gains, and so forth.

Whether one looks at taxes payable or taxes payable plus taxes deferred, foreign taxes as a percentage of foreign book income usually exceed U.S. taxes as a percentage of U.S. book income. For the six petroleum companies, foreign taxes payable are almost 70 percent of foreign book income, or more than twice the proportion for U.S. taxes. These foreign income taxes consist largely of taxes paid to oil-exporting

26. Because depreciation allowances for tax purposes are accelerated compared to those used in reporting book income to shareholders, corporations deduct from their book income taxes paid and taxes deferred. The figure (taxes payable or taxes payable plus taxes deferred) that gives the better picture of a firm's tax burden is a conceptual problem, not only a technical one.

Table 6-1. Income Tax and Financial Ratios for Selected American Petroleum and Manufacturing Multinationals, 1974

| Multinational and rank according to sales | Tax payable as percentage of before-tax income | | Tax payable plus tax deferred as percentage of before-tax income | | U.S. tax as percentage of global tax | | U.S. before-tax income as percentage of global before-tax income | U.S. assets as percentage of global assets | U.S. sales as percentage of global sales |
	U.S. tax: U.S. income (1)	Foreign tax: foreign income (2)	U.S. tax: U.S. income (3)	Foreign tax: foreign income (4)	Payable (5)	Payable plus deferred (6)	(7)	(8)	(9)
Petroleum companies									
Exxon (1)	33.4	78.2	34.9	78.8	8.1	8.3	17.0	54.2	n.a.
Texaco (4)	8.6	49.9	14.4	52.3	3.7	5.8	18.2	48.0	n.a.
Mobile Oil (5)	18.3	75.0	23.9	79.3	3.5	4.2	12.8	45.4	n.a.
Standard Oil of California (6)	20.8	49.6	14.6	50.2	11.1	7.9	22.9	n.a.	34.2
Gulf Oil (7)	47.0	78.8	21.8	80.2	8.4	4.8	13.3	n.a.	60.7
Marathon Oil (60)	43.0	79.8	36.2	79.8	14.2	12.3	21.7	n.a.	59.5
Average[a]	28.5	68.6	24.3	70.1	8.1	7.1	17.7	49.2	51.5
Manufacturing companies									
General Motors (2)	23.2	55.8	41.4	48.0	72.2	84.3	86.2	69.8	72.9
Ford Motors (3)	-18.6	55.6	15.5	64.1	-55.9	20.7	51.9	76.9	64.6
General Electric (8)	n.a.	n.a.	n.a.	n.a.	77.9	79.4	n.a.	n.a.	n.a.
International Business Machines (9)	51.3	46.9	47.5	45.5	53.1	52.0	50.9	58.0	53.1

Company									
International Telephone and Telegraph (10)	19.7	49.2	13.7	60.4	19.0	11.7	36.9	n.a.	49.2
Union Carbide (22)	25.2	49.7	30.7	54.2	41.8	44.4	58.6	n.a.	65.7
Dow Chemical (27)	n.a.	n.a.	n.a.	n.a.	61.1	63.3	n.a.	n.a.	53.0
Procter and Gamble (28)	43.1	39.4	47.1	44.7	73.3	72.6	71.5	n.a.	n.a.
Eastman Kodak (32)	39.8	45.1	41.1	48.3	73.0	72.3	75.4	66.6	63.2
Caterpillar Tractor (36)	n.a.	n.a.	n.a.	n.a.	77.8	77.4	n.a.	n.a.	81.4
Xerox (41)	50.6	38.3	53.1	47.6	58.0	53.9	51.1	51.4	58.0
Monsanto (43)	n.a.	n.a.	n.a.	n.a.	75.9	75.8	n.a.	60.7	71.4
W. R. Grace (44)	n.a.	n.a.	n.a.	n.a.	36.0	41.7	n.a.	63.5	62.4
Continental Can (52)	n.a.	n.a.	n.a.	n.a.	84.9	70.1	n.a.	n.a.	91.7
Minnesota Mining and Manufacturing (59)	41.7	41.3	45.7	41.3	61.1	63.2	60.8	8.27	n.a.
Honeywell (68)	-3.5	22.5	41.5	17.6	-25.9	75.3	56.8	50.2	59.2
Sperry-Rand (70)	39.5	32.7	44.7	47.0	51.9	45.9	47.2	76.0	n.a.
Consolidated Production Corp., Int. (71)	38.4	41.9	40.9	47.7	41.4	39.9	43.6	n.a.	50.3
Coca Cola (74)	n.a.	n.a.	n.a.	n.a.	26.2	28.3	n.a.	58.8	59.0
Uniroyal (82)	24.5	42.2	38.4	42.9	33.7	43.9	46.7	n.a.	67.6
National Cash Register (97)	n.a.	n.a.	n.a.	n.a.	23.2	37.3	n.a.	52.5	48.7
Johnson and Johnson (99)	40.0	39.7	41.1	43.7	48.7	46.9	48.5	n.a.	58.7
Warner Lambert (102)	n.a.	n.a.	n.a.	n.a.	38.2	40.6	n.a.	n.a.	57.0
Borg-Warner (108)	28.8	45.2	24.6	41.6	59.4	57.7	69.7	n.a.	72.5
American Standard (117)	40.2	60.7	59.8	55.1	56.6	68.1	66.3	n.a.	54.7
National Lead (124)	50.3	38.7	30.1	42.7	43.8	29.7	37.5	n.a.	80.6

Table 6-1 (continued)

Multinational and rank according to sales	Tax payable as percentage of before-tax income		Tax payable plus tax deferred as percentage of before-tax income		U.S. tax as percentage of global tax		U.S. before-tax income as percentage of global before-tax income	U.S. assets as percentage of global assets	U.S. sales as percentage of global sales
	U.S. tax: U.S. income (1)	Foreign tax: foreign income (2)	U.S. tax: U.S. income (3)	Foreign tax: foreign income (4)	Payable (5)	Payable plus deferred (6)	(7)	(8)	(9)
Pfizer (130)	−18.8	37.8	17.2	41.2	−20.9	12.6	25.7	53.7	47.0
Burroughs (134)	31.2	40.1	46.2	32.4	61.4	74.5	67.2	62.0	63.4
H. J. Heinz (139)	23.8	43.3	26.2	48.3	39.3	39.0	54.1	57.0	58.7
Merck (152)	n.a.	n.a.	n.a.	n.a.	77.4	77.8	n.a.	n.a.	55.0
Gillette (160)	53.2	42.1	52.4	40.9	43.8	44.2	34.8	n.a.	49.5
Crown Cork and Seal (248)	42.5	46.7	43.7	46.7	58.2	61.9	59.6	n.a.	n.a.
Schering-Plough (266)	n.a.	n.a.	n.a.	n.a.	73.8	73.4	n.a.	n.a.	55.7
Chesebrough-Ponds (309)	44.4	37.6	46.4	37.6	73.9	74.7	70.5	n.a.	68.7
Norton (311)	26.3	29.0	39.7	36.7	36.3	40.5	38.6	n.a.	55.1
Miles Laboratories (420)	n.a.	n.a.	n.a.	n.a.	20.4	20.4	n.a.	n.a.	74.8
Average[a]	30.7	42.2	38.7	44.6	46.4	53.2	54.4	62.8	62.2
Average, all companies[a]	30.3	47.5	35.8	49.7	40.9	46.6	47.1	60.5	61.3

Sources: 1974 Securities and Exchange Commission 10-K forms filed by individual corporations; global income, sales, and assets from consolidated income statements and balance sheets; most tax data from notes to income statements or supplementary notes to 10-K reports; most foreign income, sales, and assets from text of reports. Data do not include state and local taxes; Canadian data were subtracted where necessary by assuming values at 10 percent of total. Negative entries indicate excess tax credits, which can be applied to taxes for an earlier or a later year. Sales rank from "The Fortune Directory of the 500 Largest Industrial Corporations," *Fortune*, vol. 91 (May 1975).

n.a. Not available.

a. Averages based on companies for which data are available.

countries and perhaps should not be counted as income taxes. But even when we turn to manufacturing companies, foreign taxes are still comparatively larger. Income taxes paid average 42.2 percent of book income overseas versus 30.7 percent in the United States, which is a substantial differential. This differential is narrowed, but hardly eliminated, when taxes deferred are included in the measured tax burden. Foreign taxes payable or deferred average 44.6 percent of foreign book income, compared to 38.7 percent in the United States. Although one can find counterexamples (for example, IBM and Xerox), American corporations do seem to pay heavier taxes on their foreign investment income than they do on their domestic investment income.

The total taxes paid at home or abroad depend not only on domestic and foreign tax laws but also on how much income accrues in each jurisdiction. Reported income reflects the inherent profitability of domestic and foreign investment as well as the allocation of income and expenses within the multinational corporation. If a multinational has some leeway in determining the transfer price for components manufactured in the United States and sold to a foreign affiliate, a high transfer price will increase reported U.S. book income and diminish foreign book income. To determine how income and taxes are allocated between U.S. parents and their foreign affiliates, we have computed the ratios of U.S. taxes, book income, assets, and sales to the global amounts.

In table 6-1, columns 5 and 6 show U.S. taxes payable in 1974 as a percentage of global taxes payable and U.S. taxes payable or deferred as a percentage of the comparable global total, respectively. For the six petroleum companies, U.S. taxes average only 7–8 percent of the global total, using either tax measure. Among the manufacturers, the U.S. share is considerably higher: the thirty-six companies surveyed paid 46.4 percent of their global taxes to the United States, while taxes paid plus taxes deferred in the United States were 53.2 percent of the global total. In short, these large multinational manufacturers pay approximately half of their total taxes to the U.S. Treasury and half to overseas tax authorities. This is less than the U.S. share of the book income of the firms, as shown in column 7, because foreign income taxes are comparatively higher than American.

Although corporations do not consistently report the national distribution of their sales or assets, enough do to draw tentative conclusions about foreign versus domestic rates of return. The three petroleum companies publishing the necessary statistics had 49.2 percent of their assets and 51.5 percent of their sales in the United States. Fifteen manufacturers reported U.S. assets averaging 62.8 percent of global assets, while U.S. sales averaged 62.2 percent of global sales for thirty-one of them. Thus, in manufacturing as well as petroleum, the U.S. share of taxes and book income is smaller than its apparent share of either assets or sales. The pretax return on assets or sales appears to be higher for foreign affiliates than for their U.S. parents, even though average tax burdens would seem to favor allocating income to the U.S. parents rather than their foreign affiliates.

This may simply suggest that foreign investment has heretofore been more profitable than domestic investment. Or the allocation of income may favor foreign affiliates at the expense of U.S. parents; as we see below, average tax burdens may be a poor indicator of the additional taxes payable when taxable income is increased via transfer pricing. But, whatever the cause, the statistics in table 6-1 show foreign affiliates reporting higher book rates of return than their U.S. parents.

We must investigate foreign tax practices in greater detail to understand how and why American firms may end up paying higher taxes on foreign affiliate income than they do on domestic income. This is a tall order, because statutory income tax rates vary substantially from one country to another. Worse, so do depreciation allowances, treatments of capital gains, provisions for carrying losses forward or backward, and so on. One approach is to use Department of Commerce data on foreign income taxes as a percentage of American affiliates' book income, which indicate that manufacturing affiliates paid 42.0 percent of book income in income taxes in 1966 and 40.1 percent in 1970.[27] The problem in using these statistics is that one cannot be sure what the comparable U.S. tax rate was. Book income usually exceeds taxable income because of the generous tax treatment of depreciation, but the size of that differential is hard to determine.

The next best solution is a measure of foreign tax payments as a percentage of foreign affiliate income, using the Internal Revenue Service definitions of income. Fortunately, such estimates are available. When American corporations compute their allowable foreign tax credit, they must state the ratio of current dividends to current earnings using U.S. Internal Revenue Code definitions of income. M. E. Kyrouz, working for

27. *Survey of Current Business,* vol. 54 (May 1974), table 7, p. 36.

the international tax staff of the U.S. Treasury, analyzed corporate tax returns for 1968 and computed realized tax rates for manufacturing affiliates in most foreign countries.[28]

We show in column 1 of table 6-2 Kyrouz's realized tax rates (expressed per thousand dollars of taxable income) for manufacturing affiliates in twenty-four countries for which we could obtain the necessary dividend payout ratios. Thus, for example, the Canadian affiliates of American firms paid an average of $428 in Canadian income taxes per thousand dollars taxable income.

If the affiliates reinvest all their earnings, they would pay no taxes beyond those shown in column 1 because of the U.S. policy of deferral. But when dividends are paid out, they are subject first to a dividend withholding tax collected by the foreign country and, at least potentially, to income taxes in the United States. The dividend withholding taxes are payments over and above the regular income taxes on foreign affiliate income. In the second column, we show the withholding tax rates which various countries applied to dividends paid to U.S. investors in 1968, and in the third column the portion of after-tax earnings paid out as dividends by American manufacturing affiliates. Using these three columns, we compute in column 4 the withholding taxes on dividends paid to foreign governments per thousand dollars pretax income. By adding the income taxes in column 1 to the withholding taxes in column 4, we obtain the total taxes paid to the foreign government, as shown in column 5.

We should pause here a moment and look at the figures in column 5. Foreign income and withholding taxes frequently amount to 40 percent to 50 percent of the foreign affiliates' earnings. If we use the total earnings from each country (see column 10) to get a weighted average of countries' tax rates, we see (column 5) that U.S.-owned manufacturing affiliates paid foreign taxes averaging 43.8 percent of their pretax income in 1968. While many low-tax countries (such as Taiwan, Singapore, and Ireland) are excluded from table 6-2 for lack of dividend data, the aggregate earnings of all excluded countries amounted to only 4.3 percent of the worldwide total in 1968. Thus, even if these countries collected no income or dividend withholding taxes, the global average could drop only to 41.9 percent of pretax income. Although American investors may not have religiously used the Internal Revenue Code definitions of income in computing foreign tax credits, we are probably safe in conclud-

28. See source note, table 6-2.

Table 6-2. Foreign Tax Rates on American Manufacturing Multinationals, Selected Countries, 1968

Ratio per thousand dollars of taxable income

Country	Realized foreign income tax[a] (1)	Foreign withholding tax rate (2)	Dividend payout rate (3)	Foreign withholding tax paid[b] (4)	Foreign tax paid[c] (5)	U.S. tax liability[d] (6)	Foreign tax credit[e] (7)	Tax credit deficit[f] (8)	Global tax[g] (9)	Global earnings (10)
Developed										
Canada	428	0.15	0.394	34	462	189	203	−13	449	0.267
United Kingdom	386	0.15	0.520	48	434	250	249	1	435	0.176
Belgium	344	0.15	0.340	33	377	163	151	13	390	0.018
France	480	0.05	0.674	18	498	324	341	−18	480	0.035
Germany	430	0.15	0.711	61	491	341	367	−25	466	0.105
Italy	411	0.05	0.755	22	433	362	333	30	463	0.019
Netherlands	345	0.05	0.725	24	369	348	274	74	443	0.020
Denmark	325	0.05	0.750	25	350	360	269	91	441	0.002
Norway	458	0.10	0.250	14	472	120	128	−8	464	0.002
Sweden	431	0.05	0.777	22	453	373	357	16	469	0.004
Switzerland	222	0.05	0.441	17	239	212	115	97	336	0.017
Japan	415	0.10	0.322	19	434	155	153	2	436	0.051
Australia	406	0.15	0.411	37	443	197	204	−6	436	0.056
New Zealand	487	0.05	0.076	2	489	37	39	−3	486	0.005
South Africa	358	0.15	0.567	55	413	272	258	15	427	0.015

Less developed

	(1)	(2)	(3)	(4)	(5)	(6)	(7)	(8)	(9)	(10)
Mexico	422	0.20	0.473	55	477	131	170	−39	438	0.038
Panama	139	0.10	0.882	76	215	365	182	183	398	0.007
Argentina	217	0.12	0.605	57	274	227	160	68	342	0.030
Brazil	300	0.25	0.643	113	413	216	248	−32	381	0.049
Chile	330	0.40	0.428	115	445	138	210	−72	373	0.003
Peru	321	0.30	0.800	163	484	261	337	−77	407	0.002
Venezuela	300	0.15	0.314	33	333	106	99	7	340	0.021
India	570	0.257	0.833	92	662	172	303	−131	531	0.005
Philippines	296	0.35	0.880	217	513	297	400	−103	410	0.010
Average, weighted by dividends	387	0.150	0.533	52	439	247	253	−5	434	…
Average, weighted by earnings	391	0.148	0.511	47	438	230	235	−5	433	…

Sources: Estimates of realized foreign income and withholding tax rates (columns 1 and 2) from M. E. Kyrouz, "Foreign Tax Rates and Tax Bases," *National Tax Journal*, vol. 28, no. 1 (March 1975), pp. 62–66; 1968 dividend payout ratios (column 3) and global earnings (column 10) calculated from *Survey of Current Business*, vol. 54 (August 1974), pp. 20–21.

a. Based on pretax income.
b. Before-tax income, minus foreign income tax paid (column 1), times dividend payout rate (column 3), times withholding tax rate (column 2).
c. Calculated by adding income tax (column 1) and withholding tax (column 4).
d. For developed countries, subject to grossing, the liability is 48 percent of dividend payout rate (column 3) times $1,000 before-tax income. For less-developed countries, exempt until 1976 from grossing, the liability is 48 percent of foreign affiliate income after income taxes, times dividend payout rate.
e. For developed countries, credit is dividend payout rate, times realized foreign income tax, plus foreign withholding taxes paid. For less-developed countries, credit is ratio of income after the income tax to income before that tax, times income tax, times the dividend payout rate, plus foreign withholding taxes paid.
f. Tax credit is U.S. tax liability (column 6), minus tax credit (column 7); figures are rounded.
g. Tax is foreign tax (column 5), plus tax credit (column 8).

ing that foreign income and withholding taxes exceed 40 percent of the affiliates' taxable income.

Despite the severe differences in national tax laws, accounting rules, sample coverage, and dates, the various sources of tax information indicate that foreign taxes equal 40–45 percent of affiliates' income. Our limited sample of twenty-four large manufacturers in table 6-1 had foreign taxes amounting to 42.2 percent of the foreign affiliates' book income. The Commerce Department survey found that foreign income taxes averaged 42 percent of manufacturing affiliates' book income before taxes in 1966 and 40.1 percent in 1970. Using Kyrouz's statistics on realized income tax rates in 1968, plus other statistics on dividend payout ratios, we find that foreign taxes amounted to 43.8 percent of affiliates' pretax income, using U.S. Internal Revenue Code definitions.[29]

Having described foreign taxation of American investments abroad, we can now focus on U.S. taxes on their income. In column 6 of table 6-2 we show the taxes that would be due in the United States were it not for the foreign tax credit. This tentative tax liability is based solely on the dividends paid out; U.S. taxes on earnings retained by the foreign affiliates are deferred. Before 1976, for the developing countries the tentative tax liability in the United States equaled 48 percent of the dividend paid by the affiliate. A Philippine affiliate paying a $620 dividend (88 percent of $704 after-tax earnings) would generate a tentative U.S. tax liability of $297 (48 percent of $620). For developed countries, dividends must be grossed up by the portion of the foreign income tax corresponding to the paid-out dividend, which is equivalent to basing the U.S. tax on pretax income multiplied by the dividend payout rate. For example, the $189 tentative U.S. tax liability on Canadian-source income equals 48 percent (the U.S. tax rate) of 39.4 percent (the dividend payout rate shown in column 3) of each thousand dollars in pretax income.

29. We reject the notably lower rate in Robert B. Stobaugh, "The U.S. Economy and the Deferral of U.S. Income Tax on Foreign Earnings" (Cambridge, Massachusetts: Management Analysis Center, 1975; processed), p. 3-1. Stobaugh's analysis of the impact of deferral is predicated on a foreign income tax rate of only 33 percent of the foreign affiliates' income before taxes, a Commerce Department estimate for affiliates whose foreign taxes were less than 48 percent of their taxable income. The apparent rationale for excluding affiliates paying higher taxes was that they would be unaffected by the repeal of deferral. But the majority of manufacturing investors used the overall method of calculating foreign tax credit, so high taxes from one affiliate are averaged with low taxes from another. Commerce Department statistics based on all manufacturing affiliates are sounder than those used by Stobaugh.

Next we come to the foreign tax credit. For dividend income, the tax credit equals the foreign income taxes allocable to the dividend plus the withholding tax applied directly to the dividend. To take the Canadian case as our example again, the foreign tax credit would amount to 39.4 percent (the dividend payout rate) of $428 (Canadian income taxes paid), or $169, plus the $34 in Canadian withholding taxes. The foreign tax credits from the less-developed countries were less because of the exemption from grossing up (repealed in 1976). In the Philippine example, the $400 tax credit equals $217 for the withholding tax plus $183 of the income tax (88 percent of $296 times 1 − 0.296). As we can see by comparing column 6 to column 7, as often as not, the tentative U.S. tax liability is fully offset by a foreign tax credit. The weighted average of foreign tax credits for the twenty-four countries shown in table 6-2 exceeds that of tentative U.S. taxes by $5.

What happens next depends on how the American investor calculates the limitation of its foreign tax credit. If it elects the per-country method (which it could do until 1976), it would pay the difference between the tentative tax liability and the applicable foreign tax credit whenever that difference were positive. Thus no additional taxes would be paid on Canadian-source income, but an additional $1 per thousand dollars of U.K.-source income would be payable to the U.S. Treasury. If the investor elects the overall method, it can match its total foreign tax credits from all countries against its total tentative tax liability. The negative figures in column 8 can be used to offset the positive ones. If the investor has an overall surplus of foreign tax credits, it pays no additional taxes in the United States. We can then refer back to column 5 to determine the global tax burden on foreign affiliate income, for the United States has imposed no additional taxes. If the investor has an overall deficit of foreign tax credits, it must pay to the U.S. Treasury the difference between the total tentative tax liability and total foreign tax credits.

Perhaps the most meaningful way of showing the consequences of an overall deficit of foreign tax credits is to ask what would happen if foreign affiliates in various countries generated an additional thousand dollars in taxable income and paid additional foreign taxes and dividends at the rates shown in columns 1 through 5. In the Canadian case, a foreign tax credit $13 larger than the tentative tax liability would be generated, and the American investor could reduce its U.S. taxes on other foreign income by that amount. In the U.K. case, however, the foreign tax credit is less than the increased tentative tax liability, and the

U.S. investor would increase its U.S. taxes by one dollar. Column 8 thus displays the U.S. tax on foreign affiliate income for a corporation having an overall deficit of tax credits. If we add the tax credit deficit in column 8 to the total foreign taxes in column 5, we can calculate the global tax burden on the additional foreign-source income. In some instances that global burden exceeds the foreign burden, in others it falls short.

The conclusion is that the total taxes imposed on each foreign affiliate's income depend not just on the income and withholding taxes imposed directly on that income but on the American investor's global tax situation. If the investor has sufficient overall tax credits, no U.S. taxes are paid on any foreign-source income, not even that from low-tax countries. Income from various countries is taxed at the rates shown in column 5. If the investor has insufficient tax credits, however, the global tax burden includes a U.S. adjustment, shown in column 8. The total tax burden on income from low-tax countries is increased, while that on income from high-tax countries is decreased. U.S. tax policy, if it has any impact at all, serves to increase the global tax burden slightly and to smooth the variation in tax burdens on income from different countries.

What use can we make of the calculations in table 6-2? What can we learn from knowing that the global tax burden on income from various countries is as we show it in column 5 or column 9? In answering these questions, we must distinguish between transfer pricing and location-of-investment issues. By transfer-pricing issues, we mean the flexibility that American multinationals may have in setting prices for intrafirm exports and imports; in levying charges for research and development, head-office expenses, trademarks, and goodwill; in using debt or equity in advancing funds to overseas affiliates; in charging interest on intrafirm loans; and in otherwise allocating income within the multinational firm. These are very complex decisions. Foreign exchange controls, exchange rate uncertainties, limits on profit repatriation, and the firm's internal accounting rules, and tax considerations influence firms' internal accounts strategy.[30]

30. That tax avoidance does affect various intrafirm accounts has been shown by Sidney Robbins and Robert B. Stobaugh, *Money in the Multinational Enterprise* (Basic Books, 1973), pp. 28 and 77; George F. Kopits, "Dividend Remittance Behavior Within the International Firm: A Cross-Country Analysis," *Review of Economics and Statistics*, vol. 54 (August 1972), pp. 339–42; and George F. Kopits, "Intrafirm Royalties Crossing Frontiers and Transfer Pricing Behavior" (November 1974; processed).

Tax authorities both in the United States and abroad try to constrain firms' flexibility in exporting locally taxable income. Ordinary income subject to no special deductions or credits is taxed in the United States at a rate of $480 per thousand dollars of income. If the tax rates shown in columns 5 and 9 are tolerable approximations of the taxes due on additional foreign affiliate income, then the net tax benefit of allocating income to overseas affiliates would be $480, less those rates. In some cases (for example, France), the benefit may be negative, and the American multinational transferring income to such an affiliate would pay more foreign income and withholding taxes than it would have paid in U.S. income taxes. In other cases, the tax benefits of allocating income to overseas affiliates are positive, but small. Nontax considerations may dominate intracompany accounting practices. But when foreign tax rates are substantially below American, as they are in Switzerland and Panama, the tax savings from shifting income may be substantial. Since the tax rates shown in columns 5 and 9 average slightly less than $480, we conclude that on average an American investor has a weak tax incentive to allocate taxable income to most overseas affiliates but substantial incentive to transfer income to low-tax affiliates.[31]

If we consider where the investment is made, the differential in tax rates may be even smaller. Real investment in the United States benefits from an investment tax credit, from the asset depreciation range acceleration of depreciation allowances, and, perhaps, from the use of a domestic international sales corporation. Unlike other elements in the definition of taxable income, these allowances are not extended to foreign source income and are not, as a consequence, reflected in Kyrouz's realized tax rates.

Adjusting the U.S. tax rate to account for investment tax credit or accelerated depreciation can be complex, because the tax savings are concentrated in the early years of the investment rather than spread evenly over its lifetime. Consider the investment tax credit. From 1962 to 1966, 1967 to 1969, and 1971 to 1975, 7 percent of expenditures on qualifying machinery and equipment could be deducted from current U.S. taxes. The investment tax credit serves to reduce the initial capital outlay and, thus, to raise the rate of return on domestic investment. The

31. This conclusion assumes that, for one reason or another, such income would not be treated as base-company income, which under subpart F is subject to current U.S. taxation rather than deferral.

same effect could be achieved by reducing the tax on the investment income. The size of the comparable reduction in the income tax rate depends on several factors, such as the coverage of the investment tax credit or the rules for depreciating new investment. The 7 percent investment tax credit provides roughly the same stimulus to domestic manufacturing investment as a reduction in the corporate income tax from 48 percent to 46 percent.[32] If investors can use the asset depreciation range, also, to shorten the depreciation life of investment by 20 percent, manufacturing investment would be further stimulated; the boost would be the same as lowering the income tax rate from 46 percent to 45 percent. If the rough assumptions behind these calculations are sound, we should conclude that the investment tax credit and the use of the asset depreciation range virtually equalizes the average tax burden on domestic and foreign investment. Although individual corporations may have strong tax incentives to locate certain types of investments in certain foreign countries, the average tax incentive to invest abroad rather than in the United States is minimal.

If the choice is between investing abroad to serve the local market and investing in the United States for export, tax considerations may favor the

32. Hufbauer, "The Taxation of Export Profits," pp. 43–60, derives a formula for the tax-cost-of-capital index: $I = 1 - uz - f/1 - u$, in which I is the index, u is the nominal tax rate, z is the present value of depreciation deductions from taxable income, and f is the present value of the investment tax credit or similar subsidy.

This index measures the proportion by which a tax system increases the pretax return on capital necessary to generate any given aftertax return. We assume, somewhat arbitrarily, that 50 percent of all new investment (including that in inventories and other current assets) is depreciable and that Hufbauer's estimate of z (.547) applies to those investments. Thus, our estimate of .274 is half of Hufbauer's. These estimates do not include the use of ADR allowances. If u is 48 percent and there is no investment tax credit, f equals zero and I equals 1.67. If a 7 percent tax credit applicable to 40 percent of total investment is introduced, then f equals 2.8 percent (40 percent of 7 percent), and I drops to 1.62. By taking the total differential of the formula for I, we show that reducing u from 48 percent to 46 percent would have a comparable impact on I.

Determining the impact of ADR requires additional assumptions: Hufbauer's estimate of the present value of z follows from a 10 percent rate of discount, an investment with a 13-year depreciable life, and the use of the straight-line method of depreciation. If ADR shortens the depreciable life by 20 percent, to 10.4 years, it increases the present value of future depreciation to .605 times the current capital outlay. Because we assume that only 50 percent of total investment is depreciable, our estimate of z increases from .274 to .303. By accelerating the depreciation deductions, ADR further reduces the tax cost of capital from 1.62 to 1.59; a comparable reduction in I could also be achieved by further reducing the income tax from 46 percent to 45 percent.

latter. If the American investor establishes a domestic international sales corporation to receive export commissions, it can defer indefinitely at least one-quarter of its income from U.S. taxation. The combination of a 7 percent investment tax credit, ADR depreciation allowances, and the use of a DISC can reduce realized U.S. taxes from 48 percent to 33.8 percent (75 percent of 45 percent) of pretax income.

In summary, the most striking feature of the existing tax system is its complexity and, consequently, the variation of effective rates of taxation from one corporation to another and from one country to another. Of the twenty-four companies reporting foreign tax and income statistics, American Standard pays 60.7 percent of its foreign affiliates' book income in foreign taxes, while Honeywell pays only 22.5 percent in foreign taxes (see table 6-1). For the twenty-four countries examined, foreign income and withholding taxes average 66.2 percent of taxable income in India and 21.5 percent in Panama. In averaging these tax burdens across countries, we compute a typical tax burden of 43.8 percent for 1968 (see table 6-2). Because this rate is less than the 48 percent statutory rate in the United States, we conclude that American corporations might have a weak incentive to allocate taxable income to foreign, rather than American, affiliates. The high income and withholding taxes in Canada and most countries in Western Europe discourage allocating income to those affiliates, whereas the low tax rates in certain (particularly developing) countries may attract taxable income to them.

When the issue shifts from transfer pricing to the location of investment, tax differentials narrow further. The investment tax credit and the ADR, which apply only to domestic investment, offer inducements to invest in the United States rather than abroad. Furthermore, if the manufactures are destined for export, a DISC can reduce the U.S. tax rate by one-fourth, more than enough to tilt the tax bias toward investing in the United States. Despite the widespread view that current U.S. tax policy encourages American corporations to allocate income and investment to overseas affiliates, that bias is true only in exceptional cases.

Possible Changes in U.S. Tax Policy

We turn now to an analysis of the effects of possible changes in U.S. tax policy, singly or in combination, on the location of new investment, the level of taxes paid at home and abroad, corporate profitability, and other items of potential concern. Although one inevitably prejudges certain issues in drawing up the list of changes to be considered, we scanned a long menu: eliminating deferral, going back to the per-country method of calculating the foreign tax credit, extending the domestic investment tax credit to foreign expenditures on qualifying machinery and equipment, repealing DISC, increasing R&D charges against foreign-source income, and replacing the foreign tax credit with a simple deduction.

Repealing Deferral

Under current tax policy, an American investor's tentative tax liability and offsetting tax credit are based on the dividends it receives, which are typically a third to a half of its affiliates' total earnings. As long as foreign income and withholding taxes average less than 48 percent of the affiliates' earnings (which occurred in eighteen out of twenty-four countries represented in column 5 of table 6-2), American investors benefit from deferral. Were deferral eliminated and all foreign earnings subject to U.S. taxes, the effective rate of taxation on those earnings would be elevated to 48 percent.

Assuming that American investors could continue to use the overall method of calculating allowable foreign tax credits, the tax burden on income from various countries would increase by $480 minus the amount shown in column 5 or 9 of table 6-2. Taxes on income from a Canadian affiliate would be increased by $18 per thousand dollars of pretax income for an investor with a current overall surplus of tax credits, and by $31 per thousand dollars for an investor with an overall deficit. Since the earnings-weighted average of foreign taxes across all twenty-four countries in 1968 was 43.8 percent, repealing deferral would have raised an American investor's taxes by over 4 percent of foreign affiliate earnings before taxes in that year.

Between 1968 and 1974, foreign earnings of manufacturing affiliates increased substantially and dividend payout ratios declined from 51 percent to 40 percent.[33] Even if foreign income and withholding tax rates remained constant, the decline in the dividend payout ratio alone would have reduced the average tax burden on foreign affiliate earnings from 43.8 percent to 42.7 percent. By this reckoning, repealing deferral might

33. *Survey of Current Business,* vol. 54 (August 1974), pp. 20–21; and ibid., vol. 55 (October 1975), table 4.

cost American investors 5–6 percent of their foreign affiliates' earnings in 1974, hardly a trivial increase.

While the preceding estimates give a rough impression of the gross impact of eliminating deferral, they take no account of the multinationals' response to the increased taxes on foreign affiliate earnings. Any resulting cutback in foreign investment not only reduces taxable income and revenues but also the flow of investable funds from parent to affiliate and, thus, the global investment strategy. Telling a coherent story, much less a realistic one, about the consequences of any tax change requires a fully specified model of multinational investment behavior. Most analyses stop here, for it is difficult to estimate the probable impact on investment patterns, profitability, and the like.

In an effort to present the entire picture, we developed a microeconomic model of investment behavior to simulate the impact of changing various aspects of American tax policy. While the model necessarily simplifies and distorts real-life behavior, it does allow us to trace some of the important implications of U.S. policy. Although the impact of any tax reform, such as repealing deferral, may vary substantially from one investor to another, we believe that our analysis yields objective, if crude, estimates of the typical consequences for a large multinational manufacturer.[34]

Although we tried to keep our microeconomic analysis as simple as possible, incorporating the essential features of U.S. tax policy makes even the most simplistic model complex. Rather than incorporating the formal analysis into the text, we summarize its critical features here and refer interested readers to appendix B. The model simulates the behavior of a large manufacturer with ongoing operations at home and abroad. We ignore exporting and assume that foreign and domestic investment opportunities are independent of each other. The primary link between foreign and domestic investment derives from their competition for the multinational's investable funds. While the multinational can supplement its own cash flow with borrowed funds in financing its global investment, we assume that the investor must pay higher interest costs the more it seeks to borrow.

These assumptions constrain the predicted impact of any tax change, such as the elimination of deferral. Since eliminating deferral raises taxes

34. We do not attempt to simulate the impact of tax changes on mining, shipping, or any other nonmanufacturing industries.

on foreign affiliates' income, the investor becomes less willing to invest its own funds overseas. Domestic U.S. investment will be substituted for foreign investment whenever the tax burden on the latter is increased. Furthermore, higher taxes leave the investor with lower investable funds worldwide. While firms can increase their borrowing, they will find it growing more costly, so global investments fall when taxes increase. The net impact of a tax change is a combination of a substitution effect (for example, domestic investment rising and foreign investment falling) and a liquidity effect (for example, global investment falling). While the size of the substitution and liquidity effects depends on the elasticities of investment demand and other parameters, their existence is assumed by the very nature of our analysis. As in all simulation models, the conclusions are the product of the underlying assumptions.

Our analysis incorporates many of the essential features of intrafirm financial behavior: the use of debt and equity in transferring funds to overseas affiliates; interest payments on outstanding debt; head-office, royalty, and other intrafirm charges; and intrafirm dividend payments. As we show in appendix B, tax considerations affect optimal intrafirm financial behavior. That financial behavior, in turn, modifies the impact of tax policy. For instance, the substitution of debt for equity in financing foreign investment mitigates the impact of any tax change on foreign investment. This is the inevitable consequence of allowing firms to deduct interest costs and taxing only the return on equity. It is difficult to know how much flexibility American investors have in changing their intrafirm accounting practices and how much they would use that flexibility to avoid the burden of a tax change. Accordingly, most of the estimates developed below assume that American investors maintain constant rates for charging head-office, research and development, and other joint expenses back to their affiliates and that they maintain constant dividend payout ratios. In cases considered below, where a U.S. tax policy would encourage multinationals to manipulate these financial ratios, we indicate what those changes are and what their consequences would be.

While certain of our model's parameters could be estimated easily (for example, dividend payout ratios, debt-equity ratios), others could not. In particular, the responsiveness of foreign or domestic levels of investment to changes in the cost of capital, or of interest rates to the volume of borrowing, cannot be ascertained. These parameters are critical: the more elastic the investment opportunities and the supply of investable funds, the greater the impact of tax changes on foreign and domestic investing. In the end we specify what seems to be reasonable values for these critical parameters and proceed with our calculations. But the mathematical nature of our analysis hardly compensates for the lack of accurate information about investment and borrowing opportunities.

Our estimates of the impact of repealing deferral on American manufacturing investors (the model does not suit other industries well) are shown in table 6-3.[35] These figures represent our best judgment of what would have happened if all foreign affiliate earnings, not just dividends, had been subject to U.S. taxation in 1974. Because of the increased tax on foreign investment income, the multinational manufacturer would substitute domestic for foreign investment. We estimate that the current rate of U.S. investment (in property, plant, equipment, inventories, and so on) would have risen by $1,429 million, or 3.9 percent more than the actual value. Likewise, new foreign investment would have fallen by $1,549 million, or 8.5 percent of its actual value. Note that foreign investment would have fallen by more than domestic investment would have risen. This is the liquidity effect: higher global taxes lead to lower global investment. Note, too, that the impact of eliminating deferral on the capital outflow from the U.S. parent to its foreign affiliates is significantly larger than its impact on foreign or domestic capital formation. This reflects our implicit assumption that American investors would have financed more of their foreign investment and less of their domestic investment with locally borrowed funds than they actually did. Changing U.S. tax policy may have more of an impact on the location of borrowing than on the location of real investment.

Table 6-3 shows how eliminating deferral might have altered the distribution of 1974 pretax earnings among foreign governments, the U.S. Treasury, and American investors. The principal gainer would have been the U.S. Treasury; the foreign affiliates' retained earnings would have been taxable, and domestic investment and income would have been stimulated. The big losers would have been the American multinationals, whose consolidated after-tax earnings would have been reduced by

35. Our simulation model was refined and its parameters reevaluated over the course of its development. Accordingly, these estimates may not be the same as those in earlier reports on our research. We regret possible confusion but believe that the comments and criticisms we received on earlier versions were too important to ignore.

Table 6-3. *Estimated Effect of Eliminating Deferral on American Manufacturing Multinationals, 1974*

Millions of dollars unless otherwise stated

		Change	
Item	Initial valueᵃ	Amount	Percentage
Domestic investment	36,400	1,429	3.9
Foreign investment	18,300	−1,549	−8.5
Net capital outflow	2,710	−2,466	−91.0
Consolidated after-tax profits	15,194	−534	−3.5
U.S. taxes	6,005	545	9.1
Foreign taxes	5,001	−80	−1.6

Source: See appendix B. Data previously appeared in Thomas Horst, "American Taxation of Multinational Firms," *American Economic Review*, vol. 67, p. 383.

a. Figures for domestic investment are estimates of the 1974 increase in total assets (short- and long-term) of parent corporations of American manufacturing multinationals. Figures for foreign investment are estimates of the 1974 increase in total assets of the foreign affiliates of the multinationals. Figures for net capital outflow represent the 1974 new capital outflow from parent corporations to their foreign affiliates. Figures for consolidated after-tax profits are the 1974 profits after taxes of American multinationals. Figures for U.S. taxes include 1974 income taxes on both domestic and foreign-source income. Figures for foreign taxes include taxes on affiliates' income plus withholding taxes on interest, dividends, and all other intrafirm charges.

roughly the increase in U.S. taxes. Foreign income and withholding taxes fell slightly, because foreign investment was cut back and foreign borrowing costs increased. Notice, finally, that increasing taxes is a negative-sum game: the gains to the U.S. Treasury are outweighed by the combined losses to the American investors and to the foreign treasuries. This conclusion follows from our assumption that American investors are partially dependent on their own retained earnings to finance new investment and generate new earnings.

The preceding analysis presumes that the United States could repeal deferral without any change in foreign tax laws or tax rates. But foreign governments might react to the potential loss of investment and revenues, at a minimum, by eliminating their present tax incentives for U.S. investors and thus raising their effective tax rate to the normal rate of corporate tax. The host countries might even retaliate by treating the total earnings of American affiliates as presumed dividend distributions, and thereby subjecting them to the dividend withholding tax.[36] Because this

36. Dan Throop Smith, "Taxation of Foreign Business Income: The Changing Objectives," *Taxation of Foreign Income by the United States and Other Countries* (Tax Institute of America, 1966), pp. 241–55 and Department of the Treasury, *U.S. Taxation of the Undistributed Income of Controlled Foreign Corporations* (April 1976), p. 76. A separate but similar problem arises regarding nonrepatriable

scenario may be as plausibly pessimistic as our prior presumption (no foreign retaliation) was optimistic, let us trace its implications.

The bottom line of table 6-2 indicates that foreign income taxes averaged 39.1 percent and dividend withholding taxes 14.8 percent of foreign affiliate earnings. If these withholding taxes were applied to all earnings, total foreign taxes would have averaged 48.1 percent of the foreign affiliates' income. (The effective tax rate would equal .391 + .148 (1 − .391) = .481.) If so, the multinationals' foreign and domestic investment, the intrafirm flow of funds, and after-tax earnings would remain almost as shown in table 6-3. These two scenarios differ in who collects the higher taxes, for now the foreign government would, through its withholding tax, capture a significant portion of the $566 million tax gain we attribute to the United States. So, while the United States would still gain new investment, it would capture only a small portion of the higher taxes paid by the multinationals.

We use our model to estimate the impact of eliminating deferral on American investor's current rates of domestic and foreign investment, after-tax earnings, and foreign and domestic taxes but have not projected our findings over a long period of time. Stobaugh has made a long-run analysis, which concludes that the long-run consequences of eliminating deferral reverse the short-run effects.[37] Let us contrast his analysis with ours.

Stobaugh's analysis rests on certain critical assumptions: multinationals will not invest more at home when the tax on foreign investment income increases; the rate of new foreign investment is strictly limited by the after-tax earnings on existing assets; new foreign investment has a cumulative impact on the cost-competitiveness of U.S. overseas investment, a learning-by-doing effect. The net product of these assumptions is a rigid link between the after-tax earnings on existing investment and the growth and profitability of future investment. While our own findings,

---

earnings, such as those completely blocked by host-country exchange controls or those discouraged by steeply graduated remittance taxes (as in Brazil). In such instances, the parent firm could not finance its tax payments from the subsidiary whose earnings were being taxed. It would not be possible to grant blanket exceptions for such earnings, for host countries would be encouraged to levy them. Exceptions should probably be made in specific cases (as they are now for branch earnings, where the identical problem occasionally arises).

37. Stobaugh, "The U.S. Economy and the Deferral of U.S. Income Tax on Foreign Earnings," esp. chap. 5.

if extrapolated into the future, suggest the same divergence between short-run and long-run effects, the projected turning point would not come nearly as early.

Calculating Foreign Credit by Per-Country Method

With the passage of the Tax Reform Act of 1976, all U.S. investors must use the overall method of calculating their allowable foreign tax credit. Because the overwhelming majority of manufacturers preferred the overall to the per-country method, this change will have a minimal impact on manufacturing investors. A case can be made, however, against the overall method: if a U.S. multinational has excess foreign tax credits from high-tax countries, it will have a tax incentive to allocate income to and locate production in countries with low tax rates, tax holidays, liberal depreciation allowance, or other tax incentives. In short, the overall limitations and deferral are objectionable for the same reasons.

The virtue of the overall limitation is that it is simpler to administer than the per-country limitation:[38] determination of a company's U.S. tax liability does not hinge on transfer prices for transactions between two foreign affiliates. However, the benefits of the per-country limitation could be had at a lower administrative cost if foreign-source income were put into two baskets, a high-tax basket and a low-tax basket, and if two separate foreign tax credit limitations applied. Then the only transactions whose transfer prices would need close monitoring would be those between high-tax and low-tax countries (like Irish exports to France).

Extending the Investment Tax Credit to Foreign Income

If deferral were eliminated, the realized rate of taxation on foreign affiliate earnings would climb to 48 percent. Because domestic investment was eligible for a 7 percent investment tax credit in 1975 and a 10 percent credit thereafter, the tax changes analyzed above would clearly tilt the tax incentives toward investing in the United States. If the objective of U.S. tax policy is to equalize the tax burden on foreign and domestic in-

---

38. Department of the Treasury, *U.S. Taxation of the Undistributed Income of Controlled Foreign Corporations* (April 1976), p. 61.

Table 6-4. *Estimated Effect of Extending a 7 Percent Investment Tax Credit to New Investments of Affiliates of American Manufacturing Multinationals, 1974*

Millions of dollars unless otherwise stated

Item	Initial value[a]	Change with tax credit alone		Change with tax credit plus elimination of deferral[b]	
		Amount	Percentage	Amount	Percentage[c]
Domestic investment	37,829	−1,182	−3.1	247	0.7
Foreign investment	16,751	2,103	12.6	554	3.0
Intrafirm flow of funds	244	1,776	727.9	−690	−25.5
Consolidated after-tax income	14,659	442	3.0	−92	−0.6
U.S. taxes	6,573	−457	−7.0	88	1.5
Foreign taxes	4,921	54	1.1	−24	−0.5

Source: See appendix B.
a. After elimination of deferral. For definition of each value, see table 6-3, note a.
b. See table 6-3.
c. Based on initial values, table 6-3.

vestment, the foreign tax credit must include a credit for new investment by the foreign affiliate.[39]

We use our microeconomic model to simulate the impact of extending a 7 percent investment tax credit to foreign manufacturing affiliates' investment in 1974, assuming that 40 percent of total investment would qualify under the definitions currently in use regarding domestic investment. Table 6-4 shows these effects (assuming that deferral were eliminated) and the combined impact of both tax changes. The primary impact of extending the investment tax credit would, of course, be to stimulate foreign affiliates' investment spending. We estimate that such expenditures would rise by $2.1 billion, which would be more than enough to reverse the impact of eliminating deferral. While this addi-

39. Capital-export neutrality could be achieved by eliminating the investment tax credit (and the asset depreciation range) altogether. This is a much larger step than extending it to foreign investment, however, and raises questions concerning U.S. domestic economic policy, which are not considered in this volume.

The original investment tax credit (1962) was viewed as temporary and, indeed, has been removed and restored twice since that time. More recently, however, it has come to be viewed as a permanent part of U.S. tax policy. In 1976 Congress did consider making it permanent, and President Carter proposed such a step in early 1978. Any future suspension, however, should apply to foreign as well as domestic investment.

tional change would depress domestic investment, it would still be higher than before the tax changes. Note that the combined impact of eliminating deferral and extending the investment tax credit is to expand global investment; the investment tax credit has a comparatively larger impact on investment spending than deferral has.

Extending the investment tax credit (even at 7 percent) to foreign investment income largely offsets the impact of eliminating deferral and on corporate income, U.S. taxes, and foreign taxes. The U.S. Treasury would have collected 1.5 percent more in corporate income taxes from manufacturing investors than it actually did in 1974, while corporate income after taxes and foreign taxes would each have fallen by less than 1 percent. The combined tax changes necessary to equalize the tax burdens on foreign and domestic investment income would, thus, have a minimal impact on the aggregate balance between foreign and domestic investment. While individual corporations or countries may feel more of the effects than others, the aggregate impact is apt to be small.

Repealing DISC

When the domestic international sales corporation legislation was passed in 1971, its primary justification was to promote U.S. exports and reverse a growing balance-of-payments deficit. Its supporters argued that DISCs are necessary to give American exporters tax advantages approaching those enjoyed by their foreign competitors and to offset the impact of deferral in encouraging American firms to produce overseas. As noted above, the use of a DISC effectively reduces the tax on income from exporting by one-fourth. Without the investment tax credit, the effective tax on export income would be reduced from 48 percent to 36 percent; with a 7 percent investment tax credit, the tax burden would be diminished to 34.5 percent.

The Tax Reform Act of 1976 limited DISC benefits to U.S. exports over and above a base value. This base value until 1980 is 67 percent of the average value of a corporation's exports during the four-year interval 1972–75; in 1980 the base period shifts forward by one year (1973–76) and continues shifting forward in each succeeding year. If a corporation's annual exports during the base period average, for example, 50 percent of its current exports, then the base value would be 33.5 percent (67 percent of 50 percent). Under the new legislation, the U.S. exporter would be deemed to have distributed dividends from its DISC equal to 33.5 percent of the DISC's earnings plus half of the remaining 66.5 percent, or a total of 66.75 percent. Under the original DISC legislation, only 50 percent of DISC earnings were deemed to be distributed and, thus, subject to U.S. taxation. Rather than trying to incorporate DISC into our microeconomic model, we drew on a similarly motivated analysis of the consequences of the old and the new DISC legislation.[40] Our conclusions are:

1. The rate of return on DISC-assisted export sales was 17.3 percent in 1974, more than twice the comparable 8.4 percent return on domestic sales. Because export income is taxed at a lower rate than domestic income, we have prima facie evidence that some portion of DISC tax savings were retained by U.S. exporters as profits after taxes, rather than passed on to foreign importers through lower export prices. Our best estimate is that one-half to three-fourths of the tax savings made available by DISC were passed on through lower export prices and that the remaining one-half to one-quarter was retained by U.S. exporters. (A primary source of uncertainty in this estimate is exporters' ability to allocate deductible expenses, such as interest, depreciation, even labor and materials, to domestic, rather than export, sales.)

2. The best available estimate of the elasticity of foreign demand for U.S. manufactured exports implies that a 1 percent reduction in export prices expands the volume of U.S. exports by 2.85 percent and the value by 1.85 percent. Combining that elasticity with our estimate that DISCs reduced export prices by 2.5 percent in DISC-year 1974 (roughly, calendar year 1973) and the fact that DISC-assisted exports amounted to $44 billion, we conclude that U.S. exports were $2.1 billion higher in DISC-year 1974 than they otherwise would have been. This gain represents less than 3 percent of contemporary U.S. exports. By contrast, the 15 percent depreciation of the U.S. dollar against foreign currencies between 1971 and 1974 would have contributed more than ten times the DISC contribution to U.S. export growth.

These conclusions characterize the immediate impact of DISCs, rather

40. Thomas Horst and Thomas Pugel, "The Impact of DISC on the Prices and Profitability of U.S. Exports," *Journal of Public Economics,* vol. 7 (February 1977), pp. 73–87.

than the long-run, general-equilibrium effects. In this instance, however, the long-run effects are particularly hard to ignore. Exchange rates have been far freer to fluctuate since 1971. Under a flexible exchange rate system, the DISC-induced increase in exports tends to appreciate the value of the dollar in foreign exchange markets, which makes it harder for DISC nonusers to export from the United States and easier for foreign producers (including the foreign subsidiaries of U.S. companies) to export to the United States. Exchange-rate adjustments may partially or fully offset the immediate impact of DISCs. Thus, we conclude that DISCs add far less to net U.S. production, investment, or the balance of payments than proponents claim, and that DISCs overcompensate for the tax advantages of deferral, in most instances.

Increasing Charges for Joint Expenses

As noted in table 6-1, American investors report higher earnings and pay higher taxes abroad than they do in the United States. While the differential may be due to faster growth and less competition in foreign countries, it may also reflect intrafirm accounting practices. In 1973, for example, head-office, royalty, R&D, and all other such charges amounted to just over 1 percent of foreign manufacturing affiliates' total sales.[41] Determining what expenses should be prorated among foreign and domestic affiliates (all research and development? only basic research?) and what basis should be used in prorating such expenses (sales? assets? employment?) is fraught with peril, and we have no way of knowing exactly what such intrafirm charges should be.

The historically low charges for R&D and other joint expenses finally led the Treasury Department to issue new guidelines for sections 861 and 863 of the Internal Revenue Code. These sections guide the allocation of joint costs among foreign and domestic affiliates for the purpose of determining the overall limitation on the foreign tax credit. Unless an investor's total foreign tax credits are less than its allowable maximum, the new guidelines raise taxes paid to the U.S. Treasury.

The impact of the new guidelines on a corporation depend crucially on how much R&D and other such charges against foreign-source income

41. *Survey of Current Business,* vol. 55 (August 1975), p. 23; and ibid., vol. 55 (October 1975), p. 49.

can be increased. Once again, let us consider two very different scenarios: first, that the new guidelines succeed in inducing U.S. manufacturers to double their current charges for R&D, head-office expenses, and so on. (We do not mean to imply that a doubling of charges is likely or reasonable but to establish a benchmark for judging the possible significance of the Treasury Department guidelines.) Our microeconomic model indicates that the impact on foreign and domestic investments would be as indicated in table 6-5. As one can see, real capital formation at home and abroad would be affected only marginally. The primary impact would be to shift taxable income and, thus, tax payments from the foreign affiliates to the U.S. parents. Since the 48 percent U.S. rate exceeds the current realized foreign income tax rate, the global tax burden on American investors goes up slightly, and consolidated after-tax earnings fall by 1 percent.

Our second scenario assumes that foreign tax authorities will not permit any increase in R&D or other intrafirm charges.[42] If the U.S. parent must nonetheless reallocate expenses for U.S. tax purposes, its allowable foreign tax credit will fall. Unless the investor starts with a deficit of foreign tax credits (that is, is paying fewer foreign income and withholding taxes than the maximum that can be credited), its U.S. tax payment will increase. Whether we call this disputed income foreign or domestic, it will be subject to double taxation.

Since the tax increase is likely to be proportional to a firm's foreign investment, the new guidelines would have exactly the opposite effect to extending the investment tax credit to foreign-source income: U.S. taxes would increase in proportion to foreign investment. If the new guidelines doubled R&D and other such charges to foreign affiliates, but no new deductions were allowed overseas, we estimate that the changes shown in the last two columns of table 6-5 would have occurred. Because foreign investment is subject to implicit double taxation, it falls by $3 billion (17 percent of its 1974 value), and U.S. tax collections increase by almost $1 billion, but the gain comes at the multinationals' expense rather than the foreign governments'. Foreign governments can thus protect their tax base only at the cost of discouraging American-owned investments.

42. For example, Canada in the early 1970s disallowed deductions for interest paid to related companies whenever the debt-equity roster of the affiliate exceeded 3:1. Similar limits might be placed on the other types of intracompany transfers.

Table 6-5. *Estimated Effect of Doubling Head-Office, R&D, and Other Intrafirm Service Charges by American Manufacturing Multinationals, 1974*

Millions of dollars unless otherwise stated

Item	Initial value[a]	Higher deductions allowed by foreign tax authorities		Higher deductions not allowed by foreign tax authorities	
		Amount change	Percentage change	Amount change	Percentage change
Domestic investment	36,400	149	0.4	1,393	3.8
Foreign investment	18,300	−332	−1.8	−3,087	−16.9
Net capital outflow	2,710	444	16.4	−2,718	−100.3
Consolidated after-tax income	15,194	−142	−0.9	−992	−6.5
U.S. taxes	6,005	688	11.5	981	16.3
Foreign taxes	5,001	−592	−11.8	−84	−1.7

Source: See appendix B. Table previously appeared in Thomas Horst, "American Taxation of Multinational Firms," *American Economic Review*, vol. 67, p. 384.

a. For definition of each value, see table 6-3, note a.

b. Assumes that charges are raised from 1.1 percent to 2.2 percent of foreign subsidiaries' total assets and that the foreign government allows higher deductions from the subsidiaries' taxable income.

c. Assumes that charges are raised from 1.1 percent to 2.2 percent of foreign subsidiaries' total assets.

Replacing Foreign Tax Credit with Simple Deduction

The AFL-CIO advocates eliminating the foreign tax credit altogether and merely allowing American investors to deduct foreign income and withholding taxes from their foreign-source income. Foreign-source income would, thus, be taxed twice (first by the foreign government and then again by the United States), achieving national neutrality. We use our microeconomic model to determine what would have happened in 1974 in the absence of the foreign tax credit; our tentative conclusions are tabulated in table 6-6.

Our analysis indicates that U.S. manufacturing investors would not only stop sending new capital overseas but also repatriate substantial sums already invested. While the rate of new investment by overseas affiliates would be slashed by more than half, foreign operations would continue to expand, albeit at a greatly reduced rate, as long as the subsidiaries could tap local capital markets. Domestic investment by the U.S. parents would increase by $9 billion, or just over 25 percent of the parents' current rate. Despite the substantial substitution of domestic for

Table 6-6. *Estimated Effect of Repealing Deferral and the Foreign Tax Credit and Allowing a Deduction for Foreign Taxes Paid by American Manufacturing Multinationals, 1974*
Millions of dollars unless otherwise stated

		Change	
Item	*Initial value*[a]	*Amount*	*Percentage*
Domestic investment	36,400	9,291	25.5
Foreign investment	18,300	−10,283	−56.2
Net capital outflow	2,710	−15,725	−580.3
Consolidated after-tax income	15,149	−2,983	−19.7
U.S. taxes	6,005	3,028	50.4
Foreign taxes	5,001	−504	−10.1

Source: See appendix B. Data previously appeared in Thomas Horst, "American Taxation of Multinational Firms," *American Economic Review*, vol. 67, p. 386.
a. For definition of each value, see table 6-3, note a.

foreign investment, the multinationals would still end up paying $3 billion in additional taxes to the U.S. government, which would reduce their consolidated after-tax income by almost a fifth.[43] It is worth noting that if U.S. investors are prevented from repatriating past capital outflows, by, inter alia, the unwillingness of host countries to accept such changes in their own balance-of-payments positions, the substitution of domestic for foreign investment would be greatly truncated. In fact, if net capital outflows must remain positive, domestic investment would actually fall: the higher U.S. taxes paid by the parent would have a greater impact on its domestic investment than the limited substitution of domestic for foreign investment. All of this is to say that the gain in domestic investment should not be taken for granted.

Because the tax consequences of the foreign tax credit are so large, the multinationals would doubtless seek other ways of minimizing the impact of its loss. Some corporations would surely reincorporate overseas.[44] Many would divest themselves of subsidiaries, although this might

43. Other analysts predict much larger effects: $7.5 billion (Department of Commerce); $3.3 billion in 1970, probably rising to about $7 billion by 1975 (Peggy B. Musgrave); and $6.7 billion (International Economic Policy Association, IEPA). These results are summarized in the IEPA testimony, *Tax Reforms,* Hearings before the House Ways and Means Committee, 94:1 (GPO, 1975), pt. 3, p. 2027.
44. J. L. Kramer and G. C. Hufbauer, "Higher U.S. Taxation Could Prompt Changes in the Multinational Corporate Structure," *International Tax Journal*, vol. 1 (Summer 1975), pp. 301–24.

be difficult with many erstwhile subsidiaries for sale. Most investors would search for ways to pare their equity investment to a minimum while maintaining effective control over their subsidiaries' operations. Management service contracts, which have become common in the resource extraction industries, could spread through other industrial sectors. The quantitative significance of these responses is impossible to estimate, but they might mitigate the impact of losing the foreign tax credit.

Summary and Conclusions

In theory, the United States taxes foreign-source income but in practice most U.S. manufacturing investors pay little or no U.S. taxes on income earned abroad. The foreign tax credit is usually sufficient to offset U.S. taxes tentatively due on foreign-source income. Foreign investment in some countries qualifies for tax holidays or is otherwise spared from taxation, but in Canada and most countries of Western Europe the combined income tax and dividend withholding tax produce an effective tax rate comparable to that of the United States. Although exact statistics are hard to find, the typical foreign manufacturing affiliate appears to pay 40–45 percent of its pretax income to foreign governments, a rate as high as or higher than the rate U.S. firms pay to the U.S. government on their domestic income. Despite the well-publicized exceptions, as a general rule multinationals do not escape taxation by investing overseas.

The broad objective of U.S. tax policy should be, we believe, to equalize the tax burden on foreign and domestic income (the standard of capital export neutrality). Although the full implications of repealing the foreign tax credit and striving for national neutrality are difficult to assess, the evasive tactics of the multinationals and the protective reactions of foreign governments are likely to deprive the United States of many of the expected benefits. At the other extreme, matching the exemption for foreign income offered by some foreign governments in the hope of achieving competitive neutrality seems clearly inconsistent with broad U.S. interests.

In the aggregate, U.S. tax policy is closer to capital export neutrality than commonly supposed. Deferral gives foreign investment only a small advantage, which is offset by the denial of the investment tax credit and the ADR acceleration of depreciation. But when the retained earnings of an affiliate in a low-tax country avoid U.S. taxation through deferral, while its dividends are sheltered by excess tax credits from high-tax countries, assertions of aggregate neutrality have a hollow ring.

Neutrality at a low level of aggregation can be achieved by modifying the overall limitation (without necessarily reinstating the per-country limitation of the 1950s). Dividing countries into high-tax and low-tax categories and imposing separate limitations on the foreign tax credits in each category would correct the worst feature of the overall limitation. Only transfer prices involving transactions between a high-tax country and a low-tax country would need to be closely scrutinized, for reallocations of income among high-tax countries or among low-tax countries are of little concern to the Internal Revenue Service.

Although their aggregate effects are likely to be small, we nonetheless believe that these changes should be made. The political controversy over multinationals is heightened by the widespread belief that U.S. tax policy implicitly encourages American manufacturers to export jobs, and although that belief is largely unfounded, exceptions do exist. Some investors do have strong tax incentives to invest in low-tax countries, and those incentives would be largely eliminated by the tax changes we propose. Furthermore, the deferral of U.S. taxes on foreign-source income helps justify domestic international sales corporations, which serve little purpose in a world of flexible exchange rates. Finally, as long as deferral is granted, manipulative transfer pricing is encouraged, and tax havens must be attacked with the cumbersome rules defining base-company income.

Perhaps the messiest issue confronting policymakers is allocating taxable income within the multinational enterprise. Foreign affiliates tend to earn higher returns on sales and assets than their U.S. parents earn, and the differential may be partly due to low charges for R&D and other joint expenses incurred by the parent. Unfortunately, pinpointing this issue is easier than solving it. Increasing R&D and other such charges is a zero-sum or negative-sum game: U.S. tax gains must come from the multinationals or from foreign tax authorities. The new guidelines for sections 861 through 864 of the Internal Revenue Code are welcome steps in the right direction. Whether they have the desired effect of increased R&D and other such charges against foreign subsidiaries' taxable income remains, of course, to be seen. But some unilateral action by the United States was and is necessary. Without pressure from the United States, the multinationals have little incentive to propose (or foreign treasuries to accept) new or higher charges. As we note, foreign governments can protect their tax base by refusing to permit any new charges, but in doing so participate in the double taxation that makes local investment less attractive.

Ultimately, the only satisfactory solution to the problem of allocating income within the multinational firm may be international use of formulas based on national sales, assets, payrolls, or some other stable base.[45] Such formulas could be incorporated into bilateral tax treaties, and accepted by both home and host countries, if supported by agreement on accounting concepts and on standards against which the activities of the firms could be assessed. If foreign governments are not ready to accept formula allocations of income, the United States might still use such formulas in deciding when to apply new guidelines to sections 861–864 of the Internal Revenue Code. For example, a company whose transfer pricing system allocates global income in rough proportion to sales or assets might be spared new allocations in any one area, such as R&D expenses. By looking at the net outcome of all transactions, rather than the merits of each, the United States may have a better chance of collecting a higher share of the taxes on multinational income without producing double taxation in the process.

45. See Brannon, "National Shares of Multicompany Income"; and Peggy B. Musgrave, "International Tax Base Division and the Multinational Corporation," *Public Finance*, vol. 27 (1972).

CHAPTER SEVEN

Industry Structure, Competition, and Antitrust

THE PRECEDING CHAPTERS address the areas where foreign investment is widely thought to have the greatest impact on the U.S. economy: the volume and composition of exports and imports, the balance of payments, the employment and earnings of U.S. labor, the taxes collected or uncollected by the U.S. Treasury, and the terms of U.S. access to foreign natural resources. All these matters have been widely debated and a consensus reached that, if nothing else, they are key issues.

By contrast, the impact of U.S. investments abroad on the structure and performance of U.S. domestic industry has been largely ignored, perhaps because the issue is subtle and complex. While most of the foreign countries in which American multinationals invest appreciate the competitive advantages of U.S.-based investors over locally owned firms, few observers consider that these investments may in turn give the U.S. parents significant advantages over their domestic U.S. competitors. In chapter five, we analyze how the increasing collaboration between extractive multinationals and host-country governments is already strengthening the oligopoly structure of some critical industries (including oil and aluminum), and threatens to replicate the process in general unless new policy measures are taken by the United States to interrupt the trend. This chapter presents evidence that foreign investment by U.S. manufacturers has significantly increased their insulation from effective competition in the United States.

213

The chapter has three sections. The first reviews the considerable literature on why firms invest abroad and the much more limited research on the impact of those investments on domestic industry structure. The second presents our evidence that direct investments abroad have given U.S.-based investors significant competitive advantages over their domestic competitors, and thereby rendered U.S. industries less competitively balanced. The implications for U.S. antitrust policy, the traditional instrument to attack problems of market structure and performance, are explored in the third section. We conclude that the principal challenge to U.S. antitrust policy is not the oft-noted need for greater bilateral or multilateral cooperation among national antitrust authorities but the all too familiar problem of dealing with legitimately acquired monopoly positions. Foreign investment aggravates a traditional challenge to antitrust policy, but, as we argue below, offers new opportunities for fashioning effective remedies to these disorders.

A Review of the Literature

The Domestic Origins of Foreign Investment

Stephen Hymer's 1960 study was the first to demonstrate that foreign *direct* investment could not be coupled with *portfolio* investments in a unified theory of international capital flows.[1] While portfolio flows might be adequately explained by differentials in rates of return, direct investment belonged more to the theory of industrial organization, the analysis of market imperfections. Normally a firm or an individual might want to own assets located abroad but have little interest in controlling their use. Foreign investments are subject to different and unfamiliar laws and possible discriminatory treatment at the hands of foreign government, banks, and other institutions. While the rate of return abroad may be high enough to compensate the foreign investor for the risk of owning the asset, controlling that asset is only asking for trouble.

If firms were to invest abroad, then they must have some advantage over foreign competitors or some reason to avoid arm's-length buying from or selling to foreign firms. In natural-resource extraction, the advantage might come in coordinating the vertical stages of production and

1. *International Operations of National Firms: A Study of Direct Foreign Investment* (Massachusetts Institute of Technology Press, 1976).

thereby eliminating the risk of single-stage operations and the necessity to haggle over intermediate prices. In manufacturing investments, the advantage might come from a well-designed product or the rights conferred by a patent.

Hymer was particularly struck by the similarity between the motives for investing abroad and Joe S. Bain's list of barriers to entry in American industry.[2] Bain argued that traditional industrial organization analysis placed too much emphasis on the ability or inability of sellers to collude in raising prices and too little on the ability of new competition to enter the industry and undercut established prices. In fact, the only way a monopolist or oligopolist could keep prices above a competitive level for very long would be by constructing barriers to new competition.[3] According to Bain's taxonomy, entry barriers could be put into one of three categories:[4]

1. *Economies of scale.* Economies of scale, if they are significant relative to the aggregate size of the market, may permit established firms to maintain artificially large price-cost margins without attracting new competition. New producers may be reluctant to enter the market on a limited scale, knowing that their costs will be comparatively high. Entering the market on a large scale may bring the cost down but may also depress prices to make entry unprofitable for everyone, including the entrant. Established firms keep prices high, knowing that small-scale entry is unprofitable and large-scale entry self-defeating.

2. *Absolute cost advantage.* These advantages, by definition, are maintained by established firms over new entrants regardless of the scale of production. If established firms control the richest natural resource deposits, they earn higher profits than new entrants working marginal holdings. Likewise, if established firms succeed in patenting special machinery or superior processes, they enjoy an advantage over new producers as long as the advantage is protected by patents, secrecy, or other safeguards of commercial property.

3. *Product-differentiation advantages.* These advantages arise not from lower costs but from an ability to sell at a higher price than would-be competitors. The product itself may be protected by a patent on which the firm is earning an economic rent. Likewise, two products may be physi-

2. *Barriers to New Competition* (Harvard University Press, 1956).
3. Ibid., pp. 2–4.
4. Ibid., pp. 15–16.

cally equivalent, but consumers familiar with one brand may be unwilling to take a chance on another unless it is much cheaper. Superficial and real differences between products may be heightened by advertising, more convenient delivery or distribution, or better follow-up servicing. Although these product-differentiating activities may generate additional costs for the manufacturer, they too may reap substantial economies of scale. Whether one wants to consider the economies of large-scale advertising, sales promotion, distribution, and the like, as product-differentiation advantages or economies of scale, their ability to make entry difficult cannot be denied. Established firms may consistently earn higher than competitive profits, even taking into account the costs of product differentiation.

Hymer supported his thesis that foreign investment was based on market imperfections with a variety of evidence. He showed that foreign investing is not a common practice in all industries but is highly concentrated in a few large firms (for example, the Seven Sisters of the American petroleum industry were the source of nearly a third of all American investments at that time), which in turn are centered in a few, oligopolistic industries (as indicated by high seller-concentration ratios). Furthermore, since the barriers to entry in the United States were much the same as abroad, Hymer noted that American multinationals often confronted foreign multinationals, such as Shell in the petroleum industry, Imperial Chemical Industries in chemicals, Lever Brothers in household detergents, Nestlé in food products, or Dunlop in rubber.[5]

That Hymer's conclusions seem so obvious in retrospect bears real testimony to their power. Since the thesis touches upon so many important issues, much of the research done in the last fifteen years can be seen as a refinement or an extension of it. However, Hymer raised as many questions as he answered. Quite apart from the obvious and unavoidable deficiencies in his data, he was vague on several critical issues. For in-

5. Hymer reasoned that entry barriers provide a necessary, but by no means sufficient, basis for foreign expansion. An alternative to foreign investment is licensing a foreign-owned firm, which spares the investor the risk of foreign operations. But licensing has its own disadvantages—a royalty rate must be negotiated with the licensee, American antitrust laws may proscribe certain uses of the license, circumstances may change to the detriment of the licensor and to the advantage of the licensee, or the foreign firm may acquire the expertise to become a future competitor. Hence, although licensing is frequently undertaken where investment is not a real option (as in most industries in Japan), a firm usually prefers to invest.

stance, while no one would dispute the relevance of Bain's list of entry barriers to foreign investing, Hymer was vague on the correspondence between the two. Are all entry barriers also incentives to invest abroad? Or vice versa? To put this critical question into more concrete terms, Bain's ranking of selected American industries by the height of their aggregate entry barriers are listed below.[6]

Industries with very high entry barriers are automobiles, cigarettes, fountain pens ("quality" grade), liquor, tractors, and typewriters.

Industries with substantial entry barriers are copper, farm machines (large, complex), petroleum refining, shoes (high-priced men's and specialties), soap, and steel.

Industries with moderate-to-low entry barriers are canned fruits and vegetables, cement, farm machinery (small, simple), flour, fountain pens (low-priced), gypsum products, meat packing, metal containers, rayon, shoes (women's and low-priced men's), and tires and tubes.

These same industries, ranked by their foreign investment positions, correlate to a large degree with this listing. (See table 3-2.) However, the correlation is by no means perfect. For instance, neither steel nor shoe manufacturers approach equally ranked petroleum and soap producers in terms of foreign investment, while the manufacturers of metal containers and tires and tubes with moderate-to-low entry barriers have substantial foreign operations. With the perspective of hindsight, we can see that Hymer pointed the way without preempting the field.

The next significant link between domestic industry structure and foreign direct investment was forged by Raymond Vernon, whose product-cycle hypothesis is summarized in chapter three.[7] The U.S. economy, Vernon noted, is marked by high wage rates and personal incomes, which bias American technology toward labor-saving and leisure-supporting innovations. Because U.S. research and development was largely devoted

6. Bain, *Barriers to New Competition*, p. 170.
7. See Raymond Vernon, "International Investment and International Trade in the Product Cycle," *Quarterly Journal of Economics*, vol. 80 (May 1966), pp. 190–207; William Gruber, Dileep Mehta, and Raymond Vernon, "The R&D Factor in International Trade and International Investment of United States Industries," *Journal of Political Economy*, vol. 75 (February 1967), pp. 20–37; and Raymond Vernon, *Sovereignty at Bay: The Multinational Spread of U.S. Enterprises* (Basic Books, 1971). Vernon's first application of the product-cycle theory, interestingly enough, is his analysis of New York City and its economic relation to the rest of the United States (*Metropolis, 1985*, Harvard University Press, 1960).

to such efforts, both U.S. exports and the follow-up investments were markedly higher in American industries spending heavily on R&D (such as chemicals, electrical and nonelectrical machinery, and transportation equipment) than in industries with more stagnant products or processes.

While R&D effort is not closely correlated with heavy use of capital (which helps explain Leontief's paradox that U.S. imports were more capital-intensive than U.S. exports),[8] the technologically advanced industries were often dominated by a few large firms. Among oligopolists, long-run prospects are judged more by current market shares than by short-run rates of return. This oligopolistic emphasis on market shares affects foreign investment behavior by making each and every investor highly sensitive to what its competitors are doing. A new investment by anyone threatens the stability of an oligopoly by raising the spectre of one competitor gaining access to cheaper raw materials or untapped foreign technology. American exporters and investors, in their anxiety to maintain their competitive positions, undertake parallel behavior in matching each other's overseas investments more consciously than firms in less concentrated industries.

Charles Kindleberger probably did more than anyone else to publicize the industrial organization aspects of American investments abroad. In addition to arguing Hymer's thesis and supplementing it with his own evidence, Kindleberger introduced Lamfalussy's notion of defensive motives for investing.[9] A defensive investment offers a less than adequate rate of return on its own, but prevents outright losses on other investments. Kindleberger argues that such was often the case with foreign investments where overseas production was necessary to "defend" a foreign market threatened by tariffs or exchange controls suddenly imposed by foreign governments. Other authors extend the defensive label to situations in which foreign markets were threatened by foreign and American

8. Wassily Leontief, "Domestic Production and Foreign Trade: The American Capital Position Re-examined," in the American Economic Association, *Readings in International Economics* (Richard D. Irwin, 1968), pp. 503–27.

9. Charles Kindleberger, *American Business Abroad: Six Lectures on Direct Investment* (Yale University Press, 1969), especially lecture 1; and Alexander Lamfalussy, *Investment and Growth in Mature Economies* (London: Macmillan, 1961). Defensive investing is quite rational and entirely consistent with profit-maximizing behavior. The supposed below-average rate of return is an accounting illusion, for the true rate of return would include the potential loss on past investments if the new investments were not undertaken. (Kindleberger was Hymer's thesis advisor at Massachusetts Institute of Technology.)

competitors willing to invest locally and thereby forcing everyone else to do likewise.

Hymer and Kindleberger repeatedly stressed the proposition that foreign direct investment analysis belongs to the theory of industrial organization, but Richard Caves deserves credit for his serious and systematic efforts to link the two bodies of literature.[10] According to the industrial organization literature, an industry will earn higher than normal profits over an extended period of time only if the firms are few enough in number to recognize the folly of cutting prices and if they have some way of keeping new competition from entering the industry. While there are many barriers to entry, not all lend themselves to foreign investing. With horizontal foreign investments (that is, where the foreign subsidiary produces the same computers, chemicals, or farm machinery in the foreign country that the parent does at home), product differentiation tends to be the critical element of market structure. Such product differentiation is usually based on technology or design, either of which may be protected by patents and transferred to the subsidiary. With vertical investments (that is, where the foreign subsidiary extracts and processes crude oil, bauxite, or bananas for export back to the parent firm), product differentiation is usually irrelevant, but high seller concentration in the home country is crucial. In these industries, control over scarce natural resources at home and abroad is itself an important barrier to new competition.

This part of Caves's contribution is essentially a precise formulation of Hymer's thesis. Caves begins to break new ground, however, in pushing the analogy between a national industry consisting of several more or less distinct regional markets and a global industry consisting of several more or less distinct national markets. Just as the latitude for regional producers to raise prices depends on the threat of entry by established firms in other regions, so too does the latitude of national firms depend upon the potential competition from foreigners. Unlike the de novo firm, the new entrant from another region or another country has certain advantages. Having developed a product for its home market, it avoids many

10. Richard E. Caves, "International Corporations: The Industrial Economics of Foreign Investment," *Economica*, vol. 38 (February 1971), pp. 1–27; "Industrial Organization," in J. H. Dunning, ed., *Economic Analysis and the Multinational Enterprise* (London: Allen & Unwin, 1974); and "Causes of Direct Investment: Foreign Firms' Shares in Canadian and United Kingdom Manufacturing Industries," *Review of Economics and Statistics*, vol. 56 (August 1974), pp. 279–93.

220   *American Multinationals and American Interests*

of the start-up costs the novice cannot. Or if the economies of scale are highly concentrated at one stage of the production process, the established firm may be able to produce the critical component at home and everything else abroad. If successful entry depends on high cash outlays for capital equipment, local advertising, or a distribution network, the foreign investor can use his credit rating in the home market. Finally, if the foreign investment is exceedingly risky, the established firm includes the new investment with its old ones in a single, risk-sharing pool. The relevance of particular entry barriers to the foreign investment process depends on how location-specific they are: a patent that can be worked in numerous locations provides an excellent basis for investing abroad, while a network of warehouses and deliverymen may be no help whatsoever.

American firms have an easier time entering certain foreign product markets than do new, local firms, and once into the market they may show less respect for traditional modes of behavior and market shares than local firms do. Because tacit collusion depends on mutual recognition of collaborative focal points, the foreign investor out of ignorance is more likely to step on toes, trigger price wars, and so on. And since the foreigner may be importing more of his components and using his home technology, he may have a different cost structure from his foreign competitors; when firms have different cost structures, collusive agreements are harder to effect. Finally, the foreign investor is initially less enmeshed in a tangle of relations with local banks, labor unions, and government bureaucracies; it is less susceptible to pressure to collude from these quarters.

Caves concludes that, from a competitive point of view, foreign subsidiaries are thus a mixed bag as far as host countries are concerned. On the positive side, their ability to hurdle high entry barriers and their propensity for rivalrous behavior upset local, entrenched oligopolies. On the negative side, they divert competition away from price cutting and toward advertising and other forms of brand differentiation. In addition, they may provoke defensive mergers among their local competitors, and they may participate in such mergers themselves, further limiting the scope for competition.[11] Whether American investment makes foreign markets more or

11. Of the total growth of assets of American multinationals in Brazil and Mexico from 1960 through 1972, an estimated 23.9 percent and 19.8 percent, respectively, derived from acquisitions of existing firms. Richard S. Newfarmer and Willard F. Mueller, *Multinational Corporations in Brazil and Mexico: Structural Sources of*

less competitive thus depends on the balance between competitive and anticompetitive effects, which in practice can cut either way.

Thomas Horst investigated empirically the characteristics distinguishing American multinational firms from the general population of American manufacturers.[12] The differences between multinationals and non-multinationals were partitioned into two groups: differences within the same industry, and differences between industries. Within an industry, the only consistent difference is that multinationals tend to be larger than nonmultinationals. The different propensity for foreign investing between industries was not a question of size but of technological intensity, of natural resource requirements combined with seller concentration in the U.S. market, and of the total capital required to establish a foreign subsidiary. Capital requirements have a double-barreled effect on the foreign investment process: in industries where economies of scale are substantial (for example, aluminum smelting or automobiles), smaller American firms may be reluctant to establish a foreign factory, but larger American firms, which make the investments, have an advantage over small competitors in the foreign market.

The analysis of foreign investment propensities in different industries was considerably extended by Dale Orr, Richard Caves, and Harry G. Baumann.[13] Orr focused on foreign (American, British, and so forth) penetration of Canadian industry and found that the foreign share was larger in industries marked by high R&D spending, high advertising, large firm size, and the absence of regional market segmentation. He argued that regionally segmented markets are marked by high transport costs and/or the need for specific knowledge of local market conditions. As Hymer would have predicted, domestic Canadian firms have a decided advantage over foreign investors in such industries.

Caves's research, concurrent with and independent of Orr's, investi-

---

Economic and Noneconomic Power (Government Printing Office, 1975), pp. 70, 123. The "dependencia" analysts argue that collusion takes place between the multinational enterprises and local capitalists even without formal mergers (see chap. 10).

12. "The Firm and Industry Determinants of the Decision to Invest Abroad: An Empirical Study," *Review of Economics and Statistics*, vol. 54 (August 1972), pp. 258–66.

13. Orr, "Foreign Control and Foreign Penetration in the Canadian Manufacturing Industries" (1973; processed); Caves, "Causes of Direct Investment"; and Baumann, "The Determinants of the Pattern of Foreign Direct Investment: Some Hypotheses Reconsidered" (1974; processed).

222 *American Multinationals and American Interests*

gated foreign ownership in both Canada and Great Britain. Like Orr, Caves found that foreign penetration of the Canadian market is high in industries marked by high advertising and R&D expenditures and large firm size. Pursuing a hypothesis advanced by Eastman and Stykolt, and seconded by McManus,[14] Caves compared foreign ownership patterns in Canada to multiplant ownership in the United States. Although the extent of multiplant operations depends in part on advertising, research and development, and average firm size, Caves showed that multiplant activity nonetheless had some additional explanatory power in accounting for American investments in Canada. Because multiplant operations did not prove significant in analyzing the British data, Caves concluded that American companies can extend the economies of bulk purchasing and/or distribution to their Canadian but not to their British operations.

An alternative interpretation is suggested by Baumann's research, which indicates that the multiplant measure is highly correlated with seller concentration in the U.S. market (that is, the industries in which most plants are operated by multiplant firms tend to be dominated by a few large firms). Although Baumann interprets seller concentration as measuring economies of firm size, its traditional interpretation as a measure of oligopolistic interdependence seems highly relevant. Of all the foreign bases from which a successful attack on the American market might be launched, Canada may be the most threatening to an American oligopoly. American investments in highly concentrated Canadian industries may be preemptive strikes against sources of new competition and not just attempts to reap North American economies of firm size. Regrettably, the collinearity between multiplant operations and seller concentration makes it difficult to choose between the two hypotheses.

The role of oligopolistic interdependence, apart from the underlying elements of industry structure that might have given rise to an oligopoly, was studied by Frederick Knickerbocker.[15] Unlike the studies considered above, which are concerned with foreign market penetration by U.S. corporations, Knickerbocker's concern was for the dynamics of the foreign investment process and especially for the propensity of oligopolistic firms

14. See Harry C. Eastman and Stefan Stykolt, *The Tariff and Competition in Canada* (St. Martin's Press, 1967); and John C. McManus, "The Theory of the International Firm," in G. Paquet, ed., *The Multinational Firm and the Nation State* (Collier-Macmillan Canada, Ltd., 1972), pp. 66–93.

15. *Oligopolistic Reaction and Multinational Enterprise* (Harvard University Graduate School of Business Administration, 1973).

to quickly match the investment patterns of rival firms. Following the thinking of Hymer, Vernon, and Kindleberger, Knickerbocker reasons that firms in highly concentrated industries, perceiving their own mutual dependence, feel threatened when one makes a new investment abroad. They fear that the new investor may get a leg up on the foreign market or, worse, develop a new technology or find a cheaper source of supply, which can be used in the home market. Rather than take a chance, they match the original investment. So when one firm invests abroad, it sets off a chain reaction of investments by its rivals in the U.S. market.

Knickerbocker's Entry Concentration Index (ECI), a measure of American firms' propensity to duplicate quickly each other's new foreign investments, is the centerpiece of his analysis.[16] His most striking result comes from comparing an industry's ECI with its seller concentration ratio in the domestic U.S. market, as depicted in figure 7-1. An increase in an industry's concentration ratio is associated with an increase in its ECI, at least up until the largest eight firms account for approximately two-thirds of the U.S. market. For high seller concentration ratios, however, the ECI seems to decline, which Knickerbocker attributes to the ability of the tightest oligopolies to restrain their foreign investment plans and thereby to avoid overcrowding.

Knickerbocker turned to domestic industrial organization analysis and found further support for his line of analysis. In one of Frederic M. Scherer's articles is evidence that domestic American plant and equipment expenditures were considerably more volatile in highly concentrated industries than in less concentrated ones, which lends further credibility to Knickerbocker's finding of entry-bunching abroad.[17] In an earlier article Scherer demonstrates that R&D effort increases with seller concentration to the point of moderate concentration; beyond that, R&D effort

16. Knickerbocker based the index on Harvard School of Business Administration data on the date, country, and industry of all foreign manufacturing investments of 187 American multinationals. The index for a particular industry is the proportion of all subsidiaries established between 1947 and 1970 in the three, five, or seven year period of maximal activity, the indexes for twenty-one countries being averaged to get the industry mean. While this measure represents an artful use of the available data, it does not reflect the behavior of other American firms nor of all foreign firms, nor does it distinguish large, developed countries (Canada, United Kingdom, and Western Europe) from small, less-developed countries.

17. "Market Structure and the Stability of Investment," *American Economic Review*, vol. 59 (May 1969), pp. 72–79.

Figure 7-1. *Relation between Entry Concentration and Seller Concentration, Eight Largest Firms in Industry*

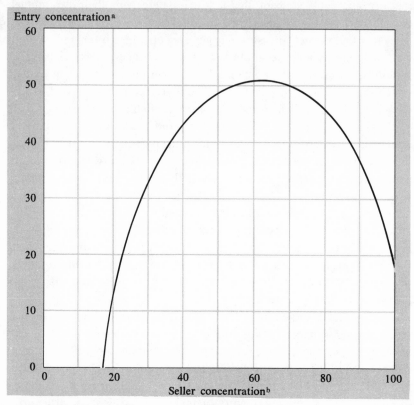

Source: Regression equation based on Frederick T. Knickerbocker, *Oligopolistic Reaction and Multinational Enterprise* (Harvard University Press, 1973), table 3-12.
a. Proportion of foreign subsidiaries formed in most intensive three-year interval, 1947–70.
b. Proportion of industry shipments by eight largest firms.

seems to decline.[18] Scherer's explanation of this curvilinear relation stresses the ability of oligopolists to restrain costly and offsetting expenditures. If they can limit their R&D effort to their mutual advantage, why not their foreign investment behavior? Finally, the finding of both Scherer and Knickerbocker that highly concentrated industries were capable of closer coordination than low and moderately concentrated industries is consistent with Bain's original view that industry profitability, the name of

18. Frederic M. Scherer, "Market Structure and the Employment of Scientists and Engineers," *American Economic Review*, vol. 57 (June 1967), pp. 524–31.

the game, increased with seller concentration, but only at the highest levels.[19]

Feedback Effects on U.S. Industrial Structure

All of these studies view foreign investment behavior as an outgrowth of domestic industry structure. Whether the issue is the origin of American competitive strength in world markets, the extent of American penetration of foreign markets, or the timing of oligopolists' investments, conditions at home determined behavior abroad. Quite recently, a few authors raised the obverse question: What impact do foreign operations have on U.S. industry?

Benjamin I. Cohen investigated the impact of foreign operations on the stability of American firms' earnings and sales.[20] Working with a sample of 233 large firms, Cohen explored the year-to-year variation in both earnings and sales around either their mean or their trend over the years 1961–69. Controlling as best he could for the size, diversity, and principal industry of the firm, he found that both earnings and sales fluctuations were reduced by foreign investment. Since economic conditions in different countries do not go up and down in perfect unison, Cohen concluded that foreign investing provided American firms with an effective way of stabilizing their global earnings.

Alan K. Severn and Martin M. Laurence explored the contributions of R&D spending and foreign investing to corporate profitability.[21] Naturally enough, they found that foreign investors tend to spend more and earn

19. Joe S. Bain, "Relation of Profit Rate to Industry Concentration: American Manufacturing, 1936–1940," *Quarterly Journal of Economics*, vol. 65 (August 1951), pp. 293–324. Knickerbocker did not try to discover whether the lemming instincts of oligopolists lead to greater American penetration of foreign markets or merely to more and smaller shares in an unchanged market. Until better data and analytical methods are available, caution must be exercised in equating the number of foreign subsidiaries with the total volume of American investments, let alone relating them to American and host-country economies.

20. *Foreign Investment by U.S. Corporations as a Way of Reducing Risk*, Economic Growth Center discussion paper no. 151 (Yale University, 1972). The increasing synchronization of the major national economies in the early 1970s, however, may have reduced this particular attraction of foreign investment to American firms.

21. "Direct Investment, Research Intensity, and Profitability," Division of International Finance discussion paper no. 30 (Board of Governors of the Federal Reserve System, May 31, 1973; processed).

more than firms without investments abroad. Even if the only link between foreign investing and profitability were their joint dependence on R&D effort, this result would obtain. The authors accordingly set out to discover whether foreign investing makes any separate and independent contribution to firm profitability, or whether it merely allows a firm to spread its R&D over a larger sales base.

Their findings were mixed. By regressing a firm's rate of profits on the R&D level for its industry and on one or the other proxy for its foreign investment position, Severn and Laurence obtained a consistently positive coefficient on the R&D measure and a positive coefficient on one of the foreign investment measures but not on the other. They conclude that foreign investment makes no direct contribution to profitability but does allow firms to spread their R&D costs over a larger base.

However, Severn and Laurence's conclusion does not follow from their analysis. The sign and significance of the R&D variable measure the contribution of R&D to domestic profitability, holding the level of foreign investment constant; the sign and significance of the foreign investment variable indicate its contribution to profitability, holding R&D constant. If foreign investment allows a multinational firm to spread R&D costs over a larger sales base, as Severn and Laurence conclude, then the foreign investment term, and not the R&D term, should have been significant. Firms with more foreign investment can spread their R&D costs further and thereby enjoy higher profits.

The impact of foreign investing on corporate profitability is also explored in Thomas Horst's investigation of the food-processing industry.[22] Firms with foreign operations did indeed earn a higher rate of return than firms without such operations, and that differential could not be fully attributed to advertising expenditures, distribution requirements, and other structural elements of the food-processing industry. But the difference might well be due to a higher return on foreign operations than on domestic operations, especially because 1970, the year for which the data were taken, was a bad one domestically. Foreign operations were clearly buoying the consolidated rate of return. What could not be determined was whether these multinational firms were also earning a higher rate of return on their domestic operations than their domestic competitors were.

---

22. *At Home Abroad: A Study of the Domestic and Foreign Operations of the American Food-Processing Industry* (Ballinger, 1974), chap. 5.

If so, foreign operations would be something more than a mere stabilizer of corporate performance. This is precisely the issue we take up below.

Raymond Vernon has added to the debate by noting that the degree of concentration of world production in several industries characterized as "mature oligopolies" (aluminum smelting, automobiles, copper, petroleum production and refining, pulp and paper, zinc) declined over the period 1950–70.[23] He recognizes, however, that the decline does not necessarily mean that competition in world markets increased. Because this decrease in global concentration reflects more the rapid growth of European and Japanese firms outside the United States and less the corresponding deterioration in U.S. concentration, the tangible benefits for the United States may be small. But as foreign producers become increasingly significant in the U.S. economy, they may yet bring real benefits to the United States.

Finally, Richard J. Barnet and Ronald E. Müller argue that the corporate globalization process has led to an acceleration in industrial and financial concentration of the U.S. domestic sector.[24] How so? Between the late 1950s or early 1960s and the 1970s the share of foreign profits in the U.S. corporate total grew from 7 to 13 percent, plant and equipment expenditures from about 9 percent to approximately 25 percent, sales from 7 to 13 percent.[25] Likewise, between 1955 and 1970 the Fortune 500s share of employment, profits, and assets grew from 40 to 70 percent of the total for U.S. manufacturing. These two phenomena are closely linked, according to Barnet and Müller, because the multinationals are simultaneously conglomerates and oligopolists in their individual product markets. As conglomerates, they can employ their financial, technological, and marketing resources developed in one market to cross-subsidize their expansion in another. Just as conglomerates expanded their market shares and drove undiversified firms from the market, so will multinational firms drive out domestic firms.

Barnet and Müller's argument, whatever its intuitive appeal, is on shaky grounds empirically. Over the last two decades, when the aggregate share of U.S. manufacturing controlled by the largest 50 (or 200 or 500)

23. "Competition Policy Toward Multinational Corporations," *American Economic Review*, vol. 64 (May 1974), pp. 277–80.
24. *Global Reach: The Power of the Multinational Corporations* (Simon and Schuster, 1974), esp. chap. 10.
25. Ibid., pp. 260–61. For our own estimates, see tables 1-1, 1-2, and 1-3.

rose dramatically, the share of individual product markets controlled by the top four or eight firms maintained a more or less constant average.[26] Since concentration ratios for individual markets are better indicators of oligopolists' ability to coordinate prices or to exclude smaller rivals from the market, one must be wary of aggregate concentration ratios. Their usefulness depends on the importance of cross-subsidization, on firms' ability to marshall the resources from one market for use in another. Despite Müller's claim that cross-subsidization within a conglomerate is a basic practice of modern corporate life, its economic significance has been hard to demonstrate.[27] In fact, Stephen A. Rhoades recently concluded that conglomerate diversification (such as ITT's acquisition of Continental Baking) may be counterproductive. "This suggests that more widespread diversification . . . may lead to inefficiencies in production, distribution, and management that outweigh the positive effect of diversification."[28] If the experience of the conglomerates were any indication, one would probably have little to fear from the multinationals.

Barnet and Müller's mistake, we believe, lies not in their final conclusion, that multinationals enjoy substantive advantages over their domestic competitors, but in their basing that conclusion on the experience of conglomerates. Unless two activities are closely linked in their technology, their distributional requirements, or in some other respect, the benefits of merger may be small and may even be outweighed by a variety of intangible costs. The ability to shift funds, head-office management, and other highly fungible resources is no great advantage.

Multinationals benefit, as we argue below, from their ability to economize on nonfungible resources. Capital and general managerial skills are probably the least of their advantages. Technological and industry-specific managerial know-how are the greatest. Multinational firms have been notable for the narrowness of their product lines, given their large size, particularly before the merger movement took on international di-

26. See, for example, Frederic M. Scherer, *Industrial Market Structure and Economic Performance* (Rand McNally, 1970), p. 63.

27. Ronald Müller, "The Political Economy of Global Corporations and National Stabilization Policy: A Diagnostic on the Need for Social Planning" (December 1974; processed), p. 7.

28. "A Further Evaluation of the Effect of Diversification on Industry Profit Performance," *Review of Economics and Statistics,* vol. 56 (November 1974), pp. 557–59.

mensions in the 1960s.[29] Having found good opportunities for growth abroad, they had less need for conglomerate acquisitions and mergers. The experience of conglomerate firms in diversifying into one product market after another bears only a superficial resemblance to that of the multinationals investing in one country after another.

Conclusions

The main conclusions of industrial organization research on foreign direct investment can be easily summarized. Several authors show that foreign investment is the product of domestic industry structure. Hymer stressed the relevance of Bain's barriers to entry; Vernon emphasized the technological basis of American exporting and investing; Caves argued the case for product differentiation, which narrowed the Hymer argument and broadened the Vernon thesis.

Within any given industry, the multinationals are almost always the leading domestic producers. Seller concentration is difficult to disentangle from the technological requirements, the advertising effort, and the economies of scale that limit competition to begin with. Knickerbocker's study links concentration to the timing, but not the magnitude, of American investments abroad. While there may be room for further research, understanding the domestic origins of foreign direct investment has come a long way in the last fifteen years.

Understanding of the consequences—as opposed to the causes—of foreign investment is still rather primitive. Cohen's research shows that foreign investing stabilized corporate earnings, at least in the 1960s. Severn and Laurence raised the critical issue of whether foreign investing makes any independent contribution to corporate profitability, but their findings are inconclusive. Barnet and Müller argue that multinationals may use their foreign operations to cross-subsidize their domestic activities, but the advantages allegedly reaped by the conglomerates from analogous opportunities proved illusory. Obviously, an understanding of the domestic consequences of American investments abroad is a long way off.

29. Caves, "International Corporations: The Industrial Economics of Foreign Investment," notes that "product diversification across national boundaries is almost unknown" (p. 3).

Figure 7-2. *Principal Relations among Domestic Industry Structure,
Foreign Investment, and Industry Performance According to Three
Analytical Methods*

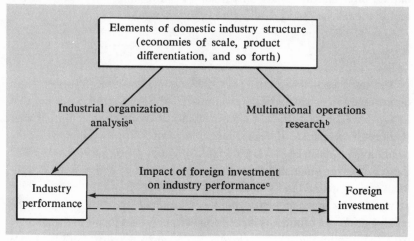

a. As set forth by Joe S. Bain and others. See text.
b. As set forth by Stephen Hymer and others. See text.
c. New empirical evidence set forth by authors. See text.

New Empirical Evidence

As is apparent from this review of the literature, industrial organization
research focused largely on the causes rather than the consequences of
American investments abroad. But what are the implications of these investments for industrial structure in the United States? Do they directly
or indirectly boost the market power of the multinationals at home?

The nature of this question, and the difficulties in answering it, are
portrayed in figure 7-2. Conventional industrial organization analysis relates economies of scale, the extent of brand differentiation, method of
distribution, and other elements of domestic industrial structure, to excess of price over cost of production, to technological progressiveness,
and to other dimensions of industry performance. The objective is to show
that the hallmarks of monopoly or oligopoly (high profits or high concentration of sales among a handful of large firms) are to be found in those
very industries where economies of scale, advertising effort, and other
barriers to new competition bulk large.

COMPETITION AND ANTITRUST   231

The literature on international investment stresses the importance of these same elements of domestic industry structure in generating direct investments abroad. For example, technological know-how (protected by patents and secrecy but easily transferred to a foreign affiliate) is a well-recognized determinant of foreign investment. Because the barriers to new competition at home turn out to be inducements to invest abroad, multinational firms typically enjoy oligopoly positions in their domestic markets.

Our objective, as distinct from that of either industrial organization analysis or the foreign investment literature reviewed above, is to assess the direct impact of foreign investment on domestic market performance. Foreign investment and oligopoly power go hand in hand. But is oligopoly power enhanced significantly and substantially by foreign investment? Or, putting the question somewhat differently, does foreign direct investment constitute a separate and significant barrier to entry into the domestic market? Unfortunately, foreign investment and domestic market power have a common dependence on the elements of industry structure. This common relationship plus the obverse relationship to the one being investigated—the possible stimulating effect of domestic market power on foreign investment—must be separated from the effect of particular concern here.

Industrial organization analysis, despite its tendency to ignore international influences on domestic product markets, offers a broad context in which to assess the significance of foreign investment. Until the 1950s, such analysis reasoned that market power was based on the size of firms either in dollar terms or in market share. A firm with a dominant market position could raise its price unilaterally, as could a small group whose collective position was strong. Seller concentration ratios, such as the proportion of industry sales made by the four leading firms, were and still are a common way of measuring market power. Bain shifted the focus of analysis by reasoning that such power would be vacuous unless a monopolist or the oligopolists also had some way of keeping new competition from entering the industry and undercutting their prices. Economic history is indeed replete with grand mergers and elaborate cartels destroyed by new competition attracted by high prices. Oligopolists threatened with new competition need only a little foresight or hindsight to perceive the folly of raising prices.

A corollary of the importance of entry barriers in generating real market power is the inadequacy of firm size or seller concentration as an index of such power. The two may be highly correlated, since economies of scale and other entry barriers tend to produce large firms and high concentration ratios. Likewise, firms with market power may prefer to maximize their market share by driving rivals from the industry rather than by keeping prices and profits high. But the equation between power and size is too inexact to rely on; too many industrial brontosauruses exist for one to assume that whatever is big must be powerful or that whatever is growing must be getting more powerful. Industrial organization analysis has increasingly relied upon price-cost margins and rates of return as measures of monopoly power.

Although rates of return are routinely used by industrial organization economists as an indicator of market power, this practice often provokes objection and criticism.[30] If a firm's rate of return is the difference between its price and its cost, are high profits a reflection of high prices or low costs? *In any particular case,* one cannot know. Even casual comparisons of firms' performance reveal that some firms are more efficient than others, better managed than others, or just luckier than others. High profits do not necessarily imply control over the price charged to customers.

Most industrial organization economists would argue, however, that ability and good luck are to be found in all industries, not just those enjoying economies of scale, patent protection, or extensive brand differentiation. Despite the more or less random variation in firms' profitability, a statistically significant correlation between industries' profitability and the barriers to new competition may be observed. Differences in firms' luck or innate ability may average out when firms are grouped into industries or may remain in the unexplained residual of the statistical analysis. That barriers to entry offer only a partial explanation of why some firms or

30. The published income and balance-sheet statistics are poor sources for research. The unpublished depreciation rules, inventory valuation, and other accounting practices may have a profound effect on the apparent profitability of a corporation. But while deficiencies in the data can blur an underlying relation, they may not obscure it altogether. Industrial organization analysts have successfully demonstrated the link between industrial structure and price or profit performance, using different sets of data, each with its own deficiencies. For a review, see Leonard W. Weiss, "The Concentration-Profits Relationship and Antitrust," in Harvey J. Goldschmid and others, eds., *Industrial Concentration: The New Learning* (Little, Brown, 1974), pp. 184–233.

some industries are more profitable than others should be readily conceded, but that concession in no way diminishes the value of showing a statistically strong and significant link between the two.

Although phrases like "market power," "oligopoly," and "barriers to competition" are often pejorative, implying that public policy should make every effort to be rid of them, in actual practice the common cures may be worse than the diseases. For instance, economies of scale at any stage in the production and distribution process may allow firms to economize on labor and capital and free it for employment elsewhere. In an economist's utopia, firms would pass on these savings to buyers through lower prices and retain for themselves and their employees only a competitive rate of return. In the real world, however, firms pass on only what their corporate interests require. Designing an antitrust policy or regulatory procedures to force firms to pass on such savings without having unwanted side effects (high administrative costs, red tape, lost initiative, and so on) is no easy task. So, without abandoning the lexicon of industrial organization analysis, we do reserve judgment on the policy implications until we explore the remedies.

The outline of this empirical section is straightforward. In the following sections we explore in greater detail our reasons for supposing, a priori, that foreign investment may contribute to domestic market power, and vice versa. Next we explore the origins of and limitations on the data available for testing our hypotheses. After that, we present a research design for properly analyzing these data; then we turn to the econometric results.

Foreign Investment as a Determinant of Domestic Market Power

As established by the literature reviewed above, American multinationals are bigger than their purely domestic competitors and enjoy larger market shares, are more likely to be found in industries where competition is highly imperfect and based on product differentiation, and are rewarded by smaller year-to-year fluctuations in their consolidated earnings. What we want to find out is whether the domestic market power of these multinational firms is further reinforced by their overseas investment; whether by virtue of their foreign operations they earn a higher domestic rate of return than their domestic competitors. Judging from their apparent reasons for investing abroad, the possibility that foreign investment benefits domestic operations must be taken seriously. Consider the potential benefits:

1. *Vertical integration.* A substantial portion of American foreign investments constitutes vertical integration of production or distribution across national boundaries. In the petroleum, copper, aluminum, steel, and other resource-intensive industries, large American processors and refiners sought to develop and control natural resources. Likewise, the thousands of sales, service, and assembly operations that American manufacturers established in foreign countries, often as a prelude to full-scale manufacturing, constitute forward integration. For American firms to benefit from vertical integration across countries, not only must the American operations be protected in one way or another from new competition but so, too, must the foreign operations. Only when both stages of production are protected is there any real complementarity between domestic and foreign investment. An ideal example is petroleum exploration, extraction, transportation, refining, and marketing, each of which may be subject to substantial economies of scale. Likewise, the design, production, sales, and servicing of a complicated machine require close coordination and planning. In each instance, an American manufacturer who has integrated across national boundaries may enjoy substantial advantages over one who has not and who can participate in foreign markets only through arm's-length trading or licensing. Whether one calls this a vertical integration advantage or a foreign investment advantage is purely semantics, but under either guise an integrated multinational firm may enjoy advantages over its nonintegrated domestic rivals.

2. *Spreading joint costs.* A firm operating in two or more national markets may be able to spread joint overhead costs over a larger production and sales base than a domestic firm. Technological know-how obtained through research and development is a prime example, although other managerial, marketing, engineering, and financial services may qualify as well. If the size of R&D and other joint programs is fixed at some "take-it-or-leave-it" level, then a multinational firm can charge a portion of these common costs to its overseas affiliates, while a domestic firm, by definition, cannot. If the size of such programs is variable, with larger programs yielding greater benefits, then a multinational firm can afford to spend, and will want to spend, more on R&D in dollar terms (though not necessarily as a percentage of total sales or assets) than its domestic competitors can or will. Although exporting or licensing foreign producers

allows domestic firms partial relief from the constraints of the domestic market, that relief is apt to be incomplete. The primary conclusion of chapter three was that foreign investment does not consistently displace (or promote) U.S. exports, which implies that exporting is not always a viable alternative to foreign investing for spreading joint costs. Likewise, patent licenses or contracts for know-how and management services are often costly to negotiate and costly to police. A contract is nothing more than a license to sue and, in an international context, to sue in the foreigner's courts. So, while all forms of international commerce have potential significance, foreign investment merits attention in its own right.

3. *Portfolio diversification.* As Cohen and several other writers have noted, international investment allows firms to diversify their investment portfolios across national economies, just as domestic diversification allows such spreading across industries. While portfolio theory tells us that new investment opportunities allow firms to raise their aggregate returns and/or reduce their aggregate risk, the consequences for the domestic return on domestic investment are uncertain. Foreign investment may encourage American firms to make riskier but more rewarding domestic investments than they otherwise would. But then again, they may not. An optimal strategy may be to choose only safe, low-yield, domestic investments and take the big risks abroad. The most one can say is that portfolio diversification may lead to a higher expected rate of return on domestic investments.

4. *Tax considerations.* Certain features of U.S. taxation of foreign-source income (see chapter six) may heighten a multinational's advantage over its domestic rivals. Although the tax incentives to allocate global income to foreign affiliates rather than the U.S. parent are generally small, there have been notable exceptions to the rule, especially in the past. The economies of spreading the joint costs of R&D may be greater, paradoxically enough, when those costs are not spread evenly in the financial accounts. As noted in chapter six, the generally low charges for R&D by U.S. parents to their foreign affiliates led the U.S. Treasury to issue new and more stringent guidelines for differentiating foreign from domestic income. While tax avoidance has probably not been a major source of competitive advantage, it may have reinforced other, more palpable, benefits of foreign investment.

Although this list of potential advantages hardly exhausts the possibilities, it probably covers the more significant ones. Notice that each of these advantages has its domestic counterpart. Vertical integration is common within the United States and cost-spreading and portfolio diversification are common across regional markets or separate product lines. Since some states have corporate income taxes, national firms may be able to avoid some taxes that regional firms in high-tax states cannot. But, although this list may have nothing unique to foreign investing on it, the size of the benefits may be particularly large in a foreign context. Natural resources and cheap labor may be in greater abundance in foreign countries than within the United States; the benefits of spreading costs and diversifying portfolios may be much larger in moving into new foreign countries than into new product lines; tax rates may differ more from one country to another than from one state to another. If so, these old advantages may take on new significance.

For foreign investment to provide a significant advantage for multinational firms over their domestic rivals in U.S. product markets, there must be some substantial obstacle to the domestic firms' establishing their own foreign investments. Why don't all firms go multinational if the benefits are so large? The answer lies with the nature of foreign investment opportunities. At the outset, foreign investing can be quite risky. Although established multinationals are often the picture of financial health, they may have written off substantial entry costs and investment losses against past income. Firms that tried and failed to establish foreign market positions are, by definition, excluded from a list of multinationals, just as are those whose investments were expropriated by foreign government. While events may have been kind to those firms willing to take the foreign plunge before everyone knew the water was fine, it is easy to see why conservative firms stuck to domestic markets. The barriers to foreign investing—the size of the required investments, the uncertainty about the eventual return, the lag between sowing and harvesting—are thus comparable to the barriers to domestic competition—advertising, R&D, and so on.

Finally, the inherent ambiguity of distinguishing domestic from foreign profits must be acknowledged. Whether the advantage is based on vertical integration, spreading joint costs, portfolio diversification, or tax avoidance, foreign and domestic operations are complementary; the benefits of the combination cannot be unambiguously attributed to either foreign or domestic operations. Consider, for example, the benefits of a common R&D program undertaken by the parent firm in the United States. What share of the R&D budget should be charged to the foreign affiliate? What share to domestic operations? Since operations everywhere may benefit from the fruits of that research, it hardly seems fair to make the parent pay the whole bill, or for that matter, even what it would have paid had there been no foreign affiliates. Why not charge the foreign affiliates what they would have paid had there been no parent? The only fair procedure is to allocate joint costs in proportion to the parent's or the affiliate's share of the global sales or production of the corporation.

Alas, a multinational firm's allocation of profits may be based on tax avoidance, bookkeeping convenience, historical precedent or some other consideration than giving credit where credit is due. To prove that foreign investments are important to domestic operations, some of the benefits must be included in domestic profits. Indeed, it is altogether appropriate to include in domestic profits some fraction of the profits on trade between parent and affiliates, the portion of R&D and head-office costs charged to foreign affiliates, and other income from foreign operations, for these are the domestic benefits of foreign investment. That the division of the benefits of multinational operations between foreign and domestic operations is arbitrary is no excuse to ignore it, though it complicates analysis of the relation between the two.

Domestic Market Power as a Determinant of Foreign Direct Investment

Distinguishing cause from effect is a continuing challenge to industrial organization analysis. For simplicity's sake it is assumed that economies of scale, product differentiation, and other elements of industry structure determine the rate of return, the technical progressiveness and efficiency of the industry, and other aspects of industry performance. But these, of course, are only analytical simplifications. In actual practice, oligopolistic firms may channel their excess profits into new technology and more advertising, thereby affecting the structure of the industry. A study of the 1950–65 R&D and profit histories of 111 large firms shows that high R&D led to high profits, and vice versa.[31] Another study shows that high advertising may be both cause and effect of high rates of return in the

31. Ben Branch, "Research and Development Activity and Profitability: A Distributed Lag Analysis," *Journal of Political Economy*, vol. 82 (September/October 1974), pp. 999–1011.

food-processing industry: the Del Monte, Quaker Oats, and General Mills mergers produced consolidation of brands and a new emphasis on advertising and marketing; but advertising, itself, produced substantial market positions for H. J. Heinz, William Wrigley, Jr., and W. K. Kellogg.[32]

There is reason to believe that foreign investing, also, may be an effect as well as a cause of domestic market power. American firms that individually or collectively dominate their domestic product markets often find continued domestic expansion less and less rewarding. While small firms can lower prices or increase advertising without retaliation by competitors, large firms cannot. Even if domestic competitors are unwilling or unable to retaliate in kind, they may complain to the Justice Department or the Federal Trade Commission and instigate an antitrust investigation. Frustrated in the attempt to continue growing in their original market, large firms may turn not only to diversification within the United States but also to new markets abroad. In this sense, expansion abroad is an alternative to conglomeration at home.

Whether the potential impact of domestic market power on foreign investment is a major or minor obstacle to showing the impact of foreign investment on domestic market power is hard to judge. The willingness of domestic competitors to retaliate against price cutting or more aggressive marketing, or the eagerness of the Justice Department or the Federal Trade Commission to bring antitrust charges, may depend more on the size of the firm or on its market share than on its profits. Taking account of firm size or industry concentration reduces the apparent impact of domestic profitability on foreign investment levels.

In fact, once size is accounted for, the only reason to suppose that more profitable firms will invest more abroad is that internal liquidity stimulates expansion generally and foreign investment in particular. But Alan K. Severn's analysis of intrafirm financial flows concludes that an extra dollar invested by an American parent in its overseas affiliate would generate only a 10–15-cent increase in the foreign affiliate's total assets (the other 85–90 cents apparently being used to reduce external liabilities).[33] So, while the impact of domestic profitability on the rate of foreign investment

32. Horst, *At Home Abroad,* chap. 3.
33. "Investment and Financial Behavior of American Direct Investors in Manufacturing," in Fritz Machlup and others, eds., *International Mobility and Movement of Capital* (New York: National Bureau of Economic Research, 1972), pp. 380–90.

cannot be ignored, it is not likely the primary source of the strong statistical relation described below.

Empirical Results

To see whether foreign investing may give American multinationals a competitive advantage over domestic firms in U.S. product markets, we proceeded as follows. First, we used the Internal Revenue Service's *Statistics of Income* to find out how much American corporations of different sizes in different industries earned on their domestic investments between 1965 and 1971. Then we gathered comparable statistics on firms' advertising expenditures, employment of scientific personnel, average size, and other attributes. Finally, we used multiple regression analysis to measure the contributions of these industry attributes to both domestic profitability and to the firms' foreign investment positions and, more important, to see whether even holding these factors constant, higher domestic profits are associated with more foreign investment. While even the complex regression analysis cannot tell which is cause and which effect, it is hard to believe that the increasingly strong statistical relation between foreign investing and domestic profitability that emerges could be caused by the pressure of domestic liquidity on foreign investment alone.

The data employed are essentially the same as those used in chapter three. Rather than analyzing industry totals, however, the data are further disaggregated into asset-size classes. Each of the seventy-five industries (meatpacking, dairy processing, fruit and vegetable canning and preserving, and so on) is disaggregated into asset-size classes (meatpackers with more than $1 billion in total assets, meatpackers with $250 million to $1 billion in total assets, and so on). Although we would prefer to use statistics from individual tax returns (which are unavailable), these data give some indication of how profitability and foreign investment vary within a given industry as well as between different industries.

As noted in chapter three, the Internal Revenue Service statistics do not include the foreign assets or sales of American subsidiaries but only the dividends received and foreign tax credits claimed by the American parents. Likewise, the total assets of the American parents include their net investment in their overseas affiliates but do not show it separately. Nevertheless, our foreign investment proxy (foreign dividends plus tax credits divided by total assets) behaves well in actual practice. Table 3-2 ranks the seventy-five industries by the foreign investment proxy. The industries on the top are those heavily committed to foreign investment, while those at the bottom are hardly known for large domestic operations much less multinational business. When these seventy-five industries are further disaggregated by asset-size class, foreign dividends and tax credits are, as expected, concentrated within each industry in the largest size classes. Even in the technologically advanced or high-advertising industries, where medium-sized firms earn some foreign dividends and claim some tax credits, the tendency is for large firms to have a high ratio of foreign dividends and tax credits to total assets. Because this pattern accords so closely with that found in earlier studies using more readily defensible statistics for foreign investment, we are entitled to some confidence in our foreign investment proxy.

Our goal is not to develop a new foreign investment proxy for its own sake but to relate that proxy to American firms' rate of return on their domestic operations. Rates of returns are measured by firms' income before taxes plus interest paid on debt minus foreign dividends and tax credits, all deflated by total assets. By grouping the interest on debt with the return on equity, the effect of high or low debt-equity ratios on corporations' net income can be ignored. Foreign dividends and tax credits are subtracted from net income to avoid any spurious relation between the two primary variables. Unfortunately, the parent's foreign assets cannot be subtracted from its total assets to see what the domestic return on domestic assets is, but this bias only makes it more difficult to show that foreign investment contributes to domestic profitability.

Before the regression analysis is discussed, some cross-tabulations of the foreign investment and domestic profitability data will be helpful. In table 7-1, each group of firms (a group being those firms in the same asset-size class and the same industry) is classified according to whether their foreign dividends plus tax credits equaled 1 percent or more of total assets (multinationals), whether their advertising expenditures were more than 5 percent of total assets, whether industry's employment of scientists and engineers was more than 5 percent of their 1970 total employment; and whether their total assets exceeded $250 million. The table shows the foreign investment proxy (foreign dividends plus tax credits deflated by total assets) and the domestic profitability measure (net income before taxes plus interest on debt less foreign dividends and tax credits, all deflated by total assets) for 1966 and for 1970 for various categories of

Table 7-1. *Foreign and Domestic Returns, Multinational Firms and Domestic Firms, as Percentage of Total Assets, by Level of Advertising, Level of Technology, and Size of Firm, 1966 and 1970*

Industry character- istic[a]	Multinational firms[b]				Domestic firms			
	Foreign return[c]		Domestic return[d]		Foreign return		Domestic return	
	1966	*1970*	*1966*	*1970*	*1966*	*1970*	*1966*	*1970*
Advertising								
High	3.6	4.3	17.0	14.3	0.2	0.3	13.8	10.8
Low	1.8	2.2	13.0	8.1	0.1	0.2	11.4	6.6
Technology								
High	2.4	3.1	16.7	11.0	0.3	0.3	13.2	5.7
Low	2.3	2.4	12.6	8.7	0.1	0.2	11.5	7.1
Size of firm[e]								
Large	3.3	3.1	14.9	9.7	0.3	0.4	11.6	6.2
Small	2.0	1.7	13.8	9.6	0.1	0.1	11.7	7.3

Sources: *U.S. Census Bureau, 1970 Census of Population, Occupation by Industry*, PC(2)-7B (GPO, 1973).

a. Definitions: high advertisers spend more than 5 percent of total assets on advertising; high technology industries employ scientists and engineers in excess of 5 percent of total employment; large firms have assets of more than $250 million.

b. Multinational firms are those whose foreign dividends and tax credits exceed 1 percent of total assets.

c. Foreign dividends plus tax credits divided by total assets.

d. Net income before taxes, plus interest paid on debt, minus foreign dividends and tax credits, divided by total assets.

e. The differential between large and small firms in 1970 and the decline in foreign return for domestic firms between 1966 and 1970 are illusions. Through mergers, inflation, and real growth between 1966 and 1970, a substantial number of firms passed the $250 million mark. Since foreign investing increases more than proportionately with firm size, a big change in composition reduces average foreign dividends and tax credits in both groups.

firms. In 1966, the firms with high foreign investment proxies and high expenditures on advertising reported foreign dividends and tax credits equal to 3.6 percent of total assets and domestic returns equal to 17 percent of total assets; those with high foreign investment but low advertising reported foreign dividends and tax credits equal to 1.8 percent and domestic returns amounting to 13 percent of total assets.

As one can see by comparing the pairs of statistics, high advertising consistently implies high foreign dividends and tax credits (for example, for the multinational groups of firms in 1966, 3.6 percent, versus 1.8 percent for low advertising) and high domestic returns (for example, for these same groups in 1966, 17 percent versus 13 percent). The association between high technology and either foreign investment or domestic profitability is somewhat weaker and less consistent than that based on advertising. Large firm size is closely associated with more foreign investment but not with higher domestic returns. These results, while interesting, only confirm those already obtained from existing foreign investment and industrial organization studies. Also apparent in table 7-1 is the correlation between foreign investing and domestic profitability, holding advertising, technology, and firm size more or less constant: among high-advertising groups, the multinationals earned 17 percent domestic return on total assets in 1966 versus 13.8 percent for domestic groups; among low advertisers, the multinationals earned 13 percent versus 11.4 percent for the domestics. In fact, for all three types of firm in both years, multinationals averaged significantly higher domestic returns than domestic firms.

Multiple regression analysis was used to isolate the relation between the foreign investment proxy and domestic profitability, for only then is the association apparent between the two variables, holding all others constant.[34] Table 7-2 presents the regression results based on data from 1965

34. Two obstacles occur in applying ordinary least-squares regression techniques to the data. (1) The foreign investment proxy tends to be skewed, with most groups of firms showing little or no foreign dividends and tax credits and a few groups having substantial receipts. Asymmetric distribution violates two assumptions for applying and interpreting linear regression results. First, the apparent relation between foreign investing and each of the several characteristics (advertising, technology, firm size, and so forth) is approximately linear at high values of foreign investment but flattens as the foreign investment value approaches zero (its lower limit). Furthermore, since the values of the foreign investment proxy cannot fall below zero, low values are bunched more closely than high ones. (In technical language, the relation is heteroscedastic—having unequal standard deviations.) The simplest, albeit rough, solution is to work with a nonlinear transformation, such as the square root. Such a transformation unbends the curvilinear relation between the proxy and the variables while generating a more uniform distribution of the unexplained residuals. (Experiments with other nonlinear transformations produce similar results but often only with complex manipulations and interpretations, so only the results of the simpler, square-root transformations are included here.) To make the equation for foreign investment comparable to domestic net returns, both sets of equations are based on the square root of the proxy. (2) The groups of small firms show much greater variability in their domestic earnings than the large firms. It may be that large firms use their market power to stabilize (not just maximize) profits; or the IRS sampling of the returns of small firms may be incomplete. But the major source of heteroscedasticity seems to be the uneven size of the groups. Many classes of the firms characterized as small are populated by firms whose collective importance is small. The simplest remedy is first to assume that the standard deviation of the residual varies inversely with the group's share of its industry's total assets and then to apply generalized least squares. This procedure is equivalent to giving different weights to the different groups (in this instance, giving each group a weight in proportion to its contribution to its industry's total assets). Thus, the correction gives more credit to the more important groups of firms, a correction with intuitive appeal. Estimates from the equation for domestic net returns should be comparable to the equation for foreign investment, so that the direct and indirect contributions of each

through 1971, where the square root of foreign dividends plus tax credits deflated by parents' assets is the dependent variable. Each row of figures describes a regression equation for a paricular year. The coefficients of explanatory variables are in columns, the t statistics in parentheses below them. Although these equations combine interindustry and intraindustry effects, examination of the underlying data reveals that advertising and technology intensities set one industry off from another (the technology variable did not, of course, differ from one group to another within an industry), whereas firm size is critical within an industry but not between industries. Within any given industry the large firms clearly tend to be the foreign investors, but in some industries (meatpacking, ferrous metals, aircraft assembly), average firm size is large but foreign dividends and tax credits are small. In all but those with the least foreign investment, the leading firms usually have significant foreign operations; but only in the high-technology and the high-advertising industries do medium-sized firms match the foreign operations of the leaders. Small firms (for example, firms with $25 million or less in total assets) rarely have foreign dividends or tax credits of any significance, regardless of industry. The similarities between our findings and those in the literature surveyed above are striking, especially considering the superficial problems with the foreign investment proxy.

Table 7-3 presents equations with domestic net return deflated by parent's assets as the dependent variable and the square root of foreign dividends and tax credits similarly deflated as one of the independent variables. As the reader can see, each equation in table 7-2 has its counterpart in table 7-3. Unlike foreign operations, which grew steadily and profitably over 1965–71, the domestic U.S. market grew at a snail's pace, and corporate profit rates were in nearly steady decline. Domestic earnings plus interest paid on debt net of foreign dividends and tax credits declined from 12.1 percent in 1966 to 7.4 percent in 1970, a drop of almost 40 percent of the initial value. American firms with foreign operations were obviously

---

characteristic can be calculated. Therefore, these weights are also applied to the foreign investment equation. (In addition, it should be noted that the logarithm of average asset size is used. In the first set of equations, the square root of the foreign investment proxy is regressed on advertising, technology, and the log of asset size. In the second set of equations, domestic profits is regressed on the square root of foreign investment, advertising, technology, and the log of asset size. In both sets of equations, the observations are weighed by the share of that group's contribution to its industry's total assets.)

Table 7-2. *Foreign Investment*[a] *Equations, 1965–71*

Year	Number of groups	Intercept	Coefficients of independent variables[b]			Summary statistics[c]	
			Advertising	Technology	Assets	R^2	F
1965	548	−0.032 (−8.6)	0.24 (9.0)	0.17 (6.6)	0.008 (10.3)	0.56	235.0
1966	706	−0.029 (−10.2)	0.31 (14.4)	0.13 (5.4)	0.007 (12.0)	0.58	326.0
1967	640	−0.07 (−11.2)	0.67 (13.4)	0.37 (7.2)	0.023 (16.2)	0.74	603.0
1968	646	−0.10 (−12.6)	0.69 (14.3)	0.29 (6.4)	0.023 (17.2)	0.76	692.0
1969	732	−0.10 (−12.4)	0.62 (12.4)	0.35 (8.2)	0.023 (17.1)	0.76	761.0
1970	736	−0.09 (−10.7)	0.75 (12.5)	0.55 (11.8)	0.020 (14.2)	0.75	737.0
1971	570	−0.09 (−9.4)	0.89 (13.4)	0.36 (7.3)	0.026 (14.2)	0.80	735.0

Source: See table 7-1.

a. Dependent variable is the square root of the foreign investment proxy: foreign dividends plus tax credits deflated by total assets.

b. Advertising expenditures are deflated by parent's total assets. Technology is share of a group's or an industry's scientists and engineers employed in 1970 (held constant within an industry and from year to year). Assets are the log of total group assets, using firm average. The numbers in parentheses are t ratios.

c. R^2 not corrected for degrees of freedom.

fortunate, as the portfolio diversification motive suggests, in having a source of earnings free of the burden of domestic recession.

As table 7-3 indicates, multinational firms are twice blessed. In addition to the foreign dividends and tax credits received, the positive and statistically significant coefficient of foreign investment indicates that foreign investing raised domestic profits net of foreign dividends and tax credits. Between the mid-1960s and the early 1970s, the size of this contribution increased slightly. More spectacularly, its t statistic went from marginal values around 2.0 to highly significant values around 8.0. The contribution of domestic advertising underwent a comparable increase in statistical significance, while that of technology and firm size declined substantially and even turned negative and significant. These patterns of changing size and significance indicate that declining domestic profits had an uneven incidence. While virtually every category of firm suffered (see table 7-1) some suffered much less than others. The most fortunate, or the least cursed, were those who advertised heavily and, better yet, had substantial foreign operations. High-technology firms and large firms without foreign operations, by way of contrast, suffered the most, while similar firms with foreign operations appear to have fared no better or no worse than average. As is apparent from an examination of the underlying data, the statistical significance of foreign investment rests on differences within industries: *multinationals tend to be more profitable, even ignoring their foreign dividends and tax credits, than domestic firms in the same industry*. Although one might imagine that this reflects some other economy of firm size, the regression analysis clearly prefers the foreign-investment explanation to the firm-size explanation of these profit differentials.

To get some feeling for how big or small the contribution of foreign investing to domestic profitability can be, consider the extreme values. At one end are the thousands of small firms with no foreign dividends or tax credits. At opposite extremes are the group whose 1966 foreign dividends and tax credits averaged 7 percent of total assets and the group whose 1970 foreign receipts and credits equaled 14 percent of its total assets. The econometric estimates suggest that these groups' domestic earnings are further increased by an additional 5 percentage points and 8 percentage points, respectively.[35] Or if one takes a value of the foreign investment

35. Estimated by taking the square root of the proxy and multiplying it by the regression coefficient of the square root of the proxy in the domestic profitability equation.

Table 7-3. *Domestic Profitability Equations, 1965–71*

		Coefficients of independent variables[b]					Summary statistics[c]	
Year	Number of groups	Intercept[a]	Foreign investment	Advertising	Technology	Assets	R^2	F
1965	548	0.08 (10.7)	0.20 (2.3)	0.42 (6.9)	0.25 (4.3)	0.001 (0.3)	0.77	464.0
1966	706	0.10 (13.6)	0.22 (2.4)	0.39 (6.4)	0.39 (6.6)	−0.003 (−1.5)	0.76	556.0
1967	640	0.11 (15.1)	0.22 (5.4)	0.44 (7.8)	0.20 (3.8)	−0.009 (−5.1)	0.75	476.0
1968	646	0.13 (13.3)	0.22 (4.7)	0.53 (8.2)	0.21 (4.0)	−0.010 (−5.6)	0.74	466.0
1969	732	0.11 (12.8)	0.31 (8.3)	0.52 (9.3)	0.08 (1.6)	−0.010 (−6.1)	0.74	510.0
1970	736	0.07 (8.9)	0.26 (8.1)	0.81 (14.3)	−0.05 (−1.2)	−0.006 (−4.0)	0.71	446.0
1971	570	0.09 (11.0)	0.28 (8.6)	0.65 (10.8)	−0.09 (−2.1)	−0.009 (−5.5)	0.77	468.0

Source: See table 7-1.
a. Domestic profitability: domestic net return deflated by parents' assets. The numbers in parentheses are t ratios.
b. For explanation of variables, see notes a and b, table 7-2.
c. R^2 not corrected for degrees of freedom.

proxy equal to 2.2 percent (the mean value for the firms designated multinational) the apparent contribution of their foreign operations to their domestic net returns is approximately 3 percentage points, almost a third of the total. Although only a fraction of American corporations have substantial foreign operations (and are, thus, able to benefit from spreading joint costs, and so on, across national boundaries), our results indicate that the benefits to these few may, nonetheless, be substantial.

Tables 7-2 and 7-3 also point up significant differences among the elements of domestic industry structure as incentives to invest abroad and as barriers to new competition. Advertising alone is consistently large and statistically significant in the two roles. The employment of scientists and engineers, which characterizes firms with substantial foreign dividends and tax credits, deteriorates substantially in its role as a barrier to entry. Firm size, which makes a clear-cut distinction between multinationals and domestics within the typical industry, seems to detract only from domestic net profits.

Summary

This section raises the question of the impact of American investments abroad on the investing firm's U.S. market power. Although market power is an elusive concept, industrial organization analysis seems to offer the best context in which to try to measure it and to assess its relation to foreign direct investment. Foreign investment offers established multinational firms substantial opportunities for backward integration to cheap labor and raw materials and forward integration to new markets, for spreading costs (R&D, head-office, and others) across a larger sales base, for portfolio diversification across national boundaries with its attendant opportunities for raising returns and reducing risks, and, perhaps, for avoiding U.S. taxes. Foreign investing is also subject to the high fixed costs, considerable uncertainty, and long lag between investment and return characteristic of barriers to new competition.

Using simple averages, cross-tabulations, and multivariate regression equations, we find a clear, positive, and consistently significant relation between firms' foreign investment positions and their domestic profits, net of foreign returns. This relation persists even when we control statistically for the extraneous influences of advertising, technology, and firm size. If anything, the relation grew stronger over the 1965–71 interval. Hence we conclude that foreign direct investment by U.S.-based multinational enterprises adds significantly to their power in the domestic markets of the United States.

U.S. Antitrust Policy and American Business Abroad

As both the review of the literature and our own empirical research show, domestic market power in the United States and direct investments abroad go hand in hand. They are inextricably linked through their common parents, the elements of domestic industry structure; through the ability of foreign investment itself to impede new entry into domestic product markets; and through the propensity of oligopolists to turn to foreign markets for further growth and profits. In trying to mitigate domestic market power, the U.S. government should thus pay close attention to foreign direct investment by U.S.-based firms.

In doing so, it can turn to several policy tools: taxation, direct regulation, antitrust, and so on. In singling out antitrust policy, we do not deny the relevance (and, in selected cases, the critical importance) of other policies for checking domestic market distortions. Given the need to assign particular policy instruments to particular policy objectives, however, it is natural to devote antitrust policy to the broad objective of maintaining competition. This section explores the success of U.S. antitrust laws in dealing with anticompetitive behavior rooted in foreign direct investment. Should antitrust policy be modified in any significant way to cope with foreign investment problems? Is an assist from other policies necessary?

Before answering these questions, current antitrust policy must be assessed. While one need not be an antitrust attorney to appreciate the issues, familiarity with the statutes and leading cases is essential. Accordingly, this section begins with a general review of existing U.S. policy, but particularly as applied to foreign direct investment. Proposals for reforming international antitrust policies are presented and our own conclusions given.

Domestic Antitrust Policy[36]

Because the case law of U.S. antitrust policy as applied to the foreign operations of U.S. business is very thin in places, much of what is now

36. Discussion of legal precedents draws on Scherer's excellent text, *Industrial Market Structure and Economic Performance,* chaps. 18–21.

deemed illegal in an international setting depends upon domestic precedents. Domestic policy is based both on common law and on five U.S. statutes: the Sherman Act of 1890, the Clayton and the Federal Trade Commission Acts of 1914, the Robinson-Patman Act of 1936, and the Celler-Kefauver Act of 1950. These acts separately or together prohibit: (a) contracts, combinations, and conspiracies in restraint of trade; (b) monopolization, attempts to monopolize, and conspiracies to monopolize trade or commerce within the United States or between the United States and foreign countries; (c) price discrimination that substantially lessens competition or that tends to create a monopoly; (d) tying clauses and exclusive-dealing agreements that adversely affect competition;[37] (e) mergers lessening competition substantially; and (f) interlocking directorates among competing firms.

Price-Fixing

To understand the real nature of U.S. antitrust policy, one must look beyond the language of the statutes to the cases. In the area of price-fixing and related attempts to limit production and share markets, antitrust authorities have enjoyed their greatest successes. In a series of decisions culminating in *United States* v. *Socony-Vacuum Oil Co. et al.,*[38] the courts decided that price-fixing and similar conspiracies are illegal per se; that is, the prosecutor or civil plaintiff need only prove the existence of such an agreement for the consequent harmful effects to be presumed. Included under per se violations are not only price-fixing agreements but also agreements to restrict output, to assign areas or specific customers to individual sellers, to adhere to standard pricing formulas, and to punish competitors who do not abide by the norms.

The only important exception to these per se rules derives from the rights of a patent holder to impose price, output, and market restrictions on a valid patent license. Normally, a patent licensor has the right to grant exclusive territories, set prices and quality standards, and limit production to enhance the commercial value of the patent. But even these exemptions are far from absolute. Patent licenses may not be the pretext for otherwise illegal restraints of trade. The hard question, which must be

37. A tying clause requires that a customer who buys a product from a supplier (a computer, for example) buys a second product from the same supplier (punch cards, for example). An exclusive-dealing agreement requires a dealer (of automobiles, for example) to handle no competing products.

38. 310 U.S. 150, 218–221 (1940).

answered on a case-by-case basis, is whether particular restraints represents a legitimate extension of the basic rights conferred by the patent or whether illegitimate restraints on trade are built around a patent license or group of licenses. In legal jargon, this is the ancillary doctrine. A patent license may also violate antitrust laws when it is part of a cross-licensing arrangement, where all other parties are excluded from participation. Such agreements may constitute a conspiracy to monopolize commerce by the cross-licensing parties. Patent rights confer a partial, not an absolute, exemption from antitrust prosecution.

Monopolization

Price-fixing violations are considerably easier to detect, prosecute, and prevent than monopolization, largely because the first falls under the per se rule while the latter is subject to the "rule of reason." In two early cases, the Supreme Court ruled that monopolization consists of two elements, the actual acquisition of a monopoly position and the intent to acquire that position and exclude rivals.[39] Each of these elements presents a formidable burden of proof. One must anguish over how large a market share constitutes a monopoly position and, more important, how narrowly or broadly "market" should be defined. In actual practice both the product range (high octane gasoline? gasoline? refined petroleum products? energy sources?) and the geographical boundaries (Kirkland Street? Cambridge? Greater Boston? Massachusetts? the Northeastern States? continental United States?) of "the" market must be delimited. Although the definition of the market depends on the ease with which buyers and sellers can substitute other products or buy in other areas, actual definitions are inherently arbitrary.

Even more difficult questions arise in proving intent, the second element of monopolization. While no court demands direct evidence on the motivation of the accused, they are very cautious about inferring intent from behavior (which is no easy task, in any event). In Standard Oil's case, intent to monopolize was inferred from its acquiring 120 former rivals, securing discriminatory freight rates and rebates from the railroads, foreclosing crude oil supplies by buying up pipelines and refusing to handle competitors' shipments, conducting business espionage, and engaging in

39. *United States* v. *Standard Oil Co. of New Jersey et al.*, 173 Fed. 177 (1909) and 221 U.S. 1 (1911); and *United States* v. *American Tobacco Co.*, 221 U.S. 106 (1911).

predatory pricing. Likewise, American Tobacco excluded rivals from access to tobacco wholesalers, cornered the leaf tobacco market, bought out more than 250 rivals, and sold "fighting brands" in rivals' local markets until each rival sold its business.

Such obviously predatory behavior contrasts sharply with that of U.S. Steel in two cases that the government lost.[40] Like Standard Oil and American Tobacco, U.S. Steel gained its dominant market position by acquiring erstwhile competitors. But unlike the former two, U.S. Steel engaged in no predatory practices. Quite to the contrary, U.S. Steel actively cultivated the goodwill of its competitors. E. H. Gary, the chairman of U.S. Steel, regularly had his "rivals" over to dinner and, in setting steel prices (the dinners were free), always kept the levels high enough to allow the competitors to survive and even prosper. This obvious lack of predatory intent led to the Supreme Court's oft-quoted finding that "the law does not make mere size an offense or the existence of unexerted power an offense. It . . . requires overt acts. . . . It does not compel competition nor require all that is possible."[41]

Matters thus stood until *United States* v. *Aluminum Company of America et al.*[42] Having resolved the issue of market share against Alcoa, the court turned to the intent. Had Alcoa's market position been "thrust upon" the company, or had the company succeeded by virtue of superior "skills, foresight, or industry," Alcoa would have been absolved. The intent to monopolize was, however, inferred from Alcoa's building up bauxite reserves, electrical power supplies, and refining capacity well in advance of demand:

It was not inevitable that it should always anticipate increases in the demand for ingot and be prepared to supply them. Nothing compelled it to keep doubling and redoubling its capacity before others entered the field. It insists that it never excluded competitors; but we can think of no more effective exclusion than progressively to embrace each new opportunity as it opened, and to face every newcomer with new capacity already geared into a great organization, having the advantage of experience, trade connections and the elite of personnel.[43]

This reasoning was broadly supported in two subsequent and closely

40. *United States* v. *United States Steel Corporation et al.*, 223 Fed. 55 (1915) and 251 U.S. 417 (1920).
41. Ibid. at 451.
42. 148 F.2d 416 (1945), p. 431.
43. Ibid. at 430.

252 American Multinationals and American Interests

related decisions.[44] The A&P Tea Company was convicted of a criminal conspiracy to monopolize food retailing, even though its national share was less than 10 percent, and its share of local markets exceeded 40 percent in only a handful of relatively small cities. A&P's intent to monopolize was inferred from its refusal to buy from suppliers who did not offer preferential discounts, by threatening to manufacture its own food products when price concessions were not tendered, and by reducing prices in areas where competition was stiffest. Likewise, United Shoe Machinery refused to sell, rather than lease, certain machines, lowered prices on machines where competition was strong and raised them where patent protection was absolute, and priced machines in such a way as to create a strong incentive for customers to use the full line.[45] In these cases the intent to monopolize was inferred from the aggressive behavior of a firm gaining or maintaining a monopoly position.

As in the Alcoa and A&P cases, monopoly position may be buttressed by control over critical inputs or support services. In *United States* v. *Yellow Cab Company et al.*,[46] the Checker Cab Manufacturing Company was accused of foreclosing the taxicab market by compelling its taxicab-operating subsidiaries to buy exclusively from the parent. In *United States* v. *Columbia Steel Company et al.*,[47] the Justice Department tried to prevent U.S. Steel from acquiring a structural steel and steel plate fabricator. Although the Justice Department lost both cases for failing to show that a substantial portion of the relevant market had been foreclosed, the principle of monopolization through vertical integration was established.

Little new case law has been established in the last twenty years. Successful prosecutions have come in cases involving illegalities other than monopolization; some important suits were lost or dropped for insufficient evidence; others were settled by a consent decree.[48] Whether or not mo-

44. *United States* v. *New York Great Atlantic and Pacific Tea Company, Inc. et al.*, 67 F. Supp. 626 (1946) and 1973 F.2d 79 (1949).
45. *United States* v. *United Shoe Machinery Corporation*, 110 F. Supp. 295 (1953) and 347 U.S. 521 (1954). Compulsory leasing was objectionable because of the severe financing requirements it imposes on competitors to match the terms of the lease.
46. 332 U.S. 218 (1947).
47. 334 U.S. 495 (1948).
48. A consent decree is a negotiated compromise to which the Justice Department and the defendants agree. If accepted by the courts, it binds the future activities of the defendants but protects them from further prosecution by the government.

nopolization policy has served the country well is a hotly debated issue. Generally speaking, antitrust policy has two separate objectives: to protect small firms from unfair trade practices and to bring the fruits of competition (lower prices, better products) to consumers. While everyone wants fair competition, inefficient producers are threatened when competition becomes aggressive. Lower prices may wipe out smaller firms. The antitrust ideal is the Sisyphus myth: much effort but no lasting success for any single producer.

What is unsettling about U.S. monopolization policy is that when low prices threaten inefficient firms the courts frequently protect other producers rather than consumers. Alcoa and A&P were in some sense victims of their own success, U.S. Steel the beneficiary of its own high-price policy. The reluctance of the Justice Department to bring a case against General Motors, based on its exclusive-dealing contracts with its franchised dealers, may be based on General Motors' willingness to keep car prices high enough for smaller firms to survive.[49] A better policy, in the minds of many economists, would be to attack entry barriers directly and not worry so much about the actual number of firms in an industry or the size of their market shares. In an industry where barriers to new competition are low, even a monopolist must charge a competitive price.

In commenting on monopolization policy, we should also note its uneven incidence. Firms producing traditional, standardized products with few economies of scale are sitting ducks compared to those with technically complex products or substantial economies of scale. With standardized products, markets are easier to delimit, and predatory tactics are easier to distinguish from good business practice. Even if the evidential requirements can be met, judges are reluctant to tamper with companies whose technology they comprehend only imperfectly, or whose production enjoys substantial economies of scale. While some restraint is obviously prudent, the Justice Department in bringing cases, and the courts in deciding them, may consistently have been too conservative in avoiding difficult cases.[50]

Whether consent decrees remedy the original evil must be judged case by case. Since a consent decree negotiated before a trial begins does not constitute an admission of guilt by the defendants, it cannot be used as precedent or as prima facie evidence in subsequent litigation (such as private antitrust suits for triple damages).

49. Scherer, *Industrial Market Structure and Economic Performance*, p. 464.

50. Richard A. Posner, "A Statistical Study of Antitrust Enforcement," *Journal of Law and Economics*, vol. 13 (October 1970), pp. 365–419.

Mergers and Acquisitions

Antitrust policy toward mergers and acquisitions falls between price-fixing and monopolization in terms of its standards of evidence, burdens of proof, and so on. Mergers and acquisitions, according to the Clayton Act of 1914 as amended by the Celler-Kefauver Act of 1950, are illegal "where in any line of commerce in any section of the country, the effect of such acquisition may be substantially to lessen competition, or to tend to create a monopoly." More important, Congress in passing the Celler-Kefauver Act expressed its clear intention that the provision be rigorously enforced. The Federal Trade Commission and the Justice Department have taken Congress at its word, and the courts have cooperated in construing liberally the definitions of markets.

Here, too, one must look to the case legacy to understand the scope of the law. In 1957 the Supreme Court upheld the Justice Department's request that du Pont divest itself of its 23 percent stock interest in General Motors, on the grounds that a substantial portion of the market for synthetic fabrics and lacquers had been foreclosed to du Pont's competition.[51] In 1958 a district court blocked Bethlehem Steel's acquisition of Youngstown Sheet and Tube, even though the combined shares of the two firms were barely 20 percent of domestic consumption.[52] In 1962 the Supreme Court endorsed a lower court's decision blocking a merger of Brown Shoe Company and G. R. Kinney Company, where the two companies together had less than 5 percent of the national market in either shoe manufacturing or shoe retailing.[53] The threat to competition was found by treating each city of more than 10,000 people as a separate retail market and by regarding 8 percent of Kinney shoes supplied by Brown after the aborted merger a substantial lessening of competition. In *United States* v. *Von's Grocery Company et al.*,[54] the Supreme Court blocked a merger between two retail grocery chains, even though the two together accounted for only 7.5 percent of area retail sales. The difference in standards between monopolization and merger cases could not be more dramatic.

The success of the Federal Trade Commission and the Justice Depart-

51. *United States* v. *E. I. du Pont de Nemours and Company et al.*, 353 U.S. 586 (1957).
52. *United States* v. *Bethlehem Steel Corporation et al.*, 168 F. Supp. 576 (1958).
53. *Brown Shoe Company* v. *United States*, 370 U.S. 294 (1962).
54. 384 U.S. 270 (1966).

ment in attacking horizontal and vertical mergers is clearly revealed in the sharp decline in this type of merger in the United States over the last twenty-five years. The merger movement has not, however, been halted. Rather, it has been diverted to conglomerate and foreign acquisitions. Foreign acquisitions are discussed below; as for conglomerate mergers, the only opposition has come in cases in which the two firms had something in common, that is, where the term conglomerate was something of a misnomer. In some cases, the two firms were not direct competitors but sold in different geographical markets. In these and other cases, one or both firms were potential entrants into the other's market, and the merger might have substantially lessened potential competition.

This doctrine of potential competition has also been applied to joint ventures by independent companies. In *United States* v. *Penn-Olin Chemical Company et al.*,[55] the Justice Department sued to prevent the Pennsalt Chemicals Corporation and Olin Mathieson Corporation from forming a joint venture to produce sodium chlorate in the southeastern United States. Although the Justice Department eventually lost for failing to show that *both* companies might have entered the market, along the way the Supreme Court endorsed the principle that such a showing would have been sufficient to block the merger.

Antitrust and Foreign Investment[56]

Against this backdrop of domestic antitrust policy, the nature and extent of the policy's application to foreign investment is more easily understood. With respect to foreign commerce in general, U.S. antitrust policy has three separate objectives: (a) to eliminate unreasonable restraints on U.S. exports and imports; (b) to encourage foreign firms to enter the U.S. market; and (c) to prevent U.S. or foreign firms from restraining commerce in the United States through their foreign operations.

The most notable aspect of these objectives, as far as we are concerned, is that not one of them pertains directly to foreign investment. The foreign

55. 217 F. Supp. 110 (1963), 378 U.S. 158 (1964), 246 F. Supp. 917 (1965), and 88 S. Ct. 502 (1967).

56. This section draws on Kingman Brewster, Jr., *Antitrust and American Business Abroad* (McGraw-Hill, 1958). For current treatment see Wilbur Lindsay Fugate, *Foreign Commerce and the Antitrust Laws*, 2nd. ed. (Little, Brown, 1973).

commerce included under the Sherman Act is export and import trade but not capital services, technology, or any other intangible. This means that American subsidiaries engaged solely in the domestic commerce of a foreign country are quite free, as far as the United States is concerned, to join foreign cartels, drive foreign competitors from the industry using the most predatory of tactics, or engage in any other practice. While U.S. restraint may well be self-serving—by increasing the earnings of U.S.-based multinationals—the basis of that restraint is the desire to avoid extraterritorial application of U.S. laws. For better or worse, the presumption is that foreign governments have sole jurisdiction over their own internal commerce and can implement that jurisdiction effectively.

But the fact that antitrust policy has no direct concern with foreign investment hardly implies that such investment escapes U.S. antitrust scrutiny altogether. Foreign subsidiaries joining foreign cartels might agree to illegal restraints on the export trade of their American parents or on exports to and investments in the United States by foreign competitors, which is covered by the U.S. statutes. Likewise, two or more American firms may restrain their competitive behavior within the U.S. markets through their foreign investments (for example, through joint ventures supplying both parents with some critical natural resource). Because American-owned subsidiaries influence U.S. exports and imports in a variety of ways, and because they indirectly affect the extent of competition within domestic product markets, they come under U.S. antitrust scrutiny.

Of course, international commerce is subject to overlapping national jurisdictions. Conflicts of national laws, perhaps reflecting conflicts of national interests, are possible. An obvious case would be one in which a large American company, extracting a foreign natural resource, helped maintain a high and stable price for the natural resource. In chapter five, we note with concern a tendency for companies to collude with host-country governments to that end, thereby enhancing the likelihood of such outcomes. President Figueres of Costa Rica is said to have defended monopolization by United Fruit because it would stabilize Costa Rica's banana industry.[57]

Such conflicts may be inevitable. Were countries to refrain from regulating their foreign commerce altogether, such commerce would go en-

---

57. A. Berle in address to the American Management Association Meeting, New York, May 25, 1955; Berle's speech is quoted in Brewster, *Antitrust and American Business Abroad*, p. 42.

tirely unregulated. Were countries to regulate only their exports and not their imports, or vice versa, they would leave themselves open to foreign exploitation. Antitrust policy is not alone, of course, in creating conflicts of national laws and interest; tariffs, import and export quotas, balance-of-payments controls, foreign exchange regulations, tax laws, and other national policies raise analogous problems. What we really want to know is how frequent and severe are the conflicts of national laws stemming from U.S. antitrust policy and how well does current U.S. policy serve American interests, both in and out of conflict situations.

Price-Fixing and International Cartels

Before the Second World War, U.S. antitrust applied to foreign commerce more on paper than in practice. International cartels flourished during the 1920s and 1930s. Although U.S. antitrust policy prevented U.S. firms from openly participating in these cartels, the firms joined secretly or tacitly cooperated with them.[58] To take one of many examples: the Aluminum Company of America, which until 1945 was *the* aluminum company of America, did not join the European aluminum cartel directly but participated through its wholly owned Canadian subsidiary, Alcan. When the Justice Department saw through this transparent strategem and lodged an objection, Alcoa distributed its Alcan shares to Alcoa shareholders. Since Alcoa shares were held by the Davis and Mellon families and their foundations, Alcoa did not give up control of its subsidiary. The common control of the American and Canadian companies manifested itself in adjacent corporate offices in New York City and in the fact that the president of Alcan was the brother of the president of Alcoa. Although Alcoa did not participate directly in the cartel, it respected the commitments made by Alcan on its behalf.[59]

With the advent of the Second World War, the United States developed a critical need to free its corporations from the cartel restrictions they had so willingly accepted a few years before. An enthusiastic assistant attorney general for antitrust, Thurman Arnold, revived the Sherman Act (which became known as the "Thurman Act"). Although many cases

58. See George W. Stocking and Myron W. Watkins, *Cartels in Action: Case Studies in International Business Diplomacy* (New York: Twentieth Century Fund, 1946).
59. Ibid., pp. 255–60.

were settled quietly with consent decrees, the few fought through to the Supreme Court formed the leading precedents for international antitrust as we know it today. *United States* v. *Aluminum Company of America*[60] is a landmark in two respects. First, it clearly establishes the principle that U.S. courts can regulate conspiracies conducted outside the United States that have direct and foreseeable economic consequences inside the United States. While questions of fact (how directly did the accused participate in the conspiracy? how immediate was the restraint on U.S. commerce?) and problems of gathering evidence or effecting a remedy remain, the principle is firmly established. Second, Alcoa's monopoly of aluminum ingot production was based in part on ownership of foreign bauxite and hydroelectric sites.

United States v. *National Lead Company et al.*[61] dismissed the perennial argument that U.S. firms must be free to participate in foreign cartels to claim their share of world markets. The judge ruled:

> The second line of evidence is that American producers cannot do business successfully in a cartelized world except on cartel terms; and that, to abstain from such business, would amount to a greater restraint on trade than is involved in joining the cartel. . . . The validity of this argument has been the subject of congressional inquiry. . . . That kind of inquiry, rather than a judicial one, is appropriate to the evaluation of the merits of the proposition. For the courts it is conclusive that Congress has not yet validated such a solution to the problem. Until it does, private agreement and combination and private regulation may not substitute for legislation. Only Congress, not the courts, may grant the required immunity.[62]

---

60. 148 F.2d 416, 429 (2 Cir., 1945). It never went to the Supreme Court. The case took so long to prepare and adjudicate that, by the time it was appealed to the Supreme Court, there were not enough justices uninvolved in this and related cases to form a quorum. A special panel of three judges from the District Court of Appeals served as the court of final appeal.

61. 63 F. Supp. 513 (S.D.N.Y. 1945), aff'd, 332 U.S. 319 (1947).

62. 63 F. Supp. 513, pp. 525–526. Congress has granted immunity in only two cases: Webb-Pomerene export associations and international patent licensing agreements. The Webb-Pomerene Act, enacted in 1919, exempts from the Sherman Act "an association entered into for the sole purpose of engaging in export trade" that "is not in restraint of the export trade of any domestic competitor"; nor can it "enter into any agreement, understanding, or conspiracy, or do any act which artificially or intentionally enhances or depresses prices within the United States . . . or otherwise restrains trade therein" (40 Stat. 517). In practice, these associations have not been widely used, partly because the Federal Trade Commission and the courts exclude individually owned and jointly owned foreign subsidiaries. A Webb association, therefore, cannot follow export success with a foreign subsidiary nor regulate

In short, the per se illegality of price-fixing, market-allocating, and other "naked" restraints of trade apply to foreign commerce and not just to domestic commerce. Although Judge Rifkind ruled that only Congress could grant immunity from antitrust laws, he went on to ridicule the substance of the argument:

Judicial intervention to break up a combination in restraint of trade is not in itself a restraint of trade, although for a time the established channels of commerce may be disarranged. To prohibit adherence to conspiratorial trade restraints hampers trade in about the same way that the prohibition against the circulation of counterfeit money hampers it. *It may prevent the consummation of a particular transaction but in the long run it frees business from private regimentation and secures it against those who would trammel it.*[63]

Monopolization, Mergers, and Foreign Investment

Monopolization of a local market in a foreign country is perfectly legal under U.S. antitrust laws. Whether the foreign government will tolerate the monopolization is, of course, another matter. In theory, a U.S. firm can be charged with monopolizing U.S. export or import commerce in some commodity, but as a practical matter, such power would probably be matched by or based on similar power in domestic commerce.

In *United States* v. *Aluminum Company of America* the Justice Department put primary emphasis on Alcoa's monopoly of domestic ingot production rather than on its exports or imports of bauxite, alumina, or aluminum. Likewise, the Federal Trade Commission, in a complaint that Xerox monopolized the U.S. market for dry copiers, charged that Xerox had conspired with Rank-Xerox (jointly owned by Xerox and the Rank Organisation, a British concern) to limit Xerox's export markets. But the consent decree the Federal Trade Commission negotiated with Xerox sought only to modify Xerox's domestic business practices, not its foreign

---

the subsidiaries of members. Since firms view foreign investing as a natural development of exporting, they may be discouraged from exporting. Indeed, Webb-Pomerene, by legitimizing export controls for raw materials such as sulphur and phosphate rock, make it difficult for the United States to challenge (especially in the courts) export controls of others, such as OPEC. The right of the patent holder to issue a foreign license to work the patent depends, as in domestic cases, on the ancillary doctrine—whether it is a pretext for an otherwise illegal restraint of trade or is necessary to protect the legitimate interests of the licensor or licensee.

63. 63 F. Supp. 513, 531 (italics added).

operations.[64] This emphasis on the domestic aspects of monopolization reflects both a greater concern for domestic market conditions and the greater ease in gathering information, obtaining expert testimony, and otherwise prosecuting domestically based cases. But given the close link between monopolies in domestic and foreign commerce, an attack on the former may be tantamount to an attack on the latter.

The tendency of monopolization of domestic and foreign commerce to be closely linked and the preference of the Justice Department and the Federal Trade Commission to tackle the domestic violations mean, of course, that all the liabilities of domestic monopolization policy outlined above carry over to foreign monopolization. A firm conspiring with other U.S. or foreign rivals to raise prices and restrict foreign commerce would be liable to prosecution, as would one aggressively undercutting competitors' prices. But if the global monopoly is built up gradually without the aid of cartels, cross-licensing, mergers, or acquisitions, the antitrust authorities would probably not object. A firm buying out a foreign rival and then eliminating trade between the two countries may be guilty of an antitrust violation, but one forming its own subsidiary and then eliminating its own trade is not. Such anomalies are inherent in the current U.S. approach to monopolization.

Whereas the Sherman Act applies to domestic and foreign commerce, the Clayton and Celler-Kefauver Acts, which deal explicitly with mergers, acquisitions, and joint ventures, apply only to the lessening of competition "in any section of the country." This limitation does not mean, however, that the acquisition of a foreign firm by an American investor, a joint venture by two American investors, or a joint venture by an American and a foreign firm, are outside the reach of U.S. antitrust law. Part of the Justice Department's case in *United States* v. *Imperial Chemical Industries, Ltd.*,[65] was that a Canadian subsidiary, jointly owned by ICI and du Pont unreasonably restricted du Pont's exports to Canada. And when ICI and du Pont were convicted of conspiracy to monopolize, the court ordered that their joint venture be dissolved.

---

64. U.S. Federal Trade Commission, "FTC Proposed Complaint Alleges Xerox Monopolized Office Copier Industry," *Federal Trade Commission News* (December 12, 1972). The consent decree was accepted by the Federal Trade Commission in 1975. See *Trade Reg. Rep.*, no. 188 (August 4, 1975).

65. 100 F. Supp. 504, 559 (1951).

Although the Clayton and Celler-Kefauver Acts prohibit acquisitions and mergers only if they limit domestic competition, foreign acquisitions may still be subject to challenge under the doctrine of potential competition in the United States. In *United States* v. *Joseph Schlitz Brewing Company et al.*,[66] Schlitz's proposed acquisition of John Labatt, Ltd., a Canadian brewer, was challenged on the grounds that a small California brewer owned by Labatt was a competitor of Schlitz and that Labatt was a potential entrant on a larger scale into the U.S. market. As a general rule, the only foreign acquisitions likely to encounter antitrust challenges are those in which leading American producers want to acquire credible foreign entrants into the U.S. industry.

Problems of Jurisdiction and Remedy

As the Alcoa case establishes, a U.S. investor cannot escape antitrust scrutiny by traveling abroad or by working through foreign subsidiaries. The clear jurisdiction of U.S. courts over the parent firms greatly facilitates the collection of documents and information necessary for antitrust proceedings. Although American courts find it difficult and often impossible to break up foreign cartels that restrain U.S. import trade, it is difficult for U.S. firms to join those cartels without explicit or implicit antitrust immunity. The failure of the pervasive interwar cartels to reappear after the Second World War is due in no small part to the unilateral opposition of U.S. antitrust policy.

In antitrust cases, determination of guilt or innocence is prior to and independent of the fashioning of a remedy. Once a firm is convicted of an antitrust violation, the courts have wide discretion in imposing cease-and-desist orders, fines, compulsory patent licensing, or divestiture of assets. If the offense has a substantial foreign component, the U.S. courts may well require a foreign remedy. And this may create problems.

United States v. *Imperial Chemical Industries, Ltd.*, once again, is a good case in point.[67] Having found du Pont and ICI guilty of monopolizing domestic and foreign commerce in certain chemicals through their extensive cross-licensing agreement, the U.S. judge wished to order compul-

---

66. 253 F. Supp. 129 (1966) and 385 U.S. 37 (1966).
67. This summary is based on Fugate, *Foreign Commerce and the Antitrust Laws*, pp. 129–34.

sory licensing of the misused patents. In deference to ICI's foreignness, he did not order compulsory licensing of its foreign patents, but he did order such licensing for ICI's American patents and for du Pont's domestic and foreign patents. The problem arose with du Pont's British patents, for du Pont had given an exclusive license to ICI, and ICI in turn had passed on these rights to a subsidiary, British Nylon Spinners, in which ICI held a 51 percent stock interest. British Nylon Spinners sued in British courts to prevent its parent, ICI, from licensing other British manufacturers, as ordered by the American judge. In short, the American antitrust decree was in conflict with the terms of a British contract between ICI and its subsidiary, British Nylon Spinners.

In ordering compulsory licensing of du Pont's foreign patents, the American judge noted that some of the patents had been passed from ICI to British Nylon Spinners, its own affiliate, *after* the Justice Department began proceedings. The action thus appeared to be an effort to evade prosecution. The British judge, who ruled in favor of British Nylon Spinners and against the American judge, did so not because the American judge had overreached his jurisdiction, but because he, the British judge, found that British Nylon Spinners was not a party to nor had any knowledge of the illegal conspiracy between du Pont and ICI. In short, the British judge appeared willing to accept the principle on which the American judge was acting but not the facts. Given that some of the patents were transferred after the cross-licensing arrangements were challenged and that ICI held a majority interest in British Nylon Spinners, the finding that British Nylon Spinners had no knowledge of the conspiracy is mysterious, to say the least. The American judge, having tried and failed to obtain British support, relieved du Pont of its obligation to license all applicants who wanted to use its American patents.

Because of the lack of any similar cases over the last twenty years, the ICI case is often cited as an example of the difficulties for even the largest country in applying its antitrust laws to international business. But the fundamental point is that the conspiracy between du Pont and ICI was undone. Although both corporations were free in the end to exploit their patents unilaterally, the monopolistic synergy of cross-licensing was lost. So while the international dimensions of the case forced the court to abandon its preferred remedy, an effective solution to the ultimate problem was nonetheless found.

An Evaluation and Policy Conclusions

Several economists and political scientists argue that U.S. antitrust policy, like other national policies pursued unilaterally in a world of multinational firms, is becoming impotent.[68] It is true that the Justice Department can do little or nothing about the Organization of Petroleum Exporting Countries or South African controls over gold and diamond exports. Although the effect on U.S. foreign commerce may be profound, U.S. jurisdiction is nominal at best, as long as the foreigners keep their operations outside the United States.

But grouping the difficulties of applying U.S. antitrust laws to American foreign investors, with those of foreign commerce generally, is inappropriate. American multinational firms are sitting ducks. These firms can make life more difficult for the antitrust authorities by moving unlawful activities offshore, but the substantial domestic operations of the parent firm make international flight impossible should the Justice Department or the Federal Trade Commission discover what transpired. A small country whose natural resources or domestic market are limited cannot be so sanguine about its jurisdiction over a multinational firm, but the United States has comparatively little cause for concern.

Over the last ten years, there has been a flurry of interest in multilateral approaches to international antitrust problems. Goldberg and Kindleberger urge that the provisions of the abortive International Trade Organization pertaining to restrictive trade practices be resuscitated in the form of a General Agreement on International Corporations.[69] More recently, the United Nations has begun work on an international antitrust agreement.[70] At least three motivations are involved: some of the proponents of an international antitrust code hope that it could provide more

68. See, for example, George W. Ball, "Cosmocorp: The Importance of Being Stateless," *Columbia Journal of World Business*, vol. 2 (November–December 1967), pp. 25–30; Paul M. Goldberg and Charles P. Kindleberger, "Toward a GATT for Investment: A Proposal for Supervision of the International Corporation," *Law and Policy in International Business*, vol. 2 (Summer 1970), pp. 295–325; and Vernon, "Competition Policy Toward Multinational Corporations," p. 280.

69. Goldberg and Kindleberger, "Toward a GATT for Investment."

70. United Nations Economic and Social Council, "The Impact of Multinational Corporations on the Development Process and International Relations," E/5500/Add. 1 (June 1974; processed).

effective power against the alleged abuses of multinationals; some see it as reducing the intergovernmental friction that arises when the antitrust authorities of a single nation attack corporate activities occurring within another country; and some want to protect the firms against the inconsistencies that inevitably occur as a result of different national antitrust philosophies, laws, and practices.

Agreement among all countries on a meaningful treaty is difficult to envision now, however, because restrictive trade practices sufficiently serve national economic interests to offset the costs, particularly in the developing countries. Countries that individually or collectively control a significant proportion of world natural resources may benefit from restricting exports and raising prices, just as capital-exporting countries may benefit from allowing their multinational firms to monopolize local product markets. What all nations want, of course, is for others to eliminate restrictive practices, unilaterally. The world as a whole might be a better place to live if all trade restrictions were eliminated, but certain key countries (Saudi Arabia, Kuwait, South Africa, for example) could lose substantially. And without their participation many other countries, including the United States, have less incentive to act.

International cooperation between the United States and other developed countries, either bilaterally or through the Organisation for Economic Co-operation and Development, appears much more feasible. Both the European Economic Community (EEC) collectively and some of its members individually (particularly West Germany), seem disillusioned with industrial policies, which, stripped to their essence, promote monopoly in the hope of making domestic firms more competitive in world markets. The EEC, in fact, has developed an approach to antitrust which is tougher than that of many of its individual member states and may be tougher than that of the United States.[71] And the United States recently signed a formal agreement with Germany on antitrust consultation and exchanges of data and is discussing similar arrangements with several other countries. The United States benefits from such exchanges in three ways: it can increasingly draw on foreign information and expertise in bringing future antitrust cases itself; it can more easily mute foreign opposition (and problems for the multinationals) to its own antitrust efforts

71. Sigmund Timberg, "An International Antitrust Convention: A Proposal to Harmonize Conflicting National Policies Towards the Multinational Corporation," *Journal of International Law and Economics,* vol. 8 (December 1973), pp. 157–84.

whenever there is a potential jurisdiction clash; and, most important, it can encourage other countries to adopt stronger antitrust policies. Hence the growing international coordination of national antitrust policies should proceed as rapidly as possible.

As noted above, the Justice Department and the Federal Trade Commission have effective jurisdiction over U.S.-based multinational corporations. Concern for the foreign investment activities of these firms should be focused on the inadequacies of the monopolization provisions of the Sherman Act and on possibilities for reform. While price-fixing, market-sharing, cross-licensing, mergers, and joint ventures all play roles in the domestic and international development of our multinational firms, even without such practices multinational firms would still exercise market power, both domestically and internationally. The origins of the multinationals' power are their economies of scale in production, in raising capital, in distribution, in advertising and in research and development as well as the legal protection afforded them as holders of patents, copyrights, trademarks, trade secrets, and mineral rights. And, except for the monopolization provisions of the Sherman Act, that power is beyond the reach of U.S. antitrust policy.

Market power based on underlying economies of size and technological or managerial leadership, rather than on predatory tactics, presents real difficulties for antitrust policy. First is the economic dilemma: monopoly or oligopoly may be the price of efficiency and innovation. In the Alcoa case, the court was unwilling to split up Alcoa for fear of losing substantial economies of scale in production and in research and development. And even when Kaiser and Reynolds were created (by forbidding Alcoa to bid on aluminum smelters built by the government during the Second World War), Alcoa remained the dominant firm in a highly concentrated industry. Likewise, the court was unwilling to divide United Shoe Machinery into separate units, for the company's production was concentrated in a single plant. Here, too, the remedial actions taken had little apparent impact on the industry. While the size of leading U.S. firms may be several times the minimum mandated by economic efficiency, finding ways of dividing a coherent firm into viable parts is no easy task. It is like splitting a diamond; an artful cleavage enhances the value, a clumsy one leaves a pile of chips and dust.

As if this potential conflict between more competition and greater efficiency were not enough, U.S. monopolization policy has also been saddled by a legalistic emphasis on the intent of the defendant, rather than on the economic costs or benefits of the behavior. A conspiracy between an American corporation and its overseas rivals to fix prices and divide markets is illegal per se, but a comparable conspiracy between a parent firm and its overseas affiliates is not. Although a parent and a subsidiary are separate legal entities and, thus, capable of conspiring, agreements among related companies (dubbed bathtub conspiracies) are perfectly legal. The cross-licensing and joint-venture agreement between du Pont and ICI struck down by the court would probably never have been challenged had du Pont been the American subsidiary of ICI, or ICI the British subsidiary of du Pont.[72] Schlitz's acquisition of Labatt was challenged; but General Motors' assimilation of Adam Opel, A. G., accomplished before the Celler-Kefauver Act was passed and the doctrine of potential competition developed, goes unopposed. If the ultimate objective of antitrust policy is to promote competition and/or economic efficiency, rather than to punish criminal wrongdoing (as the sparing use of the criminal provisions of the Sherman Act suggests), monopolists should be judged not by the intent but by the consequences of their behavior.

The ultimate objective of antitrust policy is to promote competition among existing producers and encourage new competition from outside. A major source of new competition in the United States today comes from imports from, and investments by, foreign producers.[73] Our own statistical analysis indicates that the differential between the high returns in technologically advanced industries and the earnings of others disappeared between 1965 and 1970, which might well be explained by the faster-than-average growth of imports in those sectors (see chapter three). As the

72. Joel Davidow, formerly chief of the Foreign Commerce Section of the Antitrust Division of the Department of Justice, reported that "No joint venture among Americans to sell abroad to foreigners has been challenged under the antitrust laws in the last twenty-five years," "Extraterritorial Application of U.S. Antitrust Law in a Changing World," paper prepared for delivery at symposium on Private Investments Abroad, Southwestern Legal Foundation International and Comparative Law Center (June 15, 1976; processed), p. 5.

73. For an analysis of why external forces are more likely to stimulate competition than internal forces, see Herbert Giersch, "Freer Trade for Higher Employment and Price Level Stability," in C. Fred Bergsten, ed., *Toward a New World Trade Policy: The Maidenhead Papers* (Lexington Books, 1975), pp. 49–69. Harry G. Johnson, "The Probable Effect of Freer Trade on Individual Countries," in ibid., p. 36, concludes that "commercial policy liberalization probably dominates any other policy change one could seriously consider" for providing additional output.

U.S. dollar depreciated in value during the 1970s, foreign producers, finding their exports priced out of the U.S. market, expanded U.S. production at a record rate.

International considerations also come to the fore when one searches for ways to make a domestic industry more competitive without making it less efficient. The avoidance of import quotas on steel products may generate as much competition as divestiture of U.S. Steel, but without a deleterious impact on economic efficiency; indeed, a substantial gain would probably result. Likewise, were the Big Three automotive producers prohibited from requiring their franchised dealers to handle their automobiles exclusively, a further competitive surge might come not just from American Motors and would-be domestic producers, but also from those British, French, and Italian manufacturers without substantial dealer networks. The recent burst of Japanese and European direct investment in the United States is only a preliminary indication of the potential of this source of new competition for American firms in their domestic markets. The Justice Department and the Federal Trade Commission, in refusing to harass foreign entrants and thereby protect established U.S. firms, probably do as much to foster competition as they achieve under any of their affirmative programs.[74]

In trying to promote effective new competition from foreign firms, the antitrust authorities should not overlook American-owned subsidiaries. Consider the following scenario. After years of litigation and appeal, the Justice Department succeeds in showing that IBM monopolizes the U.S. market for digital computers. The time has come for deciding what to do about IBM's monopoly position. A major obstacle to splitting up IBM into smaller pieces may be that IBM is a highly integrated company; it has no natural cleavages. (This, of course, is precisely what happened in *United States* v. *United Shoe Company*.) But what about IBM Europe? Under European pressure, and perhaps with economic logic, IBM Europe has become a highly integrated company. It has its own manufacturing plants for all but the largest computers, its own research programs, its own management, and so on. Were the ownership ties between parent and subsidiary severed and no contractual obligations (for example, patent license

---

74. In addition, antitrust rejection of domestic mergers allows more involvement in the U.S. market by foreign-based multinationals. Recent cases include the takeover of Sinclair by British Petroleum after it was denied to ARCO and the takeover of First Western Financial by Lloyd's Bank, which was denied to Wells Fargo.

restrictions) put in their stead, IBM Europe would be a credible new entrant for the U.S. market. In short, without having to build new factories, train new managers, create new legal entities, and so on, a new and credible entrant into the U.S. market would be born. IBM Europe might not be able to compete immediately with its erstwhile parent at the very frontiers of computer technology, but the infusion of a relatively small number of added personnel (attracted perhaps from European computer firms without such a strong foundation or perhaps from the parent IBM) could well enable it to do so in a relatively short period of time.

Other possible cases include the major Canadian and European subsidiaries of the Big Three automotive manufacturers, the leading farm equipment manufacturers, and the chemical processors. Economies of scale in existing and contemplated R&D programs could be protected by allowing the erstwhile affiliates to cross-license each other, but without any market restrictions written into the licenses. Considerable care would have to be given, of course, to eliminating any artificial restrictions on the affiliates' ability to enter each others' home market. Interlocking directorates and common ownership of significant blocks of shares would have to be explicitly forbidden.

This proposal is not unprecedented. Alcoa, in its attempt to circumvent the antitrust restrictions on U.S. participation in foreign cartels, voluntarily distributed its shares in its Canadian subsidiary to its shareholders. Because Alcoa shares were so closely held by the Mellon and Davis families, however, Alcoa and Alcan remained under unified leadership. As part of the remedy to Alcoa's monopoly of the U.S. aluminum market, its shareholders were ordered to divest themselves of their shares in either Alcoa or Alcan.[75] In two steps, the first voluntary and the second not, Alcoa's Canadian subsidiary became its competitor in world aluminum markets.

Considerations beyond U.S. antitrust objectives are involved in any decision to require such divestiture of existing foreign affiliates. National security factors could be involved in cases regarding high-technology companies, such as IBM. The international financial ramifications would depend on the nature of the required divestiture; for example, a parent corporation whose shares were widely owned might cede effective control of an erstwhile subsidiary with minimal impact on the balance of payments

75. *United States* v. *Aluminum Company of America et al.*, 91 F.Supp.333 (S.D.N.Y. 1950).

by distributing its shares in the subsidiary to its own shareholders. Foreign policy considerations might also come into play. Would France really prefer an independent IBM Europe to a subsidiary linked directly to Armonk? Would West Germany really prefer a European company centered in France to an American-owned subsidiary? These issues could become stumbling blocks to divestiture of U.S.-owned subsidiaries.

The question often arises of whether a vigorous antitrust policy really benefits the United States. Schumpeter's famous hypothesis, that monopoly or oligopoly are prerequisites for technological innovation, is often linked to the argument that strong technology and marketing know-how are the primary sources of U.S. competitiveness in world markets.[76] Economists have examined Schumpeter's hypothesis in much depth, however, and the general consensus is that a limited amount of monopoly power may be necessary to induce firms to undertake substantial R&D programs but that high levels of concentration are unnecessary and, perhaps, counterproductive.[77] Among the formidable competitors in world markets are the industrial Davids, not just the Goliaths. Antitrust policy, including limitations on foreign direct investment, may even promote technological effort.[78]

Finally, one cannot ignore the possibility that a tough U.S. antitrust policy, in its pursuit of more domestic competition objectives, could undermine the strength of U.S. firms in world markets. American multinationals do enjoy some degree of monopoly power in certain lines of international trade and investment, and the United States may derive some national benefits from the exercise of that power. For this reason, and some of the others just cited, the national costs and benefits of antitrust decrees should clearly be judged on a case-by-case basis.

On balance, however, we believe that a strong antitrust policy is consistent with the national welfare of the United States and that such a policy will increasingly require the antitrust authorities to look explicitly at the foreign activities of American firms, both as potential sources of excess

76. Joseph Schumpeter, *Capitalism, Socialism and Democracy*, 3rd ed. (Harper and Row, 1950), chap. 7.

77. Scherer, *Industrial Market Structure and Economic Performance*, chap. 17.

78. Even where the size and productivity of the R&D program depend on spreading its costs and benefits across a global sales base, joint ventures and cross-licensing arrangements are an alternative to foreign direct investment. Such arrangements, especially when there are no territorial restrictions, may be more consistent with American interests.

market power and as potential remedies in demonstrated monopoly situations. Why? First, by following a strong policy domestically and internationally and encouraging others to follow suit, the United States may gain much more than it could by setting the opposite example. It has taken a long time and there have been many setbacks, but recent developments in the OECD, the Commission of the EEC, West Germany, and elsewhere, suggest that other countries are growing disillusioned with national policies that promote monopoly in the hope of reaping competitive advantages in world markets. This skepticism should be encouraged, for it reinforces support for U.S. antitrust policy and helps promote true competition in world markets.[79] In addition, this growing convergence of national attitudes toward antitrust policy has virtually eliminated concern in other countries over the extraterritorial application of U.S. antitrust law, which, triggered by the activities of multinational enterprises, was once a frequent source of intergovernmental conflict.

But even if other countries are unwilling or slow to emulate such an approach, our analysis earlier in this chapter suggests that the benefits to the United States of allowing U.S. firms to obtain and preserve excessive market power abroad must be weighed against the costs to American consumers of the activity. Cooperation and collusion built up in one national arena have a way of spilling over quickly into others. It is difficult, and probably impossible, to design an antitrust policy that maximizes the multinationals' ability to exploit foreign markets and minimizes their ability to do the same to American consumers. Thus we firmly reject proposals to relax the U.S. antitrust laws—allegedly to improve the international competitiveness of American firms—on the grounds that it is impossible to segment the foreign and domestic markets.

In addition, a relaxed antitrust policy could have adverse effects on the distribution of income both between the United States and other countries and within the United States. Unlike a domestic monopoly, whose profits may be taxed by the federal and state governments or shared with labor through higher wages, a foreign subsidiary's monopoly brings few tax benefits. (The United States currently collects virtually no taxes on U.S.

79. Davidow, "Extraterritorial Application of U.S. Antitrust Law in a Changing World," p. 3, concludes that "U.S. antitrust laws have been one of our most successful exports," noting that twenty-one of the twenty-nine OECD countries have "begun to develop significant antitrust programs" and even that "a number of developing nations have turned to American antitrust principles as a model for their laws."

investment abroad, and our policy proposals, while they seek to redress the balance to some extent, stop well short of taxing foreign investment at the same rate as domestic investment.) Thus the benefits of U.S. monopoly power in foreign markets accrue largely to the multinationals and their shareholders and to the governments (and perhaps the workers) of foreign countries, while the cost of domestic monopoly is borne by the U.S. population as a whole.

We conclude, then, that the largest problems faced by the United States in limiting anticompetitive behavior affecting her foreign and domestic commerce involve primarily foreign-based firms and cartels rather than American multinationals. In terms of gaining effective jurisdiction, gathering evidence, and implementing remedies, U.S. multinationals are, comparatively speaking, easy prey for U.S. antitrust authorities.

The major antitrust problem involving U.S. multinationals lies with U.S. monopolization policy. The traditional approach emphasizes the intent of the monopolist, and thereby tends to protect other producers rather than consumers. While the legalistic emphasis on intent can be legislated away (or even judicially interpreted away), a potential trade-off between monopoly and efficiency may remain. In looking for an escape from this dilemma, antitrust authorities should be looking more and more to foreign sources, including the subsidiaries of American multinationals, for effective competition. And while the courts must continue to be careful not to sacrifice substantial economies in ordering divestiture, costs and benefits can and should be carefully weighted on a case-by-case basis. From a purely nationalistic perspective, an antitrust policy that seeks to check the oligopoly power of U.S.-based firms in world markets could be extremely beneficial to the United States.

Beyond such changes in its own national policy, the United States should intensify its efforts to develop international antitrust agreements. The growing convergence of views on the subject among at least the major industrialized countries suggests that such an effort might well be successful. Indeed, the guidelines for multinational enterprises adopted by the OECD in June 1976 reveal that consensus to an impressive degree and provide useful first steps toward a more far-reaching agreement.[80]

80. OECD, news release A (76) 20 (June 21, 1976; processed), pp. 9–10.

CHAPTER EIGHT

The Systemic Effects of
Multinational Enterprises

MULTINATIONAL ENTERPRISES have become such a major factor in the world economy that they can importantly affect the functioning of the entire international economic order: the monetary system, the trading system, the international distribution of income (including the distribution between industrialized and developing countries), and perhaps even world growth and price stability. The United States has a major stake in the effective functioning of all these components of the international economic order, because of both its deep external economic involvement and the impact of international economics on world political relations. Hence, U.S. national interests are importantly affected by the impact of multinational enterprises on the international economic system, and any analysis of U.S. interests must include an appraisal of those effects. These systemic effects of multinational enterprises are conceptually distinct from their direct effects on U.S. trade flows and the U.S. balance of payments, although the two are of course closely related.[1]

---

1. The discussion on monetary systemic effects draws on C. Fred Bergsten, *The Dilemmas of the Dollar: The Economics and Politics of United States International Monetary Policy* (New York University Press for the Council on Foreign Relations, 1975). For an analysis of the political ramifications see C. Fred Bergsten and Lawrence B. Krause (eds.), *World Politics and International Economics* (Brookings Institution, 1975), section 1.

Multinational Enterprises and the International Monetary System

The questions of traditional focus concerning the international monetary role of multinational enterprises are whether their financial capabilities enable them to alter decisively the pattern of exchange rates among currencies and whether they in fact bring about changes in that pattern through speculation in the foreign exchange markets.[2] A closely related question is whether the liquid cash flows of multinational enterprises across national borders have become so big that national monetary policies have been rendered impotent. Of particular concern in the United States has been the charge that U.S.-based multinational enterprises played a major role in the devaluations of the dollar in 1971 and 1973.

The primary question from the standpoint of U.S. national interests is whether the dollar devaluations, the entire array of exchange-rate changes in recent years, and the widespread adoption of more flexible exchange rates are desirable. The U.S. government obviously thinks so, and there is no significant domestic opinion to the contrary. The realignment of late 1971 was wholly triggered by the economic policy initiatives of the United States.[3] The realignment of early 1973 was clearly pushed by the United States. And the United States has firmly resisted any restoration of convertibility for the dollar into U.S. reserve assets, strongly preferring the regime of managed flexibility of exchange rates that has evolved instead.

To be sure, the two devaluations plus the further depreciation in mid-

2. Richard J. Barnet and Ronald E. Müller, *Global Reach: The Power of the Multinational Corporations* (Simon and Schuster, 1974), claim that "global corporations and global banks now dominate the international flow of money" (p. 283). Their support for the contention refers primarily to banks, however, and they offer no explanation why international capital flows are any larger as a result of the multinationalization of individual banks.

3. There remains a view that the U.S. actions of 1971, particularly the cessation of convertibility of the dollar into U.S. reserve assets, were forced by foreign demands for gold. However, there is no evidence of escalation of such demands. The policy was determined almost wholly by U.S. national objectives, primarily the elimination of the adverse effects of the dollar's overvaluation on U.S. jobs and its role in stimulating protectionist trade policies. See C. Fred Bergsten, "The New Economics and U.S. Foreign Policy," *Foreign Affairs*, vol. 50 (January 1972), esp. pp. 200–09.

1973 played a major role in accelerating the pace of U.S. inflation.[4] But this additional inflation represented an inevitable if belated payment for the excesses of U.S. economic policy in the late 1960s. Part of the inflationary effects associated with the Vietnam War were exported through the growing overvaluation of the dollar, which resulted from the continued willingness of foreign monetary authorities and private citizens to add to their dollar balances. This systemic overvaluation of the dollar, in turn, made inevitable the devaluations of the early 1970s. It was most unfortunate for the United States that the devaluations intensified an already highly inflationary situation, but there was no way to avoid them without further erosion of the competitive position of the United States in international trade.

The United States and all other countries have two interests in the international monetary system, both in terms of their direct economic interests and broader systemic concerns. One is to avoid excessive and extended balance-of-payments disequilibria. Indeed, the entire debate over international monetary reform has been a search for the best means to achieve that objective, as it became increasingly clear that the system created at Bretton Woods contained no effective mechanism for achieving payments adjustment. To the extent that multinational enterprises push the international monetary arrangements toward equilibrium exchange rates and an effective balance-of-payments adjustment process (as the data presented below suggest to be the case), they serve the national interests of all countries.

The second interest is in reducing the external constraint on internal economic policies. During this period, when governments are accepting an ever-growing list of policy responsibilities, external constraints are particularly deplored. To be sure, no monetary regime can or should eliminate the effects of international transactions on individual countries in today's highly interdependent world economy. But flexible exchange rates restore at least a measure of autonomy for domestic policy, especially

4. *The 1975 Joint Economic Report,* Joint Economic Committee, 94:1 (Government Printing Office, 1975), pp. 65–66, concludes that each percentage point of trade-weighted dollar depreciation adds about 0.2 percentage point to the consumer price index. On this basis, the 15–20 percent drop in the value of the dollar from August 1971 through 1974 raised U.S. prices by 3–4 percentage points, about half the increase in overall consumer prices (from 4.3 percent in 1971 to 11.0 percent in 1974).

monetary policy. These considerations are particularly important for the United States, for which external constraints would prove more costly than for most other countries. This is because external transactions play a smaller role in the U.S. economy than in the economy of any other major market economy, so internal macroeconomic policy (the only alternative to exchange rate changes to achieve lasting adjustment) has less leverage over the balance of payments for the United States than for others. Hence, multinational enterprises also serve U.S. interests, on this count, to the extent that they push the international monetary system in the direction of greater flexibility of exchange rates.

It is universally agreed that devaluation of the dollar was necessary in the early 1970s, both for internal U.S. reasons and to reduce the instability of the dollar-based international monetary system. There remains some debate over whether the amount of the devaluations and the subsequent fluctuations in the exchange rate were precisely correct. There are also debates over the process through which the devaluations occurred, the massive market speculation that preceded them, and the heavy-handed negotiating tactics of the U.S. government in 1971. But there is widespread concurrence that the devaluations were necessary, were within the right order of magnitude, and, given the inertia that dominates most governmental decisionmaking, particularly in international monetary affairs, probably would not have occurred in the absence of major market pressure.

At least partly as a result of the exchange-rate realignments, the U.S. trade balance improved over $7.3 billion in 1973, moving from its largest deficit in peacetime history into a small surplus. Despite an increase of almost $17 billion in the cost of imported oil, the trade balance fell by only about $6.3 billion in 1974, suggesting an improvement of at least $8 billion (allowing for the feedback effects on exports of the increase in oil payments) in the rest of the U.S. trade balance, on top of the improvement in 1973. There was further improvement of $14 billion in 1975, bringing the total for the three years (excluding the increase in the price of imported oil) to around $30 billion.[5] This swing in the external accounts added about two percentage points to the gross national product, keeping the deepest recession of the postwar period from going even deeper. To be

5. Calculated from *Survey of Current Business*, vol. 56 (June 1976), pp. 40–43.

sure, factors other than the exchange-rate changes helped the U.S. trade balance during the period.[6] But those changes were a major cause of the dramatic swing in the U.S. competitive position. Hence any forces that helped promote the exchange-rate realignments made an important contribution to both the national interests of the United States and to the effective functioning of the international economic system.

Somewhat more controversial is managed flexibility of exchange rates, adopted by all major countries to replace the Bretton Woods system of more rigidly fixed parities.[7] And one of the key forces that pushed the world to accept flexible rates, that finally stemmed the recurrent foreign exchange crises of ever-growing magnitude, was the massive and growing international capital flows, much of which are often attributed to multinational enterprises.

There are only four ways in which national monetary authorities can respond to disequilibria in their balance-of-payments positions: (1) financing the imbalances through their international reserves or the extension of credits; (2) internal economic adjustment to the external imbalances; (3) the application of controls to selected international transactions; and (4) changes in the exchange rate. Most observers agree that controls are an ineffective adjustment option, which at best suppress disequilibria and may well exacerbate them. There is also widespread agreement that few countries either should or will target their internal economic and social goals solely toward the requirements of external balance, as the traditional rules of the gold standard require, though appropriate domestic policies are always necessary to support the objectives of exchange-rate changes.

The primary debate is whether to let exchange-rate fluctuations absorb most of the pressure created by international monetary disequilibria or whether to offset at least part of those disequilibria, particularly those

6. For example, agricultural exports increased sharply when production fell in other countries. However, the exchange rate may also have been a factor; see G. Edward Schuh, "The Exchange Rate and U.S. Agriculture," *American Journal of Agricultural Economics*, vol. 56 (February 1974), pp. 1–13.

7. *Proceedings and Documents of the United Nations Monetary and Financial Conference, Bretton Woods, New Hampshire July 1–22, 1944*, vol. 1 (GPO, 1948). Joint Statement 4, par. 2, states "no change in the par value of a member's currency shall be made by the Fund without the country's approval. Member countries agree not to propose a change in the parity of their currency unless they consider it appropriate to the correction of a fundamental disequilibrium. Changes shall be made only with the approval of the Fund," p. 37.

parts identifiably caused by short-term flows, through financing instead of adjustment. Those who emphasize financing argue that trade balances and other fundamental economic transactions should not be affected by "hot money" movements (as they are when the "hot money" movements alter exchange rates), and that most short-term flows will shortly reverse themselves, in any event. Those who advocate maximum flexibility for exchange rates, on the other hand, regard such money movements as accurate market signals of needed adjustment, or at least as better indicators than the judgments of government officials, and, as more likely, under efforts to maintain fixed exchange rates, to cumulate than to reverse themselves. Flexibility also preserves at least a measure of autonomy for domestic (particularly monetary) policy, which no amount of international financing can provide under fixed rates.

The truth probably lies somewhere in between these two interpretations. The Bretton Woods regime, based on fixed exchange rates and the dollar, collapsed largely because it proved unable to effect the exchange-rate changes (or other modes of adjustment) needed to correct the massive balance-of-payments disequilibria that developed in the late 1960s and early 1970s, and because it gave no evidence of being able to maintain any new set of equilibrium positions. At the same time, imperfections in the foreign exchange markets do seem to produce exaggerated swings in exchange rates over given short-term periods, in large measure through the mechanism of the same short-term capital flows that have correctly signaled the proper direction for adjustment measures on numerous occasions. Speculation is probably stabilizing in the long run but may often prove destabilizing in the short run. In addition, monetary policy clearly has more, though by no means total, domestic leverage under flexible exchange rates than under fixed exchange rates.

The best international monetary system at the present stage of world economic history is thus probably one of managed flexibility of exchange rates, the kind of regime toward which the world is evolving. To the extent that multinational enterprises have pushed the world in this direction (and have reduced the proclivity of national authorities to try to adjust by applying controls to selected international transactions), they have served a useful purpose. The firms were of course not motivated by such an objective, and most of them were indeed apprehensive over the loss of apparent exchange-rate stability; nevertheless, the results were beneficial for both their private interests and the broader national interests of the

United States and other countries. The importance of this contribution by multinational enterprises depends on their importance in the foreign exchange markets and the extent to which they use their market power.

In the most comprehensive study of the financial management of multinational enterprises, Robbins and Stobaugh conclude that the variety of factors that have heretofore motivated corporate decisionmaking in this area have generally induced the firms to overhedge against the risk of exchange-rate losses and to show relatively little interest in reaping profits from successful speculation.[8] These factors include the asymmetrical reactions of stockholders to report losses as against forgone (and thus unknowable) gains, the willingness of host governments to tolerate defensive activities but not speculative activities and, most important of all, current accounting standards.[9]

In addition, the firms must focus on the short-run effects of these accounting features because of the priority usually assigned to the results, which the firm will be able to report for the coming quarter. Corporate treasurers may hedge against further depreciation of a declining currency, even if they think it is basically undervalued, because they doubt that market sentiment will confirm the underlying trend quickly enough. Further, individual subsidiaries wish to avoid risking losses, adding to the overhedging of the corporation.[10]

To hedge against devaluation of local currencies, the firms appear to

8. Sidney M. Robbins and Robert B. Stobaugh, *Money in the Multinational Enterprise: A Study of Financial Policy* (Basic Books, 1973), chaps. 2 and 7.

9. Rita M. Rodriguez, "Management of Foreign Exchange Risk in the U.S. Multinationals" (paper prepared for presentation to the June 1964 meeting of the Western Finance Association; processed), p. 10, found that financial managers in the fifty-five firms she studied never mentioned potential gain. Accounting rules vary significantly: translation losses (those incurred in stating a subsidiary's worth in the parent's currency) sometimes are charged against current operations, but translation gains are put into a suspense account except those used to offset current or prior losses. Carrying charges may be levied on long-term debt, even those used to build plants in the country whose currency was borrowed. Some rules levy them on inventories, even those ear-marked for sale in foreign-currency terms or whose price may offset any local-currency depreciation. Robbins and Stobaugh, *Money in the Multinational Enterprise*, conclude that "executives typically use accounting principles rather than economic principles to measure the effects of devaluation or revaluation," and "that when managers adopt protective measures they are trying to minimize accounting losses rather than economic losses" (pp. 25–26).

10. James Burtle, "Some Problems in Living with a System of Flexible Exchange Rates" (paper prepared for presentation to the May 1974 Williamsburg Conference on Greater Flexibility of Exchange Rates; processed), pp. 5–8.

rely most heavily on borrowing the exposed currency and maintaining the lowest possible cash balances in it.[11] They also make some effort to prepay debts denominated in strong currencies and to delay conversions into threatened currencies, through manipulating intracorporate accounts (the typical leads and lags). Multinational enterprises do not usually rely on the forward exchange market, though they may turn to it when a crisis develops and exposure remains. And they can be expected to worry less about hedging against devaluations of the dollar than against devaluations of other currencies, because their consolidated accounts are stated in dollars, and most of their foreign assets gain rather than lose dollar value when the dollar depreciates.

The most exhaustive effort to uncover data on this subject was undertaken in 1974 by the Subcommittee on Multinational Corporations of the Senate Foreign Relations Committee. The subcommittee developed original data on the foreign exchange transactions of the parents and subsidiaries of fifty-six major U.S.-based multinational enterprises during the first quarter of 1973 (the height of the crisis period). It compared these to the same classes of transactions in the first quarter of 1972 and to similar activities (during both time periods) of a control group of twenty-seven U.S. subsidiaries of foreign-based multinational enterprises, trading companies, and smaller firms.[12] Some of the main findings for the period between the first quarter of 1972 and the first quarter of 1973 follow.

1. The U.S.-based firms in the sample increased their liquid holdings of strong currencies (marks, Swiss francs, guilders, yen) by about $1 billion (60 percent), raising the share of those currencies in their total portfolios from about 20 percent to over 25 percent. About half the buildup came during the crisis months of February and March 1973.[13] (The control group, mainly U.S. subsidiaries of non-U.S. multinational enterprises, tripled their liquid nondollar assets—an increase of over $500 million— and cut their dollar holdings in absolute terms. They also cut their dollar

11. This paragraph summarizes the findings of chap. 7 of Robbins and Stobaugh, *Money in the Multinational Enterprise.* On p. 139 they provide a useful list of the various hedging methods.

12. *Multinational Corporations in the Dollar-Devaluation Crisis: Report on a Questionnaire,* prepared by the staff of the Subcommittee on Multinational Corporations of the Senate Foreign Relations Committee, 94:1 (GPO, 1975).

13. The devaluation effectively took place on February 9, 1973. The dollar further depreciated after that time, however.

billings, from more than 95 percent to less than 75 percent of their total billings, in favor of billings in strong currencies.)

2. The foreign subsidiaries of U.S.-based firms increased the dollar share of their payments to third parties (outside the corporate structure of their own multinational enterprise) from 13.7 percent in 1972 to 18.1 percent in 1973, presumably to lighten their dollar balances.

3. Multinational enterprises increased their long-term dollar-denominated debt to foreigners by 29 percent (about $1 billion) and cut their strong currency debt by 3 percent.[14]

4. Recorded outflows for foreign direct investment itself were about $1 billion more than might have been expected (also the case in 1971), and an important share of the huge "errors and omissions" (which were in fact the major component of the balance-of-payments deficit in each period) must have been due to corporate leads and lags.[15]

5. American multinational enterprises, as a group (according to their SEC reports), made no net use of the forward exchange markets to speculate against the dollar. Indeed, only 86 of the 139 firms (including the control group) entered the forward markets at all. On balance, the group's forward activities strengthened the dollar, although some individual firms did sell dollars forward during the crisis period.

6. Multinational enterprises as a group did not pursue the other possible routes to hedge against the dollar. They showed no significant short-term dollar borrowings to build their liabilities in the weak currency. Nor was there any noticeable change in the timing of dividend, royalty, or fee payments. Third parties actually reduced their strong-currency debts to multinational enterprises, suggesting that the multinational enterprises either bet wrong or are not so powerful, after all.

Hence, the firms did in fact take a series of steps, over a fairly protracted period of time, to protect themselves against dollar devaluation. But the study shows that some of the firms bet wrong, that there was competition within multinational enterprises to put the exchange risks on

14. These data were derived from Securities and Exchange Commission reports, which the companies filed with the subcommittee. They are supported by Office of Foreign Direct Investment data, cited by the subcommittee, which show that the nondollar debt of all U.S. foreign direct investors dropped in 1972 from 34.6 percent to 32.4 percent of their total debt (*Multinational Corporations in the Dollar-Devaluation Crisis,* p. 74).

15. Some of these flows may have become the source of the increased liquid holdings mentioned above, however, so the figures cannot simply be cumulated.

other members of the same corporate family, and that the firms did not generate great pressure on the exchange markets at the height of the crisis. It also suggests that the U.S. subsidiaries of foreign-based multinational enterprises speculated much more actively against the dollar during the crisis period than did U.S.-based multinational enterprises.

Thus the several findings of the Senate Foreign Relations Subcommittee mesh with the stated predilections of the firms. This similarity is particularly noteworthy, because the Robbins-Stobaugh analysis derives from a period of fixed exchange rates, when the overwhelming concern of multinational enterprises was with devaluations against the dollar. The subcommittee study covered a period when the United States had already moved some distance toward more movable exchange rates; a period that featured revaluations against the dollar.

Even if this picture accurately represents the past, it still conveys a quite powerful (and, in our view, constructive) monetary role for multinational enterprises. If it is true that multinational enterprises now account for even 25 percent of world nonagricultural trade, their weekly billings alone amount to over $3 billion. Thus a speedup or slowdown of two or three weeks in payments or receipts by even a small number of firms (and even in the face of active intervention by central banks) could have a major impact on the foreign exchange markets, most of which are quite thin.[16]

Legitimate concern could also be expressed about a possible increase in the impact of multinational enterprises on the money markets. Accounting standards could become more symmetrical, as they already have to a

16. The Tariff Commission, *Implications of Multinational Firms for World Trade and Investment and for U.S. Trade and Labor,* a report to the Senate Committee on Finance (GPO, 1973), p. 8, gives a misleading impression when it compares multinational liquid balances of $268 billion with central bank reserves. First, a large part of their assets are not readily available to the firms; Benjamin Klein, "The Role of U.S. Multinational Corporations in Recent Exchange Crises," Occasional Paper no. 6 (Washington: Center for Multinational Studies, December 1974; processed), pp. 2–5, notes that only $115 billion is owned by nonfinancial U.S. corporations (the usual term for multinational enterprises), and only $14 billion of that can be quickly mobilized, in any event, because most of it is inventories and receivables. Second, and even more important, central banks in countries with surpluses can buy foreign exchange coming into the country indefinitely (and thereby defend the existing exchange rate) simply by creating more local currency. As indicated in the text, the Senate Subcommittee on Multinational Corporations found a movement of only about $1 billion for all multinationals covered (including those based outside the United States) during the 1973 period.

large extent for central banks, which might encourage more active speculation.[17] Multinational enterprises could become more sophisticated,
looking to reap currency gains as well as to avoid currency losses, an evolution that has apparently already transpired for some private banks,
notably in continental Western Europe, with a few widely publicized unhappy results.

Two important considerations run counter to these possibilities, however. One is the finding of Robbins and Stobaugh that larger and more
experienced multinational enterprises, for a variety of structural reasons,
take a more relaxed attitude toward exchange losses than smaller or even
medium-sized firms.[18] As multinational enterprises continue to grow, their
anxiety about exchange-rate issues in general could thus be expected to
decline. Second, the advent of more flexible exchange rates goes far toward eliminating those situations (the one-way bets when a devaluation is
clearly imminent) in which multinational enterprises are likely to turn
heavily to the forward exchange markets. And they make far more difficult the whole business of trying to profit from exchange-rate fluctuations.
At the same time, more flexible rates enhance the chance for multinational
enterprises to play a socially useful role in the exchange markets by becoming the stabilizing speculators, which, according to economic theory,
permit a system of flexible rates to run smoothly.

So we conclude that, by simply pursuing their corporate interests, multinational enterprises deserve a significant share of the credit for prodding
governments to accept the international monetary reforms of the recent
past and can play a continuing useful role in the future. At the same time,
both because of their size and because of structural factors (asymmetrical
accounting practices and the pressure of showing profits for the current

17. Accounting asymmetries made many central banks unwilling to accept flexible exchange rates, which constantly change not only the local-currency value of
their reserve assets but the relation among these assets if they are in several national
currencies. But now most countries have procedures to establish reserves that would
credit banks with gains in their portfolios as an offset to the inevitable losses.

18. *Money in the Multinational Enterprise*, p. 133. Raymond Vernon, *Sovereignty at Bay: The Multinational Spread of U.S. Enterprises* (Basic Books, 1971),
p. 133, concurs; he generalizes that parent supervision of subsidiaries declines in all
areas as firms mature. Both books refer for support to the foreign-exchange activities
of American subsidiaries in the United Kingdom before the devaluation of 1967.
On the other hand, Rodriguez, "Management of Foreign Exchange Risk in the U.S.
Multinationals," p. 15, concludes that the "attitude of management toward foreign
exchange risk" explains their behavior better than does corporate size.

quarter in the best possible light), they have much potential for accelerating short-term swings in exchange rates, beyond the changes needed to restore equilibrium in the underlying balance-of-payments accounts. These considerations counsel national authorities to retain scope for market intervention in lieu of accepting freely flexible exchange rates (which, however, they would probably need whether or not multinational enterprises existed). Hence, the firms appear largely innocent of any charges of having subverted the international monetary system or having brought down the dollar.[19]

The Adjustment Process

A potentially more serious criticism of the effect of multinational enterprises on the international monetary system is that they may undermine the balance-of-payments adjustment process. Vernon believes "there is reason for assuming that these interaffiliate transactions are relatively insensitive to changes in exchange rates" and to all of the other traditional policy instruments used by governments, including trade controls, because "when affiliates trade with each other across an international border . . . they are less prone to shift sources in response to relative price changes."[20] He argues that multinational enterprises react so differently from the atomistic actors assumed by traditional economic theory that the conclusions of that theory, and the policy inferences drawn from it, can no longer be accepted.

Taken to this extreme, the argument espoused by Vernon suggests that the utility of the price mechanism in regulating economic activity is rapidly disappearing. This is precisely the conclusion of Barnet and

19. Similar conclusions were reached regarding American multinationals by Klein, "The Role of U.S. Multinational Corporations in Recent Exchange Crises," and Edward M. Bernstein, "Summary of the Written and Oral Statement," *Summary of the Hearings Before the Group of Eminent Persons to Study the Impact of Multinational Corporations on Development and on International Relations* (United Nations, 1974), who notes that "responsibility for disturbing the international monetary system is the least of the indictments that can be brought against the multinational corporation" (p. 18); and for British and German firms (during their exchange upheavals of 1967 and 1969–71, respectively) by W. A. P. Manser, *The Financial Role of Multinational Enterprises* (London: Associated Business Programs, 1973), pp. 127–36.

20. Raymond Vernon, "Critical Choices: The Industrial Structure of the United States and Europe" (December 1974; processed), p. 28. He subsequently adds monetary policy to the list of government measures whose efficacy is reduced by multinational enterprises.

Müller who, agreeing with Vernon that sovereignty is at bay, also share his view that multinational enterprises disrupt the international adjustment process.[21] But in their call for total governmental regulation of multinational enterprises as part of comprehensive national planning, they draw the more logical policy conclusion. Indeed Vernon, in concluding that the proper policy responses are to increase international credit (to finance payments imbalances) and to coordinate national economic policies, appears to assume that controls over multinationals are infeasible and thus to be arguing, essentially, that governments should accommodate themselves to the firms. So the point is fundamental to overall economic and social policy, not just to policies toward multinational enterprises.

It is also argued that multinational enterprises will inevitably trigger an internationalization of wage bargaining goals and practices, perhaps abetted by the multinationalization of trade unions, as discussed in chapter four. This would lead toward the equalization of real wages across national borders, destroying the money illusion needed for exchange-rate changes to achieve balance-of-payments adjustment without increasing levels of unemployment in deficit countries. Because most multinational enterprises are found in the high-productivity industries whose wage levels usually increase most rapidly and spread into less dynamic sectors, any such internationalization of real wages could also accelerate world inflation.[22] Still another consideration is that exchange-rate policy

21. *Global Reach,* pp. 283–90. Their primary evidence, however, is simply that the dollar devaluation of 1971 failed to improve the U.S. trade balance of 1972, allegedly because the foreign subsidiaries of American multinationals failed to raise the dollar price of their exports to the United States, preferring to "trim their profit margin of the moment to assure long-term stability of their market shares" (p. 287). The delayed impact of the first devaluation can of course be explained by the normal *J*-curve effect of exchange-rate changes, as explained by Helen B. Junz and Rudolf R. Rhomberg, "Price Competitiveness in Export Trade Among Industrial Countries," *American Economic Review,* vol. 63 (May 1973), pp. 412–18. As noted in the text, the U.S. trade balance did improve dramatically from 1972 through 1975 (by about $30 billion, excluding the rise in the price of oil imports). So multinationals hardly seem guilty of perverting the intended effect of the dollar devaluations. Imports from foreign subsidiaries of American multinationals (excluding those in Canada, whose exchange rate largely moved with the dollar), are a very small part of U.S. trade, anyway.

22. Geoffrey W. Maynard, "Monetary Policy" in John H. Dunning, ed., *Economic Analysis and the Multinational Enterprise* (London: Allen and Unwin, 1974), pp. 242–49. See, however, the contrary views of Lloyd Ulman, "Multinational Unionism: Incentives, Barriers, and Alternatives," *Industrial Relations,* vol. 14 (February 1975), pp. 1–31, who argues that unions in individual countries focus much more heavily on their position relative to workers in other industries within

gradually loses its power to alter relative commodity prices in an increasingly integrated world economy. Exports of intermediate products from one country become the input costs in other countries, nontraded-goods sectors shrink, and capital flows rather than trade tend to dominate balance-of-payments positions.[23]

At least tangential support for the thesis that multinational enterprises alter the balance-of-payments adjustment process is derived from recent findings that the effects of exchange-rate (and other price) changes take much longer to eventuate than had traditionally been suspected. Junz and Rhomberg, in a careful econometric study of changes in trade flows, conclude that full effects require five years and that half the total changes require three years.[24] Such increased gestation periods could be explained by the growing role of multinational enterprises. These firms are clearly reluctant to change capital budgeting plans, which are often developed in great detail for two or even three years in advance and whose revision requires both real costs and an admission of failure in foreseeing the changes that necessitate the revision. Hence, the plans may be immediately revised by large firms only in the wake of dramatic exchange-rate (or other) changes, or by small firms, which are less committed to capital budgeting and have less impact on the overall results. On this hypothesis, large multinational enterprises would respond more slowly to exchange-rate changes than theory suggests, but they would still respond. The hypothesis is very uncertain, however. There are no studies demonstrating what the period needed to effect exchange-rate changes were in the past, when multinational enterprises played a smaller role; and multinational enterprices are often viewed as responding flexibly and rapidly to such changes.

At both the microeconomic and macroeconomic levels, moreover, there are strong reasons to be skeptical of the view that multinational enterprises undermine the adjustment process. There is no compelling reason to believe that they react differently than other firms to exchange-rate (and other price) changes. Indeed, as noted, some observers believe that multinationals react *more* quickly. Vernon suggests that "when a multinational enterprise contemplates abandoning an old location for a new one in response to a change in exchange rates, it is obliged to compare the

---

their own countries than on their position relative to workers in the same industry in other countries.

23. Gary C. Hufbauer, "Multinational Corporations and the International Adjustment Process," *American Economic Review*, vol. 64 (May 1974), pp. 273–75.

24. Junz and Rhomberg, "Price Competitiveness in Export Trade Among Industrial Countries."

full cost of operating in the new location against the marginal cost of continuing in the old."[25] He thinks "it would be surprising" if similar action by independent firms were very common, because they would fear the impact of the resulting marginal pricing on their sales revenues in markets with low price elasticities of demand. But any firm must make the same comparison; it presumably would avoid jettisoning an existing plant as long as that plant could remain competitive.

Moreover, the exchange-rate changes of 1969–73 did dramatically relieve most of the major balance-of-payments pressure, including the massive U.S. deficit and the massive Japanese surplus. To be sure, the German surplus persisted, but it may be the absence of multinationalization of German firms which keeps them exporting so effectively from Germany, since they have no alternative. The quadrupling of oil prices in 1974 raised serious new balance-of-payments problems for a number of developing countries and a few major countries, notably Italy and the United Kingdom, and large deficits reappeared for the United States in 1977. However, these developments occurred wholly independent of multinational enterprises. To date, discrete parity changes and flexible exchange rates have helped restore and maintain balance-of-payments disequilibrium. No actions by multinational enterprises appear to have deflected this outcome.

Is there evidence that the actions of American multinationals contribute positively to an improvement in the balance-of-payments adjustment process? The major realignment in exchange rates that occurred from 1971 to 1973 should have had a major impact on foreign direct investment by U.S.-based firms because of the changes in comparative production costs resulting from correcting the disequilibrium, which had been building for a number of years. Even leaving aside the further depreciations of the dollar in mid-1973 and again in early 1975 (which corporate planners might have regarded as temporary and likely to be reversed), by mid-1975 the dollar declined against a trade-weighted average of all other major currencies by about 15 percent. The depreciation was about 40 percent against the currencies of several European countries and 20 percent against Japan.[26] However, the depreciation was lower if its changes vis-à-vis other individual currencies are weighted by the importance of

25. Vernon, "Critical Choices: The Industrial Structure of the United States and Europe," p. 28.

26. *Survey of Current Business*, vol. 55 (September 1975), p. 39.

Table 8-1. *U.S. Exports and Direct Investment, by Foreign Country, 1973*

Country	U.S. exports		U.S. foreign direct investment	
	Value (millions of dollars)	Share (percentage)	Value[a] (millions of dollars)	Share (percentage)
Canada	15,574	22.2	28,055	26.1
EEC[b]	12,483	17.8	19,296	18.0
Japan	8,356	11.9	2,733	2.5
United Kingdom	3,772	5.3	11,115	10.4
All others	30,070	42.8	46,069	43.0

Source: *Survey of Current Business*, vol. 54 (August 1974), pt. 2, p. 18; and ibid. (June 1974), p. 25.
a. 1973 year-end book value of outstanding stock.
b. European Economic Community six original members (Belgium, France, Italy, Luxembourg, the Netherlands, and West Germany).

other countries as recipients of foreign direct investment from the United States, rather than by their levels of trade with the United States (see table 8-1). This is because Canada and the United Kingdom weigh more heavily in U.S. investment than in trade flows, and the Canadian dollar and the pound sterling have both depreciated against the American dollar. Correspondingly, U.S. trade with Japan is much heavier than U.S. investment in Japan, and the yen has appreciated more than average against the dollar. (The trade and investment shares are about the same for the original six countries of the European Economic Community and for the developing countries as a group.)

The importance of the slightly smaller depreciation of the dollar on an investment-weighted basis than on a trade-weighted basis depends on whether U.S.-based multinational enterprises are motivated to invest in those countries primarily to sell to their local markets or to use them as bases for international marketing. If the domestic market is the major attraction (with the firm viewing its choices as exporting to the market from the United States or producing locally), the investment-weighted effects —or even just the change in the exchange rate between the dollar and that particular currency—could dominate investment planning. If the country is viewed at least partly as an export platform, the trade-weighted rate (indeed, the effective exchange rates of the two currencies weighted in terms of world trade, not bilateral trade, between it and the United States) should be more important. The local market appears to be a more important consideration in the major countries where U.S. trade and investment shares differ (Canada, Japan, and the United Kingdom), so the smaller investment-weighted depreciation of the dollar is probably more relevant for these purposes. Nevertheless, the difference is small, and a significant impact on foreign direct investment should still be expected.

It has not yet become possible to test these hypotheses empirically.[27] The exchange-rate changes could not be included in the equations in chapter three, because they occurred so recently that data for the other variables are not yet available. In any event, the normal lags both in corporate decisionmaking and in implementing those decisions make it unlikely that changes in investment plans, particularly in response to such a new consideration as exchange-rate changes, would begin to show up before 1974.[28] Hence no judgment can be rendered at this time as to whether multinational enterprises actively promote the U.S. (and global) interest in a better balance-of-payments adjustment.

U.S. International Monetary Policy

As shown in chapter one, a large number of U.S.-based firms are critically dependent for their earnings on the world market. Hence, any disruption of that market, or threatened disruption, represents a threat to their interests. Monetary arrangements lie at the heart of the international economic system, so a growing number of firms have made major efforts to promote the maintenance of a stable international monetary regime.[29]

Their stake in the stability of the international economic system appears to override their interests (at least as they perceive them) in any specific features of that system. They have not taken strong positions in favor of

27. For the beginnings of such an approach see Susan Alexander and J. Carter Murphy, "Exchange Rates and Direct International Investment," Working Paper no. 71 (Dallas: Southern Methodist University, Department of Economics, February 1975; processed).

28. There has been an increase in direct investment in the United States by foreign-based multinationals since 1971, as these theoretical considerations would suggest. As always, many factors were at play and exchange-rate changes cannot be isolated. Investment rose to over $2.5 billion in 1973 and remained at that level in 1974 and 1975 despite the world recession, whereas it had only once before reached even $1 billion (in 1970). See *Survey of Current Business*, vol. 54 (August 1974), p. 7; ibid., vol. 55 (October 1975), p. 37; and ibid., vol. 57 (October 1977), p. 27. As always, one must be cautious of equating the behavior of foreign and American multinationals. But these developments do suggest that important parts of international direct investment respond strongly to exchange-rate changes.

29. See, for example, Committee for Economic Development, *Strengthening the World Monetary System* (New York: CED, July 1973).

fixed or flexible exchange rates, special drawing rights, or gold, or the dollar. Indeed, the firms have adjusted rapidly to all alterations in the rules of the game. Their primary objective is maximum certainty as to what those rules will be.

The major specific concern of multinational enterprises about international monetary arrangements is the avoidance of quantitative barriers to the international flow of capital and goods. Thus, they usually (but not always) support liberal trade policies. In the monetary context, they support an adjustment process and financing mechanisms that limit the need for governments to apply direct controls to capital movements. Indeed, multinational enterprises began to support increased flexibility of exchange rates in the late 1960s, when they realized that resort to controls could be limited only by such an alternative means of improving the adjustment process.[30]

This propensity of multinational enterprises to promote international monetary policies that are in the national interest as well as their own was demonstrated dramatically during the most severe systemic crisis of the postwar period. Between August and December, 1971, the international components of the New Economic Policy launched by President Nixon and managed by Secretary of the Treasury John Connally (which included unilateral U.S. abrogation of its basic international commitments in both the monetary and trade areas) threatened to decisively reverse the entire postwar trend toward greater economic cooperation among the major industrialized nations.[31] By November, the absence of any progress toward a negotiated solution of the crisis was causing confidence to collapse throughout the industrialized world, which in turn was causing companies everywhere to cancel investment plans and forecasters everywhere to rapidly pare down their economic growth forecasts. There was quite clearly a real threat of international monetary and trade warfare, and, indeed, the period gave birth to the term "dirty floats."

Two factors intervened, which persuaded President Nixon to instruct

30. An important step in the conversion of businessmen (and private bankers) was the 1969–74 Bürgenstock, Switzerland, meetings, at which academic economists and exchange-market practitioners met to consider the international monetary system. See John H. Watts, "The Business View of Proposals for International Monetary Reform" in George N. Halm, ed., *Approaches to Greater Flexibility of Exchange Rates: The Bürgenstock Papers* (Princeton University Press, 1970), pp. 167–76.

31. See Bergsten, "The New Economics and U.S. Foreign Policy."

Secretary of Treasury John B. Connally (much to Connally's displeasure) to settle the crisis. One factor was the fear (transmitted by Henry A. Kissinger as a result of numerous direct appeals to him from the highest levels of European governments) that the entire Atlantic Alliance was gravely threatened.[32] The other factor was the fear (transmitted by multinational enterprises in the United States, who appealed to the President directly, through Secretary Connally, and eventually—and most effectively—through Federal Reserve Board Chairman Arthur Burns) that there would be a major setback for the U.S. economy through the impact of the crisis on international economic relations.

Hence we conclude that the American multinationals are an important source of international monetary stability, in terms of both their market behavior and their policy predilections. Their flexibility of operations, which is often regarded as a social threat, usually enables them to play a constructive role in the foreign exchange markets and adapt quickly to needed improvements in the international monetary system. Their own deep engagement in the world economy, and resulting self-interest in the maintenance of effective international monetary arrangements, strongly suggests that their role will remain positive.

Multinational Enterprises and International Trade Policy

It is clear that trade barriers are a major cause of foreign direct investment. As elaborated in chapter three, a firm can penetrate a foreign market either by exporting to it or by producing locally. Import barriers obviously tilt—and sometimes force, if they are stiff enough—the decision toward investment.[33]

Horst has shown that Canadian and European tariffs correlate in-

32. Kissinger, though still officially only the assistant to the President for national security affairs, had become the de facto secretary of state and was the only person within government with the strength to counter Connally. His strength was increased by the refusal of British Prime Minister Edward Heath to accept President Nixon's invitation to a summit conference before there had been progress in resolving the economic impasse.

33. George H. Borts, "Long-run Capital Movements," in Dunning, ed., *Economic Analysis and the Multinational Enterprise,* pp. 211–13, makes the distinction between import barriers that lead to specific incoming foreign investments and those that turn a country into a net capital importer. The latter depends on whether the foreign direct investment simply substitutes for domestic investment that would otherwise have occurred, or complements it.

versely with the share of U.S. exports in the total sales of U.S.-based firms
to those markets.[34] Indeed, host countries consciously seek to attract foreign investment by raising barriers to imports.[35] And host countries can,
through the use of tariffs and other import barriers, simultaneously replace imports with domestic production and reduce the costs of their
foreign borrowing.[36]

For American multinationals, one of the leading analysts of the subject
concludes that "tariffs and market size . . . principally motivate MNC decisionmaking."[37] A close student of continental European multinationals
agrees that "tariffs and other trade restrictions, like exchange controls,
quantitative quotas, patent-working regulations, and subsidies appear to
have been the primary influence on the decisions of European firms to
manufacture in, rather than export to, foreign markets."[38] And among the
most critical factors in the successive phases of Japanese foreign direct
investment were the protectionist policies of the developing countries that
were hosts to most of these investments in the early 1960s and the fear of
protectionism in the United States in the early 1970s.[39] Trade barriers appear to be a central influence on foreign direct investment from all major
home countries.[40]

34. Thomas Horst, "The Industrial Composition of U.S. Exports and Subsidiary
Sales to the Canadian Market," *American Economic Review,* vol. 62 (March 1972),
pp. 37–45.
35. Frank A. Southard, *American Industry in Europe* (Riverside Press, 1931),
pp. 114–16, indicates that this strategy was central to European economic policies
before 1914 and that nontariff barriers as well as tariffs were already important at
that time.
36. See W. M. Corden, "The Theory of International Trade," in Dunning, ed.,
Economic Analysis and the Multinational Enterprise, pp. 192–95. By reducing the
home-country's exports, the host-country tariff can lower the price of capital in the
home country and hence the borrowing costs of the host country. This is an application of the theory of combining optimum capital controls with optimum tariffs. It
assumes a host country of sufficient size to affect both its terms of trade and its terms
of foreign borrowing. It demonstrates that "tariffs can act as second-best taxes or
subsidies on foreign capital" (p. 195).
37. Gary Hufbauer and John G. Chilas, "Specialization by Industrial Countries:
Extent and Consequences," Herbert Giersch, ed., *The International Division of
Labour: Problems and Perspectives* (Tubingen: J. C. B. Mohr, 1974), p. 18.
38. Lawrence G. Franko, "The Origins of Multinational Manufacturing by Continental European Firms," *Business History Review,* vol. 68 (Autumn 1974), p. 301.
39. M. Y. Yoshino, "The Multinational Spread of Japanese Manufacturing Investment Since World War II," *Business History Review,* vol. 68 (Autumn 1974),
pp. 361–64 and 374–75.
40. On the other hand, a case study of the Brazilian tariff changes of 1957 dis-

Nondiscriminatory tariffs were once the traditional trade policy tool for inducing foreign direct investment. More recently, tariff discrimination (the differential treatment of imports from different countries) has become important, first within the British Commonwealth and now particularly in the European Common Market.[41] Nontariff barriers such as import quotas, government procurement preferences for local suppliers, industrial standards geared to domestic market predilections, and the whole array of industrial policies (which often inadvertently distort international trade flows) have become increasingly the focal points of national trade policies.[42] These newer forms of protection are now more likely than tariffs to induce foreign direct investment, because tariffs have been reduced to low levels in most industrialized countries, and because, as we saw in discussing capital controls and exchange-rate changes in the previous section, firms can handle price barriers but cannot circumvent quantitative limits. So the new importance of nontariff barriers probably further heightens the impact of trade policy on multinational enterprises.

Virtually every thorough case study of foreign direct investment reveals the importance of trade barriers to foreign direct investment. In his definitive survey of the literature, Hufbauer summarizes the widespread support for this view, which derives from country studies of outward investment by U.S. and British firms and incoming investment to Australia, Canada,

---

covered no effect on incoming foreign direct investment; see Robert R. Miller and Dale R. Weigel, "Factors Affecting Resource Transfer Through Direct Investment," in C. G. Alexandrides, *International Business Systems Perspectives* (Georgia State University, School of Business Administration, 1973), pp. 139–42.

41. Isaiah A. Litvak and Christopher J. Maule, "Canadian-United States Corporate Interface and Transnational Relations," *International Organization,* vol. 28 (Autumn 1974), p. 728, show that Ford of Canada invested in South Africa, Rhodesia, Australia, New Zealand, and Singapore for this reason. There is empirical debate over the impact of the common external tariff on foreign direct investment in the Common Market. Several analysts conclude that it has induced such flows: Andrew Schmitz, "The Impact of Trade Blocs on Foreign Direct Investment," *Economic Journal,* vol. 80 (September 1970), pp. 724–31; A. Schmitz and J. Bieri, "EEC Tariffs and United States Direct Investment," *European Economic Review,* vol. 3 (November 1972), pp. 259–70; and Kenneth F. Wallis, "The EEC and United States Foreign Investment: Some Empirical Evidence Re-examined," *Economic Journal,* vol. 78 (September 1968), pp. 717–19. The opposite view is taken in Anthony E. Scaperlanda and Laurence J. Mauer, "The Determinants of U.S. Direct Investment in the EEC," *American Economic Review,* vol. 59 (September 1969), pp. 558–68.

42. The best compendium remains Robert E. Baldwin, *Nontariff Distortions of International Trade* (Brookings Institution, 1970).

New Zealand, and the United States.[43] In his pioneering study of multinational enterprise decisionmaking, Aharoni finds that foreign trade barriers are the single most important factor in decisions to invest abroad.[44] Industry studies uncover the same phenomenon for chemical investments in Australia, pharmaceutical investments everywhere, and automobiles in Europe.[45] Three of the nine cases studied by Stobaugh, particularly the investment in Canada by a major U.S. rubber company, were dominated by trade barriers.[46]

The exception helps prove the case. Japan is the only major country that did not receive sizable inflows of foreign direct investment as a result of maintaining high import barriers. But this is because it maintained high barriers to investment as well, forcing foreign firms in most industries to choose between licensing their technology to Japanese firms or missing out altogether on the fastest growing major economy of the postwar period. The Japanese strategy thus went beyond those of the countries just mentioned and fostered the development of domestic capability by keeping out foreign firms as well as foreign goods.

At the same time, trade barriers hinder some types of foreign direct investment. Any investment aimed at producing for export is obviously deterred by import barriers in potential markets. Export controls may also discourage foreign direct investment.[47] Opportunities to export from for-

---

43. Gary C. Hufbauer, "The Multinational Enterprise and Direct Investment," in Peter B. Kenen, ed., *International Trade and Finance: Frontiers for Research* (Cambridge University Press, 1975), pp. 253–319.

44. Yair Aharoni, *The Foreign Investment Decision Process* (Harvard University Graduate School of Business Administration, 1966), pp. 64–65.

45. Michael Clapham, "Imperial Chemical Industries Limited: A Case Study," in C. Fred Bergsten, ed., *Toward a New World Trade Policy: The Maidenhead Papers* (Lexington Books, 1975), pp. 108–09; Robert E. Lipsey and Merle Yahr Weiss, "Exports and Foreign Investment in the Pharmaceutical Industry," National Bureau for Economic Research, Working Paper no. 87 (New York: May 1975; processed), pp. 30–31; and Louis T. Wells, Jr., "Automobiles," in Raymond Vernon, ed., *Big Business and the State: Changing Relations in Western Europe* (Harvard University Press, 1974), pp. 229–54.

46. Robert Stobaugh, *Nine Investments Abroad and Their Impact at Home* (Harvard University, Graduate School of Business Administration, 1976). In the *Harvard Business Review*, vol. 51 (September, October 1973), p. 121, Stobaugh cites "scaling a tariff wall" as the most important element in foreign investment decisions.

47. However, this issue is sometimes complicated (at least for the extractive industries) by the desire of the firms to sustain high prices by limiting output and by their desire to maintain their symbiotic relation with host countries (see chap.

eign sites are blunted by trade barriers, just as opportunities to meet local demand are promoted by them.

Thus there can be little doubt about the intimate relation between multinational enterprises and trade policies of individual countries and about the critical effect of each on the other.[48] Indeed, the only surprise is that the relation has received so little emphasis in the burgeoning literature on foreign investment during the past ten years.[49]

Beyond these aggregate conclusions, differences in national trade policies may help explain some of the puzzles concerning patterns of international investment. One reason that American and British firms tend to invest abroad more than continental European and Japanese firms may be the freer trade policies maintained by the United States and United Kingdom, particularly during the earlier postwar years, when the foreign direct investment boom began.

Aggregate tariff levels are now about the same among the major countries. Beneath the aggregates, however, a weighted average of the tariff rates of the industrialized countries other than the United States reveals that they were higher than the U.S. tariff in 130 of 200 Standard Industrial Classification categories analyzed.[50] In addition, import quotas continued to be widely used in Europe until at least the late 1950s. And the common external tariff of the European Economic Community[51] has discriminated against imports relative to internal production since 1958 (about the time that the quotas were coming off). Hence there was greater need for American manufacturing firms to invest abroad to meet foreign demand than there was for firms based in other countries.

5). For an analysis of export controls see C. Fred Bergsten, *Completing the GATT: Toward New International Rules to Govern Export Controls* (Washington: British-North American Committee, 1974).

48. The advent of multinationals has had an important impact on trade theory. See Corden, "The Theory of International Trade," pp. 180–210.

49. For example, the issue is hardly mentioned by Vernon in *Sovereignty at Bay*. Even his "A Program of Research on Foreign Direct Investment" in C. Fred Bergsten, *The Future of the International Economic Order: An Agenda for Research* (Lexington Books, 1973), examines trade theory only in terms of the new multinational actors (pp. 98–99) rather than in terms of the impact of trade policy on investment flows. Indeed, as noted above, Vernon in "Critical Choices" argues that tariffs, like exchange-rate changes and all other government policies, are becoming less effective in checking the behavior of multinationals.

50. William R. Cline and L. Hays, "Competitiveness and Disaggregated Industrial Trade Liberalization Effects" (1973; processed), table 2.

51. Belgium, France, Italy, Luxembourg, the Netherlands, and West Germany since 1958 and Denmark, Ireland, and the United Kingdom since 1972.

There is also a question as to the degree to which international trade has really been liberalized in the postwar period. Hufbauer and Chilas find that "the degree of [international] specialization attained in 1969 by the industrial nations was less than that reached in 1937"—a highly protectionist year—and "is still below the 1929 figure."[52] They conclude that "[international] specialization has increased remarkably little either between the major industrial countries or between the broad categories of manufactured goods," with the spectacular increases in international trade coming almost wholly within individual industries (where adjustment problems are easier to solve). They thus cast doubt on the degree of trade liberalization for broad economic sectors, which is central to decisions between investing abroad and exporting. Similarly, Göran Ohlin sees the proliferation of new forms of protection as a response to the reductions of tariffs and controls over capital movements, whose extent raises doubts about how much net liberalization has taken place.[53]

On this reading, it is the explosion of international investment that has been the main driving force of increasing international economic interdependence in the postwar period. And if there has been little net trade liberalization, the freer trade stance the United States maintained in the early postwar period might in fact persist, at least partly explaining the higher proclivity of U.S. firms (compared to European or Japanese firms) to invest abroad. This conclusion derives support from the testimony of a number of foreign companies that, beginning in the early 1970s, they decided to invest in the United States because they feared that the United States might adopt widespread import controls.

These conclusions mesh with those concerning exchange-rate relations. For much of the postwar period, the United States had a tendency toward both an overvalued dollar and low import barriers. The relatively more liberal trade policy of the United States may have declined in the late 1960s, but the dollar was then becoming increasingly overvalued. So these two factors, which are not usually highlighted in analyses of multinational enterprises, may help explain the high level of foreign direct investment by U.S.-based firms relative to foreign direct investment by foreign-based firms.

Another question regarding the pattern of foreign direct investment is why the multinationalization of U.S.-based manufacturing firms takes

52. "Specialization by Industrial Countries," pp. 5–6.
53. "National Industrial Policies and International Trade" in Bergsten, ed., *Toward a New World Trade Policy*, p. 180.

place most heavily toward the lower end of industrial size.[54] Table 3-2 ranks U.S. industries in order of their degree of internationalization. It shows that the five categories of textile industries are in the bottom third of U.S. industries on this measure and that the two steel industry categories are in the lower half. The least internationalized industry is shipbuilding. On the other hand, the fifteen most internationalized industries include computers and office machines, photographic equipment, optical goods, communication equipment, and automobiles. More generally, our regression analyses, like those of many other observers, disclose a high positive correlation between technological prowess and foreign direct investment by U.S.-based firms.

One explanation lies in the different structure of trade protectionism in the different industrial countries. The United States has most heavily protected its lagging industries, both through higher tariffs and import quotas.[55] By contrast, a significant share of European and Japanese import barriers represent protection of their nascent high-technology industries, largely through nontariff barriers such as government procurement practices and other devices of industrial policy. To be sure, there is European (and now Japanese) protection in low-technology industries, such as textiles. But, in relative terms, foreign protection tilts more toward the high-technology end of the spectrum.

American industries thus opt for (and often receive) import protection toward the low end of the product cycle and face import protection in other countries toward the top of the product cycle.[56] In part, this pattern reflects national differences in comparative advantage. To some extent, it could thus be viewed as simply intensifying or accelerating shifts in the location of international production, which would occur anyway.

54. This pattern is stressed by Kiyoshi Kojima, "A Macroeconomic Theory of Foreign Direct Investment," in Bergsten, ed., *Toward a New World Trade Policy*, pp. 75–100. All home countries of course have multinational enterprises in the extractive industries, which complement home-country production rather than substitute for it.

55. J. H. Cheh, "United States Concessions in the Kennedy Round and Short-Run Labor Adjustment Costs," *Journal of International Economics*, vol. 4 (November 1974), concludes that the low tariff reductions in this round are associated with "declining industries, and industries with a high proportion of unskilled or old workers" p. 323.

56. These U.S. trade barriers in turn are related to some of the foreign direct investment by foreign-based multinationals. Japanese-based textile firms, for example, accelerated the pace of their foreign investments to get around the "voluntary" restraints forced by the U.S. government on textile exports from Japan to the United States.

But the nearly total absence of foreign direct investment by such U.S. industries as steel and textiles, compared with most other U.S. industries, and the relative lack of foreign direct investment by foreign-based (except British) industries in high-technology industries, suggest that the quantitative impact of the different structures of trade policy are central. The U.S. pattern is trade protection at the bottom of the product cycle and foreign direct investment at the top, while the continental European and Japanese pattern has been trade protection at the top and foreign direct investment at the bottom.

In a careful study of trade patterns based on the relatively realistic assumptions of two factors of production and many traded commodities, William P. Travis in fact concludes that "seemingly moderate duties are in fact prohibitive of trade even as between countries with widely different relative capital and labor endowments" (p. 103), and that "the *U.S.* tariff prohibits the exchange of capital-intensive for labor-intensive products" (p. 87).[57] If this were true, it would mean that U.S. firms in capital-intensive industries (which are usually, though not always, high-technology industries) could meet foreign demand only by investing where the market was. In such a situation, foreign trade barriers would explain the bulk of the foreign direct investment by U.S.-based firms. Travis goes too far, but his analysis reaffirms the importance of both the level and structure of trade barriers to foreign investment.

Thus there is a close interaction between multinational enterprises and trade policy, in structure as well as aggregate level. Asymmetries in structure and level among national trade barriers help explain asymmetries in structure and level of foreign direct investment between U.S.-based multinational enterprises and foreign-based multinational enterprises. The future of trade policy, in turn, can have an important effect on the magnitude and composition of foreign direct investment.

Implications for World Trade Policy

It is widely assumed that multinational enterprises are a major force for the liberalization of international trade. The analysis above suggests a more nuanced conclusion, however. Indeed, multinational enterprises may support protectionism in host countries. Import barriers induce in-

57. "Production, Trade, and Protection When There Are Many Commodities and Two Factors," *American Economic Review,* vol. 62 (March 1972). That such trade does exist derives from "special U.S. skills" and other technological factors that "filter through the tariff, which is revised only from time to time" (p. 104).

ward investment. Most host countries seek investments they feel promote
their national interests or can be channeled into doing so. In view of the
problems facing many countries in expanding exports rapidly enough to
support their overall balance-of-payments positions, the option of inducing import-substituting foreign investment remains attractive. Most host
countries now seek foreign investors who will export as well; but a protected domestic market may often be a necessary starting point, both for
economic reasons (to achieve adequate scale of production and to cover
start-up costs) and to entice the firm to undertake the venture in the first
place. Hence, the investment option as embodied by multinational enterprises provides an increased inducement to host countries both to attract
multinational enterprises and to get them to accept performance requirements determined by host governments.

Once foreign investment is in place, the plot thickens. Whether or not
pledges are made, the firm, like many firms in any economy, may seek
protection to help it maintain its market position against import competition.[58] It will almost certainly oppose reductions in the trade barriers behind which it invested in the first place. (It will also oppose reductions in
nontrade barriers, such as the local-content rules levied by Brazil and
other host countries in the automotive industry, described in chapter
nine.) Indeed, this is perhaps one of the most egregious features of the
dependencia syndrome, which posits that collusion between foreign and
domestic capitalists in developing economies distorts the path of economic development.

Protectionist efforts by foreign subsidiaries of multinational enterprises
are much more likely in developing than in industrial host countries, for
two reasons. The first is simply that any individual multinational enterprise tends to have more political clout in a smaller, less-developed country. The second is that the firms recognize the closer relation between the
trade policies of industrial countries and the United States, and most of

58. Several examples from Canada in the 1930s are discussed in Herbert Marshall, Frank Southard, and Kenneth Taylor, *Canadian-American Industry: A Study
in International Investment* (Yale University Press, 1936), p. 275. "In general" they
conclude "the management of American-owned plants in Canada will be found supporting a protectionist tariff policy." More recently, in 1975 General Motors persuaded Australia to set tight import quotas for Japanese automobiles while allowing
General Motors to import parts duty-free from Japan "so that it could avoid firing
its Australian auto workers." The sales director for General Motors Australia com-
mented that this turn of events "puts us in the best marketing position we've been
in during the postwar years." *Journal of Commerce,* March 31, 1975.

them wish to avoid the creation of import barriers in their home country, which happens to be the richest market in the world.[59]

Protectionism in the United States would limit the chance for multinational enterprises to sell to the United States from their foreign subsidiaries. It would raise the cost of other imports to their U.S. plants. It could trigger protectionism in other countries, which could hurt the sizable exports of most of the parent firms in the United States. Worst of all, from their perspective, it could perhaps spill over into controls against foreign investment itself. The imposition of U.S. import barriers, or even significant threats thereof, would induce foreign-based multinational enterprises to invest in the United States, which U.S.-based multinational enterprises fear would enable the foreign-based firms to compete more effectively in their home market.

So American multinationals are strong supporters of liberal trade policies for the United States. This is of critical importance, since most of the traditional sources of support for freer U.S. trade (foreign policy concerns, organized labor, the agricultural community) have weakened in recent years.[60] Indeed, one acute observer concludes that "U.S. trade policy is now the product primarily of the political pressures from transnational enterprises on the one hand and organized labour on the other" and that "where these interests are in conflict in particular industries, the evidence suggests that the former will usually win out, and liberal trade policies will be pursued."[61]

The multinational enterprises were decisive in turning back the threats embodied in the "Mills bill" of 1970 (H.R. 18970), the import surcharge imposed on August 15, 1971, as part of President Nixon's new economic policy,[62] and the Burke-Hartke bill in 1972 (H.R. 14052).

59. For similar reasons of policy interaction, American multinationals have led the fight against U.S. restrictions on foreign investment in the United States. Some even opposed the application of U.S. countervailing duties against Michelin's subsidized exports to the United States from its plant in Canada (see chap. 3) out of concern for their investments in France.

60. See C. Fred Bergsten, "Crisis in U.S. Trade Policy," *Foreign Affairs*, vol. 49 (July 1971), pp. 619–35.

61. G. K. Helleiner, "Transnational Enterprises and the New Political Economy of U.S. Trade Policy" (Toronto: April 1976; processed), p. 18. Of course, industry and labor often join forces in seeking protection or free trade; Helleiner notes that multinationalization of an industry can split them, although such splits are only partially evident so far, even in the automobile industry.

62. *Imposition of Supplemental Duty for Balance of Payments Purposes*, Proclamation 4074, 85 Stat. 926.

Multinational firms would almost certainly subordinate free trade to maximum freedom (and, indeed, government support) for their foreign investment activities, if forced by U.S. political pressure to choose. Such a choice seemed to be present in the debate over the Burke-Hartke approach (which linked trade issues with taxation of foreign income) and in the early stages of the congressional deliberations in 1973 on what eventually became the Trade Act of 1974. During those debates, the firms revealed their preference for favorable investment policies, particularly in the tax area, over liberal trade policies. In addition, they did not always support paying the price of liberal trade policies (for example, adequate programs of trade adjustment assistance).

But, on the whole, multinational enterprises are an important and effective force in support of international trade policies (as well as monetary policies) which are socially desirable for the United States. The efforts of multinationals to promote policies of freer trade in the United States are strongest for those products of direct interest to them.[63] For example, over strong opposition from labor, multinationals successfully supported the U.S.-Canadian automotive pact and resisted repeal of sections 806.30 and 807.00 of the Tariff Schedule, which permit duty-free entry of inputs originating in the United States and which are ideally suited to multinational production. Both the level and the trend of U.S. protection are much more liberal for goods in which intrafirm trade is important. Those industries significantly protected (such as textiles and dairy products) or which were until recently (such as steel and meat) are notably nonmultinational. So the existence of multinational enterprises affects the level and structure of U.S. trade barriers, just as the profile of trade policy affects the flow of foreign direct investment.

The Outlook for the Future

If import barriers induce foreign direct investment, and thereby tempt multinational enterprises to support a continuation of such antisocial policies in host countries, would the elimination of barriers improve the social performance of multinational enterprises? If so, those who doubt the desirability of foreign direct investment should promote the liberalization of international trade.

63. Data in this paragraph drawn from Helleiner, "Transnational Enterprises and the New Political Economy of U.S. Trade Policy," pp. 13–14.

Certainly, reduction of import barriers would eliminate an important stimulus to many types of past investment. And a commitment to avoid reimposing them would preclude some of the antisocial effects of multinational enterprises (and local firms), which are a legitimate source of concern to host-country nationals.

At the same time, however, trade liberalization would open new vistas for multinational enterprises, which might then extend their foreign direct investment. With trade barriers removed, or even significantly reduced, multinational enterprises would be better able to pursue strategies of worldwide sourcing and worldwide marketing from single locations. Drawing on his analysis of intensity of trade among the regions of the United States, Hufbauer predicts that corporations might embark on a global "wave of rationalization" in the future but that the "prognosis critically depends on the continued relaxation of trade barriers."[64]

So trade liberalization would not necessarily reduce the pace of foreign direct investment, ceteris paribus, and could even increase it. The nature of foreign direct investment would then be less dictated by market imperfections. It would tend more closely to follow traditional lines of comparative advantage. As a result, it should be more economic and hence more widely sought. It would then be less likely to cause conflicts, between governments and between firms and governments, because there would be fewer reasons to believe that investments are triggered by the overt efforts of individual countries to capture economic benefits for themselves at the expense of other countries. With one critical caveat (see below), liberalization of trade barriers could represent a major policy step toward defusing the problems, both economic and political, surrounding multinational enterprises.

The Pace of Change

The potential further expansion of multinational enterprises highlights what is probably the major systemic problem they have caused: a dramatic increase in the pace of change, particularly the transmission of comparative advantage among nations. The costs of adjustment to change have traditionally been ignored in most economic analyses, partly because they were assumed to be quite small and readily offset by macroeconomic policy.

64. "The Multinational Enterprise and Direct Investment," p. 271.

One recent analysis concludes, however, that the increase in imports which would accompany elimination of U.S. tariffs and several import quotas could produce 1.5 million job changes over five years and levy a discounted present cost on the entire economy of perhaps $2 billion.[65] The adjustment costs of simply eliminating tariffs in five import-sensitive U.S. industries are estimated at $283–$578 million.[66] Both estimates assume full employment and cover only the transition costs as displaced workers move from one job to another. Such costs of changes in international production patterns are thus by no means trivial in macroeconomic terms, let alone in terms of the individuals involved, though they represent only a small offset to the benefits to the United States of the posited trade liberalization.

It is quite probable that multinational enterprises accelerate the pace of change in international production patterns. Their ability to move quickly to exploit new production opportunities, by taking advantage of their better pool of information and their more rapid decisionmaking, constitutes much of the rationale for their existence. To the extent that they move quickly, they perforce accelerate the timetable for adjustment by other factors of production, notably labor.

Whether acceleration of change increases total costs of adjustment is a more difficult question to answer. In traditional economic terms, the pace of adjustment makes little difference to its aggregate cost. As in the case of the international monetary system, major benefits may result from forcing the pace of change if the alternative is resistance to the inevitable, as is often the case.

In practice, however, economic growth usually permits a smooth adjustment to economic dislocation over time. Both analyses of the U.S. costs of adjusting to free trade, cited above, assume full employment throughout, which is more likely to be true over the course of an entire business cycle than in any single year. In social and personal terms, adjustment is usually less costly if spaced out. And it becomes increasingly difficult for governments (and other potential countervailing forces) to cope as the process accelerates.

65. Stephen P. Magee, "The Welfare Effects of Restrictions on U.S. Trade," *Brookings Papers on Economic Activity, 3:1972,* pp. 678–83.
66. Robert Baldwin and John H. Mutti, "Policy Issues in Adjustment Assistance: The United States," in Helen Hughes, ed., *Prospects for Partnership: Industrialization and Trade Policies in the 1970s* (Johns Hopkins University Press, 1973), pp. 158–62.

Of course, the benefits to the United States from foreign investment presumably accelerate pari passu with the costs. An immediate question is whether multinational enterprises accelerate the opportunities for adjustment at the same time they accelerate the need for adjustment. If they were creating as many new jobs in a given geographical (perhaps subnational) region as they were moving out, directly or indirectly, their net effect would likely be beneficial or, at worst, neutral.

Another key variable is government policy response. The accelerated pace of change triggered by multinational enterprises could improve government performance, as it helped produce the exchange-rate changes of 1971–73 and the acceptance of greater flexibility of exchange rates. It could also help initiate better programs of adjustment assistance (and may have been at least marginally involved in doing so in the late 1960s).[67] On the other hand, groups adversely affected by the speedup could pressure the government into measures with negative social impact, such as barriers to imports or capital flows.

As a result, the drive to develop countervailing forces to multinational enterprises has intensified as transmitting activities speed up. Hufbauer readily recognizes that a world of free trade, within which multinational enterprises can fully rationalize global production, is possible only if accompanied by either much faster migration of workers or effective programs of adjustment assistance.[68] Faster migration is, in practice, highly unlikely, and indeed appears now to be slowing in Europe. Hence better adjustment is clearly called for as a political response to the acceleration of change induced by multinational enterprises.[69]

Summary

Multinational enterprises appear, on the basis of current evidence, to contribute significantly to the effectiveness of international monetary ar-

67. The U.S. trade adjustment assistance program legislated in 1962 lay dormant for many years. A key reason for its implementation in 1969 was the pressure for trade protectionism, which was in turn related to charges that multinational enterprises were exporting jobs, especially those whose foreign subsidiaries were exporting back to the United States (as in the consumer electronics industry, whose workers were among the most ardent advocates of import controls within the AFL-CIO).

68. "The Multinational Enterprise and Direct Investment," p. 273.

69. See chap. 13 for discussion of this alternative, including who should pay for it.

rangements, to the maintenance of liberal U.S. trade policies, and thus to these important national interests of the United States. They propelled the monetary system toward exchange-rate changes that serve to eliminate the balance-of-payments disequilibria which plagued international economic relations and the U.S. economy in the late 1960s and early 1970s and toward a system that provides the greatest promise for avoiding the development of major new disequilibria. They worked hard, and so far successfully, to promote national policies in both the monetary and trade areas that would produce cooperative systemic arrangements rather than nationalistic confrontations and even conflict. These are best illustrated by their efforts to end the monetary crisis of late 1971 and to head off trade protectionism from 1972 through 1974.

At the same time, the structural characteristics of multinational enterprises raise three major problems for the international economic system. First, their proclivity to invest behind trade (and other) barriers suggests that they will oppose trade liberalization by those countries. The systemic effects of such positions may be limited when they are adopted in the poorer developing countries but can be significant when adopted in developed countries (such as Canada and in Western Europe) and even in more successful developing countries (such as Brazil).

Second, the rapidity with which the firms change their operations accelerates the pace of international economic change and the dislocations, at both the macroeconomic and microeconomic levels, that often follow. Dislocations require government policies of assistance to the specific dislocated factors and adequate control over the macroeconomic effects through such devices as maintaining a capability to intervene in the foreign exchange markets.

Third, it is possible that the focus of multinational enterprises on long-term oligopoly considerations undermines the international balance-of-payments adjustment process, whether that process relies on exchange rates or on other means to achieve the changes in relative prices required for balance-of-payments equilibria. We doubt such a phenomenon. Nevertheless, the issue requires further research before a judgment can be made about it with great confidence.

A final conclusion is that import barriers increase the level (and perhaps the aggregate level) of at least some types of foreign direct investment, alter the structure of foreign direct investment, and promote protectionist attitudes in host countries. Hence an elimination of those barriers would eliminate some of the problems associated with multinational enterprises, such as U.S. penetration of high-technology industries in other countries and the concerns of developing countries about anti-social lobbying effects of multinational enterprises. Our analysis of the interactions between foreign direct investment and international trade reinforce our view that both U.S. and global interests will be served by maximum liberalization of international trade and national policies that smooth the adjustment of all sectors of society to the increase in trade flows which would result.

Foreign Policy

CHAPTER NINE

A Framework for the Analysis of Foreign Policy

THE EFFECT of American multinationals on the national interest is far broader than their effect on the national economy. Multinational corporations affect the distribution of power, the level of tension, and the structure of relations between home and host countries. We need, therefore, a theoretical framework for understanding the impact of foreign investors on both the foreign policy interests of the United States (whether, for example, they increase or decrease America's power, enhance or undermine its security) and on the international system in which American policymakers must act.

The Historical Setting

In the decade and a half following the Second World War, an axiom of American policy was support for direct foreign investment of American companies because of their purported contribution to the American national interest. Free capital flows were integral to the vision of a liberal world order that would allocate resources efficiently and prevent a repetition of the global and domestic economic depression and political fragmentation of the 1930s.[1] Indeed, restoration of an open multilateral

1. Cordell Hull, *The Memoirs of Cordell Hull*, vol. 1 (Macmillan, 1948), reasoned that "unhampered trade dovetailed with peace; high tariffs, trade barriers, and unfair economic competition, with war . . . if we could get a freer flow of trade—

economic system ranked alongside "no more Munichs" as a cornerstone of postwar U.S. foreign policy.

At that time, trade was clearly a more important issue than private direct investment. But the view that the welfare of all, and the particular interests of the United States, required a world of open economic borders permeated the efforts of both the Truman and Eisenhower administrations to persuade hesitant U.S. corporations to expand their operations abroad. Those efforts were justified on the basis of their contribution to global welfare and security, which would enable host countries to raise their standard of living and move toward prosperity and peace.[2] They were justified on the basis of their contribution to U.S. welfare and security: providing access to raw materials, which Clark Clifford and James Forrestal, among others, thought the United States was running out of; promoting the export of manufactured products to a dollar-short world; securing political allies among the recipient countries in a prosperous interdependent world economy.[3] They were justified on the basis of their contribution to domestic stability and their strengthening of American business at home; and of their serving as demonstration by example "that the way of economic life which goes by the name of private enterprise is the sound and true gospel."[4] The arguments in favor of an international system open to both trade and investment appealed, simultane-

---

freer in the sense of fewer discriminations and obstructions—so that one country would not be deadly jealous of another and the living standards of all countries might rise . . . we might have a reasonable chance for lasting peace" (p. 81). Given America's technological lead and potential productiveness, the creation of a liberal international system, he realized, had the additional attraction of assuring the United States of a position "at the head of the column of nations in finance and industrial efficiency and capacity" (p. 126). These views, according to Hull, lasted throughout his twelve years as secretary of state.

2. Harry S. Truman, State of the Union Message, January 4, 1950, *Public Papers of the Presidents: Harry S. Truman, 1950* (GPO, 1965) pp. 4–5; Dwight D. Eisenhower, *Mandate for Change 1953–1956* (Doubleday, 1963), p. 421.

3. Walter Millis, ed., *The Forrestal Diaries* (Viking, 1951), p. 358. Clark Clifford contributed to an early draft of the Truman Doctrine but was dissuaded from phrasing it in those terms by Dean Acheson and George Marshall. See Dean Acheson, *Present at the Creation* (Norton, 1969), p. 221.

4. Merwin L. Bohan, "Understanding Inter-American Economic Problems," *Department of State Bulletin*, vol. 30 (June 7, 1954), p. 876. James Forrestal made similar comments to the Truman cabinet: "I said that the real need was the appointment of ambassadors with some business experience and background as well as negotiating skill, who would vigorously and continuously push the interests of American business." Millis, *The Forrestal Diaries*, p. 358.

ously, to the motifs of global idealism, American economic benefit, and the ideology of free enterprise, that traditionally have been combined in American foreign policy.

Advocates of a liberal world order did not suggest that support for American investment be conditional upon any particular distribution of benefits from the investment. Nor, indeed, did they expect that the political and economic harmony of their vision might depend upon that distribution. Of course, they were wrong. Foreign investment carries with it an extraordinary amount of tension and controversy over the distribution of benefits. Indeed, there are only two conditions under which the economics and politics of distribution might be ignored: one, near-perfect competition in the industries where foreign investment occurs; two, a world in which the costs of economic nationalism for host countries are prohibitive because of either limited economic options or a belief that American political and economic hegemony is eternal.

Near-perfect competition, from the point of view of the host country, would maximize short-term (static) economic welfare. The investor could not exercise discretion about the distribution of benefits except according to the principle of comparative advantage; in other words, a foreign private investor would behave the same as a local private investor. But, even with perfect competition, foreign investment does not necessarily maximize the host's long-term (dynamic) economic welfare or equate private with social costs, which require government intervention in the local economy and, consequently, a host government with the ability to overcome the power of entrenched groups (foreign or indigenous) interested in preserving the status quo.

From the point of view of the United States, as a large, richly endowed home country, an international economic system open to foreign investment under a condition of near-perfect competition would simultaneously optimize the use of its resources and strengthen its position in relation to other countries. But even then the home-country government could add optimum foreign investment controls (analogous to an optimum tariff) in the hope of using its monopoly power as supplier of capital, management, or technology to improve its relative and absolute position at the expense of other states.

The enthusiasm for the analogy to free trade and the confusion of "free enterprise" with "perfect competition" made the rhetoric of businessmen and policymakers in the United States sound as if American policy toward foreign direct investment were predicated upon the assumption of atomistic competition in industries where the investments might take place. In addition, there is no evidence that the United States ever seriously considered optimum investment controls. Rather, given its fear for the national security if the restrictive controls of the 1930s were reinstituted, it adopted a liberal stance toward trade and investment and pressed other nations to do likewise.

But the association of foreign direct investment and highly competitive industries does not fit well with fact or with theory. American companies that grew to multinational dimension in the postwar period are in highly concentrated industries.[5] And, from a theoretical point of view, direct investment would probably never take place under conditions of perfect competition. Capital might flow across borders, seeking the highest interest rate, but it would be under the direct control of the parent only if the firm hoped to exploit some special advantage not accessible to local enterpreneurs—only if the investment were associated with some barrier to entry that rendered the traditional model largely inapplicable.

Imperfect competition undermines the liberal vision of economic and political harmony among home, host, and investor interests and makes that vision appear either naive or hypocritical. To the extent there is monopoly power within an industry, foreign investors enjoy discretion about distribution between home and host countries of the benefits of their investments (employment, taxes, exports). Both home and host, therefore, have an interest in forcing or enticing the investor to do something he would not otherwise do, so as to tilt the benefits toward them. With imperfect competition, then, conflict between home and host coun-

5. *Survey of Current Business,* vol. 40 (September 1960), pp. 20–23, reveals that 64 percent of the $29.7 billion in American foreign direct investment accumulated by 1959 was in petroleum, mining, chemicals, transport, metals, and nonelectric machinery. James W. Vaupel and Joan P. Curhan, *The Making of Multinational Enterprise* (Harvard University Graduate School of Business Administration, 1969), show that, from 1946 to 1961, the ten industrial sectors with the most new foreign subsidiaries are, in order: drugs, industrial chemicals, plastics and synthetics, other fabricated metal products, soaps and cosmetics, motor vehicles and related equipment, other electrical machinery, construction machinery, stone/clay/concrete products, and refined petroleum. According to Joe S. Bain, *International Differences in Industrial Structure: Eight Nations in the 1950s* (Yale University Press, 1966), pp. 70–71, these industrial categories are highly concentrated. For example, 1954 four-firm concentration ratios exceed 50 percent for nearly every subcategory in mining, metals, chemicals, and transport; half of them exceed 75 percent. Economy wide, 1954 manufacturing concentration exceeds 50 percent in only 23.3 percent of the industrial sectors and 75 percent in only 9.2 percent.

tries is inevitable unless both sides agree to let the investor do as he pleases or unless one side acquiesces, by choice or by necessity, in the attempt of the other to maximize its gains jointly with the investor.

The United States did not question the liberal vision as long as the magnitude of American foreign investment was small and other countries had little choice but either accept foreign investment on terms proposed by Americans or do without. American policies and American encouragement for American foreign investment were formed when host governments could do little to induce multinationals to exercise their oligopolistic discretion on behalf of host-country goals. First, host countries had limited capabilities for duplicating or even monitoring the activities of foreign investors; second, competition among foreign investors for entry into host-country industries was low, and the alternatives to multinationals' capital, management, and technology were limited; third, few American companies were exposed to threat or damage if they did not comply with host-country demands; and fourth, host governments did not want to disturb close political relations with the United States. These circumstances are rapidly changing. In short, during the formative period of American policies and attitudes toward American multinationals, the "invisible hand" that seemed to reconcile public and private, home and host interests, making the best option for one the best option for all, was the result of the quasi-monopoly power held by U.S. investors in particular and by the United States in general, not the perfect competition and apolitical international system envisioned by Adam Smith. As the invisible hand itself disappears and the magnitude of American foreign investment expands, policymakers need a new framework to relate the operations of American multinationals to American national interests. No longer can unequivocal support (let alone subsidy) for all American investments abroad be justified in the hope that such investments will benefit home and host countries and increase global welfare. Rather, American policy must be based on a calculation of whether the activities of U.S. multinationals will contribute to American national interests or to the interests of other countries where they operate at U.S. expense, when trade-offs between home and host countries are unavoidable and important welfare or security interests of the United States are at stake.

Will what is best for General Motors be best for the United States as the company extends its interests multinationally? How much discretion will American companies retain as they expand abroad? Under what conditions will they become hostage to host countries, putting their oligopoly power at the service of an ever greater array of host government objectives?

There have been four attempts to relate, in a systematic fashion, the activities of multinational corporations to the economic and political interests of the home country: neoimperialist, neomercantilist, sovereignty at bay, and global reach. The first two postulate that the growth of multinationals represents an extension of the power of the home country at the expense (when there is a trade-off) of the host countries. They differ over how much narrow class interest predominates over the public interest in the formation of foreign policy in the home state. The sovereignty-at-bay and global-reach schools of thought postulate that the growth of multinationals represents an extension of their own power at the expense of the power of both home and host countries. They differ over whether multinationals transform the international system for good or for ill. Each view makes predictions about the prospects for tension or harmony between governments struggling to remain sovereign and about the evolution of the structure of dependence or interdependence among them. Each approach has unique strengths and important insights. None is adequate for the future. In this chapter, after a discussion of these models, we present a new model for answering the questions, and in the chapters that follow, we suggest appropriate policy implications.

The Neoimperialist Interpretation[6]

The neoimperialist analysis of the relation between the private interests of American multinationals and the public interests of the United States

6. See Gabriel Kolko, *The Politics of War: The World and United States Foreign Policy, 1943–1945* (Random House, 1969); Joyce Kolko and Gabriel Kolko, *The Limits of Power: The World and United States Foreign Policy 1945–1954* (Harper, 1970); Harry Magdoff, *The Age of Imperialism: The Economics of U.S. Foreign Policy* (Monthly Review Press, 1969); Stephen Hymer, "The Multinational Corporation and the Law of Uneven Development," in Jagdish N. Bhagwati, ed., *Economics and World Order: From the 1970s to the 1980s* (Macmillan, 1972); K. T. Fann and Donald C. Hodges, eds., *Readings in U.S. Imperialism* (Porter Sargent, 1971); Ernest Mandel, *Europe versus America: Contradictions of Imperialism* (Monthly Review Press, 1970); William Appleman Williams, *The Tragedy of American Diplomacy*, rev. ed. (Dell, 1972); Richard D. Wolff, "Modern Imperialism: The View from the Metropolis," and Arthur MacEwan, "Economics of Imperialism: Discussion," *American Economic Review*, vol. 60 (May 1970); Harry Magdoff, "The Logic of Imperialism," *Social Policy*, vol. 1 (September–October 1970).

rejects the notion of pluralist democracy in the United States. The national interest is synonymous with the interests of American business groups with growing stakes in activities outside the country's borders, not, to be sure, in each and every instance of foreign policy, but in its broad design. Neither government nor policymakers have autonomy in the conduct of foreign policy, except within narrow margins dictated by these groups. As a consequence, any redirection of America's postwar drive to create an international environment receptive to the spread of American business, any abandoning of the defense of the assets and earnings of existing American multinationals, would require a fundamental restructuring of American society.

The neoimperialist school also rejects the liberal notion that an open international economic system is a normatively or politically neutral construct in which foreign investment enables host countries to share the skills of the "center" to the benefit of all. Instead, multinationals have been the agents of American imperialism, producing and maintaining a pattern of inequality and dependency among states. Their operations ensure that the centers of power and decision are located in a few cities of the developed countries—New York, London, Tokyo—while the rest of the world is consigned to lower kinds of economic activity and lower orders of power, status, and income.[7] In the developing countries, the penetration of foreign investment allows host countries to develop only in ways that enable them to respond ever more perfectly to the needs of the home countries. It creates local elites that, fearful of losing a status that is dependent upon the presence of the foreigners, refuse to challenge the privileged position of American multinationals in their societies. Neoimperialists see the American government and American-based multinationals marching hand-in-hand to dominate the world, and often succeeding.

For the future, the Kautskyite branch of neoimperialists predicts a global division of labor in which Europe and Japan act as junior partners inside the American empire, while the Third World becomes efficiently subjugated within a global division of labor. The Leninists, however, predict increasing conflict among the capitalist states and increasing upheaval among the underprivileged states because of inequality and dependency created by the domination of multinational corporations.

7. See Hymer, "The Multinational Corporation and the Law of Uneven Development."

Economic Determinism

The more deterministic of the neoimperialists focus, for the explanation of American foreign policy, on those statements by American policy-makers who have collapsed their motivation into a single expression of economic necessity. James Forrestal, for example, feared that the structure of American industry would be threatened if American access to Middle Eastern oil were endangered.[8] He defended the Truman Doctrine in terms of the need for access to foreign sources of raw materials: "What we are talking is raw materials and we haven't got them. . . . That is the only thing that makes any impression on me at all."[9] Dean Acheson, while undersecretary of state, tried to persuade an isolationist congressional committee that to keep the levels of employment, production, and income growing, the United States would have to find outlets abroad for production and investment.

Such attitudes convince the neoimperialist school that, as long as the economic structure is capitalist, the American government must have an expansionist foreign policy to protect the access of American business to foreign markets and foreign natural resources and to ensure an outlet for surplus capital. The economic hypotheses upon which this argument is based, however, do not stand up well to empirical testing. There is no evidence of a worsening in the distribution of income in the United States over the past three decades, no crisis of underconsumption, and no decline in profitable opportunities for domestic investment (in the aggregate), all of which might push surplus capital abroad.[10] Nearly 70 percent of American foreign investment has gone to other developed areas, where capital is abundant, rather than to the capital-deficient developing areas.[11] The prospect of raw materials shortages is a recent phenomenon, related to host-country leverage over foreign investors—a shift in bargaining power opposite to that predicted by neoimperialist analysis.

8. Specifically, Forrestal warned that the denial of Middle Eastern supplies would force Americans to convert to four-cylinder automobiles. Millis, *The Forrestal Diaries,* p. 358. Thirty years later, after a history of abundance of oil in the U.S. market, Forrestal is being proven right.

9. Quotation according to Paul Shields, *San Francisco Chronicle,* March 19, 1947, cited in Richard J. Barnet, *Roots of War* (Atheneum, 1972), p. 162.

10. See Benjamin J. Cohen, *The Question of Imperialism: The Political Economy of Dominance and Dependence* (Basic Books, 1973), chap. 4; and chap. 4 of this book.

11. *Survey of Current Business,* vol. 54 (August 1974), pt. 2, pp. 18–21.

The proposition that the structure of the postwar economic system was determined by the institutional necessities of capitalism in general or by American monopoly capitalism in specific began to be contradicted by the evidence shortly after the end of the Second World War. Rather than confirming the marxist prediction of chronic underconsumption in advanced capitalist societies, the boom in consumption surprised those on both the left and the right who expected a return to depression. The strength of demand for American manufactures at home and abroad forced prominent American officials (representing the summit of the business-government elite) to apologize repeatedly to the country's trading partners for delays in making delivery on exports. William L. Clayton, a millionaire cotton merchant serving as assistant secretary of state for economic affairs, told the Latin Americans as early as the Chapultepec Conference of 1945 that the United States faced an extremely difficult problem in providing goods to countries that had accumulated hard currency during the war.[12] Winthrop Aldrich, president of the Chase National Bank and advisor to President Truman on international economic policy, led a commercial mission through Latin America in 1947 to explain the North American difficulties in responding to the needs of the developing world with capital, credits, or exports.[13] Rather than looking for markets abroad, the United States maintained export controls on many products through the end of the Korean War in an effort to moderate inflation at home.

The need for raw materials does not explain American policy any better than the need for markets or the need for outlets for capital. The abundance of supply at home and abroad in the first decade after the end of the war, irrespective of the Paley Commission's prediction that the United States would have to rely on rising levels of imports, led to "almost continuous threats of tariff increases or other restrictions" against countries exporting petroleum, copper, lead, zinc, and other commodities that were inundating markets and threatening producers in the United States.[14]

12. *Department of State Bulletin*, vol. 12 (March 4, 1945), pp. 334–38. Clayton was brought to the State Department by Edward Stettinius to help shape international economic policy. Clayton typifies how, from the radical perspective, corporate views were translated directly into postwar foreign policies. Yet he recognized early the limits of America's need for markets, especially in the developing countries.

13. Aldrich had been appointed Chairman of the Committee for Financing Foreign Trade by Truman in 1946. He later backed Thomas Dewey.

14. *Department of State Bulletin*, vol. 21 (July 19, 1954), pp. 80–81.

Stockpiling was begun not to protect against long-term scarcity but to support domestic prices for strategic commodities; to reduce the impact of abundance.[15] The International Trade Organization (proposed in 1945 to complement the General Agreement on Tariffs and Trade but rejected by the Congress in the late 1940s) focused on excessive raw materials supplies and falling prices.[16] And Dean Acheson characterized the declining terms of trade for natural resources as the single recurrent feature of U.S.-Latin American relations.[17]

At the microeconomic level, Bethlehem Steel and U.S. Steel did not begin developing foreign sources of iron ore with any vigor until the end of the Korean War.[18] Copper-producing and petroleum-producing countries were menaced by protectionist senators, not the insatiable appetite of the metropolis.[19] Only intensive lobbying by Anaconda and Kennecott (to enable them to sell their foreign copper at home) kept the U.S. copper tariff suspended for the major part of the 1945–60 period.[20] Oil producers with sources overseas were less successful in securing access to the U.S. market, where they met first informal and then formal import quotas.[21]

Power Elite

But the neoimperialist identification of the American interest with the interests of American multinationals need not depend, in accounting for

15. See Robert Harrison Wagner, *United States Policy Toward Latin America: A Study in Domestic and International Politics* (Stanford University Press, 1970), chaps. 2 and 4, and Percy Bidwell, *Raw Materials: A Study of American Policy* (Harper for the Council on Foreign Relations, 1958), p. 29.

16. C. Fred Bergsten, *Completing the GATT: Toward New International Rules to Govern Export Controls* (Washington, D.C.: British–North American Committee, 1974), p. 4.

17. Acheson, *Present at the Creation*, pp. 496–98.

18. Mira Wilkins, *The Maturing of Multinational Enterprise: American Business Abroad from 1914 to 1970* (Harvard University Press, 1974), p. 306.

19. The efforts of Senator Wallace F. Bennett of Utah to reimpose the four-cent tariff on copper (amounting, at times, to more than 25 percent of the price of refined copper) were particularly resented in Latin America. See *Boletín Minero* (Santiago de Chile: National Mining Society, June 1949).

20. See James L. McCarthy, "The American Copper Industry, 1947–1955," *Yale Economic Essays,* vol. 4 (Spring 1964), p. 98.

21. See M. A. Adelman, *The World Petroleum Market* (Johns Hopkins University Press for Resources for the Future, 1972), pp. 154–55.

the past or in predicting the future, upon economic determinism within the capitalist system. A power elite hypothesis predicts the same outcome. That is, the protection of the business stake abroad and the preservation of the investment option for the future might be a permanent basis for American foreign policy, because these are also the objectives of an elite that dominates American politics. From Franklin Roosevelt's mobilization of prominent Republicans (Henry Stimson, Robert Lovett, and John H. McCloy) to give bipartisan leadership to the war effort, until 1960, 60 percent of high-level posts, deputy assistant secretary or above, in the State, War and Defense, Treasury, and Commerce Departments, and in the White House, were filled by men from backgrounds in international finance, business, or law.[22] Forty-five individuals from large corporations, investment banks, or law firms accounted for 32 percent of all posts. Three investment banks (Dillon, Read, and Co., the Detroit Bank, and Brown Brothers Harriman) accounted for forty posts. Three law firms (Sullivan and Cromwell, Carter, Ledyard and Gilburn, and Coudert Brothers) filled twenty-nine posts.[23] After 1960, the composition of America's foreign policy leadership did not change greatly. In short, Dean Acheson's "spacious environment for free societies" and James Forrestal's "world in which a capitalistic-democratic method can continue" became

22. Gabriel Kolko, *The Roots of American Foreign Policy* (Beacon, 1969), pp. 1–26.

23. Barnet, *Roots of War,* found that "if we look at the men who have held the very top positions, the Secretaries and Under Secretaries of State and Defense, the Secretaries of the three services, the Chairman of the Atomic Energy Commission, and the Director of the CIA, we find that out of ninety-one individuals who held these offices during the period between 1940 and 1967, seventy of them were from the ranks of big business or high finance, including eight out of ten Secretaries of Defense, seven out of eight Secretaries of the Air Force, every Secretary of the Navy, eight out of nine Secretaries of the Army, every Deputy Secretary of Defense, three out of five Directors of the CIA, and three out of five Chairmen of the Atomic Energy Commission," p. 179.

In *Men Who Govern* (Brookings, 1967), pp. 38, 132, David Stanley, Dean Mann, and Jameson Doig show that in the Truman administration 20 percent of the top 180 federal officeholders came from business (60 percent from corporations in the *Fortune* 500) and 22 percent from law; in the Eisenhower administration 34 percent came from business (56 percent from corporations in the *Fortune* 500) and 26 percent from law; in the Kennedy administration, 17 percent came from business (65 percent from corporations in the *Fortune* 500) and 25 percent from law; in the Johnson administration, 20 percent came from business (61 percent from corporations in the *Fortune* 500) and 20 percent from law (pp. 38, 132).

a world where such policy was determined by a small number of men from a narrow class background.[24]

Domestic Consensus in Postwar America

But from the formative period through the 1960s there is little evidence that any prominent political groups in the United States felt that the global interest, the national interest, or the interests of their constituencies would be hurt by American foreign investment. Henry Wallace was harsh in his criticism of Truman's hardening line toward the Soviet Union, but he supported a classic open door approach to trade and investment.[25] So did many isolationists, who claimed to be otherwise opposed to foreign treaties and political entanglements.[26] The American liberal community,

24. For Acheson's view see *Present at the Creation,* pp. 492–97; for Forrestal's statement, see Millis, *The Forrestal Diaries,* p. 127.

25. For this reason, Wallace, the hero of the old left came under attack from the new left. See Ronald Radosh and Leonard P. Iggio, "Henry A. Wallace and the Open Door," in Thomas G. Paterson, ed., *Cold War Critics: Alternatives to American Foreign Policy in the Truman Years* (Quadrangle Books, 1971), pp. 76–113.

26. Robert Taft, however, steadily opposed the open door policy and government subsidies to American business abroad, because he traced the causes of the Depression not to insufficient aggregate demand but to excessive lending abroad by Eastern financiers, which the foreigners then failed to repay. He was also skeptical of the ability of direct foreign investment to improve the material conditions of the masses in other parts of the world or to promote representative government. "I am a little troubled by this theory of exporting capital so that we own billions of dollars of property all over the world—haven't we experienced that that has created hard feelings? We have been absentee landlords and they are always accusing us of exploiting people. . . . Today in Cuba, the fact that we have invested large sums of money . . . is the principal argument of the tremendously growing communistic movement in Cuba today"; *Bretton Woods Agreement Act,* Hearings before the Senate Banking and Currency Committee, 79:1 (GPO, 1945), p. 98. Besides Taft, black critics of colonialism appear to be the only consistent critics of the open door. See Mark Solomon, "Black Critics of Colonialism and the Cold War," in Paterson, *Cold War Critics,* pp. 205–39.

Isolationists feared foreign political commitments, multilateral organizations that might be controlled by others (the United Nations, International Monetary Fund, World Bank), and losing the option of raising tariffs. But opposition to programs that promoted American exports and private direct investment was scarce. The predominantly midwestern conservatives who united behind Taft or Republican Senate Whip Kenneth Wherry to oppose Bretton Woods Agreements Act, the British loan of 1946, and the United Nations Participation Act of 1945, nevertheless supported the Export-Import Bank expansion bill as a way of increasing American penetration of foreign markets, especially in Latin America, and a plan for European

which supports public aid and government loans more vigorously than the conservatives, also supported foreign investment as a central element in U.S. foreign policy.[27] The Alliance for Progress was built on the contribution of American private companies. The leaders of American labor in both the AFL-CIO and the UAW worked strenuously until the late 1960s to convince their constituencies that an international economy open to trade and investment served the political and economic interests of the United States.[28]

The consensus does not reveal a fraudulent democratic process, a perverted pluralism, a false consciousness. As long as there were little or no welfare, security, and adjustment costs traceable to foreign investment, American labor and its political supporters lacked significant self-interest to challenge the economic and political justifications for a liberal economic system. American foreign economic policy, therefore, adequately represented the interests of labor as well as the desires of international business.

Labor's perception of its own interests has now changed, and it claims that the foreign operations of American companies create unemployment in the United States. In aggregate terms this does not appear to be the case (see chapter four). But the adjustment costs from the spectacular rise in American investments (as well as from international trade) fall heavily on organized labor and will continue to in the future. At the same time, labor's bargaining power is threatened by the multinationalization of American firms. Hence, its turn toward restrictionism and protectionism may be a feature of domestic politics for some time to come.

---

reconstruction (advanced by Christian Herter at a lower level of aid than Truman desired) if the reconstruction program were carried out throughout a public corporation, run by businessmen, and independent of the Democratic administration. See also Ronald Radosh, *Prophets on the Right: Profiles of Conservative Critics of American Globalism* (Simon and Schuster, 1975); Richard M. Freeland, *The Truman Doctrine and the Origins of McCarthyism: Foreign Policy, Domestic Politics and Internal Security 1946–48* (Knopf, 1972); and Selig Adler, *The Isolationist Impulse: Its Twentieth Century Reaction* (Abelard-Schuman, 1957).

27. See Robert H. Swansbrough, *The Embattled Colossus: Economic Nationalism and United States Investors in Latin America* (University of Florida Press, 1976); Arthur M. Schlesinger, *A Thousand Days: John F. Kennedy in the White House* (Houghton Mifflin, 1965).

28. See Ronald Radosh, *American Labor and United States Foreign Policy* (Random House, 1969); Frederick S. Dunn, *Peace-Making and the Settlement with Japan* (Princeton University Press, 1963), p. 158; and Gus Tyler, "Labor's Multinational Pains," *Foreign Policy,* no. 12 (Fall 1973), pp. 113–32.

322 *American Multinationals and American Interests*

In addition, other groups in American society have changed their attitudes toward private business and foreign involvement. Tax reformers challenge the tax treatment provided the firms. Others see foreign direct investment engaging the United States in destructive foreign adventures. Recent U.S. policy and legislation reduce, at least modestly, the traditional proinvestment tilt, so that the degree of political change necessary for a new policy approach falls considerably short of the death and transfiguration of American society envisioned in the neoimperialist model. Despite the fact that large American companies (the "power elite") may continue to have a strong—even, in light of their already heavy commitments, growing—private interest in foreign expansion, the outcome of the domestic pressure shaping international economic policy seems much more problematic (for better or for worse) for the next decade than it has been in the last three.[29]

Changes in Host-Country Power

As for the hierarchical structure of exploitation that the neoimperialist school postulates, it has begun to show cracks as the bargaining strength of host countries increases at the expense of foreign investors and their home countries. This change is part of a shift in power from multinationals to host governments that is cumulative, irreversible, and speeding up all the time. This movement runs directly counter to the neoimperialist position.

To be sure, these new power relations may trigger confrontation and economic conflict between home and host countries and, perhaps, among home countries as well. But the conflict will not be based on automatic home-country support for the multinationals, which the power-elite theory predicts. The neoimperialist model successfully accounts for the attempts by a few vulnerable investors to resist host-country pressure by appealing to their home governments for backing. But it ignores the possibility that investors might try to prolong their lives not by seeking extraterritorial diplomatic support but by responding to the wishes of their hosts, even

29. For the reason why individual manufacturing firms may feel an intense need to expand abroad, see Theodore H. Moran, "Foreign Expansion as an 'Institutional Necessity' for U.S. Corporate Capitalism: The Search for a Radical Model," *World Politics*, vol. 25 (April 1973), pp. 369–86. Whether or not their interests will be translated into American policy, however, depends upon the strength of countervailing pressure in the policymaking process.

at the expense of the home country. And it ignores the inevitable result of that process: home-country intervention against the coalition of host-country governments and captive multinationals.

As competition among investors of different nationalities has risen, any strategy other than accommodation has proved increasingly counterproductive. In Iran, the United States did help Great Britain in organizing a blockade against Mossadeq between 1951 and 1953, after he nationalized the operations of the Anglo-Iranian Oil Company; and, under the pretext of keeping the petroleum reserves from falling into the hands of the Soviets, the United States did help overthrow the Mossadeq government.[30] In Guatemala, the Eisenhower administration did back the position of United Fruit Company and its political supporters in Washington (in contrast to the sympathetic American stance toward social reform in post-1952 Bolivia where few American investors were involved), isolated Arbenz, and overthrew him when he turned to the Soviet Union for protection.[31] But there was already a foretaste in the Iranian confrontation of the strength that competition among investors in imperfectly competitive industries could give to economic nationalists. As Great Britain and the United States struggled to maintain a united front against the demands of Mossadeq, W. Alton Jones, president of Cities Service Oil Corporation, suddenly appeared in Teheran, willing to act as refiner and distributor of nationalized Iranian crude, which would have propelled Cities Service from the position of a small independent refiner into the ranks of the major integrated oil companies. Jones was dissuaded from pursuing his purpose, although his very presence "aroused British suspicions . . . and enhanced Mossadeq's obduracy."[32] Mossadeq never got the chance that Qaddafi did.

30. On the nationalization of the Anglo-Iranian Oil Company, see David Wise and Thomas B. Ross, *The Invisible Government* (Random House, 1964); Acheson, *Present at the Creation;* Anthony Eden, *Full Circle: The Memoirs of Anthony Eden* (Houghton Mifflin, 1960). For details of the CIA involvement, see Charles J. V. Murphy, "Uncloaking the CIA," *Fortune,* vol. 91 (June 1975).

31. According to Richard Adams, *Crucifixion by Power: Essays on Guatemalan National Social Structure, 1944–1966* (University of Texas Press, 1970), pp. 185–94, communists occupied important posts in the Arbenz government, especially in the land reform administration. The issue on which members of the press and the Congress challenged Secretary of State John Foster Dulles was whether a soft-line approach might have wooed Arbenz from communist influence and kept him from looking to Czechoslovakia for arms.

32. Acheson, *Present at the Creation,* p. 681.

The Neomercantilist Interpretation

The neomercantilist analysis of the relation between American investors and American national interests exhibits many of the same weaknesses as the neoimperialist approach.[33] It dismisses the impact of pluralist politics on the definition of the national interest and assumes that foreign investors will be responsive to the needs of the home rather than the host country. This school sees the nation-state (rather than the capitalist class) as a unitary actor and postulates that the government uses the activities of businesses abroad to advance the interests of the state.[34]

Nationalism and International Trade

For neomercantilists, anarchism is the natural condition of international relations, since countries will always strive with each other for relative advantage. In such an environment, the "high politics" of national power and national security take precedence over the "low politics" of economic welfare. Foreign economic policy is subordinate to national security policy. The promotion of international economic power and domestic prosperity are only aspects of the larger objective of preserving national strength in relation to other states.

In the neomercantilist perspective, the spread of American multinationals cannot be understood apart from the international political order created by the United States at the end of the Second World War, in competition with the Soviet Union, to bring host countries into its orbit of influence. An open international economic system may in fact provide economic gains to all its members. But maximizing global economic efficiency, or even domestic economic welfare, has never provided sufficient motivation for nation-states to accept liberal trading and investment arrangements. Stable, open international economic systems of the past were

33. Contemporary mercantilists (or neomercantilists) do not identify their position with protectionism in trade. Rather they define mercantilism as the subservience of economic policy to the goal of exercising national power, a goal justified in military, ideological, and humanitarian terms but frequently pursued as an end itself.

34. In contrast to most other neomercantilists, Robert Gilpin, *U.S. Power and the Multinational Corporation* (Basic Books, 1975) uses a pluralist model of U.S. policymaking, asserting that international business groups in the United States (as, earlier, in Great Britain) may force the state to follow policies that are not in the broader national interest.

creations of imperial powers, which enforced the rules of liberalism in trade and investment because those rules helped consolidate both their economic and political power in the international system.

Conversely, the rules of liberalism have been accepted by subdominant powers only so long as the cost (political, military, or economic) of pursuing a more autonomous course was insupportable. This was true during the half century following the abolition of the British Corn Laws in 1846, when the British Empire went from global preeminence into relative decline. It has been equally true in the post-World War II period, when America began by dictating the trade, monetary, and investment relations for the rest of the world that best served its own national interest and then lost the power to set the rules.

As the security bonds that characterize the bipolar confrontation of the cold war weaken, the traditional goal of nation-states—namely, to enhance their security and power relative to other nation-states—will, according to neomercantilists, reassert itself. The international system will become more heterogeneous, more nationalistic, and perhaps more protectionist. States will be more prone to close their borders, individually or on a regional basis, rather than tolerate a massive foreign presence. In contrast to the exuberant expansion of American multinationals with implicit or explicit government support, in the first two decades of the postwar period, a counteroffensive on the part of other governments to limit or even roll back the American invasion may be a central feature of the era that replaces the Pax Americana. This reaction will be reinforced by the reluctance of the United States to allow non-American investors to buy up the so-called commanding heights of the American economy.

Neomercantilists tend to draw their evidence from relations among the developed states rather than from developing countries, as the neoimperialists do.[35] They argue that American postwar policy toward Europe and Japan demonstrates (contra the radicals) that the "high politics" of national security prevailed over the "low politics" of American economic welfare in general, and over the interests of American business in particular. The United States underwrote the reconstruction of European

35. They counsel non-American host countries to build up independent industrial and technological bases and their own multinationals to challenge American investors. But non-American multinationals, like American multinationals, respond less and less to the preferences of their own home governments. For evidence, see chapter 11.

societies, through the Marshall Plan, as a bulwark against the Soviet Union and sponsored the formation of the Common Market to eliminate the problem of a revitalized Germany at the cost of discrimination against U.S. exports and the creation (in the long run) of an economic rival to the United States. American policymakers permitted the Japanese to exclude direct foreign investment from their economy while allowing the Japanese access to the American market in exchange for American bases in Japan and Okinawa. Here too the ultimate effect of U.S. security policy (only dimly perceived at the beginning) was to create a major competitor to the American business community.

The Evidence Against

But these illustrations do not withstand close scrutiny in historical terms. Even less are they guides to analyzing the relation between corporate and national interests in the future. The international banking and investment community in the United States was clearly more concerned about the danger of Japan's collapse in the short run than the challenge of its economic revival in the long run. When the peace treaty was being negotiated (1951), Japan accounted for only 1.9 percent of all American imports, concentrated in sewing machines, toys, glassware, and china.[36] American policymakers, though concerned with the threat of a rejuvenated Japanese merchant marine to the American shipping industry, never had the anxiety that their counterparts did in Great Britain, Australia, and New Zealand that Japan might one day be a commercial threat.[37] Given the unavailability of American capital and management to underwrite the reconstruction of Japan, the indifference of James Forrestal or John Foster Dulles to the de-zaibatsu efforts of the American government (the reversal of which ultimately permitted the protection and recartelization of Japanese industry) equally suited their views as Wall Street capitalists and as national security managers.[38] They, like the leaders of the AF of L and the CIO,[39] predicted that rising U.S. exports and declining

36. Jerome B. Cohen, "Economic Problems of Free Japan," Princeton University Center for International Studies (1952; processed), pp. 67–68.

37. Dunn, *Peace-Making and the Settlement with Japan*, pp. 150–64.

38. Millis, *The Forrestal Diaries*, p. 328; on Dulles, see Chitoshi Yanaga, *Big Business in Japanese Politics* (Yale University Press, 1968), chap. 9.

39. *Proceedings of the Thirteenth Constitutional Convention of the Congress of Industrial Organizations* (New York: 1951), p. 487.

U.S. taxes (to pay for the occupation) would be the primary results of speeding Japan's economic recovery.

With regard to the Common Market, American business and labor anticipated that the economic growth it stimulated would create more trade with the United States than it diverted; that it, more than any other feasible policy, would lead to a larger market for American exports (even with discrimination). Moreover, the American government insisted, as a condition of U.S. support for the Treaty of Rome, that subsidiaries of American multinationals be treated as national firms, providing a gap in the tariff walls for American investors. In a double sense, American policy was clearly not a trade-off between corporate and national interests.

Thus, when American policy toward Europe and Japan was formed during the cold war period, the American business community believed that the greatest threat to individual corporate interests would also be the greatest threat to national security interests. The alternative, against which the neomercantilist school measures the validity of its perspective, namely, that American investors push for short-term private gains at the expense of national security, is simply implausible. The interests of an international business community, fearing the expansion of Soviet influence, predict the same kind of policy response as the interests of a global power trying to deal with the instability caused by the collapse of Germany and Japan.[40] The "high politics" of America's national security

40. Overdetermination largely accounts for the inconclusiveness of the revisionist debate about the origins of the cold war. It is not enough for one side to demonstrate that the great majority of American policymakers during the period came from a particular class background. Nor is it sufficient for the other side to refute the "economic necessity" of expansionism, as Robert W. Tucker does (*The Radical Left and American Foreign Policy,* Johns Hopkins University Press, 1971). One must also ask whether American leaders without corporate ties or corporate socialization would have defined the country's security needs differently. There is no doubt that hypothetical elites trying to maximize the power of, say, an international proletariat in other than a nation-state environment would have advocated dramatically different policies. But did the actual policymakers behave in a way that policymakers who pursued only the welfare and security interests of the United States would not have? For example, would the latter have accepted boundaries for the postwar noncommunist order that excluded the countries of Eastern Europe or would they have insisted on more extensive frontiers? And if they had acted in a more restrained manner, would this have proved (in revisionist terms) that they were free of the conditioning of capitalism or simply more skillful at traditional statecraft? Without a clear divergence between long-run corporate interests and long-run national interests, revisionists face a severe methodological hurdle—separating class bias from inept realpolitik. One must also ask, of course, whether such a hypothetical noninter-

were the "high politics" of America's international business as well; the two-track approach to politics and economics was built on a single roadbed.[41]

DIVERGING INTERESTS. But the strategic needs of American business and the strategic needs of the United States will not necessarily continue to overlap as American multinationals extend their operations farther. Some companies and some industries will find their interests diverge completely from American interests. For others, there will be more congruence. The supposition of the neomercantilist school, that the spread of American multinationals is identical with the extension of American national power, depends on the circumstances of the past. The neomercantilist school is surely justified in anticipating the resurgence of the assertion of national sovereignty among host governments as the conditions that surrounded the early American postwar hegemony disappear. But their arguments do not support the simultaneous decline of American multinationals as the environment that encouraged them changes. Our analysis suggests that with the relative decline of American political and economic power, American multinationals may not recede. Rather, they (like the multinationals of other home countries) will survive as self-interested institutions, adapting to the changing pattern of pressure by putting the use of their oligopoly power increasingly at the service of diverse national claimants.[42]

---

national capitalist elite could have avoided the domestic (noneconomic) political pressure—for example, the competition between Republican and Democratic parties for the East European ethnic vote—that pushed the country toward confrontation with the Soviet Union.

41. The important analytical distinction is really between the past and the present. In the past American business leaders saw a fundamental compatibility between the requirements of national security and the requirements of their own maximum corporate growth abroad, which they may not see now. For the two-track distinction, see Richard N. Cooper, "Trade Policy is Foreign Policy," *Foreign Policy,* no. 9 (Winter 1972–73), pp. 18–36.

42. Analysts have rightly pointed out that American multinationals have never (despite proud pronouncements to the contrary) become anational institutions in terms of ownership or management. A survey of the seventy-one U.S. corporations with the largest foreign activity in 1966 showed that, while total foreign employment in the companies reached 33 percent, only 1.6 percent of the top management (30 of 1,815 executives) were non-American. Kenneth Simmonds, "Multinational? Well, Not Quite," *Columbia Journal of World Business* (Fall 1966), p. 118. A study of 1,029 directors of companies in the Harvard Business School's sample of 187 multinationals revealed only nineteen foreigners, of whom fourteen were Canadian or British. (See Raymond Vernon, *Sovereignty at Bay: The Multinational Spread of*

The hypothesis that, in a crisis, the United States as home country could force its companies to do its bidding overseas is dubious. In the few instances where it worked, the cumulative effect might be to reduce America's power to react (or, more precisely, to raise the cost, economically and politically, of reacting) even in a crisis. Moreover, in the post-cold-war period, as the "high politics" of national security become blurred, dissatisfaction with the activities of American multinationals among influential groups at home could precipitate a reaction of restrictionism and protectionism that would be inimical to the long-term economic, political, and security interests of the United States.

Sovereignty-at-Bay Interpretation

For the sovereignty-at-bay and the global-reach schools, the focus shifts from multinational corporations as extensions of the power of the home country to multinational corporations as independent forces constraining the actions of all the states they touch.[43]

From the sovereignty-at-bay perspective, four nonpolitical variables laid the basis for the expansion of multinational corporations in the postwar period: the decline in the cost of international transportation, the decline in the cost of international communication, the rise in logistical efficiency in managing complex organizations, and the rise in the cost of generating and launching major industrial innovations. All four trends are predicted to continue. In this setting, the ability of multinationals to provide goods and services more efficiently than the available alternatives is both the necessary and the sufficient explanation for their spread.

Multinationals as an Anational Force

Furthermore, although multinationals (European and Japanese as well as American) may have been used in the past to advance particular interests of their home governments, according to the sovereignty-at-bay school they are all now becoming apolitical, anational institutions. Be-

---

U.S. Enterprises, Basic Books, 1971, p. 146.) Control of the key activities does not require majority ownership, or, indeed, any.

43. See Vernon, Sovereignty at Bay; Robert O. Keohane and Joseph S. Nye, Jr., eds., Transnational Relations and World Politics (Harvard University Press, 1971).

cause they must key their activities to the behavior of rivals in the international arena, they are forced to dissociate themselves from the political and economic objectives of both home and host countries. At the same time, this increase of competition among foreign investors pushes multinational behavior, even among large and relatively concentrated businesses, toward maximizing global economic welfare. The share that any particular government (home or host) receives of the rising global welfare, then, depends upon its natural factor endowment and international comparative advantage.

Unlike the liberal vision of harmony, however, the process of global development via multinational corporations is not expected by the sovereignty-at-bay school to occur without conflict. On the contrary, the profound importance that multinational corporations hold for American national interests, and for the evolution of the international system, is the result of the economic and political tension they arouse. The reaction against the spread of these private, independent centers of economic power, operating according to supranational strategies, comes from at least three directions: from governments that want more control over the domestic economy; from local economic groups that want to compete with the multinationals; and from host-country leaders who want to seize the issue of foreign penetration to gain some advantage in local politics.

Four factors, however, make restrictive or exclusionary policies untenable (at least as a sustained response). First, the economic and technological benefits for the populace of host countries are likely to be too great to permit governments to do without the activities of multinationals. Second, regulation is certain to be ineffective, and frequently counterproductive, when confined to single states acting on their own. Third, in an interdependent world, the mutual vulnerability of countries to retaliation against their own investors (or commerce) deters effective nationalistic action. Finally, multinational executives, whose interests would be damaged by barriers and obstacles that impede the operations of foreign investors, form transnational alliances and become "the new globalists," the "advance men" of "economic one-worldism" who "wear the robes of diplomats."[44] Separately or in combination, these four factors are pre-

44. William I. Spencer (president, First National City Corporation), "The New Globalists" (speech delivered to the American Chamber of Commerce, Frankfurt, Germany, September 6, 1972), quoted in Samuel P. Huntington, "Transnational Organizations in World Politics," *World Politics*, vol. 25 (April 1973), p. 363.

dicted to offset the psychic satisfaction sought in narrow nationalistic responses.

Supranational Regulation

There remains, therefore, only one method to combine the benefits of international investment with the desire for sovereign control. That is supranational regulation. How this might transform the international system is suggested with widely differing degrees of certainty and enthusiasm, widely differing views on what international control of corporate-state interaction would look like, and widely differing predictions about the degree of political spillover. The researchers associated with the Harvard project on multinational enterprises suggest that international regulation will be hesitant and piecemeal, that multinational corporations will themselves be the object of control by a global regulatory body formed by governments exercising sovereignty on behalf of their populations, and that other political spillover effects may be minimal.[45]

Others in the economic and business community assert that the implications for political transformation will be more dramatic, with acts of nationalism by individual states being the object of control. In this scenario, the goal would be to provide multinationals with maximum freedom to operate unimpeded. George W. Ball, for example, argues that "the nation-state is a very old-fashioned idea and badly adapted to serve the needs of our present complex world," and that the only way the world's populations can take advantage of the benefits that multinationals have to offer is by "modernizing the world's political structure."[46] Harry G. Johnson postulates that "the fundamental problem of the future is the conflict between the political forces of nationalism and the economic forces pressing for world economic integration."[47] At the moment, he continues, nationalism may appear to be ascendant but "in the longer run economic forces are likely to predominate over political, and may indeed

45. See Vernon, *Sovereignty at Bay,* chap. 8; Raymond Vernon, "Economic Sovereignty at Bay," *Foreign Affairs,* vol. 47 (October 1968), pp. 110–22; and Raymond Vernon, "The Multinational Enterprise: Power Versus Sovereignty," *Foreign Affairs,* vol. 49 (July 1971), pp. 736–51.
46. "The Promise of the Multinational Corporation" (speech delivered to the New York Chamber of Commerce), reprinted in *Fortune,* vol. 75 (June 1967), p. 80.
47. *International Economic Questions Facing Britain, The United States, and Canada in the 1970's* (London: British North American Committee, 1970), p. 24.

332   *American Multinationals and American Interests*

come to do so before the end of this decade. Ultimately, a world federal government will appear to be the only rational method for coping with the world's economic problems."

Nevertheless, the desire for the benefits of multinational corporations and the desire to exercise effective national sovereignty are projected to head in a single direction; sovereignty at bay in individual nations will lead to the pooling of sovereignty among nations; sovereignty at bay in the face of the continuing penetration and cross-penetration of multinational corporations will lead to the obsolescence of the nation-state.

The Argument Against

But will economic nationalism be too costly and too ineffective for individual governments to pursue without cooperating in a global effort to regulate multinational corporate activities? There are five (nonexclusive) reasons to believe that the assertion of national sovereignty may not initially take the form of international regulation projected by the sovereignty-at-bay school. First, in a world where multinational corporations are global oligopolies exercising substantial discretion in the conduct of international activities, bargaining by an individual state to get those corporations to serve its goals may not involve any economic losses at all to the state; the result may simply be collusion, active or tacit, between host governments and firms, their disagreements limited to how to divide up the spoils. Second, in a world where multinational corporations are global oligopolies exercising substantial discretion in the conduct of international activities and where other host countries are exerting pressure to get multinational corporations to serve their goals, a state that does not push as hard as it can to serve its own national interests may find itself a loser. Third, in the industrial centers of Europe, Japan, and some of the developing countries, economic security and the exercise of sovereignty may be perceived to be worth potential losses in efficiency. Fourth, the gains to a single state from a nationalistic policy may be greater than its loss of a share of global welfare. Fifth, the joint regulation of multinationals at some level other than global (for example, by a producer's cartel or by regional groups such as the Andean Pact and the European Community) may better reconcile sovereign and economic interests for some states than the worldwide coordination of national policies.

If these conditions hold, economic nationalism is a rationally self-interested approach. The resulting struggle among nations to tilt in their direction the distribution of benefits generated by multinationals suggests a potential for fragmentation and disintegration in the international system quite at odds with the kind of cooperation and harmony envisioned by some proponents of the sovereignty-at-bay school. Far from finding that the enormous growth of multinationals places sovereignty at bay, we conclude that the rivalries among them increase their vulnerability to government pressure in the countries where they operate and may produce a battlefield strewn with both economic distortions and political conflict.

The significance of multinationals for the structure of the international system, then, is not as independent centers of private economic power, limiting the sovereignty of all they touch, but as a means for nation-states to exercise national power.[48] Instead of pooled sovereignty, we predict nationalistic struggles to seize maximum advantage for individual nations from multinational corporations, leading, in the extreme, to investment wars, unless the United States arms itself with new policy tools to alter the calculus of self-interest on the part of investors and countries alike and then takes a leadership role in formulating and enforcing policies of cooperation.

Global-Reach Interpretation

Like the sovereignty-at-bay approach, the global-reach school concludes that the power of multinational corporations is growing at the expense of both home and host countries. According to Richard J. Barnet and Ronald E. Müller, multinationals are striving by conscious design to become anational entities (although they are still likely, when in trouble, to seek to use their home governments in subtle or covert ways to undermine the attacks of nationalists).[49] But in contrast to the optimism of the sovereignty-at-bay school that foreign investors promote global economic welfare and political harmony, the global-reach school holds that multinationals stifle competition, cartelize world markets, worsen income

48. See Huntington, "Transnational Organizations in World Politics."
49. *Global Reach: The Power of Multinational Corporations* (Simon and Schuster, 1974). Page references in the following paragraphs are to this edition.

distribution, and create poverty in home and host societies alike. Further, American multinationals export jobs from the United States, destroy jobs in host countries, and refuse to develop new labor-intensive technologies to take advantage of the factor proportions in developing countries.

Barnet and Müller recognize, however, that foreign-investor relations with the Third World may be at a point of change, because the developed countries need the natural resources and cheap labor of the developing countries. In their chapter "The Power of the Poor" one glimpses the beginnings of a theory of host-country bargaining power: they relate Europe and Japan's economic recovery to the improved terms on which host countries do business—their demands for sealed-bid contracts and disclosure. But Barnet and Müller go on to refute this finding by claiming that the "global oligopolies develop ever greater and more concentrated power through various forms of 'cross-subsidization' " (p. 220)—that they use their power in one sector of the economy to acquire power in another. Nor do the authors seek to reconcile the contradiction between their correct assessment that the firms go to developing countries to employ cheap labor and their claim that the multinationals raise levels of unemployment wherever they go.

The impact of multinational corporations on the international economic and political system, from the global-reach perspective, is malign in the extreme. Multinationals negate the workings of international markets through their use of transfer pricing, dominate the international flow of money through unrecorded transactions, and deny to even the largest countries (Germany, the United States) the macroeconomic tools to restore stability (p. 285). Multinationals are responsible for antagonism between developed and the developing countries and divisiveness between the rich and the poor everywhere. In short, they "act as disturbers of the peace on a global scale" (p. 367).

Barnet and Müller would remedy these problems through international disclosure of corporate activities, investment by American companies at home rather than abroad, national development planning, local community control, and worker sovereignty. The targets would be an internal and international redistribution of income in favor of the poorest 60 percent of the world's population and a move toward self-sufficiency in raw materials and manufactured goods for the United States. The result would not be isolationism, according to them. Rather, it would prepare Americans to act as global citizens.

The Evidence Against

Aside from the internal inconsistencies among its policy proposals, there are other weaknesses in global-reach theory.[50] Our investigation leads us to be highly skeptical of its conclusions on unemployment and distribution of income in the United States and about corporate concentration worldwide (although we find that foreign investment by American firms does increase oligopoly power in the United States). Furthermore, the power of host governments to impose new demands on the foreign-based multinationals is increasing over time and will continue to do so.

The conflicts that multinational corporations provoke among the countries where they invest can be turned into opportunities for cooperation through measures far less disruptive than Barnet and Müller propose. We argue in chapter eight that, on balance, multinationals act as a major force propelling nation-states (including the United States) to take a long-range view of their national interests in terms of a smoothly functioning international system. Severe restrictions on the ability of American firms to operate abroad—even restrictions much less stringent than Barnet and Müller envision—would deprive host countries of advantages they have become accustomed to, and would reduce global economic welfare to the detriment of even the poorest 60 percent. The need to face trade-offs between home and host in the distribution of benefits from multinationals cannot be avoided. Radical populism (no matter how generously phrased) could in fact fuel the drive toward U.S. isolationism and nationalism.

The New Setting

During the first decade and a half of the postwar period, the question of whose national interests American investors would serve as a by-product of pursuing their own self-interest was not a problem for American policymakers. Other countries could neither duplicate nor do without the

50. How could comprehensive national planning coexist with local community control? How could a reduction of investment by American firms promote the welfare of the poorest groups abroad? How could U.S. self-sufficiency be squared with being a good global citizen? Barnet and Müller (ibid.) do not reconcile these contradictions, and thus useful material in the analytical chapters has received less attention than it deserves.

services of American investors, American companies had few assets and earnings abroad, in comparison to what they had in the United States, competition among potential investors was small, and host governments were usually not willing to risk political conflict with the United States. But these special conditions are rapidly disappearing and with them the basis for uncritically equating the interests of American multinationals with American interests.

INTERNATIONAL POLITICAL CHANGE. First, the political basis of international economic relations has changed. The relaxation of cold war tensions means that no host country, be it a member of NATO or a developing country, needs to constrain its economic policies and objectives to avoid tension with its protector, the United States. Confrontation with an American-based firm will not jeopardize its security. (In times of high bipolar tension, exposed countries formerly were unable to express concern over even nonsecurity issues for fear of jeopardizing their security relation.) In addition, escape from the security dilemma enables other home countries to support home-based multinationals, which, by competing with American multinationals, provide new options for host countries. Partly because of this decline in the international leverage of the United States and partly because of the rise in scope for nationalistic expression in host countries, American multinationals are increasingly reluctant to appeal to the U.S. government to defend them in disputes with host countries, which further emboldens host countries in pushing for their demands.

INTERNATIONAL ECONOMIC CHANGE. Second, the resurgence of national economies and firms throughout the industralized world provides host countries with more economic options. For one, more benefits can be exacted from American multinationals because European-based and Japanese-based multinationals are frequently waiting in the wings to step in if an opportunity arises.[51] Then, again, to help them overcome late entry into the race for international markets and sources of production, non-American multinationals are often more flexible in meeting the desires of host countries.[52]

51. One example of the difference this can make, even for some of the poorest of host countries, is recounted in Robert L. Curry, Jr. and Donald Rothchild, "On Economic Bargaining Between African Governments and Multi-national Companies," *Journal of Modern African Studies*, vol. 12 (June 1974), esp. p. 182.

52. M. Y. Yoshino, "Japanese Foreign Direct Investment" (Harvard University Graduate School of Business Administration, 1972; processed), pp. 32–42, makes this point explicitly about Japanese firms.

Furthermore, there are alternatives to foreign direct investment, itself. The private international capital market in recent years has provided billions of dollars of credits to developing countries. Technology is available through licensing, particularly for countries with large markets, which foreign-based firms want to participate in even if it means compromising their own preference. Management is available under contractual arrangements with both multinationals and independent firms. In some industries, to be sure, the offer of these functions in one bundle (the multinational enterprise) is a more attractive package, and host countries vary in their ability to unbundle the package. But the growth of real options, in both geographical and functional terms, greatly strengthens host countries in pursuing their own national interests.

GROWTH OF SOCIAL GOALS. Third, governments have assumed responsibility for a broader array of economic and social policy goals, raising the need for the benefits which multinationals can provide if they are properly harnessed. Outside forces, including trade flows as well as multinational investment flows, must be channeled so as not to disrupt plans. In addition, the excess of policy targets over policy instruments compels these governments to find additional sources of help and to devise policies that can direct foreign investment to support domestic objectives.

GROWTH OF HOST-COUNTRY SKILLS. Fourth, the competence of host countries to deal effectively with multinationals has progressed tremendously. Development over two decades has generated an educated and trained elite in developing as well as industrialized countries. Experience in dealing with multinationals provides them with the expertise to deal with the most skillful firms. When indigenous talent is unavailable or too thin to handle all of the investment applications, outside consultants are available. The new United Nations program on multinationals provides such assistance. Cooperation among host countries helps them cope effectively with multinational enterprises. Producers' associations share information on the activities of the companies, which at a minimum reduces the possibility that the countries can be played off against each other and may enable the countries to develop a consistent general strategy for controlling the companies while allowing them to perform the roles (such as marketing and allocation of production) that will promote host-country goals.[53] Investment control by host countries are in fact becoming an im-

53. OPEC's history is traced in Abdul Amir Q. Kubbah, *OPEC, Past and Present* (Vienna: Petro-Economic Research Centre, 1974); on the International Bauxite Agreement, see C. Fred Bergsten, "A Second OPEC in Bauxite," *Challenge* (July/

portant transnational factor in international economic and political relations. Active communication and seminars have sprung up among these officials, particularly throughout the developing world.

Host-Country Attitudes

As a result of these shifts in political and economic conditions, the past decade and a half has witnessed the intensification of efforts on the part of host countries to harness foreign multinationals to a broad spectrum of national tasks. Until about ten years ago, the attitudes of most countries toward incoming investment were clear-cut and dogmatic. They either welcomed it with open arms or were skeptical in the extreme. The welcomers included most of Western Europe, the white Commonwealth (including Canada and Australia), and most of the nonsocialist developing countries (including the oil exporting countries). The main skeptics were the communist countries, countries oriented toward socialism (such as India), and Japan. In most cases, attitudes toward foreign direct investment paralleled national attitudes toward private enterprise in general: market-oriented countries liked foreign as well as domestic private investment, socialist-oriented countries disliked both. Japan was the most notable exception to this generalization, distinguishing throughout the postwar period between domestic and foreign enterprises (and goods) rather than between private and state enterprises. France periodically followed the Japanese pattern (although in a more selective manner) and is the most difficult major country to classify among the welcomers and the skeptics.

During the last decade, the dichotomy in host-country attitudes has given way to a remarkable convergence. All but the most rigid of the skeptics, primarily the Asian communist countries (including Albania), have significantly liberalized their attitudes toward foreign direct investment. The most dramatic changes of attitude have come in the Soviet Union and several Eastern European countries (particularly Rumania, Hungary, and Czechoslovakia), which now actively seek it.

At the same time, the welcomers of the past have become skeptical.

August 1976); and on the Intergovernmental Council of Copper Exporting Countries see Karen A. Mingst, "Cooperation or Illusion: An Examination of the Intergovernmental Council of Copper Exporting Countries," *International Organization*, vol. 30 (Spring 1976), pp. 263–87.

Canada and Australia offer the most dramatic examples of this turnabout, adopting detailed national legislation and creating government agencies to regulate the flow of inward investment. For developing countries, the traditional love-hate approach to foreign investors has remained unchanged on the verbal level, but host-country policies governing multinationals have become stricter, more selective, and more effective. Even the industrialized host countries of Western Europe, including those whose ideology is traditionally laissez-faire (such as Germany) and those whose role as home countries makes them chary of tight governmental surveillance of multinationals (especially the United Kingdom and the Netherlands), are part of this trend.

The result is that countries no longer simply ask themselves whether they want foreign direct investment or not but pursue, instead, a two-track policy of first attracting investment (through the use of tax and other inducements, if necessary) and then harnessing it to assure that it will promote their national interests. To be sure, the balance of bargaining power has tilted further for some countries than for others. Japan and Brazil have booming internal markets; Canada and Australia, a wealth of industrial raw materials; OPEC countries have oil; and Mexico, Taiwan, Korea, and Singapore can produce semimanufactured goods with high efficiency at low wages. But even such low-developed countries as Papua New Guinea and Botswana struck remarkably favorable deals with such sophisticated firms as Rio Tinto Zinc and Amax, respectively.

Host-Country Rhetoric

This increasing exercise of countervailing power by host countries is a cardinal element in the declining salience of le défi Americain as a domestic political issue in Western Europe, Canada, and Australia. However, it is not yet reflected in either the rhetoric or the policies of the developing host countries. There, charges that multinationals are either entities unto themselves, socially responsible to no one, or merely the latest tools of American imperialist exploitation, have, if anything, escalated. These countries continue to use international forums to press for new countervailing powers.

In our view, several factors explain the contradiction between the postures of less-developed host countries and the realities. The most important is the tactical advantage they gain by keeping the multinationals and their home countries on the defensive. This advantage is manifest in the ongoing discussion about controlling multinationals—but not host countries—through international organizations. It is also apparent in the more general effort of the Third World to achieve a "new international economic order" by, in part, playing on First World guilt that its institutions, including multinational enterprises, have exploited the developing countries. Keeping home countries on the defensive may keep them from perceiving the reality, that host-country control of multinationals can have adverse effects on the national interests of home countries.

Part of the difference between rhetoric and reality stems from domestic and international bureaucratic considerations within the developing countries. The leverage over incoming multinationals is exercised by the finance and other economic ministries, whereas the policies for the United Nations and other forums are developed by ministries of foreign affairs. Hence economic reality may not be quickly translated into political rhetoric.

In addition, policies in the international institutions, especially the United Nations, are often implemented by uninstructed delegations, who therefore simply repeat the words of the past even though realities have changed dramatically. This tendency fuses with the international politics of the Third World, which adopts a common position that the most strident countries will accept. In the interests of rhetorical solidarity, as opposed to pragmatic action (in which it is more difficult to maintain a solid front), the politically oriented participants in debates in the United Nations and elsewhere will thus tend to castigate the multinational enterprises.

A further explanation is the usual lag in perceptions of reality. Most trends are observed only when enough time has passed that watersheds can be clearly observed. Particularly in light of the lags in the availability of data, it is fully understandable that most of the conventional wisdom about the power of multinational enterprises and the weakness of host countries continues to dominate thinking in many parts of the world. These lags in perception are fueled, of course, by proclamations in the United States that sovereignty is at bay and that the firms can exercise an unfettered global reach.

A final factor may be an understandable lack of confidence on the part of host countries that, despite the impressive series of steps they have in fact undertaken, they will be able to maintain effective countervailing power. Even now, some developing countries lack the ability to implement their own performance requirements, an important shortcoming in the exercise of host-country power.[54] And it is certainly true that any number of outside events could reduce the leverage of host countries. Prolonged and deep world recession could force host countries to accept the terms offered by prospective investors. Coordination of host-country interests may not prove sustainable; particularly in tough economic periods, local capitalists and even government officials may once more "sell out" to the multinationals. A recrudescence of cold war could again make them dependent on the United States for their security and less able to exercise independence vis-à-vis American-based firms if the United States chose to make that a consideration. New technological breakthroughs, either to use materials more effectively or to use alternatives, could weaken the commodity power of OPEC and its emulators. If several home countries restrict the spread of their corporations, host countries would have fewer alternatives. If governments decided together to control the Eurocredit markets, they could limit another source of independence for hosts. Multinationals could devise new strategies to foil the efforts of the host countries, perhaps by engaging their home-country governments to defend them more effectively than in the past.

Hence, there are legitimate reasons to question whether the countervailing power of host-country governments is permanent. However, two changes that have enabled them to exercise greater control seem irreversible: the greater competence of host-country nationals and the increased economic capability of other industralized countries to provide competition for American multinationals. We doubt that any of the events listed in the last paragraph will occur to a sufficient degree to reverse the process. Nevertheless, the possibility that host countries could lose ground, combined with the factors mentioned earlier, suggests why the rhetoric of

54. Examples are provided in Richard D. Robinson, "National Efforts to Establish Guidelines for the Behavior of Multinational Firms" (report prepared for the U.S. Labor Department; processed), esp. pp. 0.35 and 1.22; and in Lynn Mytelka, "Direct Foreign Investment, Technology Transfer and Andean Integration" (paper prepared for delivery at the 1976 meeting of the International Political Science Association; processed), p. 26. Robinson also concludes, however, that private foreign investors "see an increasing effort to introduce an effective monitoring system in all host countries" (p. 24).

dependencia continues into an era of countervailing power. And the lament that sovereignty is at bay masks the reality of sovereignty reemergent.

The Goals of Host Countries

The objectives of host countries vis-à-vis multinational enterprises can be grouped in three categories. One is domestic economic goals, which go well beyond expanding the gross national product to specific concerns such as reducing unemployment and expanding domestic research and development. A second is external economic goals, primarily improving the balance of payments. A third is assuring that multinationals will respond effectively to host-country policies by localizing management control over the multinationals.[55]

Domestic Economic Goals

The most important domestic objective has been jobs. In the developing world, host countries tend to concentrate on expanding domestic value-added. In developed countries, host governments place more emphasis on regional planning to bring jobs to lagging areas. Canada, Great Britain, France, and Sweden have experimented as much as Mexico, Brazil, and Singapore with methods to induce foreign companies to enter areas where they can train and utilize unemployed workers. No less important, they pursue this objective by making it extremely difficult for investors to lay off workers. Sizable requirements for severance pay, far greater than in the United States, make production shutdowns extremely costly in Germany, the Netherlands, and other European countries. American multinationals have been unable to declare bankruptcy or even give away their Italian subsidiaries, because unemployment would result.

55. Details for five Asian and eight Latin American countries can be found in Robinson, "National Efforts to Establish Guidelines for the Behavior of Multinational Firms," which concludes that "little evidence emerged . . . of a fear by governments that they could not control these firms," that several countries included in the study (notably Brazil, Malaysia, and the Philippines) "are pushing fairly rapidly toward effective control of the foreign direct investor," that "sovereignty is not at bay," and that in the long run "entry control systems are very likely to produce massive conflict of interest" (p. 0.35–.36).

Table 9-1. *Factors in the Approval of Sixty-three Foreign Investments,
Canada, April 1974–March 1975 and April 1975–May 1975*

| | Investments assessed by each factor | | | |
| | April 1974–March 1975 | | April–May 1975 | |
Factor	Number	Percentage	Number	Percentage
Compatibility with industrial and economic policies	61	96.8	14	100.0
Improved productivity and industrial efficiency	46	73.0	11	78.1
Increased employment	43	68.3	13	92.3
New investment	36	57.1	12	85.7
Canadian participation (as shareholders/ directors/managers)	34	54.0	7	50.0
Improved product variety and innovation	30	47.6	6	42.9
Enhanced technological development	29	46.0	6	42.9
Increased resource processing or use of Canadian goods and services	26	41.3	8	56.8
Other benefits (increased employee benefits; employee training)	24	38.1	n.a.	n.a.
Additional exports	22	34.9	6	42.9
Beneficial impact on competition	19	30.2	5	35.5
Indirect benefits (vendor undertakings)	4	6.3	n.a.	n.a.

Sources: Foreign Investment Review Agency of Canada, *Annual Report 1974–1975* (Ottawa: Information Canada, 1975), p. 36; and additional information provided to authors by the Foreign Investment Review Agency of Canada.
n.a. Not available.

In the Foreign Investment Review Act of Canada, employment is in the first of the five categories of factors that must be shown for an investment to be approved (see table 9-1).[56] The Foreign Investment Act of Mexico lists the creation of employment fourth among the seventeen criteria to be applied by its Foreign Investment Commission to certain applications.

A classic example of host-country demand for increased value-added was reported by Thomas Murphy, vice-chairman of General Motors.

56. In its *Annual Report 1974/75* (Ottawa: Information Canada, 1975), p. 1, the Foreign Review Investment Agency concludes that the first year of federal government screening brought in 7,000 new jobs (and over $500 million in new investment). Twenty of the ninety-two resolved applications were either rejected or withdrawn because they could not demonstrate that they would be of "significant benefit to Canada." From its implementation in April 1974 until October 15, 1975, the act applied only to foreign takeovers of Canadian firms. From the latter date, however, it has also applied to direct investments by firms not previously present in Canada and to expansion into "unrelated businesses" by foreign-controlled Canadian companies.

"Typically, a developing country, for national policy reasons, will establish so-called local content regulations, which require assembly and manufacturing facilities to follow a time schedule leading ultimately to producing a vehicle entirely from local sources. . . . Our operations are working within official guidelines and in close cooperation with the official planning authorities of the host countries [although] *in the absence of national development policies, a country's motor vehicle demands could be met at lower costs through imports.*"[57] General Motors justified its decision to proceed in Brazil, within such rules, on three grounds.[58] First, it had "an established assembly operation" there. This suggests that the concept of the obsolescing bargain, explored in chapter five, applies to manufacturing facilities as well as raw materials. Second, Brazil had excellent market potential. (In the face of similar local content requirements, General Motors withdrew from India, Pakistan, and Peru, though it met requirements and continued to operate "in many more" countries than it departed.) Third, it was highly probable that other foreign producers would accept the requirements and stay. The competition among eight foreign firms for the Brazilian market, in fact, provided immense leverage to the government of Brazil.[59]

The Brazilian example demonstrates clearly how successful a host country can be in harnessing even the most powerful multinationals (General Motors was, until 1975, the largest corporation in the world) to promote their national interests. It also demonstrates how host-country industrial or employment policies can force a multinational to invest locally. In this case, the policy goes one step beyond inducing the investment: it structures much of the economic impact of the investment, through detailed performance criteria.

The example demonstrates two other modern realities: the lemming

57. Informal verbatim transcript of meeting, *The United Nations Group of Eminent Persons* (September 11, 1973; processed), pp. 57–63; emphasis added.
58. Author interviews with General Motors officials.
59. Kenneth Mericle, in "The Brazilian Motor Vehicle Industry," a study prepared for U.S. Labor Department, summarized in Massachusetts Institute of Technology, Notes on International Business Research, no. 10 (August 1975; processed), notes that the Brazilian government had "tremendous bargaining power [which enabled it] to channel investments and bargain over the nature of the projects" (p. 24). He lists seventeen major export incentives offered by the government, including complete exemption from all federal income taxes and a 30 percent credit against local taxes (pp. 68–77) and calculates that the total export subsidy offered by the government amounts to 39 percent of the total value of the exports (p. 79).

instinct of multinationals (indeed, only an international cartel of the firms, hardly a happy alternative, could have prevented them competing to defend their market positions); and the adverse consequences to home countries from their home-based firms' pursuit of corporate objectives.

In addition, this particular example shows how host-country policies can trigger home-country reaction. During the congressional debate on energy legislation in early 1975, with the U.S. auto industry in its deepest slump of the postwar period and facing an unprecedented loss of market share to imports (above 20 percent for the first time), U.S. labor and part of the U.S. auto industry proposed to emulate the value-added practices of Brazil and other host countries.

External Economic Goals

Host countries have a variety of external economic targets: expanding exports, limiting imports, maximizing incoming capital, and limiting outgoing capital through repatriation of earnings and capital. But while domestic policies have narrowed their focus from general pursuit of growth to specific pursuit of jobs, balance-of-payments policies have broadened their perspective from import substitution and limits on repatriation to the more promising avenues of export expansion and maximum incoming investment capital.

Export expansion is in fact a central focus of many host-country policies toward foreign direct investment. Since increased exports usually mean increased jobs, such efforts support the primary internal economic goal as well as the external one. They are linked, for example, in the first criterion of the Canadian Foreign Investment Review Act. American-based firms already export more than their local counterparts in the United Kingdom, Australia, and Canada.[60] Some developing countries seek to expand exports through regional integration schemes. Central to the success of these schemes is harnessing foreign investors to their objectives, by avoiding competition for investment and, more positively, by using investment to promote programs that seek equitable distribution of industry.

60. Donald T. Brash, *American Investment in Australian Industry* (Canberra: Australian National University Press, 1966), chap. 9; A. E. Safarian, *Foreign Ownership of Canadian Industry* (Toronto: McGraw-Hill, 1966), pp. 273–75; and John H. Dunning, *The Role of American Investment in the British Economy*, Political and Economic Planning Broadsheet 507 (London: PEP, February 1969).

Developing countries have the largest and most explicit export requirements. India requires that 60 percent of output be exported within three years. Argentina requires a progressive increase in the share of output sold abroad. Taiwan permits foreign direct investment only to produce exports, except for products otherwise totally unavailable in the domestic market. Brazil levies minimum export quotas on firms in the automotive sector. In the socialist bloc, Rumania insists that virtually all production be exported, mainly for hard currencies. The countries in East Europe, like their counterparts in the European Economic Community, give preference to firms that promise to strengthen their balance of payments.

Some countries offer sizable inducements to firms that will establish export platforms. Ireland's program of direct grants and fifteen-year tax holidays gives foreign investors a base to penetrate the European community.[61] Tunisia's investment code, enacted in 1972, exempts export industries from all Tunisian taxes and currency restrictions. A less expensive device to influence multinational behavior is the lure of exemption from other performance requirements, most notable that majority ownership be vested in local interests. Despite their zeal to avoid foreign ownership, the countries of the Andean Common Market exempt new investors from having to take minority positions (and existing investors from disinvesting) if they export 80 percent of their production. Mexico permits subsidiaries to be wholly owned if they wholly export their output. Korea waives its requirement that foreign owners take minority positions if production is solely for export. India bars foreign equity ownership above 40 percent except for firms exporting at least 80 percent of their output; it permits full ownership for firms providing high employment and high technology, as well.

In some cases the goal is improving the quality of exports and expanding export of high-technology goods. In the early 1970s, for example, Canada prohibited Control Data Corporation from competing for government contracts unless it helped Canada achieve a trade balance in that sector, both by exporting and by substituting for imports.[62] In the developing world, host governments use foreign firms to hurdle the barriers to entry into multinational marketing. In other cases the external target is

61. For a detail account see Frank Long, "Foreign Direct Investment in an Underdeveloped European Economy—The Republic of Ireland," *World Development*, vol. 4 (January 1976), pp. 59–84.
62. See the remarks by Jean-Luc Pepin, Minister of Industry, Trade and Commerce, press conference (Control Data Corporation, May 14, 1970; processed).

raising the price of exports by using natural resource companies to help implement the price increases host authorities decree, by requiring that raw materials be exported in processed form, or by requiring that intra-corporate prices be shifted in their favor.

Finally, host-country efforts to fortify the capital account of their balance of payments have intensified. A number of host countries now systematically require incoming investors to bring capital with them. No long-term capital is available to multinationals in Bangladesh or in countries that are members of the Andean Pact. Explicit government permission is needed to borrow locally in India. Brazil and Argentina frequently limit foreign access to domestic capital. These efforts have followed American moves in past decade (1965–74) to support its own balance-of-payments positions by limiting the availability of U.S. capital to American multinationals. While the program did cut outgoing capital, it deterred little actual investment, simply shifting financing to, primarily, the Eurodollar market. Australia and Canada reacted immediately by requiring American multinationals to finance a large share of their investments with imported capital. Australia levied a similar requirement on multinational enterprises based in the United Kingdom, which launched a program like that of the United States at about the same time. These are among the first examples of major policy conflict between home and host countries via multinational enterprises, in this instance because of their efforts to improve or defend immediate balance-of-payments positions.

On the other side of the balance-of-payments equation, limits on repatriation of capital and earnings are becoming increasingly sophisticated and remain widespread.[63] A related step is legislating limits on intracorporate payments for technology, which many host countries suspect have been excessive in the past. A large number of host countries, in both the industrialized and developing worlds (the Andean countries, Argentina, Brazil, France, India, Israel, Japan, Mexico, Pakistan, Spain, and Yugoslavia) have tightened their rules or have tightened surveillance of existing rules. A prototype is Mexico's 1973 Law on the Transfer of Technology, which bars requirements on local subsidiaries to purchase from the licensor and to desist from exporting to third countries. President Echeverria originally claimed that the law would save Mexico at least

63. Repatriation includes not only remittance to the home country but remittance to a subsidiary in a third country, either for investment there or elsewhere or to take advantage of a tax haven.

$80 million over the succeeding ten years, but Mexican officials in 1975 raised their estimate "several times higher."[64] A sample of firms in other Latin American countries reveals that vigorous policy efforts have enabled Colombia and Peru to reduce their royalty payments as a percentage of gross sales to 3.6 and 4.7 percent, respectively.[65]

Harnessing the Multinationals

The third major host-country objective has been as much political as economic: assuring effective domestic control over the firms to avoid both disruption of domestic policy goals and charges of selling out to the foreigners. It is becoming clear to an increasing number of host countries that control does not require ownership, nor does ownership assure control.[66] Yet for symbolic as well as real economic reasons, local authorities continue to put a high premium on the appearance of control that comes with various kinds of domestic ownership: minority joint ventures, majority joint ventures, compulsory sale of stock on national exchanges, worker participation, and systematic divestment over a specified period of time.

A large and growing list of countries—including India, Mexico, Morocco, Bangladesh, Rumania, and Yugoslavia—limit foreign investors to minority positions (except, as noted, for firms exporting all or most of their production). Multinationals, however, continue to expand despite the changes in the nature of their involvement.[67]

64. "Licensing: A Revolt Against 'Exorbitant' Fees," *Business Week,* July 14, 1975, p. 69.
65. Mytelka, "Direct Foreign Investment, Technology Transfer and Andean Integration," p. 62. Some firms, however, admit that they circumvented the limitations on royalty payments at least partially by increasing their dividend repatriations.
66. John Fayerweather, *Foreign Investment in Canada: Prospects for National Policy* (White Plains, N.Y: M. E. Sharpe, 1973), pp. 143–44, traces the evolution of Canadian pressures from the original quest for ownership to the contemporary effort to assert control. Douglas Bennett and Kenneth Sharpe, in "Controlling the Multinationals: The Ill Logic of Mexicanization" (Temple University and Swarthmore College, February 1977; processed), find that local ownership requirements achieved almost no benefits for the host country except as a bargaining chip to trade for better performance on other objectives.
67. In Mexico, for example, a number of American multinationals—including Chrysler, Continental Can, Del Monte, du Pont, Ford, Gillette, Monsanto, Pennsalt, Sterling Drug, and Upjohn (but not General Electric and Purina)—initiated efforts to form joint ventures shortly after enactment of a new foreign investment law in 1973 to obtain the tax and other incentives reserved for mexicanized opera-

There are important differences in the degree to which host countries seek to capture benefits from incoming foreign direct investment, at least as recorded in their official statements of national policy. Canada approves investments covered by the Foreign Investment Review Act only if they promise substantial benefits to Canada. Australia now permits all investments not contrary to the national interest.[68] So do the Comecon countries. The Commission of the European Communities suggests a neutral criterion of simply avoiding adverse effects on member states.[69] The Third World runs the gamut from requiring demonstration of "substantial benefits" to "avoiding adverse effects." There are also major differences among host countries in the intensity of their scrutiny. Some look at every application in detail.[70] Some focus only on the biggest investments or those in the most sensitive sectors (however defined). A few use their powers only on a standby basis.

But selectivity is everywhere the keynote; from the mass of investments available to the host country, only those likely to promote its national objectives will be permitted. And there is a clear general trend toward negotiating the terms of entry to extract as many benefits as possible without discouraging the investment. An investment proposal initially unacceptable because of inadequate benefits for the host country may suddenly

---

tions (Alan Riding, "Mexico Again Seeks Foreign Investing," *New York Times,* December 26, 1974). Indeed, foreign investment in Mexico declined in 1971–72 and then rose after passage of the new law. And a thorough study of the impact of Decision 24 of the Andean Group, initially regarded with total hostility by American multinationals, concludes that even it "has not been an obstacle to continued direct foreign investment," indeed, "American investment in manufacturing in Peru was maintained and it rose dramatically in Colombia and Venezuela since the implementation of Decision 24"; Mytelka, "Direct Foreign Investment, Technology Transfer and Andean Integration," pp. 66–68. The rise in investment is partly because Decision 24 is not of great consequence relative to the national measures of Andean Group members.

68. The Australian Liberal Party, returned to power in late 1975, was widely viewed as softer toward incoming foreign direct investment. However, it announced on April 1, 1976, the creation of a Foreign Investment Review Board to examine, inter alia, all foreign proposals to establish Australian businesses of $1 million and over, detailed criteria for judging proposals, and a directive to the review board for making investments conform with the national interest.

69. Commission of the European Communities, *Multinational Undertakings and the Community,* Bulletin of the European Communities, supplement 15/73, p. 8.

70. Robinson, "National Efforts to Establish Guidelines for the Behavior of Multinational Firms," p. 0.4, finds that the Philippines has "the most complex entry system in the world . . . [based on a] highly sophisticated set of objective criteria."

become acceptable because the firm agrees to generate more jobs and exports. Virtually all host countries have set up explicit machinery to bargain for them.

American Interests

The bargaining process does not always give host governments all they demand.[71] Nor does it have a known positive or negative aggregate effect on global economic welfare (the next two chapters emphasize the highly differentiated impact of this bargaining process on welfare and efficiency). However, a large number of cases have effects that are clearly negative on important American economic interests.

The major implication for the United States is that, although American subsidiaries account for a swelling share of world output and world trade and world investment, there is an empty chair at the negotiations. No one represents American interests broader than those of the firms themselves. This situation risks significant economic costs to the United States, international political conflict between the United States and host countries, and domestic political repercussions, which could tilt public opinion—already hostile to foreign direct investment—against a continued liberal approach to international investment.

For the Future

The response of multinationals to the rising demands of host-country authorities has undergone a dramatic change in the past decade and a half, from obstinate and self-righteous rejection, to acceptance, and beyond that, sometimes to active collaboration with host governments. In some cases, local demands are economically rational, from a corporate point of view, and push the firms toward greater use of low-cost labor, greater processing at the production site, and greater diversification in the sourcing of components. In some cases, locale makes no difference, and firms respond to host-country demands to ensure the continuance of their welcome. In other cases, costs of host-country demands are not economically

---

71. Useful bargaining models can be found in Stefan H. Robock and Kenneth Simmonds, *International Business and Multinational Enterprises* (Richard D. Irwin, 1973), esp. part 3 and chap. 16; and Paul Streeten, "The Multinational Enterprise and the Theory of Development Policy," *World Development*, vol. 1 (October 1973).

rational but are wholly or partially offset by tax incentives, trade restrictions, import protection, or other market distortions. But in all cases, the firms are inclined to follow the path of least resistance, the principle of expediency.

In the future the strength of host countries to make American investors serve national objectives will gain at the expense of the home country given the following: (a) continued growth of international competition among investors and other sources of the factor inputs traditionally supplied by multinationals; (b) continued growth, in either absolute or relative terms, of American multinational earnings and assets in countries outside of the United States; (c) continued growth in host-country skill in monitoring and analyzing multinational corporate activities; (d) the internal development of host countries and the subsequent decline in the cost of forgoing the services of foreign investors; (e) continual decline in the political or security risk to host countries of taking actions that harm private American interests.

As competition in a particular industry increases, whether from foreign or domestic sources, the bargaining power of any given multinational declines. Hence the opportunity costs of making nationalistic demands on investors decline for a country, while the opportunity costs of not responding to nationalistic demands rise for the investors. As the distribution of assets and earnings of a particular multinational spreads, the opportunity costs of not responding to the demands of hosts rise in comparison to the opportunity costs of not responding to the needs of the home country. The corporate calculation for how to survive and how to maximize profits over the long run must include a judgment on corporate vulnerability to the demands of the assorted governments where the company operates, as well as judgments based on classical comparative advantage. We predict that, as these variables change, the extent of investor vulnerability to the demands of host countries, in general, will rise.[72]

The steady growth of host-country countervailing power will have an international impact similar to the national impact that Galbraith predicted as national governments moved to counter national firms.[73] But

72. In making such a calculation, one must, of course, hold constant the countries' economic characteristics (for example, size and growth of market, strength of balance of payments, and cost of labor).

73. John Kenneth Galbraith, *American Capitalism: The Concept of Countervailing Power* (Houghton Mifflin, 1952), esp. chap. 9.

the concept of countervailing power contains a basic flaw if it includes only two parties pushing the market toward equilibrium. Just as business and labor, in Galbraith's equation, could collude rather than compete and thus together divert income from consumers, so could the equilibrium of host country and multinational simply result in two-party joint maximization that adversely affects the home country, the third actor in this particular drama.

In the light of the evolution of bargaining power, the casual inattention of the United States to the ability of host countries to force American investors to put their oligopoly power at the service of host-country goals is no longer defensible. Rather, American policy must be prepared to deal with unstable, imperfect competition among international investors, in an environment where the welfare and security interests of American multinationals lead to actions that do not necessarily serve the welfare and security interests of the United States. Yet the United States is not now prepared to identify and defend its national interests in the struggle over the uses of multinational corporate power. It is not prepared to channel the activities of American multinationals in ways that serve national interests, nor to control them when they do not so serve, nor to lead the way toward international coordination of foreign investment policies.

Under some conditions, the United States may find itself virtually powerless to influence the operations of American companies abroad, even when its vital welfare or security issues are at stake. We have had a brief and moderate taste of that in the energy crisis following the October 1973 war in the Middle East.[74] For such cases, the United States must develop policies to safeguard its own interests directly and not indirectly through incentives, pressure, or invective aimed at its companies abroad. Under some conditions, the United States should be prepared to provide effective disincentives to foreign investment when it can be demonstrated that substantive damage will result for American welfare and security and that better alternatives are available. Under other conditions, there may be no alternative that causes less damage to the American economy. Or

74. For example, a radio announcement of King Faisal's decision to impose an oil embargo on the United States was enough to propel Frank Jungers, chairman and chief executive officer of Aramco, to order a cutback larger than the percentage demanded by Faisal, just for good measure. "The important thing," according to Jungers, "was to give the immediate image of being *with* the government, not trying to fight it." Allan T. Demaree, "Aramco is a Lesson in the Management of Chaos," *Fortune*, vol. 89 (February 1974), pp. 58–65

the potential damage to the American economy from any adverse distribution of investment benefits may be so small in absolute terms, or so small in relation to the political benefits, that the United States will want to absorb the economic costs. But, for foreign policy as well as economic reasons, the United States must develop policies toward foreign direct investment that will enable it to choose among these options and effectively promote its national interests.

CHAPTER TEN

The Developing Countries

ALTHOUGH ONLY A FRACTION of American overseas investment is in the developing countries, its effect on the American interest is the most highly charged.[1] For one, there is no consensus what effect multinationals have on these countries' own interests—whether investment stimulates desirable development or is a means for the industrial countries to exploit them through a process of cumulative dependence. Second, there is no consensus on the effect of these multinationals on American domestic welfare or foreign policy goals—whether multinational–host-country alliances undermine the U.S. industrial base, or, if such alliances are not formed and their relation is adversary, whether the United States is drawn into their disputes against its own best interests.

Multinationals caused few problems for the United States as long as their involvement with host-country goals was low and the balance of power between them tilted toward investors. When the multinationals had greater power than host countries, the U.S. government could disregard the way they jointly maximized their interests, anticipating that most conflicts would be settled quietly and to the satisfaction of the former and that the political and economic costs would be low. As those conditions change, particularly as host countries throughout the developing (as well as industrialized) world assert themselves in their relations with multinationals, the U.S. response must change. American policy must be aimed at preserving the advantages of the international transfer of scarce cor-

1. At the end of 1975, 26.2 percent of the outstanding book value of U.S. foreign direct investment was in the developing countries; the figure is 24.1 percent when petroleum is excluded. *Survey of Current Business*, vol. 56 (August 1976), p. 46.

porate resources, avoiding the political tensions of recurrent investment disputes, and striking a balance among its interests in domestic welfare, international efficiency, and development in the poorer countries.

Multinationals and Development

Traditional theory posits that foreign direct investment contributes positively to development.[2] It brings to those societies most in need of them capital, technology, and management and marketing skills. In addition to the direct income effects, jobs are created and government tax revenues, which can be used for further development, are augmented. The balance-of-payments constraints on development, chronic in many poorer countries, are eased by the infusion of capital, by the substitution of domestic production for imports, and by the expansion of exports. Supporters of this view correlate the sizable flows of direct investment with both the economic progress of postwar Western Europe and the more recent success stories in Third World countries such as Taiwan and Korea.

In 1966, sales of American multinationals accounted for almost 14 percent of the gross domestic product of Latin America.[3] Currently, majority-owned affiliates of foreign-based multinationals compose 50 percent of the manufacturing sectors of Brazil and Mexico.[4] In the extractive industries, multinationals provide large amounts of foreign exchange and tax revenues to those countries endowed with copper, bauxite, tin, iron ore, oil, and other industrial commodities, and the share of the oligopoly rents going to the host countries is constantly rising.

On the other hand, foreign capital, directly invested, represents only about one-quarter of the financial flow over the past twenty years to developing countries; it was matched in most years by other types of private

2. For a comprehensive treatment of this view see Grant L. Reuber and others, *Private Foreign Investment in Development* (Clarendon, 1973).

3. Herbert K. May, "The Contributions of U.S. Private Investment to Latin America's Growth," summary (New York: Council for Latin America, 1970; processed). At the end of 1973, 83 percent of all U.S. foreign direct investment in manufacturing industries in developing countries was in Latin America. The bulk of the rest was in the Far East; *Survey of Current Business*, vol. 54 (August 1974), p. 19.

4. R. Newfarmer and Willard F. Mueller, *Multinational Corporations in Brazil and Mexico: Structural Sources of Economic and Noneconomic Power*, Report to the Senate Foreign Relations Committee (GPO, 1975), pp. 54, 107.

capital (notably portfolio investment and export credits).[5] And multi-nationals provide no more than about half of 1 percent of all jobs in the developing world.

U.S. Policy

Official postwar U.S. policy, largely accepting traditional analysis, promotes foreign direct investment as a major aspect of its foreign assistance program. The program's most straightforward tool is government insurance and guarantees for foreign direct investment (see chapter two). Beyond OPIC and its predecessors, are indirect U.S. policies that promote foreign direct investment in the developing countries.

Tax policy is the major case in point. Deferral of taxation of foreign income until it is repatriated and the overall option for calculating the foreign tax credit encourage foreign direct investment in low-tax countries. In turn, these ratify the tax incentives offered by many developing countries to attract investments. Profits from disinvestments in developing countries may be treated as capital gains rather than as regular income. Permission for foreign investors to offset domestic profits with losses from their foreign branches probably encourages investment in developing countries more than in developed countries. And full tax deductibility for expropriation losses is, of course, important to investments in that part of the world. In the past, the use of tax policy to promote such investment was even more widespread. A tax regulation treating royalty payments as foreign direct taxes, creditable against U.S. tax liabilities, was explicitly adopted in the early 1950s to provide aid to oil-producing countries in the Middle East. From 1962 until 1975, corporations in less-developed countries were exempt from the limitations on tax deferral of foreign income from subsidiaries in tax haven countries covered by the Internal Revenue Code.[6] They have also (until 1976) been exempt from the requirement that foreign dividends be grossed up to calculate U.S. tax liability. Finally, since 1942 tax preferences have been offered to western hemisphere trade corporations to encourage investment in Latin America. This will be phased out by 1980.

American import policy and American leadership in reducing trade

5. Organisation for Economic Co-operation and Development, *Development Co-operation: 1975 Review* (Paris: OECD, 1975), p. 217.
6. 26 U.S.C. 955.

barriers in all countries promote both investment in the developing countries and exports from them. A liberal trade system is a requisite for many kinds of investment in the poorer countries, particularly for their use as export platforms for worldwide sourcing, the practice of a growing number of multinationals. Two specific aspects of U.S. trade policy directly encourage investment in the developing countries. One permitting duty-free importation of the final products made abroad from American-made components (sections 806.30 and 807 of the Tariff Code) encourages assembly operations in other countries. The original target was aircraft produced in Europe with American components, but the industries most affected now are electronics and toymaking in Mexico and the Far East. Second is the system of generalized preference, in force since January 1, 1976, which provides duty-free importation for many manufactured and semimanufactured products for at least ten years and thus encourages foreign direct investment in those sectors in eligible developing countries.[7]

Evaluating Development

In recent years, the contribution of multinationals to the development of poor countries has been called into question.[8] According to the antagonists to investment, multinationals take out of developing countries more than they put in; and thus, if annual repatriations of earnings exceed

7. See G. K. Helleiner, "Manufactured Exports from Less-Developed Countries and Multinational Firms," *Economic Journal,* vol. 83 (1973), pp. 21–47. Controls over capital outflows to finance foreign direct investment, maintained from 1965 through 1973 for balance-of-payments purposes, espoused preferential treatment for developing countries. Such treatment had little effect on levels of foreign direct investment but simply shifted the sources from the United States to other countries. To the extent that the financing was shifted to developing countries, their imports of foreign capital (but also future outflows to repay such borrowings) were reduced. Data that would permit analysis of the extent of the shift are not available.

8. Richard J. Barnet and Ronald E. Müller, *Global Reach: The Power of the Multinational Corporations* (Simon and Schuster, 1974), esp. chaps. 6 and 7; and two papers in Jagdish N. Bhagwati, ed., *Economics and World Order From the 1970s to the 1990s* (MacMillan, 1972): Stephen Hymer, "The Multinational Corporation and the Law of Uneven Development," and Oswaldo Sunkel, "Underdevelopment in Latin America: Toward the Year 2000." See also Constantine V. Vaitsos, "Employment Effects of Foreign Direct Investment in Developing Countries," in Edgar O. Edwards, ed., *Employment in Developing Nations* (Columbia University Press, 1974), pp. 331–49, and "Income Distribution and Welfare Considerations," in John H. Dunning, ed., *Economic Analysis and the Multinational Enterprise* (London: Allen and Unwin, 1974), pp. 300–41.

annual infusions of new foreign capital, multinationals undermine balance-of-payments positions. They increase unemployment by using capital-intensive techniques developed for their own labor-scarce, high-wage economies, rather than labor-intensive techniques thought to be more appropriate for developing countries. They promote unequal income distribution, because local high-income groups strengthen their positions through alliances with foreign investors. Economic growth itself may be stunted, both short and long term, because the foreign firms drain away local capital and brain power that could otherwise create strong indigenous industries. In addition, they generate, through their advertising, consumption patterns inappropriate for countries at early stages of development; and they limit the countries' technological progress by doing the bulk of their research and development elsewhere.

To evaluate the contribution of multinational corporations to development one needs to specify the alternative against which to measure their behavior. Dependency theory points in the direction of a hypothetical state agency to duplicate the services multinationals perform, at less cost in terms of local resources.

But traditional analysis tends to the opposite extreme, where the alternative to a given investment is assumed to be no investment at all. Within this framework, the most ambitious efforts to develop empirical conclusions yield mixed results. A study of manufacturing investments in five countries (India, Philippines, Ghana, Guatemala, and Argentina) commissioned by the Organisation for Economic Development and Cooperation shows the effects of foreign investment on national income (and thus on government revenues) to be generally positive.[9] By contrast, the effects on the balance of payments were generally negative and the net

9. H. C. Bos, Martin Sanders, and Carlo Secchi, *Private Foreign Investment in Developing Countries* (Boston: D. Reidel, 1974). Many of these results are inherent in the Bos model. The study takes a purely historical view of the capital flows associated with foreign direct investment, simply netting inflows and repatriation in each year against each other, which virtually assures a negative balance-of-payments result. It posits an inverse relation between income and the balance of payments, on the grounds that ex ante balance-of-payments deficits make resources available for development and on the assumption that the deficits will be met in ways that do not check growth, which in turn virtually assures a positive reading on gross national product and government revenues. Other shortcomings include the absence of price data and the assumption of constant capacity utilization in both the foreign and domestic sectors. Lack of adequate empirical data also forces the authors to make numerous assumptions concerning key parameters.

income effect of foreign direct investment was in each case less than the value added directly by such investment, implying that its indirect effects were negative on the gross national product. The magnitudes of each effect differed significantly from country to country (and from sector to sector within some countries), and results with signs opposite the general outcome appeared for some sectors in some countries.

Using a different approach, Paul Streeten compares net benefits over five to seven years in the late 1960s, in relation to the net benefits of either importing the products or obtaining the capital in nonequity forms (with technology and other factors constant).[10] In terms of balance-of-payments effects, the overwhelming number of firms exported more foreign exchange than they earned. The export performance of the overall sample was unimpressive. Only fifty-eight of the firms generated capital flow into the host country. And 40 percent of the firms imported over 30 percent of the value of their sales, while nearly 60 percent of the firms imported over 20 percent.

The net effect in Streeten's analysis, essentially an efficiency effect, rests on the assumption that someone else would undertake the production in the absence of the foreign investor. The analysis reveals wide differences among the different countries. For Kenya, the average income effect was 12.7 percent of sales, with foreign majority firms outperforming the single foreign minority firm. In Jamaica, with only foreign-owned subsidiaries in the sample, the effect was 7 percent of sales. The Indian sample indicated an even smaller effect on income: the average for the entire sample was 1.3 percent of sales, with foreign-owned plants much superior to either joint ventures or domestically owned firms, both of which yielded negative income effects. The overall income effect for Iran was 5.6 percent, once again with foreign-owned firms significantly outperforming minority or totally domestic ventures. For both Colombia and Malaysia, however, the effects were negative, averaging −1.5 percent and −4.5 percent, respectively. In both countries, joint ventures significantly outperformed foreign-owned projects. In addition to the sizable variations between countries, a firm-by-firm breakdown within the countries showed remarkable range.

The Bos and Streeten approaches show some marked differences in

10. Paul Streeten and Sanjaya Lall, *The Flow of Financial Resources: Private Foreign Investment, Main Findings of a Study of Private Foreign Investment in Selected Developing Countries,* UN Doc. TD/B/C-3/111, May 1973.

their appraisals of the impact of foreign direct investment on host-country income. Bos found positive effects for all countries, while Streeten found a negative impact in two of his six. In terms of balance-of-payments effects, the quite different Streeten and Bos approaches yield the same result, that foreign direct investment has a negative impact.[11] Their aggregate conclusions were similar for India, the only country common to the two studies, but Bos found that joint ventures performed better than foreign majority-owned plants, while Streeten reached an opposite conclusion. The comparability of the two studies is severely limited, however, by their use of different methodologies, countries, and companies.

While the Streeten findings suggest that a sizable number of subsidiaries yield negative net social income effects, it must be remembered that within this framework none of the benefits of foreign direct investment commonly classified as externalities are captured; that highly uncertain values must be put on nontradable factors; and that effects of specific projects on macroeconomic variables, such as prices and national income, are not covered. Given the diversity of his own results, Streeten concludes that projects need to be evaluated individually to judge their potential social value. This observation is particularly important when considering the balance of bargaining power between foreign investors and host countries and the shift of that power away from the foreigner over time (which, depending upon industry characteristics, enables local authorities to harness multinationals).

Distribution of Income

Three issues relating to the role of multinationals, beyond simply their effect on the gross national product of poor countries, are particularly significant: their impact on the distribution of income, their use of appropriate technology, and their effect on consumer tastes. Traditional theory predicts that direct foreign investment will equalize rather than

11. However, OPIC data suggest that the 132 projects assisted by that agency during fiscal year 1976 will have a positive effect of $722 million annually on the balance-of-payments positions of recipient countries, with import substitution ($837 million) plus exports generated ($434 million) exceeding production inputs ($279 million) and outgoing capital ($270 million). These projects are, of course, supported because of their positive developmental effects. See "U.S. and Developmental Effects Data Output Sheet for Groups of OPIC Assisted Investors," report no. 18 (Overseas Private Investment Corporation, September 8, 1976; processed).

concentrate income in the host country by creating new jobs (more than
it displaces), by raising the demand for labor (and hence its wages), and
by lowering the return to capital. But to arrive at such conclusions, the
analyst must make three crucial assumptions: that the foreign investment
adds to total domestic investment; that there is full employment; and that
foreign and domestic producers utilize technologies equally labor intensive. If these assumptions do not hold, then the impact of multinational
activities on local income distribution is highly problematic and, as we
shall see, extraordinarily difficult to measure.

There are two reasons why multinational corporations might not add
to domestic capital formation. They may borrow locally rather than bring
capital into the country. They may monopolize the host country's best
investment opportunities, to the detriment of state companies and private
capitalists, who may then send their capital abroad (licitly or illicitly)
rather than invest in less promising projects at home.[12] It is frequently
hypothesized, in fact, that foreign firms enjoy preferential treatment in
borrowing locally from host-country financial institutions. In periods of
economic expansion, when all countries restrict credit markets to control
inflation, foreign subsidiaries get a more generous ration of host-country
loans to expand operations than domestic firms do. In periods of economic contraction, when financial institutions are hesitant to maintain
their credit exposure in businesses that could go bankrupt, the foreign
subsidiaries receive more sympathetic service than their domestic counterparts. Thus multinationals may have a comparative advantage in borrowing locally, which is a disincentive to their bringing capital into the country and reinforces their ability to capture the best domestic investment
opportunities.

There have been no systematic efforts to test whether multinationals
enjoy preferential treatment from local financial institutions. However,
foreign investments do appear to generate a significant proportion of their
capital requirements locally. Funds from the United States are typically
only 20–25 percent of those used annually by American multinationals in
developing countries (see table 10-1). Some is borrowed in third coun-

12. Albert O. Hirschman, "How to Divest in Latin America, and Why," *Essays
in International Finance,* no. 76 (Princeton, N.J.: Princeton University Economics
Department, November 1969). Hirschman argues that eliminating local firms might
result in unfavorable externalities, such as stifling domestic entrepreneurship or reducing national investment.

Table 10-1. *Sources of Funds, American Manufacturing Investments in Developing Countries, 1966–72*
Percentage

Year	Retained earnings	Depre- ciation	Other	U.S. funds	Debt from affiliates	Debt from foreign sources	Foreign equity
			All developing countries				
1966	25	25	−2	20	4	26	2
1967	12	32	−5	25	2	29	4
1968	18	21	1	8	2	44	4
1969	15	24	n.a.	31	1	27	3
1970	7	33	3	13	7	36	2
1971	13	40	9	21	−4	24	−4
1972	13	22	n.a.	24	2	37	2
			Latin America				
1966	32	29	−1	9	1	30	1
1967	11	40	−8	23	3	27	4
1968	17	23	n.a.	9	3	44	4
1969	14	24	n.a.	33	1	26	2
1970	2	33	4	14	5	40	3
1971	13	48	11	23	−7	19	−7
1972	12	21	n.a.	26	n.a.	39	2

Source: From author calculations based on *Survey of Current Business*, vol. 55 (July 1975), p. 31.
n.a. Not available.

tries, particularly the Eurobond and Eurocredit markets, but in one sample of seventy-two new investments and sixty expansions in developing countries in 1975–76, one-sixth of their non-U.S. funding came from local sources.[13] In addition, a large share of the investment funds generated through depreciation and local earnings, which together account for over 40 percent of total cash flow, can be regarded as coming from local savings. But in the aggregate, multinationals almost certainly provide a net addition to the capital stock of host countries, and via this mechanism have some progressive impact on domestic income distribution.

The possibility of an adverse effect on income distribution from foreign investment also arises if there is chronic unemployment in the host-country labor market. Under the assumption of full employment, foreign investment increases the efficient use of host-country resources and frees

13. "U.S. and Developmental Effects Data Output Sheet for Groups of OPIC Assisted Investors," p. 2.

Table 10-2. *Foreign Direct Investment and Annual Growth Rates of Personal Income in Twelve Developing Countries*

Country and period	Foreign direct investment per capita (dollars)	Percentage annual growth, each income bracket		
		Upper 20 percent	Middle 40 percent	Lower 40 percent
		Improving distribution		
Taiwan (1953–61)	11	4.5	9.1	12.1
Sri Lanka (1963–70)	12	3.1	6.2	8.3
Colombia (1964–70)	36	5.6	7.3	7.0
El Salvador (1961–69)	24	4.1	10.5	5.3
Philippines (1961–71)	21	4.9	6.4	5.0
Peru (1961–71)	62	4.7	7.5	3.2
		Deteriorating distribution		
Panama (1960–69)	586	8.8	9.2	3.2
Korea (1964–70)	3	10.6	7.8	9.3
Brazil (1960–70)	41	8.4	4.8	5.2
India (1954–64)	3	5.1	3.9	3.9
Mexico (1963–69)	36	8.0	7.0	6.6
Venezuela (1962–70)	357	7.9	4.1	3.7

Sources: Hollis Chenery, *Redistribution with Growth: Policies to Improve Income Distribution in Developing Countries* (London: Oxford University Press, 1974), p. 42; foreign direct investment figures are from Grant L. Reuber and others, *Private Foreign Investment in Development* (Clarendon Press, 1973), pp. 209–93.

the labor it displaces for more productive employment elsewhere in the economy. If there is permanent unemployment or underemployment in the host country, however, foreign investment may simply bid up the wages for a small domestic labor elite while consigning a greater number of workers to the ranks of the marginados.[14]

Empirically, the issue is cloudy. In terms of simple correlation, there is no apparent relation between per capita investment levels and domestic income structure (see table 10-2). Countries whose income distribution has improved most rapidly (Taiwan and Sri Lanka) host relatively little foreign direct investment on a per capita basis. At the other extreme, two of the countries with the largest per capita levels of foreign direct investment in the developing world (Venezuela and Panama) experienced deterioration in their patterns of income distribution. Of the six countries where income distribution deteriorated, two were among the highest re-

14. William R. Cline, "Distribution and Development: A Survey of the Literature," *Journal of Development Economics*, vol. 1 (1974), p. 372.

cipients, two were among the lowest, and two (Brazil and Mexico) were in the middle. And even Taiwan and Sri Lanka adopted wholly different approaches to the issue in recent years.

To judge net impact of foreign investment on host-country income distribution, one must examine how the host government uses its potential bargaining power vis-a-vis the foreign firms.[15] It may use performance requirements and tax revenues for welfare and development projects that equalize domestic income. Or it may use them to subsidize the middle and upper classes or the military, in ways that worsen domestic income distribution. Again, host government policy plays a central role in determining the impact of American multinationals on host countries, and thus relations between those countries and the United States.

Appropriate Technology

One charge against multinational corporations is that they use technology that is capital intensive in countries where unemployment and underemployment are major problems. This allegation poses a dilemma for the analyst: on the one hand, foreign firms do typically use production techniques developed in an environment where they economized on labor; on the other hand, profit-maximizing goals should, logically, cause firms to take advantage of local factor endowments (employing relatively more labor if labor is abundant).

There are three complementary explanations for the inappropriate technology phenomenon.[16] First, one may hypothesize that foreign firms in a new environment do not in fact compare the marginal costs of one production technique (for example, a capital-intensive technique) with the marginal costs of another production technique (for example, a labor-

15. See Irma Adelman and Cynthia Taft Morris, *Economic Growth and Social Equity in Developing Countries* (Stanford University Press, 1973), esp. pp. 160–97. After analyzing the impact of twenty-seven variables on income distribution in developing countries, they conclude that economic growth affects distribution adversely unless the national government promotes (or at least permits) such prodistributional institutions as primary and vocational schools and a strong labor movement. Whether foreign companies influence host-country redistributive policies positively, negatively, or neutrally, is a question of great controversy and little empirical exploration.

16. Walter A. Chudson and Louis T. Wells, Jr., *The Acquisition of Technology from Multinational Corporations by Developing Countries*, UN Doc. ST/ESA/12, 1974.

intensive technique) when contemplating the establishment of a local plant. Rather they compare the marginal cost of a known technique with the total cost of designing a new process. Under such conditions, the use of techniques that do not use local factors most efficiently is consistent with profit maximizing behavior, although it deviates from both economic optimality and the behavior of local firms.

A second explanation may lie in the desire of governments throughout the developing world for the newest and latest production techniques, coupled with an incentive structure (accelerated depreciation, duty-free imports of equipment, and so on) that encourages the choice of capital-intensive technologies.[17] Many countries, for example, restrict or forbid the importation of secondhand equipment even though it is less capital intensive than newer machines.[18]

A third explanation may be that what appear as inappropriate production processes are not inappropriate at all because of hidden costs associated with the supervision of large work forces.[19] These hidden costs are not reflected in simple comparisons of relative wage rates. By adopting a capital-intensive technology, foreign managers may be trying, implicitly or explicitly, to economize on scarce supervisory skills or overhead costs. Whether local entrepreneurs would behave differently depends on whether they had special expertise in managing a large number of workers in a factory or cottage industry. If they did not, then the penetration of foreign

17. From a transcript of statements by Jacques Maisonrouge of International Business Machines and Irving Shapiro of du Pont to the United Nations Group of Eminent Persons (New York, September 1973; processed), pp. 13–18 and 21, respectively.

18. Chudson and Wells, *The Acquisition of Technology from Multinational Corporations by Developing Countries,* found secondhand machinery in less than 10 percent of the plants surveyed in Indonesia. W. Paul Strassman, *Technological Change and Economic Development: The Manufacturing Experience of Mexico and Puerto Rico* (Cornell University Press, 1968), p. 207, found secondhand equipment in more than half the plants he studied in Puerto Rico and Mexico, where government policy was ambiguous.

19. R. Hal Mason, *The Transfer of Technology and the Factor Proportions Problem: The Philippines and Mexico,* report no. 10 (New York: United Nations Institute for Training and Research, 1972); Howard Pack, "The Substitution of Labor for Capital in Kenyan Manufacturing" (U.S. Agency for International Development, 1972; processed); International Labour Organization, *Employment, Incomes, and Equality: A Strategy for Increasing Productive Employment in Kenya* (Geneva: I.L.O., 1972), esp. pp. 133–51; International Labour Organisation, *Automation in Developing Countries* (Geneva: I.L.O., 1972).

investors into the local market would, for economic reasons, drive them in the direction of greater capital intensity.

These three possibilities should not lead one to conclude that multinationals lock host countries into a socially wasteful structure of production. Several studies indicate that corporate preference for the capital-intensive techniques of the home country is heavily influenced by competition in the host-country market. Wayne A. Yeoman found, for example, that the more price elastic the demand for an American multinational's products in a low-wage country (that is, the greater the price competition), the more its host-country production technique differs in labor intensity from the technique used in the United States.[20] A study by Louis T. Wells shows that foreign-owned firms that compete primarily on the basis of price in a developing country are more likely to use labor-intensive techniques than those that compete primarily on the basis of brand names.[21] Furthermore, multinationals that set up foreign production facilities to export textiles or electronics to markets in developed countries are generally driven by price competition to locate their labor-intensive stages in the Third World. This suggests that to the extent host-country authorities encourage competition among foreign investors or between foreign investors and local firms, they encourage multinationals to use labor-intensive production technologies. And efficient use of local resources could be further facilitated by allowing economic rather than prestige considerations to dictate host-country policy toward the use of old or secondhand equipment.

Furthermore, once such labor-intensive technology is developed in one part of a multinational system, its use may spread rapidly throughout the corporations' network in the Third World. Ford's low-cost "modern Model T" (the Fiera), for example, is designed to be produced in small job shops where brake presses and simple welding jigs replace the stamping dies and automated equipment that make upwards of two hundred welds simultaneously in Ford's U.S. plants. The company decided to use this type of production technology as an experiment; if it is successful in

20. "Selection of Production Processes for the Manufacturing Subsidiaries of U.S. Based Multinational Corporations" (Harvard University Graduate School of Business Administration, 1968; processed). Price elasticities of demand are, of course, extremely difficult to quantify, particularly in developing countries.

21. Louis T. Wells, Jr., "Economic Man and Engineering Man: Choice in a Low-Wage Country," *Public Policy*, vol. 21, pp. 330–31.

the first plant, in the Philippines, it can be subsequently introduced throughout the Asia-Pacific region.[22]

Nevertheless, the fact that the real costs of supervising large work groups may be higher than the simple cost of wages leads one to be pessimistic about the ability of multinationals, under even the best of circumstances, to provide a massive solution to the problems of unemployment and underemployment in developing countries. Some of the criticism leveled against multinationals may be in answer to the inflated claims of defenders of the corporations. Majority-owned affiliates of American-based manufacturing firms employed approximately 525,000 workers in the developing countries in 1966, a number which probably rose to between 1 million and 1.5 million in 1975 (see table 10-3). A hypothetical increase in labor intensity of 50 percent would add "only" 500,000 to 750,000 jobs, compared with more than 100 million workers estimated to be unemployed or underemployed in the developing countries (excluding China) in 1970. Should one view the glass as 1/100 full or 99/100 empty?

Consumer Tastes

As foreign companies try to expand the market for home-country products to the Third World, their advertising will portray the tastes and the consumption ethic of the home country in a positive light. Conversely, advertising may tend to denigrate local customs—urging, for example, formula feeding of infants rather than breast feeding, or mechanized, high-fertilizer, high-pesticide farming rather than labor-intensive, conventional methods.

There is no evidence to demonstrate, however, that the marketing efforts of foreign firms portray different norms, or portray them more effectively, than local firms that also profit from such consumption patterns. Thus the issue that local authorities confront is not so much the particular question of cultural dependency as it is the general question of whether to protect the local population from certain values of which they disapprove. The options for public policy range from the relatively easy (requiring firms to prove the benefits claimed in their advertising, or publicizing the advantages of alternatives to the advertised way or prod-

22. Chalmers Goyert, "Ford in Asia: A Case Study" (Dearborn, Michigan: 1974, processed), pp. 13–22.

Table 10-3. *Four Estimates of Employment Created in Developing Countries by American Multinationals, 1966, 1970, 1973, 1975*

	Alternative estimates			
Year	(1)	(2)	(3)	(4)
1966	525,000	525,000	547,267	n.a.
1970	723,017	864,800	758,800	758,800
1973	871,607	1,503,000	1,318,800	1,178,769
1975	970,667	n.a.	n.a.	n.a.

Sources: U.S. Commerce Department, *U.S. Direct Investment Abroad, 1966*, pt. 2 (GPO, 1970), p. 190; William G. Tyler, "Employment Generation and the Promotion of Manufactured Exports in Less Developed Countries: Some Suggestive Evidence," in Herbert Giersch, ed., *The International Division of Labour: Problems and Perspectives* (J. C. B. Mohr, 1974), pp. 363–72. For alternative 1, average absolute increase per year was calculated for 1966–70 by applying the growth rate of the sample data for 1970 to the universe data for 1966 and projecting to 1973 and 1975. For alternative 2, 1966 sales/employee ratios were applied to estimates of sales for 1970 and 1973. For alternative 3, average 1966 and 1970 sales/employee ratios for Brazil and Mexico were applied to total sales for 1966 and 1970. Ratio for 1970 was applied to sales for 1973. For alternative 4, average 1966 and 1970 sales/employee ratios were projected to 1973 and applied to 1973 sales.
n.a. Not available.

uct) to the more difficult (a government effort to counter the lure of a high-consumption lifestyle). While most countries find the latter unacceptably intrusive, democratic governments as well as undemocratic governments have begun to try to limit the spread of affluent or wasteful or environmentally dangerous patterns of living. The exchange of information about successful policies in these states could provide governments of developing countries with a variety of tools to strengthen values that they consider worthy of preservation.

An Assessment

This review indicates serious limitations in existing knowledge concerning the impact of foreign direct investment on development. The bulk of economic theory and the limited empirical work that has been done suggest that its aggregate effects are usually positive on national income, jobs, and government revenues in the host countries. However, the contribution of the firms to development, on these criteria, could be improved further through (a) actions of their own (for example, adaptation of their production processes to local factors), (b) host-country policies toward investment (for example, reduce incentives to capital-intense processes), and (c) host-country policies in general (for example, toward more equitable income distribution). And major doubts remain about the impact of foreign direct investment on both the capital and current accounts of host-country balance-of-payments positions.

The Ascendance of Host Countries

The combination of oligopolistic firms and nationalistic host countries indicates that the contribution of foreign direct investment to development will turn increasingly on explicit negotiations between firms and host governments. What determines the bargaining power of developing countries with respect to multinational enterprises, and how has it evolved over time? Game theory analysis of foreign-investor–host-country relations provides only the beginnings of an answer. It depicts the balance of bargaining power between multinationals and local authorities as an exercise in joint maximization. Each has threats to make and benefits to offer as it seeks to increase its returns from the investment process. The total to be divided is seldom independent of how the shares are distributed. Collaborative solutions can expand the size of the pie and increase the absolute returns of both sides, a proposition those theorists that concentrate on international dependency usually admit, although for them the gain received in well-played bargaining sessions may still come at the expense of options for autonomy in the future.[23]

But the idea of joint maximization is essentially static. To understand the underlying trends or cycles in foreign-investor–host-country relations, it is necessary to formulate some idea of the evolution of the balance of power between them. Chapter five hypothesizes that the ability of host countries to influence the actions of foreign investors is a function of five variables: (1) its ability to monitor investor and industry behavior; (2) the cost of duplicating, or forgoing, what the foreign investor offers; (3)

23. Dependency theorists are reluctant to compare the impact of a foreign investment with what would happen if that investment did not take place. They compare an actual investment with their hypothetical ideal, for example a domestic socialist agency providing the same (or better) services while capturing all the rent for national development. Another hypothetical ideal (now widely discredited) is a national bourgeoisie to perform similar functions and to provide progressive social change, as well. For overview and general theories see Oswaldo Sunkel, "Big Business and 'Dependencia': A Latin American View," *Foreign Affairs,* vol. 50 (April 1972), pp. 517–31; and Helio Jaguaribe, *Political Development: A General Theory and a Latin American Case Study* (Harper and Row, 1973), and *Economic and Political Development,* rev. ed. (Harvard University Press, 1962).

competition within the industry; (4) the vulnerability of the foreigner's assets and earnings to adverse treatment by the host government; and (5) the ability of the host country to discount the international political tension caused by investment disputes.[24] This provides the framework for a dynamic model of the balance of power between the foreign investor and the host country.

The Era of Investor Power

For the first decade and a half of the postwar period, foreign corporations were virtually the sole source of capital, technology, and managerial expertise for the developing world. Despite the beginnings of import-substituting industrialization (especially in Latin America), their skills could be duplicated at the local level only with great loss in efficiency, if at all. The home governments of potential investors, moreover, structured the activities of multilateral lending agencies to prevent the emergence of alternatives to private direct investment (for example, preventing the World Bank from extending loans for projects where private investment was available); made the doctrine of growth via private enterprise a central element in security and aid relation; and reinforced via their tax systems (for example, deferral) the tax subsidies offered by developing countries to direct investors.

At the same time, the push of foreign-based companies into the developing world was relatively weak and the competition among new entrants feeble in the extreme. France and Great Britain did not add appreciably to their numbers of foreign subsidiaries (even in their colonies or former colonies plus Argentina) until after 1955. Germany and Japan did not begin strong investment drives until a decade later. European and Japanese investors established 254 new subsidiaries (for a total of 529) in the Third World between 1946 and 1959 (about one-sixth of the 1,549

24. In addition, for each investment project, taken individually, there is a sixth variable: uncertainty. When uncertainty is great (for example, before the project is producing), the bargaining strength of the investor is also great. As the uncertainty dissipates, the bargaining strength is attenuated. This model draws on Raymond Vernon, *Sovereignty at Bay: The Multinational Spread of U.S. Enterprises* (Basic Books, 1971); Louis T. Wells, Jr., *The Evolution of Concession Agreements in Developing Countries,* Economic Development Reports, No. 117 (Cambridge, Massachusetts: Harvard Development Advisory Service, 1969); and Theodore H. Moran, *Multinational Corporations and the Politics of Dependence: Copper in Chile* (Princeton University Press, 1974).

subsidiaries they subsequently established from 1959 to 1970).[25] Between 1945 and 1955, 525 new American subsidiaries (for a total of 1,062) were established in Asia, Africa, South America, and the Middle East (many more than the Europeans and Japanese but less than half the 1,324 created in the subsequent decade).[26]

The exposure of individual companies was low, except those in natural resources, plantations, and utilities. Host countries could neither threaten nor bargain effectively. When one did attract foreign companies to set up local operations, it was not in a position to place stringent requirements on corporate behavior. And few developing countries, in any case, had the expertise to structure procedures for accounting, taxes, and reporting.

In natural resources, host-country tax rates for petroleum, copper, bauxite, iron ore, and sulphur seldom rose above 50 percent, and were frequently below the U.S. rate despite the foreign tax credit. Concession contracts or development agreements covered long periods of time, from forty years to perpetuity. They not only permitted the investment incentives common to developed countries (for example, accelerated depreciation, the expensing of development outlays, and, in some cases, percentage depletion in the calculation of taxable income at the local level), they also frequently included conditions that host authorities must have been ill equipped to analyze, such as depreciation and tax deduction of reserves for replacement of the same asset, tax holidays, capital expenditure write-offs, and loss carry-forwards running in sequence rather than concurrently.[27] The parent corporations enjoyed wide latitude in arranging transfer pricing and interaffiliate transactions to suit their needs. Host-country limitations on the deduction for interest charged to subsidiaries by parent corporations, for example, do not begin to appear in concession agreements until the mid-1960s.

Moreover, because the foreign companies could not be removed, replaced, or even threatened without great risk to the local economy, they

25. Calculated from James W. Vaupel and Joan P. Curhan, *The World's Multinational Enterprises: A Sourcebook of Tables* (Harvard University Graduate School of Business Administration, 1973), pp. 64–71.

26. James W. Vaupel and Joan P. Curhan, *The Making of Multinational Enterprise* (Harvard University Graduate School of Business Administration, 1969), pp. 123, 125, 129. These calculations do not include investments in South Africa, Rhodesia, Australia, New Zealand, Japan, or Turkey.

27. For examples from Asia, Africa, and Latin America, see Wells, *The Evolution of Concession Agreements in Developing Countries.*

tended to exercise de facto sovereignty over the pricing and marketing of output. They transmitted to the host governments the wishes of the consumer states, rather than vice versa, during the heavy demands of the Second World War and Korean War, setting prices and volumes for industrial commodities in collaboration with consumer governments at substantial cost to host countries. In 1950 the United States treated Chile no differently than Belgium treated the Congo (which was then its colony) when it failed to invite Chile to meetings where the Allies set the price for the output of Chilean mines.[28] But it did invite Anaconda and Kennecott.

In manufacturing, much of the evidence for the first fifteen years of the postwar period is from the automotive, electrical machinery, and electronics industries in Latin America.[29] Foreign (predominantly American) investors were initially invited to move behind local tariff walls to aid the process of import-substituting industrialization begun during the Depression and the Second World War. They began by opening plants to assemble components imported from the parent or from traditional suppliers in the United States. There were few specifications as to local value added and little supervision of transfer pricing, technology sharing, or other interaffiliate transactions.[30] Not until 1955 did Mexico, a pioneer in using foreign investment for industrial development, revise its basic investment law to favor foreigners who produced locally, rather than those who imported and assembled. Jack Baranson estimates that the domestic

28. Moran, *Multinational Corporations and the Politics of Dependence*, p. 63.

29. See Rafael Izquierdo, "Protectionism in Mexico," in Raymond Vernon, ed., *Public Policy and Private Enterprise in Mexico* (Harvard University Press, 1964); Merle Kling, *A Mexican Interest Group in Action* (Prentice-Hall, 1961); Raymond Vernon, *The Dilemma of Mexico's Development* (Harvard University Press, 1963); Mira Wilkins, *The Maturing of Multinational Enterprise: American Business Abroad from 1914 to 1970* (Harvard University Press, 1974); Harry K. Wright, *Foreign Enterprise in Mexico: Laws and Policies* (University of North Carolina Press, 1971); *Multinational Corporations,* a compendium of papers prepared for the Subcommittee on International Trade, Senate Finance Committee (GPO, 1973); See Jack Baranson, *Manufacturing Problems in India: The Cummins Diesel Engine Experience* (Syracuse University Press, 1967); Michael Kidron, *Foreign Investments in India* (London: Oxford University Press, 1965).

30. Technology sharing, transfer pricing, and other interaffiliate transactions (including restrictive business agreements) are among the last areas to be subjected to close national scrutiny. Studies of 409 licensing agreements in five Andean Pact countries in 1971 show that almost 80 percent forbade the local company the use of the technology of the foreign parent to produce exports. UN Conference on Trade and Development, *Transfer of Technology* (Santiago: UNCTAD, December 29, 1971).

content of automobiles manufactured in Latin America in 1957 averaged 30 percent.[31] In electronics, Rafael Izquierdo finds that as late as 1959 Mexican-made parts accounted for no more than 20 percent of the cost of materials for foreign firms.[32] As in natural resources, host governments did not have the bargaining strength to demand tighter terms nor the public institutions to administer them. This laid the basis for Latin America's ambivalent attitude toward foreign investment that began to bedevil relations with the United States during the Eisenhower administration: their desire for ever greater amounts of U.S. private capital was coupled with resentment at the asymmetry of bargaining power when they tried to entice the investor in.

Decline of Investor Power

The appearance of economic nationalism in the first decade and a half of the postwar period was frequently attributed in the United States to waves and outbursts of emotion, "resentments against the United States" on the part of "uncontrolled and politically rebellious groups," and "Communist influence" in "unstable regions where revolutions and rioting were not uncommon," as President Eisenhower generalized from the case of Guatemala.[33]

But by the 1960s, the relations between foreign investors and host governments began to follow a regular, even predictable, pattern. After entering on terms largely dictated by themselves, American companies experienced mounting pressure to make more of a contribution to host-country goals. Once foreign investments were sunk, markets explored, and projects producing, local authorities found that they could use the subsidiary as a hostage to levy new requirements on the parent. Domestic requirements for employment and for tax-financed government services created an incentive to strengthen the expertise within host-country bureaucracies in international tax law, corporate accounting, and industrial analysis that could be used in negotiating with foreign companies.

31. "Integrated Automobiles for Latin America?" *Finance and Development Quarterly*, No. 4 (1968), p. 26.
32. "Protectionism in Mexico," p. 283.
33. Dwight D. Eisenhower, *Mandate for Change: 1953–1956* (Doubleday, 1963), p. 421.

As competition among investors increased, as alternative sources of external inputs developed (for example, the Eurocredit markets), and as local development proceeded, the cost of nationalistic demands declined both in absolute terms and in relation to the corresponding rewards in local politics. Sometimes crudely, and sometimes with great sophistication, governments in the developing world began to play foreign companies off against one another, a process that increased when European and Japanese investors began to make offers countering established U.S. companies.[34] For host countries to honor contracts with American companies long after the balance of power allowed them to push for new benefits, required them to ignore the domestic pressure that accompanied social mobilization, urbanization, and industrialization after the Second World War. Some governments, especially military dictatorships in Latin America, could do this in the 1950s. Few regimes of any type could do so in the 1960s.

Changes in Host-Country Policy

Beneath the rhetoric of dependency and exploitation, therefore, host-country policies have proceeded simultaneously along two tracks: inducing foreign investments, and then harnessing them to host-country goals. These goals fall into four categories: (1) domestic economic objectives, such as reducing unemployment or raising tax revenues; (2) external economic objectives, such as improving the balance of payments or breaking into new markets; (3) national ownership of certain economic activities; and (4) indigenous managerial control over certain economic activities.

As we observe in chapter five, the obsolescing bargain in natural resources attracts foreign companies with favorable concessions and then demands renegotiation once the investments are made. These renegotiations bring host countries more local refining or processing, more trained nationals for supervisory and managerial roles, greater shares of operating

34. Louis T. Wells, "Social Cost/Benefit Analysis for MNCs," *Harvard Business Review*, vol. 53 (March–April 1975), concludes, however, that "in most instances the multinational businessman lags far behind the host government's analysts in understanding the evaluation techniques" of social cost/benefit analysis, but that, once he does, "in many cases a project can be saved by modifying it so that it better meets the government's objectives" (pp. 40, 154).

revenues, greater ownership for domestic agencies or individuals, and greater control over production, pricing, and marketing.[35] New foreign investments at the production stage repeat the pattern of older projects (differing only according to the priorities of host-country governments— a trade-off of lower revenues for greater ownership, or vice versa), except that the process has speeded up over time. In one decade, Peru has been able to match many of the terms for copper extraction that Chile spent four decades gaining. In five years, Ecuador has been able to demand revisions in its petroleum agreements (even before the energy crisis) that Venezuela struggled with for half a century.

This process has not paused for the development of indigenous expertise in the industry. In 1973–74, Papua New Guinea, without a strong negotiating capability of its own, used competing teams of consultants from the Harvard Business School, Australia, and the Peruvian Ministry of Mines to develop its negotiating strategy with foreign companies in the country's nascent copper industry.[36] Nor has the specter of the 1950s— the fear of spoiling the investment climate—deterred host governments from demanding renegotiation of major concessions or from nationalizing the companies if they proved recalcitrant. When President Eduardo Frei reneged on a two-year-old agreement with Anaconda in 1969, even before the company's $135 million expansion was complete, the parent's management was unable to get a single American company to make the ritual "chilling effect" pronouncement to bolster Anaconda's bargaining position.[37] And in Peru, the American business community tried to persuade the Nixon administration to take a soft line toward the IPC dispute (the

---

35. In one case, a multinational, itself (Booker McConnell) undertook the renegotiation of the agreement (Commonwealth Sugar Agreement, on behalf of Guyana). See Isaiah A. Litvak and Christopher J. Maule, "Foreign Corporate Social Responsibility in Less Developed Economies," *Journal of World Trade Law*, vol. 9 (March/April 1975), p. 131.

36. For the Bougainville mine, the government in Port Moresby chose the formula of the Australian experts over the recommendations of the Harvard consultant and denounced the latter. For the OK Tedi mine, the government stuck with the recommendations of the Peruvian group but eventually drove Kennecott, the prospective investor, away. See Raymond F. Mikesell, *Foreign Investment in Copper Mining: Case Studies of Mines in Peru and Papua New Guinea* (Johns Hopkins University Press for Resources for the Future, 1975), pp. 5–6.

37. Author interview with Charles Brinkerhoff, chairman, Anaconda Co., New York, July 1, 1970.

International Petroleum Corporation was a subsidiary of Standard Oil Company of New Jersey) after the military government took over the company in 1968.[38] The other American investors considered their own home government a bigger threat than the Peruvian government to the investment climate in Peru!

In manufacturing industries, American companies found themselves in the early 1960s accused by host countries of being responsible for the problems associated with import-substituting industrialization. With a combination of threats, tax incentives, and harassment for noncompliance, they were required to buy more inputs locally, train supervisory personnel, take on local partners, and fill export quotas.[39] In the automobile industry, for example, estimates of local content rise from 30 percent for Latin America in 1957 to 70 percent in 1967.[40] With the expansion of the automotive market during that decade, the rate of growth for value added in the host countries averaged nearly 33 percent per year. Requirements varied from country to country: American automakers were forced to increase the local content of vehicles to more than 60 percent in Mexico, 95 percent in Argentina, and 100 percent in Brazil. As local goals were reached, Argentina restricted the introduction of new lines to firms willing to increase automotive exports. Mexico tied the importation of components, dollar for dollar, to the vaue of exports. Brazil limited market expansion to investors willing to commit themselves to an export program of $400 million over a ten-year period. Stiff competition from Volkswagen (which outpaced the American companies in Mexico and Brazil) and Fiat (which outpaced them in Argentina), plus the entry of Toyota and Datsun, put the American companies under strong pressure to comply. Chrysler, for example, exported $80 million worth of equipment from Mexico in 1975, including 48,000 engines, 650,000 con-

38. Jessica Pernitz Einhorn, *Expropriation Politics* (Lexington Books, 1974); and author interviews with the management of the major companies involved (1973–74).

39. Reuber and others, *Private Foreign Investment in Development*, pp. 120–34, found that developing countries frequently mix tax and trade restrictions, requirements, subsidies, and incentives with such overlap that it is difficult to calculate the net financial impact on broad categories of firms.

40. Baranson, "Integrated Automobiles for Latin America?", p. 26. See also H. W. Gage, "General Motors in Latin America" (Aspen, Colo.: Council on Religion and International Affairs, 1973; processed); Organization of American States, *Sectoral Study of Transnational Enterprises in Latin America* (Washington, D.C.: OAS, 1974).

densers for air conditioners, and a line of finished trucks.[41] Similarly, General Motors has been pushed to export Terex off-highway equipment from its Brazilian plant at Belo Horizonte. As noted in chapter nine, the reaction of U.S. labor to the success of these host-country policies in the Third World demonstrates that there is a risk of investment wars akin to the trade wars of the past.

This pattern of host-country pressure is by no means limited to the automobile industry. There is evidence of a similar cycle—moving from value-added requirements to exports—in the electronics, electrical machinery, office equipment, food processing, rubber, chemical, petrochemical, pharmaceutical, and household goods industries.[42] Clearly host countries have been more successful in inducing foreign investors to meet some objectives than others: the growth of domestic value added and the penetration of world markets have progressed substantially; the development of labor-intensive technologies and the surrender of ownership or managerial control have advanced more slowly.

Foreign investors appear to resist the demand for local ownership in proportion to the extent they wish to integrate a particular subsidiary with their broad international corporate network. The need to ensure production to specification and the need to meet operational timetables, plus the need to allocate markets within the firm, raise the parents' preference for total (or at least majority) ownership and control. Thus host countries have had to choose, in some cases, between the promise of favorable export behavior and more participation in the decision-making of the subsidiary.[43] Evidence from Mexico suggests that the

41. "Multinationals Find the Going Rougher," *Business Week,* July 14, 1975.

42. See, for example, the statements by Clark Equipment Company, Champion Spark Plug Company, Owens-Illinois, Armstrong Cork Company, Manufacturing Chemists Association, Union Carbide, and the Emergency Committee for American Trade, in *Multinational Corporations,* papers submitted to the Subcommittee on International Trade, Senate Finance Committee.

43. For evidence about what kinds of firms can most easily "tolerate" joint ventures, see Lawrence G. Franko, *Joint Venture Survival in Multinational Corporations* (Praeger, 1971); and Louis T. Wells, Jr., "The Multinational Business Enterprise: What Kind of International Organization?" in Robert O. Keohane and Joseph S. Nye, Jr., eds., *Transnational Relations and World Politics* (Harvard University Press, 1971). Franko suggests, however, that multinational firms that are organized into worldwide product divisions tolerate local ownership better than those that have centralized geographical divisions within the corporation. Perhaps because they value the local expertise of joint-venture partners in introducing new products, such firms in 1966 had local partners in 30 percent of their foreign manufacturing operations.

country benefits most when it chooses economic performance over ownership.[44]

Nevertheless, there is a definite trend toward a sharing of ownership and control in foreign manufacturing ventures. The Harvard Business School sample of 187 American multinationals formed 487 joint ventures in manufacturing (27 percent of new manufacturing subsidiaries) in the developing countries from 1958 to 1968, and significantly decreased the share of ownership in 81 established operations.[45] In the prior decade they had formed 147 joint ventures (16 percent of new manufacturing subsidiaries) and significantly decreased the share of ownership in 16 more. Competition among foreign firms again played a major role. Both Ford and General Motors resisted joint ventures in Latin America longer than many American investors in other industries but finally succumbed in Asia because their European and Japanese competitors were willing to allow local participation in Korea, Thailand, and the Philippines. The trend is being reinforced by arrangements that investors accept in Eastern Europe. Dow Chemical, for example (which once balked at giving Chile 51 percent of its Chilean operations and ended, in 1973, being taken over), in 1975 signed an agreement with a Yugoslav state company for a petrochemical complex in which Dow would have only 49 percent ownership.[46]

Success of Host-Country Policy

Certainly not all host-country demands have been met, even in part. General Motors, for example, withdrew from Peru in 1970 (as it had earlier from India and Pakistan) rather than comply with a decree re-

44. Douglas Bennett and Kenneth Sharpe, "Controlling the Multinationals: The Ill Logic of Mexicanization," Temple University and Swarthmore College (February 1977; processed).

45. Vaupel and Curhan, *The Making of Multinational Enterprise*, pp. 122, 243, 511.

46. "Dow, Yugoslavia Sign Accord to Build Plant," *Washington Post,* February 15, 1975. Dow executives report that their relations with the marxist administrators had been "most encouraging" until they refused the request for 51 percent government ownership; Herbert E. Meyer, "Dow Picks up the Pieces in Chile," *Fortune,* vol. 89 (April 1974), pp. 142, 145. Romania and Poland insisted on buy-back clauses, which require investors and licensors to market local products abroad. See *Business Week,* July 14, 1975, p. 64, and Marshall Goldman, *Détente and Dollars: Doing Business with the Soviet's* (Basic Books, 1975), chap. 5.

quiring 70 percent local content, the elimination of engine imports within three years, and the sale of 51 percent of the company's shares to Peruvians within one year.[47]

But even from the failures, host countries learn how best to get foreign investors to serve host-country needs. From observing the problems of the Andean Pact (and aided by outside experts), the ASEAN nations (Thailand, Malaysia, Singapore, Indonesia, and the Philippines) constructed regional regulations more likely to induce foreign companies to respond to their complementation objectives than the Latin American effort.[48]

Successful nationalistic actions, moreover, generate a clear demonstration effect. On the basis of Constantine Vaitsos' pioneering work on transfer pricing in the pharmaceutical, rubber, chemical, and electrical industries in Colombia in the late 1960s (demonstrating, for example, that American drug companies, spurred on by Colombian price controls and limitations on dividend remittances, kept their profit margins low in Colombia by importing tetracycline at ten times the quotation in the U.S. market) pricing policy in the international pharmaceutical industry was revolutionized. Indeed, the need to scrutinize interaffiliate transactions has become a cause célèbre worldwide.[49] But subsequent studies are inconclusive about which countries (home, host, or neither—because of tax havens and other third countries) gain from transfer pricing. In a sample of 257 foreign firms representing 25 percent of Latin America's manufactured exports, Ronald Müller and Richard Morgenstern found that wholly

47. Gage, "General Motors in Latin America."

48. Thomas W. Allen, "Policies of Asian Countries Towards Direct Foreign Investment," *SEADAG Papers on Problems of Development in Southeast Asia* (New York: Southeast Asia Development Advisory Group, 1973); Richard D. Robinson, "National Efforts to Establish Guidelines for the Behavior of Multinational Corporations," a study prepared for U.S. Labor Department (1975; processed); and author interviews with some of the advisers involved, 1974–75.

49. Constantine V. Vaitsos, "Interaffiliate Charges by Transnational Corporations and Intercountry Income Distribution" (Harvard University, 1972; processed); According to Vaitsos, provisions in the Andean Pact (1970) covering transfer pricing and payments for technology were directly reflected in Argentina law the following year (Law no. 19.231 of 1971) and Mexican law two years later (1972): Constantine V. Vaitsos, "The Changing Policies of Latin American Governments Toward Economic Development and Direct Foreign Investments" (March 1973; processed). Information on changes in drug pricing came from author interviews with officials at Eli Lilly and Pfizer, 1974–75.

owned subsidiaries selling to affiliates in other Latin American countries systematically underinvoiced the value of their exports in relation to firms exporting to unrelated buyers.[50] They hypothesize that tax havens and free ports in the Caribbean were the profit centers for such transfer-pricing strategies. Partly because of the inconclusiveness of the evidence, the pressure for fuller disclosure of interaffiliate transactions has escalated.

In other areas of corporate regulation, there has been a similar demonstration effect. Retroactive licensing controls to curb payments in royalties and fees spread rapidly from Latin America (Brazil, Mexico, Argentina, and the Andean Pact countries) to Spain, Yugoslavia, India, Pakistan, and Israel. Mexico's 1973 Law on the Transfer of Technology required foreign investors to rewrite 5,000 existing contracts and pared royalties on 1,500 new contracts from the 5–15 percent range to less than 3 percent in the majority of cases.[51] The creation of an agency in the United Nations to collect data and exchange information on multinational corporations may speed the spread of such techniques and intensify the pressure to make multinational operations known.

Some investors will doubtless be relatively immune from this process. Where technology is complex, rapidly changing, and tightly held—such as computers—the shift of bargaining power toward developing (and other) host countries will proceed least rapidly. The Mexican commission that regulates transfer of technology, for example, approved royalties higher than 3 percent for products with high R&D costs, while holding retailers' fees for trademarks on brand names (in cosmetics and food processing) to as little as 1 percent. International Business Machines (IBM) maintains a straight 10 percent royalty for use of technology, despite the efforts of host countries to reduce it.[52] Other industries with products at the beginning of the product cycle may be able to offset vul-

50. Ronald Müller and Richard Morgenstern, "Multinational Corporations and Balance of Payments Impacts in LDC's: An Econometric Analysis of Export Pricing Behavior," *KYKLOS,* April 1974, pp. 304–21. Müller and Morgenstern's analysis does not reveal, however, whether foreign-owned subsidiaries undercharge their sister affiliates for intrafirm exports or merely export smaller quantities than locally owned firms. Thus, whether their's is further evidence of abusive transfer pricing is inconclusive.

51. *Business Week,* July 14, 1975, p. 69.

52. R. A. Bennett, "IBM in Latin America," in Jon P. Gunnemann, ed., *The Nation-State and Transnational Corporations in Conflict* (Praeger, 1975); and author interviews with IBM management, 1974–75.

nerability in older, more mature product lines.[53] But the most reasonable prediction is that new investment projects in the Third and Fourth Worlds will replicate the pattern of earlier ones. In this process, the charges of exploitation and dependencia, real in the sense that host countries have to pay high prices for valuable goods and services at early points in the bargaining cycle, serve the function of a self-denying prophecy.[54]

Effect on the United States

Even before the Eisenhower administration left office, the flexing of bargaining muscle in the Third World provoked both sympathy and outrage in Washington.[55] Washington began to divide into hardliners and softliners about the proper American stance toward economic nationalists when U.S. investors found their contracts broken and their interests threatened. The debate ever since has been conducted in moralistic and legalistic terms: for one side, accommodation of American investors to host-country demands is good, and defense of property rights or rights of contract is considered intransigent; for the other side, sanctity of contract is good, host-government assertion of national sovereignty considered ir-

53. For example, American petrochemical companies in Brazil may be trading an unattractive arrangement for the production of chlorine for a profitable arrangement for the production of polyurethane foam (TDI). Peter Evans, "Testing the New Alliance: The Brazilian State, the Multinationals and the Launching of the Polo Petroquímico at Camaçari, Bahia" (Brown University, February 1976; processed).

54. The observation that bargaining power shifts over time toward host-country governments in no way implies that host governments will necessarily reallocate the benefits of that shift internally in ways that improve domestic income distribution. But it does suggest that the host governments themselves should be held responsible for not exercising their power to redistribute income, through domestic tax or welfare programs (rather than foreign investors, for not "giving" them the power). At the same time, the hypothesis that some foreign companies (for example, in labor-intensive export industries such as electronics or textiles) exert strong pressure to retard local labor organizing or to prop up repressive governments should be tested carefully. One would expect foreign firms producing products for domestic consumption, however, to be in favor of an income distribution that would enlarge the market for their goods.

55. Milton Eisenhower, *U.S.-Latin American Relations: Report to the President,* U.S. State Department (1953); and Christopher Mitchell, "Dominance and Fragmentation in U.S. Latin American Policy," in Julio Cotler and Richard R. Fagen, eds., *Latin America and the United States: The Changing Political Realities* (Stanford University Press, 1974), pp. 176–204.

responsible. But the hard-line/soft-line dichotomy obscures the fundamental shift in the balance of power between investor and host country and precludes an analysis of the impact of that shift on American welfare and security, an analysis that is needed even when there is a successful accommodation—perhaps particularly when there is successful accommodation—because of the implied collusion between host countries and multinational enterprises.

The economic impact of the shift in bargaining power in natural resource industries is analyzed in chapter five. Control over pricing and marketing for most major raw industrial commodities exported from developing countries passed to the governments of these countries: bauxite, in 1974, was the last, following copper, petroleum, sulphur, natural gas, tin, zinc, and iron ore. In the long run, only competition—not the parent company or the parent company's government—will restrain host countries in setting prices. But large equity investments are now vulnerable to either nationalization or heavy taxes, discouraging new investments, and thus discouraging competition. Thus there is no way for the United States to avoid the costs and insecurities engendered by host-country power as long as the system of direct equity investment is the primary vehicle for developing industrial raw materials.

In manufacturing, the shift in bargaining power from foreign investors to host countries has a more ambiguous effect on the United States. In one class of cases, economic nationalism has forced American companies to play the role of the Schumpeterian entrepreneur, establishing infant industries and expanding them to a size where economies of scale are present, developing local suppliers and aiding them to become efficient, and producing in the end an internationally competitive product. For example, the development of "border" industries in textiles and electronics in Korea, Taiwan, and Mexico came after American firms, enticed there to manufacture substitutes for imports, were led to discover the hosts' comparative advantage in the labor-intensive stages of production and thus were encouraged to export. Insofar as host-country nationalism has forced multinationals to find out more quickly where comparative advantage lies, it has led to greater global economic welfare.

The result for the United States, under most assumptions, would be positive in these cases. The shift in the share of value added (and the share of employment) to the Third World would be more than offset by lower prices for American consumers and a more efficient allocation of resources in the United States. The central problem for the United States would then be the adjustment costs borne by particular groups in American society (especially unskilled labor) that should, in the public interest, be offset by a generous and effective adjustment assistance program.

There is a second class of manufacturing cases, however, in which the assertion of economic nationalism has had the opposite effect, leading to economic costs for the United States that have not been compensated for by increases in efficiency. The insistence of eight Latin American countries to have their own automobile industries, for example, has simply proliferated inefficient plants. The production of cars, trucks, and buses is highly sensitive to economies of scale, with 220,000 to 240,000 units per year being the most efficient number of each fully assembled vehicle type.[56] Yet by 1970 there were approximately seventy foreign-owned plants in Latin America, producing over 200 basic models, with an average annual run of 10,000 vehicles per plant. Chile had the most notorious case of fragmentation, with 16,000 vehicles turned out by nineteen firms.[57] Yet not a single automotive item was added to the list for tariff concessions within the Latin America Free Trade Association between 1961 and 1968.[58]

There are similar examples among foreign investments in the consumer appliance, industrial machinery, chemical, and petrochemical industries, where economies of scale are clearly not reached in the local economy and local suppliers are not competitive. Instead, host governments have encouraged inefficient operations to multiply, siphoning employment from the home countries of the foreign investors to the local economy (or, in some cases, third countries) and imposing higher costs on local consumers. Protected behind high tariff walls, the investors themselves may be quite content with the market distortions—indeed, in some cases, demand such distortions as a condition of entry—to the detriment of the home country, of the world economy, and ultimately, of the host country, itself.

Most manufacturing investments, however, are neither wholly successful nor unsuccessful but are inefficient when the investment is made, while

56. Baranson, "Integrated Automobiles for Latin America?"
57. The Allende regime tried to reduce this fragmentation and rationalize production in the automobile industry. The military regime has continued in this direction.
58. Baranson, "Integrated Automobiles for Latin America?", p. 25.

having possibilities for improvement with time. For example, a prediction in 1967 that American automobile companies would be able eventually to produce internationally competitive products in Mexico or Argentina had to confront the fact that locally manufactured parts then cost, on the average, 119 percent more than imports in Mexico (with 63 percent local content required) and 210 percent more than imports in Argentina (with 83 percent local content required).[59] Yet, by the early 1970s, the companies were exporting successfully from both countries; in 1973, the United States alone imported from Mexico $20 million worth of cars, trucks, and buses and $45 million worth of automotive parts.[60] But such outcomes are uncertain, even when American companies begin with plants of a scale sufficient for maximum efficiency and enjoy a potential comparative advantage in local factors of production. For example, the Asian subsidiaries of General Motors were recently trying to decide whether to commit themselves to buying transmissions from a large new General Motors facility in the Philippines or from alternative company sources in Europe and the United States.[61] The impact on the American economy of this third class of cases may begin in the negative, move toward the positive along the lines of the infant industry model, but, in any case, carry great uncertainty about the final outcome.

Even if it were possible to estimate the net economic effect on the United States of the Third World's use of multinational manufacturers to serve their national goals, such a global calculation would be of limited value for the purposes of American policy. The only alternative against which the effect could be measured would be in a world in which economic nationalism did not exist, in which the shift in bargaining power never took place. But the United States cannot turn back the clock to its post-World War II position of hegemony. The only useful measure from the point of view of current U.S. policy is whether the United States would be better or worse off if American companies did not take part in such investment projects. In the first class of cases, the United States would be worse off, unless it could (and wanted to) devise controls on American

59. Ibid.; and World Bank Report, *Automotive Industries in Developing Countries,* EC-162 (Washington, D.C.: IBRD, 1968).

60. Statement of Motor Vehicle Manufacturers Association of the United States, Inc., in *Oversight Hearings on Impact of Motor Vehicle Imports on Employment in the United States,* Hearings before the Subcommittee on Labor Standards of the House Education and Labor Committee, 94:1 (GPO, 1975), p. 60.

61. Author interviews with General Motors management, 1974–75.

investors analogous to an optimum tariff, which would increase U.S. welfare at the expense of everybody else. In the second class of cases, the United States would be better off if the American firms stayed out. In the third group of cases, the United States would have to make a highly uncertain judgment about the net impact over time.

The very uncertainty of the results from any given manufacturing investment, however, suggests three major conclusions for American policy. First, given the diversity of cases, a policy of across-the-board support for all American investors under all circumstances is a particularly inefficient way to stimulate global welfare. Second, given the range of effects on the economy, such a policy is a particularly inappropriate way to increase U.S. domestic welfare and nonwelfare objectives. Third, given the difficulty of making reliable calculations of the economic effect of a particular investment, an across-the-board policy could not be fine-tuned to enhance any economic welfare or other objectives of the United States. The implications of these limitations are analyzed in the final section of this chapter.

Political Relations

The model presented in this chapter predicts that investor-host interaction will inevitably be unstable over time as bargaining conditions change and relative bargaining strengths are transformed. To argue that there should not be an ongoing process of adjustment—because of the "sanctity" of the original contract—is only to argue that agreements should be frozen on terms favorable to the foreign investors. It is not surprising, therefore, that the probability of finding legal rigor over the course of investment agreements is low.[62] Foreign investors have consistently respected contracts negotiated under circumstances favorable to themselves. Host governments have, with equal consistency, brought pressure to readjust such contracts when circumstances have changed in their favor.

The problem with these swings in the balance of power, from a political point of view, is that they generate extraordinary tension and extreme

---

62. Such a prediction is not unique to investor-host relations. The probability is low for any contractual relation where there are vast asymmetries in bargaining power, with abrupt shifts from side to side.

perceptions of injustice on both sides.[63] Although the great majority of the resulting investment disputes are settled by mutual accommodation at the local level without any appeal for extraterritorial support, the incidence of cases in which accommodation fails is far from random. And it cannot all be traced to personal or ideological idiosyncracies on the part of the management of the companies involved.

In number, size, and impact on U.S. relations with the developing countries, the failure of local accommodation has involved, almost exclusively, investors with three characteristics: high fixed capital costs, undifferentiated products, and slowly changing technology. Industries that fit into this group include natural resources, plantation agriculture, and utilities. Here, once the investment is sunk, the shift in the balance of power away from the foreign investor is the most abrupt and most extreme. In contrast to manufacturing, where marketing skills, new technologies, and a credible threat to withdraw help them keep their bargaining strength, investors in these three types of industry have a lot to lose and little local leverage. A Library of Congress study shows that five of seven significant foreign expropriations between the end of the Second World War and the early 1960s were either utilities or plantations; two involved natural resources; none were manufacturing firms.[64] A State Department survey in 1970 of pending foreign expropriations and nationalizations found twenty-three in natural resources (accounting for

63. As is argued for extractive industries (chap. 5), the balance of power between a home-government investor, and a host government would pass through the same evolution, unless (a) the home government does not extract as high a return as its control over technology and risk allows (that is, the home government acts as an aid-giving institution); or (b) it operates on a production-sharing rather than profit basis, acceptable to the host government (ceteris paribus) because no direct foreign ownership is involved. Soviet natural-resource companies adopted the second option, eschewing direct foreign ownership in, for example, the Dabele bauxite project in Guinea. In manufacturing, Soviet joint stock companies (for example, Konela in Finland, Konela-Norge-Bil of Norway, Scaldia-Volga of Belgium, and Matreco-Bil of Sweden) embody the first option, incorporating hidden Soviet subsidies. Soviet manufacturing activity in the Third World is rare, with most companies (for example, WAATEGO in Nigeria, Marinexport in Morocco, or Ethso in Ethiopia) being fundamentally trading companies. Goldman, *Détente and Dollars,* chap. 5 and app. 3.

64. *Expropriation of American-Owned Property by Foreign Governments in the Twentieth Century,* prepared by the Legislative Reference Service for the House Committee on Foreign Affairs (GPO, 1963).

$845 million or 97 percent of all appraised claims); three were utilities and plantations (accounting for $27 million or 2.5 percent of appraised claims); and eight were manufacturing companies (accounting for less than one-half of 1 percent of appraised claims).[65]

Protecting American Investments

The vulnerability of American companies with large fixed investments and limited local bargaining power began to present the U.S. government in the late 1950s with what was diagnosed as a dilemma. There was an unsettlingly strong correlation between governments that were most open to popular pressure for reform and an unstable life for established U.S. investors. The dilemma was between good relations with nationalistic governments (especially ones democratically elected) and defending the interests of American companies whose private investments were threatened. As long as support for private companies abroad could be wrapped in the mantle of U.S. security (linking the fate of American companies to the fate of the nation) American investors had some chance of support from the diverse centers of government power in Washington (as in the case of United Fruit in Guatemala). But, from the late 1950s onward, the defense of the private interests of American investors when no military threat was involved—and when host-country nationalists were cast as progressive reformers—split both Republican and Democratic parties.[66] Richard Nixon's trip to Caracas in 1958 (in the midst of which President Eisenhower was required to put U.S. paratroopers on alert for a possible rescue of his vice president from crowds that identified the United States with the former dictator, General Pérez Jiménez) revealed in dramatic fashion the diplomatic hazards of giving unequivocal support to governments whose primary credential as allies was the tranquility they offered American companies.[67] The appearance of Fidel Castro raised the

65. U.S. State Department, "Pending Expropriation Cases Involving United States Property Abroad" (May 8, 1971; processed).
66. Jerome Levinson and Juan de Onís, *The Alliance that Lost Its Way: A Critical Report on the Alliance for Progress* (Quadrangle Books, 1970).
67. After this incident, U.S. policymakers began to assess the need for a fundamental reorientation in U.S. relations with Latin America. See Milton Eisenhower, *The Wine is Bitter: The United States and Latin America* (Doubleday, 1963); and Richard M. Nixon, *Six Crises* (Doubleday, 1962), pp. 183–235.

specter of a revolutionary alternative to the status quo if the United States did not actively support "reformist" regimes.[68]

With the election of the Kennedy administration in 1960, uncertainty about Washington reaction to the dilemma presented vulnerable American investors with a problem inconceivable to an analyst of the neo-imperialist school: how to defend their holdings independent of how American policymakers defined the national interest. There were two possibilities: rejuvenate an economic version of the big stick to supply pressure on their behalf even if such pressure conflicted with other foreign policy objectives; or construct transnational alliances to spread their risks and defend their interests, no matter what policy the government adopted.[69] The first strategy represented an attempt to influence the foreign policymaking process rather than dominate the definition of foreign policy goals. The second represented an attempt to reshape the international environment in which American foreign policy would have to be carried out. In either case, their strategy aimed at self-protection without having to pass the test of what best served the public good. With the balance of power moving fundamentally against them, it was far too uncertain to leave the defense of their particular interests to statesmen, who, no matter what their socioeconomic background, might be reflecting upon the national interest.

The first strategy depended upon the ability of beleaguered companies to build a coalition of sympathetic public officials in the fragmented U.S. political system who would support the defense of individual private investors whether or not that defense undermined other policy objectives. Supporters did not argue that such a policy had to pass the test of whether

68. Our model of the shift in the balance of power toward host authorities suggests that "good treatment" for American investors is a most tenuous basis for choosing particular countries as political allies, and the American business community appears to agree. In response to the question "Please indicate the relative importance you believe the U.S. should attach, in general, to the following policy objectives in its involvement with underdeveloped countries," the response of 1,059 vice presidents of the 500 largest U.S. corporations and financial institutions gave lowest priority (a mean of 5.7 on a scale of 1 to 7) to "a government which allows broad opportunities for American business investment." They awarded highest priority (a mean of 2.3 on the same scale), however, to "a stable government capable of preserving internal order." Bruce M. Russett and Elizabeth C. Hanson, *Interest and Ideology: The Foreign Policy Beliefs of American Businessmen* (W. H. Freeman, 1975), p. 276.

69. On transnational relations and international politics, see Keohane and Nye, *Transnational Relations and World Politics;* and Samuel P. Huntington, "Transnational Organizations in World Politics," *World Politics,* vol. 25 (April 1973).

it contributed to the overall economic or political welfare of the United States. Rather, they justified their approach by analogy to a citizen's right to government protection as he traveled abroad. "It has always been my concept that one of the duties of the U.S. government is to protect the reasonable, fair, equitable rights of American citizens abroad," Bourke Hickenlooper explained to his colleagues in the U.S. Senate, "but the State Department and the administration are not exercising vigorous care or attention to see to it that the traditional protection given to their rights—not the unusual or extraordinary territorial rights, but merely the basic rights of American citizens abroad—is being afforded American citizens."[70]

The Hickenlooper amendment (76 Stat. 260–61) was introduced at the urging of Harold Geneen, president of International Telephone and Telegraph, whose utility subsidiaries were under fire in Brazil and Argentina.[71] It specifically denied the President the right to waive the requirement to cut off aid to countries that expropriated U.S. companies, even if the cutoff adversely affected the national interest. Shortly after the amendment was passed in 1962, a moderate government in Nicaragua was threatened with its application for proposing a land reform law (one of the primary aims of the Alliance for Progress) that could have included some of United Fruit's plantations. The following year (1963), the Hickenlooper amendment was broadened to include any case in which a government repudiated or nullified an existing contract with a U.S. investor (77 Stat. 387). This put the U.S. government explicitly in the role of trying to force other countries to do business with U.S. companies on terms reflecting bargaining strength long since gone, whenever those companies decided they were tired of playing the game of obsolescing bargain. Senator Hickenlooper said the change was directed at Argentina, where Arturo Frondizi had been overthrown for refusing to renegotiate contracts with seven U.S. oil companies, and where the new president, Arturo Illía, had just carried out a campaign commitment to void the contracts altogether.[72] In the same year, but without formal invocation of the Hicken-

70. *Congressional Record,* October 2, 1962, p. 21615. Hickenlooper was by no means alone in his advocacy of such legislation. Other congressmen supported similar legislation.

71. Levinson and de Onís, *The Alliance That Lost Its Way,* p. 144.

72. For background on the conflicts between the American oil companies and a series of governments in Argentina, see Gertrude G. Edwards, "The Frondizi Contracts and Petroleum Self-Sufficiency in Argentina," in Raymond F. Mikesell and

looper amendment, aid to Peru was cut for three years in an effort to force Fernando Belaunde Terry to settle a dispute with the International Petroleum Corporation on terms acceptable to Standard of New Jersey.[73] Belaunde was precisely the kind of popular reformer envisioned by the framers of the Alliance for Progress as worthy of U.S. support. He was overthrown in 1968 because of the terms on which he finally settled with IPC.

A Policy that Failed

That multinationals pressed for congressional actions is the best evidence that they no longer counted on any administration to defend their interests. But congressional actions—the Hickenlooper amendment and, in 1972, the Gonzalez amendment (86 Stat. 59), which requires the American representative in the Inter-American Development Bank to vote against loans to countries that expropriate American property—produced, in many ways, the worst of all possible worlds. They led to political tension between the United States and the developing world (even countries not directly affected) and to Third World charges of American economic aggression. The political price has not been compensated for, even in part, by gains for the United States in other welfare or security areas. They have not kept oligopoly rents from flowing, in growing measure, to the treasuries of resource exporting governments. They have not ensured sovereignty to American multinationals over production and marketing decisions. They have not created an investment climate conducive to expanding the productive capacity of developing nations. In Latin America, the crises in natural resource, plantation agriculture, and utility industries—predictable with or without the Hickenlooper and Gonzalez amendments—have given an unhappy constancy to poor inter-American relations despite periodic rephrasings of the desire for good neighborliness.

Finally, the Hickenlooper and Gonzalez amendments have not even been a success on their own terms: protecting the private interests of

William Bartsch, eds., *Foreign Investment in the Petroleum and Mineral Industries: Case Studies of Investor-Host Country Relations* (Johns Hopkins University Press, 1971), pp. 157–215.

73. On the IPC case in Peru, see Richard Goodwin, "Letter from Peru," *The New Yorker,* May 17, 1969, pp. 41–109; Levinson and de Onís, *The Alliance that Lost Its Way,* pp. 146–56.

established American investors. The only noticeable result of U.S. government pressure on behalf of American oil companies in Argentina in the mid-1960s was a demand that Ambassador Robert McClintock be sent home.[74] The decade of conflict over IPC in Peru ended in the expropriation of the La Brea y Parinas oil field without formal provisions for compensation.[75] In Jamaica, when Ambassador Vincent de Roulet's efforts to defend Alcoa, Reynolds, Kaiser, Anaconda, and Revere became publicly known, he was declared persona non grata, and the attack on the American aluminum companies intensified.[76] By 1970, roughly three-fourths of American investors in Latin America considered the Hickenlooper and the Gonzalez amendments counterproductive and favored their repeal.[77]

In several prominent cases, Latin American governments have in fact been able to exercise influence in the decentralized U.S. political system with more skill than their corporate counterparts. After a twenty-year fight to keep the Mexican postwar concessions of Pan American Sulphur and Texas Gulf Sulphur intact, the parent companies and their supporters in the U.S. Senate were beaten at their own game by the government of President Díaz Ordaz.[78] In the mid-sixties the Mexican minister of national properties and the minister of industry and commerce mobilized

74. Edwards, "The Frondizi Contracts and Petroleum Self-Sufficiency in Argentina," pp. 174–75.
75. The United States government, however, gave Exxon a portion of the compensation it had negotiated on behalf of other nationalized companies.
76. See "Jamaica Asks Recall of U.S. Ambassador," *Washington Post*, July 21, 1973; and "A High-Risk Policy in Jamaica," *Washington Post*, July 25, 1973.
77. Council of the America's survey of members, 1970. The council represents 90 percent of U.S. investors in Latin America. Although 76 percent favored repeal of the amendments, a breakdown of the responses indicates that extractive industries make up a small proportion of the responding group. Of the fifteen extractive companies, 47 percent responded that the Hickenlooper amendment had not outlived its usefulness. In contrast, of the forty-eight manufacturing companies, 21 percent felt that the amendment had not outlived its usefulness. Forty-two percent of the manufacturers and 20 percent of the extractive companies rated the danger of expropriation as low. See Robert H. Swansbrough, *The Embattled Colossus: Economic Nationalism and United States Investors in Latin America* (University of Florida Press, 1976), pp. 195, 211.
78. See Miguel Wionczek, "Foreign-Owned Export-Oriented Enclave in a Rapidly Industrializing Economy: Sulphur Mining in Mexico," in Raymond F. Mikesell, ed., "Robbing the Gringo—The Outrage in Mexican Sulphur Turns Back the Clock," *Barron's*, May 3, 1965; "Robbing the Gringo II: Pasco's Fate Flashes a Warning to Investors in Mexico," *Barron's*, October 10, 1966.

enough support in the New York financial community and the U.S. Congress to reverse Senator Russell Long's moves to cut aid, credit, and the quota for sugar for Mexico. Instead, the sulphur companies by 1966 found themselves under intense pressure in the United States as well as in Mexico to mexicanize and set up local fertilizer operations as a condition for remaining in the Mexican market. Similarly, when Eduardo Frei nationalized Anaconda in 1969, Chile's Christian Democrats had so thoroughly prepared their allies in the Washington foreign policy establishment that the company's management was isolated when it looked for support, even from a Republican administration.[79] Anaconda's board of directors had no choice but to agree to a formula for compensation that represented the biggest loss in estimated future earnings since Mossadeq nationalized the oil in Iran.

The Companies React

As a consequence of their growing vulnerability, the largest U.S. utility investors, American and Foreign Power and International Telephone and Telegraph, have divested themselves of utility holdings and diversified into the more secure manufacturing and service industries (not, however, without a few parting shots by ITT against economic nationalists).[80] Some American plantation owners headed in the same direction.[81] United Brands (the former United Fruit) reduced its banana acreage in Guatemala, Costa Rica, and Panama in the course of the 1960s, buying instead from independent farmers in a competitive open market and taking its profits at the distribution stage of the industry. The decision of American

79. Moran, *Multinational Corporations and the Politics of Dependence,* chap. 5.
80. For a list of American and foreign powers' divestments in Latin America, see Wilkins, *The Maturing of Multinational Enterprise,* p. 362.
81. For evidence from tropical agriculture, see Theodore H. Moran, "New Deal or Raw Deal in Raw Materials," *Foreign Policy,* no. 5 (Winter, 1971–72), pp. 119–36; Henry Arthur, James Hovck, and George Beckford, *Tropical Agribusiness: Structures and Adjustments—Bananas* (Harvard University Press, 1968). For successful moves out of estate ownership in sugar and vegetable production, see Ray Vicker, "New Partners: Multinational Firms Help Poorer Nations to Boost Food Output," *Wall Street Journal,* March 18, 1975. The rubber plantations of Goodyear, U.S. Rubber, and Firestone in South Asia and Africa suffered many of the same problems as the tropical agriculture plantations (including nationalization of Goodyear and U.S. Rubber in Indonesia under Sukarno). The parent companies have not, however, moved in the direction of local divestiture. (See Wilkins, *The Maturing of Multinational Enterprise,* p. 371.)

banana marketers against exclusive reliance on sources owned by the parent—in favor of helping to multiply the number of alternative suppliers from whom the parent could buy—placed a severe constraint on the ability of exporting governments to increase their revenues (at the expense of U.S. consumers) through an export tax in 1973–74. This is precisely the policy of dealing with the sources rather than the consequences of oligopoly, that we advocate in chapter five.

The vulnerability of American natural resource companies under continuing direct equity arrangements makes them, therefore, prime candidates for generating political tension between the United States and the host countries in the future. The decline in the perception of a security threat from revolution in the Third and Fourth Worlds leaves such investors as the best organized and best financed domestic constituency trying to influence relations with countries from Botswana or Papua New Guinea to the Dominican Republic. The Gonzalez amendment gives the Congress power to wield a big stick on their behalf, despite the decline in bilateral aid. Although the Hickenlooper and Gonzalez amendments should be repealed, to get rid of international political tension, especially with Congress more actively influencing foreign policy, it is necessary to get rid of the underlying problem: direct ownership of foreign natural resources by American companies that have no viable method of defending themselves once they have sunk hundreds of millions of dollars in a successful operation.

The corporate strategy of building transnational alliances in marketing and finance to offset their increasing vulnerability is an attempt by natural resource companies to protect themselves, analogous to that of manufacturers who produce specialized components in diverse offshore plants.[82] The strategy is to leave host governments no place to sell nationalized output. More than that, it attempts to cut the government off from sources of international finance. The success of this strategy does not depend on the influence of business at any level of the U.S. government. Rather, it relies on the creation of private pressure that could raise the cost of nationalization to host governments irrespective of the policy stance of the U.S. government.

82. For evidence of this strategy in oil, natural gas, copper, and nickel industries, see Theodore H. Moran, "Transnational Strategies of Protection and Defense by Multinational Corporations: Spreading the Risk and Raising the Cost for Nationalization in Natural Resources," *International Organization,* vol. 27 (Spring 1973), pp. 273–87.

To make it effective, the corporations must abandon the conventional notion of foreign investment as a single package that the parent company commits, with the entire burden of risk on its own corporate shoulders. Instead, in the late 1960s, American companies in the copper, petroleum, natural gas, and nickel industries initiated a process of unbundling corporate services, separating the provision of capital from the provision of management skills, the provision of production technology, and the provision of marketing experience. They spread the risk of capital commitment by securing loans (in the subsidiary's name) from customers or by selling collection rights on contracts outstanding to financial intermediaries. As a consequence, fewer of their own assets were exposed to nationalization, and a broad array of creditors stood ready to bring pressure against a nationalistic government. In addition, they wrote long-term contracts with major users for the output of vulnerable subsidiaries, so that a nationalization threat would disrupt the markets of Europe, Japan, and the United States, simultaneously.

Finally, the firms initiated lawsuits in the courts of consuming countries to block the marketing efforts of the agencies that had taken over their properties. Thus, even if these agencies could maintain output at prenationalization levels, the former owners could block sales by suing customers who bought the output. Kennecott used this strategy to impound cargoes of copper sold by the Chilean government in France, Italy, and Germany.[83] Occidental Petroleum, Bunker Hunt, Texaco, and Standard Oil Company of California made a similar effort with regard to oil from disrupted properties in Libya.[84] In 1973, the New England Petroleum Corporation, for example, had to pass on extra costs and the prospect of brownouts to utilities in the Northeast because of the threat of legal action by Texaco and SoCal against delivery of "hot" Libyan crude. Legal disputes about acts of state, the valuation of equity, and the subtraction of excess-profits taxes from awards of compensation, have rendered this strategy effective in hindering the delivery of output to consumers but not in giving security to direct investors.

American natural resource companies, finding American hard-line

83. For details see Kennecott Copper Corporation, *Confiscation of El Teniente*, supplement no. 3 (New York: Kennecott, 1972); and ibid., supplement no. 4 (May 1973).

84. *Multinational Corporations and United States Foreign Policy*, Hearings before the Senate Foreign Relations Committee, 93:1, 93:2 (GPO, 1974), pt. 5.

policies undependable and ineffective and its soft-line, or flexible, policies nothing more than negotiation for the surrender of their holdings took the defense of their assets into their own hands. Their strategies, however, carry the prospect of generating further political tensions and economic cost for producer and consumer states but not much prospect of creating efficient and competitive natural resource markets. And no approach has been developed to enable them to transfer their valuable capabilities to developing countries in a way that gives them adequate protection and that channels their instincts for self-preservation in a direction that does not damage the interests of the countries that rely on the output. But only through such a new approach will there be much chance of improving the impact of foreign direct investment on U.S. relations with the developing world.

Policy Implications

Our analyses in earlier chapters, as well as in this one, conclude that in neither manufacturing nor raw materials could the United States place general restrictions on the operations of American multinationals—including their operations in the developing countries—without substantial losses in U.S. economic welfare, global economic efficiency, and development abroad. But we also see major difficulties in policies that blindly support American-based firms. What is needed is a set of policies toward the foreign investments of American firms that best serve the American interests in its own economic welfare, in world development, and in relations of mutual respect between developed and developing nations.

Domestic Economic Interests

A policy toward manufacturing investors directed as narrowly as possible toward maximizing domestic economic interests would include two components: (a) neutrality toward operations that were established strictly according to considerations of international comparative advantage; and (b) checks on operations that were not so established, by which host countries attracted investment through direct subsidies, trade restrictions, or other market distortions.

Global Economic Interests

How might such a policy be modified to reflect an American interest in encouraging long-range industrial development in the Third and Fourth Worlds? Present U.S. efforts are a poor guide. There is no evidence that indiscriminate tax-policy support (such as deferral, the no grossing up provision of the past, and the western hemisphere trading corporations) induce American investors to contribute more to the development process than they would in the absence of such measures. These policies may even decrease the revenues available to host countries or increase the flow to tax-haven repositories. They reward projects that detract from the efficient allocation of resources as well as those that enhance it. Rather than across-the-board tax and other support, a more efficient approach would be to encourage the establishment of manufacturing activities in the poorest countries, perhaps in specified industries that have the greatest prospects for supporting developmental objectives.

The market distortions caused by host governments when they lure foreign investment could be checked by international rules. In the absence of agreed-on rules, the United States should retaliate bilaterally against such distortions. Similarly, it could countervail against performance requirements that cause demonstrable injury to U.S. economic interests. The exception would be the poorest countries of the Fourth World, which could be exempt from the imposition of such penalties. Drawing up the list of countries where American companies would be eligible for tax incentives and production direction from host governments requires a balancing of concern for the industrial development of the middle range of developing countries (for example, Nigeria and Indonesia) with the resulting loss of job opportunities and other economic benefits in the United States.

Foreign Policy Interests

Minimizing the political tensions between the United States and the host countries that result from the activities of American manufacturers does not require further modifications in the policy outlined above. It would, of course, be utopian to suggest that the presence of American companies in the most technologically advanced, most rapidly growing, industrial sectors of developing countries could completely avoid suspicion and resentment. Indeed, our model of bargaining power predicts recurrent cycles of tension and instability as new investments are made or new products are introduced and as other investments or products mature. But the desire of host countries for the benefits of the technology and marketing of foreign manufacturing companies, and the ability of the companies to retain bargaining strength through their control over that technology and marketing, tend to keep their interaction manageable at the local level. We have seen that investment disputes involving manufacturers seldom escalate to the point of producing confrontations between the United States and the host country. Expropriations have been relatively few and are likely to become still fewer because of the growing skill of host countries to harness the firms to their own objectives—to expropriate the profit rather than the property. And American government pressure on behalf of American companies has been, if anything, counterproductive. Simple repeal of the Hickenlooper and Gonzalez amendments would be responsive to the demands of the developing countries that the United States end its "economic aggression." And it would be consistent with our principle that the foreign operations of American companies not be given favored treatment by the U.S. government.

In natural resources, these steps are not enough to protect American economic and political interests. There is no way to avoid the cost to the U.S. economy or to the international economy of the shift in power from foreign companies to host governments without separating American skills and technology from direct equity ownership to spur producer competition.[85] In terms of political relations, the end of direct foreign ownership in natural resources, by removing American companies from the sensitive position of exercising property rights over the national patrimony

---

85. Higher prices for primary products are no more desirable when set by developing countries. Ninety percent of Third World natural-resource exports are from countries that account for less than one-fourth of the Third World's population. Sixty-one of 103 developing countries have no more than a minuscule mineral sector. With regard to commodities in general, 60 percent of the total moving in world trade (excluding oil) originate in developed, not developing, countries. Higher commodity prices result in an income shift from the periphery to the center, and, within the periphery, from poorer countries to richer countries. Moreover, within all countries, commodity inflation hits the poor, the old, the unskilled, and the unorganized disproportionately, resulting in a distribution of income that favors the haves over the have-nots. See Jack Barkenbus and Dennis Pirages, "The Future of Mineral Interdependence: Myth and Reality" (paper prepared for delivery at the 1975 annual meeting of the American Political Science Association; processed).

in foreign countries, would resolve for the U.S. government the dilemma of defending or abandoning them as they became increasingly vulnerable. It would eliminate the main source of investment disputes in Latin America and prevent the problem from developing elsewhere. Hence, the economic and foreign policy interests of the United States require discouragement of equity investment in the extractive industries, espeically in the developing countries. Differences between the United States and those countries would clearly remain but would be much more manageable.

International Accords

The prospects for formulating codes of conduct or principles of international regulation acceptable to home countries, host countries, and multinational corporations—and thus for moving away from the tension, instability, and suspicion associated with foreign investment in the Third and Fourth Worlds—are extraordinarily limited at this time.[86] The enthusiasm in some quarters for codes of conduct masks fundamentally different conceptions of who is going to be controlled, who is going to do the controlling, and what the purpose of the controls will be. If disputes between investors and developing countries, or between governments of home and host countries, arose from some kind of "bad behavior" on the part of American multinationals, then proposals for a code of "good conduct" and international "rules of the game" might hold some promise. The corporate proposition, "tell us what the rules are, and we'll follow them," taken at face value, indicates a willingness to adapt to local requirements of acceptable behavior in return for stability in local operations. But most investment disputes come not from "bad behavior" but from both sides trying to take advantage of, but not be trapped by, dramatically changing asymmetries of bargaining power. Few responsible

86. See Robert O. Keohane and Van D. Ooms, "The Multinational Firm and International Regulation," in C. Fred Bergsten and Lawrence B. Krause, eds., *World Politics and International Economics* (Brookings Institution, 1975); Don Wallace, Jr., ed., *International Control of Investment: The Dusseldorf Conference on Multinational Corporations* (Praeger, 1974); Jack Behrman, "Control of the Multinational Enterprise: Why? What? Who? and How?" (paper prepared for delivery at 1973 conference on multinational business and government relations, Graduate School of Management, UCLA; processed).

corporate officials would commit large amounts of their companies' resources, at great risk and under great uncertainty, without taking advantage of whatever bargaining strength they have. Few responsible political leaders in the developing countries would give up the chance to eventually redress that asymmetrical relation, after the uncertainty is dissipated and the risk reduced. If they did, their political opposition would not. Unless one postulates a world of unopposed puppet governments in the developing nations, which do not try to harness foreign companies to national goals, foreign-investor–host-country disputes will be a regular and largely inevitable accompaniment of the investment process.

Multinational corporate executives who speak approvingly of a GATT for investment really want to protect themselves from the ravages of the obsolescing bargain. For them, international regulation means restraints on host governments' exercise of sovereign power after the investments are successfully producing. Leaders of the developing countries who speak approvingly of rules of conduct really want to avoid paying the price for scarce business skills offered at high risk at the beginning of an operation. For them, international regulation means restraints on foreign investors' exercise of corporate strength at the time of entry. Popular governments in the Third and Fourth Worlds could not credibly bind themselves in the way investors desire, even if they wanted to. And multinational corporations would never make the initial investments under uncertainty if they were constrained in the way host countries desire. For these reasons, we suggest that investor-host relations be allowed to run their normal, cyclical course at the local level in manufacturing with no threat of home-country intervention, and be completely restructured as outlined above in natural resources.

As this dialectical process moves along, however, it lays the basis, in true Hegelian fashion, for far-reaching international agreements among home-country authorities, host-country authorities, and multinational corporate authorities. As developing countries become more skillful in getting multinationals to tilt the distribution of benefits in their favor, home countries develop a parallel interest in safeguarding their own interests. Thus, as traditional problems recede in importance, new problems take their place. Both sides must then see to it that the activities of all three actors become transparent, a move multinationals may resist as long as they benefit from secrecy but which they will share as demands from all directions begin to constitute multiple "dips" into corporate treasuries. Greater harmonization of investment policies, which would follow greater disclosure, would avoid destructive investment wars over distribution of the benefits from multinational operations. We outline proposals for such harmonization in chapter thirteen.

CHAPTER ELEVEN

The Industrialized Countries

WHAT IS THE RELATION between American policies toward foreign investment by American companies and broader U.S. national interests in Europe, Japan, and the Soviet Union? Should such policies be shaped, for strategic reasons, according to criteria different from a simple calculation of what would maximize U.S. economic welfare? Does the United States have a political interest in supporting the spread of American multinationals into Europe and Japan, now that their economic recovery is long since past, the legacy of American hegemony is accepted (at most) with ambivalence, and the world is moving from bipolar hostility to a more diffuse and pluralistic balance of power? Does the United States have a political interest in promoting the spread of American multinationals into the Soviet Union or in retarding it?

The political value of American foreign investment in Europe and Japan has undergone a profound metamorphosis in the past thirty years. During the cold war, American policy toward U.S. investors was part of the high politics of national security that thrust American interests outward, multiplying commitments and responsibilities abroad. American companies were supposed to speed the development of Europe and Japan, spread the capitalist way of life, and pull the recipient countries closer to the United States. Within this setting, tax benefits, government insurance, and political support for the overseas expansion of American businesses grew—haphazardly but steadily—in the postwar period.

But as the cold war declined in intensity, the fear in industrial countries of foreign control and technological dependence grew, rendering the political rationale for American direct foreign investment problematic. The

Japanese, anyway, rejected it from the start, refusing to let American military guarantees be translated into direct economic penetration into Japan. European reaction to le défi americain came later and has been more ambiguous. Is it consistent, now, with its proclaimed intent to pull back from the globalism of the cold war period, for the United States to promote the penetration of Europe and Japan by American multinationals? Does not the United States, rather, have a political interest not only in avoiding the subsidization of foreign direct investment into Europe and Japan but even in restraining it, thereby removing decisionmaking on many sovereign issues from the boardrooms of U.S. corporations? Does not the United States also have an interest in pushing Europe and Japan toward reliance on their own corporations (even if at some cost in efficiency) in the interest of their prosperity and stability?

In the final section of this book we make specific proposals that are, in some respects, fundamentally different from the former blanket encouragement of the proliferation of American subsidiaries abroad. But the political basis of these proposals does not correspond to the idea of devolution in the international system, which would bring about a much smaller world role for the United States. Our objective, to the contrary, is to provide a new basis for a constructive—and cooperative—role of leadership for the United States.

The mercantile idea, which led Europe and Japan to believe that their own corporations would create an economic and technological foundation for autonomous and responsible roles in international affairs, made sense when multinational companies functioned as extensions of the home country. The shift in the balance of pressure on multinationals (away from home countries) now casts doubt on that premise, however, and has profound implications for American-European and American-Japanese relations and for the transition from an international order held together by American hegemony to a pluralistic system characterized by equivalence and reciprocity. We are skeptical about the economic underpinning for the devolution of U.S. power and responsibility, even in a post-cold-war world, and, therefore, on political as well as economic grounds, propose American investment policies, which will lead the United States not into a distant, autonomous pattern of interaction with Europe and Japan but will be the basis for a moderate and constructive U.S. engagement in the affairs of Europe and Asia.

The contribution of American multinationals to American-Soviet relations has been regarded with either high hope or great cynicism. On the one hand, American investment could either create links through which the U.S. government could manipulate Soviet behavior when vital political interests came into conflict or create an interdependency, which would reinforce the prospect for détente. On the other hand, it could strengthen Soviet totalitarian rule at home and produce a corporate lobby in the United States that, for the sake of corporate gain, would urge the sacrifice of political interests. American investment in the Soviet Union brings to the fore two issues that appear constantly in our analysis: the proclivity of American companies to become hostage to the wishes of the host rather than the home country; and the need for the U.S. government to carefully separate the national interests of the country from the particular interests of the companies. Unless the U.S. government establishes a mechanism to coordinate American multinationals' dealings with the Soviet Union, it may lose many of the economic as well as political benefits of détente.

From the first hints of relaxation in the cold war and the first signs of sustained European economic recovery, two visions of U.S.-European relations have competed for the allegiance of policymakers on both sides of the Atlantic: the original Atlantic idea, in which European unification would go hand in hand with closer transatlantic community; and a rival European idea—associated with Charles de Gaulle but extending beyond both de Gaulle and France—in which European cohesion would have priority over the unity of the Atlantic community as a whole, with the aim of limiting American influence and producing greater European autonomy.[1] The debate about the desirability of American investment, and the proper European response to it, plays an important role in each of these perspectives.

The Atlantic Idea

The Atlantic idea was, in part, a child of the cold war. It was born of the desire to prevent the Soviet Union from filling the vacuum left by the defeat of Germany and the weakness of the other European powers. To support the effort at containment, private capital flows (along with the public funds supplied in the Marshall Plan) could strengthen the countries of Europe against the possibility of aggression from without or subversion from within. But the Atlantic idea embodied a broader strategic

1. Harold van B. Cleveland, *The Atlantic Idea and Its European Rivals* (McGraw-Hill, 1966).

vision as well.[2] It sprang from the recognition that the United States could not hope to avoid the consequences (economic as well as military) of the kind of deterioration of relations among the major powers in Europe that had led to the First and Second World Wars.[3] This required an American commitment to turn away from isolationism and to play an active role in (and, at least initially, bear a disproportionate share of the costs of) maintaining a system in which Europe would be secure and stable. Within this context, American investment had the effect (not clearly foreseen at the beginning) of creating a web of private ties and interests, which helped prevent a turn back to isolationism on the part of the United States. From the late 1950s through the 1960s, it produced an influential domestic constituency, which provided some guarantee of American involvement in, and commitment to, European security.

The notion that American investment could help integrate the Atlantic community under American leadership fit easily into the plan for temporary support for European revival and was not broadly challenged on economic grounds as long as the flow of private U.S. investment was small.[4] With the signing of the Treaty of Rome in 1957,[5] the devaluation

2. The revisionist perspective on the role of American economic interests in the cold war (see chap. 9) does not take into account the strategic need for American involvement in European affairs, thus undermining its usefulness as a guide for future U.S. policy.

3. The idea that the United States should encourage the export of equity capital as well as credits to stimulate trade was novel. See Mira Wilkins, *The Maturing of Multinational Enterprise: American Business Abroad from 1914 to 1970* (Harvard University Press, 1974). As Wilkins points out, the Truman administration's conviction that "private enterprise ought to export capital, technology, skills, and management" (p. 289), to Europe was in marked contrast to the attitude of the U.S. government at the end of the First World War, which then and throughout the 1920s was against overseas investment by American companies in European manufacturing, lest it create competition and thereby hurt U.S. exports. By the late 1940s, foreign investment was seen as trade-creating rather than trade-replacing, and private capital flows found favor because they meshed with U.S. political objectives.

4. From 1946 through 1957, the value of direct American investment grew about 6 percent a year, from $2 billion to $4.15 billion, with the following concessions at the end of the period: Great Britain, $1.97 billion; France, $0.46 billion; Germany, $0.58 billion; Italy, $0.25 billion. *Survey of Current Business,* vol. 29 (November 1949), p. 20; and ibid., vol. 40 (September 1960), p. 20.

5. *Treaty Establishing the European Economic Community and Connected Documents* (English translation: Publishing Services of the European Communities, 1962). The treaty was signed in Rome, March 25, 1957, by the representatives of Belgium, France, Germany, Italy, Luxembourg, and the Netherlands. The six participating states had all ratified the treaty by January 1, 1958.

of the French franc in 1957, and the restoration of external convertibility for the Six plus Great Britain in 1958, direct investment by American companies took a quantum leap forward.[6] The promise of European status for American subsidiaries located anywhere in the EEC provided a method for supplying rapidly expanding markets protected by the common external tariff. From 1958 to 1967, intra-Community trade doubled as a share of its total trade, growing at an average annual rate of 28.4 percent and expanding three times as fast as imports from outside countries. The book value of American investment in Europe jumped from $4.15 billion at the end of 1957 to $24.52 billion in 1970, or about 600 percent.[7] By the mid-1960s, the European invasion by American multinationals gave rise in Europe to three concerns: the threat of technological dependence, the fear of industrial dominance, and the prospect of losing control over national economic planning.[8]

European Dependence on American Technology

Viewed in strictly economic terms, the objection to American investment represented, at best, a selective view of reality. The United States in the 1960s spent four times as much on research and development as the countries of Western Europe—three to four times as much per capita and double the percentage of gross national product.[9] American multinationals received more R&D grants and subsidies from the U.S. government than

6. The growth rate for the preceding five years was 14.2 percent. In the 1958–67 period, EEC imports from third countries increased 10 percent a year, versus 9.4 percent a year in the earlier period. Dennis Swann, *The Economics of the Common Market*, 3rd ed. (Penguin, 1975), p. 73.

7. *Survey of Current Business*, vol. 52 (November 1972), pp. 24, 30.

8. Jack N. Behrman, *National Interests and the Multinational Enterprise: Tensions Among the North Atlantic Countries* (Prentice-Hall, 1970). See also Francis Williams, *The American Invasion* (London: Anthony Blond, 1962); Edward A. McCreary, *The Americanization of Europe* (Doubleday, 1964); James McMillan and Bernard Harris, *The American Take-Over of Britain* (London: Frewin, 1968); Christopher Layton, *Trans-Atlantic Investments* (Boulogne-sur-Seine: The Atlantic Institute, 1966), and *European Advanced Technology: A Programme for Integration* (London: Allen and Unwin, 1969); Christopher Tugendhat, *The Multinationals* (Random House, 1972).

9. The United States spent 3.1 percent of its gross national product on research and development ($94 per capita); Britain, 2.2 percent ($34 per capita); France, 1.5 percent ($24 per capita); and Germany, 1.3 percent ($20 per capita). C. Freeman and A. Young, *The Research and Development Effort in Western Europe, North America and the Soviet Union* (Paris: OECD, 1965), p. 71.

European firms received from theirs, and U.S. firms spent more in the aggregate than their European counterparts. And when they invested in Europe, they tended to concentrate their activities in R&D-intensive industries. This brought to European consumers the benefits of technology without the burden of paying for government-sponsored research. But at the same time it stimulated the brain drain: scientifically and technically trained Europeans going to work for American companies. The combination of the smaller R&D effort in Europe (both public and private) and the brain drain raised the specter of an expanding technology gap between European companies and their American competitors.[10]

The technology issue was compounded by the prospect of the most successful sectors of the European economies—the so-called commanding heights—falling under foreign ownership. The most sensitive cases were General Electric's first attempts to buy into France's Machines Bull; Chrysler's try for Great Britain's Rootes Motors in 1964; and the purchase of Deutsch Erdöl AG and Aral AG (Germany) by Texaco, Inc. and Socony-Mobil Oil Company in 1966. Between 1958 and 1967, about 43 percent of new entries into Europe by American companies were acquisitions.[11] In some cases the European firms were near bankruptcy when the Americans bought them out. In all cases, the acquisitions freed European resources for uses where they could be employed more efficiently (including the purchase of stock in the American companies). But these benefits had to be weighed against the long-term economic and political effects of having American corporations preempt the development of in-

10. Jean-Jacques Servan-Schreiber, *The American Challenge* (Avon, 1969); Raymond Vernon, "International Investment and International Trade in the Product Cycle," *Quarterly Journal of Economics*, vol. 80 (May 1966). A large number of innovations in the industries where American companies were strong (even in electronics, which Servan-Schreiber called "the base upon which the next stage of industrial development depends," p. 42) moved rapidly through the product cycle into standardized production that could be imitated locally without massive research and development. But this was small consolation if it meant that Europe would be constantly scrambling to catch up to the Americans. Without an indigenous R&D capacity and an industrial structure to convert discoveries into commercial products, the threat remained that the countries of Europe might constantly lag behind American technology. For a thoughtful analysis of the question of whether major powers should specialize in technology, see Robert Gilpin, *France in the Age of the Scientific State* (Princeton University Press, 1968).

11. James W. Vaupel and Joan P. Curhan, *The Making of Multinational Enterprise* (Harvard University Graduate School of Business Administration, 1969), p. 254.

dependent national companies across important sectors of the local economy.

Moreover, even if the mode of entry of American investors could have been controlled, the possibility of American predominance remained. The rate of growth of American investment was higher than the corresponding increase in fixed assets in the private sectors of most European countries. In Great Britain it was double that of private domestic fixed assets for the entire decade of the 1960s.[12] Between 1957 and 1963, all American manufacturing corporations increased their sales nearly four times faster than all British manufacturing firms.[13] American multinationals were clearly focusing their activities in the most rapidly growing local industries, a trend that could lead, as Harold Wilson phrased it, to American "domination or, in the last resort, subjugation."[14]

American foreign investment throughout the 1960s was heavily concentrated in Great Britain, but its growth rate (from lower starting points) was more dramatic on the continent: 19 percent a year in Germany and 15 percent a year in France, in comparison to 12 percent a year in Great Britain.[15] To Europeans, the projection that the trend would continue was reinforced by deficits in the American balance of payments and an increasingly overvalued dollar. The capital controls introduced in the mid-1960s by the United States to help its balance of payments changed the sources of financing for the American multinationals but not the rate of investment. American companies began to use European capital to buy up European firms. The effect of the overvalued dollar in motivating American firms to produce abroad rather than to export—and in allowing them to do it by buying European assets cheaply—is not empirically clear. But the frustration of many Europeans at not being able to stop America's "deficits without tears" was keen. The European Community Industries Union (UNICE) appraised foreign investment in the Common Market in 1967 and warned that entire sectors of the economies of Europe might become dependent on decisions made by Americans.[16] Even Germany

12. Economist Intelligence Unit, *The Growth and Spread of Multinational Companies* (London: Economist Intelligence Unit, 1971), p. 58.

13. John Dunning and M. Preston, *Washington Post,* January 21, 1968.

14. Speech delivered to English-Speaking Union, November 30, 1966; processed. Text from *EFTA Reporter* (January 9, 1967), p. 14.

15. Calculations based on *Survey of Current Business,* vol. 40 (September 1960), p. 20; and ibid., vol. 52 (November 1972), p. 30.

16. Cited in Behrman, *National Interests and the Multinational Enterprise,* p. 37.

(normally averse to governmental economic controls) suggested an upper limit on American penetration.

American Control of European Economies

Besides creating problems of technological dependence and foreign ownership in the industrial sector, American multinational corporations in Europe exacerbated the loss of control that accompanied the opening of borders within the Common Market in the 1960s. The problems American investors caused for national planners varied with the importance of economic planning in each country, but certain problems affected all of them, even those, like Germany and Great Britain, that relied on market forces for domestic adjustments. Through their access to foreign borrowing and manipulation of interaffiliate transactions (internal loans, leads and lags in international payment, and transfer pricing), multinationals could avoid the control of credit by national authorities and minimize national tax liabilities.[17] These methods were available to all multinationals, of course, not just to American firms, but there were some indications (and a broad presumption) that, when conditions were unfavorable, the American companies were less willing than national companies to help local authorities control prices or maintain employment.

The most celebrated examples of foreign ownership, technological dependence, and loss of control over macroeconomic policy were in France. In 1962 the Frigidaire Sales Corporation plant at Gennevilliers abruptly closed. In the same year, several hundred workers at a Remington Rand Corporation plant near Lyon were laid off at the insistence of a cable from the U.S. headquarters. In 1966 IBM-France was refused U.S. State Department permission to sell computers to the French government (the United States wished to retard France's nuclear program and pressure it into signing the test ban treaty). American investors disregarded the Comissariat du Plan guideline on channelling credit, part of the country's indicative planning. But the challenge represented by American multinationals was felt in all the major capitals of Europe and caused concern among both "good Europeans" as well as nationalistic citizens in Ger-

---

17. Donald Macamso and Robert G. Hawkins, "The Avoidance of Restrictive Monetary Policies in Host Countries by Multinational Firms," Discussion Paper in international investment and business studies, no. 25 (University of Reading, February 1976; processed).

many, England, and Italy, sympathetic to the philosophies of de Gaulle. The complaints presented only one side of the impact of American multinationals on European development; U.S. investors did broaden the European tax base, strengthen European balance-of-payments positions, create European employment, raise European wages, and provide Europe with benefits of technology. But they also brought into focus a fundamental strategic question that had to be dealt with on its own terms: Might the economic policies adopted to promote the political goals of European independence and self-confidence have, in the long run, the opposite effect, consigning Europe to the position of a permanent satellite of the United States? This concern was rendered particularly acute and particularly galling when some of the most articulate internationalist American observers proclaimed its inevitability.[18]

The European Idea

The United States approached the strategic issues raised by American investment in Europe the same way it approached the strategic issues raised by the nuclear guarantee: by reducing the political question (Who controls?) to a technical question (What is the most efficient way of allocating resources?). On the basis of casual inspection, American analysts suggested that, as a result of American investments, Europeans were enjoying better products, more competition, higher wages, and more rapid economic change than they would have without them. Any other choice could be justified only in terms of psychic income, which, in this debate has a pejorative connotation.

If the idea of an Atlantic community held the same appeal in the mid-1960s that it held a decade and a half earlier, Europeans might have been satisfied with a cost-benefit analysis of American investment that relegated noneconomic considerations to the realm of psychological gratification. Within the confines of the Atlantic idea, American ownership of European subsidiaries was, after all, a legitimate manifestation of transatlantic integration, and technological dependence was perfectly consistent with international specialization. And they might have been satisfied, then, with the American solution: changing the characterization of the

18. See, for example, Zbigniew Brzezinski, *Between Two Ages: America's Role in the Technetronic Era* (Viking, 1970).

Atlantic idea from community to partnership without making any substantive change in those policies (economic and military) that ensured American predominance.

But the European desire to turn their own recovery into a partnership with the United States required more than a change in rhetoric. It signified that many Europeans were no longer satisfied with the pretense of equality or a relation in which American leadership was accepted without question. The questions about national power, national control, and national autonomy, provoked by the penetration of American businesses, raised political issues that required political responses. In economic affairs, as in military policy, the United States could not find a technical solution that made the fundamental political problem disappear. That political question was: Within the Atlantic relationship, who would lead and who would follow?

Gaullism

The European idea followed logically from two premises: first, that U.S. and European national interests would diverge over time; second, that the countries of Europe should have alternatives to American preferences when those divergences became significant. De Gaulle's mistrust of an international arrangement that left defense of its national interest to the discretion of other states began with the Suez crisis of 1956 (if not with the Yalta agreements more than a decade earlier). In 1956 President Eisenhower and his secretary of state, John Foster Dulles, had refused to support the British-French-Israeli invasion of Egypt and threatened to order American oil companies to hold back Europe's oil supplies unless the British and French withdrew.[19] This scenario was one de Gaulle (and others) feared would be repeated in other peripheral areas—North Africa, Southeast Asia, the Middle East—where there were fundamental differences among the interests of the major powers.

Furthermore, even in areas where common security interests were acknowledged, the reliability of American commitments, in the Gaullist view, became more uncertain during the 1960s. As American cities became vulnerable to Soviet nuclear weapons, the idea that the United States

19. Townsend Hoopes, *The Devil and John Foster Dulles* (Atlantic Monthly Press, 1973), p. 387.

would risk war to protect Europe diminished in credibility. French strategists argued that their fate should not depend (as it did under the Atlantic alliance) on America's willingness to invite self-destruction.[20] The growth of American assets in Europe, from the Gaullist perspective, would neither reduce European military vulnerability nor enhance the ability of the European states to influence their own destiny. The rising penetration of American businesses might create a domestic constituency in the United States committed to European affairs, as the Atlanticists hoped, but such a commitment was not readily transferable into a nuclear guarantee.[21]

Gaullist military doctrine, in fact, received relatively little support in Europe. The British drew the opposite conclusion from the Suez experience: that they would never again launch a major military action in the face of American opposition.[22] Their financial difficulties kept them to this maxim throughout the 1960s, even after the United States canceled the Skybolt project and dropped the idea of multilateral nuclear force. Though the Gaullist military theory appealed to some German strategists (like Franz Josef Strauss), it left Germany, ultimately, with the choice between an Atlantic alliance headed by the United States or a European alliance headed by France.[23] When the choice had to be made, German leaders chose Atlanticism, despite painful berating from the French for their dependence on the Americans.

But the fear of permanent subordination to the United States remained. From the European point of view, the lack of military, economic, and technological capabilities posed a triple threat: the possible sacrifice of European interests in a major cold war confrontation if détente failed; U.S.-Soviet condominium over issues that vitally concerned them if dé-

20. André Beaufre, "Nuclear Deterrence and World Strategy," in Karl H. Cerny and Henry W. Briefs, eds., *NATO in Quest of Cohesion* (Praeger, 1965), p. 221; Pierre M. Gallois, "U.S. Strategy and the Defense of Europe," *Orbis,* vol. 7 (Summer 1963), pp. 226–49.

21. Such an appraisal may have been correct on the narrow issue of whether American investment made the nuclear guarantee any more credible. But American investment did make a stable, cooperative international system more important to the United States than its short-term nationalistic objectives, and in this way ensured the dependability of American policy, a necessary condition for de Gaulle's independence.

22. Hoopes, *The Devil and John Foster Dulles,* p. 392.

23. Franz Josef Strauss, *Challenge and Response: A Programme for Europe* (Weidenfeld and Nicolson, 1969).

tente succeeded; and no option of independent maneuver between the superpowers in pursuit of their own diplomatic and economic interests.

Economic Independence

During the sixties, a European economic base, not dependent on American companies but which would use the vast scientific and technical skills in individual countries, grew more appealing. And despite their differences in philosophy and style, France, Great Britain, and Germany, responded to the idea in similar ways.[24] One, they encouraged mergers and consolidations among local companies in high-technology industries, mature-technology industries, and natural resources to become large national companies—national champions that could compete with American multinationals, both locally and abroad. Two, they sponsored research and development to broaden the indigenous technological base. And three, when buying goods and services, their public agencies gave preference to national companies. In addition, political spokesmen in all three countries and in the bureaucracy of the EEC proposed measures from time to time to limit and control the activities of American multinationals in Europe. But these latter initiatives, as we shall see, bore little fruit.

FRANCE. France, of course, took the lead in the formation of national champions.[25] In 1964, de Gaulle announced a long-term policy to reduce foreign companies' share in importing, refining, and distributing oil and gas. And, supported by government subsidies (France's fifth economic plan, 1966–70), three French groups—Enterprise de Recherches et d'Activités Pétrolières (ERAP), Compagnie Française des Pétroles (CFP), and ANTAR—gained control of more than half the domestic market by the early 1970s. Special efforts were made to strengthen capabilities in electronics, aircraft, and nuclear engineering. The plan Calcul, for computers, became the model for using public resources to gain inde-

24. See Raymond Vernon, ed., *Big Business and the State: Changing Relations in Western Europe* (Harvard University Press, 1974); Layton, *Trans-Atlantic Investments;* Behrman, *National Interests and the Multinational Enterprise;* Geoffrey Denton, Murray Forsyth, and Malcolm MacLennan, *Economic Planning and Policies in Britain, France, and Germany* (Praeger, 1968); Andrew Shonfield, *Modern Capitalism: The Changing Balance of Public and Private Power* (London: Oxford University Press, 1965).

25. See Charles-Albert Michalet, "France," in Vernon, ed., *Big Business and the State,* pp. 105–26; John H. McArthur and Bruce R. Scott, *Industrial Planning in France* (Harvard University, Graduate School of Business Administration, 1969).

pendence from American technology. Compagnie Internationale pour l'Informatique (CII), the chosen national champion, was set up in 1966, and to strengthen it, the government promised it would supply most of the state's data-processing equipment.[26] In chemicals, the encouragement of mergers among private firms (Pechiney and Saint Gobain in 1961, Ugine and Kuhlmann in 1966, and Saint Gobain and Pont à Mousson in 1969) produced national champions without state support. In the automobile industry, France had both government-owned (Renault) and privately owned (Citroën) champions. To encourage innovation, the state began in 1965 to subsidize half the cost of new industrial processes. The French also scrutinized the method of entry of American firms, squashing acquisitions by Westinghouse Electric Corporation, International Telephone and Telegraph Corporation, H. J. Heinz, and Helena Rubinstein, Incorporated, to name a few.

GREAT BRITAIN.[27] Great Britain's efforts to stimulate a new generation of national champions to compete effectively against American multinationals (as British Petroleum Company, Limited, Unilever, Limited, and others already did) antedate its entry into the Common Market by at least a decade. In 1961, in an abrupt break with the Tory tradition of considering national planning anathema, Harold Macmillan set up the National Economic Development Office to produce proposals for medium-range industrial rejuvenation, similar to the policy studies undertaken in the Commissariat du Plan of France. The Labor party extended the effort at industrial planning with the creation of the Ministry of Technology (1964) and the Industrial Reorganization Corporation (1966) to foster domestic research and development. These institutions encouraged corporate restructuring through the merger of local companies: British Motor Corporation, Limited with Leyland Motors, Limited; English Electric with General Electric Company, Limited (of Great Britain). Among other projects, they sponsored the consolidation of a group of small companies into International Computers, Limited (ICL), to compete with IBM. They supported research and aided mergers in the aircraft industry. They supplied aid for the construction of three British aluminum smelters.

26. The cost was larger than would have been required three years earlier to rescue Machines Bull from General Electric. See Michalet, "France," pp. 111–12; and Nicholas Jéquier, "Computers," in Vernon, ed., Big Business and the State, pp. 214–16.

27. See Trevor Smith, "The United Kingdom," in Vernon, ed., Big Business and the State, pp. 87–104; Layton, Trans-Atlantic Investments.

And they subsidized the conversion in the machine tool industry to numerically controlled operations. The British government, like the French, favored national champions with purchasing policy, allowing public authorities to purchase ICL computers, for example, even though they cost as much as 25 percent more than comparable American equipment.

GERMANY.[28] The Germans, traditionally even more reluctant than the British to engage in national planning, became concerned about competing internationally because of the inflation of the early 1960s, the slowing of their economic miracle, and the fear of technological inferiority in comparison to American industry. Within the Christian Democratic party, Walter Hallstein (president of the EEC commission) led the fight in favor of the French planning model, while Ludwig Erhard fought for a more laissez-faire policy. After 1966, when the CDU-SPD grand coalition, headed by Kurt Kiesinger, replaced the Erhard government, and Karl Schiller became finance minister, public programs were initiated to underwrite German research and development. Federal authorities (a) awarded preferential purchase contracts to national champions in the heavy electrical, telecommunications, and computer industries (Siemens Aktiengesellschaft, Allgemeine Elektricitaets Gesellschaft, Telefunken, SEL, and Nixdorf) to gain a measure of independence from American companies; (b) gave a tax subsidy (16 percent in 1969) for investments using major industrial innovations; (c) directly sponsored research in aerospace, electronics, and nuclear energy; (d) and gave a six-year subsidy to a joint venture of seven German oil companies to try to supply 25 percent of the country's crude oil demand. Private sector mergers were officially encouraged, and between 1967 and 1973 the federal government policy was "to remove obstacles which stand in the way of concentration of enterprises . . . blocked by cartel law, so that the development of firms of optimum size will not be hindered."[29]

THE COMMUNITY. When European governments tried to act together, competition for the benefits of American investment thwarted their efforts

---

28. This section is drawn from Georg H. Küster, "Germany," pp. 64–86; and Jéquier, "Computers," p. 218, in Vernon, ed., *Big Business and the State.*

29. Federal Cartel Office, report of 1967, quoted in Küster, "Germany," p. 79. From 1966 to 1970, the cartel office recorded 646 mergers in German industry, already the most concentrated in Europe. This was more than one-and-a-half times the number (404) in the entire decade 1958–68. Most significant was the horizontal concentration among companies whose sales exceeded a billion deutsche marks, with 116 cases recorded between 1966 and 1970.

to draw up a policy that would be ratified by EEC members.[30] For example, when General Motors Corporation encountered stiff French requirements for an assembly plant in Strasbourg, it negotiated a more favorable agreement with the Belgian government for a plant at Antwerp and exported the vehicles to France, duty free.[31] Thus to create employment, especially in depressed areas, European governments underbid each other for foreign investments, heightening the feeling that American multinationals constituted a threat to European sovereignty.[32]

Despite the large size of its combined market, the EEC has in fact been less effective than Japan, Canada, Brazil, or some large Third World countries, in controlling American investors.[33] Indeed, it is curious that Europe opted to develop national or pan-European champions rather than simply to harness American multinationals. The answer probably lies in the timing of the American "invasion," combined with the security relation between the two areas. Europe was the major target of foreign direct investment in the postwar boom, which occurred at a time when host countries, even in Europe, were not powerful enough to cope effectively. In addition, Europe was wholly dependent on America for its security in a world of cold war and could not risk not meeting this most critical national need for possible political (or even economic) benefits. And because of its geographical position, Europe is, of course, more ex-

30. The contradiction between the desire for a strong centralized industrial policy for Europe and the unwillingness to cede sovereignty to obtain it was particularly pronounced in the French position. See Alfred Grosser, "Europe: Community of Malaise," *Foreign Policy*, no. 15 (Summer 1974), pp. 171–72.

31. The Belgian government underwrote a $50 million loan to General Motors to cover half the costs of the new Antwerp plant, thus supporting the contention that the European governments were willing to undercut each other to get American investment. Layton, *Trans-Atlantic Investments*, pp. 62–63.

32. A more recent example of a member country successfully offering extraordinary incentives to attract American investors is Ireland. For example, aided by a fifteen-year exemption from Irish taxes and direct grants from the Irish government, foreign drug firms invested $200 million between 1973 and 1975. Exports of pharmaceuticals and "fine chemicals" (pesticides, steroids) grew 300 percent, to $140 million annually, in the period 1971–75 (*Wall Street Journal*, March 31, 1975). For a complete listing of the Irish incentives and an analysis of their effects in the early 1970s, see Frank Long, "Foreign Direct Investment in an Underdeveloped European Economy—The Republic of Ireland," *World Development*, vol. 4 (January 1976), pp. 59–84.

33. A useful list of the policies of European countries is tabulated in J. J. Boddewyn, "Western European Policies Toward U.S. Investors," nos. 93–95 (New York University: *The Bulletin*, March 1974), pp. 34–35.

American Multinationals and American Interests

posed to security threats than are Canada, Japan, or most developing countries. Thus the paradox that galls Europeans: far "weaker" countries than they have coped far better with American multinationals, because these countries are less exposed to security threats and because they faced the challenge of the multinationals later, when many more options existed and the security dilemma was less acute.

AMERICAN RESPONSE. Thus by nationalistic effort in individual countries, even good Europeans in Britain, France, and Germany hoped to use their wealth and talent to make a cohesive and self-reliant community, with options in world affairs other than economic and political subservience to the United States. This process is considered by many strategists as working to American political advantage, as well. "Until Europe knows the reality of roughly equivalent power," George W. Ball argued in 1968, "Europeans will never risk the full acceptance of a partnership relation. They are quite aware that a junior partner has little to say about the affairs of a firm, and unless they feel equal in fact they will be likely to regard partnership as a Yankee device designed to induce them to serve as bush-beaters and gun-bearers in support of United States policies—including policies of which they are skeptical and in the making of which they have had little voice."[34]

Is there a political rationale, therefore, for the United States to abandon its enthusiasm for supporting the penetration of Europe by American investors? Should the United States reconstruct its policies toward American multinationals to reflect closer allegiance to the European goals of autonomy and self-reliance?

The Future of Atlantic Relations

The debate about how the United States might reorder its relations with Europe, and how it might structure its policy toward American investment to contribute to that reordering, should be informed by a prediction of where European efforts to create alternatives to dependence on American corporations are likely to lead: To greater European integration? To less integration? To a stronger economic sovereignty?

The literature on the political dimensions of the transatlantic relationship is notably obscure on these questions. Few analysts suggest that

34. *The Discipline of Power* (Little, Brown, 1968), p. 61.

Europe wants to do completely without American expertise in, for example, computers. Fewer still imagine that Europe could avoid losses in economic efficiency as it moves toward independence of American corporations. But many assume that, in the process of becoming economically and technologically autonomous, Europe will move along the functionalist path of Jean Monnet and Robert Schuman toward an integrated and self-confident political community. Economic costs for Europeans would be traded for, and compensated by, political gains for Europe. Neither the evidence from the past nor our analysis of the contemporary shift in the balance of pressure on international companies, however, offers much support for this assumption.

The Extractive Industries

In natural resources, especially petroleum, the creation of national champions in Europe to avoid dependence on American (or Anglo-Saxon) multinationals has increased, rather than decreased, the potential for divisiveness among the countries of the European community.[35] Unable to decide on a Europe-wide allocation system acceptable to their domestic constituencies during the oil crisis of 1973–74, governments that had national oil companies publicly and privately pressured them to favor their home markets. The oil committee of the Organisation for Economic Co-operation and Development, which had been set up after the 1956 Suez crisis but whose mandate had not been tested during the Six Day War of 1967 (when an attempted oil embargo fell apart), was not allowed to activate its distribution plan. Fearful that they might lose their "friendly" status with the Arab producers, the British and the French insisted that the OECD take no cooperative action. Furthermore, by refusing to supply the required data, they sabotaged those minimal measures which could have been agreed on by the EEC Council of Ministers. Only the ability of the large oil companies, European as well as American, to keep themselves immune from the demands of the governments where they marketed their products—to play the detested role of being accountable to no one but themselves—kept the conflict among the EEC countries from growing to unmanageable proportions.

The aim of France and Italy in supporting the growth of their national

35. See, for example, Romano Prodi and Alberto Clô, "Europe," *Daedalus* (Fall 1975), pp. 91–112.

oil companies during the 1950s (like Britain and the Netherlands before them) was to secure their access to sources of supply at the production stage. The easiest strategy to get a larger share of the oil business—which Ente Nazionale Idrocarburi (ENI), ERAP, and CFP followed, as did American independents such as Occidental Petroleum Corporation, Continental Oil Company, and Bunker Hunt—was to underbid the established majors for concessions in the most promising areas of North Africa and the Middle East. As chapter five pointed out, this gave their companies initial access to the oil but in the process strengthened the bargaining position of the producing countries, leading to higher taxes and greater host-government influence over corporate decisions.

During the oil crisis and embargo of 1973–74, however, the national oil companies of the European states evidently could not give the consumers of their home countries preferential prices. And though they did have the option of favoring certain markets with preferential allocations, either by routing oil unevenly among nonembargoed countries or by rerouting oil from nonembargoed to embargoed countries, the evidence indicates that European oil companies behaved like the American majors, acting so as to equalize the suffering and thus favoring neither Europe, generally, nor their home countries. When Prime Minister Heath asked British Petroleum to give preferential volume to the British market, its management refused, saying that (despite 48 percent government ownership) it would adhere to contractual obligations, rather than to "instructions from their stockholders."[36] Together with the American companies, British Petroleum and Royal Dutch Shell rerouted oil to favor the embargoed countries (Holland and the United States). According to the calculations of Robert Stobaugh, the differences in shortfall for Europe, Japan, and the United States were small.[37]

But will oil companies in the future have such independence in arranging allocations? A source of leverage against their home governments is

36. Robert B. Stobaugh, "The Oil Companies in Crisis," *Daedalus* (Fall 1975), p. 189.
37. Ibid., pp. 190–95. Stobaugh argues that French negotiations with Algeria produced an order from Sonatrach to CFP and Elf-ERAP to send their entire output to France, irrespective of other commitments. Those negotiations led Algeria to order non-French companies not to cut back their deliveries of Algerian oil to France. Stobaugh estimates, however, that the shortfall in France was worse than in either the United Kingdom or Germany, relative to the quantity forecast for the embargo period.

their potential to embarass the government in its external political relations by demanding to be told publicly which countries they should shortchange to favor the home market.[38] By nationalizing a recalcitrant company, however, a government could allocate oil without revealing who is being discriminated against. And, with periodic crises in many raw-materials industries in the scenarios of the future (see chapter five), home countries will be more likely to take this course, thus undermining the role multinationals play in keeping competition for supplies from leading to open political animosity. Without a prior political agreement on allocations in time of scarcity, backed by sufficient domestic consensus to enforce it, the creation of national companies in Europe and the search by individual European countries for special relations with exporting countries only accentuate intra-EC differences.

In such a nationalistic world, the United States and Japan might be constrained to defend their national interests by adopting equally nationalistic controls over their multinationals. Indeed, they might have to, to avoid being shortchanged during a period of short supply. Political tension, even open hostility, among industrialized countries would be inevitable.

Manufacturing Multinationals

As alternatives to American multinationals, national manufacturing champions are not as potentially divisive of the Community—or of U.S.-Europe relations—as are national natural resource companies. But there are elements of the same paradox: the *prerequisite* for national firms to serve pan-European economic needs is the very political willingness to submerge individual national sovereignties (and the belief that they will stay submerged) that the process has as its *goal*. But the paradox here is crueler: even given such a political willingness, it is doubtful that successful pan-European multinational champions could behave differently from their American competitors or add to the self-confidence and self-reliance of the European Community.

Originally, the spread of American manufacturing firms in Europe was perceived as a challenge to many Europeans because only the Americans

38. Louis Turner, "The European Community: Factors of Disintegration—Politics of the Energy Crisis," *International Affairs*, vol. 50 (July 1974), p. 411.

appeared to be taking advantage of the Common Market, rationalizing production and marketing on a Community-wide scale. European firms, by contrast, seemed wedded to their own national economies. One obstacle to their spreading within Europe, which did not hinder the Americans to as great an extent, was the lack of a uniform company law, of uniform standards, of uniform patent regulations, of uniform treatment of debt.[39] Even if a common industrial policy were adopted by the Community's Council of Ministers and ratified by member countries, it would have to be supplemented by far-reaching programs for pooling R&D efforts within Europe and for opening public procurement to nondiscriminatory bidding by European national champions. Thus, for European companies to achieve the scale advantages that American companies enjoy in the U.S. market (and which they transferred to their operations in Europe), requires first, a major commitment to closer political as well as economic unification.

Such a commitment was one of the dramatic achievements of the late 1960s. But it did not eliminate two extraordinarily troublesome demands: first, none of the major governments wanted their firms excluded from the most advanced, high-technology industries; second, all governments (especially the French) wanted a "just return" of the benefits from joint projects in proportion to their contribution. These two demands pushed the pan-European companies in the direction of cross-border mergers "in which one national identity is not swallowed by the other, but both share in something larger."[40]

The weakness of such mergers is in reconciling the demands for national identity and national reward with the potential advantages of scale in the Common Market. Attempts at government-to-government collaboration in high-technology manufacturing, such as the Concorde or the Airbus, resulted only in temporary consolidation of research efforts and producing organizations.[41] While these projects undoubtedly reduced some cost of duplication, their structures put them at a disadvantage com-

---

39. For discussions of the difficulties of promoting intra-European mergers, with special emphasis on the case of Agfa-Gevaert, see Layton, *European Advanced Technology,* chap. 15; Frank Vogl, *German Business After the Economic Miracle* (John Wiley and Sons, 1973), pp. 110, 145, 200–02.

40. Layton, *European Advanced Technology,* p. 250.

41. See M. S. Hochmuth, "Aerospace," and Raymond Vernon, "Enterprise and Government in Western Europe," in Vernon, ed., *Big Business and the State,* pp. 148–69.

pared to American competitors in terms of their speed and efficiency in responding to the market. Consequently, keeping joint projects afloat requires permanent government subsidies. Such subsidies would have to be approved on a case-by-case basis and would likely perpetuate their competitive disadvantage in relation to American companies. Furthermore, the few European partnerships that have been arranged across national boundaries (Dunlop-Pirelli and Fiat-Citroën prior to its demise) have been largely agreements to split markets rather than genuine efforts to stimulate innovation, to take risks in the development of new products, or to explore new demand.[42] On the basis of the evidence, there is little reason to expect that such cooperative arrangements will produce the cascading benefits needed to overcome the obstacles to ever higher levels of European integration.

On the contrary, the desire of European companies to take advantage of economies of scale exerts a strong counterpull to the ideal of self-reliance for Europe. In those sectors where the Europeans have been most worried about technological dependence—computers, telecommunications, nuclear power, and aerospace—the easiest way to compete in the European market has been to form alliances with strong American multinationals. The French and Belgian shareholders of Jeumont-Schneider, for example, fought for a merger with Westinghouse Electric Corporation to improve the company's position for selling electrical equipment throughout Europe.[43] The merger of France's CII with Honeywell Incorporated-Machines Bull, rather than with Siemens Aktiengesellschaft of Germany, is a more recent example.

Merger with an American multinational has occurred where a "European solution" was not available for bailing out an ailing national firm. But it also has a strong attraction for a healthy firm, because it allows the European company to specialize in research and development; it alleviates the fear of having the national champion (of France, for example) swallowed up not by a pan-European champion but by the national champion of another European country (for example, Germany), and it offers ac-

42. Vernon, "Enterprise and Government in Western Europe," pp. 18–19.
43. The Jeumont-Schneider-Westinghouse merger was vetoed in 1968 by de Gaulle. In creating the joint venture (Framatome) that now has a virtual monopoly in the sensitive field of nuclear power in France, the Schneider holding company followed a path it had already explored with Westinghouse. Patricia High Painton, "A Belgian Baron Fights for His Corporate Domain in France," Fortune, vol. 92 (August 1975), pp. 170–80.

cess to the American market. Even in the sensitive field of military aircraft, the ability of General Dynamics and Northrup to dangle joint production agreements in front of Sabca (Belgian), Fairey (Belgian), and Fokker-VKW (Dutch), gave an incentive besides price and performance to choose the American F-16 fighter over the Mirage F-1. In the winning package, General Dynamics allowed European purchasers to build locally 40 percent of the parts (by cost) of the European version of the F-16, 10 percent of the parts for planes bought by the United States, and 15 percent of the parts for planes bought elsewhere.[44]

Even if these problems were growing pains on the way to a sustained European collaboration and the creation of genuine European champions, the result is an empty victory. The rationale for pan-European champions, like the rationale for European national champions, is that such firms better serve the national interest than foreign firms and would be more likely to respond to national policies. The justification for such a belief is hard to discover. National champions in Europe that have joined the ranks of American multinationals have done so by responding successfully to the same calculus of opportunities and threats as their American and Japanese counterparts. In the process, they have experienced the same shift of bargaining power from foreign investor to host country, and from home government to host government.

In the automobile industry, for example, the relations of the major European car manufacturers with the Third World parallel those of Ford Motor Company and General Motors Corporation.[45] The European companies began with vehicle assembly in Latin America and North Africa, behind tariff walls built to encourage import-substituting industrialization. So as not to lose these protected markets, the manufacturers gradually yielded to host-government demands to expand the local content of their final product. Finally, faced with a combination of host-country pressure to export and competition from other multinationals, which were using low-wage export platforms to penetrate markets in developed countries, they began to export both parts and final products from the developing

44. "Belgium Joins Others, Picks U.S.-Built F-16," *Wall Street Journal*, June 9, 1975.

45. Louis T. Wells, Jr., "Automobiles," in Vernon, ed., *Big Business and the State*, pp. 250–51; Executive Secretariat for Economic and Social Affairs, Organization of American States, *Sectoral Study of Transnational Enterprises in Latin America: The Automotive Industry*, SG/Ser. G. 42/3 (1974).

world to their own home markets. In this evolution, they transferred large portions of their production out of the home country, into the Third World.

In the early 1970s, output from the Volkswagen plant in Brazil and Fiat's in Spain equaled about one-fourth of their totals in their home countries.[46] Renault had plants in eighteen countries. In 1975, Fiat assured authorities in Minas Gerais, Brazil that it would build a 200,000 vehicle-per-year, $582 million plant, despite massive layoffs in Italy.[47] Furthermore, as part of the Brazilian requirements, Fiat will have to export from Belo Horizonte, jeopardizing its role as Italy's largest exporter. During 1974–75, British Leyland in Nigeria, France's Berliet in Algeria, and Britain's Rolls Royce in Egypt were persuaded to maintain or expand production, although they were cutting back production at home.[48] In short, to maintain their positions in foreign markets and to stay competitive in their home markets, European champions are driven to emulate American multinationals, whether or not that behavior meshes with the desires of home-country officials.

The same tension—between the corporation's desire to enhance long-term profits and the home country's desire to protect its share of the value-added by the firm—is evident in the movement of European companies into the North American market. Michelin's decision to build tire factories in Nova Scotia and South Carolina in 1969–70 was an exception only because it happened to take place during a period of strong demand for automotive products.[49] Volkswagen's plan to establish a major plant in South Carolina, however, stimulated sentiments in Germany similar to those in the United States that motivated the Burke-Hartke bill (see chapter eight). Partly because of Rudolph Leiding's determination to improve Volkswagen's profit base by expanding operations abroad (in the United

46. Wells, "Automobiles," p. 247.
47. Marvin Howe, "Brazilian State Pins Hope on Cars," *New York Times,* February 16, 1975; Robert Ball, "Europe's Auto Crack-up Is Worse Than Ours," *Fortune,* vol. 91 (May 1975), pp. 180–85, 256–59. Minas Gerais attracted Fiat with a package of incentives (designed by Arthur D. Little) that included low-cost land and a 25.6 percent rebate on the state sales tax for up to five years.
48. *Journal of Commerce,* July 25, 1975; and industry sources.
49. By 1974, all but seventeen of Michelin's forty-five plants were outside of France. Within Europe, however, Michelin had not had to lay off workers for more than thirty years. Robert Ball, "The Michelin Man Rolls Into Akron's Backyard," *Fortune,* vol. 90 (December 1974), p. 139.

States and Brazil), he was deposed as president of the company in 1974 by representatives of labor and German government interests.[50]

As with American multinationals, it is not clear whether European corporations' growth in direct foreign investment increases global economic efficiency or the economic welfare of the home country, nor is it clear whether it is motivated by threats and incentives of the host country (including the United States). But it is clear that the growth of European multinationals is not a solution to their governments' loss of control over American investors. Rather, it will probably aggravate the problem.

Thus, the efforts of the Common Market countries to avoid economic and technological dependence upon the United States (as a prelude to stepping out from the shadow of American hegemony) do not presage a cohesive, confident, self-reliant Europe. They do not promise to provide a focal point for further European integration nor a means for European governments to control their common national destinies. They indicate, at best, that the drift that has characterized European integration since the late 1960s will continue. And, with energy shortages or other natural-resource crises, such efforts may lead to further fragmentation and disintegration within the European Community.

Japan and America

Because Japan tightly limits foreign investment, American direct investment has not played the role in American-Japanese relations that it has in American-European relations. Indeed, Japan's is a story of development success achieved without foreign direct investment. There have been occasional U.S. efforts to push Japan to liberalize its investment policy, most notably in the late 1960s when the Japanese economic miracle became a magnet for U.S. firms in many industries (and when dollar overvaluation and yen undervaluation were reaching the point of greatest imbalance). But the issue did not become central to their relations. The United States was then restraining capital outflows, particularly to industrialized countries, as its balance-of-payments deficits reached a peak

---

50. "Change of Command: In the Wake of Bitter Executive Feuds, VW Prepares to Welcome a New Leader," _Wall Street Journal,_ January 10, 1975. Leiding had been Volkswagen's chief executive in Brazil before moving to higher management levels in Germany.

and attached a higher priority to other economic matters, including the textile industry and the growing disparity in bilateral trade between the two countries. Thus, investment in Japan, although growing from 1.4 percent of total American investment in 1965 to 2.5 percent in 1973, is still low, and Japan has no equivalent to le défi americain.

American policy on foreign investment affects American-Japanese relations primarily in terms of how that policy affects the structure and functioning of the international economic system, which is crucial to Japan. The way the pressure structure—of host countries and international competitors on all multinational corporations—has evolved circumscribes the role that Japan will play in the international system even more sharply than it does the role of Europe. To have an impact on U.S.-Japanese relations, therefore, American policies toward foreign investment by American multinationals should aim not at changing the behavior of U.S. companies operating within Japan but rather at moderating the divisive political consequences of this global pressure.

Despite frequent domestic criticism of U.S.-Japanese security arrangements, the factions in Japan's Liberal Democratic Party, in the civil service, and in the business community, that have ruled the country's political life since the Allied occupation, have never followed the European path of searching out a more independent and assertive foreign policy posture. On the contrary, their reaction to periodic American shoves toward a more active international role has been to try to keep themselves snugly in a secure and tranquil "special relationship" with the United States.[51]

The controversy generated in both countries by this exaggerated quiescence in world affairs grew as the disparity between Japan's international economic role and its political (and military) role increased.[52] Within Japan, those who advocate a low profile in international affairs argue that

51. Opposition to dependence on the United States has now grown within the Liberal Democratic Party as well as within opposition parties. See Ralph N. Clough, *East Asia and U.S. Security* (Brookings Institution, 1975), p. 109.
52. See Kei Wakaizumi, "Japan's Dilemma: To Act or Not to Act," *Foreign Policy*, no. 16 (Fall 1974), pp. 30–47; Priscilla Clapp and Morton H. Halperin, eds., *United States-Japanese Relations: The 1970's* (Harvard University Press, 1974); Robert E. Osgood, *The Weary and the Wary: U.S. and Japanese Security Policies in Transition* (Johns Hopkins University Press, 1972); Zbigniew Brzezinski, *The Fragile Blossom: Crisis and Change in Japan* (Harper and Row, 1972); Henry Owen, ed., *The Next Phase in Foreign Policy* (Brookings Institution, 1973); Edwin O. Reischauer, *The United States and Japan*, 3rd ed. (Harvard University Press, 1970).

the domestic political situation is too fragile and the Japanese capacity for singleminded endeavor too great to risk moving toward greater participation in international politics. It also might suggest to its neighbors (Russia and China as well as the more vulnerable developing countries of East Asia and Southeast Asia) a replication of the expansionism of the 1930s. Those who urge a more positive stance for Japan take the position that the benefits of U.S. guardianship are waning while the costs are rising, and that the country's peculiar combination of economic strength and economic vulnerability makes a more active political role inevitable. If Japan does not move in this direction now, according to the latter view, it will find itself having to make decisions during future crises with the same lack of experience and with less flexibility than it has now.

For the United States, the conventional formula for sponsoring the return of Japan to full membership in international society became intolerably ambiguous as Japan's growth in the 1960s moved it toward the ranks of the economic superpowers. Was Japan's role to be global, or merely regional? Should it be political as well as economic? If political, what was its proper military posture?

Debate over these questions was sharpened by the widespread feeling among American business and labor that Japan had been getting a free ride at U.S. expense for a long time: it devoted less than 1 percent of its gross national product to national defense (in comparison to America's 7–10 percent), while enjoying the U.S. nuclear umbrella and the U.S. security commitment to South Korea. And it used the savings to undermine the position of American industry and labor. The Nixon "shocks" of July–August 1971 (announcing the visit to China and devaluing the dollar) were, in form and substance, a victory not only for American strategists who felt that Japan should be pushed out of the nest and forced to fly but also for American economic groups who wanted to redress the economic imbalance.

The wisdom of encouraging Japan to play a more active role in international affairs has been defended in Washington by those who see the country's growth to superpower status as inevitable (despite the energy crisis) and its politics as stable.[53] It has been challenged by others, to

53. See Herman Kahn, *The Emerging Japanese Superstate: Challenge and Response* (Prentice-Hall, 1970); and Norman Macrae, "Pacific Century, 1975–2075?," *The Economist*, January 4, 1975, pp. 15–35. Macrae is optimistic that Japanese political stability will remain even if, as he expects, a Socialist-led coalition replaces the Liberal Democratic Party.

whom Japan is a "fragile blossom," with economy and polity vulnerable to a highly unstable evolution.[54] According to the latter interpretation, the potential rivalry between the United States and Japan for markets and resources is so strong that a restructuring of the "special" political relation might be hard to keep within bounds. A deterioration in their political and economic interaction would surely undermine both countries' security arrangements. And once American guarantees came into doubt, Japan's preferred stance of unarmed neutrality (happo-yabure or "defenseless on all sides") might soon prove untenable, upsetting the balance of power in Asia.[55]

Analysis of how American policies toward investment might contribute to the preferred evolution in U.S.-Japanese relations (as in the case of U.S.-European relations) should begin by projecting how new demands on all multinationals, including Japanese, will affect Japan's ability to provide for its own needs. The domestic stability in Japan that is crucial to either maintaining its passive international stance or moving toward a moderate and responsible exercise of international power, is founded on the ability of Japanese business, through their international activities, to provide for the country's economic welfare and security. That foundation may now be severely shaken.

Japanese Access to Raw Materials[56]

The country's economic vulnerability is most evident, of course, in raw materials. Japanese economic growth depended in the past on a reasonably competitive, smoothly functioning, and nondiscriminatory system to

54. Reischauer, *The United States and Japan;* and Brzezinski, *The Fragile Blossom.*

55. The Japanese expression is from Saburo Okita, "National Resource Dependency and Japanese Foreign Policy," *Foreign Affairs,* vol. 52 (July 1974), pp. 714–24. The Socialist Party in Japan also traditionally advocates a policy of unarmed neutrality.

56. See M. Y. Yoshino, "Japanese Foreign Direct Investment" (Harvard University Graduate School of Business Administration, 1972; processed); "Japan—New Giant in the Minerals Industry," *Engineering and Mining Journal,* vol. 172 (November 1971); Lawrence B. Krause, "Evolution of Foreign Direct Investment: The United States and Japan," in Jerome B. Cohen, ed., *Pacific Partnership: United States-Japan Trade—Prospects and Recommendations for the Seventies* (Lexington Books, 1972); and Yoshi Tsurumi, *The Japanese Are Coming: A Multinational Interaction of Firms and Politics* (Ballinger, 1976), chap. 3.

supply natural resources that kept material costs relatively low and enabled business to exploit the low wages and high productivity of its labor force. In the 1940s and 1950s, when the absolute size of the demand for raw materials was small, Japanese businesses could rely almost entirely on purchases in the open market, occasionally supplemented by long-term contracts (primarily for petroleum) from the major foreign companies. This strategy gave processors flexibility and allowed them to devote their scarce capital to build refining and fabricating capacity in Japan, while other investors (frequently American) bore the economic uncertainties and political risks associated with large lump-sum natural resource investments. And Japan remained safely insulated from the tension associated with ownership of subsoil rights in the Third World, while its traditional suppliers tried to forget the memory of Japanese expansionism into the Greater East-Asian Co-Prosperity Sphere.[57]

However, in the 1960s, as Japan's need for natural resources soared and its demand became a sizable share of global consumption, the country had to use more aggressive policies to ensure sufficient flows of raw materials at acceptable prices. The aim of its policies—long-term contracts and direct equity investment in the production stage—was to tie up output far in advance. Insofar as these policies have succeeded in assuring access at reasonable prices, however, it has been as a by-product, rather than as a direct consequence, of official policy efforts and in contradiction to stated policy objectives.

OIL. Although Japan made an initial foray into direct ownership in 1961 with the foundation of the Arabian Oil Company to exploit concessions from the Saudi Arabian and Kuwaiti governments, more than 90 percent of its oil imports continued to be supplied by foreign companies.[58] In an effort to become more independent, the government founded a petroleum development corporation in 1967 to invest up to 75 percent of the equity required for exploration and to lend up to 50 percent of the total required for development (with no repayment in case of failure).[59] Because of the corporation's support, in the late 1960s several Japanese groups (including refiners, end users, trading companies, and financial in-

57. For background on Japanese expansionism in the 1930s, see James B. Crowley, *Japan's Quest for Autonomy: National Security and Foreign Policy 1930–1938* (Princeton University Press, 1966).
58. On Japanese oil policy, see Yoshino, "Japanese Foreign Direct Investment"; Yoshi Tsurumi, "Japan," *Daedalus* (Fall 1975), pp. 113–27.
59. Yoshino, "Japanese Foreign Direct Investment," pp. 12–13, 16.

stitutions) began moving upstream to the production stage. The country's first major venture into equity ownership occurred in 1973 with the purchase of the Abu Dhabi Oil Company.[60]

MINERALS. Encouraged by their government, Japanese copper and iron ore smelters and refiners began to change in the 1960s from spot purchases to ten- or fifteen-year contracts for large portions of the output of mines in Canada, Australia, South America, and South Asia. By concentrating their purchasing power rather than competing with one another for output, Japanese firms on some occasions paid lower prices (especially for Australian iron ore) than those in other world markets.

Later, direct equity ownership was seen as a better means of achieving the same results. Undertaken "for the purpose of securing stable mineral resources over a long period of time," according to Mitsuo Aikyo, president of Mitsubishi Metal Corporation, Japanese mining companies began bringing the Musoshi copper mine in Zaire and the Mamut copper mine in Malaysia into production in the early 1970s.[61] At the same time, they undertook direct investments in the zinc industry in Peru, in the copper industry in Chile and Ethiopia, and in the nickel industry in Australia, and initiated joint ventures with American aluminum companies in Africa, Brazil, and the South Pacific.

The assertion of economic nationalism among producers in the Third World, and the shift toward resource diplomacy in Australia in the late 1960s, demonstrate how unreliable was the expectation that Japanese buyers could tie up large amounts of raw materials with long-term contracts at prices significantly below world market levels. As noted in chapter five, the federal government of Australia, in a constitutional reversal, began in 1965 to refuse to grant export licenses for iron ore from concessions already negotiated by the state governments unless prices were raised to match higher quotations available elsewhere. Similarly, the major copper-producing countries, meeting in Lusaka in 1967, decided to create a producers' price for their output—whether or not it was under long-term contract—pegged to the quotation on the London Metals Exchange.

Thus, Japan has had to retreat from the goal of ensuring itself a fixed amount of output at a fixed price to the goal of having a fixed amount at

60. Tsurumi, *The Japanese Are Coming*, p. 44.
61. Mitsuo Aikyo, in "Japanese Enterprises Moving Towards Multinationalization," in *Industria*, p. 40.

a variable price. But, as chapter five argues, even this objective can be achieved only as long as the exporting governments have neither the power nor the will to cut back production with the aim of boosting prices or imposing a selective embargo on consumers.

The same reduction of expectations, in the face of the economic nationalism of exporting governments, will accompany the Japanese foray into direct equity investment at the production stage. In addition, direct equity investment exposes the Japanese to the tensions of foreign ownership of subsoil resources and to the problems of the division of oligopoly rents. The energy crisis of 1973 revealed to the Japanese, as to other consumers, the vacuity of the assumption that direct ownership could ensure access to supplies when the exporting governments had the potential to wield market power selectively. The massive investment of almost $800 million in Abu Dhabi in 1972 came just in time to demonstrate that Japanese equity had little to do with whether the country would have a place on the "preferred list" of oil purchasers.

Japanese government support for national companies operating overseas, by multiplying the number and diversity of suppliers and increasing the availability of capacity, helped solve the problem of access to natural resources, although this was not the primary goal of the policy. Japanese policy focused on the expansion of new output rather than on the maximization of private profits at the production stage, and access was a byproduct of the earlier search, not the result of mature investments.

Japan began in the mid-1960s to write long-term contracts for minerals that could be used by suppliers to finance new sources of production. Frequently, the Japanese supplied a large part of the financing themselves. They did not limit themselves to established oligopoly members, nor to Japanese mining companies. Long-term Japanese contracts for copper metal or copper concentrates were used as collateral to provide capital between 1966 and 1973 for fourteen new mines in nine countries, bringing into the industry ten companies and three countries (plus the province of British Columbia in Canada) that had not been significant copper producers before.[62] Iron ore contracts for output developed (in most cases)

62. The new mines are Lornex, Port Hardy, Valley Copper, and Fox Lake in British Columbia; Rio Blanco and Sagasca in Chile; Bougainville in Papua New Guinea; Ertzberg in Indonesia; Mamut in Malaysia; Musoshi and Shaba in Zaire; Cuajone in Peru; Gunpowder in Australia; and Cerro Colorado in Panama. "Copper—Japan's Largest Metal Import," *Engineering and Mining Journal*, vol. 172 (November 1971), p. 105; and industry sources.

with loans from Japanese companies (eight large projects in Southeast Asia, six in Australia, six in Africa, six in Latin America, and five in South Asia) created more than a dozen new companies in seven countries that had not been major iron ore producers before.[63] Thus, the Japanese attempts to tie up future output had the side effect of keeping the copper and iron ore industries relatively competitive during the late 1960s and early 1970s. Given the desire of exporting governments to push up prices, competition among suppliers was the major force countervailing oligopoly power at the production stage.

Hence Japan has already taken the path we recommend for the United States: maximizing the volume and geographical diversity of output in natural resource industries, with less concern for maximizing the share of the rents accruing from those industries to home companies. Japan's leadership is entirely natural, since it is the country most vulnerable to high prices and insecure access of natural resources. Even so, there remains in Tokyo a myth that "Japan, Inc." can develop captive sources of raw materials through direct investment (in emulation of the traditional practices of the United States and Europe) but avoid the adverse political and economic consequences by maintaining friendly relations with the exporting governments. We would hope that Japan abandon totally the idea of direct ownership in favor of policies aimed more explicitly at the problem of producer concentration and market power. Whether it follows this course, and when, probably depends on the direction the United States itself moves.

Japanese Manufacturing Multinationals

The stability of Japan's political system has depended not only on a stable natural resource supply system whose future is now precarious but also on a strategy for manufacturing industries that may be increasingly

63. Southeast Asia: the Dungun, Rompin, and Sungei Gau projects in Malaysia; the Philex, Larap, Filmag, Morong, and Leyte projects in the Philippines. Australia: the Hamersley, Goldworthy, Mt. Newman, Savage, Whyalla, and Robe River projects. Africa: Cassinga in Angola; Miferma in Mauritania; LAMCO in Liberia; Marampa in Sierra Leone; and Palabora and Swaziland in South Africa. Latin America: Itabira and Carajas in Brazil; Marcona in Peru; Algarrobo and Santa Fe in Chile; and Hierro Patagónico in Argentina. In South Asia: Dempo, Foment, and Salgaoncare in Goa; and Kiriburu and Bailadila in India. "Iron and Steel—Japan's Bellwether," *Engineering and Mining Journal*, vol. 172 (November 1971), pp. 101–03; and industry sources.

vulnerable to international pressure, which Japanese companies now cannot protect themselves against. The initial success of Japanese governments in providing rapid economic growth and full employment depended upon low labor costs, toleration of industrial pollution, and an increasingly undervalued exchange rate for the yen. As wage rates rose, as tolerance for pollution declined, and as revaluation and flexible exchange rates eliminated any monetary advantage for production in Japan, foreign investment allowed Japanese manufacturers to maintain the competitiveness of their exports.

Japanese investment in overseas manufacturing operations went through the same sequence as American and European investment.[64] In the late 1950s and early 1960s, Japan set up production facilities to serve the local markets in countries, such as Korea and Taiwan, that had erected trade barriers to stimulate import substituting industrialization. Japanese companies then realized the possibility of using such locations as export platforms to supply the major consumer markets (including Japan). The movement of American and European competitors into the same low-wage centers locked Japanese firms into this strategy. In 1971 the leading Japanese firms in the synthetic fiber, textile, electronics, electric, automobile, truck, and steel (galvanized iron sheets) industries each had at least ten overseas manufacturing subsidiaries.[65] Since then, the revaluation of the yen has reinforced this process. Competition among companies for access to export platforms forces the companies to favor host countries rather than home countries in percentage of local content, arrangement of transfer pricing, and other practices.

These practices do not necessarily portend good relations with those countries of Asia and Latin America that are hosts to increasing numbers of Japanese manufacturing plants, however.[66] Although some analysts see in the apparent willingness of Japanese investors to form joint ventures or take minority shares in foreign operations evidence that they would blend unobtrusively into the local environment and thus avoid the tensions that

64. See Yoshino, "Japanese Foreign Direct Investment"; Krause, "Evolution of Foreign Direct Investment"; Tsurumi, *The Japanese Are Coming,* chaps. 4, 9; Jun Nishikawa, "Toward Economic Independence of Southeast Asia," *The Developing Economies,* vol. 11 (December 1973); and Donald R. Sherk, "Foreign Investment in Asia: Cooperation and Conflict Between the United States and Japan" (Federal Reserve Bank of San Francisco, October 1973; processed).
65. Tsurumi, *The Japanese Are Coming,* p. 73.
66. See Tsurumi, *The Japanese Are Coming,* chaps. 8, 9.

have plagued investors of other nationalities, joint ventures and minority roles belong to only a brief phase of the investment cycle in manufacturing. Yoshi Tsurumi finds that as Japanese investors switch from making goods for local markets to making goods or components for export, there is a dramatic turning away from their tolerance for joint ventures with nationals. As in the case of American firms, the need to control quality and to coordinate marketing brings about a strong preference for total control, or at least majority ownership. This preference is reinforced by ringi-seide: consensus decisionmaking plus management that rises through ranks (which inhibits, as well, host-country nationals from becoming managers). Thus, conflicts for Japanese foreign policy arising from investor-host disputes are likely to increase rather than diminish.

The sequence of Japanese manufacturing investments, from foreign assembly for local markets to foreign production for export, did not produce strains with the Japanese economy as long as the domestic growth rate was greater than 10 percent a year and employment was high. Under those conditions Japanese planners enthusiastically encouraged the export of industry, congestion, and pollution. There were cases during this period in which local electronics and textile suppliers within Japan went bankrupt and workers became unemployed, as major firms moved to Korea or Hong Kong.[67] But within the large industrial conglomerates, workers displaced by runaway plants were absorbed elsewhere in the firms, preserving the social contract between workers and management and maintaining the tradition of corporate loyalty.

If Japanese domestic growth were to regain a 10 percent annual rate and continue at that rate indefinitely (as some predict), corporate strategy may never become a divisive political issue.[68] With less favorable growth rates, however, a corporate strategy of investing in offshore export platforms may mean unemployment and the eventual destruction of the corporate tradition of worker welfare. Furthermore, Japan spends less money, in the aggregate, on research and development than either France or Germany and spends only about a third as much per scientist or technician.[69] It is estimated that one-tenth of Japan's manufacturing activity uses for-

67. Author interview with Yoshi Tsurumi, January 1975. He reports that the management of the small subcontractors typically took salary cuts with the workers—eventually going bankrupt—thus preserving the tradition of paternalism.
68. See Macrae, "Pacific Century, 1975–2075?"
69. Ibid. But massive spending would drain the capital available for social and environmental improvements, thus generating more domestic discontent.

eign technology; and, in the more advanced sectors, about one-fourth.[70] As production at the low end of the product cycle is moved to foreign locations, adapted technology may be insufficient to generate enough new growth to take its place, even during the expansionary phase of the business cycle. And there will not be a large enough indigenous R&D effort to fill the gap with production processes at the high end of the product cycle.

The role of Japan in the emerging international system turns closely on whether Japanese democracy survives the exposure of the Japanese economy to fluctuations in the international business cycle. If Japanese business lays off workers and exports jobs, class and social conflict are certain to increase. Crises and shortages in natural resources can weaken the social fabric of the country. The consequences of dealing with the problem through a political shift toward authoritarianism (of either left or right) are not likely to be limited to Japan, if only because all other Asian powers would look for—and fear—a revival of militarism in Japanese foreign policy.

In short, the emerging environment for Japanese multinationals suggests unpropitious conditions for Japanese domestic stability, and, consequently, for the devolution of power and responsibility on Japan. It also suggests that the stability of the international system that replaces the era of American hegemony will still be based on the ability and willingness of the United States to stay constructively engaged in the affairs of Europe and Asia. U.S. policies, although they cannot lessen the pressure on multinationals, may be able to resolve common problems through cooperation that helps the international system to evolve in the direction of moderate pluralism.

The International System

The simple mercantilistic notion that national companies could be made to function in their international operations as arms of the home state—relatively free to serve national needs and ensure national security—cannot survive in the face of the changing balance of pressure on multinationals. The demise of this possibility complicates the problem of how to move from a world dominated by a single power in the West to a world of muted pluralism.

70. James C. Abegglen, ed., *Business Strategies for Japan* (Tokyo: Sophia University, 1970), p. 118.

The vision of an orderly devolution of power and responsibility in the post-cold-war era is founded on the assumption that Europe and Japan can use their wealth and talent to become stable, self-reliant, political actors in the international system. The struggle between home and host governments over the distribution of the benefits produced by multinational corporations (whatever their nationality) magnifies the difficulty of that task and makes the outcome much less certain. This observation is not another premature obituary for the European community nor one more announcement of approaching autumn for Japan's "fragile blossom." But it does suggest that the economies of Japan and Europe may be too vulnerable and the self-confidence of their polities too scant for them to be able to easily propose the initiatives or take the risks for the common interest, which a nonhegemonic system requires. The assertion that an American retreat from the effort to exert leadership in economic, political, and military affairs would provide a good setting for devolution was a better indication of dissatisfaction with the way the United States was exercising its (waning) powers in the late 1960s and early 1970s than it was a prediction about how smoothly and comfortably the system could function without any leadership at all.

Indeed, the readiness of American policymakers to believe that fundamental external conditions were favorable to the emergence of strong, self-reliant allies in Europe and Japan fed the dissatisfaction. It increased the willingness of the United States to confront Europe or Japan with unilateral proposals. It inflated the expectation that they should respond in a rapid, coherent manner. And it aggravated the tendency to resort to old-fashioned techniques of manipulation if the response proved craven. Our analysis suggests that there will be a continuation of this kind of interaction if the assumptions and expectations about devolution remain, even as the statesmen involved change.

The energy crisis and oil embargo of 1973–74 dealt a severe blow to those who, in the late 1960s and early 1970s, were urging that an American abandonment of its imperial pretensions would be the welcome (and necessary) prelude to the development of a new order built upon equivalence and reciprocity. But the economic base on which the major powers must build a new structure of political relations is vulnerable not only to oil supply or to a crisis in energy. Rather, the crisis is only a graphic reminder that the touted interdependence of the modern world—the sensitivity of the welfare of one country to changes in the welfare of others—is extraordinarily fragile and the potential for serious deterioration in the structure is great. An apt analogy might be the twilight of the British hegemonial system (before and after the First World War), in which the recognition of mutual dependence was not strong enough to prevent the competition and rivalry that led to the disintegration of relations among the great powers.[71] The retreat of the dominant state from its leadership role did not produce by itself an orderly devolution of power and responsibility in world affairs. Neither the promise of mutual benefit nor the threat of mutual loss propelled the major powers, acting individually, to guide the international system toward a new stable balance. If the United States in the present period were to turn either to isolationism or belligerent nationalism, in a way that magnifies the sense of vulnerability and insecurity in Europe and Asia, it could risk a similar fragmentation, if not disintegration, in the international system.

That possibility is not remote. Behind official American commitment to its alliances and pledges around the world is a public that is less committed to internationalism than at any time in the last three decades, that is more concerned (and dissatisfied) with domestic economic issues and less confident that its leaders can solve them. The number of internationalists (those who agree that the United States should take into account the views of its allies, that it should defend West Europe and Japan, that it should not go its own way) dropped from 65 percent in 1964 to 59 percent in 1968, 56 percent in 1972, 41 percent in 1974 and 37 percent in 1976. Those agreeing with the assertion that "the United States should mind its own business internationally and let other countries get along as best they can on their own" rose from 18 percent in 1964 to 41 percent in 1976.[72] In contrast to statements by President Nixon, President Ford, and Secretary of State Henry Kissinger that the disenchantment with America's traditional foreign policy role was limited to the "liberal Eastern establishment," these demographic opinion surveys indicate that the shift toward isolationism has taken place throughout the population and is most pronounced among those with little education, low to middle incomes, midwesterners, westerners, and nonurban residents. Moreover, at the

71. See Charles P. Kindleberger, *The World in Depression: 1929–1939* (University of California Press, 1973).

72. See Lloyd A. Free, "The International Attitudes of Americans," in Donald R. Lesh, ed., *A Nation Observed: Perspectives on America's World Role* (Washington, D.C.: Potomac Associates, 1974), pp. 147–48; and William Watts and Lloyd A. Free, "Nationalism, Not Isolationism," *Foreign Policy*, no. 24 (Fall 1976), p. 17.

same time that internationalist sentiments dropped, the impetus to both nationalism and unilateralism among the American public increased.

This is particularly ominous because it comes at a time when the attentive public for foreign policy is more split on international involvement, military engagement, and the role of the United States in world affairs than at any time since the end of the Second World War.[73] Not only particular policies, but the basic goals and assumptions of American foreign policy, are losing acceptance. Labor, of course, has become actively hostile to liberal internationalism, especially in trade and investment matters (unlike its position before the late 1960s).

At the least, with the decline of a clear military threat from the Soviet Union, the formation of foreign policy will become more like the formation of domestic policy, with parochial economic interests having an impact impossible during the era of cold war confrontation. More disturbing, these splits and dissatisfactions offer the possibility of a dramatic break with the traditional pattern of American politics, in which the established parties compete for the center of the American electorate. They open the door, according to analysts of voting behavior, to competition among extreme groups for the allegiance of lower-class and lower middle-class voters, who are not bound by party identification, who are increasingly mistrustful of public leadership, and to whom the more appealing stances appear to be isolationism, protectionism, militarism, nationalism, and unilateralism.[74]

There is less excuse, in an abstract sense, for the United States to refuse to take risks or bear burdens in the common interest than there is for Europe or Japan. The relative military security of the United States and the size and self-contained nature of the American economy make it structurally easier for the country to act responsibly in the international sys-

73. William Schneider, "Public Opinion: The Beginning of Ideology?" *Foreign Policy*, no. 17 (Winter 1974–75), pp. 88–120. In the past, Schneider argues, there has traditionally been "a critical margin of support for foreign policy decisions among the educated elite" (p. 92). Over the past decade, however, the divergence of views on America's proper role in international affairs has fractured "the consensus within the stratum of the electorate traditionally most responsive to leaders' initiatives" (p. 93). The cleavages are most clearly defined among the better-educated, with liberals being more isolationist, antimilitary, and prodétente, than conservatives. This split is particularly noticeable between generations, with age groups over sixty years old and under thirty years old differing by 35 percent (in comparison, for example, to 10 percent for the same groups of noncollege voters); see p. 96.
74. Ibid.

tem. But where will the domestic support for an active and liberal, but moderate, internationalism come from? Within the United States, the constituency with the strongest interest in involvement rather than isolationism, in restraint rather than aggressive nationalism, is the international investment community.[75] In 1971–72, it was the countervailing force that ultimately prevailed over Secretary of Treasury John Connally's impatience with Europe and his apparent willingness to risk ruining the international system for parochial American interests.[76] In Japan, where the U.S. investment community was less directly involved and transnational ties less strong, there was no similar force to moderate the shocks of 1971–73 (including the import surcharge and soybean embargo). American business, whose relations with Japan were predominantly trading rather than investment and which felt that Japan had been taking unfair advantage of America's generosity in defense and economic affairs for some time, pushed the government toward harsh and abrupt action rather than restraining it.

One might conclude, therefore, that the United States has a political interest in continuing to support the spread of American multinationals in Europe and Japan. We feel, however, that continued American policies of overt support for foreign investment by U.S. companies ultimately will weaken, rather than strengthen, the ability of multinationals to function transnationally as a force for stability and moderation in the relations among nations. Such policies legitimize the hostility of American labor toward American investors. They arouse the antagonism of business groups in host countries, who see them as giving Americans a competitive advantage. And, when matched by similar support on the part of other governments for their own multinationals, they might ultimately inspire local labor movements to react along the lines of the Burke-Hartke bill. Thus we advocate a neutral U.S. policy toward foreign direct investment for the political purpose of helping defuse across-the-board campaigns, both abroad and in the United States itself, against American multinationals, as well as for the economic reasons addressed in part two of this volume. Such an approach would provide the best possible basis for trans-

75. Failure to appreciate this fact is the major defect in many critical appraisals that argue that multinational corporations destabilize the international system; for example, Richard J. Barnet and Ronald E. Müller, *Global Reach: The Power of the Multinational Corporations* (Simon and Schuster, 1974).

76. For the flavor of Connally's approach, see William Safire, *Before the Fall: An Inside View of the Pre-Watergate White House* (Doubleday, 1975), p. 514.

national action to inspire cooperative (rather than narrowly self-interested) relations between the United States and Europe and the United States and Japan.

In addition, we advocate new international initiatives by the United States to better mesh the policies toward foreign direct investment of the several important home countries, all of which are in the industralized world; to help moderate the centrifugal forces which threaten relations among home countries; and to stimulate the search for common solutions to common problems. For example, we propose in chapter five that the Overseas Private Investment Corporation develop joint programs with its counterparts in the other home countries, to push firms to move from direct equity investment to management or service contracts in the natural resources industries. We predict that this will increase the flow of capital to the producing countries, increase the dependability and availability of output to all consumers in all phases of the business cycle, and remove multinational corporations from their unstable position under traditional ownership arrangements. Hence, it would lessen the potential for conflict between producer and consumer states and push their interaction toward multilateral relations, rather than special relations and spheres of influence. In turn, scrambles among the industrialized countries for preferential access to resources and "special deals"—which could disrupt overall U.S. foreign policy—could be avoided.[77] And when accompanied by international stockpiling (either by the importing countries together, as with the International Energy Agency, or by importing and producing countries together), by efforts to negotiate prohibitions against export controls, and by a provisional allocation scheme for times of shortage, such an American policy would reflect as well a continuing commitment to provide for the security of Europe and Japan.

In manufacturing, an American move to offset the efforts of other countries (notably industrialized and developing host countries, but home countries as well) to force or entice foreign investors to serve their national goals has immediate zero-sum connotations for the rest of the world. But, for that reason, it provides an ideal occasion to begin to negotiate agreements with Europe and Japan that address the economic issues discussed in part two. Such agreements would define what constitutes both legitimate inducements to tilt the benefits of foreign investments toward

77. Helmut Schmidt, "The Struggle for the World Product," *Foreign Affairs,* vol. 52 (April 1974).

any one nation, and legitimate checks on the activities of the multinational enterprises. The objective would be to push governments and firms to accept comparative costs as the governing principle of investment decisions, to make explicit exceptions (for example, for certain classes of developing countries), to place limits on the competition among states in bidding for the favors of multinational corporations, and to reduce the likelihood of protectionism against the output from offshore subsidiaries. The OECD Council made a promising start in this direction, with its decision of June 1976 on national treatment and international investment incentives and disincentives. But this decision only began to touch the central issues.[78]

Ensuring access to natural resources is central to the evolution of relations among Europe, Japan, and the United States. Establishing procedures to control runaway plants and prevent investment wars is also important. In these areas, as in other areas of economic, political, and military policy, the United States is likely to find, in the post-cold-war period, that a responsibility for international order will be thrust upon it, for better or worse.

The Soviet Union: Linkage and Détente

A special problem for U.S. foreign policy arises in connection with investment by American multinationals in the communist countries.[79] The issue is most important vis-à-vis the Soviet Union, but similar issues arise in relation to the Eastern European countries.

78. Press release/A(76)20, Organisation for Economic Co-operation and Development, June 21, 1976.

79. See Marshall Goldman, *Détente and Dollars: Doing Business with the Soviets* (Basic Books, 1975); Samuel Pisar, *Coexistence and Commerce: Guidelines for Transactions between East and West* (McGraw-Hill, 1970); John P. Hardt and George D. Holliday, *U.S.-Soviet Commercial Relations: The Interplay of Economics, Technology Transfer, and Diplomacy,* prepared for the Subcommittee on National Security and Scientific Developments, House Committee on Foreign Affairs (GPO, 1973); John P. Hardt, George D. Holliday, and Young C. Kim, *Western Investment in Communist Economies: A Selected Survey on Economic Interdependence,* prepared for Subcommittee on Multinational Corporations, Senate Committee on Foreign Relations (GPO, 1974); Alec Nove, "Can We Buy Détente?" *New York Times Magazine* (October 13, 1974); Franklyn D. Holzman and Robert Legvold, "The Economics and Politics of East-West Relations," in C. Fred Bergsten and Lawrence B. Krause, eds., *World Politics and International Economics* (Brookings Institution, 1975), pp. 275–320.

Since the late 1960s, détente has become mixed with confrontation as the basis of U.S. policy toward the Soviet Union. When properly viewed as a gradual accommodation to each other's interests within a framework of continued competition, détente leads both countries to search for links among their overlapping interests. By developing and implementing such trade-offs, each can pursue its own national interests within a climate of accommodation in which world peace and stability are strengthened. Each must, of course, gain approximately as much as it gives, in terms of its narrow national interests, to satisfy domestic opponents of détente that the policy is in the national interest.[80]

The major objectives the United States seeks through détente are strategic and political: Soviet help in reducing tensions in key trouble spots around the world, now most notably the Middle East; limitations on strategic armaments; cuts in conventional forces in Europe; and, through the intervention of the Congress, liberalization of Soviet policy toward Jewish emigration. The Soviet Union also has obvious interests in reducing world tension and limiting strategic arms, and hence there is the possibility of self-contained negotiation in these areas. Further, it has demonstrated other political interests in détente, such as ratification of Europe's postwar borders through the Conference of European Security and Co-operation.

In addition, many experienced American observers of the Soviet Union believe that economic needs are among the most important of its motivations in pursuing détente.[81] Since the 1970 events in Poland, the Kremlin leadership may be aware of the risk of political instability, even in a controlled society, when popular demands for improved economic conditions (including adequate food supplies) are not met. At the same time, in its bid to position itself in all parts of the world to counter the U.S. presence, the Soviet Union is steadily increasing its strategic and conventional armaments. The Soviet economy has not grown rapidly enough to meet both its consumption and investment needs, and its leadership is confronted with the dilemma of opting for one over the other, and risking, with either choice, major internal problems (including the unseating of the leader-

80. Regarding the Soviet side see Richard Rosecrance, "Détente or Entente?" *Foreign Affairs*, vol. 53 (April 1975), especially pp. 469–74.
81. See, for example, Marshall Shulman, "Toward A Western Philosophy of Coexistence," *Foreign Affairs*, vol. 52 (October 1973), especially pp. 43–44 and 55–56. Shulman recommends a steady but controlled increase in U.S. economic involvement with the Soviet Union, with transfers of higher technology deferred until later stages of the process to keep the Soviets interested in maintaining détente.

ship). This dilemma provides the rationale for a third option: a sharp increase in economic contacts with the west, particularly the United States, to tap sufficient foreign resources to tide the Soviet Union over the present difficult period.

These resources could be sought in several forms. Imports could be expanded, both to provide additional consumer goods for Soviet society and better capital equipment to improve the Soviet's own output of such goods. But the balance-of-payments position of the Soviet Union remains chronically weak and its foreign exchange reserves, low. Sizable and sustained increases in imports would have to be financed either by increased credits abroad or by increased Soviet exports. An increase in exports would require both a considerable improvement in the quality of Soviet output and marketing, and, at least in the United States, liberalization of the traditional, discriminatory tariff barriers against purchases from the Soviet Union.

Perhaps of greatest importance to Soviet economic plans is the availability of western—particularly American—technology. The Soviet Union is rich in both material and human resources, yet its productivity remains disappointingly low. Improved methods are needed in many areas; production (especially in agriculture), transportation, finance, and management. An infusion of better technology is viewed by the Soviets as the best, perhaps only, route to real economic self-sufficiency in the foreseeable future—both through more efficient use of resources and through a growth in exports sufficient to erode the balance-of-payments constraint.

These desiderata led the Soviets to seek to increase their relations with American multinationals. The firms combine a number of the elements sought by the U.S.S.R.: technology, capital, marketing skills, and political clout in Washington for the support of liberal policies toward the Soviet Union. Furthermore, the Soviets are in a strong position to offer an attractive investment climate. Labor is cheap and there are no strikes or unions. The potential market is vast. Raw materials are available. There is no threat of expropriation.

But Soviet policymakers also had to persuade the U.S. government to remove its controls on their dealings with the firms. This, then, became a major Soviet goal in the détente process. Its success was expressed first in the gradual relaxation of U.S. export controls in 1970–71 and finally in the establishment of a joint U.S.-U.S.S.R. commercial commission following the Nixon-Brezhnev summit of May 1972. Since then, investments have expanded steadily in a variety of industries, despite the cooling of the atmosphere brought about by the Angola problem and the American 1976 election campaign, and despite passage of the Jackson amendment to the Trade Act of 1974 (88 Stat. 2056) which resulted in Soviet repudiation of parts of the commercial agreement.

The United States has three major interests in the expansion of its economic ties with the Soviet Union. One is the immediate economic benefits of increased trade and earnings on foreign investments. However, these returns are likely to remain small no matter what happens with détente. Before the U.S.-Soviet wheat deal of 1974, American exports to the Soviet Union were half the size of U.S. trade with Mexico.[82] Periodic droughts and poor harvests in the Russian heartland require periodic purchases of huge amounts of foreign grain, so the Soviet balance of payments may well remain too weak to sustain large remittances of profits and royalties. American natural resource companies operating under coproduction agreements and receiving, as payment, shares of the output to market abroad may not be affected by the balance-of-payments problem. But American manufacturing multinationals, unless they can sell in the west large amounts of Soviet manufactures (which, except in the heavy machinery sector, have never been attractive to western customers), may find that their hard-currency rewards for penetrating Soviet markets are meager.

Even in raw materials investment, the benefits to the United States are likely to be slow in coming. Most of the largest potential projects (the Yakutsk coal or natural gas fields, the Yudokan copper deposits, the Tyumen oil field, or the Urengoi natural gas reserves) are located in inaccessible parts of East or West Siberia where labor is in short supply and transportation costs high. Moreover, Soviet insistence on repaying development loans only after production begins and its reluctance to give financial information to foreigners will retard the opening of these resources. Finally, uncertainty about the dependability of the Soviets in honoring long-term supply contracts could deter large-scale investments.

On the other hand, the Soviets have a history of good conduct in international economic affairs. Their recurrent need to come to western markets for wheat, corn, and soybeans should be an incentive to good commercial behavior. They have a record as cheaters in natural resource cartels, undercutting the oligopoly price in aluminum and petroleum, as

82. For the dimensions of U.S.-Soviet trade, see Goldman, *Détente and Dollars*.

long as the latter could be concealed from OPEC.[83] But even though they could significantly expand exports of oil, natural gas, copper, coal, chrome, zinc, timber, platinum, and palladium, the payoffs to the United States from raw materials projects may only appear far in the future.

Second, expanded economic relations might, over time, develop the same kind of societal interdependencies which now mark relations between the United States and Western Europe. This could reduce hostilities between the superpowers and improve the prospects for the maintenance of world peace. On the other hand, some commentators doubt the evolution of such effects. They note that active economic relations have not in the past prevented conflict (for example, between Germany and France), that the level of U.S.-Soviet economic relations will never be sizable enough to deter either country from risking them if its political interests are involved, that external economic resources may enable the Soviets to postpone internal economic reforms and hence delay convergence with western societies, and that, in any event, centralized Soviet control will inevitably limit the impact of any such interdependencies on Soviet policy.

Indeed, some argue that economic détente will always put the United States at a bargaining disadvantage in view of the greater impact of lobbies in Washington than in Moscow. For many individual American firms, the impetus to establish a subsidiary in the Soviet Union is extremely strong. The Soviet bureaucracy has a long history of favoring particular foreign corporations or individuals over long periods of time (for example, Armand Hammer, Pullman, Ford, General Electric, International Harvester, and Chase Manhattan Bank). To get in on the ground floor in establishing close contacts with Soviet officials and to avoid being preempted by other multinationals, American investors have been willing to compete fiercely to get into Soviet markets. In political terms, this has meant that the American business community has done an abrupt turnabout, from hostility toward the Soviet Union to lobbying for relaxation of restrictions on economic contacts with the Soviet Union. In economic terms, it has meant that American companies have considered initial investment projects as loss leaders to be made up in subsequent years, or as

83. For Soviet dumping of aluminum at cut-rate prices, see Zuhayr Mikdashi, *Business and Government in Extractive Industries* (Cornell University Press, 1975). For Soviet willingness to act as a conduit for OPEC countries (for example, Iraq) who wanted to expand oil output during 1973–74, see Marshall Goldman, "The Soviet Union," *Daedalus* (Fall 1975), pp. 137–38.

raffle tickets on the chance for a privileged place if the economic prospects brighten. Such behavior allowed Soviet authorities to play foreign companies off against one another and led to charges in the United States that American companies want détente at any price and are selling their technology for "nothing" (that is, at marginal cost after years of public and private R&D in the United States).[84] It is clear that economic détente will produce societal interdependencies, but it is unclear whether these interdependencies will do much to support either world peace or the more narrow interests of the United States.

Third, the Soviet desire for increased economic relations provides the United States with a potential lever in the overall détente process. It is possible that the United States might be able to use this lever to achieve some of its major political goals. An important asymmetry appears in the two countries at this point, however. The Soviet government controls all of the issues in détente, both political and economic. Its centralized structure of economic management enables it to exploit effectively the competition among American (and other) multinationals, in pursuit of its purely economic objectives. Although the U.S. government largely controls the political and strategic issues, it clearly does not control all of the economic issues, most notably those concerning the activities of multinational enterprises. This gap in the ability of the U.S. government to manage the economics of détente is particularly important, since the Congress has severely circumscribed the administration's control of the other key economic variables: export credits and the extension of most-favored-nation treatment. The role of the multinationals thus looms large in U.S.-Soviet economic relations, which in turn loom large in U.S.-Soviet relations, in general.

Hence there is a strong case, in terms of both the political and economic interests of the United States, for effective U.S. government control over the activities of American multinationals in the Soviet Union, and indeed throughout the communist world. To be sure, informal controls now exist. Many firms considering investing in the U.S.S.R. contact Washington before they act. In addition, the U.S. government must still license any exports of machinery or technology from the United States (though not from the foreign subsidiaries of American firms). But many projects, in-

84. For the argument that direct investment by American companies provides the Soviet Union with hostage capital, or with a pro-Soviet lobby in the U.S. political system, see "Prepared Statement of Gregory Grossman," in *Soviet Economic Outlook,* Hearings before the Joint Economic Committee, 93:1 (GPO, 1973), p. 143.

cluding some of the largest, proceed with little or no coordination with overall U.S. policy. And much of the high-level government attention paid the issue consists simply of exhorting the Soviet Union to provide an open door to American investors. There is now no government control over these important levers of détente, either substantive actions of the firms or, often of equal importance, their timing.

The relation between foreign investment by American companies and American policy toward the Soviet Union thus involves a dialectic between two of the central themes developed in this chapter. On the one hand, the potential economic benefits of multinational corporate investment and the potential political influence of the multinational corporations may be significant forces in restraining the narrow nationalistic and antagonistic impulses of both home and host countries. On the other hand, multinational corporations can become hostages to host-country interests and, if left unsupervised, may act as ambassadors of host-country rather than home-country policies.

These issues are particularly acute in the case of the penetration of American multinationals into the Soviet Union, because the process is being encouraged by both the United States and the Soviet Union for explicitly political reasons and because the Soviet government, with monopolist-monopsonist authority over the operations of foreign companies, is in a strong position to exploit the competition among multinational firms (for economic advantage) and the decentralized structure of the U.S. political system (for political advantage). Properly supervised by the American government, American multinationals can be an important tool in managing relations with the Soviet Union in an era of détente. Left to themselves, American multinationals may let many of the economic and political benefits of détente slip away.[85]

85. Raymond Vernon thus notes that "The distribution of the economic benefits from détente may be so unbalanced as to threaten the process of détente itself" and regards the most important question that proponents of economic détente must answer is "how far the United States is prepared to centralize and control its trade with the Soviet Union in order to ensure that the interaction between the two economies brings adequate benefits to the U.S. side." See his "Apparatchiks and Entrepreneurs: U.S.-Soviet Economic Relations," *Foreign Affairs*, vol. 52 (January 1974), pp. 250 and 261.

PART FOUR

Toward a New American Policy

CHAPTER TWELVE

Foundations for a New Policy

OUR CONCLUSIONS in parts one and two of this volume present a mixed picture of the impact of American multinationals on the economy and foreign policy of the United States. On the positive side, multinationals generally enhance global economic welfare—some of which accrues directly to the United States—by shifting the location of production according to comparative advantage. They contribute modestly to improving international monetary arrangements, for their transactions push countries toward equilibrium exchange rates and have hastened the adoption of a system of more flexible exchange rates. Multinationals generally promote development in the poorer countries by injecting new resources, thereby reducing both unemployment and technological shortcomings. And in general, they have supported a responsible foreign policy.

There are also some costs. First, foreign investment appears to increase the firms' U.S. market power. Second, extractive multinationals with equity involvement in natural resources find it difficult to support the national interest of the United States as an importing country, difficult to maximize output of natural resources, and difficult to diversify geographical origin. Third, tax revenues are lost to the United States because (within limits) firms can arbitrarily allocate their costs between home and host countries.

In two of the most hotly debated areas—jobs and foreign policy—the multinationals' impact on the United States is mixed. Their investments seem, on balance, neither to create nor to destroy an appreciable number of American jobs. They have little net effect on U.S. balance of trade or balance of payments. There is no discernible impact on the distribution of

449

income, nor is there reason to believe that there will be any. The firms seem to play only a small direct role in U.S. relations with other industrialized countries. Their effect on U.S. relations with developing countries must be assessed by weighing their contributions to development against concerns that their activities reinforce market imperfections. And they probably have only a small net impact on world trade policy, as their support for a liberal U.S. approach is partially offset by their support for a protectionist approach for some host countries.

It is clearly impossible to draw up a neat balance sheet of these conclusions and thus to determine whether foreign direct investment by American multinationals is good or bad for the country. Besides the problem of defining the national interest, many of the conclusions are qualitative. Many must be hedged. Indeed, one of our principal findings is that foreign direct investment is an extremely heterogeneous phenomenon. With respect to jobs and market concentration, for example, major differences exist among and within manufacturing industries.

Generalizations (including ours) about effects of foreign direct investment thus must be treated with extreme care, as must calls for sweeping policy approaches. From both narrow and broad perspectives on American national interests, there is no case for blanket restrictions on foreign direct investment and no case for blanket support, let alone subsidies. The imperialist and mercantilist schools are wrong in their belief that American multinationals and the American government together bring great benefits to the United States at the expense of host countries. The AFL-CIO and the multinationals err in attributing pervasive ills or vast virtues, respectively, to foreign direct investment. The sovereignty-at-bay and global-reach schools are wrong in their conclusions that the firms are dominant actors for good or ill, respectively, in both home and host countries. The beliefs of each of these groups on the effect of foreign direct investment on the welfare of home and host countries are shown below:

Group	Home countries	Host countries
Imperialist	positive	negative
Mercantilist	positive	negative
Sovereignty-at-bay	positive	positive
Multinationals	positive	positive
Global-reach	negative	negative
AFL-CIO	negative	positive

An alternative is to support investments that offer benefits for the United States and discourage those that appear negative. We recommend such an alternative for investments that maximize output of raw materials or enhance the development of poor countries. But as a general rule, a fine tuning of U.S. policy toward direct investment is difficult to do well. Selective policies, such as DISC, invite pleading for favoritism by vested interests. The broader national interest is often badly served by such programs. Indeed, a finely tuned policy is inconceivable without fundamental changes in our basic economic system, changes that cannot be justified by the need for better policy control over American multinationals.[1]

At present, U.S. policy toward foreign direct investment has much less impact on the national interest than is usually supposed. Tax policy is essentially neutral: the foreign tax credit simply avoids double taxation of the same income; deferral and the overall method for calculating the foreign tax credit promote foreign investment, but in the aggregate they are offset by the investment tax credit and the asset depreciation range, which favor domestic investment. The insurance and guaranty programs of the Overseas Private Investment Corporation pay for themselves. The U.S. government's use of American multinationals as instruments of foreign policy through the extraterritorial application of U.S. law (affecting such issues as trade with China and Cuba) has declined. This declining intervention has even extended to the congressional limits on U.S. foreign aid policy embodied in the Hickenlooper and Gonzalez amendments.

Principles for U.S. Policy

Future policy should be explicitly neutral toward foreign direct investment, neither encouraging nor discouraging it. Foreign direct investment should be guided to the maximum extent by market forces; the goal should be the maximization of global welfare. Other national policy instruments can more properly be directed at equitable distribution of world wealth

1. If the United States were to adopt the comprehensive economic and social planning advocated by Richard J. Barnet and Ronald E. Müller, *Global Reach: The Power of the Multinational Corporations* (Simon and Schuster, 1974), esp. chap 13, it would obviously include comprehensive regulation of multinational enterprises. Barnet and Müller, however, do not examine the need for such planning nor the problems associated with it.

and income among countries and among the people within countries.[2] Neutrality does not mean noninvolvement by the U.S. government in the affairs of American multinationals. First, the government must provide the proper economic and political environment for multinational firms. For example, any sizable and prolonged distortion of exchange-rates skews the flow of foreign direct investment and its effects on different countries. Protectionist trade policies induce investments that market forces alone would never support. A laissez-faire antitrust policy may permit accumulation of excessive market power.[3] Hostility between producers and consumers of raw materials disrupts productive investment in the extractive industries. Inadequate policies toward development in the poorer countries pervert the impact of foreign direct investment on income distribution, foreign exchange positions, and other such concerns.

Second, in the absence of international rules regulating national policies toward direct investment, the United States has an affirmative obligation to protect U.S. national interests from the adverse impact of other countries' policies. Host-country governments induce multinationals to locate in their countries by offering tax breaks and other incentives. They play an increasingly major role in determining the ongoing production plans of U.S.-owned subsidiaries.

Other governments attract plants and production with export subsidies and import quotas. In the past, virtually no one in the U.S. government paid attention to the negotiations between American multinationals and host-country governments, let alone their effects on the U.S. economy.

Other home countries may seek to provide their multinationals competitive advantage over American multinationals. Earlier chapters review a number of such cases in both raw materials (direct support by European governments for European oil multinationals) and manufacturing (ex-

2. James W. McKie, ed., *Social Responsibility and the Business Predicament* (Brookings Institution, 1974), summarizes a Brookings conference on the social responsibility of business that concluded that business "cannot accept general responsibility for problems that lie any appreciable distance outside its traditional economic concerns; that is, maximizing efficiency and growth" (p. 15). Indeed, McKie concludes that the ability of a government to use a multinational for its own purposes is a major "test of adequate political development" for a country (p. 15).

3. Stefan H. Robock bases "The Case for Home Country Controls Over Multinational Firms," *Columbia Journal of World Business,* vol. 9 (Summer 1974), p. 75, "on the reality that the goals of the multinational firm and the goals of its home country are not identical," on such issues as accumulation of excessive market power.

emption from domestic taxation of export income in some European countries). Thus, the U.S. government may need to counter intervention by both home and host governments in the foreign direct investment process.

Third, the U.S. government may have a responsibility to help counter the adverse effects on particular sectors of U.S. society of policies adopted for the benefit of that society as a whole. The Department of Defense actively helps firms, workers, and communities hurt by changes in military procurement. Likewise, trade adjustment assistance provides all three sectors with financial support and training for new endeavors.[4] A program could be enacted to pursue similar goals for dislocations caused by particular foreign direct investments.

Beyond these three government responsibilities toward foreign direct investment and its impact on U.S. interests, there are several areas where changes in U.S. policies could enhance the contribution of such investment to important national objectives. New governmental approaches could alter the behavior of extractive multinationals in ways that would enhance the prospect of adequate investment in industrial raw materials. Antitrust policy should consider the international activities of American multinationals much more comprehensively, both in terms of their impact on domestic market power and in terms of providing a potential source of new competition for U.S. producers. American negotiating leverage with the Soviet Union could be enhanced by more active policies toward the American multinationals that seek business there. Overall U.S. relations with the Third and Fourth Worlds would be improved by more sensitive policies toward the developmental impact of foreign direct investment.

In most of these areas, the economic and foreign policy interests of the United States lead in similar directions. Pushing the extractive multinationals toward nonequity forms of involvement with producing countries, for example, should both expand output and reduce political tension. Maintaining the present balance in tax treatment between domestic and foreign income avoids distortions in the decision between investing at home or abroad and avoids, also, the conflicts with host countries that would result if U.S. policy were consciously to encourage or discourage foreign direct investment. A program of investment adjustment assistance

4. Detailed case studies can be found in Charles R. Frank, Jr., with the assistance of Stephanie Levinson, *Foreign Trade and Domestic Aid* (Brookings Institution, 1977).

would avoid domestic economic dislocation and facilitate the investments sought by host countries.

In some cases, however, economic and foreign policy considerations will clash. An immediate conflict between the host country and the United States would come with any overt U.S. reaction to the host's investment incentives or its performance requirements. An antitrust policy that explicitly regulated the foreign activities of American multinationals would also ruffle feathers in other countries. The United States must tread carefully between the domestic and foreign constituencies involved in all foreign direct investment issues. Other countries must be consulted both when domestic considerations are given priority and when long-run international considerations are involved; internal groups must be kept apprised of developments when external concerns are deemed to be overriding.

More broadly, virtually every aspect of a comprehensive U.S. policy toward foreign direct investment must comprise both domestic and international measures. The international nature of the issue limits the extent to which either type of action, alone, can be satisfactory or effective. This principle does not preclude the need for unilateral steps by the United States in some cases. They may be necessary to galvanize other countries toward serious negotiations on international arrangements, for they give credence to the possibility that the United States may otherwise "go it alone." Domestic actions should be structured, however, so that they can be folded into international arrangements, when and if they are negotiated.[5]

At the international level, two types of collaboration are needed, among home countries and between home countries and host countries. Some policy objectives can be met through agreements or informal cooperation among home countries. An important example is harmonization of the tax treatment of foreign income; another is cooperation to enhance the contribution of foreign direct investment to expanding world output

5. There are precedents in the trade field. For example, section 122(d)(3) of the Trade Act of 1974 authorizes the President to discriminate in applying an import surcharge to protect the U.S. balance of payments; but "after such time when there enters into force for the United States new rules regarding the application of surcharges as part of a reform of internationally agreed balance-of-payments adjustment procedures, the exemption [from MFN treatment] shall be applied consistently with such new international rules" (88 Stat. 1989).

of industrial raw materials. Indeed, home-country collaboration would be helpful in virtually every policy area and is far easier to achieve than global agreements for three reasons. First, they have similar approaches to multinational firms because of their general sympathies for private enterprise and market-oriented economic policies, and they have basically harmonious relations. These contrast with the *dirigiste* economic policies of socialist countries and many developing countries and with the politically tense relations between them and home countries. Second, host-country attacks on home countries, both directly and through their multinationals, tend to push home countries together if only for defensive reasons. (Home countries are, broadly speaking, in the industrialized North, so the issue is an important component of the North-South debate despite the fact that all Northern countries are also hosts to multinationals, and that some see themselves primarily as hosts.) Third, eleven countries account for virtually all of the world's outgoing foreign direct investment, simplifying considerably the complexities of the negotiating process. Meaningful home-country cooperation was presaged in 1976 by their ability to take the initial negotiating steps through the Organisation for Economic Cooperation and Development. However, since the United States is the home country for close to half of total foreign direct investment, it will clearly have to take the lead if such cooperation is to proceed.

International arrangements are also needed between home and host countries. Indeed, issues likely to be the most internationally significant both economically and politically—such as incentives offered by host governments to multinationals and the performance levels they require of them—can be handled satisfactorily only through such arrangements. Actions by home countries, as a group, affect host countries, and if taken without involving host countries, they may intensify tension between the two groups, which, in turn, can both cause substantive problems among home countries and make them more difficult to solve.

Furthermore, many home countries are also major host countries. The United States is the world's second largest host country (after Canada) as well as the largest home country. Foreign direct investment within the United States has aroused concern about a "Japanese invasion" in the early seventies and an "Arab invasion" in the mid-seventies. These concerns proved largely unfounded—and must have been quite strange, anyway, to a world that for three decades had witnessed an "American

456   *American Multinationals and American Interests*

invasion"—but U.S. policy toward foreign direct investment must nevertheless consider its role as host as well as home country.

The United Kingdom and Germany are also both home and host countries and would be reluctant to compartmentalize their roles in working out and implementing international agreements. They would obviously seek to balance their interests on the two sides of the equation. Hence it will probably be necessary to mesh home-country and host-country interests even in working out arrangements limited to home countries, as indeed the OECD did in 1973–76.

The objectives of international arrangements are twofold. One is to limit the unilateral involvement of governments, both home and host, in the process of foreign direct investment. Such involvement distorts the process and raises both economic and political difficulties for some or all of the parties involved. Indeed, much of the case for the unilateral involvement of the U.S. government relates to the need to counter interventions by other governments. International agreement on the acceptable scope for such involvement would clearly be the best means for achieving this objective.

The other goal is to limit the activities of the multinationals, again for both economic and political reasons.[6] There are cases in which the limited, national jurisdictions of individual governments make it difficult for them to exercise effective countervailing power; allocation of tax revenue, for example, or the threat of excess market power. Because of their limitations, governments should recognize their interest in agreeing on common rules. The very magnitude of foreign direct investment, both in absolute terms and relative to even the largest economies, assures that both home and host countries will realize their potential to disrupt economic and political developments and thus will view it as a perennial source of political tension within countries and among them.

It is clear that national governments will never forgo their unilateral authority to control private investors unless they are convinced that such control can be exercised, where necessary, at the international level. In-

6. Raymond F. Vernon, "Foreign Operations," in McKie, *Social Responsibility and the Business Predicament,* rightly concludes that multinational business itself will not seriously consider international rules to govern its activities "unless and until the unilateral and uncoordinated acts of numerous national governments seem seriously to threaten the vitality of the multinational enterprises. Then, a system of multinational public control may be seen as the lesser threat" (p. 310). It is the argument of this book that such a threat is rapidly approaching.

deed, the European countries insisted on just such linkage during the OECD effort. They required agreement on a code of conduct for the firms not only as quid pro quo for the U.S. request for reaffirmation of the principle of national treatment for multinational enterprises, but also as a barrier to the use of incentives and disincentives to foreign direct investment. The developing countries feel even more strongly about such linkage. In short, effective *international* countervailing power is necessary if individual countries are to be expected to limit their exercise of *national* countervailing power.

The Analogy to Trade Policy

To a large extent, these policy principles emulate the principles that came to govern international trade relations in the postwar period. Those policies derived largely from the disastrous events of the 1930s. During the interwar years, trade wars erupted as individual nations sought to tilt the benefits of trade flows—then the primary means of international economic exchange—in their direction. To do so, they adopted several types of policies. To reduce unemployment, countries barred imports through quotas, raised import prices through tariffs, and subsidized exports. When supply shortages arose in the late 1930s, export quotas were enacted to keep goods at home. Initial moves in one country quickly spread to others. Private firms contributed to the conflict, by forming cartels and by dumping their products on depressed world markets; these steps too were met by retaliation, including antidumping duties. As a result, the Great Depression was broadened and deepened,[7] totalitarianism increased in several countries, and political relations among nations deteriorated further.

The postwar economic order was thus structured to include comprehensive national policies and international rules for governing trade among nations. The basic objective of those rules was to provide the maximum scope for market forces to determine trade flows. Import quotas were largely prohibited; if tariffs were raised, other countries were given

7. See particularly Ragnar Nurkse, *International Currency Experience: Lessons of the Inter-war Period* (League of Nations, 1944) and Hal B. Lary and Associates, *The United States in the World Economy*, U.S. Department of Commerce, Economic Series no. 23 (Government Printing Office, 1943).

the explicit right to retaliate. Both export subsidies and export controls were also prohibited, though with many more exceptions. The initial steps were (a) preventing the creation of new barriers to trade and (b) requiring public notification, by the responsible governments, of existing barriers.

Subsequently, trade was to be liberalized in a series of negotiations governed by two basic principles: most-favored-nation treatment, through which all countries were to be treated equally and regional blocs discouraged; and reciprocity, to assure that all countries benefited equally from the liberalizations. A standing international organization, the General Agreement on Tariffs and Trade (GATT), was created to enforce the new rules and provide a forum for multilateral surveillance over the trade policies of member countries. Any country aggrieved by the trade measures of another had the right to protest through the GATT and, in the absence of adequate compensation through corresponding reductions in barriers to its other exports, to retaliate.[8]

The rules to check import controls have been notably successful in avoiding anything approaching the clashes of the interwar years and in contributing to the unparalleled economic progress of the first postwar generation.[9] Tariffs declined dramatically during the postwar period. So, too, did the use of import quotas. For most of the period, trade issues remained largely separate from the high politics of security issues, both internationally and within most national governments.[10]

To be sure, the rules and institutions governing international trade have not been perfect. The concerns of the developing countries have received inadequate attention, although they too have benefited from the steady liberalization of world trade. Methods of controlling nontariff barriers to trade, such as import quotas, commodity agreements, and orderly marketing agreements, have been slow in developing.[11] Nevertheless, the experience of the past thirty years demonstrates the immense value of interna-

8. Detailed description and analysis of the GATT can be found in John Jackson, *World Trade and the Law of GATT* (Bobbs-Merrill, 1969).

9. For a recent review see Gerard and Victoria Curzon, "The Management of Trade Relations in the GATT," in Andrew Shonfeld, ed., *International Economic Relations of the Western World 1959–1971* (London: Oxford University Press, 1976), pp. 143–241.

10. Richard N. Cooper, "Trade Policy is Foreign Policy," *Foreign Policy*, no. 9 (Winter 1972–73), pp. 18–36.

11. See Robert E. Baldwin, *Nontariff Distortions of International Trade* (Brookings Institution, 1970).

tional rules and institutions in checking economic costs and economic and political conflicts that arise from international economic exchange.

Our basically liberal trade policy does admit some apparent exceptions. When foreign countries provide export subsidies or foreign exporters dump their goods on the American market, the United States will retaliate. Likewise, import barriers can be raised when the national security is threatened or when domestic industries are injured. But these exceptions represent less a retreat from a basic principle and more a safety valve to relieve the occasionally intolerable pressure of a free trade policy.

Both of these avenues to import relief require those seeking protection to meet clear criteria through standardized procedures, and as a result, there has been relatively little deviation from the basic trend toward freer trade. The major deviations have occurred, in fact, through the negotiations of "voluntary" export restraints with foreign countries, which enabled several administrations to circumvent the procedural and substantive requirements installed by the Congress as the basis of U.S. trade policy. To be sure, political pressure affects the outcome even when the objective procedures are followed. But, on the whole, these rules and procedures provide a rational policy framework within which the United States, contrary to its history and the expectations of many observers, maintains an essentially liberal trade policy and world leadership in free international economic exchange.

A major innovation was added to U.S. trade policy in the Trade Expansion Act of 1962, which authorizes the President to give "trade adjustment assistance" to workers or firms injured by imports, in lieu of erecting barriers to the imports. This program is based on the principle that individual sectors of society should be compensated for the adverse effects on them of policies adopted to promote the national interest.[12] In 1974, assistance was also authorized for communities adversely affected by imports.

The problems created by foreign direct investment are quite similar to those of international trade. Multinationals determine the patterns of both trade and investment; their restrictive practices affect both. For example,

12. This program was ineffective in its early years, however, for a variety of reasons. It was greatly liberalized by the Trade Act of 1974, and in the first year over $200 million was spent to implement it, more than four times that spent in the previous thirteen years of the program. For a thorough analysis of how the program could be made to work effectively see Frank, *Foreign Trade and Domestic Aid.*

parent firms may limit their subsidiaries' exports and require them to purchase components or raw materials from the parent (or vice versa). In addition, government policies play an increasingly important role in determining investment flows. Some of these measures include trade policies—tariffs or quotas on imported goods to induce import-substituting investment. Tax incentives are similar to export subsidies; both seek to increase domestic investment and employment at the expense of economic activity abroad. The minimum export quotas imposed by host countries are an even closer analogue to export subsidies, since both directly aim to improve trade balance. Value-added requirements force firms wishing to sell locally to produce locally, but these requirements are wholly uncovered by the rules governing international trade. In sum, host and home countries seek to tilt the benefits of international investment in their directions, just as in the past they sought to tilt the benefits of trade through import and export measures.

Two leading students of foreign direct investment believe that such trade policies are now "the biggest nontariff barrier to international trade."[13] In this sense, trade and investment are inextricably linked in the world economy of the 1970s. New national policies and international rules to govern the foreign investment policies of both host and home countries are badly needed.[14] Without them, conflict among nations could produce investment wars akin to the trade wars of the 1930s.[15]

13. A. E. Safarian and Joel Bell, "Issues Raised by National Control of the Multinational Corporation," *Columbia Journal of World Business* (Winter 1973), p. 16.

14. Paul M. Goldberg and Charles P. Kindleberger, "Toward a GATT for Investment: A Proposal for Supervision of the International Corporation," *Law and Policy in International Business*, vol. 2 (Summer 1970), pp. 295–325, proposed a General Agreement on International Corporations (GAIC). Their proposal, however, was limited in its range, providing only a forum and procedures rather than firm rules and obligations. It explicitly ignored most host-country concerns and implicitly ignored all home-country concerns and the potential of a clash between the policies of home and host governments.

15. See C. Fred Bergsten, "Coming Investment Wars?" *Foreign Affairs*, vol. 53 (October 1974). John Dunning, "The Future of the Multinational Enterprise," *Lloyd's Bank Review*, no. 113 (July 1974), pp. 15–32, likens the current investment situation to the trade situation of the 1930s, both home and host countries pursuing unilateral investment policies, as they did trade policies, then. He predicts that they will go through a phase of bilateral policies before arriving at the multilateral measures needed to avoid the risk that international production will "seize up" as did trade in the 1930s. See also David Robertson, "International Regulations for Multinational Enterprises," *Pacific Community*, vol. 6 (January 1975), pp. 300–13.

CHAPTER THIRTEEN

Proposals for a New Policy

THE FOREGOING ANALYSIS of the ways American multinationals affect the United States, economically and politically, leads us to conclude that American policy needs reform in six specific areas: taxation; compensation for domestic workers, firms or communities hurt by foreign investment; antitrust; insurance and guarantees through the Overseas Private Investment Corporation (OPIC); host-country expropriation; and investment in the Soviet Union. In addition to these six specific areas, other broad areas of U.S. international economic policy should be reconsidered in view of the increasing importance of multinational corporations. Of particular concern are international monetary and trading arrangements, access to imported raw materials, and the economic development of the poorest countries. Virtually all these issues call for both national and international initiatives by the United States.

Taxation of Foreign Income

As a general rule, U.S. tax policy should be neutral, seeking neither to promote nor to discourage American corporations from investing abroad. As we saw in chapter six, current tax policy provides a surprisingly close approximation to neutrality, at least in the aggregate.

The foreign tax credit, viewed by some as an unwarranted subsidy to foreign investment, has become the generally accepted method for eliminating international double taxation by countries taxing the worldwide income of domestic citizens or residents. Having found in the course of

461

this study no reason for either exempting foreign income from taxation or for subjecting it to double taxation, and seeing no realistic alternative to the foreign tax credit in this regard, we believe that the credit should remain the cornerstone of U.S. tax policy.

The neutrality of current U.S. tax policy is, however, almost an accident. In most developed countries, income and dividend withholding taxes combine to give a rate of income taxation approximating that in the United States. Although many developing and some developed countries have very low effective tax rates, the collective importance of these low-tax countries is still too small to have a substantial impact on the overall foreign taxes paid by American multinationals. The benefit of deferral is smaller than most people seem to believe and is roughly offset by the failure of foreign investment to qualify for the domestic investment tax credit or the ADR (asset depreciation range) acceleration of class-life depreciation.

Current U.S. tax policy is, moreover, neutral in the aggregate, but not in individual cases. Under the overall method of calculating the limitation on the foreign tax credit, U.S. investors can combine taxes paid in high-tax countries with those in low-tax countries. German taxes, for example, can be used to shelter South Korean income from U.S. taxation. Thus, the *dividends* from low-tax countries are sheltered from U.S. taxation by tax-credit averaging, while the *retained earnings* are protected by deferral. In this sense, the statement that U.S. tax policy is already roughly neutral has a hollow ring.

For political as well as economic reasons, U.S. policy should seek neutrality at a lower level of aggregation than it now achieves. Accordingly, the proposals outlined below would repeal deferral and would impose separate limitations for high-tax countries and for low-tax countries but would extend the investment tax credit and ADR to foreign investment in each group of countries. The net effect of all these changes taken together would be to eliminate the tax incentive to invest in, or transfer taxable income to, low-tax countries.

Deferral

Eliminating deferral is a critical first step toward eradicating the ability of taxes to divert new investment to low-tax countries. Although the United States has a real interest in allowing U.S. investors to locate new investment where wage and other costs can be minimized, it has no interest in reinforcing those economic incentives with artificial tax advantages. Investments which would not be undertaken but for the tax savings should be discouraged.

Eliminating deferral would also have a salutary effect on transfer-pricing practices. A modern multinational has myriad transactions with foreign affiliates: multinational sourcing of production has created a substantial flow of intracompany exports; captive insurance companies are increasingly used to collect premiums from, and insure risks of, the national affiliates of a single enterprise; patents, trade secrets, brand names, and other intangibles are sold or licensed within the same multinational family. Section 482 of the Internal Revenue Code allows the Service to challenge the transfer prices used in these intrafirm transactions when those prices diverge from an arm's-length standard. But with so many transactions to scrutinize and with market prices for nonmarket transactions so difficult to determine, the opportunities for tax avoidance are large and growing. If deferral were eliminated and earnings subject to the same rate of taxation wherever they arose, the incentive to manipulate transfer prices to the detriment of U.S. tax payments would be substantially reduced.

As long as foreign income is taxed less than domestic income, U.S. corporations also have an incentive to borrow in U.S. capital markets and finance foreign investment with U.S. equity, rather than locally borrowed funds. Interest deducted from U.S. income saves more taxes worldwide than an identical deduction against a lesser taxed foreign subsidiary's income. By shifting the location of new borrowings to foreign subsidiaries, eliminating deferral will indirectly raise U.S. tax revenues.

The Overall Method of Limiting the Foreign Tax Credit

A limitation on the foreign tax credit prevents multinational corporations from using foreign tax credits to avoid paying U.S. taxes on their domestic, U.S. income. Few features of U.S. tax policy have undergone more frequent changes than the method of calculating this limitation. From 1961 to 1975, U.S. corporations could choose between a separate limitation for each country in which they earned income and a single, overall limitation. In 1975, the per-country option was repealed for petroleum companies to prevent their writing North Sea (and other) drilling costs off against domestic, U.S. income while simultaneously claiming a full foreign tax credit for payments to OPEC countries.[1] In 1976, all investors lost the per-country option (except hard-mineral companies, which will retain the option until 1980).[2]

Exclusive reliance on an overall limitation was, we believe, a step in the wrong direction. The primary virtue of a per-country limitation was that excess tax credits from one country could not be used to shelter from U.S. taxation income from another country. The averaging under an overall limitation protects low-tax dividends from taxation, just as deferral protects low-tax retained earnings from taxation. Thus, the overall limitation is objectionable for the same reasons that deferral is.

The overall limitation was not the only way, or even the best way, of preventing the oil companies from deducting foreign drilling and development costs from domestic, U.S. income. Like other investments, these costs can and should be capitalized and amortized over the life of the relevant investment (in this case, the foreign oil field). With a proper matching of income and deductions, the per-country limitation need not have come under the attack it did.

A more telling objection to the per-country limitation is its administrative complexity. A company (and the Internal Revenue Service auditor) must determine the exact national origin of all foreign income. Transfer prices for transactions among all the foreign affiliates, not just between the U.S. parent and its overseas subsidiaries, must conform to an arm's-length standard. Whether the companies or the Internal Revenue Service have the personnel to administer this system fairly and effectively is debatable.

The problem is not as severe, however, as it might appear. Foreign-source income need not be put into a separate basket for each country, but only into a high-tax basket and a low-tax basket. German income could be grouped with French income in a high-tax basket, while South Korean income is put with Taiwanese income in a low-tax basket. The only transactions whose transfer prices must be carefully scrutinized are those between a high-tax and a low-tax country (for example, tax-exempt exports from Ireland to other Common Market countries, or insurance premiums from high-tax countries to an affiliate in the Bahamas). For all

1. See the Tax Reduction Act of 1975, 89 Stat. 54.
2. Tax Reform Act of 1976, 90 Stat. 1620–1624.

intents and purposes, this two-basket approach would work as well as the more cumbersome per-country method.

Finally, an argument in favor of keeping both deferral and the overall limitation is that their repeal would be matched by an increase in foreign taxes. What does the United States gain, it is often asked, from encouraging foreign countries to increase their taxes on U.S. investors? The answer is that neither of our recommendations are based primarily on a direct revenue gain for the U.S. Treasury. Our ultimate objective is to eliminate the impact of taxes on the location of new investment or the allocation of taxable income among countries. Only in certain cases, such as development-promoting investments in the poorest of the developing countries, does the United States want to keep the foreign tax rate low. But these special cases can be better addressed through the specific measures discussed below than by allowing deferral and the overall limitation for all investments, regardless of location or type.

DISC, the Investment Tax Credit, and ADR

The provision for domestic international sales corporations (DISC) was introduced in 1971 as part of President Nixon's New Economic Policy. It was scaled down in 1976, and in early 1978 President Carter proposed its elimination. DISC was originally rationalized as necessary not only to remedy a large balance-of-trade deficit but also to offset the impact of deferral on an American multinational's choice between foreign and domestic production. Since 1971, the balance of trade has cycled from deficit to surplus to deficit to surplus and now back to deficit again. According to a recent Treasury Department study,[3] however, DISC added only $1.0–$2.5 billion to U.S. exports in 1974, at a total tax cost of $1.2 billion. In view of the high cost and limited benefits of DISC, repealing deferral would provide more than adequate justification for repealing DISC.

If deferral were repealed and the overall limitation modified, the balance of tax incentives would clearly favor investing in the United States rather than overseas: domestic investment qualifies for the investment tax credit and the ADR acceleration of depreciation, while foreign investment

3. U.S. Treasury Department, *The Operation and Effect of the Domestic International Sales Legislation, 1975 Annual Report* (April 1977).

does not. To achieve a neutral tax system, not one biased toward investment in the United States, foreign investment should qualify for the investment tax credit and ADR.

The two-basket method described above would apply, also, to the extension of the investment tax credit and ADR to foreign investment. Foreign countries would be put into the high-tax or the low-tax category by comparing foreign to U.S. taxes for the typical American investor. For simplicity, the designation of countries might apply to all U.S. investors, rather than depending on each company's tax situation. The net result of separating high-tax countries from low-tax countries in this way would be to exempt the income from high-tax countries from further U.S. taxation, while extending to low-tax countries the benefits of the investment tax credit and ADR, but not the larger benefits of deferral and tax-credit averaging. This system would achieve an important dimension of tax neutrality that our current system does not.

Promoting Specific U.S. Objectives

In two specific areas, access to raw materials and aiding development of the poorer countries, the United States may need to deviate from its general principle of tax neutrality. The cardinal U.S. goal in raw materials is to expand output and diversify existing sources of supply. Equity investments by American multinationals in producing raw materials appears, however, to increase the instability of the foreign investment climate and to undercut the ultimate objective (see chapter five). By contrast, nonequity commitments, such as management service contracts, better serve the national interest. Accordingly, genuine service income should continue to qualify for a full foreign tax credit subject only to the limitation outlined above, but the credit for taxes on equity investments should be gradually phased out.

With respect to promoting economic development of the poorest countries, we recommend some form of tax sparing. Tax sparing is not necessary for the more advanced developing countries, which have little trouble attracting U.S. investment. But the poorest countries of the Fourth World need all the help they can get, including tax sparing. Tax sparing could take several forms: credit for taxes forgiven by the foreign government, reassignment of the country from the low-tax to the high-tax category (presuming the low-tax category would otherwise be appropriate), and/

or the continuation of deferral. The particular form of tax sparing should be tailored to individual countries through appropriate bilateral tax treaties.

An Escape Clause for Foreign Direct Investment

Our analysis throughout this volume concludes that, on balance, foreign direct investment by American multinationals is not adverse to most aggregate U.S. economic interests. However, it indicates that there are numerous criteria, including employment and the balance of payments, on which specific foreign direct investments may be adverse to particular U.S. interests. Within the general policy of continued freedom for foreign direct investment, a mechanism to assess the impact of specific investments on such variables and to provide policy responses in selected cases is needed. No such mechanism exists today.

Such a mechanism should provide explicit criteria against which to judge whether a foreign direct investment (a) enhances or hurts the aggregate national interest and (b) injures particular domestic interests. It should contain procedural safeguards to assure that all interested parties have an opportunity to present their views before an impartial, technically competent, fact-finding agency. The escape clause, a central feature of U.S. trade policy for over forty years, provides an apt precedent for what is needed regarding foreign direct investment.[4] Within the context of a basically liberal trade policy, individual U.S. firms or workers can petition for temporary relief from increased imports. They submit the factual and analytical justification for their case to the U.S. International Trade Commission (formerly the Tariff Commission), which hears the views of interested parties—importers, consumers, and the U.S. representatives of the foreign exporters—and reports to the President (a) whether they believe the petitioners have in fact been injured by imports or are threatened with such injury and (b) if so, what remedy should be applied. Trade laws spell out the criteria against which injury is tested; for example, "with respect to serious injury, the significant idling of productive facilities in the industry, the inability of a significant number of firms to operate at a rea-

4. This approach was first suggested in C. Fred Bergsten, "The Multinational Firm: Bane or Boon?, Discussion," *Journal of Finance*, vol. 28, no. 2 (May 1973), pp. 461–62.

468 *American Multinationals and American Interests*

sonable level of profit, and significant unemployment or underemployment within the industry; with respect to threat of serious injury, a decline in sales, a higher and growing inventory, and a downward trend in production, profits, wages, or employment (or increasing underemployment) in the domestic industry concerned."[5]

When the commission finds that the imports have in fact caused injury, it forwards its analysis and recommendation to the White House. Final decisions are left to the President, on the grounds that only he is in a position to judge the impact of trade restrictions on the overall U.S. economy and on overall U.S. foreign policy.[6] Since 1962, the President has had three choices in acting on injury findings by the commission: do nothing; impose new import barriers; and/or provide adjustment assistance to the injured firms, workers, or communities. Import barriers erected under the escape clause are temporary, although renewable.[7]

Trade adjustment assistance already applies to some adjustment problems arising from foreign direct investment. The program treats imports into the United States from the foreign subsidiaries of American multinationals like all other imports. The Trade Act of 1974, in authorizing assistance for communities (but not for workers or firms), made them eligible upon a determination by the Secretary of Commerce "that the transfer of firms or subdivisions of firms located in such area to foreign countries have contributed importantly to the total or partial separations or threats thereof."[8]

There is a recent precedent for such coverage. Export displacement was an explicit trigger for assistance under the Automotive Products Trade

5. Trade Act of 1974, 88 Stat. 2012; chap. 1 of Title II of the Trade Act of 1974, Public Law 93–618 (88 Stat. 2011–18) spells out the entire escape clause process. It changes several parallel provisions of the Trade Expansion Act of 1962, particularly by reducing the degree to which imports must be shown to cause the injury to U.S. parties and by eliminating the requirement that the import increases must be caused by U.S. trade concessions.

6. As part of the trend toward closer congressional oversight of the President's conduct of foreign policy, however, the Trade Act of 1974 requires the President to justify any differences, in terms of the national economic interest, between his decisions and the recommendations of the International Trade Commission. The act authorizes the Congress to impose the commission's recommendation by a simple majority vote of both houses within ninety days.

7. Under the Trade Act of 1974, relief can extend for five years. Phasing out begins after three years "to the extent feasible," with one three-year extension permitted (88 Stat. 2017).

8. 88 Stat. 2036.

Act of 1965, which authorized U.S. participation in the U.S.-Canada auto agreement. That agreement, which covered most trade in automobiles and automotive parts between the United States and Canada, sought to head off the kind of conflict that is a focus of concern in this book. It was recognized that U.S. jobs might be lost as a result of the industrial restructuring, both because of increased imports into the United States and reduced U.S. exports to Canada. The United Auto Workers conditioned their agreement to the pact on an adjustment assistance program, which covered both exports and imports.

Hence, an extension of adjustment assistance to cover the various dislocations which may be caused by foreign direct investment simply represents a logical extension of existing policy. Important differences between the policy problems raised by foreign direct investment and those raised by imports exist, to be sure. But the trade escape clause affords an excellent model, within the framework of a liberal policy, for limiting individual investments adverse to important U.S. interests. The process could work as follows:

A group that believes it is injured or threatened with injury by a foreign direct investment by a U.S.-based firm could appeal to the International Trade Commission. Petitioners would include groups of workers who believe their jobs are being exported; communities hurt as the result of transfers of production; and other firms in the industry that feel they may be compelled to invest abroad to remain competitive but if given assistance may remain competitive without investing abroad.[9]

To provide time for injury petitions to be filed before a particular foreign direct investment actually took place, the "early warning" called for in section 283 of the Trade Act of 1974 (88 Stat. 2041) should be made mandatory, as it was in the Senate version of that legislation and as it is in several other countries. Section 283 calls on firms relocating in foreign countries (a) to provide at least sixty days' advance notice to their workers, to the Secretary of Labor, and to the Secretary of Commerce "before moving productive facilities from the United States to a foreign country";

9. This option could check, probably to the benefit of all firms involved, what we call the lemming tendency of U.S. firms to follow each other abroad (see chap. 7). Such understandable follow-the-leader behavior may be positive in terms of individual firms but, in specific cases, may be negative in terms of overall U.S. interests. Data demonstrating this effect can be found in Frederick T. Knickerbocker, *Oligopolistic Reaction and Multinational Enterprise* (Harvard Business School, Division of Research, 1973).

(b) to apply for adjustment assistance themselves; and (c) either to offer new jobs within the United States to their workers or to help them relocate where jobs exist. Notification should also be required for sizable expansion of existing foreign plants.

The International Trade Commission would analyze whether the specific foreign direct investment would cause or threaten injury to the petitioners. In so doing, it would assess the effect of the investment on such economic factors as those in the trade escape clause: unemployment or underemployment, idling of capacity or inadequate profit levels. It should also assess several other factors germane to foreign direct investment, such as the effects on the U.S. balance of payments and the long-term competitiveness of the U.S. economy. The International Trade Commission has already developed expertise on these issues through its analyses of multinational enterprises as well as through its work on traditional trade issues.

The Commission would report its findings to the President, including recommendations for action when its findings substantiate an injury claim. The proposals should be acted on within a reasonable period of time (probably ninety days for each of the two stages of the process), to avoid unnecessarily thwarting the investing firm's effort to maintain or improve its competitive position.[10] Several types of policy remedies would be available to the President:

1. If the foreign direct investment promotes the national interest but adversely affects the interests of specific groups, the investment would proceed and the government could finance adjustment assistance for those groups. Such cases would include investments that enable firms to gain access to new technology, to penetrate markets otherwise unavailable due to trade or other barriers, or to remain competitive (and thus perhaps maintain markets for some U.S. exports) in light of the investment decisions of foreign firms.

2. If the foreign direct investment appears to have little net impact on the national interest, but an adverse impact on the interests of specific groups (notably its own workers, or those in supporting industries or communities), it should be permitted if the firm itself would finance adjustment assistance.[11]

10. It would thus be desirable to increase the requirement for advance notification to 180 days, to increase the probability of dealing with cases of an ex ante basis.
11. The idea was originally proposed by the United Auto Workers; see Nat

3. If the foreign direct investment appears to unduly speed the pace of change needed for U.S. industry to remain globally competitive, it could be delayed (if the complaint were brought ex ante) or reduced in magnitude. The case (discussed in chapter three) of an American electronics firm investing in Taiwan in anticipation of Japanese penetration of the U.S. market five years later, may be such an example.

4. If the foreign direct investment appears extremely injurious to the national interest, it could be permanently blocked or disinvestment could be required.

The proposed escape clause would cover both prospective investments and those already undertaken. It would, of course, be desirable for all escape clause actions to be triggered before an investment took place. Indeed, the policy options available to the President would be circumscribed once the investment had taken place: capital costs would have been incurred, and foreign relations could be strained by action against a committed investment. On the other hand, prior restraints would be based not on actual injury but on threat of injury, which is hard to substantiate.

Implementing and even institutionalizing this new escape clause risks international conflict. The U.S. government might block an investment in a host country that played by the new rules and that, therefore, feels unjustly harmed by the U.S. action. Because of the possibility of problems like this, the United States should also seek agreement on an international safeguard mechanism. We suggested earlier that international rules ban investment-inducing tax subsidies by both home countries and host countries. Countries restricting investment flows without justification should also compensate countries injured as a result of the restriction or accept retaliation.[12] As in the case of trade, the existence of such international

---

Weinberg, "A Labor Approach to International Corporations" in C. Fred Bergsten, ed., *Toward a New World Trade Policy: The Maidenhead Papers* (Lexington Books, 1975), pp. 143–44. Our analyses in chap. 3 suggest that a great many cases might fit this category and, indeed, a number of firms already internalize such costs.

12. Since most home governments cannot generate investment in a particular host country, in view of the free enterprise nature of their economies, retaliation would probably play a bigger role in this area than it does in trade, where a country raising import barriers for one product can lower them for another. Both compensation and retaliation should probably encompass measures outside the area of foreign direct investment, itself. If, to protect jobs, the United States were to block an investment in Brazil by a U.S. automobile company, it could compensate by, for example, accepting Brazilian export subsidies for shoes, cutting the U.S. tariff on shoes, or accepting Brazilian investment incentives to U.S. tractor manufacturers.

rules would help guard against capricious use of the escape clause by the United States or other countries.

Negotiations on these international rules, as on most others proposed in this chapter, might prove time-consuming, so the United States should adopt its own escape clause. That legislation, however, should both direct the President to seek negotiations on international rules and require that the U.S. safeguards conform to those rules once negotiated.

As in the case of the safeguard mechanism that governs trade flows,[13] certain exceptions to the prohibition of restrictions would be allowed. Such exceptions would apply both to the policies of home and host countries toward foreign direct investment and to their actions regarding specific investment flows. National security would clearly be one exception, balance-of-payments concerns another.[14] Investments in the Fourth World might also be exempt from surveillance.

Antitrust

Only on the issue of antitrust does the U.S. government have the legislative authority to deal with the effects of outward foreign direct investment on the U.S. economy. As noted in chapter seven, however, the focus of that policy needs to be altered from the *intent* to monopolize to the *effect* of such monopolization. In addition, much greater antitrust attention should be directed toward foreign expansion, because it appears to increase profits above the corporate average and, hence, has the potential to create excessive market concentration within the United States.

Government policy toward foreign direct investment should thus include far greater surveillance by the Antitrust Division of the Justice Department and the Federal Trade Commission over the foreign direct investments of U.S.-based firms. Such surveillance should encompass analyses of past foreign direct investments as well as an ongoing appraisal of new steps, since the more mature investments may be least beneficial to the U.S. economy.

13. *Basic Instruments and Selected Documents,* vol. 1 (Geneva: GATT, May 1952), p. 47.

14. See C. Fred Bergsten, "Reforming the GATT: The Use of Trade Measures for Balance-of-Payments Purposes," *Journal of International Economics,* vol. 7 (February 1977), pp. 1–18.

Antitrust policy should also be alert to the fact that spinning off foreign subsidiaries is a possible remedy for excess domestic market power. For example, spin-off of IBM Europe from IBM might significantly increase competition in the computer market, both globally and in the United States. Spin-offs of the major foreign subsidiaries of General Motors Corporation, Ford Motor Company, and Chrysler Corporation could do the same in the automobile industry. (Any restrictive arrangements between the new entities would, of course, be prohibited and entry into each other's markets should be facilitated.) In specific cases, objectives beyond antitrust must be considered. But such spin-offs, in addition to promoting global economic welfare, would serve the U.S. foreign policy interest of inducing firms to pursue joint ventures and cross-licensing agreements, rather than majority equity investments. We thus recommend that antitrust be placed high on the agenda for international negotiations. An initiative by the United States, as the home country of the largest number of firms affected, is the most likely route to multilateral action.

At the same time, attitudes toward restrictive business practices in other home countries—especially France and Japan—render progress uncertain. Hence, a more immediate possibility might be bilateral cooperation between the U.S. antitrust authorities and their counterparts in countries with similar views. Bilateral cooperation has already begun with Canada and Germany. Even though the differences among industrialized countries seem to be narrowing, as many adopt tougher policies and stronger antitrust laws, multilateral accords should be viewed as an ultimate, rather than a proximate, objective. In the meantime, the United States should pursue its own vigorous policy. To limit adverse international repercussions, it should accept the proposal of the UN Group of Eminent Persons to condition final actions on subsequent consultations with the governments affected by the action, as indeed it largely does already under a 1967 resolution of the OECD.

Government Insurance of Foreign Direct Investment

Government insurance and guaranty programs, as now implemented through the Overseas Private Investment Corporation (OPIC), represent the most direct involvement of the U.S. government in the process of foreign direct investment. The stated rationale of these programs is to promote economic development in countries friendly to the United States. In practice, however, they have gone the way of most foreign aid programs and now serve a melange of interests, including straightforward commercial interests of individual American firms. Largely as a result of this increasing confusion over its purposes, Congress in 1974 mandated the privatization of OPIC—the devolution of most of its functions to private enterprise—by the end of the decade.

The OPIC program, like any government effort, can be justified only if it supports clear-cut national interests of the United States as a whole. One of the principles underlying our policy proposals is that foreign direct investment promotes the U.S. interest in the development of the poor countries and should not otherwise receive general support. On this criterion, the OPIC program is at least superior to tax subsidies, because it encourages selectivity. But the policy issue is whether OPIC's selection of projects does in fact promote U.S. national interests. In principle, OPIC insures projects that provide significant benefit to a less-developed country and that cause no adverse effects for the United States. It argues that investments it insures contribute to U.S. employment and the U.S. balance of payments, which in some cases is difficult to reconcile with their contributions to the development of the host country, at least on these same criteria.[15]

We see a need for four changes in OPIC policy to improve the contribution of American multinationals to U.S. national interests. First, OPIC should resume its original mission, by limiting its developmental activities to a small group of host countries. Only the forty or so countries of the Fourth World should be eligible. The new middle class of countries, the Third World, is capable of attracting foreign direct investment in the amounts they want, in the sectors where they want it, and in an area matching their national objectives. They need no active support from the U.S. government.

At the same time, the poorest countries (mainly in South Asia, Africa, and the Caribbean basin) may for some time continue to need traditional

15. It is possible for both the United States and the host countries to gain jobs from the same investment, but our analysis in chap. 3 reveals that substitution is at least as possible. It is even more difficult for both home and host countries to obtain balance-of-payments improvement from a given investment; third countries could experience the concomitant losses, but their own "OPIC" programs—which taken together exceed the U.S. program, and in the case of Japan is growing faster than the U.S. program—enables them to recoup those losses.

assistance—including assistance in attracting foreign direct investment—to promote their development. OPIC should selectively insure investments that seem likely to promote development in these countries. Development would be defined by the host country itself, and OPIC's focus would be on particular industries, even particular production processes, in terms of specific developmental results (for example, their prospects for creating new jobs). OPIC is experienced in evaluating such investments on a case-by-case basis and thus is one of the most promising tools for promoting development through foreign direct investment. The list of eligible countries should be continually reviewed, and "graduates" from the Fourth World to the Third, now able to fend for themselves in attracting investment, should be ineligible. During 1977, OPIC adopted new policies which indicated an intention to move sharply in this direction.

Second, OPIC insurance and guarantees should be used actively to promote the U.S. national interest in one area: assuring access to imported raw materials. As chapter five shows, maximizing world output and diversifying its location are the only realistic policies for reducing the risks to the United States of both real and contrived shortages. These objectives require more investment in natural resources, through means least likely to cause an interruption in the availability of supplies as a result of the inevitable host-country temptations to change the terms of the deal once the multinational enterprise has sunk its capital and technology. Other U.S. interests—maximizing over time the U.S. share of the rents accruing from the production of foreign resources, avoiding the budgetary and political costs of undercompensated expropriations—are also served by maximizing the stability of a given foreign direct investment.

Hence the U.S. government should use OPIC to promote expansion and diversification of world output of raw materials through the various forms of service and management contracts, instead of equity positions. OPIC already insists on joint ventures in some cases and has insured at least one sizable service contract. It should actively solicit such projects in all countries, not just those of the Fourth World, and indeed began to do so during 1977.

Such efforts should be coordinated with OPIC counterparts in other countries that are net importers of a given raw material. (Sixteen industrialized countries now sponsor such institutions.) Coordination would reduce the costs to each country by avoiding duplicate efforts in the same raw material. It would reduce the risk of conflict among home countries, which is probably more serious here than for most other aspects of foreign direct investment, because the basic competition is for raw materials rather than corporate earnings.[16] And it would increase the costs to a host country of reneging on an agreed deal, since doing so would require it to "take on" government institutions in several consumer countries. This proposal pursues much the same objective as the International Resources Bank, suggested officially by the United States in 1976, but would be far easier to inaugurate and far more flexible to implement.

Chapter five demonstrates that it is chimerical for any one country to think that it has preferred access to foreign raw materials because its firms are involved in their exploitation or even their processing. Hence there is no national loss in internationalizing the search for this particular aspect of economic security. Indeed, it could be an important component of an overall joint strategy by consuming countries for assuring access to imported raw materials at reasonable prices. Cooperation in a number of areas already exists between OPIC and its counterparts in other home countries, so collaboration in a new area, if based on high-level policy decisions among the governments involved, should be relatively easy to work out.

Third, OPIC could be the institutional basis for the new overall U.S. policy toward foreign direct investment set forth in this book. Certain functional issues would be handled primarily through other agencies: the Treasury Department, for example, would administer any changes in the tax treatment of multinational enterprises. But OPIC provides the strongest capability in the U.S. government regarding foreign direct investment. It has built up a great deal of experience in judging the effects of specific investments on both the home and host country. It has actively negotiated on a wide range of issues with other home countries. It has negotiated even more actively with host countries, both before the investment (to make agreements within which its programs can operate) and after expropriations have occurred. The mixed public-private character of OPIC's board of directors would help assure that the inevitable difficulties the proposed policies would create, for a while, in the relation between the government and private investors would be fully discussed. Its staff is the largest and most knowledgeable in the federal government regarding multinational enterprises. The experience it has developed in handling hundreds of ap-

16. See Helmut Schmidt, "The Struggle for the Global Product," *Foreign Affairs,* vol. 52, no. 3 (April 1974), pp. 437–51.

plications for assistance and a number of claims for compensation (most of them executed quite skillfully) gives it a unique basis for the broader role, which must be filled somewhere in Washington.

The president of OPIC should become, simultaneously, the President's Special Representative for Foreign Direct Investment Policy, on the model of the President's Special Representative for Trade Negotiations (STR) as created by the Trade Expansion Act of 1962 and upgraded by the Trade Act of 1974.[17] The special representative would chair an intragovernmental committee of all departments and agencies with responsibilities for foreign direct investment policy, would be the channel to the President for policy recommendations, and would serve as the chief U.S. representative in negotiations for new international rules. The same reasons that motivated the creation of STR apply here: giving the leadership role to the Department of State would downplay domestic economic interests, while giving the role to the Treasury Department (or any other economic agency) would underrepresent foreign policy interests. Any such policy area as foreign direct investment (which meshes economic and foreign policy interests on a number of specific issues) can be managed effectively only from the executive office of the President. Investment policy would in turn be meshed with overall U.S. foreign economic policy through the special representative's participation in whatever mechanism existed for that purpose.

Fourth, the congressional mandate of 1974 to privatize OPIC should be rescinded. That action was fully understandable in view of the confusion in OPIC goals and operations. But it is wholly incompatible with the new and broadened role for OPIC envisaged in these proposals. Some privatization would remain, de facto, because exclusion of Third World countries from eligibility for OPIC insurance means that their coverage would have to be provided by the private sector. But the basic congressional purpose of phasing out the agency would be reversed under the policy approach proposed here.

Indeed, privatization would no longer be feasible, because our proposals increase the prospect that OPIC would need financial support from the federal budget. To date, OPIC insurance premiums cover its expenses

17. 88 Stat. 1999. James Theberge, "A Mineral Raw Materials Action Program," *Foreign Policy*, no. 17 (Winter 1974–75), p. 76, proposed the institution of a Special Representative for Foreign Investment Dispute Settlement in the executive office of the President to deal with that particular aspect of foreign direct investment policy.

(including payments on expropriation and other claims) and even enable it to build a small reserve. But OPIC's own data reveal that the high insurance rates necessary to achieve these results deter firms from pursuing worthwhile development projects. Promoting investments in the Fourth World and in the extractive industries would increase OPIC's exposure to losses and may require it to dip modestly into the public treasury. We believe that the proposed programs will promote important national interests and, therefore, that such expenditures are justified.

Expropriation

In the past, nationalization without adequate compensation has been one of the most important issues for U.S. policy toward American multinationals. For the future, however, the phenomenon is likely to be much less pervasive.

First, host countries are increasingly sophisticated in harnessing multinational enterprises to their national interests. They have less need for ownership and instead of expropriating the property, expropriate the profit. Second, American multinationals are decreasingly likely to call on the U.S. government for help, even when they are expropriated. This is true for a variety of reasons, including the increasing flexibility of the firms in both preempting and responding to expropriation actions (see chapter five) and the intensification of the firms' problems when they politicize the issue. Most of the private sector agrees, in fact, that the worst of all worlds—further hostility from the host country and no real help for the expropriated company from the home country—results whenever the United States invokes the Hickenlooper or Gonzalez amendments. This is one reason those amendments have been all but repealed in a de facto sense and should be repealed de jure. Third, experience shows that the business climate is the most effective deterrent, and response, to expropriation. Host countries suffer adverse economic effects through market anticipation and response to expropriation, and these effects have far greater impact than anything home countries could do. Host countries may accept such effects and proceed for reasons they consider overriding; but it is the market effect that will give them pause, if anything does.

Nevertheless, U.S. policy should seek to reduce still further the likelihood that uncompensated expropriations will occur. As indicated in the discussion of OPIC, one way to do so in the extractive industries, where the problem is most acute, is by eliminating the equity component of U.S. corporate activity abroad. Equity ownership in foreign firms does not promote U.S. national interests. Indeed, in most cases equity participation hurts the national interest by destabilizing the entire investment relation, which, in turn, jeopardizes the flow of raw materials and hurts U.S. relations with the host country.

When expropriations do occur, U.S. policy should continue to accept them when compensation is "prompt, adequate, and effective." The key issue, of course, is the definition of those terms, whether fair compensation is book value, market value, going concern, replacement value, or some other concept. So long as there are no international rules, the government's judgment on what, in each case, is prompt, adequate, and effective compensation should be based on an objective analysis by OPIC, which would consider the views of all interested parties, including the government of the host country. Because OPIC now makes such analyses when drawn into expropriation cases through its insurance program, it has developed considerable expertise and objectivity. Its involvement in other expropriation cases would clearly indicate to host countries that the U.S. government will not automatically side with the firm and, indeed, that it well might question not only the propriety of the firm's action but whether the expropriation was in any sense unjustified. The quiet involvement practiced by OPIC has in a number of cases both promoted an equitable settlement and avoided international politicization of the issue.

The U.S. government should, at the same time, continue to disapprove of clear violations by sovereign governments of legal commitments undertaken in good faith. It should not extend foreign direct investment insurance or guarantees to firms investing in the confiscating country until adequate compensation is provided. The United States should increase the firms' scope of action by seeking international agreement on a "hot products" convention, through which expropriated companies could sue in the courts of all participating countries for possession of output delivered from, or payment rendered to, state companies which had not provided fair compensation. Beyond these steps, it should assess each situation as it arises and alter—or not alter—its policy toward the country in question as appears to be most effective at the time. The U.S. government should not be bound, however, to cut off aid, vote against loans, or deny trade preferences to countries that expropriate U.S. firms.

Investment in the Soviet Union

A final foreign policy issue, as demonstrated in chapter eleven, is the need for broader U.S. government control over the involvement of American multinationals in the communist countries, primarily the Soviet Union. The economic gains to the United States through such investments are small, particularly since the Soviets exercise total control over the terms of the investments—perhaps the ultimate expression of host-country power. The long-run political implications of the increased interdependence between the two societies, which might be fostered by foreign investment, are ambiguous in terms of U.S. national interests.

The primary consideration, which should determine U.S. policy in this area, is the asymmetrical nature of the interaction. The Soviet government controls all aspects of Soviet involvement in détente, but one of the largest elements of U.S. involvement—and one of the elements of greatest interest to the Soviets—occurs through the private sector, largely outside the control of the American government. The need for more government oversight of these activities is intensified by the tight restrictions placed by the Congress on U.S. loans to the Soviets through the Export-Import Bank and on increased U.S.-Soviet trade, both of which magnify the role of multinational enterprises in overall U.S.-Soviet economic relations.

Hence, the government should require licensing for all activities of American multinationals in the Soviet Union (and other communist countries) and grant such licenses on the basis of political as well as economic considerations. Such a policy represents simply an extension of the Export Administration Act of 1969, which requires licenses for exports of some U.S. technology and goods to the communist countries. To be sure, the perennial problem of export controls would arise. Firms in other countries, including subsidiaries of U.S.-based firms, could simply replace firms located in the United States in carrying out many of the same transactions. This possibility would not vitiate the benefits to the United States of a unilateral control policy, however. In some instances, the Soviet Union is interested in technology that can only be provided by the parent companies. Moreover, the Soviet Union is interested in the political implications—as well as the economic—of direct involvement by U.S. firms in their economy.

Nevertheless, since the United States appears to gain political benefits only in cases where American firms are clearly superior, or where the Soviet Union seeks participation of U.S. firms for political reasons, the new U.S. law covering foreign direct investment in communist countries should permit restriction only in cases where the same inputs cannot be provided from other sources, including the foreign subsidiaries of U.S. firms. Such a provision would be identical to the one governing export controls, which was added to the Export Administration Act in 1974. To increase the effectiveness of such a policy, however, the United States should explore with the other home countries of multinational enterprises the possibility of joint control over the multinationals' involvement in the communist countries.

Changes in Broader U.S. Economic Policies

As we stress throughout this book, several issues raised by foreign direct investment could be dealt with most effectively through policies outside the arena of foreign direct investment, per se. Four such policies are most important: international monetary policy, trade policy, U.S. policy regarding access to raw materials, and U.S. support for development in the poorer countries.

International Monetary Policy

Three aspects of multinational enterprise activities relating to international monetary affairs are outlined in chapter eight: their alleged speculation in the foreign exchange markets, their "use" by the U.S. government to improve the U.S. balance of payments, and their possible resistance to the balance-of-payments adjustment process. In each case, a better solution seemed to be improving the international monetary system rather than regulating multinational enterprises. Indeed, the advent of managed flexibility of exchange rates, since March 1973, largely mutes the issue of currency speculation by multinationals. And this fundamental improvement in the balance-of-payments adjustment process, by greatly reducing U.S. proclivity for controlling foreign direct investment for balance-of-payments purposes, alleviates several sources of friction, including the extraterritorial application of home-country policies.

The more serious issue is the impact of multinational enterprises on the adjustment process. Some argue that these firms do not respond to price changes and other incentives, as do the atomistic actors of traditional economic theory, and therefore may undermine the effectiveness of traditional economic policies.

Unfortunately, the evidence on this critical subject is skimpy. Experience with exchange-rate changes is still limited. The apparent macroeconomic responses to exchange-rate changes have clearly promoted balance-of-payments equilibrium. And these macroeconomic responses are heavily weighted by the microeconomic responses of the large multinational enterprises, which play a major role in both world trade and international capital flows. The anecdotal evidence is that multinational firms do react to changes in exchange rates in ways that support the adjustment effort.

Additional research is clearly needed. Differences between multinational enterprises and national firms in their responsiveness to traditional policy measures, both internal and international, need much closer analysis. But the conclusion will likely be that the international monetary problems allegedly caused by multinational enterprises can best be remedied by changes in the international monetary system, rather than by measures aimed directly at multinational enterprises.

Trade Policy

Trade policy could play an important role in dealing with some of the problems, both proved and alleged, caused by multinational enterprises. Many foreign direct investments are initially motivated by high tariffs and nontariff barriers, and the vested interest of such investors in maintaining those barriers can distort host-country economic policies.[18] Freer trade could thus serve a number of policy objectives vis-à-vis multinational enterprises, as well as its usual purposes of maximizing world welfare and avoiding international trade conflicts. The dismantling of trade barriers would eliminate the necessity of investing abroad for many industries in

18. For a persuasive argument to this effect in the context of relations between industrialized and developing countries see Carlos F. Díaz-Alejandro, "North-South Relations: The Economic Component" in C. Fred Bergsten and Lawrence B. Krause, eds., *World Politics and International Economics* (Brookings Institution, 1975), pp. 213–41.

many countries, particularly in developing countries.[19] The concomitant reduction in the discriminatory effect of the European Community's common external tariff would additionally reduce the incentives for U.S. foreign direct investment in Europe. The freest trade possible would maximize world welfare, by allowing multinational enterprises to rationalize production with minimal market distortions.

Vigorously enforcing GATT rules and tightening some of them could also be helpful. Export subsidies, now barred by GATT, are an important inducement to investment in many countries. The threat of export controls induces investment by industries requiring assured access to raw materials, yet such controls are in principle outlawed by GATT. The current multilateral trade negotiation (MTN) intends to deal with reform of GATT rules as well as liberalization of trade barriers.

In essence, all steps toward the elimination of trade barriers and distortions would help defuse issues raised by foreign direct investment. Such barriers and distortions trigger investments that would not take place under competitive conditions and, hence, raise problems for both home and host countries. This is one of the clearest areas where government actions can distort the investment process. They add to the case for a strong U.S. initiative, in the MTN and elsewhere, to liberalize and make more equitable the rules of international trade.

Access to Raw Materials

American multinationals cannot be relied upon to provide the United States with assured access to raw materials at reasonable prices (see chapter five). Host-country control over these resources are limited only by the competition in the industry and the availability of substitutes, not by the parent corporations. The need to commit large sums of capital in a fixed investment, with the inevitability of an obsolescing bargain once the operation is successful, limits the ability of American business to keep such industries competitive under the present system of direct equity in-

19. Developing countries could thus promote their stated objective of reducing their reliance on multinational enterprises by reducing their trade barriers. Many host countries now derive their power over multinational enterprises by combining the carrot of trade protection with the stick of performance requirements. Hence the proposed limitations on such investment regulations should have the beneficial side effect of promoting more liberal trade policies in host countries.

vestment. Thus, the role of American companies in supplying raw materials from abroad has been transformed in two ways: first, the investor cannot assure the United States preferential treatment in terms of supply or price during a period of shortage; second, the direct investment process is becoming dysfunctional in ensuring that shortages do not occur.

We propose, therefore, a major reconstruction of the way technology and managerial skills are transferred from American companies. The principal objective is for management and service contracts to replace direct equity investment. The capital would be provided in the form of debt from final consumers or from factoring (selling collection rights to a financial intermediary at a discount). The aim would be to make all multinational companies less vulnerable to becoming the hostages of host governments after the projects are on-stream, less likely to play the role of tax collectors on behalf of host countries, and more able to expand production capacity in the face of economic nationalism among exporting states. The United States could accomplish this end by barring OPIC coverage for equity investors in natural resource projects while encouraging it for companies operating on management or service contracts and by phasing out the credit for taxes on equity investments.

To protect the interests of the creditors who provide the capital for the new state-owned natural resource companies, the United States should seek agreement on a "hot products" convention. The convention would authorize creditors to sue in signatories' courts for possession of either the output delivered from or payment rendered to the state companies that were in default. OPIC insurance could cover the loans of American financial institutions to encourage their participation and to provide the U.S. government with a tool for channeling funds to the countries and the resource sectors where they would have the greatest influence in increasing competition.

Such changes in U.S. policy toward the extractive multinationals would, however, only partly assure U.S. access to imported raw materials. In addition, the United States could build economic security stockpiles for particularly sensitive products. It could seek agreement among the major importing countries to construct and manage such stockpiles together, which, to some extent, has been done for oil. It could negotiate commodity arrangements with the producing countries. And it could pursue wide-ranging trade agreements through which industrial countries guarantee access to their markets and commodity producers guarantee access to their supplies.[20] New approaches toward the extractive multinationals, however, should be an important element of any such overall policy.

Development

The United States has a major interest in the economic and social development of the poorer countries. This interest derives both from the immediate impact of its development policies on overall U.S. relations with those countries and from the major U.S. interest in an effectively functioning world economy, which is possible only if the international economic order is equitable as well as efficient and thus actively supports the developmental efforts of the less-developed countries.

Foreign direct investment is neither the panacea for underdevelopment, as claimed by proponents, nor a bogey as claimed by its opponents. Indeed, the effect of foreign direct investment on development is difficult to pinpoint. Present U.S. policy is now largely neutral toward foreign direct investment in the developing countries. Some U.S. tax provisions, particularly deferral and the overall method for calculating the tax credit, support the tax incentives used by many developing countries to attract foreign direct investment. (Indeed, they are necessary to permit their implementation.) But the investment tax credit and several other provisions of the tax code discriminate against such investment. OPIC was created to promote foreign direct investment in the developing countries, but the program in recent years has drifted from that purpose. When the United States restricted capital outflows to finance foreign direct investment, for balance-of-payments purposes, the preferential treatment nominally provided for the developing countries had little impact.

Indeed, current U.S. policy tends to support flows to the richer of the poor countries; it does little to channel investment to the countries in the Fourth World, which most need it. Current policy does not discriminate among industries; in fact, OPIC tends to promote investments in sectors that boost U.S. exports, which may not provide maximum help for the host country. The programs do not focus on specific development goals, such as reduction of unemployment and better income distribution.

Hence any U.S. program that seeks to support development through foreign direct investment must become much more selective. It should be

20. For details see C. Fred Bergsten, "The Response to the Third World," *Foreign Policy*, no. 17 (Winter 1974–75), pp. 3–34.

limited to the countries of the Fourth World—primarily in South Asia, Central America, and sub-Saharan Africa. It should seek to promote sectors, such as agriculture, that are the priorities of the recipients. It should seek to promote techniques, such as labor-intensive technologies, that help development. To the extent possible, such support should be multilateral.

A number of the proposals we have already made would help promote these objectives. The overseas extension of the investment tax credit would promote investment in new productive equipment. An escape clause and an expanded adjustment assistance program would facilitate investment in developing (and other) countries by getting around protectionist restrictions. Eliminating the Hickenlooper and Gonzalez amendments and the exclusion of expropriators from eligibility for generalized tariff preferences would remove what are perhaps the largest U.S. policy barriers to effective investment relations between the United States and developing countries. Active U.S. support for nonequity investment in the extractive industries should both expand the flow of investment and reduce its destabilizing political effects.

Beyond this, there are several U.S. policies that could directly promote development. First, as suggested above, OPIC should abandon the attempt to support U.S. economic interests in its program of insuring investments in the Fourth World and return to its original goal of supporting development there. Close attention would need to be paid to the sectors and techniques of particular investments, as well as their aggregate level. OPIC should work closely with the development officials of the host countries in determining which projects to support.

Second, the poorest countries should be exempt from prohibition of investment incentives and performance requirements (part of the proposed international regime for foreign direct investment; see next section). The economic and political impact on the United States of such steps by these countries is relatively slight and should be accepted as part of the U.S. contribution to their development. The key issue here is the list of eligible countries. At present, it should include only those designated most seriously affected by the increase in oil prices and world recession, and it should be constantly revised to eliminate countries that advance their levels of development.

Third, the United States could negotiate bilateral tax treaties with Fourth World countries to provide for U.S. sparing of their tax incentives to foreign direct investment. This approach would substitute an eclectic treatment, in terms of countries and potentially sectors, for the present generalized treatment which, in terms of its impact on development, may be quite wasteful of resources both in the United States and in the developing countries. The traditional opposition to tax sparing might be reduced if it were limited to the poorest countries and incorporated into the new policy proposed here. If the overall tax package we propose is not adopted—so that deferral remains and the investment tax credit continues to apply only to domestic investment—an alternative would be extension of that credit to the poorest countries or implementation of a special tax credit for investments there (perhaps modeled on the "Boggs bill," described earlier).

Needless to say, proposals relating to foreign direct investment should be only a small part of overall U.S. development policy. Policies on trade, aid, energy, and commodity issues are at least as important. Nevertheless, the proposed investment policies and measures aimed specifically at development can add significantly to overall U.S. support for what is now a central aim of international economics and politics.

A New International Regime for Multinational Enterprises

The evidence throughout this volume makes clear that the activities of multinational enterprises cause international problems of two types. First, they raise the threat of investment wars—primarily between home and host countries but also among home countries and among host countries—because these countries increasingly seek to tilt the benefits of foreign direct investment in their national directions. Incentives and disincentives for investment, performance requirements, and scrambles for raw materials, are among the causes of such wars. (Specific measures to prevent them have already been discussed.) Second, multinational enterprises often escape the jurisdiction of any single country, causing a nation to try to escape the limitation on its jurisdiction and embroiling it in a conflict over extraterritoriality with another country. International cooperation can check many of these conflicts. We have already made proposals on antitrust and taxation of foreign income by home countries in this context.

Some of the international arrangements needed to deal with these two problems can be made by home countries alone, acting solely in their roles as home countries. Some require action by both home and host countries. In actuality, however, every home country, including the United States, is also an important host country. For practical purposes, the interests of both home and host will thus have to be considered together in constructing any major international arrangements. Conceptually, however, some international steps can be taken solely from the home-country side of the investment equation, while others require more explicit meshing of home-country and host-country concerns.

Our policy recommendations would be reinforced if home countries undertook the following five steps:

1. *Harmonization of their taxation of foreign income.* This would enable each home country to avoid the problems caused by deferral (or its equivalents), without adversely affecting the competitive position of firms based in any single country. All should retain their foreign tax credits and harmonize the methods of their calculations. Each country that extends tax incentives to domestic investment, such as the investment tax credit in the United States, should extend them to foreign investment as well.

2. *Joint action to get host countries to limit the use of tax subsidies and other subsidies to foreign direct investment.* These subsidies distort the allocation of capital and generate conflict. Such joint action could take the form of countervailing duties, like those now imposed by importing countries injured by export subsidies.

3. *Coordination of their investment insurance to promote more investment in raw materials* by pushing the extractive multinationals toward nonequity forms of involvement.

4. *Agreement on a "hot products" convention,* under which nationals of any signatory country could sue in the courts of any other signatory country where output is sold by a defaulting debtor.

5. *Coordination of tight restraints on multinational activities in communist countries,* especially the Soviet Union.

The same number of international arrangements need to be instituted among home and host countries, together:

1. *A safeguard mechanism by which home countries could bar, limit, or delay a foreign direct investment because of its adverse internal effects* (according to agreed criteria). Host countries have a stake in the definition and implementation of the criteria, which may affect investments they desire.

2. *Procedures to govern the active extension of home-country antitrust policy to the foreign subsidiaries of a multinational firm.* The procedures may include collaboration between the home and host countries on antitrust activities or home-country consultations with the host government concerning an action being considered. Long-run efforts to create internationally agreed antitrust concepts and regulatory procedures should also begin.

3. *Machinery for the settlement of disputes caused by expropriations by host countries and extraterritorial activities by home countries.*

4. *Limitations on the use of tax incentives to foreign direct investment by both home and host countries.*

5. *Methods to allocate tax income among all countries served by a multinational enterprise,* such as acceptance of common transfer-pricing standards.

Beyond these issues, several others require new international rules and institutional arrangements. The most important in terms of potential conflict among governments—and the most difficult to regulate—are performance requirements levied on the firms by host governments (and also, in some cases, by home governments). These measures include quantitative and qualitative job quotas, minimum export quotas, efforts to diversify and upgrade the export mix, value-added (local content) requirements, requirements on capital inflows, and limitations on capital outflows, as well as the more traditional requirements for import substitution and local ownership.

These requirements are often cloaked in the guise of more general policy objectives, such as regional development schemes or general labor policies. It should not be permissible, however, to justify either investment incentives or performance requirements because "they are also available to domestic firms." This issue is recurrent in trade policy and is handled in a straightforward way: it is fine for Canada to transfer jobs from Quebec to Nova Scotia by subsidizing investment in the latter, but Canada will be subject to countervailing duties if it tries to transfer jobs from Akron to Nova Scotia by such means. The principle is not whether the discrimination is against or in favor of the foreign-based firm—indeed, in this case, it would be of greater concern to the home country if its firm received discriminatorily *favorable* treatment. The principle is whether the policy has the effect of exporting the host-country's problems to other countries;

such measures should be barred except where justified under exceptions to the rules, and foreign retaliation should be authorized.[21]

Many of these devices are designed to circumvent existing international rules. For example, the value-added requirements applied to the automobile industry by a large number of host countries have the same effect as import quotas but escape international proscription—and risk of retaliation—because they apply to local production rather than to international trade. The GATT rules limit export subsidies and at least refer to export controls that limit the level of a country's sales abroad; but they do not address the *minimum* export quotas required of firms by governments of some host countries (nor the export targets set for U.S.-based firms by the U.S. government under its "voluntary" balance-of-payments program during 1965–67). At the same time, some of the restrictions on capital flows—such as host-country rules governing capital inflows and limiting repatriation of profits and even capital and home-country (especially U.S. and British) restraints on outflows and encouragement of repatriation—run counter to at least the spirit of the International Monetary Fund and OECD rules governing exchange restrictions.

The first step to deal with these problems is a negotiated standstill among home and host countries on the adoption of investment incentives and performance requirements. The first purpose of the GATT was to check escalation of existing tariff barriers to trade, with its second task the more difficult one of reducing those that already existed. We recommend a similar sequence in the new regime to govern international investment.

Indeed, one of the first tasks of the new international organization would be to compile an inventory of existing government policies toward foreign direct investment, which would be the basis for policing the standstill and a starting point for negotiating their liberalization. In the 1930s, the absence of general knowledge of national trade policies contributed to the proliferation of the beggar-thy-neighbor policies that were adopted; indeed, it is only since the creation of the GATT that governments have had an obligation to notify each other of changes in their trade policies,

21. This conclusion is strengthened by the finding of John H. Dunning and George N. Yannopoulos, "Multinational Enterprises and Regional Development: An Exploratory Paper," University of Reading discussion papers in international investment and business studies, no. 21 (April 1975; processed), that multinational enterprises in practice are often better able to take advantage of nominally nondiscriminatory investment incentives than are domestic firms.

let alone to consult on them internationally. Dozens of examples of distorting government policies, by both home and host countries, are cited in this book, but it is clear that our research has only scratched the surface. Collection of data on government policies toward multinational enterprises should thus proceed simultaneously with collection of data on multinational enterprises themselves.[22]

In addition to performance requirements, other issues must be dealt with by means of international arrangements. Antitrust policy is one, and has been discussed earlier in this chapter. Another issue is transfer pricing, which has led to a number of abuses.[23] Both host and home countries are often victimized by this practice, the only "national" beneficiaries usually being tax havens, where the profits from both hosts and homes go. The only remedy that does not raise major problems of extraterritoriality is intergovernmental agreement on arm's-length pricing practices, with vigorous national enforcement by all countries. The international equivalent of section 482 of the U.S. Internal Revenue Code has already been discussed by the industrialized countries in the OECD. Standardization of international accounting principles could be worked out by the private accounting profession and submitted to governments for adoption.[24]

In addition, multinational enterprises should be required by governments of all countries in which they operate to make data on their activities in *all* countries publicly available. At a minimum, such publicity would prevent blatantly contradictory stories being told in different countries. More broadly, it would improve the capabilities of all governments to deal with multinational enterprises. It should thus significantly reduce the tension multinational enterprises cause in many countries. Indeed, both effi-

22. The approach of the United Nations Commission on Transnational Enterprises, in collecting data on the firms but ignoring data on the government policies, is dangerously unbalanced. The Commission rejected the correct and more balanced approach suggested by the Group of Eminent Persons which spawned it.

23. Sanjaya Lall, "Transfer-Pricing by Multinational Manufacturing Firms," *Oxford Bulletin of Economics and Statistics*, vol. 35 (August 1973), pp. 173–95. Some notable abuses are cited in Ronald Müller, "Poverty is the Product," *Foreign Policy*, no. 13 (Winter 1973–74), esp. pp. 93–102.

24. Such principles are proposed in *Accounting Standards for Business Enterprises Throughout the World* (Chicago: Arthur Andersen, 1974). See also the proposal for a council for world accounting in Harvey Kapnick, *Accounting and Financial Reporting in the Public Interest*, vol. 1 (Chicago: Arthur Andersen, 1974), pp. 63–98.

ciency and equity would be promoted by assuring both the transparency of multinational practices and the transparency of the policies of host and home governments toward foreign direct investment.[25]

Still another issue in this context is the allocation of markets within a multinational family. This includes limitations on exports of subsidiaries, requirements that subsidiaries obtain their inputs from parents (and vice versa), and restrictions on technology transfer among members of the group. Such practices not only should be covered by the new international rules governing foreign direct investment but should be a major target of the proposed increase in international antitrust activity. The transparency requirements we advocate would greatly promote effective implementation of antitrust rules. This recommendation also offers a trade-off: the firms should not limit subsidiary activities and governments should not try to direct those activities.

Conclusion

We conclude that foreign direct investment by American multinationals does not have a single, preponderant net impact of any kind on the economy of the United States, the functioning of the international economic system, or the foreign policy goals of the United States. Hence we reject the views of those who either eulogize or pillory the multinational enterprises. At the intellectual level, this leads us to reject all models that heretofore dominated thinking about the phenomenon: the imperialist, mercantilist, sovereignty-at-bay, and global-reach approaches. At the policy level, we reject the calls of the AFL-CIO for blanket restrictions on foreign direct investment and of the multinationals for strong government support.

Yet, foreign direct investment has become sizable, even in terms of the overall U.S. economy. And it does have important effects on U.S. access to raw materials, tax revenues, and industrial structure. Specific investments or classes of investments can have very important effects, either

25. Statement of Ralph Nader and Mark J. Green, *United Nations Inquiry into Multinational Corporations* (September 12, 1973; processed), goes even further by calling for all countries "to formulate parallel and strict terms in their chartering mechanism covering such areas as corporate disclosure, antitrust, shareholder rights, management liabilities, and affirmative duty to report on a wide variety of matters to all nations where the firm is doing business" (p. 94).

positive or negative, on the U.S. national interest. Hence the current absence of U.S. policy toward the phenomenon is a dereliction of responsibility by the U.S. government.

We find that, whereas American multinationals generally contribute to both world welfare and the national welfare of the United States, the contribution could be increased by eliminating a number of distortions now affecting the activities of the firms. These distortions arise from a large and growing number of policies adopted by both host-country and home-country governments and from the structure and some of the behavior of the firms themselves.

In addition, we observe a number of threats (stemming partly from the proliferation of those distortions) to the continued activities of multinational enterprises. Indeed, these threats are likely to become acute during the next few years in the absence of constructive action to head them off. At the same time, there is legitimate concern in a number of quarters—both within the United States and in other countries—over the potential power of the firms to evade effective countervailing powers which seek to assure that they contribute positively to social goals. The two concerns interact, since multinational enterprises will be permitted the freedom to pursue the tasks they do best only if there is widespread confidence that their exercise of power is both legitimate and subject to effective checks in areas where it may conflict with the goals of particular nations or groups within nations.

Achievement of these objectives requires the construction of wide-ranging international policies. The thrust of these policies is to maximize global economic welfare by maximizing the scope for foreign direct investment to respond to market forces. This requires both widespread agreement that such rules are desirable and active intervention to thwart efforts by individual countries or groups to induce deviations from the norm, through either excessive restraints or excessive inducements. Such principles must apply to home and host countries, alike.

National policies that permit the U.S. government (and others) to respond effectively to problems raised or threatened by individual foreign direct investments are also needed, to deal with those cases where the social costs of unfettered corporate activity would simply be too high. Most host countries are well along toward such capability and, indeed, in some cases, may be going too far. Some home countries are moving in this direction. The United States now needs to do so to promote both its economic and foreign policy interests. The present situation, in which the U.S. national chair remains empty while an important and increasing share of world economic activity is negotiated between multinational enterprises and the governments of host countries, is untenable.

The approach to foreign direct investment and multinational enterprises that we propose should help defuse the volatile claims and counterclaims that distort both public attitudes and public policy toward the firms. For example, several of our policy recommendations would help deal with the problems for U.S. labor caused by foreign direct investment. We propose several efforts to eliminate host-country subsidies, which artificially induce investment, including the elimination of U.S. tax provisions that support some of those subsidies. We seek new measures at both the U.S. and international levels to restrain the oligopoly power of multinational enterprises, including much closer attention to them by the U.S. antitrust authorities. We would check foreign direct investments by U.S.-based firms that injure the U.S. national interest, including the interests of labor, via a new escape clause. Our proposals for adjustment assistance to workers and communities injured by foreign direct investments would alleviate the loss coming from even temporary unemployment.

New international rules are needed to head off conflicts among nations, conflicts engaged in by proxy through multinational firms and which could deteriorate into investment wars (akin to the trade wars of a past generation). Rules are needed to protect the firms from escalating and inconsistent demands of the many governments they must deal with. Rules are needed to check the firms' abuses of power, to restore their legitimacy, and to enable them to contribute effectively to world economic and political progress.

The creation of such arrangements cannot occur quickly. Indeed, it is likely to be one of the major institutional tasks of the international community for the rest of this century, just as the creation and evolution of an international structure to govern world trade and monetary arrangements was one of the major international tasks of the past quarter century. The vast size of international production relative to trade and monetary flows, and the intimate interaction of all three, require that a major effort be undertaken to accomplish the task.

A large responsibility for leadership will fall on the United States. It is the home country for half of all the foreign direct investment in the world, and thus dominates the investment market far more than any of the other major international economic markets. Its sometimes blind support for its own multinational enterprises has been a major barrier to the creation of international rules and institutions. At the same time, its lack of specific policies toward many aspects of foreign direct investment precluded any possibility of serious international initiatives.

An open and effective international economic system is integral to the achievement of U.S. economic and foreign policy objectives. Indeed, the rapidly increasing dependence of the United States on the world economy makes that need more obvious now than in the past. American multinationals are the most conspicuous components of U.S. engagement in the world economy. Active leadership by the United States to create new international rules and arrangements to govern foreign direct investment and the behavior of multinational enterprises should thus be a priority policy objective of this country.

Statistical Sources for Chapters Three, Four, and Seven

THE U.S. INTERNAL REVENUE SERVICE, *Sourcebook of Statistics of Income, Corporations, 1965 through 1971,* is available on computer tape in the U.S. National Archives. Between 1965 and 1967 the Internal Revenue Service reduced the number of manufacturing industries in its minor industry classification from over one hundred to seventy-six, and for consistency's sake we aggregated the data from the earlier years to the seventy-six-industry base. Of the latter, "chemical firms not classifiable" was dropped from our sample because it is small and cannot be matched to other data. The remaining seventy-five industries were disaggregated according to asset size (see chapter seven) and, since asset size fluctuated from year to year, the number of groups fluctuated from one year to another.

Our foreign investment proxy, the ratio of foreign dividends plus foreign tax credits to the total assets of all firms in a given industry or a given asset-size, is based on the IRS *Sourcebook.* The foreign earnings of unincorporated branches are not included in foreign dividends, but their foreign tax credits are. (Exact definitions of Internal Revenue Service classifications can be found in the appendix to their annual publication, *Statistics of Income, [year] Corporation Income Tax Returns.*)

The IRS *Sourcebook* provides information on total assets, advertising expenditures, net income before taxes, and interest paid on debt for each class of firms in each minor industry. Total assets are net of depreciation reserves and include all assets of the U.S. taxpayer, which would normally encompass an American corporation's own investment in overseas affiliates but not foreign assets financed through local foreign borrowing. Total assets thus do not consolidate the balance sheets of foreign affiliates but do consolidate the balance sheets of domestic subsidiaries.

The Internal Revenue Service minor industry classification is based on the standard enterprise classification, which can be linked to the standard industrial classification (U.S. Office of Management and Budget, *Standard Industrial Classification Manual, 1967*). See table A-1 for the concordance between the two classification systems. We used this concordance to derive industry shipments data from the annual issues of U.S. Department of Commerce, *Annual Survey of Manufactures*. Shipments statistics are based on returns from individual establishments (that is, plants) as contrasted with the IRS statistics based on corporations. Because a single corporation may have plants in different industries, the match between the two types of statistics is only approximate.

Linking industrial classifications with export and import statistics is more troublesome. Trade statistics are collected on a standard international trade classification system, which cannot be perfectly matched with the standard industrial classification, even starting from a high and moving to a low level of disaggregation. We relied upon the Bureau of the Census, *Exports of Domestic Merchandise, S.I.C. Based Products and Area Report, FT 610, Annual* and *U.S. Imports for Consumption and General Imports, S.I.C. Based Products and Area Report, FT 210, Annual* (titles vary slightly from year to year) for U.S. exports and imports between 1965 and 1971. The 1960 trade statistics were derived from a less satisfactory source, U.S. Census Bureau, *U.S. Commodity Exports and Imports as Related to Output, 1960 and 1959* (Census Bureau, 1962).

The Census Bureau's *Subject Reports* included in the *Census of Population: 1970* and *Census of Population: 1960* provide statistics on industries' employees' education, earnings, age, occupation, race, and sex. The concordance between these industries and IRS industries is close but not exact. When a Census Bureau industry matches more than one IRS industry, we assume that each of the IRS industries has the same ratio of highly educated to total employees, and so on, as other industries in the same Census class.

Industries we assessed as machinery manufacturers are:

IRS number	IRS name
3520	Farm equipment and machinery
3530	Construction, mining, and materials-handling machinery
3550	Special industry machinery
3560	General industrial machinery
3570	Office and computing machines
3598	Miscellaneous machinery
3698	Other electrical equipment and machinery
3720	Aircraft and guided missiles
3730	Ship and boat building
3798	Other transportation equipment
3810	Scientific and mechanical measuring instruments
3930	Ordnance, except guided missiles

Our unionization index is based on estimates from L. W. Weiss, unpublished appendix to "Concentration and Labor Earnings," *American Economic Review,* vol. 56 (March 1966). Because there is no comprehensive source of information on unionization by manufacturing industry, Weiss uses a variety of sources to estimate the percentage of an industry's workers in plants where a majority is covered by collective bargaining contracts. Because all such workers may not belong to a union, this measure probably overstates the percentage of workers in an industry belonging to a union (such information is much harder to gather). The unionization index is based on the Census Bureau industry classification, converted to IRS classification (see table A-1).

Table A-1. *Concordance between 1960 Internal Revenue Service Minor Industry Classification, 1967 Standard Industrial Classification, and Census Bureau Industrial Classification*

IRS number	SIC numbers	Census Bureau industries
2010	201	Meat
2020	202	Dairy
2030	203	Canning, preserving
2040	204	Grain mill
2050	205	Bakery
2060	206	Miscellaneous food preparation
2082	2082, 2083	Beverage
2084	2084, 2085	Beverage
2086	2086, 2087	Beverage
2098	207, 209	Miscellaneous food preparation
2100	21	Tobacco
2228	221, 222, 223, 226	Thread, fabric, dyeing and finishing textiles, yarn
2250	225	Knitting
2298	224, 227, 228, 229	Textiles, yarn, thread, and fabric
2310	231, 232	Apparel, accessories
2330	233, 234, 236	Apparel, accessories
2380	235, 237, 238	Apparel, accessories
2398	239	Fabricated textile products
2410	241, 242	Logging, sawmills, planing mills, millwork
2430	243	Sawmills, planing mills, millwork
2498	244, 249	Wood products
2510	251	Furniture, fixtures
2590	252, 253, 254, 259	Furniture, fixtures
2620	261, 262, 263, 266	Pulp, paper, paperboard

Table A-1 (continued)

IRS number	SIC numbers	Census Bureau industries
2698	264, 265	Paperboard containers, paper and pulp products
2711	271	Newspaper publishing and printing
2712	272	Printing, publishing, allied industries
2715	273, 274, 277	Printing, publishing, allied industries
2798	275, 276, 278, 279	Printing, publishing, allied industries
2810	281, 282	Industrial chemicals, plastics, synthetics, resins, synthetic fibers
2830	283	Drugs, medicines
2840	284	Soaps, cosmetics
2850	285	Paints, varnishes, related products
2898	286, 287, 289	Agricultural chemicals, chemicals
2910	291	Petroleum refining
2998	295, 299	Petroleum, coal products
3010	301, 302, 303, 306	Rubber products
3098	307	Plastic products
3140	314	Footwear (nonrubber)
3198	311, 312, 313, 315, 316, 317, 319	Tanned, cured, and finished leather, leather products
3210	321, 322, 323	Glass, glass products
3240	324	Cement, concrete, gypsum, plaster products
3270	327	Cement, concrete, gypsum, plaster products
3298	325, 326, 328, 329	Structural clay products, pottery, nonmetallic mineral products
3310	331, 3321, 3322, 3323, 3391	Blast furnaces, steelworks, rolling mills, primary iron and steel
3330	333, 334, 335, 336, 3392, 3399	Primary aluminum, other nonferrous industries
3410	341	Fabricated and unspecified metal products
3420	342	Cutlery, handtools, hardware
3430	343	Fabricated, and unspecified metal products

3440	344	Fabricated structural metal products
3450	345	Screw machine products
3461	3461	Metal stamping
3498	347, 348, 349	Fabricated, and unspecified metal products
3520	352	Farm machinery, equipment
3530	353	Construction and material-handling machines
3540	354	Metalworking machinery
3550	355	Other machinery
3560	356	Other machinery
3570	357	Office and accounting machines, electronic computers
3580	358	Other machinery
3598	351, 359	Other machinery
3630	363	Household appliances
3660	365, 366	Radio, television, communication equipment
3662	367	Electrical machinery
3698	361, 362, 364, 369	Electrical machinery
3710	371	Motor vehicles, motor vehicle equipment
3720	372, 1925	Aircraft and parts
3730	373	Ship and boat building and repairing
3798	374, 375, 379	Railroad equipment, mobile homes, cycles
3810	381, 382	Scientific and controlling instruments
3830	383, 384, 385	Optical and health services supplies
3860	386	Photographic equipment and supplies
3870	387	Watches, clocks, clock-operated devices
3930	191, 192	Ordnance
3990	391, 393, 394, 395, 396, 399	Miscellaneous manufacturing

Sources: See text.

Microeconomic Model

for

Chapter Six

THE EQUATIONS in appendix B set forth the microeconomic model used to simulate the impact of repealing deferral, extending the investment tax credit to foreign investment, raising R&D and other head-office charges, and replacing the foreign tax credit with a simple deduction (see chapter six). The notations used in the equations are defined in table B-1.

We assume that a multinational invests at home and abroad. The total return on each investment, R_T (net of labor and material costs but gross of interest expenses and income taxes), equals the return on past investments, R_o, plus the return on new investment, R:

(1)
$$R_T = R_o + R(I),$$

and

(2)
$$R_T^* = R_o^* + R^*(I^*),$$

where I is the rate of new investment and the asterisk (*) denotes domestic operations.

In financing new investment, the firm can borrow in foreign and domestic capital markets. We assume that both at home and abroad total borrowing costs, B_T, equal the fixed borrowing costs of outstanding debt,

502

Table B-1. *Definitions of Notation, Equations 1–80, Appendix B*

Symbol	Definition
R	Return on investment
I	Investment
L	External borrowing
B	Total external borrowing costs
F	Intrafirm capital transfer
E_R	Retained earnings
E_B	Taxable income
i_p	Interest charged on intrafirm debt
f	Proportion of F that is debt, not equity
h	Ratio of head-office, royalty, and other intrafirm charges to investment
D	Dividends
p	Dividend payout ratio
t	Rate of income taxation
T	Total income taxes
W	Total withholding taxes
w_D	Dividend withholding tax rate
w_H	Head-office and other intrafirm charges withholding tax rate
w_B	Intrafirm interest withholding tax rate
Tc	Foreign tax credit
u	Rate of investment tax credit
q	Proportion of investment qualifying for investment tax credit
h'	Head-office charges not allowed as deductions by foreign governments as a proportion of foreign investment
s_B	Share of intrafirm interest payments in total foreign-source income
s_H	Share of head-office and other intrafirm charges in total foreign-source income
s_D	Share of dividends in total foreign-source income
E_A	After-tax income
x	Binary variable, equal to unity if firm has deficit of tax credits and equal to zero if firm has surplus tax credits
Ec	Consolidated after-tax earnings
V	"Permanent" component of consolidated after-tax earnings
b	Marginal cost of external capital
r	Marginal return on investment
Z	See equations 31 and 35
ΔE_R	See equation 42
L'	See equation 44
a_{ij}	See equations 53–61
c_j	See equations 62–64
s	Binary variable equal to unity if deferral is available initially
y	Binary variable equal to unity if foreign tax credit is repealed
d_j	See equations 67–69
t_f	$t + p\,(t^* - t)$, effective global rate of taxation on foreign affiliate's income
z	Discounted present value of future depreciation allowances per dollar of current investment expenditure

B_o, plus new borrowing costs, B, which are an increasing function of new borrowing, L:

(3) $$B_T = B_o + B(L),$$

and

(4) $$B_T{}^* = B_o{}^* + B^*(L^*).$$

The firm's other source of investable funds is its own internally generated funds, which we assume consist solely of retained earnings, E_R. Rather than requiring that investment be financed locally, we allow the firm to transfer funds, F, from parent to affiliate. The affiliate's local borrowing will equal the difference between its investment and the sum of its retained earnings and funds from the parent.

(5) $$L = I - F - E_R.$$

Likewise, the parent's borrowing equals its own investment plus funds transferred to affiliate minus its own retained earnings:

(6) $$L^* = I^* + F - E_R{}^*.$$

The foreign affiliate's before-tax earnings, E_B, equals its total returns less its outside borrowing costs and less intrafirm interest and head-office charges (we include in the head-office category all royalties, R&D expenses, and other such charges):

(7) $$E_B = R_T - B_T - (i_{p_o} f_o F_o + i_p f F) - (h_o I_o + hI),$$

where i_p is the interest rate on intrafirm loans, f is the portion of intrafirm capital transfers taking the form of debt rather than equity, and h is the ratio of head-office and other such charges to total investment. The o subscript indicates the initial stock; the lack of any subscript, the current flow (for example, $h_o I_o$ represents head-office charges on existing investments, and hI, the charges on new investment).

If the foreign government taxes the affiliate's income at the rate t, and p is the proportion of after-tax earnings paid out to the parent as dividends, then total dividends, D, are

(8) $$D = p(1 - t)E_B,$$

and the affiliate's retained earnings, E_R, are

(9) $$E_R = (1 - p)(1 - t)E_B.$$

In addition to income taxes, most foreign governments collect an additional withholding tax on dividends, interest payments, and head-office charges made to overseas investors:

(10) $W = w_D D + w_B(i_{p_o} f_o F_o + i_{p} f F) + w_H(h_o I_o + hI),$

where W is total withholding taxes paid, and w_D, w_B, and w_H are the withholding tax rates for dividends, interest payments, and head-office charges, respectively.

The American parent's taxable income includes domestic investment income less domestic borrowing costs plus foreign-source income. Foreign-source income consists of interest payments, head-office charges, and the grossed up value of dividends:

(11) $E_B^* = R_T^* - B_T^* + (i_{p_o} f_o F_o + i_{p} f F) + (h_o I_o + hI) + (D/1 - t).$

That U.S. taxable income includes the dividends, but not the retained earnings, of the foreign affiliate is the essence of deferral.

The taxes actually paid to the U.S. Treasury are

(12) $T^* = t^* E_B^* - T_C^* - u^* q^* I^* - uqI + t^* h'(I_o + I),$

where t^* is the U.S. tax rate, T_C^* is the tax credit the government allows for foreign income and withholding taxes paid, u^* and u are the investment tax credits allowed on domestic and foreign investment, respectively (the latter equals zero under current policy), q^* and q are the fraction of new investment qualifying for the investment tax credit, and h' is additional head-office charges by the United States but not allowed as deductions by the foreign country. Thus, if the U.S. charges are higher than the deductions allowed by the foreign government, h is what the foreign government allows, and $h + h'$ is what the United States charges.

Under current tax policy, an American investor can claim a foreign tax credit equal to the lesser of two amounts: (1) the withholding taxes on dividends, interest, and head-office charges plus the income taxes deemed paid by the parent on repatriated dividends; and (2) the U.S. tax rate times the foreign-source income:

(13) $T_c^* = \text{minimum } \{W + tD/(1 - t), t^*[i_{p_o} f_o F_o$
$+ i_{p} f F + h_o I_o + hI + D/(1 - t)]\}.$

Notice that the firm will not have excess foreign tax credits (that is, it can claim full credit for foreign taxes paid or deemed paid) as long as the weighted average of the foreign tax rates is less than the U.S. rate:

$$(14) \qquad s_B w_B + s_H w_H + s_D[w_D(1 - t) + t] < t^*,$$

where s_B, s_H, and s_D add up to one, and are the shares of interest payments, head-office charges and grossed up dividends, respectively, in the parent's foreign-source income (the term in brackets in equation 13). While the effective foreign tax on dividend income, $w_D(1 - t) + t$, could easily exceed the U.S. tax rate, t^*, the firm may nonetheless avoid the foreign tax-credit ceiling by keeping its interest and head-office payments sufficiently high. Thus, even when an American firm invests in only one foreign country, we cannot be sure that it has excess foreign tax credits whenever the foreign income tax rate exceeds the U.S. rate.

For analytical purposes let us define a binary variable, x, which equals zero if the condition in equation 14 is satisfied and equals unity if not. Then equation 13 can be rewritten as

$$(15) \qquad T_c^* = W + tD/(1 - t) - x\{(w_B - t^*)(i_{p_o} f_o F_o + i_p f F) \\ + (w_H - t^*)(h_o I_o + hI) \\ + [w_D(1 - t) + t - t^*]D/(1 - t)\}.$$

While equation 15 looks messier than equation 13, it is far more tractable mathematically.

The parent's after-tax earnings, E_A^*, including all its foreign-source income but not the retained earnings of its affiliate, are

$$(16) \qquad E_A^* = E_B^* - T^* - W - tD/(1 - t) \\ - x\{(w_B - t^*)(i_{p_o} f_o F_o + i_p f F) \\ + (w_H - t^*)(h_o T_o + hI) \\ + [w_D(1 - t) + t - t^*]D/(1 - t)\}.$$

The consolidated, after-tax earnings, E_C, of the multinational equal the after-tax income of the parent plus the retained earnings of the affiliate:

$$(17) \qquad E_C = E_A^* + E_R.$$

Had we not introduced an investment tax credit, we would assume that the firm maximizes E_C. But the investment tax credit accrues only in the first year of the investment, so to maximize E_C as defined by equation 17, the firm should overinvest in order to reap temporary investment tax credits. We must, in short, take account of the transitional nature of the investment tax credit.

Because we do not want to go into the cost-of-capital literature, let us merely assert a finding without proof. If we could ignore capital depreciation, we could simply multiply the investment tax credit, $u^*q^*I^*$, by the marginal cost of borrowed funds, b^*, to determine the amount by which the investment tax credit could reduce the cost of borrowing. This would be a legitimate measure of the *permanent* benefit of the investment tax credit. Rather than ignoring depreciation altogether, let us assume that the tax rate and the true economic rate of depreciation are identical and that z represents the present discounted value of future depreciation expenses per dollar of investment outlay. If so, the permanent value of the investment tax credit for domestic or foreign investment is, respectively:

$$\frac{b^*u^*q^*I^*}{1-z}$$

and

$$\frac{buqI}{1-z}.$$

Consolidated after-tax earnings, E_C, includes the full investment tax credits, uqI and $u^*q^*I^*$, rather than just the permanent components discussed above. Accordingly, let us define the objective function, V, to be:

$$(18) \qquad V = E_C - uqI\left(1 - \frac{b}{1-z}\right) - u^*q^*I^*\left(1 - \frac{b^*}{1-z}\right).$$

The last two terms on the right side of equation 18 measure the temporary, noncontinuing benefit of the investment tax credit. By maximizing V rather than E_C, the multinational maximizes permanent rather than current income.

The distinction between cash flow and permanent income adds to the difficulty in specifying how much the multinational pays to its shareholders as dividends and how much it retains for reinvestment. For simplicity's sake, we assume that total retained earnings are some constant proportion, $1 - p^*$, of permanent income, V, so that

$$(19) \qquad E_R^* = (1 - p^*)V - E_R.$$

This formulation, which greatly simplifies the analysis below (some may find it hard to believe that it could be more complex), implies that current cash dividends are a constant proportion of permanent income plus the transitional component of the investment tax credit:

$$(20) \qquad D^* = E_A{}^* - E_R{}^* = p^*V$$
$$+ [1 - b^*/(1 - z)]u^*q^*I^* + [1 - b/(1 - z)]uqI.$$

What should the multinational do to maximize the permanent income from investment? Let us first show that the intrafirm financial parameters should be minimized or maximized according to straightforward tax-avoidance criteria. This is best shown by writing the formula for permanent income as

$$(21) \quad V = (1 - t^*)(R_T{}^* - B_T{}^*) + (1 - t)(R_T - B_T)$$
$$- [t^* - t + x(w_B - t^*)](i_{p_o}f_oF_o + i_pfF)$$
$$- [t^* - t + x(w_H - t^*)](h_oI_o + hI)$$
$$- \{t^* - t + x[w_D(1 - t) + t - t^*]\}(pE_R)/[(1 - t)(1 - p)]$$
$$+ b^*u^*q^*I^*/(1 - z) + buqI/(1 - z) - t^*(h_o'I_o' + h'I).$$

Equation 21, while complex, is nonetheless revealing. Since the R and B values depend only on the investment levels, external borrowing, and retained earnings, we can determine readily the optimal values for the proportions of debt to total intrafirm capital transfer, f_o and f, the interest rates on that debt, i_{p_o} and i_p, the rates for charging back head-office and like expenses, h_o and h, and the affiliate's dividend payout ratio, p. As long as the U.S. income tax rate exceeds the foreign income tax rate, all should be minimized, for all give rise to avoidable U.S. taxes. On the other hand, should the foreign income tax rate exceed that in the United States, all except the dividend payout ratio should be maximized. Dividends should be paid, but only as long as the high foreign income and withholding taxes can be fully credited, that is, only as long as the condition in equation 14 can be satisfied.

To keep the search for an optimal investment strategy manageable, we assume that the intrafirm rates, i_{p_o} and i_p, the proportions of debt in total capital transfers, f_o and f, head-office and other such charges, h_o and h, and the dividend payout ratio, p, are determined by tax considerations, financial practices, rules of thumb, force of habit, and so forth. Given these intrafirm accounting parameters, we can find the optimal level of foreign and domestic investment, of outside borrowing, and of intrafirm capital transfer. As we shall see, the optimal investment strategy depends on internal accounting parameters and not just on external investment and borrowing opportunities. And having found an optimal investment strategy for given tax laws, we can study how changes in those laws (for example, eliminating deferral) affect such things as the levels of foreign and domestic investment. Although a tax change may induce a firm to alter these ratios, our preliminary empirical estimates presume that they are fixed at their initial values.

Throughout the remainder of the analysis, we assume that the foreign investor keeps its interest and head-office charges high enough to avoid paying foreign taxes in excess of the allowable U.S. tax credit (see equation 14). If so, $x = 0$, and equation 21 can be profitably rewritten as

$$(22) \quad V = (1 - t^*)(R_T{}^* - B_T{}^* + i_{p_o} f_o F_o$$
$$+ i_p f F + h_o I_o + hI) + [1 - t - p(t^* - t)]$$
$$(R_T - B_T - i_{p_o} f_o F_o - i_p f F - h_o I_o - hI)$$
$$+ b^* u^* q^* I^* / (1 - z) + buqI / (1 - z)$$
$$- t^*(h'I + h_o' I_o).$$

The values of $t^*, i_{p_o}, i_p, f_o, f, h_o, h, p, t, u^*, q^*, u, q, h', h_o'$, and z are fixed, at least initially. Likewise, the initial stocks of foreign and domestic investment, I_o and $I_o{}^*$, foreign and domestic borrowing, L_o and $L_o{}^*$, and intrafirm capital transfers, F_o, have been determined by past decisions. This leaves the firm with only three decision variables: new foreign and domestic investment, I and I^*, and new capital transfers from parent to affiliate, F. New foreign and domestic borrowing, L and L^*, are derived from the flow-of-funds constraints (equations 5 and 6), while retained earnings, E_R and $E_R{}^*$, are determined endogenously in the context of maximizing consolidated profits. R_T, $R_T{}^*$, B_T, and $B_T{}^*$ are functions of the three control variables, I, I^*, and F, so the partial derivative of V in equation 21 with respect to F is

$$(23) \quad \delta V / \delta F = (1 - t^*)(-b^* + i_p f) + (1 - t_f)(b - i_p f)$$
$$+ (1 - t^*)b^*(\delta E_R{}^* / \delta F)$$
$$+ (1 - t_f)b(\delta E_R / \delta F) = 0,$$

where b indicates the marginal cost of capital, and $t_f = t + p(t^* - t)$ $= (1 - p)t + pt^*$, the effective global tax on foreign investment income. Since equation 19 implies that

(24) $$V = E_R^*/(1 - p^*) + E_R/(1 - p^*),$$

the last two terms in equation 23 are approximately equal to

(25) $$(1 - t^*)b^*(\delta E_R/\delta F) + (1 - t_f)b(\delta E_R/\delta F)$$
$$= (1 - t^*)b^*(1 - p^*)(\delta V/\delta F)$$

(see equation 27). With this approximation, equation 23 can be rewritten as

(26) $$\frac{\delta V}{\delta F} = \frac{(1 - t^*)(-b^* + i_pf) + (1 - t_f)(b - i_pf)}{1 - (1 - t^*)b^*(1 - p^*)} = 0.$$

The first-order condition with respect to F becomes

(27) $$(1 - t^*)b^* = (1 - t_f)b - (t^* - t_f)i_pf.$$

The first-order condition with respect to I^* is

(28) $$\delta V/\delta I^* = (1 - t^*)[r^* - b^* + b^*(\delta E_R^*/\delta I^*)] + b^*u^*q^*/(1 - z) = 0.$$

Because E_R is *not* a function of I^* (see equation 9),

(29) $$(1 - t^*)b^*(\delta E_R^*/\delta I^*) = (1 - t^*)b^*(1 - p^*)(\delta V/\delta I^*).$$

So that

(30) $$\delta V/\delta I^* = [(1 - t^*)(r^* - b^*) + b^*u^*q^*/(1 - z)]/Z^* = 0,$$

where

(31) $$Z^* = 1 - (1 - t^*)b^*(1 - p^*),$$

and the first-order condition is

(32) $$r^* - b^* = -b^*u^*q^*/(1 - t^*)(1 - z).$$

The first-order condition with respect to I is

(33) $$\delta V/\delta I = (1 - t^*)h + (1 - t_f)(r - b - h)$$
$$+ buq/(1 - z) - t^*h' + (1 - t^*)b^*(\delta E_R^*/\delta I)$$
$$+ (1 - t_f)b(\delta E_R/\delta I) = 0.$$

Using equation 24, equation 33 reduces to

(34) $\delta V/\delta I = [(1 - t^*)h + (1 - t_f)(r - b - h)$
$+ buq/(1 - z) - t^*h']/Z = 0,$

where

(35) $Z = 1 - (1 - t)b(1 - p).$

So the first-order condition reduces to

(36) $r - b = [(t^* - t_f)h - buq/(1 - z) + t^*h']/(1 - t_f).$

The three first-order conditions are, thus, given by equations 36, 32, and 27. To determine the impact of eliminating deferral or any other such change, we must take the total differentials of these three first-order conditions:

(37) $r^{*'}dI^* - b^{*'}(dI^* + dF - dE_R{}^*) + [b^*q^*/(1 - t^*)(1 - z)]du^* = 0.$

(38) $r'dI - b'(dI - dF - dE_R) + [bq/(1 - t_f)(1 - z)]\,du$
$- [t^*/(1 - t_f)]\,dh' - [(t^* - t_f)/(1 - t_f)]\,dh$
$+ \{[buq/(1 - z) - t^*h' - t^*h + h]/(1 - t_f)^2\}\,dt_f = 0.$

(39) $(1 - t^*)b^{*'}(dI^* + dF - dE_R{}^*) + (b - i_pf)\,dt_f$
$+ (t^* - t_f)\,d(i_pf) - (1 - t_f)b'(dI - dF - dE_R) = 0.$

Prime denotes the slopes of the marginal revenue and cost functions and $dt_f = (1 - p)(t^* - t)$ the amount by which eliminating deferral raises the effective tax rate on foreign investment income.

To evaluate equations 37 through 39, we must derive expressions for the differentials of E_R and $E_R{}^*$. The first is relatively straightforward. Equations 7 and 9 together imply

(40) $E_R = (1 - p)(1 - t)(R_T - B_T - i_{p_o}f_oF_o - i_pfF - h_oI_o - hI).$

The total differential of this equation is

(41) $dE_R = (1 - p)(1 - t)\left\{\left[\dfrac{t^*h' - buq/(1 - z) + (t^* - t_f)h}{1 - t_f} - h\right]dI\right.$
$\left. + (b - i_pf)dF\right\}\Big/Z + \Delta E_R,$

where

(42) $\Delta E_R = [(1 - p)(1 - t)/Z][(E_Bdp)/(1 - p) + Fd(i_pf)$
$+ Idh + F_od(i_{p_o}f_o) + I_o\,dh].$

The parent's retained earnings equal

(43) $E_R^* = (1 - p^*)(1 - t^*)(R_T^* - B_T^* + i_{p_o} f_o F_o$
$\qquad + i_p f F + h_o I_o + hI) + L' E_R$
$\qquad + (1 - p^*)[b^* u^* q^* I^*/(1 - z) + buqI/(1 - z) - t^*(h'I + h_o' I_o)],$

where

(44) $\qquad L' = [(1 - p^*)(1 - t^*)p/(1 - t)(1 - p)] - p^*.$

Before taking the total differential of the parent's retained earnings function, we note that by equation 24

(45) $\qquad \delta V/\delta I^* = [1/(1 - p^*)][\delta E_R^*/\delta I^*] = 0;$

(46) $\qquad \delta V/\delta I = [1/(1 - p^*)][(\delta E_R^*/\delta I) + (\delta E_R/\delta I)] = 0;$

(47) $\qquad \delta V/\delta F = [1/(1 - p^*)][(\delta E_R^*/\delta F) + (\delta E_R/\delta F)] = 0.$

So that

(48) $\qquad\qquad\qquad \delta E_R^*/\delta I^* = 0;$

(49) $\qquad\qquad\qquad \delta E_R^*/\delta I = -\delta E_R/\delta I;$

(50) $\qquad\qquad\qquad \delta E_R^*/\delta F = -\delta E_R/\delta F.$

According to equations 48–50 we can use equation 41 (the formula for the differential in the affiliate's retained earnings) to simplify the formula for the differential in the parent's retained earnings:

(51) $dE_R^* = -(1 - p)(1 - t)\left\{\left[\dfrac{t^* h' - buq/(1 - z) + (t^* - t_f)h}{1 - t_f} - h\right]dI\right.$

$\qquad\qquad \left. + (b - i_p f)dF\right\}\Big/ z - [(1 - p^*)E_B(dt_f)]/Z^*$

$\qquad\qquad + (1 - p^*)(1 - t^*)[F_o d(i_{p_o} f_o) + I_o dh_o$

$\qquad\qquad + Fd(i_p f) + Idh + E_B dp]/Z^*$

$\qquad\qquad + L' \Delta E_R/Z^* + (1 - p^*)[b^* q^* I^* du^*/(1 - z)$

$\qquad\qquad + bqIdu/(1 - z) - t^*(Idh' + I_o dh_o')]/Z^*.$

Equations 41 and 51 can be substituted in equations 37–39 to give

(52) $\quad \begin{bmatrix} a_{11} & a_{12} & a_{13} \\ a_{21} & a_{22} & a_{23} \\ a_{31} & a_{32} & a_{33} \end{bmatrix} \begin{bmatrix} dI^* \\ dI \\ dF \end{bmatrix} = \begin{bmatrix} c_1 \\ c_2 \\ c_3 \end{bmatrix},$

where

(53) $$a_{11} = r^{*\prime} - b^{*\prime};$$

(54) $$a_{12} = b^{*\prime}(1 - p)(1 - t)\{[buq/(1 - z) - t^*h' - (t^* - t_f)h/(1 - t_f)] + h\}/Z;$$

(55) $$a_{13} = -b^{*\prime}\{1 + [(1 - p)(1 - t)(b - i_p f)]/Z\};$$

(56) $$a_{21} = 0;$$

(57) $$a_{22} = r' - b'\left\{1 + (1 - p)(1 - t)\left[\frac{buq/(1 - z) - t^*h' - (t^* - t_f)h}{1 - t_f} + h\right]\Big/Z\right\};$$

(58) $$a_{23} = b'\{1 + [(1 - p)(1 - t)(b - i_p f)]/Z\};$$

(59) $$a_{31} = (1 - t^*)b^{*\prime};$$

(60) $$a_{32} = -(1 - t_f)b' - [(1 - t^*)b^{*\prime} + (1 - t_f)b'](1 - p)(1 - t)\{[buq/(1 - z) - t^*h' - (t^* - t_f)h/(1 - t_f)] + h\}/Z;$$

(61) $$a_{33} = [(1 - t^*)b^{*\prime} + (1 - t_f)b']\{1 + [(1 - p)(1 - t)(b - i_p f)]/Z\}.$$

(62) $$\begin{aligned} c_1 = &-b^{*\prime}\{(1 - p^*)(1 - t^*)[F_o d(i_{p_o} f_o) + F d(i_p f) \\ &+ I_o dh_o + I dh + E_B dp] + L'\Delta E_R \\ &+ (1 - p^*)(-E_B dt_f) \\ &+ b^*q^*I^*du^*/(1 - z) + bq I du/(1 - z) \\ &- t^*(I dh' + I_o dh_o')\}/Z^* \\ &- [b^*q^* du/(1 - t^*)(1 - z)]; \end{aligned}$$

(63) $$c_2 = -b'\Delta E_R + \{[t^* \, dh' + (t^* - t_f) \, dh - bq du/(1 - z)]/(1 - t_f)\} + \{[t^*h' - buq/(1 - z) + (t^*h) - h]/(1 - t_f)^2\} \, dt_f;$$

(64) $$c_3 = -(1 - t^*)c_1 - (1 - t_f)b'\Delta E_R - (b - i_p f) \, dt_f - (t^* - t_f) \, d(i_p f)b^*q^* du^*/(1 - z).$$

The terms c_1, c_2, and c_3 include changes in tax policy (for example, elimination of deferral implies $dt_f = (1 - p)(t^* - t_f)$) and changes in a firm's internal financial practices (for example, increasing head-office and royalty charges implies values of dh and/or dh_o which are positive). Using Cramer's Rule, the three equations in three unknowns represented by equation 52 can be solved, and the impact of the changes in tax policy and/or financial behavior on I^*, I, and F can be ascertained. And given the solution to that system of equations, we can also derive other measures: the impact of foreign and U.S. tax payments on the firm's consolidated after-tax earnings, and so forth.

Let us incorporate replacement of the foreign tax credit with a deduction before we obtain more general formulas. To incorporate the possible repeal of the foreign tax credit into our analysis, we must define two binary variables:

$$
(65) \quad s = \begin{cases} 0 \text{ if deferral is initially available (as above)}, \\ 1 \text{ if not}; \end{cases}
$$

and

$$
(66) \quad y = \begin{cases} 0 \text{ if the foreign tax credit remains in effect (as above)}, \\ 1 \text{ if the foreign tax credit is being eliminated}. \end{cases}
$$

To explore the effect of eliminating deferral while retaining the foreign tax credit, both s and y equal zero; t_f, the initial effective tax rate on foreign affiliate income, equals $t + p(t^* - t)$; and the change in this rate, dt_f, equals $(1 - p)(t^* - t)$. The effective tax rate after repeal of deferral is, thus, t^*, the U.S. tax rate.

To explore the additional impact of replacing the foreign tax credit with a deduction, both s and y equal unity; the initial effective tax rate, t_f, equals t^*; and eliminating the foreign tax credit is tantamount to raising the effective tax rate by the amount $dt_f = (1 - t^*)[t + w_D p(1 - t)]$.

Since t_f may initially equal either $t + p(t^* - t)$ or t^*, we do not need to modify our formulas for the a_{ij}'s given by equations 53–61. Let us however replace the three terms on the right side of equation 52 with d_1, d_2, and d_3:

$$
(67) \quad d_1 = c_1 + b^{*\prime}\{[s(t^* - t)(1 - p^*)\Delta F_R]/Z^*(1 - t)
$$
$$
- [s(t^* - t)(1 - p^*)E_B \, dp]/Z^*
$$
$$
+ y(1 - t^*)(1 - p^*)[w_B(i_{p_o}f_oF_o + i_pfF) + w_H(h_oI_o + hI)]/Z^*\};
$$

$$
(68) \quad\quad\quad\quad d_2 = c_2 + [yw_Hh/(1 - t)(1 - w_Dp)];
$$

$$
(69) \quad d_3 = -(1 - t^*)d_1 - (1 - t_f)b'\Delta E_R - [(t^* - t_f)d(i_pf)
$$
$$
+ (b - i_pf)dt_f + y(1 - t^*)w_Bi_pf] - b^*q^*du^*/(1 - z).
$$

The terms d_1 and d_2 measure the impact of higher taxes on the parent's and the affiliate's earnings available for reinvestment, while the term in brackets in the formula for d_3 measures the substitution effect.

Cramer's Rule can be used to solve for dI^*, dI, and dF. To derive the impact on the firm's consolidated after-tax earnings and on the taxes paid to foreign and U.S. governments, we first derive the impact on retained earnings: the impact on the affiliate's retained earnings is indicated by equation 41; to obtain the impact on the parent's retained earnings, we must modify equation 51:

$$
\begin{aligned}
(70) \quad E_R^* = {} & (1 - p^*)(1 - t^*)(R_T{}^* - B_T{}^* + i_{p_o}f_oF \\
& + i_pfF + h_oI_o + hI) + L'E_R \\
& + (1 - p^*)[b^*u^*q^*I^*/(1 - z) + buqI/(1 - z) \\
& - t^*(h'I + h_o'I_o)] - [s(t^* - t)(1 - p^*)E_R/(1 - t)] \\
& - y(1 - t^*)(1 - p^*)\{[t + w_Dp(1 - t)]E_B \\
& + w_B(i_{p_o}f_oF_o + i_pfF) + w_H(h_oI_o + hI)\}.
\end{aligned}
$$

The total differential is

$$
\begin{aligned}
(71) \quad dE_R^* = {} & -(1 - p)(1 - t)\left\{\left[\frac{t^*h' - buq/(1 - z) + (t^* - t_f)h}{1 - t_f} - h\right]dI \right. \\
& \left. + (b - i_pf)dF\right\}\Big/Z - [(1 - p^*)E_Bdt_f]/Z^* \\
& + (1 - p^*)(1 - t^*)[F_od(i_{p_o}f_o) + I_odh_o \\
& + Fd(i_pf) + Idh + E_Bdp]/Z^* \\
& + L'\Delta E_R/Z^* + (1 - p^*)[b^*q^*I^*du^*/(1 - z) \\
& + bqIdu/(1 - z) - t^*(Idh' + I_odh_o')]/Z^* \\
& + \{[(t^* - t)(1 - p^*)E_Bdp]/Z^* \\
& - [(t^* - t)(1 - p^*)\Delta E_R]/(1 - t)Z^*\}s \\
& - (1 - t^*)(1 - p^*)\{[w_B(i_pfF + i_{p_o}f_oF_o) \\
& + w_H(h_oI_o + hI)]y\}/Z^*.
\end{aligned}
$$

Since

$$
\begin{aligned}
(72) \quad E_C = {} & (E_R + E_R{}^*)/(1 - p^*) \\
& + [1 - buqI/(1 - z)] + [1 - b^*u^*q^*I^*/(1 - z)],
\end{aligned}
$$

the change in consolidated earnings after taxes is

$$
\begin{aligned}
(73) \quad dE_C = {} & [(dE_R + dE_R{}^*)/(1 - p^*)] + [1 - bq/(1 - z)](Idu + udI) \\
& + [1 - b^*q^*/(1 - z)](u^*dI^* + I^*du^*).
\end{aligned}
$$

To compute the impact on taxes paid, it is convenient to have the formula for the affiliate's taxable earnings:

$$(74) \qquad E_B = R_T - B_T - i_{p_o} f_o F_o - i_{p} fF - h_o I_o - hI;$$

and its differential is

$$(75) \qquad dE_B = \left[\frac{t^* h' - buq/(1 - z) + (t^* - t_f)h}{1 - t_f} - h \right] dI$$
$$+ b(dF + dE_R) - i_{p} fdF - Fd(i_{p} f)$$
$$- Idh - F_o d(i_{p_o} f_o) - I_o dh_o.$$

The total taxes collected by the foreign government equal

$$(76) \qquad T + W = [t + w_D p(1 - t)]E_B + w_B(i_{p_o} f_o F_o$$
$$+ i_{p} fF) + w_H(h_o I_o + hI).$$

So the change in foreign tax payments is

$$(77) \qquad d(T + W) = [t + w_D p(1 - t)]dE_B + w_D(1 - t)E_B dp$$
$$+ w_B[F_o d(i_{p_o} f_o) + i_{p} fdF$$
$$+ Fd(i_{p} f)] + w_H[I_o dh_o + hdI + Idh].$$

The formula for U.S. taxes is more complicated:

$$(78) \qquad T^* = t^*(R_T^* - B_T^*) + (t^* - w_B)(i_{p_o} f_o F_o$$
$$+ i_{p} fF) + (t^* - w_H)(h_o I_o + hI)$$
$$+ [t^* - t - w_D(1 - t)]pE_B - u^* q^* I^*$$
$$- uqI + t^* h'I + t^* h_o' I_o$$
$$+ s(t^* - t)(1 - p)E_B + y(1 - t^*)(T + W),$$

the total difference of which is

$$(79) \quad dT^* = t^*\{-b^* dF + b^* dE_R^* - [u^* q^* b^* dI^*/(1 - t^*)(1 - z)]\}$$
$$+ (t^* - w_B)[Fd(i_{p_o} f_o) + i_{p} fdF + Fd(i_{p} f)]$$
$$+ (t^* - w_H)(I_o dh_o + hdI + Idh)$$
$$+ E_B dt_f + [t^* - t - w_D(1 - t)](pdE_B$$
$$+ E_B dp) - u^* q^* dI^* - q^* I^* du^* - uqdI - qIdu + t^* h'dI$$
$$+ t^* Idh' + t^* I_o dh_o' + s(t^* - t)[(1 - p)dE_B - E_B dp]$$
$$+ y(1 - t^*)[w_B(i_{p_o} f_o F_o + i_{p} fF) + w_H(h_o I_o + hI)].$$

To recapitulate, the basic system of equations is

$$(80) \quad \begin{bmatrix} a_{11} & a_{12} & a_{13} \\ a_{21} & a_{22} & a_{23} \\ a_{31} & a_{32} & a_{33} \end{bmatrix} \begin{bmatrix} dI^* \\ dI \\ dF \end{bmatrix} = \begin{bmatrix} d_1 \\ d_2 \\ d_3 \end{bmatrix}$$

The formulas for the a_{ij} series are equations 53–61 and those for d_i are equations 67–69 (which incorporate equations 62–64). The value of d_i depends on what change one wishes to examine:

1. Eliminating deferral implies making $dt_f = (1 - p)(t^* - t)$ and the other differentials incorporated into d_1, d_2, and $d_3 = 0$.

2. Raising head-office charges, royalties, or other intrafirm service charges implies an appropriate, positive value for dh_o and dh, and a zero value for the other differentials. (If higher deductions are not allowed by the foreign government, then dh_o and dh are zero, and dh_o' and dh' are positive.)

3. Extending the investment tax credit to foreign investment income implies making du equal to 7 percent, or whatever the rate is.

4. Eliminating the foreign tax credit in favor of a deduction (assuming the prior repeal of deferral) implies that $t_f = t^*$, $dt_f = (1 - t^*)[t + w_D p (1 - t)]$ and that both s and y equal unity.

5. Voluntary changes in intrafirm financial ratios, such as the affiliate's dividend payout ratio or the intrafirm ratio of debt to total capital, can be simulated by setting dp, $d(i_p f)$ and $d(i_{p_o} f_o)$ equal to the intended changes. If a tax change (for example, eliminating deferral) induces a change in financial parameters, the best procedure is first to simulate the impact of eliminating deferral—computing new initial values for investment, and so on—and then to simulate the impact of the induced change.

Once the appropriate values of the d_i series have been determined, the three equations in three unknowns represented by equation 80 are solved, and the changes in dI^*, dI, and dF can be determined. And having determined these, one can use equations 49, 71, and 73 to determine the impact on consolidated after-tax earnings; equation 77 to ascertain the impact on foreign income and withholding taxes; and equation 79 to compute the effect on U.S. income tax payments.

The numerical solutions reported in tables 6-4, 6-5, 6-6, and 6-7 are based on rough estimates of the various parameters of the model. These estimates together with their sources are described in table B-2. To facilitate the calculation of numerical estimates, we have written a computer program to evaluate all formulas presented here. Copies of the program are available from the authors.

Table B-2. *Values, Definitions, and Sources of Parameters Used in Simulations*

Parameter	Value	Definition and source
b, b^*	0.09	Assumed marginal cost of externally borrowed funds for parent and affiliate, respectively.
p	0.42	Subsidiary's dividend payout ratio. According to *Survey of Current Business*, vol. 55 (October 1975), table 4, manufacturing affiliates' 1974 gross dividends-earnings ratio was 0.40. Estimate raised to approximate a 4–5 year moving average.
p^*	0.33	Parent's dividend payout ratio: ratio of all American manufacturing firms' dividends to after-tax earnings. Based on ibid.
t	0.391	Foreign income tax rate. See table 6-2, column 1.
t^*	0.48	U.S. statutory income tax rate.
E_B	10.67	Affiliate's before tax earnings. According to *Survey of Current Business*, vol. 55 (October 1975), table 11, manufacturing affiliates' 1974 after-tax earnings were $6.498 billion. Since this figure is net of income taxes, it was divided by $(1 - 0.391)$.
h, h_o	0.011	Ratio of fees and royalties, respectively, to total affiliate investment. According to ibid., table 10, manufacturing affiliates' 1974 fees and royalties were $1.855 billion. There is no reliable estimate of the total assets of U.S. manufacturing affiliates to use in deflating this figure. However, an estimate of $78 billion in total 1970 assets was obtained from *Implications of Multinational Firms for World Trade and Investment and for U.S. Trade and Labor*, prepared for the Senate Finance Committee (GPO, 1973), table 12. These assets were assumed to grow annually, 1970–74, at a rate of 16.7 percent (the growth rate of affiliate sales), bringing assets for 1974 to $170 billion. Dividing the $1.85 billion in royalties and fees by the $170 billion total assets yields 0.011.
w_D, w_H, w_B	0.15	Withholding tax rate of 15 percent applied to dividends, fees, and interest payments, respectively. See table 6-2, column 2.
F	2.71	New capital outflow from parent to affiliate. See *Survey of Current Business*, vol. 55 (October 1975), table 3.
$R_T^* - B_T^*$	12.73	Parent's domestic income before taxes. According to table 6-1, twenty-four multinational manufacturers earned 54.4 percent of book income before taxes from

Table B-2 (*continued*)

Parameter	Value	Definition and source
		domestic operations; 54.4 percent of $10.67 billion (affiliate's pretax earnings) plus x billion (domestic pretax earnings) equals $12.73 billion.
r'	-0.0025	Slope of the marginal revenue from new investment by the foreign affiliate; implies an elasticity of 2.
$r^{*\prime}$	-0.0012	Slope of the marginal revenue from new investment by parent. Elasticity of investment demand at home assumed to be same as abroad.
b'	0.0049	Slope of the marginal cost of outside capital schedule for the foreign affiliate. Elasticity assumed to be 2.
$b^{*\prime}$	0.0024	Slope of the marginal cost of outside capital schedule for parent. Elasticity assumed to be 2.
I_o	170.00	Foreign affiliate's total assets. See note for h above.
F_o	34.00	Total capital transferred from parent to affiliate. According to Sidney Robbins and Robert B. Stobaugh, *Money in the Multinational Enterprise* (Basic Books, 1973), table 4-1, 20 percent of manufacturing affiliates funds, 1966–69, were from parent firms. Estimate of $34 billion is 20 percent of the $170 billion estimate of I_o.
f, f_o	0.64	Ratio of intrafirm debt to total capital transfer for new and existing investment, respectively. Estimate from *Survey of Current Business*, vol. 55 (October 1975), table 3.
i_p, i_{p_o}	0.031	Intrafirm interest rate. Calculations of intrafirm interest payments and debt based on J. R. Nunns and G. C. Hufbauer, "Tax Payments and Tax Expenditures on International Investment and Employment," *Columbia Journal of World Business* (Summer 1975), table 2; and U.S. Office of Foreign Direct Investment, *Foreign Affiliate Financial Survey, 1966–1969* (GPO, 1971). Low average rate reflects interest-free trade credits.
I	18.30	Subsidiary's new investment in 1974. *Survey of Current Business*, vol. 56 (March 1976), table 1, indicates that manufacturing affiliates' 1974 capital expenditures on property, plant, and equipment were $11.7 billion. Figure increased by 56 percent to include short-term capital formation, based on the ratio of 1970–74 estimate increase in total assets (see note for h) and the total value of property, plant, and equipment expenditures over the same interval.
I^*	36.40	According to *Implications of Multinational Firms for World Trade and Investment and for U.S. Trade and Labor*, table 12, the 1966–70 increase in total assets of parent firms was 1.99 times that of foreign affiliates. Value of I (18.3) was multiplied by 1.99.

Table B-2 (*continued*)

Parameter	Value	Definition and source
*q**	0.40	Proportion of new investment qualifying for the domestic investment tax credit, obtained from the international tax staff of the U.S. Treasury Department. The low figure reflects the ineligibility of property, some equipment, and all current assets (inventories, accounts receivable, and so on).
*u**	0.07	Statutory rate of the investment tax credit for qualifying equipment in 1974; the rate was raised to 10 percent in 1976.
z	0.274	Present discounted value of future depreciation deductions per dollar of current total investment. Based on estimate of 0.547 total investment for U.S. manufacturing. See Gary C. Hufbauer, "The Taxation of Export Profits," *National Tax Journal*, vol. 28 (March 1975), pp. 43–60; 50 percent assumed depreciable.

Index of Names

General Index

527